fifth edition

organizational behavior

key concepts, skills & best practices

Angelo Kinicki

Arizona State University

Mel Fugate

*Southern
Methodist University*

**McGraw-Hill
Irwin**

ORGANIZATIONAL BEHAVIOR: KEY CONCEPTS, SKILLS AND BEST PRACTICES

Published by McGraw-Hill/Irwin, a business unit of The McGraw-Hill Companies, Inc., 1221 Avenue of the Americas, New York, NY, 10020. Copyright © 2012, 2009, 2008, 2006, 2003 by The McGraw-Hill Companies, Inc. All rights reserved. Printed in the United States of America. No part of this publication may be reproduced or distributed in any form or by any means, or stored in a database or retrieval system, without the prior written consent of The McGraw-Hill Companies, Inc., including, but not limited to, in any network or other electronic storage or transmission, or broadcast for distance learning.

Some ancillaries, including electronic and print components, may not be available to customers outside the United States.

This book is printed on acid-free paper.

5 6 7 8 9 0 DOW/DOW 1 0 9 8 7 6 5 4 3

ISBN 978-0-07-813720-4
MHID 0-07-813720-9

Vice president and editor-in-chief: *Brent Gordon*
Editorial director: *Paul Ducham*
Executive editor: *Michael Ablassmeir*
Executive director of development: *Ann Torbert*
Development editor: *Kelly I. Pekelder*
Editorial coordinator: *Andrea Heirendt*
Vice president and director of marketing: *Robin J. Zwettler*
Marketing director: *Amee Mosley*
Executive marketing manager: *Anke Braun Weekes*
Marketing specialist: *Elizabeth Steiner*
Vice president of editing, design, and production: *Sesha Bolisetty*
Senior project manager: *Dana M. Pauley*
Buyer II: *Debra R. Sylvester*
Senior designer: *Matt Diamond*
Senior photo research coordinator: *Jeremy Cheshareck*
Photo researcher: *Editorial Image, LLC*
Senior media project manager: *Greg Bates*
Media project manager: *Suresh Babu, Hurix Systems Pvt. Ltd.*
Cover design: *Pam Verros*
Typeface: *10.5/12 Times Roman*
Compositor: *Laserwords Private Limited*
Printer: *R. R. Donnelley*

Library of Congress Cataloging-in-Publication Data

Kinicki, Angelo.
    Organizational behavior : key concepts, skills & best practices / Angelo Kinicki,
Mel Fugate.—5th ed.
      p. cm.
    Includes index.
    ISBN-13: 978-0-07-813720-4 (alk. paper)
    ISBN-10: 0-07-813720-9 (alk. paper)
    1. Organizational behavior. I. Fugate, Mel. II. Title.
HD58.7.K5265 2012
658.3—dc23

                                       2011032566

www.mhhe.com

Less managing. More teaching. Greater learning.

 INSTRUCTORS...

Would you like your **students** to show up for class more **prepared**? *(Let's face it, class is much more fun if everyone is engaged and prepared...)*

Want ready-made application-level **interactive assignments,** student progress reporting, and auto-assignment grading? *(Less time grading means more time teaching...)*

Want an **instant view of student or class performance** relative to learning objectives? *(No more wondering if students understand...)*

Need to **collect data and generate reports** required for administration or accreditation? *(Say goodbye to manually tracking student learning outcomes...)*

Want to **record and post your lectures** for students to view online?

 With **McGraw-Hill's** *Connect*™ *Plus Management,*

INSTRUCTORS GET:

- Interactive Applications – **book-specific interactive assignments** that require students to APPLY what they've learned.

- Simple **assignment management,** allowing you to spend more time teaching.

- **Auto-graded** assignments, quizzes, and tests.

- **Detailed Visual Reporting** where student and section results can be viewed and analyzed.

- Sophisticated **online testing** capability.

- A **filtering and reporting** function that allows you to easily assign and report on materials that are correlated to accreditation standards, learning outcomes, and Bloom's taxonomy.

- An easy-to-use **lecture capture** tool.

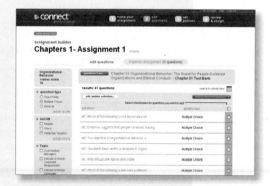

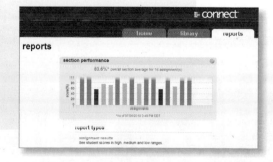

Want an online, **searchable version** of your textbook?

Wish your textbook could be **available online** while you're doing your assignments?

 ### *Connect™ Plus Management* eBook

If you choose to use *Connect™ Plus Management*, you have an affordable and searchable online version of your book integrated with your other online tools.

Connect™ Plus Management eBook offers features like:

- Topic search
- Direct links from assignments
- Adjustable text size
- Jump to page number
- Print by section

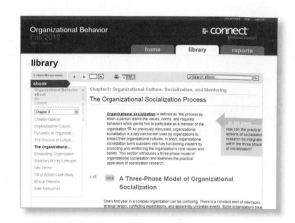

 Want to get more **value** from your textbook purchase?

Think learning management should be a bit more **interesting**?

 ### Check out the STUDENT RESOURCES section under the *Connect™* Library tab.

Here you'll find a wealth of resources designed to help you achieve your goals in the course. You'll find things like **quizzes, PowerPoints, and Internet activities** to help you study. Every student has different needs, so explore the STUDENT RESOURCES to find the materials best suited to you.

With love, gratitude, and admiration to my best friend and wife, Joyce Kinicki. Your support and love has helped me in more ways than you will ever know. Thank you for helping make dreams come true!

—AK

With love and appreciation to my dear wife, Donna. She and my wonderful family support me in everything I do. I am incredibly fortunate to have all of them in my life—thank you!

—MF

Angelo Kinicki, pictured on the right, is a professor, author, and consultant. He is a professor of management and is the recipient of the Weatherup/ Overby Chair in Leadership. He also is a Dean's Council of 100 Distinguished Scholar at the W P Carey School of Business. He joined the faculty in 1982, the year he received his doctorate in business administration from Kent State University. His primary research interests include leadership, organizational culture, organizational change,

received several awards, including a best research paper award from the Organizational Behavior (OB) division of the Academy of Management, the All Time Best Reviewer Award (1996–99) and the Excellent Reviewer Award (1997–98) from the *Academy of Management Journal,* and six teaching awards from Arizona State University (Outstanding Teaching Award—MBA and Master's Program, John W Teets Outstanding Graduate Teacher Award (2x), Outstanding Undergraduate

service as a representative at large for the Organizational Behavior division, member of the Best Paper Award committee for both the OB and Human Resources (HR) divisions, chair of the committee to select the best publication in the *Academy of Management Journal,* and program committee reviewer for the OB and HR divisions.

Angelo also is a busy international consultant and is a principal at Kinicki and Associates Inc., a management consulting firm that works with top management teams to create organizational change aimed at increasing organizational effectiveness and profitability. He has worked with many Fortune 500 firms as well as numerous entrepreneurial organizations in diverse industries. His expertise includes facilitating strategic/operational planning sessions, diagnosing the causes of organizational and work-unit problems, conducting organizational culture interventions, implementing performance management systems, designing and implementing performance appraisal systems, developing and administering surveys to assess employee attitudes, and leading management/executive education programs. He developed a 360-degree leadership feedback instrument called the Performance Management Leadership Survey (PMLS) that is used by companies throughout the United States and Europe. The survey is used to assess an individual's leadership style and to coach individuals interested in developing their leadership skills.

and multilevel issues associated with predicting organizational effectiveness. Angelo has published more than 90 articles in a variety of academic journals and is coauthor of seven textbooks (25 including revisions) that are used by hundreds of universities around the world. Several of his books have been translated into multiple languages.

Angelo is an award-winning researcher and teacher. He has

Teaching Excellence Award, Outstanding Graduate Teaching Excellence Award, and Outstanding Executive Development Teaching Excellence Award). Angelo also has served on the editorial review boards for the *Academy of Management Journal, Personnel Psychology,* the *Journal of Management,* and the *Journal of Vocational Behavior.* Angelo has been an active member of the Academy of Management, including

Angelo and his wife, Joyce, have enjoyed living in the beautiful Arizona desert for 30 years and are natives of Cleveland, Ohio. They enjoy traveling, golfing, hiking, spoiling Nala, their golden retriever, and spending time in the White Mountains.

Mel Fugate is a professor and consultant. He is an associate professor of Management and Organizations and Dunlevy Fellow in the Cox School of Business at Southern Methodist University. He teaches executive, MBA, and undergraduate courses. Prior to the Cox School he was a visiting assistant professor of Organizational Behavior at Tulane University's A.B. Freeman College of Business. He also has international teaching experience (e.g., International MBA) at EM Lyon Graduate School of Management in Lyon, France. Prior to earning his Ph.D. in Business Administration and Management from Arizona State University, Mel performed consulting services in marketing and business development and was a sales representative and manager in the pharmaceutical industry. He also has a BS in engineering and business administration from Michigan State University.

Mel's primary research interests involve employee reactions to organizational change and transitions at work. This includes but is not limited to downsizings, mergers and acquisitions, restructurings, and plant closings. He investigates employees' change-related cognitive appraisals, emotions, coping efforts, and withdrawal. Another research stream involves the development of a dispositional perspective of employability and its implications for employee careers and behavior. Current interests also include the influence of leadership and organizational culture on performance and the influence of emotions on behavior at work. He has published in and reviewed for a number of premier management and applied psychology journals, such as the *Academy of Management Journal, Academy of Management Review, Journal of Applied Psychology, Journal of Occupational and Organizational Psychology, Journal of Vocational Behavior, and Personnel Psychology*. He also served on the editorial boards of *Personnel Psychology* and the *Journal of Leadership and Organizational Studies*. Mel's research and comments have been featured in numerous media outlets: *The Wall Street Journal, The New York Times, Financial Times, Dallas Morning News,* CNN, Fox, ABC, and NBC.

His consulting work aims to enhance individual and organizational performance by utilizing a variety of practical, research-based tools related to leadership and management development, performance management, motivation, strategic talent management, organizational culture, compensation, and exceptional client service. Mel's consulting and research covers many industries (e.g., legal, energy, healthcare, information technology, and financial services). His research and consulting often overlap in the area of change management, where he assists managers in developing, implementing, and evaluating change initiatives designed to enhance employee performance and organizational competitiveness, including the integration and realignment of organizational cultures.

Mel and his wife, Donna, are both very active and enjoy fitness, traveling, live music, and catering to their sweet, savage Jack Russell "Terror," Scout Dog.

preface

The fifth edition was an important transition in the life of this textbook. It represented the end of Bob Kreitner's role as a coauthor. Bob is a great friend and a tremendous coauthor who played a major role in crafting this book into its present form. We thank Bob for this contribution. At the same time, the fifth edition is the start of Mel Fugate's tenure as a coauthor.

Mel was chosen to work on this book because he has a long track record of excellent performance across multiple professional roles. He has published over 20 academic articles in journals and books, he received three teaching awards from the Cox School of Business at Southern Methodist University, and he served on the review boards for two academic journals. Mel also brings a fresh new perspective to the book and he teaches organizational behavior to both undergraduate and graduate students. His enthusiasm and passion for teaching and researching organizational behavior will surely improve this text for both students and professors.

In our many years of teaching organizational behavior, management, and leadership to undergraduate and graduate students in various countries, we *never* had a student say, "I want a longer, more expensive textbook with more chapters." We got the message! Indeed, there is a desire for shorter and less expensive textbooks in today's fast-paced world where overload and tight budgets are a way of life. Within the field of organizational behavior, so-called "essentials" texts have attempted to satisfy this need. Too often, however, brevity has been achieved at the expense of up-to-date examples, artful layout, and learning enhancements. We believe "brief" does not have to mean short-changed, outdated, and boring.

New Standard

Kinicki and Fugate's *Organizational Behavior: Key Concepts, Skills & Best Practices,* fifth edition, represents a new standard in OB essentials textbooks. The following guiding philosophy inspired our quest for this new standard: "Create a short, up-to-date, practical, user-friendly, interesting, and engaging introduction to the field of organizational behavior." You therefore will find this book to be a lean and efficient coverage of topics recommended by the accreditation organizations AACSB International and ACBSP, all conveyed with pedagogical features found in full-length OB textbooks. Among those pedagogical enhancements are current, real-life chapter-opening cases, a rich array of contemporary in-text examples, a strong skills emphasis including Skills & Best Practices boxes throughout the text, at least one interactive exercise integrated into each chapter, a new back to the chapter-opening case feature that has students apply the text to a chapter's opening case, an appealing four-color presentation, interesting captioned photos, instructive chapter summaries, and chapter-closing Legal/Ethical Challenge exercises.

Efficient and Flexible Structure

The 16 chapters in this text are readily adaptable to traditional 15-week semesters, 10-week terms, various module formats, summer and intersessions, management development seminars, and distance learning programs via the Internet. The book begins with coverage of important topics—such as ethics, international OB, and managing diversity. The topical flow of the text then moves from micro (individuals) to macro (groups, teams, and organizations). Mixing and matching chapters (and topics within each chapter) in various combinations is not only possible but strongly encouraged to create optimum teaching/learning experiences.

A Solid Base of Fresh and Relevant Source Material

Wise grocery shoppers gauge the freshness of essential purchases such as bread and milk by checking the "sell by" dates. OB textbooks similarly need to be checked for freshness to ensure the reader's time is well spent on up-to-date and relevant theory, research, and practical examples. The fifth edition is filled with current and relevant examples from both research and practice perspectives. You will find about **339** and **171** chapter endnotes dated 2010 and 2011, respectively, indicating a thorough updating of this new edition. Our continuing commitment to a timely and relevant textbook is evidenced by the **14 (88%)** new chapter-opening cases. These cases highlight male and female role models and large and small public and private organizations around the world. Among the diverse array of organizations featured are Google, Chrysler, Tata Consultancy, the U.S. Navy, Facebook, British Petroleum, and HCL Technologies.

Every chapter contains a host of recent practical examples that highlight the application of OB theory and research. More in-depth examples are featured in boxed material labeled *Skills & Best Practices*. The fifth edition contains **50 (81%)** new Skills & Best Practices boxes from timely 2010 and 2011 material.

New and Improved Coverage

Our readers and reviewers have kindly told us how much they appreciate our efforts to keep this textbook up-to-date and relevant. Toward that end, you will find the following important new and significantly improved coverage in the fifth edition:

Chapter 1

New structure for the chapter. New material and perspectives on building social and human capital (Table 1-3). An expanded and updated section on on e-business and its implications for OB and managing people. A new section on corporate social responsibility and ethics includes suggestions on how to confront unethical behavior at work. Figure 1-4 provides a new model for OB and roadmap for the book. A new chapter-opening case based on Google, and a new legal/ethical challenge.

Chapter 2

Updated statistics regarding the four functions of organizational culture at Southwest Airlines. New organizational examples to illustrate four types of organizational culture. New Figure 2-4 that summarizes recent meta-analytic results regarding the relationship between organizational culture and organizational effectiveness. New examples to illustrate the 11 ways managers can change organizational culture. New examples to illustrate socialization techniques and mentoring along with updated research. New chapter opening case and legal/ethical challenge.

Chapter 3

New material on global mind-sets. Updated section on merging societal and organizational cultures includes current examples and a "how to" guide for becoming an "ambicultural manager." Updated research related to Hofstede and GLOBE studies. Provides new research and recommendations for successful foreign assignments and repatriation. Two new key terms—*emotional* and *informational support*. Chapter-opening case based on Tata Consultancy Services and the legal/ethical challenge are new.

Chapter 4

New coverage of how the "negativity bias" influences perceptions and the relationship between perception and counterproductive work behavior. Updated research on the impact of stereotypes and diversity within teams. New examples to illustrate the fundamental attribution bias, self-serving bias, companies that effectively manage diversity, and companies that use R. Roosevelt Thomas's generic action options for managing diversity. Updated statistics regarding demographic characteristics of the U.S. workforce and a new Table 4-2 that summarizes generational differences among employees. A new hands-on exercise that measures students' attitude toward diversity. New and updated material regarding the managerial implications of managing diversity. New chapter-opening case and legal/ethical challenge. New key term: *implicit cognition*

Chapter 5

This chapter is now organized along a continuum, based on the degree to which individual differences are fixed versus flexible: intelligence, ability, personality, core self-evaluations, attitudes, and emotions, respectively. This is illustrated in a new Figure 5-1. A new section is devoted to the concept of *core self-evaluations* (comprised of self-esteem, self-efficacy, locus of control, and emotional stability). Updated research on proactive personality and the use of personality tests. New research and examples for attitudes. Research and recommendations related to emotions and emotional intelligence are revised. Emotional contagion and emotional labor material is updated. The new chapter-opening case focuses on Mark Zuckerberg of Facebook. A new legal/ethical challenge.

Chapter 6

A new integrated model of motivation (Figure 6-1) provides a foundation for understanding the theories covered in Chapters 6 and 7. A new/revised section on job design covers the new approaches of job crafting and idiosyncratic deals. Table 6-1 outlines approaches for job crafting. A new major section on employee engagement discusses the causes and consequences of engagement and includes a new hands-on exercise measuring student engagement. New section on dual career ladders. New key terms: *job crafting, idiosyncratic deals, employee engagement, PE fit,* and *dual career ladders.*

Chapter 7

The latest research on equity theory is discussed and new examples illustrate its six key practical applications. The latest research on expectancy theory is reviewed and new examples are used to demonstrate the theory's application. Goal setting research is updated and new examples document its practical use. New chapter-opening case and legal/ethical challenge.

Chapter 8

The most current research and practical guidance on feedback is provided, such as "How to Respond to a Negative Performance Review" and how to provide "upward feedback." Organizational rewards were updated to include the concept of "total rewards." New research and guidance are provided for alternatives to money and promotions. Research is updated on pay-for-performance programs. Section on reinforcement is modified and presented differently. Figure 8-4 is a new illustration of reinforcement schedules. Both the chapter-opening case on Sprint and the legal/ethical challenge are new.

Chapter 9

Material related to group functions, development, and roles is updated with new examples. Latest research on trust is discussed and includes new recommendations for building it with others. Section on teamwork competencies and being a team player is revised and updated. Team building coverage is refreshed with new research

and recommendations. New research and examples for cross-functional and virtual teams. A new section on facilitators of team effectiveness. New key terms: *team adaptive capacity, team charters, team composition,* and *team performance strategies.* The new chapter-opening case uses Geisinger Health System as an example. Legal/ethical challenge is new.

Chapter 10

New discussion of the rational model of decision making, including a new Figure 10-1, and updated research on decision making models. New examples illustrate decision making biases, and new major section on evidence-based decision making (EBDM). The latest research on intuition is reviewed and new examples demonstrate its application. New section regarding the practical application of creativity. New section discussing a road-map to ethical decision making, including a decision tree for making ethical decisions. Updated research and examples regarding group decision-making. New chapter-opening case and legal/ethical challenge. New key terms: *decision tree, evidence based decision making (EBDM),* and *opportunity.*

Chapter 11

The discussion, research, and examples related to functional v. dysfunctional conflict are updated. Research and advice for dealing with/avoiding conflicts is reviewed. Particular attention is given to workplace incivility (e.g., bullying). Recent research and recommendations for dealing with intergroup conflict are provided. A new section on work-family conflict includes the most recent research and guidance. Specific guidance is given for implementing alternative dispute resolution (ADR). Recent Added-Value Negotiation (AVN) literature is reviewed and practical implications discussed. The new chapter-opening

case highlights the role of professional legal managers in companies. New legal/ethical challenge. New key terms: *economic value, subjective value,* and *work-family conflict.*

Chapter 12

A "how to" guide is provided for communication in job interviews. New research and examples for interpersonal (verbal and non-verbal) communications. A new section related to gender and generational communication differences and challenges includes research and recommendations. A new section focuses on information communication technologies (ICT) and their implications for OB, productivity, managing teleworkers, and the advantages and disadvantages associated with social media at work (e.g., using Facebook in your professional life). The new chapter-opening case involves Brian Dunn, the CEO of Best Buy, and his experiences and views on social media. A new legal/ethical challenge focuses on criticizing coworkers/managers/employers in social media. New key term: *social media.*

Chapter 13

Research and practice are updated for nine influence tactics. Current research, examples, and applications for the five bases of power are discussed, especially coercive, expert, and referent. Updated research and examples on employee empowerment. The scope of the organizational politics discussion is broadened to more appropriately include both negative and positive implications. A new section is included for impression management with advice on avoiding and managing bad impressions. New chapter-opening case involves Raj Gupta, former CEO of specialty chemical company Rohm & Hass. Legal/ethical challenge focuses on the influence of an elite group of bankers that control the derivatives markets.

Chapter 14

New discussion of implicit leadership theory and a new section discusses traits possessed by bad leaders. New summary Table 14-1 of positive traits associated with leadership emergence and new sections review the take-aways of Fiedler's and House's models of leadership. Two new sections cover the practical application of situational-based theories. Research on transformational leadership and emerging theories was updated, and new examples were used to illustrate these theories' practical applications. Expanded discussion of the role of followers, and new chapter-opening case and legal/ethical challenge are used. New key term: *implicit leadership theory.*

Chapter 15

New overview of organizational design and new examples to illustrate the various forms of design used by organizations. New examples of mechanistic and organic organizations. New examples used to illustrate the application of the various generic effectiveness criteria within organizations. New chapter-opening case and legal/ethical challenge. New key term: *organizational design.*

Chapter 16

New updated material and examples of the external forces of change, including a new section on the social and political pressures for change. All new material on the internal forces of change. New examples

used to illustrate a systems model of change as well as Lewin and Kotter's models of change. Material on organizational development (OD) was revamped, including a new section and Figure 16-2 to explain how OD is put into practice. New examples are used to highlight the 11 reasons people resist change. A completely revised section with new examples on strategies for overcoming resistance to change was written. Material on creating a learning organization is almost totally rewritten and includes a new Table 16-3 that outlines the reasons organizations do not learn from failure, and a new section on how to learn from success. New chapter-opening case. New key terms: *change agent* and *resilience to change.*

Chapter	Ethics	Diversity	International OB	Internet/Social Media	Teams/Teamwork
1	18–25, 28–29	5, 8–9, 13, 17	15–16	14–18, 28–29	4, 15–16
2	33–35, 40–44, 55	50, 51	39	44, 46, 52	33, 35–38, 43–51
3	64, 80	56–57, 59–66	56–68, 71–73, 76, 80	61	
4	82, 83, 89, 94, 95, 99, 109, 111–112	82, 83, 87, 89, 90, 91, 96–110		82, 92	91, 106
5	122, 133–134, 143	116–117, 122, 131	120, 124		114–115,
6	149, 167, 170	146, 152–154, 157, 159	151		146–148, 152, 154, 158, 160, 161
7	172, 173, 178, 179, 194	178		177, 178,	178, 182, 189
8	205–206, 212, 217–218, 220–221	202	208	203, 204	203
9	231, 248–249	226, 230, 231–232, 242–243, 246	233, 234, 242	227, 242–244	224–225, 226–227, 231, 234–238, 239–241, 242–243, 243–247
10	250–253, 261, 262, 270–273, 282		265	269, 279, 280	250, 251, 263, 270, 273 279
11	290, 300–302, 306	281 285, 286	291, 294 295, 300	286	286, 289, 292–294
12	332 333, 336	314–315, 318, 319, 320–321, 324–326, 328	316, 318, 321, 327, 328, 331	308–309, 311, 325, 327–334, 336	331–332
13	338 339, 344–345, 352–353, 354, 356, 360	342–345	346–347, 350, 353, 356		350, 360
14	362–363, 366–367, 369, 381–382, 392	382, 384	377, 378, 386	382	362–363, 369, 375, 380, 386–387, 389
15	416		399–400, 404, 406–407, 409 411, 413 414	404–406	394–395, 402, 406
16	423, 444		418–420, 422–423, 432, 434–435	421–422, 437	425, 431, 437, 440, 443

Emphasis on Ethics in the Fifth Edition

We have continued (and updated) two features from the fourth edition—we inserted the learning module on ethics into Chapter 1 to provide upfront coverage of this important contextual issue. We also include 11 new legal/ethical challenge cases (69%) at the end of every chapter— to set a proper moral tone for managing people at work. The 16 legal/ethical challenge cases raise contemporary ethical issues, ask tough questions, and have corresponding interpretations on our Web site at www.mhhe.com/kinickiob5e .

legal/ethical challenge

Credit-Card Issuers Have Cultures That Focus on Growth by Targeting Financially Strapped People[55]

The troubles sound familiar. Borrowers falling behind on their payments. Defaults rising. Huge swaths of loans souring. Investors getting burned. But forget the now-familiar tales of mortgages gone bad. The next horror for beaten-down financial firms is the $950 billion worth of outstanding credit-card debt—much of it toxic. . . . The consumer debt bomb is already beginning to spray shrapnel throughout the financial markets, further weakening the U.S. economy. "The next meltdown will be in credit cards," says Gregory Larkin, senior analyst at research firm Innovest Strategic Value Advisors. . . .

But some banks and credit-card companies may be exacerbating their problems. To boost profits and get ahead of coming regulation, they're hiking interest rates. But that's making it harder for consumers to keep up. . . . Sure

issuer bought by Bank of America in 2005, says her job was to develop a rapport with credit-card customers and advise them to use more of their available credit. Colleagues would often gather around her chair when she was on the phone with a customer and chant: "Sell, sell." "It was like *Boiler Room,*" says Colombo, referring to the 2000 movie about unscrupulous stock brokers. "I knew that they would probably be in debt for the rest of their lives." Unless, of course, they default.

Assume that you are member of Congress. What would you do in light of the facts in this case?

1. Create legislation that does not allow credit-card issuers to raise interest rates for those who cannot pay their bills.

McGraw-Hill *Connect Management*

Less Managing. More Teaching. Greater Learning.

McGraw-Hill *Connect Management* is an online assignment and assessment solution that connects students with the tools and resources they'll need to achieve success.

McGraw-Hill *Connect Management* helps prepare students for their future by enabling faster learning, more efficient studying, and higher retention of knowledge.

McGraw-Hill *Connect Management* Features

Connect Management offers a number of powerful tools and features to make managing assignments easier, so faculty can spend more time

teaching. With *Connect Management* students can engage with their coursework anytime and anywhere, making the learning process more accessible and efficient. *Connect Management* offers you the features described below.

Online interactives

Online Interactives are engaging tools that teach students to apply key concepts in practice. These Interactives provide them with immersive, experiential learning opportunities. Students will engage in a variety of interactive scenarios to deepen critical knowledge on key course topics. They receive immediate feedback at intermediate steps throughout each exercise, as well as comprehensive feedback at the end of the assignment. All Interactives are automatically scored and entered into the instructor gradebook.

Student progress tracking

Connect Management keeps instructors informed about how each student, section, and class is performing, allowing for more productive use of lecture and office hours. The progress-tracking function enables you to:

- View scored work immediately and track individual or group performance with assignment and grade reports.

- Access an instant view of student or class performance relative to learning objectives.

- Collect data and generate reports required by many accreditation organizations, such as AACSB.

Smart grading

When it comes to studying, time is precious. *Connect Management* helps students learn more efficiently by providing feedback and practice material when they need it, where they need it. When it comes to teaching, your time also is precious. The grading function enables you to:

- Have assignments scored automatically, giving students immediate feedback on their work and side-by-side comparisons with correct answers.

- Access and review each response; manually change grades or leave comments for students to review.

- Reinforce classroom concepts with practice tests and instant quizzes.

Simple assignment management

With *Connect Management* creating assignments is easier than ever, so you can spend more time teaching and less time managing. The assignment management function enables you to:

- Create and deliver assignments easily with selectable end-of-chapter questions and test bank items.
- Streamline lesson planning, student progress reporting, and assignment grading to make classroom management more efficient than ever.
- Go paperless with the eBook and online submission and grading of student assignments.

Instructor library

The *Connect Management* Instructor Library is your repository for additional resources to improve student engagement in and out of class. You can select and use any asset that enhances your lecture. The *Connect Management* Instructor Library includes:

- Instructor Manual
- PowerPoint files
- TestBank
- Management Asset Gallery
- eBook

Student study center

The *Connect Management* Student Study Center is the place for students to access additional resources. The Student Study Center

- Offers students quick access to lectures, practice materials, eBooks, and more.
- Provides instant practice material and study questions, easily accessible on the go.
- Gives students access to the Personalized Learning Plan described below.

Lecture capture via Tegrity Campus

Increase the attention paid to lecture discussion by decreasing the attention paid to note taking. For an additional charge Lecture Capture offers new ways for students to focus on the in-class discussion, knowing they can revisit important topics later. See below for further information

McGraw-Hill *Connect Plus Management*

McGraw-Hill reinvents the textbook learning experience for the modern student with *Connect Plus Management*. A seamless integration of an eBook and *Connect Management*, *Connect Plus Management* provides all of the *Connect Management* features plus the following:

- An integrated eBook, allowing for anytime, anywhere access to the textbook.
- Dynamic links between the problems or questions you assign to your students and the location in the eBook where that problem or question is covered.
- A powerful search function to pinpoint and connect key concepts in a snap.

In short, *Connect Management* offers you and your students powerful tools and features that optimize your time and energies, enabling you to focus on course content, teaching, and student learning. *Connect Management* also offers a wealth of content resources for both instructors and students. This state-of-the-art, thoroughly tested system supports you in preparing students for the world that awaits.

For more information about Connect, go to www.mcgrawhillconnect.com, or contact your local McGraw-Hill sales representative.

Tegrity Campus: Lectures 24/7

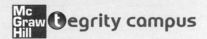

Tegrity Campus is a service that makes class time available 24/7 by automatically capturing every lecture in a searchable format for students to review when they study and complete assignments. With a simple one-click start-and-stop process, you capture all computer screens and corresponding audio. Students can replay any part of any class with easy-to-use browser-based viewing on a PC or Mac.

Educators know that the more students can see, hear, and experience class resources, the better they learn. In fact, studies prove it. With Tegrity Campus, students quickly recall key moments by using Tegrity Campus's unique search feature. This search helps students efficiently find what they need, when they need it, across an entire semester of class recordings. Help turn all your students' study time into learning moments immediately supported by your lecture.

Lecture Capture enables you to

- Record and distribute your lecture with a click of button.
- Record and index PowerPoint® presentations and anything shown on your computer so it is easily searchable, frame by frame.
- Offer access to lectures anytime and anywhere by computer, iPod, or mobile device.
- Increase intent listening and class participation by easing students' concerns about note taking. Lecture Capture will make it more likely you will see students' faces, not the tops of their heads.

To learn more about Tegrity watch a 2-minute Flash demo at http://tegritycampus.mhhe.com.

Assurance of Learning Ready

Many educational institutions today are focused on the notion of *assurance of learning,* an important element of some accreditation standards. *Organizational Behavior: Key Concepts, Skills & Best Practices* is designed specifically to support your assurance of learning initiatives with a simple, yet powerful solution.

Each test bank question for *Organizational Behavior: Key Concepts, Skills & Best Practices* maps to a specific chapter learning outcome/objective listed in the text. You can use our test bank software, EZ Test and EZ Test Online, or in *Connect Management* to easily query for learning outcomes/objectives that directly relate to the learning objectives for your course. You can then use the reporting features of EZ Test to aggregate student results in similar fashion, making the collection and presentation of assurance of learning data simple and easy.

AACSB Statement

The McGraw-Hill Companies is a proud corporate member of AACSB International. Understanding the importance and value of AACSB accreditation, *Organizational Behavior: Key Concepts, Skills & Best Practices, 5e* recognizes the curriculum guidelines detailed in the AACSB standards for business accreditation by connecting selected questions in the text and/or the test bank to the six general knowledge and skill guidelines in the AACSB standards.

The statements contained in *Organizational Behavior: Key Concepts, Skills & Best Practices, 5e* are provided only as a guide for the users of this textbook. The AACSB leaves content coverage and assessment within the purview of individual schools, the mission of the school, and the faculty. While *Organizational Behavior: Key Concepts, Skills & Best Practices, 5e* and the teaching package make no claim of any specific AACSB qualification or evaluation, we have within *Organizational Behavior: Key Concepts, Skills & Best Practices, 5e* labeled selected questions according to the six general knowledge and skills areas.

McGraw-Hill Customer Care Contact Information

At McGraw-Hill, we understand that getting the most from new technology can be challenging. That's why our services don't stop after you purchase our products. You can e-mail our product specialists 24 hours a day to get product training online. Or you can search our knowledge bank of frequently asked questions on our support website. For customer support, call **800-331-5094,** e-mail hmsupport@ mcgraw-hill.com, or visit www.mhhe .com/support. One of our technical support analysts will be able to assist you in a timely fashion.

McGraw-Hill Higher Education and Blackboard have teamed up. What does this mean for you?

1. **Your life, simplified.**   Now you and your students can access McGraw-Hill's Connect and Create right from within your Blackboard course—all with one single sign-on. Say goodbye to the days of logging in to multiple applications.

2. **Deep integration of content and tools.**   Not only do you get single sign-on with Connect and Create, you also get deep integration of McGraw-Hill content and content engines right in Blackboard. Whether you're choosing a book for your course or building Connect assignments, all the tools you need are right where you want them—inside of Blackboard.

3. **Seamless gradebooks.**   Are you tired of keeping multiple gradebooks and manually synchronizing grades into Blackboard? We thought so. When a student completes an integrated Connect assignment, the grade for that assignment automatically (and instantly) feeds your Blackboard grade center.

4. **A solution for everyone.** Whether your institution is already using Blackboard or you just want to try Blackboard on your own, we have a solution for you. McGraw-Hill and Blackboard can now offer you easy access to industry leading technology and content, whether your campus hosts it, or we do. Be sure to ask your local McGraw-Hill representative for details.

The **Best** of **Both** Worlds

Active Learning

Key Concepts, Skills & Best Practices

We have a love and passion for teaching organizational behavior in the classroom and via textbooks because it deals with the intriguing realities of working in modern organizations. Puzzling questions, insight, and surprises hide around every corner. Seeking useful insights about how and why people behave as they do in the workplace is a provocative, interesting and oftentimes fun activity. After all, to know more about organizational behavior is to know more about ourselves and life in general. We have designed this text to facilitate active learning by relying on the following tools throughout every chapter of the text:

> *"Students relate to this textbook... they thank me for choosing this book; they say it's a book they will hold onto for future use!"*
>
> —Kathleen M Foldvary, Harper College

Engage Students with Current, Relevant Cases

Brief real-world cases open every chapter with timely, relevant situations providing that needed hook to get students engaged into the chapter materials. The text's Instructor's Manual also features interpretations for each case.

> *"Excellent. These cases really seem to set the tone with relevant and interesting situations."*
>
> —Tom Myers, Champlain College

Skills and Practice

This text presents clear application of the theory presented throughout its carefully crafted narrative. Additionally, the boxed feature "Skills & Best Practices" delivers additional readings and practical application items that are designed to sharpen users' skills by either recommending how to apply a concept, theory, or model, or by giving an exemplary corporate application.

> *"Yes, it exceeds my expectations in this regard. Excellent job of linking concepts to practical application (a clear distinguishing factor of this text)."*
>
> —Karen S. Markel,
> Ph.D. SPHR
> Oakland University

SKILLS & BEST PRACTICES

Really?! I Decide How Many Hours I Work?

This title suggests employees have a choice. But most employers around the world tell employees when and how much they will work rather than ask. The Netherlands, however, provides an interesting alternative. Not only do 3 out of 4 Dutch women work part time, but many men work only four days a week. For example, Remco Vermaire is 37 and is the youngest partner at his law firm. His clients expect him to be available any minute of the day or night—*but only the four days a week that he works*. When he is "off the clock" they do not expect him to be available. This is in part because many of his clients work similarly flexible schedules. Moreover, 14 of the 33 attorneys at his firm work part time. This evidence suggests that the Dutch have particular norms related to work schedules. And as you learned in Chapter 2 norms are manifestations of a culture's underlying values.

The Dutch have managed to effectively blend traditional and modern values. While laws kept women out of the workplace for much of the 1900s, legislation in 2000 allowed all employees (men and women) to determine the number of hours they work. Employers can object if they have a compelling reason, but most challenges are not granted. Today most female-dominated jobs (e.g., nursing and education) are staffed via job sharing between two or more part-time employees. Of course, reduced schedules result in reduced income. The Dutch do not provide full-time pay for part-time work. Nevertheless, many working age people with and without kids would gladly trade money for more free time. A third of Dutch men either work part time or squeeze a full-time job into four days. More generally, 25% of workers in the Netherlands have reduced hours compared to only ten percent across the rest of Europe and the U.S.

While flexible schedules typically have been used to accommodate female employees, both in the Netherlands and elsewhere, Dutch companies now widely use flextime to attract and retain *both* male and

Personalize and Expand Key Concepts

Sixteen hands-on self-assessment exercises encourage active and thoughtful interaction rather than passive reading, and personalize the study experience for students while they evaluate their own skills, abilities, and interests in a variety of areas.

> *"Love these! They are one of the best elements of the K&K text. Students like them as well, and they like discussing their results."*
>
> —Mary Ellen Segraves, National-Louis University

HANDS-ON EXERCISE

Have You Been Adequately Socialized?

INSTRUCTIONS: Complete the following survey items by considering either your current job or one you held in the past. If you have never worked, identify a friend who is working and ask that individual to complete the questionnaire for his or her organization. Read each item and circle your response by using the rating scale shown below. Compute your total score by adding up your responses and compare it to the scoring norms.

	Strongly Disagree	Disagree	Neutral	Agree	Strongly Agree
1. I have been through a set of training experiences that are specifically designed to give newcomers a thorough knowledge of job-related skills.	1	2	3	4	5
2. This organization puts all newcomers through the same set of learning experiences.	1	2	3	4	5
3. I did not perform any of my normal job responsibilities until I was thoroughly familiar with departmental procedures and work methods.	1	2	3	4	5
4. There is a clear pattern in the way one role leads to another, or one job assignment leads to another, in this organization.	1	2	3	4	5
5. I can predict my future career path in this organization by observing other people's experiences.	1	2	3	4	5
6. Almost all of my colleagues have been supportive of me personally.	1	2	3	4	5
7. My colleagues have gone out of their way to help me adjust to this organization.	1	2	3	4	5

Ways of Building Your Human and Social Capital   TABLE 1–2

Types of Human Capital	Examples and Purposes
1. Training	Software certification to gain knowledge and skills to improve performance in current job
2. Work-based development opportunities	Job rotation (Chapter 6), shadowing, and cross-functional project teams (Chapter 9) to build your knowledge and your relationships
3. Learning activities outside of work	Fluency gained in a second language to increase opportunities within and outside of current employment
4. Career planning	Opportunities identified inside or outside of your current place of employment and assess your strengths and weaknesses
Types of Social Capital	**Examples and Purposes**
1. Internal	Mentoring relationship to provide guidance and opportunities (see Chapter 2)
	Membership in company softball team to build relationships outside of your work area
2. External	Conference attendance to meet people at other companies and learn of other job opportunities
	Join local, industry specific organizations to identify new customer (business development)

Effective Illustrations

Over 90% of the 32 instructors who reviewed this text rated the tables and graphs as *above average to excellent* in terms of their effectiveness to convey key concepts.

> *"Excellent use of tables and graphs. The graphs tend to be multi-dimensional (shadowing) and not boring, but very clear in the conveyance of important data. The cartoons were very funny and appropriate..."*
>
> —Tom Myers, Champlain College

> *"Wow! These are very well done; make for excellent slides and overall chapter discussions."*
>
> —Kathleen M Foldvary, Harper College

The Four Layers of Diversity   FIGURE 4–3

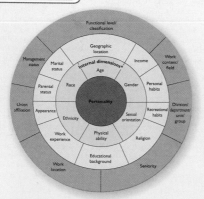

Imaginative Writing Style for Better Readability

> *"Very readable. Upbeat tone. A somewhat 'interactive style' (use of in-text questions to the reader)."*
> —Mary Ellen Segraves, National-Louis University

> *"I think that the readability of this book is excellent. Some of the examples are very rich, which gives the theory more grounding in reality."*
> —Daniel Morrell, Middle Tennessee State University

> *"Among the most readable texts on the market."*
> —Joseph C. Rode, Miami (OH) University

Up-to-Date Real-World Examples

Nothing brings material to life better than rich in-text examples featuring real companies, people, and situations. This text delivers the most current and pertinent examples of any text on the market today.

Contemporary Ethical Issues

Legal/Ethical Challenges at the end of every chapter raise contemporary issues, ask tough questions, and have corresponding interpretations in the Instructor's Manual.

> *"Thoughtfully engaged students in a more comprehensive dialogue of the issues than my text currently does surrounding ethical dilemmas."*
> —Karen S. Markel,
> Ph.D. SPHR
> Oakland University

> *"These were very good. Brief yet meaty."*
> —Daniel Morrell, Middle Tennessee State University

> *"Loved all of the situations in the chapters I reviewed."*
> —Janice S. Gates, Western Illinois University

Instructor & Student

Organizational Behavior 5e gives you all the support material you need for an enriched classroom experience.

Instructor's Resource Guide

The Instructor's Manual is a creative guide to understanding organizational behavior. It has been completely updated in order to save instructors time and support them in delivering the most effective course for their students. Each chapter includes a chapter summary, lecture outline, solution to the opening case, video resources, and much more. Each element will assist the instructor and students in maximizing the ideas, issues, concepts, and important organizational behavior approaches included in each chapter. We'd like to thank Mindy West of Arizona State University for helping us update our Instructor's Guide.

Computerized Test Bank

We've aligned our test bank with new AACSB guidelines, tagging each question according to its knowledge and skills areas. Categories include Communication, Ethics, Analytic, Technology, Diversity, and Reflective Thinking. Previous designations aligning questions with learning objectives, boxes, and features still exist as well, with over 1,200 questions from which to choose.

PowerPoint

A newly developed PowerPoint presentation created by Brad Cox of Midlands Tech allows for new functionality and variety in the classroom. With the inclusion of video usage suggestions and links to additional information, instructors have the availability to tailor their presentations to their class needs.

McGraw-Hill's Expanded Management Asset Gallery

McGraw-Hill/Irwin Management is excited to now provide a one-stop shop for our wealth of assets, making it quick and easy for instructors to locate specific materials to enhance their courses.

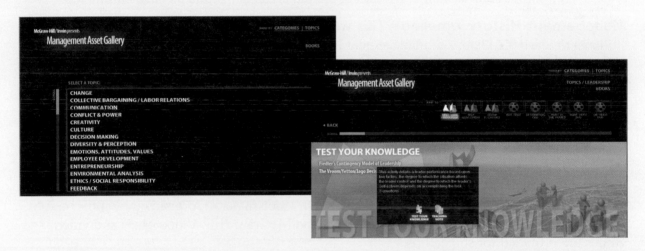

All of the following can be accessed within the Management Asset Gallery:

Manager's Hot Seat

This interactive, video-based application puts students in the manager's hot seat, builds critical thinking and decision making skills, and allows students to apply concepts to real managerial challenges. Students watch as 15 real managers apply their years of experience when confronting unscripted issues such as bullying in the workplace, cyber loafing, globalization, intergenerational work conflicts, workplace violence, and leadership versus management.

Self-Assessment Gallery   Unique among publisher-provided self assessments, our 23 self-assessments give students background information to ensure that they understand the purpose of the assessment. Students test their values, beliefs, skills, and interests in a wide variety of areas, allowing them to personally apply chapter content to their own lives and careers.

Every self-assessment is supported with PowerPoints and an instructor manual in the Management Asset Gallery, making it easy for the instructor to create an engaging classroom discussion surrounding the assessments.

Test Your Knowledge

To help reinforce students' understanding of key management concepts, Test Your Knowledge activities give students a review of the conceptual materials followed by application-based questions to work through. Students can choose practice mode, which gives them detailed feedback after each question, or test mode, which provides feedback after the entire test has been completed. Every Test Your Knowledge activity is supported by instructor notes in the Management Asset Gallery to make it easy for the instructor to create engaging classroom discussions surrounding the materials that students have completed.

Management History Timeline

This Web application allows instructors to present and students to learn the history of management in an engaging and interactive way. Management history is presented along an intuitive timeline that can be traveled through sequentially or by selected decade. With the click of a mouse, students learn the important dates, see the people who influenced the field, and understand the general management theories that have molded and shaped management as we know it today.

Video Library DVD

McGraw-Hill/Irwin offers the most comprehensive video support for the organizational behavior classroom through course library video DVDs. This discipline has library volume DVDs tailored to integrate and visually reinforce chapter concepts. The library volume DVD contains more than 40 clips! The rich video material, organized by topic, comes from sources such as PBS, NBC, BBC, SHRM, and McGraw-Hill. Video cases and video guides are provided for some clips.

Destination CEO Videos

Video clips featuring CEOs on a variety of topics. Accompanying each clip are multiple-choice questions and discussion questions to use in the classroom or assign as a quiz.

Online Learning Center (OLC)

www.mhhe.com/kinickiob5e

Find a variety of online teaching and learning tools that are designed to reinforce and build on the text content. Students will have direct access to the learning tools while instructor materials are password protected.

eBook Options

eBooks are an innovative way for students to save money and to "go green." McGraw-Hill's eBooks are typically 40% off the bookstore price. Students have the choice between an online and a downloadable CourseSmart eBook.

Through CourseSmart, students have the flexibility to access an exact replica of their textbook from any computer that has Internet service, without plug-ins or special software, via the online version, or to create a library of books on their hard drive via the downloadable version. Access to the CourseSmart eBooks lasts for one year.

Features   CourseSmart eBooks allow students to highlight, take notes, organize notes, and share the notes with other CourseSmart users. Students can also search for terms across all eBooks in their purchased CourseSmart library. CourseSmart eBooks can be printed (five pages at a time).

More info and purchase   Please visit www.coursesmart.com for more information and to purchase access to our eBooks. CourseSmart allows students to try one chapter of the eBook, free of charge, before purchase.

Create

Craft your teaching resources to match the way you teach! With McGraw-Hill Create, www.mcgrawhillcreate.com, you can easily rearrange chapters, combine material from other content sources, and quickly upload content you have written, like your course syllabus or teaching notes. Find the content you need in Create by searching through thousands of leading McGraw-Hill textbooks. Arrange your book to fit your teaching style. Create even allows you to personalize your book's appearance by selecting the cover and adding your name, school, and course information. Order a Create book and you'll receive a complimentary print review copy in three to five business days or a complimentary electronic review copy (eComp) via e-mail in about one hour. Go to www.mcgrawhillcreate.com today and register. Experience how McGraw-Hill Create empowers you to teach *your* students *your* way.

Grateful Appreciation

Our sincere thanks and gratitude go to our editor, Mike Ablassmier, and his first-rate team at McGraw-Hill/Irwin who encouraged and facilitated our pursuit of "something better." Key contributors include Kelly Pekelder, Developmental Editor; Anke Weekes, Marketing Manager; and Dana Pauley, Senior Project Manager. We would also like to thank Mindy West of Arizona State University for her work on the Instructor's Guide, Brad Cox of Midlands Tech for developing the PowerPoint presentation slides , and Floyd Ormsbee of Clarkson University for his work on Connect.

A special thank you also goes out to those colleagues who gave their comments and suggestions over the years to help us create all five editions. They are:

Abe Bakhsheshy
University of Utah

Jodi Barnes–Nelson
NC State-Raleigh

Joy Benson
University of Illinois–Springfield

Stephen C. Betts
William Paterson University

James Bishop
New Mexico State University

Linda Boozer
Suny AG & Tech College–Morrisville

Susan M. Bosco, Ph. D.
Roger Williams University Gabelli School of Business

Emilio Bruna
University of Texas at El Paso

Mark Butler
San Diego State University

Holly Buttner
University of North Carolina–Greensboro

John Byrne
St. Ambrose University

Diane Caggiano
Fitchburg State College

Dave Carmichel
Oklahoma City University

Xiao-Ping Chen
University of Washington

Jack Chirch
Hampton University

Bongsoon Cho
SUNY-Buffalo

Savannah Clay
Central Piedmont Community College

Ray Coye
DePaul University

Denise Daniels
Seattle Pacific University

Timothy Dunne
University of Missouri

Trudy F. Dunson
Gwinett Technical College

W. Gibb Dyer, Jr.
Brigham Young University

Dr. Jodie L. Ferise
University of Indianapolis School of Business

Mark Fichman
Carnegie Mellon University

Kathleen M. Foldvary
Harper College

David A. Foote
Middle Tennessee State University

Lucy Ford
Rutgers University

Thomas Gainey
State University of West Georgia

Janice S. Gates
Western Illinois University

Jacqueline Gilbert
Middle Tennessee State University

Leonard Glick
Northeastern University

Debi Griggs
Bellevue Community College

Barbara Hassell
IUPUI–Indianapolis

Hoyt Hayes
Columbia College–Columbia

Kim Hester
Arkansas State University

Chad Higgins
University of Washington

Kristin Holmberg-Wright
University of Wisconsin–Parkside

Kristine Hoover
Bowling Green State University

David Jalajas
Long Island University

Andrew Johnson
Bellevue Community College

C. Douglas Johnson
Georgia Gwinett College

Raymond Jones
University of Pittsburgh

Dong Jung
San Diego State University

Jordan Kaplan
Long Island University

John Keeling
Old Dominion University

Claire Killian
University of Wisconsin–River Falls

Howard J. Klein
The Ohio State University

Bobbie Knoblauch
Witchita State University

Todd Korol
Associate Professor Monroe Community College

Arlene S. Kreinik, Ph. D
Western Connecticut State University

Frances Kubicek
Kalamazoo Valley Community College

Gerald Levy
Franklin Career Institute

Karen S. Markel
Oakland University

Tom McDermott
Pittsburgh Technical Institute

Dr. Lisa D. McNary
North Carolina State University (College of Management)

Edward Miles
Georgia State University

Leann Mischel
Susquehanna University

Linda Morable
Richland College

Dan Morrell
Middle Tennessee State University

Tom Myers
Champlain College

Jay Nathan
St. John's University

Arlene J. Nicholas, Ph. D.
Salve Regina University

Joy Oguntebi
Rochester Institute of Technology

Regina Oneil
Suffolk University

Joseph Petrick
Wright State University

Dave Phillips
Purdue University–Westville

Christine Probett
San Diego State University

Amy Randel
Wake Forest University

Clint Relyea
Arkansas State University

Patricia Rice
Finger Lakes Community College

Joseph C. Rode
Miami (OH) University

Janet Romaine
St. Anselm College

Mary Ellen Seagraves
National-Louis University

Paula Silva
University of New Mexico

Randi Sims
Nova University

Peggy Takahashi
University of San Francisco

Jennie Carter Thomas
Belmont University

Susan C. Thompson
Champlain College

Tyra Townsend
University of Pittsburgh

Brian Usilaner
University of Maryland-University College

Matthew Valle
Elon University

Kostas Voustsas
Dickinson State University

Teresa A. Wagner
Miami University

Andrew Ward
Emory University

John Washbush
University of Wisconsin

John Watt
University of Central Arkansas

Judith U. Weisinger, Ph.D.
New Mexico State University

Ken Weidner
St. Josephs University

Scott Williams
Wright State University

Lynn Wilson
Saint Leo University

Finally, we would like to thank our wives, Joyce and Donna. Their love, support, and experience are instrumental to *everything* we do. They lift our tired spirits when needed and encourage and coach us at every turn.

This project has been a fun challenge from start to finish. Not only did we enjoy reading and learning more about the latest developments within the field of organizational behavior, but completion of this edition has deepened our friendship. We hope you enjoy this textbook. Best wishes for success and happiness!

Angelo & Mel

brief contents

contents

Part Three
Managing Group Level Factors and Social Processes   223

Chapter Nine
Effective Groups and Teams   224

Chapter Ten
Making Decisions   250

Chapter Eleven
Managing Conflict and Negotiating   284

Part Four
Managing for Organizational Effectiveness 361

part 1

Managing People Within the External and Organizational Context

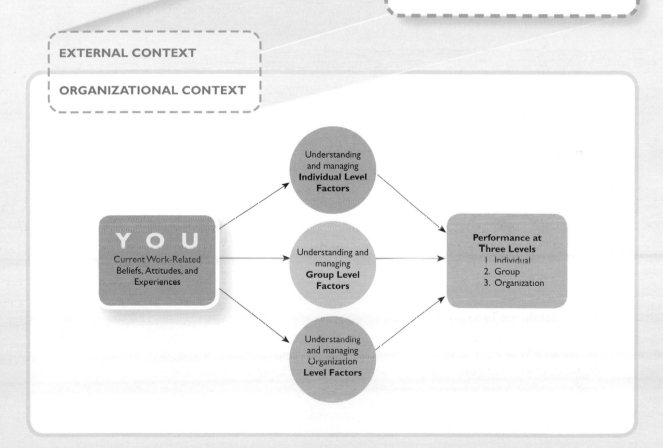

chapter 1

Needed: People-Centered Managers and Workplaces

After reading the material in this chapter, you should be able to:

LO1.1 Contrast McGregor's Theory X and Theory Y assumptions about employees.

LO1.2 Contrast human and social capital and describe three ways you can develop each.

LO1.3 Explain the impact of the positive psychology movement on the field of organizational behavior (OB).

LO1.4 Define the term *e-business,* and explain its implications for organizational behavior and managing people.

LO1.5 Describe the four levels of corporate social responsibility.

LO1.6 Explain at least three ways to improve an organization's ethical climate.

LEARNING OBJECTIVES

Why are Employees Leaving Google? What can Management do about It?

While many organizations recite a common mantra—"Our employees are our most valuable asset"— relatively few align their policies and practices with this statement. Nevertheless, employees are indeed the most valuable assets of many knowledge-based companies, whose value resides in the experience, skills, and abilities of their employees. Google, one of the hottest companies and most admired employers on the planet, is acutely aware of this fact. Google's talent (i.e., its employees) is largely responsible for the company's tremendous success to date and will largely determine the company's future success. It is no wonder then that many other companies are competing very intensely for Google's talent to drive their own growth and success.

"Google is fighting off Facebook and other fast-growing Internet companies that are approaching its staff, a reversal for a company that has long been one of Silicon Valley's hottest job destinations . . . Competition for experienced engineers . . . is especially strong as Web startups ramp up their hiring and poach from established companies like Google. Facebook and other startups have a recruiting tool that Google can no longer claim: They are private companies that haven't yet gone public, and they can lure workers with pre-IPO stock. Recruiters say Facebook and others also pay competitively, with average annual salaries for engineers typically starting at $120,000.

"'There's a huge shortage of engineers,' said Valerie Fredrickson, a recruiter in Silicon Valley. She said a recent client of hers who received a masters in engineering this spring from Stanford University got caught in a bidding war between Google, Facebook, and others. He got hired with a $125,000 salary, and is now being offered $175,000 by the companies that lost out initially. Facebook today (in late 2010) has about 1700 employees, up from 1000 a year ago. Twitter now has 300 employees, up from 99 a year ago. LinkedIn said it started the year with 450 employees and expects to end the year with 900. 'It definitely is a little easier for us right now, compared to a lot of companies' to recruit, said Colleen McCreary, the chief people officer of online gaming company Zynga Game Network. The San Francisco company said it began the year with 500 employees and now has 1250, including hires from large firms like Google and Microsoft.

"Much of the most recent hiring battles have centered on Facebook and Google. According to data from LinkedIn, 137 Facebook employees previously worked at Google. Among Google's recent departures to Facebook: Lars Rasmussen, cofounder

of Google Maps. Google Chrome architect Matthew Papakipos, Android senior product manager Eric Tseng, and top Google ad executive David Fischer also decamped to Facebook earlier this year.

"To help attract new recruits and preempt defections, Google's then-Chief Executive Officer Eric Schmidt wrote in an all hands e-mail, 'We want to continue to attract the best people to Google.' To be sure, Google is also on a hiring spree and increased its work force by 19%, or 3600 people, over the past year. To acquire some high-profile talent, Google has ramped up acquisitions of startups such as social app maker Slide Inc. And while Facebook is a huge draw now, it too has become too large for some employees who have left to start other projects.

"Hiring wars aren't uncommon in Silicon Valley, with mature tech companies long battling with

up-and-coming startups for workers. A few years ago, Google was snaring workers from Yahoo, Microsoft and others. Now, as Google's growth has slowed it is finding the tables have turned. 'Google isn't a hot place to work' and has 'become the safe place to work,' said Robert Green, who recruits engineers for startups such as Facebook.

"Google and Facebook's recruiting battles come as the two companies increasingly appear to be moving onto each other's turf. Among other things, Mr. Schmidt has spoken about adding social networking elements to Google's services. In recent days, the companies have engaged in a public war of words over data sharing practices. Google has complained that Facebook is engaging in 'data protectionism' by not allowing its users to export their friends' e-mail addresses to other websites, including Google's."[1]

HOW IMPORTANT ARE PEOPLE? Whether or not your own employers (past, present, and future) actually treat employees as valuable assets, part of the overarching mission of this book is to help you understand both *why* you should value employees and then *how* to actually do it. We contend that knowledge of organizational behavior is key to unlocking the true potential of employees and optimizing organizational performance. The chapter-opening case highlights that Google and other Internet companies understand the critical importance of employees and are betting their future success on the quality of their people.

The same is true of Southwest Airlines. As noted by Gary Kelly, the former accountant who is CEO of Southwest Airlines, "My top priority is, as it always has been at Southwest, our people." Kelly says, "If our employees love working at Southwest Airlines, everything else will fall into place."[2] Considering that Kelly has more than 35,000 employees at Southwest Airlines, he certainly has a full plate.[3]

A longer, research-based answer comes from Stanford's Jeffrey Pfeffer: "There is a substantial and rapidly expanding body of evidence, some of it quite methodologically sophisticated, that speaks to the strong connection between how firms manage their people and the economic results achieved."[4] His review of research from the United States and Germany show *people-centered practices* are strongly associated with higher profits and lower employee turnover. Seven people-centered practices in successful companies are:

1. Job security (eliminating fear of layoffs/job loss).
2. Careful hiring (emphasizing a good fit with the company culture).
3. Power to the people (via decentralization and self-managed teams).
4. Generous pay for performance.
5. Lots of training.
6. Less emphasis on status (to build a "we" feeling).
7. Trust building (through the sharing of critical information).[5]

For example, research shows that sharing information about the work group's and company's performance is associated with better financial performance, and a focus on teamwork, including training for team participation, is associated with quality improvements.[6] Importantly, the seven factors are a *package* deal, meaning they need to be utilized in a coordinated and systematic manner—not in bits and pieces.

Sadly, too many managers act counter to their declarations that people are their most important asset. Pfeffer blames a number of modern management trends and practices. One is the undue emphasis on short-term profits that preclude long-term efforts to nurture human resources. A second is excessive layoffs, when managers view people as a cost rather than as an asset, which erodes trust, commitment, and loyalty.[7] A recent survey of 42,000 people by Gallup researchers unfortunately supported Pfeffer's conclusions. Results revealed that only 33 percent of workers were engaged in their work, and a lack of engagement cost U.S. companies an estimated $350 billion a year.[8] Employee engagement is covered in detail in Chapter 6.

This lack of engagement among workers represents a tragic loss, both to society and to the global economy. We all need to accept the challenge to do better. *Fortune* magazine's annual list of "The 100 Best Companies to Work For" shows what is being done at progressive organizations that put people first. For example, SAS, a business software company in North Carolina, offers employees generous perks such as on-site medical and child care, a 66,000-square-foot-fitness center, and unlimited sick days, along with challenging and stimulating work.[9] Like SAS, many companies on *Fortune*'s "100 Best" list invest in their employees regardless of economic conditions and tend to outperform the competition in good times and bad.[10]

The mission of this book is to help increase the number of people-centered managers and organizations around the world. People-centered organizations are run by people-centered managers who utilize an organization's human, financial, technological, and other resources to compete effectively. This book introduces you to concepts and tools with which to fulfill this mission, starting in this chapter with a description of the evolution of organizational behavior (OB), including new directions in the field. This is followed by a discussion of the important topics of corporate social responsibility and ethics.

The Field of Organizational Behavior: Past and Present

Organizational behavior, **commonly referred to as OB, is an interdisciplinary field dedicated to better understanding and managing people at work.** By definition, organizational behavior is both research and application oriented. Three basic levels of analysis in OB are individual, group, and organizational. OB draws upon a diverse array of disciplines, including psychology, management, sociology, organization theory, social psychology, statistics, anthropology, general systems theory, economics, information technology, political science, vocational counseling, human stress management, psychometrics, ergonomics, decision theory, and ethics. This rich heritage has spawned many competing perspectives and theories about human behavior at work. We carefully chose some of the most useful, if not also most current, of these perspectives and included them in this book. Our choices are typically supported by research, which is presented throughout the book to help enhance your understanding and the applicability of the material.

Organizational behavior is an academic designation focused on managing people within and between individual, group, and organizational levels. Thus it is critical for success in any job and at any level. With the exception of teaching and/or research positions, OB is not an everyday job category, like those associated with functional disciplines (e.g., accounting, marketing, and finance). Students of OB typically do not get jobs in organizational behavior, per se. That said, your career success will be affected by your ability to apply OB theories and principles because they provide information needed to help you get along with and influence others.[11]

To better understand the field of OB, we describe its evolution and cover where it has been, where it is today, and some insights into where it appears to be headed. The following four topics provide an account of this evolution as well as valuable insights for understanding and managing people:

1. The human relations movement and the contingency approach.
2. The age of human and social capital.
3. The emerging field of positive organizational behavior.
4. The e-business revolution and implications for OB and managing people.

The Human Relations Movement

Prior to the 1930s, employees were largely viewed and treated simply as inputs into the production process. Then a unique combination of factors transpired that fostered the human relations movement. First, following legalization of union–management collective bargaining in the United States in 1935, management began looking for new ways to effectively deal with employees. Managers who had lost the battle to keep unions out of their factories heeded the call for better human relations and improved working conditions. Second, behavioral scientists conducting on-the-job research started calling for more attention to the "human" factor. One particular study, conducted at Western Electric's Chicago-area Hawthorne plant, was a prime stimulus for the human relations movement.

The Hawthorne Legacy   The essence of the Hawthorne studies was to manipulate a variety of workplace factors (e.g., lighting and temperature, rest breaks, length of work day, pay, and supervisory style) and measure the effects on worker performance. The host studies found varied effects on performance. However, many of the Hawthorne conclusions have turned out to be more myth than fact when reanalyzed with modern statistical techniques.[12] For instance, money, fear of unemployment during the Great Depression, managerial discipline, and high-quality raw materials—not supportive supervision—turned out to be responsible for high output in the relay assembly test room experiments.[13] Nonetheless, the Hawthorne studies and the larger human relations movement showed that data-driven research can guide managerial actions. Results also demonstrated that employee performance can be improved by attending to individual needs, supportive supervision, and group dynamics.[14] This trend persisted well into the 1950s and was spurred along by the work of Mayo and Follett.

These relay assembly test room employees in the classic Hawthorne Western Electric studies turned in record performance. Why? No one knows for certain, and debate continues today. Whatever the reason, Hawthorne gave the budding human relations movement needed research credibility.

The Writings of Mayo and Follett   Essential to the human relations movement were the writings of Elton Mayo and Mary Parker Follett. Australian-born Mayo, who headed the Harvard researchers at Hawthorne, advised managers to attend to employees' emotional needs in his 1933 classic, *The Human Problems of an Industrial Civilization.* Follett was a true pioneer, not only as a female management consultant in the male-dominated industrial world of the 1920s, but also as a writer who saw employees as complex bundles of attitudes, beliefs, and needs. Mary Parker Follett was way ahead of her time in telling managers to motivate job performance instead of merely demanding it, a "pull" rather than "push" strategy. She also built a logical bridge between political democracy and a cooperative spirit in the workplace.[15]

McGregor's Theory Y   In 1960, Douglas McGregor wrote a book entitled *The Human Side of Enterprise,* which has become an important philosophical base for the modern view of people at work.[16] Drawing upon his experience as a management consultant, McGregor formulated two sharply contrasting sets of assumptions about human nature (see Table 1–1). His Theory X assumptions were pessimistic and negative and, according to McGregor's interpretation, typical of how managers traditionally perceived employees. To help managers break with this negative tradition, McGregor formulated his ***Theory Y, a modern and positive set of assumptions about people at work.*** McGregor believed managers could accomplish more through others by viewing them as self-energized, committed, responsible, and creative beings. For example, a study of leaders in six top IT outsourcing firms showed

McGregor's Theory X and Theory Y   TABLE 1–1

Outdated (Theory X) Assumptions about People at Work	Modern (Theory Y) Assumptions about People at Work
1. Most people dislike work; they avoid it when they can.	1. Work is a natural activity, like play or rest.
2. Most people must be coerced and threatened with punishment before they will work. People require close direction when they are working.	2. People are capable of self-direction and self-control if they are committed to objectives.
3. Most people actually prefer to be directed. They tend to avoid responsibility and exhibit little ambition. They are interested only in security.	3. People generally become committed to organizational objectives if they are rewarded for doing so.
	4. The typical employee can learn to accept and seek responsibility.
	5. The typical member of the general population has imagination, ingenuity, and creativity.

SOURCE: Adapted from D McGregor, *The Human Side of Enterprise* (New York: McGraw-Hill, 1960), Ch 4.

that Theory Y behaviors positively influenced virtual team member trust, cooperation, and technology adaptation.[17]

A survey of 10,227 employees from many industries across the United States challenges managers to do a better job of acting on McGregor's Theory Y assumptions. From the employees' perspective, Theory X management practices are the major barrier to productivity improvement and employee well-being. The researcher concluded:

LO1.1

> The most noteworthy finding from our survey is that an overwhelming number of American workers—some 97%—desire work conditions known to facilitate high productivity. Workers uniformly reported—regardless of the type of organization, age, gender, pay schedule, or level in the organizational hierarchy—that they needed and wanted in their own workplaces the conditions for collaboration, commitment, and creativity research has demonstrated as necessary for both productivity and health. Just as noteworthy, however, is the finding that the actual conditions of work supplied by management are those conditions that research has identified as *competence suppressors*—procedures, policies, and practices that prevent or punish expressions of competence and most characterize unproductive organizations.[18]

The Contingency Approach to Management

The contingency approach grew from awareness that OB theories cannot be applied in all situations. The ***contingency approach* calls for using management concepts and techniques in a situationally appropriate manner, instead of trying to rely on "one best way."** In other words, don't use a hammer unless the job involves nails.

The contingency approach encourages managers to view organizational behavior within a situational context. According to this modern perspective, evolving situations, not hard-and-fast rules, determine when and where various management techniques are appropriate. Harvard's Clayton Christensen put it this way: "Many of the widely accepted principles of good management are only situationally appropriate."[19] For example, as will be discussed in Chapter 14, contingency researchers have determined that there is no single best style of leadership. Organizational behavior specialists embrace the contingency approach because it helps them realistically interrelate individuals, groups, and organizations. Moreover, the contingency approach sends a clear message to managers in today's global economy: Carefully read the situation and then apply lessons learned from published research studies,[20] observing role models, self-study and training, and personal experience in situationally appropriate ways.

New Directions in OB

Unfortunately, unsophisticated behavioral research methods caused the human relationists to embrace some naive and misleading conclusions. For example, human relationists believed in the axiom, "A satisfied employee is a hardworking employee." Subsequent research, as discussed later in this book, shows the satisfaction–performance linkage to be more complex than originally thought. Despite its shortcomings, however, the human relations movement opened the door to more progressive thinking about human nature and work. Rather than continuing to view employees as passive economic beings, managers began to see them as active social beings and took steps to create more humane work environments.[21] This evolution is reflected in the field of OB, which is a dynamic work in progress—not static and in its final form. As such, OB is being redirected and reshaped by various forces both inside and outside the discipline, including new concepts, models, and technology. In this section, we explore three general new directions for OB: human and social capital, positive organizational behavior, and the e-business implications for OB.

The Age of Human and Social Capital

Management is a lot like juggling: Everything is constantly in motion, with several things up in the air at any given time. Strategically speaking, managers juggle human, financial, material, informational, and technological resources. Each is vital to success in its own way. But jugglers remind us that some objects are rubber and some are glass. Dropped rubber objects bounce while dropped glass objects break. As more and more managers have come to realize, we cannot afford to drop the people factor (referred to in Figure 1–1 as human and social capital). Like other forms of capital (e.g., real estate, stock, facilities and equipment), both employees and their employers invest in human and social capital with the intention of reaping future returns or benefits. As we explain in the following sections, these forms of capital are useful ways of thinking about and describing employee *potential*.

What Is Human Capital? (Hint: Think BIG)   A team of human resource management authors recently offered this perspective:

"In the modern knowledge-based and service-oriented economy, the success of many firms has shifted from acquisition of tangible (physical) resources to the accumulation of intangible (human) resources."[22] ***Human capital* is the productive potential of an individual's knowledge and actions.**[23] *Potential* is the operative word in this intentionally broad definition. When you are hungry, money in your

pocket is good because it has the potential to buy a meal. Likewise, a present or future employee with the right combination of knowledge, skills, and motivation to excel represents human capital with the potential to give the organization a competitive advantage. For that reason, today's executives are very concerned about recruiting and retaining talented people, developing employees' skills, getting them fully engaged, and preparing for the day when valuable people retire or leave for another employer.[24] For example, Warren Buffett, the world-renowned investor and CEO of Berkshire Hathaway, appointed and began grooming 39 year old Todd Combs to succeed him as chief investment officer at the company. The succession plan at Berkshire, some argue, is among the most high profile in American business history due to the size and influence of the company (over $100 billion). Buffett clarified his intentions and explained his plans to split the CEO role into two positions that require different skills sets and experiences. Mr. Combs will "start small" and grow his responsibilities (e.g., the amount of Berkshire's money he invests), while Mr. Buffett continues to consider candidates to succeed him in the administrative component of his CEO role.[25]

Using Figure 1–1, describe how the types and nature of human capital required for the two roles—chief investment officer and chief administrative office—differ.

Todd Combs was chosen by legendary investor Warren Buffett to succeed him as chief investment officer at Berkshire Hathaway. What types of human and social capital will Mr Combs need to be effective in his new role?

As noted earlier, OB cuts across the individual, group, and organizational levels. This means that the value of each employee's individual human capital (e.g., knowledge, skills, and experience) accumulates to produce a company's overall human capital.[26]

What Is Social Capital?   Our focus now shifts from the individual to social units (e.g., friends, family, company, group or club, nation). Think *relationships*. **Social capital is productive potential resulting from strong relationships, goodwill, trust, and cooperative effort.**[27] Again, the word *potential* is key. Mary Meeker, for example, the former head of Morgan Stanley's global technology research and known as the "Queen of the Net" during the dot-com era of the 1990s, moved to Silicon Valley and joined a venture capital firm— Kleiner, Perkins, Caufield, & Beyers (KPCB). KPCB was an early investor in iconic Web companies such as Amazon, Google, Facebook, and Twitter. They presumably hired Meeker to utilize her extensive relationships both on Wall Street and in Silicon Valley to attract clients and money. Meeker's social capital turned out to be quite profitable because she worked with KPCB in the early 1990s to take Intuit public.[28] Saleforce.com, a customer relationship management software firm, is another good example of a company that leveraged the benefits of social capital: Forty percent of the past 1,000 employees hired were referrals of existing employees![29]

LO1.2   **How to Build Human and Social Capital**   The above discussion enables us to take the next step and provide suggestions on how to build these valuable assets. Human capital can be either *specific* to your current job (e.g., knowledge of your company's products or services) or more *generic* and serve you across jobs (e.g., Series 7 certification to sell financial products). Social capital can be either *internal* or *external* to your current organization (see Table 1–2).[30]

BACK TO THE CHAPTER-OPENING CASE

Question 1: Assume you are a Google employee. Describe what you would do to develop your internal social capital and your external social capital.

Question 2: Now, assume you will graduate from business school later this year and were fortunate enough to get a job interview with Google. Explain, in terms of human and social capital, how you would promote or sell yourself in that interview.

Both forms of capital are very important and are first and foremost the responsibility of successful employees. However, successful companies also value and invest in their employees' capital (see the Skills & Best Practices feature on page 12). The authors of this book therefore encourage you to take initiative—build your own human and social capital *and* look for employers that also will make such investments in you!

Many of the ideas discussed in this book relate directly or indirectly to building human and social capital, such as managing diversity (Chapter 2); self-efficacy and emotional intelligence (Chapter 5); goal setting (Chapter 7), positive reinforcement

Ways of Building Your Human and Social Capital   **TABLE 1–2**

Types of Human Capital	Examples and Purposes
1. Training	Software certification to gain knowledge and skills to improve performance in current job
2. Work-based development opportunities	Job rotation (Chapter 6), shadowing, and cross-functional project teams (Chapter 9) to build your knowledge and your relationships
3. Learning activities outside of work	Fluency gained in a second language to increase opportunities within and outside of current employment
4. Career planning	Opportunities identified inside or outside of your current place of employment and assess your strengths and weaknesses
Types of Social Capital	**Examples and Purposes**
1. Internal	Mentoring relationship to provide guidance and opportunities (see Chapter 2)
	Membership in company softball team to build relationships outside of your work area
2. External	Conference attendance to meet people at other companies and learn of other job opportunities
	Join local, industry-specific organizations to identify new customers (business development)

(Chapter 8); group development (Chapter 9); building trust and teamwork (Chapter 9); decision making and managing conflict (Chapters 10 and 11); communicating (Chapter 12); and leadership (Chapter 14). We challenge you to make these connections as you read this book and to identify additional ways to build your human and social capital.

The Emerging Area of Positive Organizational Behavior

OB draws heavily on the field of psychology. This often means that major shifts and trends in psychology eventually ripple through to OB. One such shift being felt in OB is the positive psychology movement. This exciting new direction promises to broaden the scope and practical relevance of OB.

Separating the Best from the Rest

The Great Recession of 2008–2010 presented companies across the globe with extreme challenges. Many didn't survive, but among those that did, some fared much better than others. Why? Geoff Colvin, an editor at *Fortune,* has a short answer—the winners invested in their people even in a down economy. This conclusion was drawn from a review of *Fortune*'s "Most Admired Companies" study conducted with the Hay Group. Their work revealed that the top three companies in any particular industry made consistent and significantly greater investments in their employees than did their competitors. Only 10% of these companies laid off employees versus 23% of their industry peers, and they were even less likely to have implemented pay or hiring freezes. They also were more likely to have explicit employee engagement and employer of choice programs. Put another way, these companies are more people-centered than their competition.

Colvin also takes aim at the common practice of treating employees as a cost. He explains that many managers cut jobs and/or employee-related benefits because they believe that Wall Street expects public companies to cut costs by reducing the head count when times are bad, and if they don't their company's stock will be punished. However, to counter this belief Colvin refers to other research that shows a *loss* in shareholder value for companies that reduce head counts for the reason of cutting costs versus those that don't.

The take away? The "Most Admired" companies put their money where their mouth is and invest in their most valuable asset—their people. These companies didn't wait for a recession to start investing in human capital, and they didn't stop such investments when the recession arrived. They instead continued to invest in their talent and reaped the rewards when the market was down, when many of their competitors were cutting "costly people." The lesson is that being people-centered and investing in human capital pays!

SOURCE: Based on G Colvin, "How Are Most Admired Companies Different? They Invest in People and Keep Them Employed— Even in a Downturn," *Fortune,* March 22, 2010, p. 82.

LO1.3   **The Positive Psychology Movement**   Much of psychology in the latter half of the 20th century was preoccupied with what was *wrong* with people! Following the traditional medical model, most researchers and practicing psychologists devoted their attention to diagnosing what was wrong with people and trying to make them better. OB research and practice often followed this same trend. However, an alternative approach gained attention at the beginning of the 21st century—positive psychology. This approach recommended focusing on human strengths and potential as a way to possibly *prevent* mental and behavioral problems and improve the general quality of life. A pair of positive psychologists described their new multilevel approach as follows:

> The field of positive psychology at the subjective level is about valued subjective experiences: well-being, contentment, and satisfaction (in the past); hope and optimism (for the future); and flow and happiness (in the present). At the individual level, it is about positive individual traits: the capacity for love and vocation, courage, interpersonal skill, aesthetic sensibility, perseverance, forgiveness, originality, future mindedness, spirituality, high talent, and wisdom. At the group level, it is about the civic virtues and the institutions that move individuals toward better citizenship: responsibility, nurturance, altruism, civility, moderation, tolerance, and work ethic.[31]

This is an extremely broad agenda for understanding and improving the human condition. However, we foresee a productive marriage between the concepts of human and social capital and the positive psychology movement, as it evolves into positive organizational behavior.

Positive Organizational Behavior: Definition and Key Dimensions

University of Nebraska OB scholar Fred Luthans defines *positive organizational behavior (POB)* as **"the study and application of positively oriented human resource strengths and psychological capacities that can be measured, developed, and effectively managed for performance improvement in today's workplace."**[32] His emphasis on the study and measurement (meaning a coherent body of theory and research evidence) clearly sets POB apart from the quick-and-easy self-improvement books commonly found on best-seller lists. POB also focuses positive psychology more narrowly on the workplace.

Luthans created the CHOSE acronym to identify five key dimensions of POB (see Table 1–3). Recent research shows that POB is positively associated with employee engagement, organizational commitment, job satisfaction, performance, well-being, and customer satisfaction.[33] Progressive managers already know the value of a positive workplace atmosphere, as evidenced by the following situations. Larsen & Tourbo, India's largest engineering company, used positive organizational behavior to develop the human capital of its employees. The company found itself needing more skilled employees to improve performance despite the large Indian population. The company operates construction schools around the country to educate and more fully realize the potential of its employees to meet this challenge.[34] This illustrates the belief that (unskilled) employees have aspirations and potential beyond their current roles, and that the company can benefit from developing them more fully.

Luthans's CHOSE Model of Key POB Dimensions   TABLE 1–3
(with cross-references to related topics in this textbook)

Confidence/self-efficacy: One's belief (confidence) in being able to successfully execute a specific task in a given context. (See Chapter 5.)

Hope: One who sets goals, figures out how to achieve them (identify pathways) and is self-motivated to accomplish them, that is, willpower and "waypower." (See Chapters 5 and 7.)

Optimism: Positive outcome expectancy and/or a positive causal attribution, but is still emotional and linked with happiness, perseverance, and success. (See Chapters 4, 5, 7, and 16.)

Subjective well-being: Beyond the emotion of happiness, how people cognitively process and evaluate their lives, in other words, the satisfaction with their lives. (See Chapters 4, 5, and 6.)

Emotional intelligence: Capacity for recognizing and managing one's own and others' emotions—self-awareness, self-motivation, being empathetic, and having social skills. (See Chapters 5, 9, 11, 12, 13, and 14.)

SOURCE: From F Luthans, "Positive Organizational Behavior: Developing and Managing Psychological Strengths," *Academy of Management Executive*, Feb. 2002, Vol. 16, No. 1, pp. 57–72. Copyright © 2002 with permission of Academy of Management via Copyright Clearance Center.

Larsen & Tourbo, a leading Indian engineering and construction company, provides schooling for its employees at many of its worksites. Bringing education to its employees not only illustrates that the company values its employees, but it also helps overcome the company's talent shortage.

The U.S. Air Force represents another good example. The Grand Forks base in North Dakota was in steep decline and its survival was uncertain. Instead of asserting more control and clamping down, leaders responded in a nontraditional fashion by implementing tools from positive psychology. The basis of their efforts was what they termed "the 5Cs": caring, connecting, committing, communicating, and celebrating. Such positively oriented efforts resulted in a dramatic turnaround in morale and performance, which leaders attributed to investing "as much in their psychological and emotional balance sheet as they do in their financial balance sheet."[35]

E-Business and Implications for OB and Managing People

Experts on the subject draw an important distinction between *e-commerce* (buying and selling goods and services over the Internet) and *e-business,* **using information communication technologies to facilitate every aspect of running a business.**[36] Today's companies are using Internet technologies to connect with employees, customers, suppliers, and other stakeholders both within and outside the organization and around the globe. Such intensive connectedness has many implications for employees and employers alike.[37] Employers are able to access markets for their products and services much more easily and efficiently and over greater distances than they did historically. Technology allows companies to have a "virtual presence" in many markets, versus a more conventional physical presence that requires offices and people. As a result, local companies often can compete nationally and internationally. Likewise, small companies can more easily compete by using software for accounting, inventory, and other important systems that give them capabilities typically available only to large companies. That means you don't necessarily have to be an industry giant to compete. For example, in early 2011 Microsoft, a perennial global juggernaut in technology, had over 88,000 employees, compared to Google with 23,000, Facebook 1,700, Zynga 1,250, and Twitter with just 300.[38] Technology has fostered many such "David versus Goliath" battles in business. Similarly dramatic implications exist for employees.

To meet their job responsibilities, employees are increasingly required to collaborate with a larger number of people inside and outside their employing organization. This scenario requires employees to influence a growing number of people over whom they have no direct authority. (Authority and other forms of power and influence are discussed in detail in Chapter 13.) Employees also use technology to expand and cultivate their social capital via professional networking sites such as LinkedIn that currently connects more than 85 million professionals globally.[39] As discussed earlier, building social capital has many benefits, such as enabling individuals to perform their current jobs better and to access future job opportunities. More generally, many jobs have fundamentally transformed in terms of how, when, and where people work. We discuss just of few of these profound changes in the following section and many more throughout the book, particularly in Chapter 12.

The Time and Location of Work   Technology allows employees to do their jobs from any location at any time. The 24/7, everywhere connectivity means that many employers no longer have dedicated office space for large percentages of their employees. IBM, for instance, estimates that approximately 40% of its employees either telecommute from home or from a client's worksite.[40] A similar scenario exists at Sabre Holdings, a worldwide travel service provider. A large percentage of its employees telecommute and/or have flexible work schedules. When employees in these companies do go to the (local) office they simply share common space with other similarly "officeless" colleagues. The people at Sabre refer to this as "hotelling,"[41] in that space does not belong to one person but is instead used temporarily, as needed, by many employees. Scenarios such as these require today's managers to select workers who have the self-discipline to work under such conditions, as well as to measure performance when they cannot directly observe their workers much of the time.

This situation potentially raises other challenges. Concern is growing that linking to the office everywhere and anytime means that workers cannot or will not ever disconnect. Managers have to be sure their people don't succumb to stress and exhaustion from being constantly tethered to their jobs. A very interesting study of more than 20,000 IBM employees in 75 countries found that office-based workers reported work-family conflicts after an average of 38 hours of work per week, in contrast to telecommuters who reported such conflicts after 57 hours. This means telecommuters work on average 19 more hours per week before noting work-family conflicts![42] What implications does this have for employees? Employers?

Technology also allows us to seemingly defy the laws of physics by being in more than one place at a time. For example, consider the futuristic situation at Hackensack University Medical Center in New Jersey:

> Doctors can tap an interval Web site to examine X-rays from a PC anywhere. Patients can use 37-inch plasma TVs in their rooms to surf the Net for information about their medical conditions. There's even a life-size robot, Mr Rounder, that doctors can control from their laptops at home. They direct the digital doc, complete with white lab coat and stethoscope, into hospital rooms and use two-way video to discuss patients' conditions.[43]

In short, organizational life will never be the same because of e-mail, e-learning, e-management, e-leadership, virtual teams, and virtual organizations.[44] You will learn more about virtual teams, virtual leadership, and virtual organizations in later chapters.

The Promise and Limits of Collaboration   Many organizations are opening their traditional walls and boundaries and collaborating with outsiders to improve their problem-solving and innovation capabilities. For example, Procter and Gamble (P&G) implemented a program—Connect and Develop (C + D)—with a goal to generate 50% of the company's innovation through external collaboration partnerships. P&G's CEO, Bob McDonald, said that since it began in 2001, "Connect and Develop has created a culture of open innovation that has already generated sustainable growth; but we know we can do more. . . . We want the best minds in the world to work with us to create big ideas that can touch and improve the lives of more consumers, in more parts of the world, more completely." [45] Such open innovation would not be possible without technology. Now P&G must effectively manage these partnerships. Among the challenges is allocating resources and rewards in ways that motivate performance and are perceived as fair by both P&G employees and their external partners (fairness is addressed in detail in Chapter 7 and performance management more generally in Chapter 8).

As in the P&G example, such changes have the potential to revolutionize many aspects of organizational life and change how business is conducted. On the one hand, it is easy to appreciate the benefits of collaborating with others if they help solve your problems (e.g., utilize customer data more effectively) or innovate (e.g., bring a new product to market). However, sharing and collaboration has limits or boundaries. Both employers and employees are reluctant to give away their "secrets" in the spirit or process of collaboration. China and other countries often require foreign companies to transfer technology to the host country in exchange for access to their markets. Both General Electric (GE) and General Motors (GM), for instance, recently signed major deals with Chinese companies. The American companies get access to the booming aviation and auto industries in China, and in exchange they need to move production and development activities to China. Despite the growth expectations from such collaboration, GE and GM executives are concerned that their Chinese partners will eventually become their competitors: Collaboration will give their partners access to their technology and other capabilities which they will use to their sole benefit in the future.[46] Thus, the promise/benefit of collaboration is clear, but with limits. The *question becomes not only what to share but how much and with whom.*

These are important considerations. The answers can determine how effectively individuals and organizations compete in the future. Jeanne Meister and Karie Willyerd, authors of *The 2020 Workplace,* contend that the key for individual and organizational success in the future is to be active, sharing members of communities, collections of people with valuable resources that are shared for each member's benefit.[47] See the Skills & Best Practices feature on page 17 for an interesting example. Before reading it, however, ask yourself: Would you be comfortable sharing all of your work—your best ideas *and* your failures? Why or why not? If you are willing to share your successes and failures, then with whom—peers, supervisors, competitors? Defend your answers.

LO1.4 **Changing Entire Industries** A less obvious but far-reaching example of e-business is found in the stock exchanges of the world. Historically, the vast majority of stock trades were conducted face to face by traders yelling on the floor of exchanges, such as the New York Stock Exchange (NYSE) and the Chicago Mercantile Exchange (CME). Now, however, large proportions or even all trades on most exchanges around the globe are made computer to computer, on servers in large warehouses located remotely to the physical exchanges. Just a few years ago nearly 70 percent of NYSE-listed stocks traded at the exchange; in 2011 less than 40 percent do.[48] Computer programs now execute trades, not people. This dramatic change accordingly requires people to play different roles and to possess different personalities and skill sets (discussed in Chapter 5). In the past, traders needed to be aggressive, effective communicators, quick thinkers, and decisive decision makers (covered in Chapter 10) to respond in real time on the floor of the exchanges. Today, however, many of the people central to trading never visit the floor of the exchange or are ever face to face with clients. They instead sit behind a computer somewhere outside the exchange,

Collaborating for a Cure

Employees from the National Institutes of Health, the Food and Drug Administration, pharmaceutical and medical device companies, nonprofit groups, and universities have collaborated to identify markers in the human brain related to the progress of Alzheimer's disease. This is a noble pursuit with potentially enormous implications; it also epitomizes the power of information communication technology, collaboration, and its effect on business and managing people. These various groups not only raise money for the cause, but they also agreed to share all other resources. For instance, to achieve their ambitious objectives they are sharing patients because no single organization has enough. Moreover, and in stark contrast to the past, the collaborators agreed that no one owns the data or can submit patent applications. Instead, all of the various parties will "share all the data, making every single finding public immediately, available to anyone with a computer anywhere in the world." This means that all techniques and results, positive and negative, are shared in real time. Such practices can greatly increase efficiency and accelerate successes (important OB outcomes sought by managers in most every industry). Scientists involved can learn from others' mistakes, not duplicate them, and devote their resources to more promising alternatives. Similar benefits could likely be achieved by applying these same practices in other industries to other objectives. Companies could build on others' successes and without having to "discover" them on their own. They wouldn't have to make the same mistakes either.

Extreme connectedness and collaboration, such as this, has significant implications for how people work and how they are managed. First, workers will likely need different skill sets and/or be willing to change. Managers in companies using open innovation need to select researchers that are willing and able to collaborate in this type of arrangement. Second, in the example above, the many scientists and businesspeople involved need to park their "egos and intellectual-property noses outside the door." This means that credit for achievement would be assigned very differently than in the past. Instead of a single scientist, single lab, or single company benefiting, credit would go to the team. How would you feel about this?

From a management perspective, how can performance be monitored and rewarded? Money, like other valuable resources (people and time), is limited. How can it be allocated within and across such a large, diverse web of contributors? Answering these questions is key to realizing the tremendous potential that super-scale collaboration can bring to bear on problem solving and innovation. Doing so allows individuals and companies to draw on the very best talent and ideas, regardless of whether they reside within or outside their own organization.

SOURCE: Based on G Kolata, "Sharing of Data Leads to Progress on Alzheimer's Disease," *The New York Times,* August 12, 2010.

conducting analyses, building models, and writing programs to execute trades automatically depending on a host of market variables. Thus, instead of success being determined by the wisdom shown on the trading floor, success is now determined by the effectiveness of a broker's analytic skills and the company's technology.

How do you think it is different managing "old-school" traders, those yelling and selling on the floor of the exchange, versus contemporary, analytical, computer-driven traders, who crunch numbers and create computer models and programs?

Web 2.0 Requires Management 2.0 The e-revolution has caused immense and permanent workplace changes. Teams and virtual networks are pushing aside the individual as the primary building block of organizations.[49] Command-and-control management has given way to participative management and empowerment.[50] Ego-centered leaders are being replaced by customer-centered leaders. Technology enables employees to exert more control over the information they send and receive: writing blogs, building relationships on social networking sites, and contributing to user-created projects like Wikipedia. This active involvement, relying heavily on user-created content, has come to be called *Web 2.0.* And now many employees are expecting to share information just as freely at work.

As a result, predicts Gary Hamel in *The Future of Management,* "Management 2.0 is going to look a lot like Web 2.0." He means managers of the future won't control the flow of information; instead, they will be expected to provide the means for employees to collaborate and share information with each other to achieve common goals. Ideally, this collaboration will bring the best ideas to the surface. The effective application of information technology can determine how well individuals and organizations compete. However, to guard against potential negative consequences—revealing trade secrets, exposing proprietary information, creating liabilities—companies and their managers need to formulate, communicate, and enforce information communication technology policies, not only for employer-owned technology but also for the employee's own equipment (e.g., smartphones).[51] As a manager, what would you do to address these challenges?

connect
www.mcgrawhillconnect.com

Go to Connect for an interactive exercise to check your knowledge on the history of OB.

Implications for OB   In *The 2020 Workplace,* Meister and Willyerd accurately summarize the OB implications of the e-business phenomenon in the following quote:

> Effective organizations in the 2020 workplace will provide "an intensely personalized, social experience to attract, develop, and engage employees across all generations and geographies. The organizations that create a competitive advantage in the 2020 workplace will do so by instituting innovative human resource practices—by first defining an authentic core set of organizational values and then augmenting these by leveraging the latest tools of the social Web to reimagine learning and development, talent management, and leadership practices."[52]

In summary, e-business and information communication technology have far-reaching effects on many OB topics discussed in this book. Look for these links as you work your way through this book.

The Ethics Challenge

connect
www.mcgrawhillconnect.com

Go to Connect for a self-assessment to determine how effective you are at ethical decision making.

Ethics **involves the study of moral issues and choices.** It is concerned with right versus wrong, good versus bad, and the many shades of gray in-between supposedly black-and-white issues. Despite the highly publicized criminal acts of now-jailed executives from the likes of Enron, Tyco, and WorldCom in the early 2000s, business ethics continue to hit new lows. This is evidenced by the imprisonment of $50 billion Ponzi schemer Bernard Madoff in 2009,[53] the ouster of Hewlett Packard's CEO Mark Hurd for an expense account scandal, and the public outrage over the (in)actions of Goldman Sachs's Lloyd Blankfein, BP's Tony Hayward, and Toyota's Akio Toyota.[54] These sad accounts highlight the need for *everyone* to join in the effort to stem this tide of unethical conduct. Research shows that "sustainable businesses are led by CEOs who take a people-centered, inclusive approach rather than a controlling, target-driven one. They are people who listen, who foster cultures in which employees are not scared to point out problems and in which staff feel they have a personal responsibility to enact corporate values, be they health and safety concerns or putting the client's interests first."[55]

Moral implications spring from virtually every decision, both on and off the job. Managers are challenged to have more imagination and the courage to do the right thing to make the world a better place. Throughout this book we will explore many of the things noted that individuals, managers, and their employing organizations can bring to bear on ethical behaviors at work, such as values and culture (Chapter 2), individual differences (Chapter 5), rewards (Chapter 8), power and influence (Chapter 13), and leadership (Chapter 14). In the process, you will learn that knowledge of OB provides numerous tools with which to better understand and manage ethical behavior at work.

To enhance your understanding of ethics within an OB context, we discuss (1) corporate social responsibility, (2) the erosion of morality, (3) seven general moral principles for managers, (4) how to improve an organization's ethical climate, and (5) a personal call to action.

A Model of Global Corporate Social Responsibility and Ethics

Corporate social responsibility (CSR) **means that corporations have obligations to others, beyond shareholders and beyond the bounds of law or contract.** CSR challenges businesses to go above and beyond just making a profit to serve the interests and needs of "stakeholders," including past and present employees, customers, suppliers, and the communities and countries in which the facilities are located. A good deal of controversy surrounds the drive for greater CSR because classical economic theory says businesses are responsible for producing goods and services to make profits, not solving the world's social, political, and environmental ills.[56] What is your opinion?

University of Georgia business ethics scholar Archie B. Carroll created a model of CSR/business ethics with the global economy and multinational corporations in mind. This model is very timely because it effectively triangulates three major trends: (1) economic globalization, (2) expanding CSR expectations, and (3) the call for improved business ethics. Carroll's model has four levels in order of increasing responsibility. Responsible organizations:

🍂**LO1.5**

Level 1–*Make a profit* consistent with expectations for international businesses to fulfill *economic responsibility.*

Level 2–*Obey the law* of host countries as well as international law to fulfill *legal responsibility.*

Level 3–*Are ethical in their practices,* taking host-country and global standards into consideration to fulfill *ethical responsibility.*

Level 4–*Are good corporate citizens,* especially as defined by the host country's expectations to fulfill *philanthropic responsibility.*[57]

BACK TO THE CHAPTER-OPENING CASE   Go to Google's corporate website at http://www.google.com/intl/en/corporate/tenthings.html and do two things:

First, describe the company's philosophy in terms of the four levels of CSR described by Carroll.

Second, assume you are a manager responsible for hiring at Google. Describe how you could use Google's approach to CSR to both attract new talent and retain existing talent.

By transforming its business practices to embrace global corporate social responsibility standards, Nike has improved its image. Does a responsible corporate reputation influence your buying decisions?

Carroll further emphasizes that each level needs to be solid. A pick-and-choose approach to CSR is inappropriate. The top level reflects "global society's expectations that business will engage in social activities that are not mandated by law nor generally expected of business in an ethical sense."[58] The spirit of Carroll's model is evident in Nike's ongoing quest to shake its sweatshop image. In the 1990s the company was charged with operating sweatshops to manufacture its shoes and clothes. From this the company learned that social responsibility needs to be more than simply a PR tool, and instead it needs to pervade policies and practices that apply to its more than 800,000 workers in 52 countries involved in the company's supply chain.[59] The company has since taken numerous actions to improve its CSR and is now seen as a leader in sustainable business practices. The company's philosophy has transformed from viewing social responsibility as a compliance or risk reduction endeavor to one of an opportunity for innovation. The company now weaves sustainability and responsibility throughout its culture, leadership, and organizational design, which is discussed in Chapter 15.[60]

An Erosion of Morality?

David Callahan, in his book *The Cheating Culture: Why More Americans Are Doing Wrong to Get Ahead,* paints this disturbing picture of modern society:

[T]he character of Americans has changed. Those values associated with the market hold sway in their most caricatured form: individualism and self-reliance have morphed into selfishness and self-absorption; competitiveness has become social Darwinism; desire for the good life has turned into materialism; aspiration has become envy. There is a growing gap between the life that many Americans want and the life they can afford—a problem that bedevils even those who would seem to have everything. Other values in our culture have been sidelined; belief in community, social responsibility, compassion for the less able or less fortunate.[61]

Does this portrayal of a "cheating culture" have merit and, if so, to what extent? Let us examine the OB research evidence for relevant insights.

Taking Local Norms and Conduct into Consideration   National culture, as we will discuss in Chapter 3, affects how people think and act about everything, including ethical issues. This reality was supported in a multination study (including the United States, Great Britain, France, Germany, Spain, Switzerland, India, China, and Australia) of management ethics. Managers from each country were asked to judge the ethicality of 12 questionable behaviors, including such things as giving and accepting gifts, passing blame, sharing confidential information, and concealing errors. Results revealed significant differences across the 10 nations in the study. That is, managers in some countries approved of practices that were frowned upon in other countries.[62] Consequently, care needs to be taken when extrapolating Callahan's characterization of American morality to other cultures. Each culture requires its own ethical analysis, taking local norms into consideration.

Ethical Lapses in the Workplace   Unethical behavior occurs at all organizational levels, although recent research indicates that senior executives tend to have significantly more positive perceptions of ethics in their organizations than do lower-level employees.[63] Perhaps that is because lower-level employees regularly witness common ethical lapses such as lying about being sick, fudging a report, bullying and sexual harassment, personal use of company equipment, and stealing company property or funds. Executives are not immune to being victims of unethical conduct, however. For example, a survey of job applicants for executive positions indicated that 64% had been misinformed about the financial condition of potential employers, and 58% of these individuals were negatively affected by the misinformation.[64] It is very likely that some of those affected individuals moved their families and left their friends only to discover the promise of a great job in a financially stable organization was a lie. (Of course, you don't need to be an executive to suffer similar consequences! Have you ever been "sold" a job?) Job applicants, for their part, also have ethical lapses. An analysis of 2.6 million background checks by ADP Screening and Selection Services revealed that "44% of applicants lied about their work histories, 41% lied about their education, and 23% falsified credentials or licenses."[65] OB can help us understand some of the causes of unethical behavior.

Intense Pressure for Results Starts Early   Pressure to perform is common in the workplace and has many sources. Perhaps most common is an individual's own desire to "look good" for their bosses, which has been identified in volumes of research as a cause of unethical behavior in lower- and mid-level employees and managers. No surprise, the pressure for results intensifies when individuals are rewarded for accomplishing their goals.[66] Other common sources of pressure are presented by Bennett Tepper, a notable researcher of undesirable work behaviors. He describes how managers pressure unethical behavior due to their own motivations to perform, perceptions that such behaviors are actually acceptable or that no consequences will occur, reward systems that incentivize unethical behaviors, and/or the physical environment facilitates such actions.[67] By fostering a pressure-cooker atmosphere for results, managers can unwittingly set the stage for unethical shortcuts by employees who seek to please and be loyal to the company.

Unfortunately, the seeds of this problem are planted early in life. A survey of 787 youngsters ages 13 to 18 found "that 44% of teens feel they're under strong pressure to succeed in school, no matter the cost. Of those, 81% believe the pressure will be the same or worse in the workplace."[68] Anonymous surveys by the Josephson Institute of almost 30,000 students from private and public high schools across the United States found 60% admittedly had cheated on a test in 2006 and 64% in 2008. Thirty-six percent reportedly had plagiarized via the Internet in 2008, up from 33% in 2006. According to the 2008 survey: "Students attending non-religious independent schools reported the lowest cheating rate (47 percent) while 63 percent of students from religious schools cheated."[69]

What can you do about questionable or unethical conduct? See the Skills & Best Practices feature on page 23 for some suggestions.

In summary, Callahan's earlier characterization of America's cheating culture is an appropriate wake up call. The challenge to improve is immense because unethical behavior is pervasive.

General Moral Principles

Management consultant and writer Kent Hodgson offers seven moral principles—"the magnificent seven"—to guide managers, and employees more generally, toward ethical work behavior (see Table 1–4). He argues that there are no absolute ethical answers for decision makers. Hodgson instead recommends that managers strive to make their actions *principled, appropriate,* and *defensible.*[70]

TABLE 1–4   The Magnificent Seven: General Moral Principles for Managers

1. *Dignity of human life: The lives of people are to be respected.* Human beings, by the fact of their existence, have value and dignity. We may not act in ways that directly intend to harm or kill an innocent person. Human beings have a right to live; we have an obligation to respect that right to life. Human life is to be preserved and treated as sacred.

2. *Autonomy: All persons are intrinsically valuable and have the right to self-determination.* We should act in ways that demonstrate each person's worth, dignity, and right to free choice. We have a right to act in ways that assert our own worth and legitimate needs. We should not use others as mere "things" or only as means to an end. Each person has an equal right to basic human liberty, compatible with a similar liberty for others.

3. *Honesty: The truth should be told to those who have a right to know it.* Honesty is also known as integrity, truth telling, and honor. One should speak and act so as to reflect the reality of the situation. Speaking and acting should mirror the way things really are. There are times when others have the right to hear the truth from us; there are times when they do not.

4. *Loyalty: Promises, contracts, and commitments should be honored.* Loyalty includes fidelity, promise keeping, keeping the public trust, good citizenship, excellence in quality of work, reliability, commitment, and honoring just laws, rules, and policies.

5. *Fairness: People should be treated justly.* One has the right to be treated fairly, impartially, and equitably. One has the obligation to treat others fairly and justly. All have the right to the necessities of life—especially those in deep need and the helpless. Justice includes equal, impartial, unbiased treatment. Fairness tolerates diversity and accepts differences in people and their ideas.

6. *Humaneness:* There are two parts: (1) *Our actions ought to accomplish good,* and (2) *we should avoid doing evil.* We should do good to others and to ourselves. We should have concern for the well-being of others; usually, we show this concern in the form of compassion, giving, kindness, serving, and caring.

7. *The common good: Actions should accomplish the "greatest good for the greatest number" of people.* One should act and speak in ways that benefit the welfare of the largest number of people, while trying to protect the rights of individuals.

SOURCE: *From Kent Hodgson, A Rock and a Hard Place: How to Make Ethical Business Decisions When the Choices Are Tough, 1992, American Management Association. Reprinted with permission of the author.*

Confronting Questionable Conduct at Work

Most of us have or will likely witness either questionable or even blatantly unethical conduct at work. Many excuses also are provided for not confronting these actions, such as: this is common practice, the incident is minor, it's not my responsibility to confront such issues, and loyal workers don't confront. While such reasons or rationalizations for not confronting unethical conduct are common, they are nevertheless excuses which can be consequential for individuals, groups, and organizations. What can you do? Below are a few suggestions:

1. **It's Business, Treat It That Way.** Ethical issues are business issues, just like costs, revenues, and employee development. Therefore, collect data and present a convincing case against the unethical conduct just as you would to develop a new product.
2. **Accept that Confronting Ethical Concerns Is Part of YOUR Job.** Whether it is explicit in your job description or not, ethics is everybody's job. If you think something is questionable then take action.
3. **You Are Who You Are.** Approach people and ethical issues in the same way you approach other matters. If you're direct, then be direct. If you're more deliberate and subtle, then approach ethical issues in the same manner. Be yourself but be sure to do something.
4. **Challenge the Rationale.** Many issues occur despite actual policy against it. If this is the case, then ask: "If what you did is common practice, then why do we have a policy forbidding it?" Alternatively, and no matter the rationale, you can ask: "Would you be willing to explain what you did and why in a meeting with our superiors or customers, or better still, during an interview on the evening news?"
5. **Use Your Lack of Seniority or Status as an Asset.** While many employees unfortunately use their junior status to avoid confronting ethical issues, being junior can instead be an advantage. It enables you to ask/say: "Because I'm new, I may have misunderstood something, but it seems to me what you've done is out of bounds or could cause problems."
6. **Consider and Explain Long-Term Consequences.** Of course many ethical issues are driven by temptations and benefits in the short-term. It therefore can be helpful to frame and explain your views in terms of long-term consequences for unethical conduct.
7. **Solutions . . . Not Just Complaints.** When confronting an issue you will likely be perceived as more helpful and taken more seriously if you provide an alternative course or solution. Doing so will also make it more difficult for the offender to disregard your complaint.

SOURCE: Based on M C Gentile, "Keeping Your Colleagues Honest," *Harvard Business Review*, March 2010.
Reprinted by permission of Harvard Business Review. Excerpt from "Keep Your Colleagues Honest," by M C Gentile, March 2010. Copyright 2010 by the Harvard Business School Publishing Corporation; all rights reserved.

How to Improve the Organization's Ethical Climate

 LO1.6

Promoting open communication and encouraging employees to speak out against questionable behavior can create a culture of integrity and result in higher performance. A Corporate Executive Board (CEB) survey of 500,000 employees from 150 global companies in 85 countries revealed that organizations that openly valued and utilized such practices produced shareholder returns 5% greater than those that did not.[71] The following suggestions provide ideas for how this can be accomplished:

- *Behave ethically yourself.* Managers are potent role models whose habits and actual behavior send clear signals about the importance of ethical conduct. Ethical behavior is a top-to-bottom proposition.

- *Screen potential employees.* Surprisingly, employers are generally lax when it comes to checking references, credentials, transcripts, and other information on applicant résumés. More diligent action in this area can screen out those given to fraud and misrepresentation. Integrity testing is fairly valid but is no panacea.[72]

- *Develop a meaningful code of ethics.* Codes of ethics can have a positive impact if they satisfy these four criteria:

  1. They are distributed to every employee.
  2. They are firmly supported by top management.
  3. They refer to *specific* practices and ethical dilemmas likely to be encountered by target employees (e.g., salespersons paying kickbacks, purchasing agents receiving payoffs, laboratory scientists doctoring data, or accountants "cooking the books").
  4. They are evenly enforced with rewards for compliance and strict penalties for noncompliance.

- *Provide ethics training.* Employees can be trained to identify and deal with ethical issues during orientation and through seminar, video, and Internet training sessions.[73]

- *Reinforce ethical behavior.* Behavior that is reinforced tends to be repeated, whereas behavior that is not reinforced tends to disappear. Ethical conduct too often is punished or ignored while unethical behavior is rewarded.

- *Create positions, units, and other structural mechanisms to deal with ethics.* Ethics needs to be an everyday affair, not a one-time announcement of a new ethical code that gets filed away and forgotten. A growing number of large companies in the United States have chief ethics officers who report directly to the CEO, thus making ethical conduct and accountability priority issues.

www.mcgrawhillconnect.com

Go to Connect for a video case to view Patagonia and how they handle social responsibility.

One can argue that effectively implementing such practices can create a *climate in which whistle-blowing becomes unnecessary.* **Whistle-blowing occurs when an employee reports a perceived unethical and/or illegal activity to a third party such as government agencies, news media, or public-interest groups.** A recent and now famous whistle-blowing case involved Cheryl Eckard, a former manager of global quality assurance for pharmaceutical giant GlaxoSmithKline. She eventually revealed to regulators and the press a number of manufacturing and safety violations.[74] Organizations can reduce the need for whistle-blowing by encouraging free and open expression of dissenting viewpoints and giving employees a voice through fair grievance procedures and/or anonymous ethics hot lines. Governor Andrew Cuomo of New York plans to utilize training as a means to manage the ethical conduct of top state administrative officials. By executive order, they must complete ethics training within the first three months of 2011.[75]

A Personal Call to Action

In the final analysis, ethics comes down to individual perception and motivation. Organizational climate, role models, structure, training, and rewards all can point employees in the right direction. But individuals first must be *morally attentive,* **meaning they faithfully consider the ethical implications of their actions and circumstances.**[76]

Second, they must *want* to do the right thing and have the courage to act. Bill George, the respected former CEO of Medtronic, the maker of life-saving devices such as heart pacemakers, gave us this call to action: "Each of us needs to determine . . . where our ethical boundaries are and, if asked to violate (them), refuse. . . . If this means refusing a direct order, we must be prepared to resign."[77] Rising to this challenge requires strong personal *values* and the *courage* to adhere to them during adversity.

www.mcgrawhillconnect.com

Go to Connect for an interactive exercise to check your knowledge concerning ethical climate.

Learning about OB: Research, Road Map, and Model

OB is a broad and growing field that draws on many academic disciplines. We use a theory→research→practice strategy to make the journey as interesting and practical as possible. For virtually all major topics in this book, we begin by presenting the underlying theoretical framework (often with graphical models showing how key variables are related) and define key terms. Next, we tap the latest research findings for valuable insights and then round out the discussion with illustrative practical examples and, when applicable, how-to-do-it advice.

Before presenting a topical model that organizes your study of OB, we provide a brief overview of the sources of OB research. This basic overview will help you evaluate the quality of conclusions provided by us and others.

Five Sources of OB Research Insights

OB gains its credibility as an academic discipline by being research driven. Scientific rigor pushes aside speculation, prejudice, and untested assumptions about workplace behavior. We systematically cite "hard" evidence from five different categories. Worthwhile evidence was obtained by drawing upon the following *priority* of research methodologies:

- *Meta-analyses.* A **meta-analysis is a statistical pooling technique that permits behavioral scientists to draw general conclusions about certain variables from many different studies.** It typically encompasses a vast number of subjects, often in the thousands. Meta-analyses are instructive because they focus on general patterns of research evidence, not fragmented bits and pieces or isolated studies. Meta-analytic results enable us to provide more generalizable conclusions.

- *Field studies.* In OB, a **field study probes individual or group processes in an organizational setting.** Because field studies involve real-life situations, their results often have immediate and practical relevance for managers.

- *Laboratory studies.* In a **laboratory study, variables are manipulated and measured in contrived situations.** College students are commonly used as subjects. The highly controlled nature of laboratory studies enhances research precision. But generalizing the results to organizational management requires caution.

- *Sample surveys.* In a **sample survey, samples of people from specified populations respond to questionnaires.** The researchers then draw conclusions about the relevant population. Generalizability of the results depends on the quality of the sampling and questioning techniques.

- *Case studies.* A **case study is an in-depth analysis of a single individual, group, or organization.** Because of their limited scope, case studies yield realistic but not very generalizable results.

A Road Map and Model for Understanding and Managing OB

The study of OB can be a wandering and overly academic journey if we overlook the need to translate OB lessons into actions that improve performance. The destination of OB therefore is improved performance across individuals, groups, and the organization as a whole. Figure 1–2 is both a model and topic road map for your journey through this book. We begin with Part 1, which provides an introduction about the context or larger external landscape in which OB occurs. Context is critically important in OB as all behavior occurs in a context. Contextual factors, such as organizational culture and the global business environment, can and do powerfully influence behavior. A particular behavior may be wonderfully effective in one context and an utter failure in another. Therefore, contextual factors always matter and must be considered when trying to understand behavior. These contextual or environmental factors are illustrated as the background in Figure 1–2, and the line represents a permeable boundary between the organization and its environment. This boundary is indeed permeable, as no organization is an island in today's highly interactive, global, and interdependent world. Beyond contextual factors, Part 1 also includes what you just learned regarding the history of OB, new directions in the field, and ethics. All of the other elements of OB depicted in the figure are influenced by and affect these contextual elements.

FIGURE 1–2   A Topical Model for What Lies Ahead

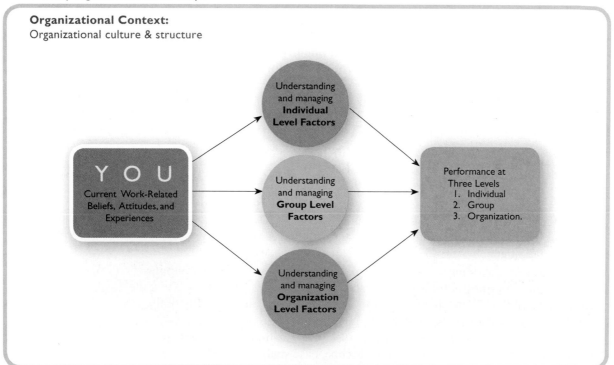

At the far left side of the figure is *you*, who enters this course with your own beliefs, attitudes, and experiences related to work. Our mission is to enrich and extend these attributes in order to enhance your ability to manage across individual, group, and organizational levels. To do this, it is necessary for you to learn about and understand the factors that influence behavior at each of these levels. The remainder of the book has the following structure: individuals (Part 2), groups and social processes (Part 3), and finally organizational processes and problems (Part 4). We end our journey in Part 5 by addressing a number of organization-level features and challenges—organizational structure, design, and effectiveness, and then managing change and organizational learning. Understanding each of these elements and how they relate to one another will enable you to effectively improve performance at all levels.

Bon voyage! Enjoy your trip through the challenging, interesting, and often surprising world of OB.

key terms

case study   25

contingency approach   7

corporate social responsibility
   (CSR)   19

e-business   14

ethics   18

field study   25

human capital   8

laboratory study   25

meta-analysis   25

morally attentive   24

organizational behavior (OB)   5

positive organizational behavior
   (POB)   13

sample survey   25

social capital   10

Theory Y   6

whistle-blowing   24

chapter summary

- *Contrast McGregor's Theory X and Theory Y assumptions about employees.* Theory X employees, according to traditional thinking, dislike work, require close supervision, and are primarily interested in security. According to the modern Theory Y view, employees are capable of self-direction, of seeking responsibility, and of being creative.

- *Contrast human and social capital, and describe three ways you can develop both.* Human capital involves *individual* characteristics and abilities; social capital involves *social* relationships. Human capital is the productive potential of an individual's knowledge and actions. Job-relevant training (e.g., your company's product/service knowledge), work-based development opportunities (e.g., a mentor), and learning activities outside of work (e.g., a second language) represent different types of human capital. Social capital is productive potential resulting from strong relationships, goodwill, trust, and cooperative effort. Social capital has two general types—internal and external to your current

employer, such as relationships with coworkers in another office and relationships with suppliers, respectively.

- *Explain the impact of the positive psychology movement on the field of OB.* Reversing psychology's long-standing preoccupation with what is wrong with people, positive psychology instead focuses on identifying and building human strengths and potential. Accordingly, Luthans recommends positive organizational behavior (POB) and identifies its basic elements with the CHOSE model. This acronym stands for Confidence/self-efficacy, Hope, Optimism, Subjective well-being, and Emotional intelligence.

- *Define the term e-business, and explain its implications for organizational behavior and managing people.* E-business involves using the Internet to more effectively and efficiently manage every aspect of a business. Because today's employees have more control over the information they can access and share, the manager's role is evolving from one of controlling information and communications into one of providing the means for collaboration and connecting people with the appropriate tasks and projects. It now is especially important for managers to find people who are disciplined self-starters and to find new and effective ways of motivating people from afar and making them feel part of the larger enterprise.

• Describe the four levels of corporate social responsibility. Carroll's model describes four levels of CSR: economic responsibility (make a profit), legal responsibility (obey the laws of host countries), ethical responsibility (be ethical considering both local and global standards),

and philanthropic responsibilities (be a good corporate citizen). Our study of ethics cuts across all levels of the organization.

• Explain how to improve an organization's ethical climate. Ethical climates are the result of interactions between individuals and the organization and can be managed by: behaving ethically, screening prospective employees, developing a code of ethics, providing ethics training, reinforcing ethical conduct, and creating positions devoted to ethics issues within the organization.

discussion questions

1. What is your personal experience with Theory X and Theory Y managers (see Table 1–1)? Which did/do you prefer? Why?
2. What are you doing to build your human and social capital?
3. As the field of positive organizational behavior (POB) evolves, what potential impacts on the practice of management do you foresee?

4. What opportunities does e-business provide for your career?
5. Think of an example of questionable or unethical conduct you've witnessed at work and *describe what was done and what could have been done* to prevent it.

legal/ethical challenge

What Is Public and What Is Personal?

The proliferation of technology has made us more connected and made life easier in many ways. For instance, the Internet certainly has made searching for jobs easier, and most people today can't even imagine searching for a job without the Web. Just as you can gather information about prospective employers more easily, which every prospective employee undoubtedly appreciates, employers too can more easily gather information about job candidates like you. And this creates a potential problem: Just because information about you is available on the Web, does that mean it is appropriate for a potential employer to consider it when evaluating you? David Kirkpatrick's *The Facebook Effect* explores many privacy issues associated with our increasing connectedness. He notes a poll of U.S. employers wherein 35% of them said they rejected candidates based on information found on social networking sites, and "provocative or inappropriate photographs

or information" was the number one reason cited.[78] Many colleges and universities are also gathering and considering such information in admission decisions.

What Would You Do?

Assume you are a job candidate or prospective student. Then assume you learned that your most desirable job or school uses any and all information they can find on the Web in making their decisions. What would you do?

1. Withdraw your application.

2. Submit your application but include a letter explaining what might be found.

3. Roll the dice and simply take what comes (i.e., do nothing and hope for the best).

4. Create and explain another course of action.

Now assume you are a recruiter or admissions officer for the company or school above. What would you do?

1. Not use information available on the Web in making your decisions.

2. Use any and all information available on the Web and tell the candidates/prospective students in advance.

3. Use any and all information available on the Web and not tell candidates/prospective students.

4. Invent something else. Discuss.

If you're looking for additional study materials, be sure to check out the Online Learning Center at

www.mhhe.com/kinickiob5e

for more information and interactivities that correspond to this chapter.

chapter 2

Organizational Culture, Socialization, and Mentoring

After reading the material in this chapter, you should be able to:

LO2.1   Discuss the layers and functions of organizational culture.

LO2.2   Describe the general types of organizational culture and their associated characteristics.

LO2.3   Summarize the process by which organizations change their cultures.

LO2.4   Describe the three phases in Feldman's model of organizational socialization.

LO2.5   Discuss the various tactics used to socialize employees.

LO2.6   Explain the four types of developmental networks derived from a developmental network model of mentoring.

Has Sergio Marchionne Gone too Far in Trying to Change Chrysler's Culture and Performance?

A decline in sales isn't the only big problem facing **Chrysler Group** LLC. Another, according to Chief Executive Sergio Marchionne, is the almost ingrained tendency to react to falling sales by slashing prices.

In Detroit, "there's almost a fanatical, maniacal interest in (market) share," Mr. Marchionne told reporters Monday on the opening day of the North American International Auto Show. But rarely, he added, has heavy discounting in pursuit of high volumes helped auto makers generate profits in the long term. . . .

For the past seven months, the 57-year-old Italian-born Canadian has been working to shake up Chrysler and move the company away from old ways that forced it into bankruptcy reorganization last year. He has ousted several veteran executives, flattened its bureaucracy and, according to people who have worked closely with Mr. Marchionne, injected an element of fear into its ranks.

One of the more frustrating problems for Mr. Marchionne has been the use of heavy rebates and other incentives to maintain sales—an issue that has plagued **General Motors Co.** and **Ford Motor Co.** over the years.

Last July, for example, when the US government offered as much as $4,500 in "cash for clunkers" rebates, Chrysler's sales chief at the time, Peter Fong, drew up a plan to offer an additional $4,500 from Chrysler, two people familiar with the matter said....

But when Mr. Marchionne found out about it, he was furious, these people said. In an August meeting with Mr. Fong and his sales team, the CEO excoriated them, saying doubling discounts amounted to "giving away margin" at a time when Chrysler was scrambling for profits, one person familiar with the details of the meeting said. "Sergio was ballistic," this person said....

Several weeks later, in September, Mr. Fong was summoned to the office of Nancy Rae, Chrysler's head of human resources, and was told his services were no longer needed, these people said....

Mr. Marchionne took the helm at Chrysler in June, when the company exited bankruptcy protection and formed an alliance with Italy's **FIAT SpA**, where he also serves as CEO and which owns about 20% of Chrysler. In November, he laid out a turn-around plan that calls for Chrysler to launch a series of small cars designed by Fiat, and envisions Chrysler breaking even in 2010 and returning to profitability by 2011.

Besides working out ways for the two companies to work together, Mr. Marchionne has tried to shake up Chrysler's plodding corporate culture....

To select his new management team, Mr. Marchionne held dozens of 15-minute interviews with Chrysler executives over several days to evaluate which ones to keep and which to push out, according to people who participated in the process.

When the process was over, Mr. Marchionne had 23 people reporting to him. Some were junior executives who had been moved up a level or two in the organization....

Many in the industry believe Mr. Marchionne has no option but to shock Chrysler out of its old ways. "The culture in Detroit is so insular, and he's going to have to throw some china against the wall," said Michael J. Jackson, chairman and CEO of AutoNation Inc., a large dealership chain....

Mr. Marchionne took an office on the fourth floor of the technology center at Chrysler's headquarters in Auburn Hills, Mich., among Chrysler's engineers, instead of an office in its adjoining executive tower. His management team began meeting weekly in a nearby conference room equipped with video gear so that Fiat executives in Italy could take part.

In these meetings, Mr. Marchionne often spelled out what he saw as Chrysler's many deficiencies: margins and vehicle quality needed to improve and better control over pricing was imperative, according to one person who has been in the sessions. Details of the discussions weren't to leave the room. Security officers even called senior executives over the summer to make sure no one was talking to reporters about the company's plans.

Mr. Marchionne, a notorious workaholic, carries five BlackBerrys and works seven days a week. He spends about one full week a month in Michigan and flies back for weekend meetings when he isn't in town.[1]

▲ **THE CHAPTER-OPENING CASE HIGHLIGHTS** the role of organizational culture in contributing to organizational effectiveness. Chrysler's culture prior to Mr. Marchionne's role as CEO clearly contributed to the company's poor performance in the marketplace. The case also highlights that an organization's culture is strongly influenced by the values and attitudes of top management, particularly the CEO.

This chapter will help you better understand how managers can use organizational culture as a competitive advantage. After defining and discussing the context of organizational culture, we examine (1) the dynamics of organizational culture, (2) the organization socialization process, and (3) the embedding of organizational culture through mentoring.

Organizational Culture: Definition and Context

Organizational culture is "the set of shared, taken-for-granted implicit assumptions that a group holds and that determines how it perceives, thinks about, and reacts to its various environments."[2] This definition highlights three important characteristics of organizational culture. First, organizational culture is passed on to new employees through the process of socialization, a topic discussed later in this chapter. Second, organizational culture influences our behavior at work. Finally, organizational culture operates at different levels.

Figure 2–1 provides a conceptual framework for reviewing the widespread impact organizational culture has on organizational behavior.[3] It also shows the linkage between this chapter—culture, socialization, and mentoring—and other key topics in this book. Figure 2–1 reveals organizational culture is shaped by four key components: the founders' values, the industry and business environment, the national culture, and the senior leaders' vision and behavior. In turn, organizational culture influences the

FIGURE 2–1   A Conceptual Framework for Understanding Organizational Culture

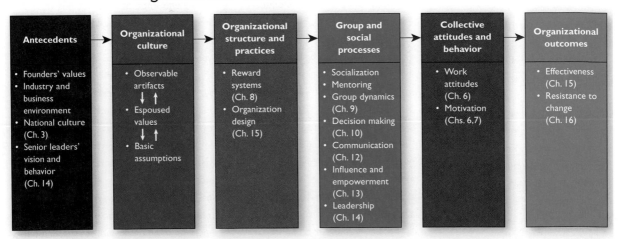

SOURCE: Adapted in part from C Ostroff, A Kinicki, and M Tamkins, "Organizational Culture and Climate," in *Handbook of Psychology*, Vol 12, eds W C Burman, D R Ligen, and R J Klimoski (New York: Wiley and Sons, 2003), pp 565–93.

type of organizational structure adopted by a company and a host of practices, policies, and procedures implemented in pursuit of organizational goals. These organizational characteristics then affect a variety of group and social processes. This sequence ultimately affects employees' attitudes and behavior and a variety of organizational outcomes. All told, Figure 2–1 reveals that organizational culture is a contextual variable influencing individual, group, and organizational behavior. This is why we are discussing organizational culture in the second chapter of your textbook.

Dynamics of Organizational Culture

To provide a better under-standing of how organizational culture is formed and used by employees, this section begins by discussing the layers of organizational culture. It then reviews the four functions of organizational culture, types of organizational culture, outcomes associated with organizational culture, and how cultures are embedded within organizations.

LO2.1

Layers of Organizational Culture

Figure 2–1 shows the three fundamental layers of organizational culture. Each level varies in terms of outward visibility and resistance to change, and each level influences another level.[4]

Observable Artifacts   At the more visible level, culture represents observable artifacts. Artifacts consist of the physical manifestation of an organization's culture. Organizational examples include acronyms, manner of dress, awards, myths and stories told about the organization, published lists of values, observable rituals and ceremonies, special parking spaces, decorations, and so on. This level also includes visible behaviors exhibited by people and groups. At Google, for example, the core design team of 16 employees has daily "stand-up" meetings. "Everyone working on the project gathers standing up, to make sure no one gets too comfortable and no time is wasted during the rapid-fire update."[5] These stand-up meetings are an artifact of Google's desire to work hard and get things done in a timely manner. Artifacts are easier to change than the less visible aspects of organizational culture.

Espoused Values   Values possess five key components. **"*Values* (1) are concepts or beliefs, (2) pertain to desirable end-states or behaviors, (3) transcend situations, (4) guide selection or evaluation of behavior and events, and (5) are ordered by relative importance."**[6] It is important to distinguish between values that are espoused versus those that are enacted.

   Espoused values **represent the explicitly stated values and norms that are preferred by an organization.** They are generally established by the founder of a new or small company and by the top management team in a larger organization. Consider, for example, the espoused values of Williams-Sonoma, Inc. (see Skills & Best Practices on page 34). At a growing number of companies, one of the espoused values is *sustainability,* which involves meeting "humanity's needs without harming future generations." Sustainability also is referred to as "being green," and Pulitzer Prize winner Thomas Friedman believes that "outgreening" other nations can renew America and defeat al-Qaeda. Others believe that outgreening can produce competitive advantage for organizations.

> **BACK TO THE CHAPTER-OPENING CASE**   Go to Chrysler's home page at
> http://www.chryslergroupllc.com/ and identify three of its key espoused values.
> Based on the chapter-opening case, to what extent is Chrysler walking the talk of
> these values? Explain.

Because espoused values constitute aspirations that are explicitly communicated to employees, managers hope that espoused values will directly influence employee behavior. Unfortunately, aspirations do not automatically produce the desired behaviors because people do not always "walk the talk."

Enacted values, **on the other hand, represent the values and norms that actually are exhibited or converted into employee behavior.** They represent the values that employees ascribe to an organization based on their observations of what occurs on a daily basis.

The enacted values may differ from the values an organization espouses. For example, Starbucks CEO Howard Schultz is trying hard to enact the company value of providing quality products and great service in response to the financial problems faced

SKILLS & BEST PRACTICES

Williams-Sonoma's Espoused Values Focus on Employees, Customers, Shareholders, Ethical Behavior, and the Environment

People First We believe the potential of our company has no limit and is driven by our associates and their imagination. We are committed to an environment that attracts, motivates, and recognizes high performance.

Customers We are here to please our customers—without them, nothing else matters.

Quality We must take pride in everything we do. From our people, to our products and in our relationships with business partners and our community, quality is our signature.

Shareholders We must provide a superior return to our shareholders. It's everyone's job.

Ethical Sourcing Williams-Sonoma, Inc., and all of its brands are committed to maintaining the highest level of integrity and honesty throughout all aspects of our business. We work to ensure that our business associates, including agents, vendors, and suppliers, share our commitment to socially responsible employment conditions.

Wood Product Sourcing Williams-Sonoma, Inc., is committed to environmental stewardship, and more specifically, to responsible wood sourcing to protect and conserve this vital natural resource integral to the health of the environment and the communities from which we source.

Paper Procurement Policy Equally important to Williams-Sonoma, Inc.'s commitment to responsible wood sourcing is our commitment to sound paper procurement practices that also ensure the sustainability of forests and other natural resources.

SOURCE: Excerpted from "Corporate Values," www.williams-sonomainc.com/careers/corporate-values.html, accessed on January 2, 2011.

by the company in 2009. He told an interviewer in 2010 that "I shut our stores for three and a half hours of retraining. People said, 'How much is that going to cost?' I had shareholders calling me and saying, 'Are you out of your mind?' I said, 'I'm doing the right thing. We are retraining our people because we have forgotten what we stand for, and that is the pursuit of an unequivocal, absolute commitment to quality.'"[8] Schultz is obviously hoping that these artifacts encourage employees to provide good service.

It is important for managers to reduce gaps between espoused and enacted values because they can significantly influence employee attitudes and organizational performance. For example, a survey administered by the Ethics Resource Center showed that employees were more likely to behave ethically when management behaved in a way that set a good ethical example and kept its promises and commitments. This finding is underscored by another recent study of 500,000 employees from more than 85 countries. Results revealed that companies experienced 10 times more misconduct when they had weak rather than strong ethical cultures.[9] Managers clearly need to walk the talk when it comes to behaving ethically.

Basic Assumptions   Basic underlying assumptions are unobservable and represent the core of organizational culture. They constitute organizational values that have become so taken for granted over time that they become assumptions that guide organizational behavior. They thus are highly resistant to change. When basic assumptions are widely held among employees, people will find behavior based on an inconsistent value inconceivable. Google, for example, is noted for its innovative culture. Employees at Google would be shocked to see management act in ways that did not value creativity and innovation.

Four Functions of Organizational Culture

As illustrated in Figure 2–2, an organization's culture fulfills four functions. To help bring these four functions to life, let us consider how each of them has taken shape at Southwest Airlines. Southwest is a particularly instructive example because it has grown to become the fourth-largest U.S. airline since its inception in 1971 and has achieved 38 consecutive years of profitability. *Fortune* ranked Southwest in the top five of the Best Companies to Work For in America from 1997 to 2000; Southwest has chosen not to participate in this ranking process since 2000. Southwest also was ranked as one of the top 50 companies committed to corporate social responsibility in 2010.[10]

1. *Give members an organizational identity.* Southwest Airlines is known as a fun place to work that values employee satisfaction and customer loyalty over corporate profits. Herb Kelleher, executive chairman, commented on this issue:

   Who comes first? The employees, customers, or shareholders? That's never been an issue to me. The employees come first. If they're happy, satisfied, dedicated, and energetic, they'll take real good care of the customers. When the customers are happy, they come back. And that makes the shareholders happy.[11]

   The company also has a catastrophe fund based on voluntary contributions for distribution to employees who are experiencing serious personal difficulties. Southwest's people-focused identity is reinforced by the fact that it is an employer of choice. For example, Southwest received 90,043 resumes and hired 831 new employees in 2009. The company also was noted as an employer of choice among college students by *Fortune*.

FIGURE 2–2   Four Functions of Organizational Culture

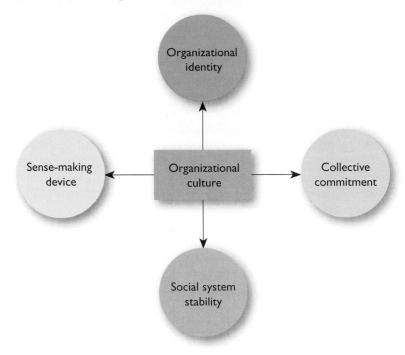

SOURCE: Adapted from discussion in L Smircich, "Concepts of Culture and Organizational Analysis," *Administrative Science Quarterly*, September 1983, pp 339–58. Reprinted with permission.

Fun and celebrating are the norm at Southwest Airlines. Colleen Barrett, president of Southwest Airlines (standing on right side) takes great pride in fostering a positive work environment. Would you like to work at Southwest?

2. *Facilitate collective commitment.* The mission of Southwest Airlines "is dedication to the highest quality of customer service delivered with a sense of warmth, friendliness, individual pride, and company spirit."[12] Southwest's nearly 35,000 employees are committed to this mission. According to the Department of Transportation's Air Travel Consumer Report, Southwest has had the fewest complaints per customer since 1987.

3. *Promote social system stability.* Social system stability reflects the extent to which the work environment is perceived as positive and reinforcing, and the extent to which conflict and change are effectively managed. Southwest is noted for its philosophy of having fun, having parties, and celebrating. For example, each city in which the firm operates is given a budget for parties. Southwest also uses a variety of performance-based awards and service awards to reinforce employees. The company's positive and enriching environment is supported by the lowest turnover rates in the airline industry and the employment of 1,164 married couples.

4. *Shape behavior by helping members make sense of their surroundings.* This function of culture helps employees understand why the organization does what it does and how it intends to accomplish its long-term goals. Keeping in mind that Southwest's leadership originally viewed ground transportation as their main competitor in 1971, employees come to understand why the airline's primary vision is to be the best primarily short-haul, low-fare, high-frequency, point-to-point carrier in the United States. Employees understand they must achieve exceptional performance, such as turning a plane in 20 minutes, because they must keep costs down in order to compete against Greyhound and the use of automobiles. In turn, the company reinforces the importance of outstanding customer service and high performance expectations by using performance-based awards and profit sharing. Employees own at least 5% of the company stock.

Types of Organizational Culture

LO2.2

Organizational behavior researchers have proposed three different frameworks to capture the various types of organizational culture: the Organizational Culture Inventory, the Competing Values Framework, and the Organizational Culture Profile. This section discusses the Competing Values Framework because it is the most widely used approach for classifying organizational culture. It also was named as one of the 40 most important frameworks in the study of organizations and has been shown to be a valid approach for classifying organizational culture.[13]

The *competing values framework (CVF)* **provides a practical way for managers to understand, measure, and change organizational culture.** It was originally developed by a team of researchers who were trying to classify different ways to assess organizational effectiveness. This research showed that measures of organizational effectiveness vary along two fundamental dimensions or axes. One axis pertains to whether an organization focuses its attention and efforts on internal dynamics and employees or outward toward its external environment and its customers and shareholders. The second is concerned with an organization's preference for flexibility and discretion or control and stability. Combining these two axes creates four types of organizational culture that are based on different core values and different sets of criteria for assessing organizational effectiveness. The CVF is shown in Figure 2–3.[14]

Figure 2–3 shows the strategic thrust associated with each cultural type along with the means used to accomplish this thrust and the resulting ends or goals pursued by each cultural type. Before beginning our exploration of the CVF, it is important to note that organizations can possess characteristics associated with each culture type. That said, however, organizations tend to have one type of culture that is more dominant than the others. Let us begin our discussion of culture types by starting in the upper left-hand quadrant of the CVF.

Clan Culture   A *clan culture* **has an internal focus and values flexibility rather than stability and control.** It resembles a family-type organization in which effectiveness is achieved by encouraging collaboration between employees. This type of culture is very "employee-focused" and strives to instill cohesion through consensus and job satisfaction and commitment through employee involvement. Clan organizations devote considerable resources to hiring and developing their employees, and they view customers as partners.

A company with a strong clan culture is Decagon Devices Inc. in Pullman, Washington. The company may be small, but senior management tries to maintain a

FIGURE 2–3   Competing Values Framework

Flexibility and discretion

Clan	Adhocracy
Thrust: Collaborate	**Thrust:** Create
Means: Cohesion, participation, communication, empowerment	**Means:** Adaptability, creativity, agility
Ends: Morale, people development, commitment	**Ends:** Innovation, growth, cutting-edge output
Hierarchy	Market
Thrust: Control	**Thrust:** Compete
Means: Capable processes, consistency, process control, measurement	**Means:** Customer focus, productivity, enhancing competitiveness
Ends: Efficiency, timeliness, smooth functioning	**Ends:** Market share, profitability, goal achievement

Internal focus and integration (left)   **External focus and differentiation** (right)

Stability and control

SOURCE: Adapted from K S Cameron, R E Quinn, J Degraff, and A V Thakor, *Competing Values Leadership* (Northampton, MA: Edward Elgar, 2006), p 32.

family atmosphere at work. The company's CEO, Tamsin Jolley, notes that "the way that we like to see it is that as we add employees we're just adding members to the family." This feeling starts with a profit-sharing program that distributes 20% of pretax profits to employees on a quarterly basis.

> Then there are day-to-day activities that bring workers closer together. Each Wednesday, some employees take turns bringing home-cooked meals to work for their colleagues. Then all the workers eat lunch together. The weekly meal is an opportunity for managers to share news about the company, introduce new employees, and teach workers how to read the company's financial statements. The company also encourages employees to socialize at work. The office has a Ping-Pong table and slot-car track, and there's a long tradition of employees playing soccer on their breaks.[15]

Decagon Devices also provides generous employee health benefits and hosts annual catered family picnics and holiday parties.

Adhocracy Culture   An *adhocracy culture* has an external focus and values flexibility. This type of culture fosters the creation of innovative products and services by being adaptable, creative, and fast to respond to changes in the marketplace. Adhocracy cultures do not rely on the type of centralized power and authority relationships that are part of market and hierarchical cultures. They empower and encourage employees to take risks, think outside the box, and experiment with new ways of getting things done. This type of culture is well suited for start-up companies, those in industries undergoing constant change, and those in mature industries that are in need of innovation to enhance growth, such as Chrysler.

Consider how these cultural characteristics are reinforced at the biopharmaceutical firm AstraZeneca. "AstraZeneca is experimenting with new ways to organize research to improve productivity. Scientists now are responsible for candidate drugs until they begin the final human trials, ending a culture of handing off early-stage products to other researchers as if on an assembly line."[16] India-based Tata group, with over 90 operating companies in more than 80 countries is another company with an adhocracy culture. "Known for its ultracheap minicar, the Nano, Tata takes innovation so seriously that it's developed an 'Innometer.' The conglomerate measures creative goals and accomplishments vs. domestic or global benchmarks while instilling a 'sense of urgency' among employees."[17] Tata was ranked as the 17th most innovative firm in the world in 2010 by *Bloomberg Businessweek*. W L Gore and Intel are two other companies that possess cultural characteristics consistent with an adhocracy.

Market Culture   A *market culture* **has a strong external focus and values stability and control.** Organizations with this culture are driven by competition and a strong desire to deliver results and accomplish goals. Because this type of culture is focused on the external environment, customers and profits take precedence over employee development and satisfaction. The major goal of managers is to drive toward productivity, profits, and customer satisfaction. Consider Richard Branson's new Virgin America airline. Branson believes that "American carriers are all very much the same, and the people who run them do not think of the customers at all. It's become a bus service." To meet customer needs, Branson's new airline uses Airbus A319 and A320 jets that are roomier, contain in-flight entertainment at every seat, Wi-Fi Internet access, and special lighting that displays 12 shades of pink, purple, and blue.[18] Time will tell whether this market culture will lead to sustainable profits.

Employees in market cultures also are expected to react fast, work hard, and deliver quality work on time. Organizations with this culture tend to reward people who deliver results. Byung Mo Ahn, president of Kia Motors, is a good example of a leader who desires to promote a market culture. He fired two senior executives from Kia Motors America in February 2008 because they were not meeting their expected sales goals. Employees from North America note that Mr. Ahn has created a very aggressive and competitive work environment. Some describe the environment as militaristic.[19] Intel is another example of a company with a market culture.

Hierarchy Culture   Control is the driving force within a hierarchical culture. The *hierarchy culture* **has an internal focus, which produces a more formalized and structured work environment, and values stability and control over flexibility.** This orientation leads to the development of reliable internal processes, extensive measurement, and the implementation of a variety of control mechanisms. Johnson & Johnson (J&J) is a good example of the value of a hierarchical culture. J&J had serious manufacturing problems in 2010 that led to recalls of children's Tylenol and other over-the-counter drugs. "A Food and Drug Administration inspection report, dated April 30, cites

Seven varieties of Tylenol infant drops were recalled by J&J. Would a hierarchical culture help or hinder the production of higher quality products?

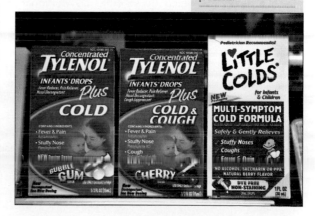

incidents of mishandling of materials, lax documentation and inadequate investigation of consumer complaints." The company estimates a loss of $600 million in 2010 and a hit to its reputation. To correct the problem, the company created "a company-wide quality team and is upgrading plants," improving plants, and training employees.[20] Time will tell if a focus on creating a hierarchical culture in its manufacturing operations will correct J&J's problems.

> **BACK TO THE CHAPTER-OPENING CASE**   Use the competing values framework to diagnose Chrysler's culture. To what extent does Chrysler possess cultural characteristics associated with clan, adhocracy, market, and hierarchy cultures?

Cultural Types Represent Competing Values   It is important to note that certain cultural types reflect opposing core values. These contradicting cultures are found along the two diagonals in Figure 2–3. For example, the clan culture—upper-left quadrant—is represented by values that emphasize an internal focus and flexibility, whereas the market culture—bottom-right quadrant—has an external focus and concern for stability and control. You can see the same conflict between an adhocracy culture that values flexibility and an external focus and a hierarchical culture that endorses stability and control along with an internal focus. Why are these contradictions important?

They are important because an organization's success may depend on its ability to possess core values that are associated with competing cultural types. While this is difficult to pull off, it can be done. 3M is a good example (see the Skills & Best Practices feature on page 40).

 **SKILLS & BEST PRACTICES**

3M Attempts to Reconcile Adhocracy and Hierarchy Cultures

3M is trying to merge competing cultural characteristics from an adhocracy with those from a hierarchy. Adhocracy-wise, 3M released 1,000 new products in 2009, and it "awards annual Genesis Grants, worth as much as $100,000, to company scientists for research. The money is allocated by their peers and is spent on projects for which 'no sensible, conventional person in the company would give money,'" says Chris Holmes, a 3M division vice president. The company has a goal to generate 30% of its revenue from products developed in the last five years. In contrast, 3M pursued a hierarchical culture by implementing quality management techniques to reduce waste and defects, and increase efficiency. Although 3M achieved better efficiency and earnings in the short run, new product revenue decreased and scientists complained that the quality initiatives were choking off innovation. One engineer quipped that "it's really tough to schedule invention." 3M's CEO, George Buckley, was made aware of these cultural conflicts and decided to reduce the conflict within company labs by decreasing hierarchical policies/procedures while simultaneously increasing those related to adhocracy. The company continues to emphasize quality and reliability in its factories. To date, results indicate a successful transition as the company achieved both its efficiency and new product revenue goals in 2010.

SOURCE: Excerpted from M Gunther, "3M's Innovation Revival," *Fortune*, September 27, 2010, pp 73–76.

Outcomes Associated with Organizational Culture

Both managers and academic researchers believe that organizational culture can be a driver of employee attitudes and organizational effectiveness and performance. To test this possibility, various measures of organizational culture have been correlated with a variety of individual and organizational outcomes. So what have we learned?

A team of researchers recently conducted a meta-analysis to answer this question. Their results were based on 93 studies involving more than 1,100 companies. Figure 2–4 summarizes results from this study by summarizing the strength of relationships between eight different organizational outcomes and the culture types of clan, adhocracy, and market: Hierarchy was not included due to a lack of research on this type.[21] Results reveal that the eight types of organizational outcomes had significant and positive relationships with clan, adhocracy, and market cultures. The majority of these relationships were of moderate strength, indicating that they are important to today's managers. Closer examination of Figure 2–4 leads to the following five conclusions:

www.mcgrawhillconnect.com

Go to Connect for a self-assessment to find out what kind of culture you prefer.

1. Organizational culture is clearly related to measures of organizational effectiveness. This reinforces the conclusion that an organization's culture can be a source of competitive advantage.

2. Employees are more satisfied and committed to organizations with clan cultures. These results suggest that employees prefer to work in organizations that value flexibility over stability and control and those that are more concerned with satisfying employees' needs than customer or shareholder desires.

3. Innovation and quality can be increased by building characteristics associated with clan, adhocracy, and market cultures into the organization.

4. An organization's financial performance (i.e., growth in profit and growth in revenue) is not very strongly related to organizational culture. Managers should not expect to increase financial performance by trying to change their organization's culture.

5. Companies with market cultures tend to have more positive organizational outcomes. Managers are encouraged to consider how they might make their cultures more market-oriented.

Researchers also have investigated the importance of organizational culture within the context of a merger. These studies indicated that mergers frequently failed due to incompatible cultures. Due to the increasing number of corporate mergers around the world, and the conclusion that 7 out of 10 mergers and acquisitions failed to meet their financial promise, managers within merged companies would be well advised to consider the role of organizational culture in creating a new organization.[22]

In summary, research underscores the significance of organizational culture. It also reinforces the need to learn more about the process of cultivating and changing an organization's culture. An organization's culture is not determined by fate. It is formed and shaped by the combination and integration of everyone who works in the organization. A change-resistant culture, for instance, can undermine the effectiveness of any type of organizational change. Although it is not an easy task to change an organization's culture, the next section provides a preliminary overview of how this might be done.

FIGURE 2–4 Correlates of Organizational Culture

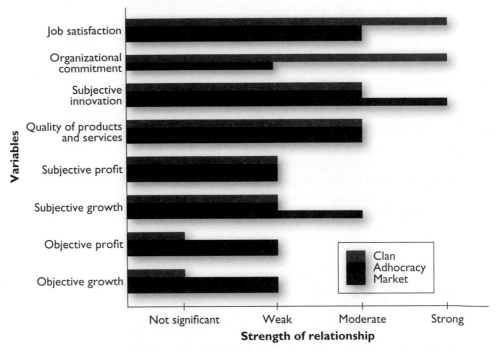

SOURCE: Derived from C Hartnell, Y Ou, and A Kinicki, 2011. Organizational Culture and Organizational Effectiveness: A Meta-Analytic Investigation of the Competing Values Framework Theoretical Suppositions. *Journal of Applied Psychology,* July 2011, pp 677–694.

LO2.3

The Process of Culture Change

We agree with the notion that leaders are the architects and developers of organizational culture, and managing organizational culture is one of the most important functions of leadership.[23] The process of culture change essentially begins with targeting one of the three layers of organizational culture—observable artifacts, espoused values, and basic assumptions. That said, culture will not change in a significant way unless managers are able to change basic underlying assumptions.[24] Edgar Schein, an OB scholar, notes that changing organizational culture involves a teaching process. That is, organizational members teach each other about the organization's preferred values, beliefs, expectations, and behaviors. This is accomplished by using one or more of the following mechanisms:[25]

1. *Formal statements of organizational philosophy, mission, vision, values, and materials used for recruiting, selection, and socialization.* Sam Walton, the founder of Walmart, established three basic beliefs or values that represent the core of the organization's culture. They are (1) respect for the individual, (2) service to our customer, and (3) striving for excellence. Further, Nucor Corp. attempts to emphasize the value it places on its people by including every employee's name on the cover of the annual report. This practice also reinforces the family-type culture the company wants to encourage.[26] Would you be attracted to work there?

This open work environment is expected to foster a more collaborative culture. Why would an open work area lead to greater collaboration?

2. *The design of physical space, work environments, and buildings.* Novartis AG in Basel, Switzerland, designed its offices to foster collaboration. This was done by using "common workspaces, sofas, soft lighting, and cappuccino machines to encourage people to talk, share ideas, and build relationships." They also invested in laptops for employees so that they would not be tied down to cubicles.[27]

3. *Slogans, language, acronyms, and sayings.* For example, Robert Mittelstaedt, dean of the W P Carey School of Business at Arizona State University, promotes his vision of having one of the best business schools in the world through the slogan "Top-of-mind business school." Employees are encouraged to engage in activities that promote the quality and reputation of the school's academic programs.

4. *Deliberate role modeling, training programs, teaching, and coaching by managers and supervisors.* Fluor Corp., one of the leading design, engineering, and contracting firms in the world, desires an ethical culture that fights corruption within the construction industry. The company, which derives more than half of its $17 billion in revenues overseas, puts all its employees through online anticorruption training sessions and teaches specialized workers, such as field operators, in person. Executives promote an open-door policy and a hot-line for reporting crimes—as well as tough penalties for violators, who receive zero tolerance for infractions.[28]

5. *Explicit rewards, status symbols (e.g., titles), and promotion criteria.* At Triage Consulting Group, employees at the same level of their career earn the same pay, but employees are eligible for merit bonuses, reinforcing the culture of achievement. The merit bonuses are partly based on coworkers' votes for who contributed most to the company's success, and the employees who received the most votes are recognized each year at the company's "State of Triage" meeting.[29]

6. *Stories, legends, and myths about key people and events.* Baptist Health Care (BHC) uses a combination of storytelling and recognition to embed clan- and market-based cultures that focus on employees and patients. "We've been able to do more and different things because of our culture, which starts with the executives who carry it to the front-line and staff," says BHC Director of People Development Scott Ginnette. "For example, throughout the year we celebrate Champions, people who have done extraordinary things in service, by sharing their stories with all employees. Every facility has its own Champions, and at the end of the year, a committee decides which Champions will be named Legends, a higher honor. The Legends are taken by limo to an offsite dinner with board members where stories are shared and the Legends are recognized."[30]

7. *The organizational activities, processes, or outcomes that leaders pay attention to, measure, and control.* When Ron Sargent took over as chief executive of Staples, he wanted to increase the focus on customer service. He started by investigating what values the office supply retailer's employees already held, and they told him they cared about helping others. Sargent used that value as the basis for developing their skill in serving customers. Staples began teaching employees more about the products they sell and now offers bonuses for team performance. Sargent also pays frequent visits to stores so he can talk directly to employees about what customers like and dislike.[31]

8. *Leader reactions to critical incidents and organizational crises.* BP's new CEO after the Gulf oil spill of 2010, Bob Dudley, responded quickly to criticism that the company valued profit and efficiency more than safety. He sent a memo to all employees indicating that "safety would be the sole criterion for rewarding employee performance in its operating business for the fourth quarter."[32] These types of rewards will need to be offered long term if the company truly wants to change employees' basic underlying assumptions.

9. *The workflow and organizational structure.* Hierarchical structures are more likely to embed an orientation toward control and authority than a flatter organization. One way that Staples enables its employees to focus on the company's commitment to customer service is by giving employees wide latitude in decision making.[33]

10. *Organizational systems and procedures.* Companies are increasingly using electronic networks to enhance collaboration among employees in order to achieve innovation, quality, and efficiency. For example, Serena Software, Inc., a California-based company with 800 employees located in 29 offices across 14 countries, encouraged its employees to sign up for Facebook for free, and to use the network as a vehicle for getting to know each other. In contrast to using a public site for networking, Dow Chemical launched its own internal social network in order to create relationships between current, past, and temporary employees.[34]

11. *Organizational goals and the associated criteria used for recruitment, selection, development, promotion, layoffs, and retirement of people.* Zappos, which was ranked as the 15th best place to work by *Fortune* in 2009, spends a great deal of time trying to hire people who will fit into their clan-based culture (see the Skills & Best Practices feature on page 45). How would you like to work at Zappos?

Zappos Works Hard to Recruit and Select People Who Fit Its Culture

Here is what Rebecca Ratner, Zappos HR director, has to say about the company's approach to recruitment and selection:

"We spend 7 to 10 hours over four occasions at happy hours, team building events, or other things outside the office. We can see them, and they can us." The process seems to be good for retention. "In 2009, we had a 20 percent turnover rate," says Ratner. That is impressive for call centers. What keeps people at Zappos? "We pay 100 percent of employee benefits," and then there's the wow factor.

"We can't ask people to wow a customer if they haven't been wowed by us," says Ratner. Zappos is so eager to wow employees and make sure who they hire is committed that they offer people $3,000 after they've been trained to walk away if they feel they and Zappos aren't a good fit. Almost no one takes the $3,000 walk-away money. But many trainees return for more Zappos training to become managers.

SOURCE: Excerpted from J Larrere, "Develop Great Leaders," *Leadership Excellence*, April 2010, p 12.

BACK TO THE CHAPTER-OPENING CASE Which of the mechanisms for changing organizational culture did Marchionne use at Chrysler? Explain.

The Organizational Socialization Process

Organizational socialization is defined as "the process by which a person learns the values, norms, and required behaviors which permit him to participate as a member of the organization."[35] As previously discussed, organizational socialization is a key mechanism used by organizations to embed their organizational cultures. In short, organizational socialization turns outsiders into fully functioning insiders by promoting and reinforcing the organization's core values and beliefs. This section introduces a three-phase model of organizational socialization and examines the practical application of socialization research.

A Three-Phase Model of Organizational Socialization

LO2.4

One's first year in a complex organization can be confusing. There is a constant swirl of new faces, strange jargon, conflicting expectations, and apparently unrelated events. Some organizations treat new members in a rather haphazard, sink-or-swim manner. More typically, though, the socialization process is characterized by a sequence of identifiable steps.

Organizational behavior researcher Daniel Feldman has proposed a three-phase model of organizational socialization that promotes deeper understanding of this important process. As illustrated in Figure 2–5, the three phases are (1) anticipatory socialization, (2) encounter, and (3) change and acquisition. Each phase has its associated

FIGURE 2–5   A Model of Organizational Socialization

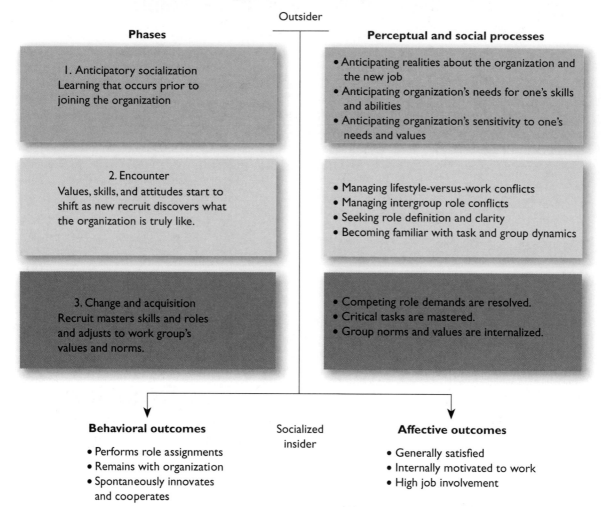

Outsider

Phases

1. Anticipatory socialization
Learning that occurs prior to
joining the organization

2. Encounter
Values, skills, and attitudes start to
shift as new recruit discovers what
the organization is truly like.

3. Change and acquisition
Recruit masters skills and roles
and adjusts to work group's
values and norms.

Perceptual and social processes

- Anticipating realities about the organization and the new job
- Anticipating organization's needs for one's skills and abilities
- Anticipating organization's sensitivity to one's needs and values

- Managing lifestyle-versus-work conflicts
- Managing intergroup role conflicts
- Seeking role definition and clarity
- Becoming familiar with task and group dynamics

- Competing role demands are resolved.
- Critical tasks are mastered.
- Group norms and values are internalized.

Behavioral outcomes

- Performs role assignments
- Remains with organization
- Spontaneously innovates and cooperates

Socialized
insider

Affective outcomes

- Generally satisfied
- Internally motivated to work
- High job involvement

SOURCE: Adapted from material in D C Feldman, "The Multiple Socialization of Organization Members," *Academy of Management Review*, April 1981, pp 309–18.

connect
www.mcgrawhillconnect.com

Go to Connect for an interactive exercise to check your understanding of the socialization process.

perceptual and social processes. Feldman's model also specifies behavioral and affective outcomes that can be used to judge how well an individual has been socialized. The entire three-phase sequence may take from a few weeks to a year to complete, depending on individual differences and the complexity of the situation.

Phase 1: Anticipatory Socialization *Anticipatory socialization* occurs **before an individual actually joins an organization.** It is represented by the information people have learned about different careers, occupations, professions, and organizations. Anticipatory socialization information comes from many sources. An organization's current employees are a powerful source of anticipatory socialization. So are the Internet and social media. For example, PricewaterhouseCoopers (PwC), the largest professional services firm in the world, uses several web-based sources to attract potential employees. "PwC's early identification strategy is supported by the pwc.tv website, *Feed Your Future* magazine (downloadable through pwc.tv; it showcases the lives and careers of PwC professionals), and Leadership Adventure (face-to-face learning programs that emphasize the PwC behaviors)".[36]

Phase 2: Encounter   This second phase begins when the employment contract has been signed. During the *encounter phase* **employees come to learn what the organization is really like.** It is a time for reconciling unmet expectations and making sense of a new work environment. Many companies use a combination of orientation and training programs to socialize employees during the encounter phase. Onboarding is one such technique. *Onboarding* **programs help employees to integrate, assimilate, and transition to new jobs by making them familiar with corporate policies, procedures, and culture and by clarifying work role expectations and responsibilities.**[37] Automatic Data Processing's (ADP) onboarding program consists of a combination of online training, classroom training, meetings with employees, written materials containing guidelines on what to expect in the first 90 days, an assimilation guide, and social networking. The company believes that these efforts are helping it to turn newcomers into fully functioning employees.[38]

Boot camp serves to quickly set expectations regarding behaviors that are expected and valued by the military. What are the pros and cons of using boot camp to socialize future soldiers?

Phase 3: Change and Acquisition   The *change and acquisition* **phase requires employees to master important tasks and roles and to adjust to their work group's values and norms.** This will only occur when employees have a clear understanding about their roles—role clarity is discussed in Chapter 9—and they are effectively integrated within the work unit. Being successful in phase 3 also necessitates that employees have a clear understanding regarding the use of social media. It is easy for you to create problems for yourself by not being aware of expectations regarding surfing, texting during meetings, and sending personal messages on company equipment. Experts suggest setting ground rules on the first day of employment, coaching employees on norms, and discussing how guidelines have changed over time.[39] Additionally, organizations such as Schlumberger, a large multinational oil company, use incentives and social gatherings to reinforce the new behaviors expected of employees.

Table 2–1 presents a list of socialization processes or tactics used by organizations to help employees through this adjustment process. Returning to Table 2–1, can you identify the socialization tactics used by Schlumberger?

Practical Application of Socialization Research

Past research suggests four practical guidelines for managing organizational socialization.

1. Managers play a key role during the encounter phase. Studies of newly hired accountants demonstrated that the frequency and type of information obtained during their first six months of employment significantly affected their job performance, their role clarity, and the extent to which they were socially integrated.[40] Managers need to help new hires integrate within the organizational culture. Consider the approach used by John Chambers, CEO of Cisco Systems.

TABLE 2–1   Socialization Tactics

LO2.5

Tactic	Description
Collective vs. individual	Collective socialization consists of grouping newcomers and exposing them to a common set of experiences rather than treating each newcomer individually and exposing him or her to more or less unique experiences.
Formal vs. informal	Formal socialization is the practice of segregating a newcomer from regular organization members during a defined socialization period versus not clearly distinguishing a newcomer from more experienced members. Army recruits must attend boot camp before they are allowed to work alongside established soldiers.
Sequential vs. random	Sequential socialization refers to a fixed progression of steps that culminate in the new role, compared to an ambiguous or dynamic progression. The socialization of doctors involves a lockstep sequence from medical school, to internship, to residency before they are allowed to practice on their own.
Fixed vs. variable	Fixed socialization provides a timetable for the assumption of the role, whereas a variable process does not. American university students typically spend one year apiece as freshmen, sophomores, juniors, and seniors.
Serial vs. disjunctive	A serial process is one in which the newcomer is socialized by an experienced member, whereas a disjunctive process does not use a role model.
Investiture vs. divestiture	Investiture refers to the affirmation of a newcomer's incoming global and specific role identities and attributes. Divestiture is the denial and stripping away of the newcomer's existing sense of self and the reconstruction of self in the organization's image. During police training, cadets are required to wear uniforms and maintain an immaculate appearance, they are addressed as "officer," and they are told they are no longer ordinary citizens but representatives of the police force.

SOURCE: Descriptions taken from B E Ashforth, *Role Transitions in Organizational Life: An Identity-Based Perspective* (Mahwah, NJ: Lawrence Erlbaum Associates, 2001), pp 149–83.

"He meets with groups of new hires to welcome them soon after they start, and at monthly breakfast meetings workers are encouraged to ask him tough questions".[41]

HANDS-ON EXERCISE

Have You Been Adequately Socialized?

INSTRUCTIONS: Complete the following survey items by considering either your current job or one you held in the past. If you have never worked, identify a friend who is working and ask that individual to complete the questionnaire for his or her organization. Read each item and circle your response by using the rating scale shown below. Compute your total score by adding up your responses and compare it to the scoring norms.

	Strongly Disagree	Disagree	Neutral	Agree	Strongly Agree
1. I have been through a set of training experiences that are specifically designed to give newcomers a thorough knowledge of job-related skills.	1	2	3	4	5
2. This organization puts all newcomers through the same set of learning experiences.	1	2	3	4	5
3. I did not perform any of my normal job responsibilities until I was thoroughly familiar with departmental procedures and work methods.	1	2	3	4	5
4. There is a clear pattern in the way one role leads to another, or one job assignment leads to another, in this organization.	1	2	3	4	5
5. I can predict my future career path in this organization by observing other people's experiences.	1	2	3	4	5
6. Almost all of my colleagues have been supportive of me personally.	1	2	3	4	5
7. My colleagues have gone out of their way to help me adjust to this organization.	1	2	3	4	5
8. I received much guidance from experienced organizational members as to how I should perform my job.	1	2	3	4	5
Total Score	___	___	___	___	___

SCORING NORMS

8–18 = Low socialization   19–29 = Moderate socialization   30–40 = High socialization

SOURCE: Adapted from survey items excerpted from D Cable and C Parsons, "Socialization Tactics and Person-Organization Fit," *Personnel Psychology,* Spring 2001, pp 1–23.

Take a moment now to complete the Hands-On Exercise on page 49. It measures the extent to which you have been socialized into your current work organization. Have you been adequately socialized? If not, you may need to find a mentor. Mentoring is discussed in the next section.

2. A recent survey showed that effective onboarding programs resulted in increased retention, productivity, and rates of task completion for new hires.[42] This reinforces the conclusion that managers should avoid a haphazard, sink-or-swim approach to organizational socialization because formalized socialization tactics positively affect new hires.[43]

3. Organizations like the U.S. Military Academy at West Point use socialization tactics to reinforce a culture that promotes ethical behavior. Managers are encouraged to consider how they might best set expectations regarding ethical behavior during all three phases of the socialization process.[44]

4. Managers should pay attention to the socialization of diverse employees. Research demonstrated that diverse employees, particularly those with disabilities, experienced different socialization activities than other newcomers. In turn, these different experiences affected their long-term success and job satisfaction.[45]

Embedding Organizational Culture through Mentoring

The modern word *mentor* derives from Mentor, the name of a wise and trusted counselor in Greek mythology. Terms typically used in connection with mentoring are *teacher, coach, sponsor,* and peer. **Mentoring is defined as the process of forming and maintaining intensive and lasting developmental relationships between a variety of developers (i.e., people who provide career and psychosocial support) and a junior person (the protégé, if male; or protégée, if female).**[46] Mentoring can serve to embed an organization's culture when developers and the protégé/protégée work in the same organization for two reasons. First, mentoring contributes to creating a sense of oneness by promoting the acceptance of the organization's core values throughout the organization. Second, the socialization aspect of mentoring also promotes a sense of membership.

Not only is mentoring important as a tactic for embedding organizational culture, but research suggests it can significantly influence the protégé/protégée's future career. For example, mentored employees performed better on the job and experienced more rapid career advancement than nonmentored employees. Mentored employees also reported higher job and career satisfaction and working on more challenging job assignments.[47] With this information in mind, this section focuses on how people can use mentoring to their advantage. We discuss the functions of mentoring, the developmental networks underlying mentoring, and the personal and organizational implications of mentoring.

Big Brothers Big Sisters is the largest volunteer mentoring network in the U.S. The organization has paired adults with children for over 100 years. A survey of former children in the program revealed that 83% obtained values and principles that influenced them throughout their lives.

Functions of Mentoring

Kathy Kram, a Boston University researcher, conducted in-depth interviews with both members of 18 pairs of senior and junior managers. As a by-product of this study, Kram identified two general functions—career and psychosocial—of the mentoring process. Five *career functions* that enhanced career development were sponsorship, exposure-and-visibility, coaching, protection, and challenging assignments. Four *psychosocial functions* were role modeling, acceptance-and-confirmation, counseling, and friendship. The psychosocial functions clarified the participants' identities and enhanced their feelings of competence.[48]

Developmental Networks Underlying Mentoring

LO2.6

Historically, it was thought that mentoring was primarily provided by one person who was called a mentor. Today, however, the changing nature of technology, organizational structures, and marketplace dynamics requires that people seek career information and support from many sources. Mentoring is currently viewed as a process in which protégés and protégées seek developmental guidance from a network of people, who are referred to as developers. McKinsey & Company tells its associates, "Build your own McKinsey." This slogan means the consulting firm expects its people to identify partners, colleagues, and subordinates who have related goals and interests so that they can help one another develop their expertise. Each McKinsey associate is thus responsible for his or her own career development—and for mentoring others.[49] As McKinsey's approach recognizes, the diversity and strength of a person's network of relationships is instrumental in obtaining the type of career assistance needed to manage his or her career. Figure 2–6 presents a developmental network typology based on integrating the diversity and strength of developmental relationships.[50]

The **diversity of developmental relationships reflects the variety of people within the network an individual uses for developmental assistance.** There are two subcomponents associated with network diversity: (1) the number of different people the person is networked with and (2) the various social systems from which the networked relationships stem (e.g., employer, school, family, community, professional associations, and religious affiliations). As shown in Figure 2–6, developmental relationship diversity ranges from low (few people or social systems) to high (multiple people or social systems). **Developmental relationship strength reflects the quality of relationships among an individual and those involved in his or her developmental network.** For example, strong ties are reflective of relationships based on frequent interactions, reciprocity, and positive affect. Weak ties, in contrast, are based more on superficial relationships. Together, the diversity and strength of developmental relationships results in four types of developmental networks (see Figure 2–6): receptive, traditional, entrepreneurial, and opportunistic.

A *receptive* developmental network is composed of a few weak ties from one social system such as an employer or a professional association. The single oval around D1 and D2 in Figure 2–6 is indicative of two developers who come from one social system. In contrast, a *traditional* network contains a few strong ties between an employee and developers that all come from one social system. An *entrepreneurial* network, which is the strongest type of developmental network, is made up of strong ties among several developers (D1–D4) who come from four different social systems. Finally, an *opportunistic* network is associated with having weak ties with multiple developers from different social systems.

FIGURE 2–6   Developmental Networks Associated with Mentoring

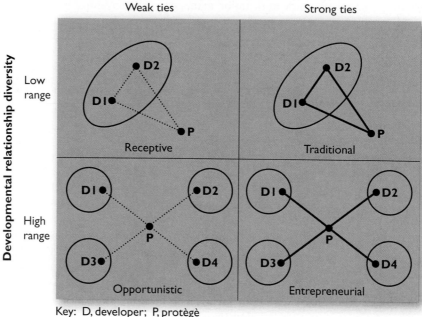

SOURCE: From *Academy of Management Review* by M Higgins and K Kram, "Reconceptualizing Mentoring at Work: A Developmental Network Perspective," April 2001, p 270. Copyright 2001 by Academy of Management. Reproduced with permission of Academy of Management via Copyright Clearance Center.

Personal and Organizational Implications

connect
www.mcgrawhillconnect.com

Go to Connect for a video case to view Pike Place Fish Market, how organizational culture affects their workers, and their mentoring program.

There are four key personal implications to consider. First, your job and career satisfaction are likely to be influenced by the consistency between your career goals and the type of developmental network at your disposal. For example, people with an entrepreneurial developmental network are more likely to experience change in their careers and to benefit from personal learning than people with receptive, traditional, and opportunistic networks. If this sounds attractive to you, you should try to increase the diversity and strength of your developmental relationships. In contrast, lower levels of job satisfaction are expected when employees have receptive developmental networks and they desire to experience career advancement in multiple organizations. Receptive developmental networks, however, can be satisfying to someone who does not desire to be promoted up the career ladder. Second, a developer's willingness to provide career and psychosocial assistance is a function of the protégé or protégée's ability, potential, and the quality of the interpersonal relationship.[51] Research also shows that the quality of the mentoring relationship is likely to be higher when the parties have common values and personality characteristics.[52] This implies that you must take ownership for enhancing your skills, abilities, and developmental networks if you desire to experience career advancement throughout your life. Third, it is important to become proficient at using social networking tools such as Twitter, LinkedIn, and Facebook. Companies like AT&T are increasingly using online tools to conduct mentoring across geographical boundaries.[53] These tools not only enable you to increase

Building an Effective Mentoring Network

1. *Invest in your relationships.* Devote the time and energy necessary to develop trust and respect in your mentors. Get to know each mentor's personality and background before plunging into specific problems.
2. *Engage in 360-degree networking.* Share information and maintain good relationships with people above, below, and at your level of the organization's hierarchy.
3. *Plan your network.* Assess what competencies you need to build, identify mentors who can help with those competencies, and change mentors as your competencies develop.
4. *Develop diverse connections.* Be open to informal and formal relationships.
5. *Agree on the process.* At the first meeting, the mentor and protégé or protégée should agree how often they will meet and how they will communicate outside the scheduled meetings.
6. *Be ready to move on.* The average mentoring relationship lasts five years. When a relationship is no longer beneficial, the parties should end it and free their time for more productive relationships.

SOURCES: Based on S C de Janasz, S E Sullivan, and V Whiting, "Mentor Networks and Career Success: Lessons for Turbulent Times," *Academy of Management Executive*, November 2003, pp 78–91; and N Anand and J Conger, "Capabilities of the Consummate Networker," *Organizational Dynamics*, 2007, pp 13–27.

the breadth of your social network, but they also can increase your productivity. Finally, you should develop a mentoring plan (see Skills & Best Practices above).

Research also supports the organizational benefits of mentoring. In addition to the obvious benefit of employee development, mentoring enhances the effectiveness of organizational communication. Specifically, mentoring increases the amount of vertical communication both up and down an organization, and it provides a mechanism for modifying or reinforcing organizational culture. An effective mentoring program can also reduce employee turnover and increase productivity. A star associate at the law firm of Milbank, Tweed, Hadley & McCloy was restless and ready to leave when a practice group leader happened to offer praise and encouragement for a job well done. The associate felt so reinforced by the partner's interest that he decided to stay with the firm after all.[54]

key terms

adhocracy culture   38
anticipatory socialization   46
change and acquisition   47
clan culture   37
competing values framework (CVF)   37
developmental relationship strength   50

diversity of developmental relationships   51
enacted values   34
encounter phase   47
espoused values   33
hierarchy culture   39
market culture   39

mentoring   50
onboarding   47
organizational culture   32
organizational socialization   45
values   33

chapter summary

- *Discuss the layers and functions of organizational culture.* The three layers of organizational culture are observable artifacts, espoused values, and basic underlying assumptions. Each layer varies in terms of outward visibility and resistance to change. Four functions of organizational culture are organizational identity, collective commitment, social system stability, and sense-making device.

- *Discuss the general types of organizational culture and their associated characteristics.* According to the competing values framework, defining culture along two axes (internal or external focus and preference for stability or flexibility) defines four types of organizational cultures. A clan culture has an internal focus and values flexibility; it achieves effectiveness through employee involvement. An adhocracy culture has an external focus and values flexibility; it emphasizes innovation and fast responses to change. A market culture has a strong external focus and values stability and control; such organizations are driven by competition and emphasize customer satisfaction. A hierarchy culture has an internal focus and values stability and control; it emphasizes formal, structured work to meet high standards.

- *Summarize the process by which organizations change their cultures.* The process essentially begins with targeting one of the three layers of organizational culture—observable artifacts, espoused values, and basic assumptions—for change. This is accomplished by using one or more of the following 11 mechanisms: (a) formal statements of organizational philosophy, mission, vision, values, and materials used for recruiting, selection, and socialization; (b) the design of physical space, work environments, and buildings; (c) slogans, language, acronyms, and sayings; (d) deliberate role modeling, training programs, teaching, and coaching by managers and supervisors; (e) explicit rewards, status symbols, and promotion criteria; (f) stories, legends, and myths about key people and events; (g) the organizational activities, processes, or outcomes that leaders pay attention to, measure, and control; (h) leader reactions to critical incidents and organizational crises; (i) the workflow and organizational structure; (j) organizational systems and procedures; and (k) organizational goals and associated criteria used for recruitment, selection, development, promotion, layoffs, and retirement of people.

- *Describe the three phases in Feldman's model of organizational socialization.* The three phases of Feldman's model are anticipatory socialization, encounter, and change and acquisition. Anticipatory socialization begins before an individual actually joins the organization. The encounter phase begins when the employment contract has been signed. Phase 3 involves the period in which employees master important tasks and resolve any role conflicts.

- *Discuss the various socialization tactics used to socialize employees.* There are six key socialization tactics. They are collective versus individual, formal versus informal, sequential versus random, fixed versus variable, serial versus disjunctive, and investiture versus divestiture (see Table 2–1). Each tactic provides organizations with two opposing options for socializing employees.

- *Explain the four types of development networks derived from a developmental network model of mentoring.* The four development networks are receptive, traditional, entrepreneurial, and opportunistic. A receptive network is composed of a few weak ties from one social system. A traditional network contains a few strong ties between an employee and developers that all come from one social system. An entrepreneurial network is made up of strong ties among developers from several social systems, and an opportunistic network is associated with having weak ties with multiple developers from different social systems.

discussion questions

1. How would you respond to someone who made the following statement? "Organizational cultures are not important as far as managers are concerned."
2. Figure 2–4 revealed that organizational culture was not strongly related to measures of financial performance. Why do you think this is the case?
3. Can you think of any organizational heroes who have influenced your work behavior? Describe them, and explain how they affected your behavior.
4. Why is socialization essential to organizational success?
5. Have you ever had a mentor? Explain how things turned out.

legal/ethical challenge

Credit-Card Issuers Have Cultures That Focus on Growth by Targeting Financially Strapped People[55]

The troubles sound familiar. Borrowers falling behind on their payments. Defaults rising. Huge swaths of loans souring. Investors getting burned. But forget the now-familiar tales of mortgages gone bad. The next horror for beaten-down financial firms is the $950 billion worth of outstanding credit-card debt—much of it toxic. . . . The consumer debt bomb is already beginning to spray shrapnel throughout the financial markets, further weakening the U.S. economy. "The next meltdown will be in credit cards," says Gregory Larkin, senior analyst at research firm Innovest Strategic Value Advisors. . . .

But some banks and credit card companies may be exacerbating their problems. To boost profits and get ahead of coming regulation, they're hiking interest rates. But that's making it harder for consumers to keep up. . . . Sure the credit-card market is just a fraction of the $11.9 trillion mortgage market. But sometimes the losses can be more painful. That's because most credit-card debt is unsecured, meaning consumers don't have to make down payments when opening up their accounts. If they stop making monthly payments and the account goes bad, there are no underlying assets for credit-card companies to recoup. With mortgages, in contrast, some banks are protected both by down payments and by the ability to recover at least some of the money by selling the property. . . .

The industry's practices during the lending boom are coming back to haunt many credit-card lenders now. Cate Colombo, a former call center staffer at MBNA, the big issuer bought by Bank of America in 2005, says her job was to develop a rapport with credit-card customers and advise them to use more of their available credit. Colleagues would often gather around her chair when she was on the phone with a customer and chant: "Sell, sell." "It was like *Boiler Room*," says Colombo, referring to the 2000 movie about unscrupulous stock brokers. "I knew that they would probably be in debt for the rest of their lives." Unless, of course, they default.

Assume that you are member of Congress. What would you do in light of the facts in this case?

1. Create legislation that does not allow credit-card issuers to raise interest rates for those who cannot pay their bills.

2. Create legislation that makes it a crime for people like Cate Colombo to entice people to spend money on a credit card when they can't afford it.

3. I would not create any legislation. Credit-card issuers and people like Cate Colombo are not to blame for our financial problems. People must be responsible for their own behavior.

4. Invent other options.

If you're looking for additional study materials, be sure to check out the Online Learning Center at

www.mhhe.com/kinickiob5e

for more information and interactivities that correspond to this chapter.

chapter 3

Developing Global Managers

After reading the material in this chapter, you should be able to:

LO3.1 Describe a global mind-set, and explain how to build its three-component forms of capital.

LO3.2 Identify and describe the nine cultural dimensions from the GLOBE project.

LO3.3 Describe the differences between individualistic cultures and collectivist cultures.

LO3.4 Demonstrate your knowledge of the distinctions between high-context versus low-context cultures and monochronic versus polychronic cultures.

LO3.5 Explain what the GLOBE project has taught us about leadership.

LO3.6 Identify an OB trouble spot for each stage of the foreign assignment cycle.

Can You Actually Hire 25,000 People in Six Months?!

For most human resources (HR) executives hiring 25,000 employees in six months is unfathomable. But this is what Tata Consultancy Services (TCS), India's leading software services company, did. The company plans to hire another 50,000 in 2011. To put this in perspective, that is approximately the same size as the entire student population of Ohio State University or the University of Florida—each had roughly 50,000 students in 2010. This daunting task is essential to compete effectively in India's information technology (IT) and outsourcing services industry. TCS was the winner of the 2010 Optimas Award for General Excellence for its ability to recruit and train a huge, multilingual workforce and to align its workforce strategy with swiftly changing business demands.

TCS is the first non-North American company to win the overall award and top prize. The IT and outsourcing giant, with nearly 175,000 employees representing 88 nationalities, in 142 offices in 42 countries, was recognized by Workforce Management for innovative recruiting and staffing programs, career development partnerships with colleges, sweeping foreign language and cross-cultural initiatives, expansion of its programs to help educate poor communities, and creation of streamlined digital systems to link people management with business strategy.

Like many other firms TCS faces pressing shortages of talented people. Traditional technical skills no longer suit burgeoning business demands, says Diane Morello, vice president of Gartner IT Consulting. She also stated, "The intersection of business models and IT requires people with varied experience, professional versatility, multidisciplined knowledge and technology understanding   a hybrid professional."

To meet such challenges TCS implements a number of noteworthy HR programs. One such program is called Ignite. It aims to expand and deepen the company's recruiting reach beyond the larger universities and cities, and beyond engineering and technology. The seven-month, high-tech, high-touch program combines electronic instruction with face-to-face contact. Women comprise 65% of program trainees. Another successful initiative involves career development partnerships with groups such as AIESEC, the largest international student organization with 50,000 members. The one-year program partners students in countries ranging from Uruguay and Ecuador to Hungary and Finland. Participants receive cross-cultural training, work with individual mentors, and meet senior management at an annual conference.

Perhaps nowhere is TCS's global response more important than in its

language and cross-cultural programs. Over the years, TCS has created a vast spectrum of classes blending learning via its intranet, the Internet, telephone, and face-to-face instruction. A few years ago in Japan, for example, TCS began an offshore center to develop bilingual training and business skills in the local culture. The program was not only implemented ahead of schedule, but TCS also estimates that it helped expand its business in Japan by more than 50% in six months.

TCS's talent development programs help ensure that associates continue to build their skills throughout their careers. TCS chief executive officer (CEO) Naratjan Chandrasekaran claims that such investments have resulted in TCS having the highest retention rate in the industry. Such efforts will be critical to TCS's long-term success. Gartner's head of India research, Partha Iyengars says, "This is one of TCS's key cultural challenges. In the United States, people in sales and marketing are the rock stars. In India it's the techies who are the rock stars. India might need to recruit

more in the United States and Europe or else how are they going to move the whole culture more to sales and marketing?"

Despite all of TCS's sophisticated HR programs designed to handle large numbers of employees, Iyengar says, the company will continue to experience the same problems organizations large and small will face in the coming years: finding and developing skilled, versatile employees. "TCS is known to be the best in training," Iyengar adds. "But if they still have a goal of achieving revenues of $10 billion by 2012 ($6.3 billion in 2010) . . . they will have to employ another 350,000 people." Ajoyendra Mukherjee, TCS's global head of HR, says: "We are very proud of the fact that in a year when the business environment was very challenging, we went ahead and recruited 38,000 people, and all of them joined TCS in the same fiscal year . . . managing this enormous growth across multiple geographies is an ongoing challenge and one that we continue to learn from and improve upon."[1]

THE CHAPTER-OPENING CASE ILLUSTRATES the challenges associated with managing growth in a major global technology services company. In addition to considering the number of people required to hire thousands of employees—the actual hiring process—consider how many new managers will be necessary! The case also underscores the importance and advantage of human capital, which we studied in Chapter 1. TCS is one of India's top three software services companies. TCS achieved this distinction and was recognized for it at least in part by taking a people-centered approach to management. Its future success no doubt depends on how well it attracts, develops, utilizes, and retains high-quality people around the world. The case also illustrates concepts related to culture in Chapter 2. TCS's clan culture values talented people and is supported by its many employee-development practices.

TCS is a global player that often competes head-to-head not only with large Indian competitors (e.g., Infosys and Wipro), but also with large American-based technology companies (e.g., IBM and Accenture). All of these companies realize that their short- and long-term success depends on their ability to manage culturally diverse workers effectively in both domestic and international markets. From the perspective of American companies, international markets are appealing because of a number of global trends.

- *Mature and slower growing domestic markets.* Emerging markets, especially the BRIC countries (Brazil, Russia, India, and China), offer much greater growth prospects than the relatively mature U.S. market.[2]

- *Foreign competition.* Likewise, foreign companies want access to the mature U.S. market as Americans are still the world's most numerous consumers. This enables them to sell higher margin products and services to customers with deeper pockets. Whether American-based or not, this results in greater competition for all companies that operate in the U.S. market.[3]

- *Globalization of capital.* Not only is human capital moving more easily across borders but so, too, is money. Investors, companies, and countries with money are looking around the globe for opportunities with greater returns. This interconnectedness was proven by the truly global nature of the recent financial crisis.[4]

- *Growing middle class.* Assuming continued economic growth in the developing world, the ranks of the global middle class are expected to triple by 2030 to 1.2 billion people, according to the World Bank. Today, more than half of that free-spending group resides in developing countries. By 2030, almost all of it, 92%, will call the developing world home.[5]

This scenario has many implications. Notably, for more than half a century Americans could take for granted that the world economy would orbit around them. No longer. Companies now must pay attention to global markets, and managers must lead employees in various parts of the world. For example, GE and Nokia established research and development centers in both China and India. Cisco Systems went so far as to establish a second headquarters in India. Such actions enable these companies to better understand these important markets.[6] If they also hire locally, then they can access the benefits of the local human and social capital.

Competition for both businesses and those seeking good-paying jobs in the global economy is an increasingly intense challenge. The purpose of this chapter is to help you move toward meeting this challenge. To do this, the chapter draws on cultural anthropology to explore the impact of culture in today's increasingly globalized organizations. We begin by discussing how to develop a global mind-set. Next, we examine key dimensions of societal culture with the goal of enhancing cross-cultural awareness. Then we review practical lessons from research into cross-cultural management. The chapter concludes by exploring the challenges of foreign assignments and ways organizations can prepare their people to meet those challenges.

Developing a Global Mind-Set

LO3.1

Managing in a global economy is as much about patterns of thinking and behavior as it is about trade agreements, goods and services, and currency exchange rates. Extended periods in a single dominant culture ingrain assumptions about how things are and should be. Today's managers, whether they work at home for a foreign-owned company or simply work with people from diverse cultural backgrounds, need to develop a global mind-set. A team of international business professors describe the competencies needed to develop a global mind-set as follows:

1. *Intellectual capital*—Knowledge of international business and ability to learn, characterized by global business savvy, cognitive complexity (ability to analyze and connect multiple elements), and cosmopolitan outlook

2. *Psychological capital*—Openness to other cultures and willingness to change, characterized by passion for diversity, thirst for adventure, and self-assurance

3. *Social capital*—Ability to form connections and bring people together, characterized by intercultural empathy, interpersonal impact, and diplomacy[7]

You can see that the first and third competencies closely relate to the concepts of human capital (e.g., knowledge and ability to learn) and social capital discussed in Chapter 1. This suggests that a global mind-set is something that you and your employer can invest in to increase your individual and organizational value in the short and long term.

> **BACK TO THE CHAPTER-OPENING CASE**   Assume you are responsible for training the many new employees at Tata Consultancy Services. Describe how you would build the three forms of capital included in a global mind-set.

The following section elaborates on how to develop a global mind-set. We do so by defining societal culture and contrasting it with organizational culture, discussing ethnocentrism, exploring ways to become a global manager, and then examining the applicability of American management theories in other cultures.

A Model of Societal and Organizational Cultures

Societal culture **involves shared values, norms, identities, and interpretations that result from common experiences of members of collectives that are transmitted over time.** Like organizational culture discussed in Chapter 2, societal culture is a social phenomenon that is shared among its members. It is this shared aspect that gives culture its power to influence behavior. Typically, when you comply with the expectations of a particular culture you are "rewarded" by its members, and when you don't comply you are "punished" in some way. Culture may be prescriptive (what people should do) and descriptive (what they actually do). Most cultural lessons are learned by observing and imitating role models—family, friends, teachers, coworkers, business leaders—as they go about their daily affairs or are observed in the media. Many factors influence societal cultures, such as economics, technology, politics, laws, ethnicities, and religion. Knowledge of such factors can enhance your global mind-set. (See the Skills & Best Practices feature on page 60 for an interesting example.)

Really?! I Decide How Many Hours I Work?

This title suggests employees have a choice. But most employers around the world tell employees when and how much they will work rather than ask. The Netherlands, however, provides an interesting alternative. Not only do 3 out of 4 Dutch women work part time, but many men work only four days a week. For example, Remco Vermaire is 37 and is the youngest partner at his law firm. His clients expect him to be available any minute of the day or night—*but only the four days a week that he works*. When he is "off the clock" they do not expect him to be available. This is in part because many of his clients work similarly flexible schedules. Moreover, 14 of the 33 attorneys at his firm work part time. This evidence suggests that the Dutch have particular norms related to work schedules. And as you learned in Chapter 2, norms are manifestations of a culture's underlying values.

The Dutch have managed to effectively blend traditional and modern values. While laws kept women out of the workplace for much of the 1900s, legislation in 2000 allowed all employees (men and women) to determine the number of hours they work. Employers can object if they have a compelling reason, but most challenges are not granted. Today most female-dominated jobs (e.g., nursing and education) are staffed via job sharing between two or more part-time employees. Of course, reduced schedules result in reduced income. The Dutch do not provide full-time pay for part-time work. Nevertheless, many working age people with and without kids would gladly trade money for more free time. A third of Dutch men either work part-time or squeeze a full-time job into four days. More generally, 25% of workers in the Netherlands have reduced hours compared to only ten percent across the rest of Europe and the U.S.

While flexible schedules typically have been used to accommodate female employees, both in the Netherlands and elsewhere, Dutch companies now widely use flextime to attract and retain *both* male and female talent in a competitive labor market. For example, Dutch Microsoft allows employees to work from anywhere anytime. This has resulted in 95% of employees working from home at least one day per week and 25% working from home four out of five days.

This scenario is summarized very well by Pia Dykstra, a member of Parliament and a well-known former Dutch news anchor: "Our part-time experience has taught us that you can organize work in a rhythm other than nine-to-five."

SOURCE: Excerpted and adapted from K Bennhold, "Dutch Professionals Work Shorter Weeks for Work-Life Balance," *The New York Times*, January 2, 2011.

Peeling the Cultural Onion Culture is difficult to grasp because it is multilayered. International management experts Fons Trompenaars (from the Netherlands) and Charles Hampden-Turner (from Britain) offer this instructive analogy in their landmark book, *Riding the Waves of Culture:*

> Culture comes in layers, like an onion. To understand it you have to peel it layer by layer. On the outer layer are the products of culture, like the soaring skyscrapers of Manhattan, pillars of private power, with congested public streets between them. These are expressions of deeper values and norms in a society that are not directly visible (values such as upward mobility, "the more-the-better," status, material success). The layers of values and norms are deeper within the "onion," and are more difficult to identify.[8]

Thus, the September 11, 2001, destruction of the New York World Trade Center towers by terrorists was as much an attack on American cultural values as it was on lives and property. That deepened the hurt and made the anger more profound for Americans and their friends around the world. In both life and business, culture is a serious matter.

Cultural Influences on Organizational Behavior   FIGURE 3–1

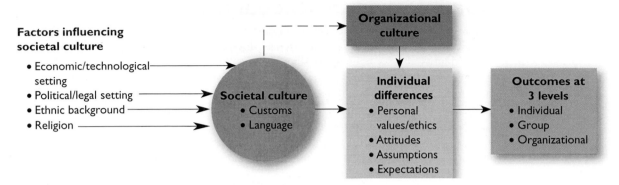

Merging Societal and Organizational Cultures   As illustrated in Figure 3–1, both organizational and societal cultures influence organizational behavior. Employees bring their societal culture to work with them in the form of customs and language. Organizational culture, a by-product of societal culture, in turn affects individual differences, such as values, ethics, attitudes, assumptions, and expectations.[9] (Individual differences are covered in Chapter 5.) These individual differences then influence behavior at the individual, group, and organizational levels.

The term *societal culture* is used here instead of national culture because the boundaries of many modern nation-states were not drawn along cultural lines. The former Soviet Union, for example, included 15 republics and more than 100 ethnic nationalities, many with their own distinct language.[10] Meanwhile, English-speaking Canadians in Vancouver are culturally closer to Americans in Seattle than to their French-speaking compatriots in Quebec.

Once inside the organization's sphere of influence, the individual is further affected by the *organization's* culture, which was discussed in Chapter 2. Mixing of societal and organizational cultures can produce interesting dynamics in multinational companies. For example, while Facebook has more than 600 million members worldwide, including more than 60% of Internet users in the United States, it has relatively few in Japan. Part of the reason is that Japan has several domestic social networking sites (e.g., Mixi and Gree), each with more than 20 million users compared to Facebook's 2 million. Another reason, however, is the stark cultural differences between Japan and the United States, and between the East and West more generally. Facebook requires all members to use their actual names and identities—no aliases. Transparency on the Web is a central value at Facebook and of founder Mark Zuckerberg. (The no-alias norm supports this value.) However, the transparency value conflicts with the Japanese value for privacy and preference for anonymity. Eighty-nine percent of Japanese mobile Web users surveyed stated they were against using their real names on the Internet. They instead commonly use pseudonyms or other names to mask their true identities. To address these differences, Facebook is trying to tailor its service to the Japanese market by allowing local translation, opening a Tokyo office, and allowing users to post their blood types (an individual characteristic with value in that culture). But little has been done so far regarding the privacy issue.[11]

To summarize, merging societal and organizational cultures is an eternal and critical challenge facing managers. Awareness and accommodation of differences is essential in order to achieve an effective fit between the two and boost performance at all levels—individual, group, and organizational. In the next section, we address a common cause of cross-cultural conflict—ethnocentrism.

Ethnocentrism: Removing a Cultural Roadblock in the Global Economy

Ethnocentrism—**the belief that one's native country, culture, language, and modes of behavior are superior to all others**—**has its roots in the dawn of civilization.** First identified as a behavioral science concept in 1906 involving the tendency of groups to reject outsiders,[12] the term *ethnocentrism* today generally has a more encompassing (national or societal) meaning. Worldwide evidence of ethnocentrism is plentiful. Militant ethnocentrism led to deadly "ethnic cleansing" in Bosnia, Kosovo, and Kenya and genocide in Rwanda, Burundi, and Sudan.

Less dramatic, but still troublesome, is ethnocentrism within managerial and organizational contexts. Experts on the subject framed the problem this way:

> [Ethnocentric managers have] a preference for putting home-country people in key positions everywhere in the world and rewarding them more handsomely for work, along with a tendency to feel that this group is more intelligent, more capable, or more reliable. . . . Ethnocentrism is often not attributable to prejudice as much as to inexperience or lack of knowledge about foreign persons and situations. This is not too surprising, since most executives know far more about employees in their home environments. As one executive put it, "At least I understand why our own managers make mistakes. With our foreigners, I never know. The foreign managers may be better. But if I can't trust a person, should I hire him or her just to prove we're multinational?"[13]

Research Insight and Dealing with Ethnocentrism   Research suggests ethnocentrism is bad for business. A survey of 918 companies with home offices in the United States (272 companies), Japan (309), and Europe (337) found ethnocentric staffing and human resource policies to be associated with increased personnel problems. Those problems included recruiting difficulties, high turnover rates, and lawsuits over personnel policies. Among the three regional samples, Japanese companies had the most ethnocentric human resource practices and the most international human resource problems.[14]

Research also shows that ethnocentrism affects managers and consumers. Expatriate managers have greater difficulties adjusting to their international assignments when their subordinates are ethnocentric.[15] It also affects consumers' purchasing decisions related to many different types of products. Interestingly, consumers prefer domestically produced goods even when the imported alternatives are cheaper and known to be better quality.[16] Now take a moment to complete the Hands-On Exercise to assess your own tendency for ethnocentrism.

Becoming a Global Manager

On any given day in today's global economy, a manager can interact with colleagues from several different countries or cultures. If they are to be effective, present and future managers in such multicultural situations need to develop a global mind-set and cross-cultural skills (see Skills & Best Practices on page 64). Developing skilled managers who move comfortably from culture to culture takes time. Consider, for example, this comment by the head of Gillette, who wants twice as many global managers on the payroll. "We could try to hire the best and the brightest, but it's the experience with Gillette that we need. About half of our [expatriates] are now on their fourth country—that kind of experience. It takes 10 years to make the kind of Gillette manager I'm talking about."[17]

How Strong Is Your Potential for Ethnocentrism?

INSTRUCTIONS: If you were born and raised or have spent most of your life in the United States, select one number from the following scale for each item. If you are from a different country or culture, substitute the country and language you most closely identify with for the terms *American* and *English,* and then rate each item.

	Strongly Disagree	Disagree	Neutral	Agree	Strongly Agree
1. I was raised in a way that was [truly] American.	1	2	3	4	5
2. Compared to how much I criticize other cultures, I criticize American culture less.	1	2	3	4	5
3. I am proud of American culture.	1	2	3	4	5
4. American culture has had a positive effect on my life.	1	2	3	4	5
5. I believe that my children should read, write, and speak [only] English.	1	2	3	4	5
6. I go to places where people are American.	1	2	3	4	5
7. I admire people who are American.	1	2	3	4	5
8. I would prefer to live in an American community.	1	2	3	4	5
9. At home, I eat [only] American food.	1	2	3	4	5
10. Overall, I am American.	1	2	3	4	5

SCORING   10–23 = Low potential for ethnocentrism
24–36 = Moderate potential for ethnocentrism
37–50 = High potential for ethnocentrism

SOURCE: Adapted from and survey items excerpted from J L Tsai, Y-W Ying, and P A Lee, "The Meaning of 'Being Chinese' and 'Being American': Variation among Chinese American Young Adults," *Journal of Cross-Cultural Psychology,* May 2000, pp 302–32.

(NOTE: Results of the Hands-On Exercise need to be interpreted cautiously because this version has not been scientifically validated; thus, it is for instructional and discussion purposes only.)

Becoming Cross-Culturally Competent

Cultural anthropologists believe you can learn interesting and valuable lessons by comparing one culture with another. Many dimensions have been suggested over the years to help contrast and compare the world's rich variety of cultures. In this section we discuss five cultural perspectives that will enhance your cross-cultural competence: basic cultural dimensions, individualism versus collectivism, high-context and low-context cultures, monochronic and polychronic time orientation, and cross-cultural leadership. Separately or together these cultural distinctions can become huge stumbling blocks when doing business across cultures. But first we need to think about cultural stereotyping and the need for *cultural intelligence.*

The Ambicultural Manager of the 21ˢᵗ Century

Notable international management scholars Ming-Jer Chen and Danny Miller coined the term *ambicultural manager* to describe those that effectively integrate Eastern and Western management knowledge and styles. Like an ambidextrous athlete (e.g., a baseball player that can bat both right- and left-handed, or a basketball player who can shoot both right- and left- handed), ambicultural managers effectively utilize their diverse knowledge and practices from multiple cultures to perform better in each. For example, a manager with experience in both China and the United States uses one to improve performance in the other, instead of simply relying on expertise in one culture at the expense of the other. Ambicultural managers therefore are a particular and cross-cultural version of contingency management studied in Chapter 1. According to Chen and Miller, ambicultural managers possess the following 10 characteristics:

1. Recognition of the shortcomings of prevailing Western and Eastern business models to meet the challenges and complexities presented by globalization
2. Openness to new ways of thinking and ability to see the benefits of other cultural and business perspectives
3. Understanding that business must balance social, geopolitical, environmental, and human needs
4. Ability to transcend divisions around the globe
5. Dedication to integrating global awareness into everyday actions
6. Emphasis on unity and morality
7. Ability to balance social good and self-interest
8. Emphasis on trust-based and legal relationships
9. Equal appreciation for teamwork and individual stars
10. Commitment to continued learning, to sharing knowledge and experience with others, and to reaching the peak of professional achievement and humanity.

SOURCE: Excerpted and adapted from M Chen and D Miller, "West Meets East: Toward an Ambicultural Approach to Management," *Academy of Management Perspectives*, November 2010, pp 17–24.

BACK TO THE CHAPTER-OPENING CASE   Answer the following questions using the 10 characteristics of ambicultural managers noted in Skills & Best Practices above.

1. Which of the 10 are most evident in TCS's approach to hiring and developing human capital?
2. Assume you are an executive vice president in charge of hiring at Tata Consultancy Services. Which 2 of the 10 characteristics do you think are most important to your performance? Explain.

Cultural Paradoxes Require Cultural Intelligence

An important qualification needs to be offered at this juncture. All of the cultural differences in this chapter and elsewhere need to be viewed as *tendencies* and *patterns* rather than as absolutes. As soon as one falls into the trap of assuming *all* Italians are this, and *all* Koreans will do that, and so on, potentially instructive generalizations become mindless stereotypes. A pair of professors with extensive foreign work experience advises, "As teachers, researchers, and managers in cross-cultural contexts, we need to recognize that our original characterizations of other cultures are best guesses that we need to modify as we gain more experience."[18] Consequently, they contend, we will be better prepared to deal with inevitable *cultural paradoxes.* By "paradox" they mean there are always exceptions to the rule—individuals who do not fit the expected cultural pattern.

An excellent example of such a paradox is Stan Shih, the founder and former CEO of Acer Group, which is currently the second-largest PC maker in the world behind HP. Shih is known as Taiwan's "godfather of IT." He is perhaps equally well known for his untraditional Chinese management philosophies and practices. For instance, he explicitly forbade his children from working in or controlling the company, arguing that he wanted to "debunk the traditional Chinese culture of 'family ruling the kingdom.'" While he founded the company, he credits Acer's success to the efforts of many and sees himself only as a representative for them. Besides, he says, the shareholders deserve for the company to be run by the very best and most qualified people. Keeping control in the family is not the way to assure this goal.[19]

Jackie Fouse is senior vice president and chief financial officer (CFO) of Celgene, a global leader in the development of treatments for cancer and immune diseases with sales of $3.6 billion in 2010. Before her position at Celgene she worked for Bunge Ltd. and before that Alcon, where she spent nine years working abroad. At each stop she added subtle skills including cultural sensitivity to her management expertise. Fouse, who is fluent in French and German, also worked for Nestlé and Swissair. She says of her many experiences, "Everything else being equal—educational background, years of experience—that was the thing more than any other that set me apart from other people."

Workers can expect to encounter many cultural paradoxes in large and culturally diverse nations (e.g., United States and Brazil) and companies. This is where the need for cultural intelligence arises.

Cultural intelligence, the ability to accurately interpret ambiguous cross-cultural situations, is an important skill in today's diverse workplaces. Two organizational behavior (OB) scholars explain:

> A person with high cultural intelligence can somehow tease out of a person's or group's behavior those features that would be true of all people and all groups, those peculiar to this person or this group, and those that are neither universal nor idiosyncratic. The vast realm that lies between those poles is culture.[20]

Those interested in developing their cultural intelligence need to first develop their *emotional intelligence,* discussed in detail in Chapter 5. They then need to be exposed to and work in ambiguous cross-cultural situations.

Nine Basic Cultural Dimensions from the GLOBE Project

LO3.2

Project GLOBE (Global Leadership and Organizational Behavior Effectiveness) is the brainchild of University of Pennsylvania professor Robert J House. It is a massive and ongoing research program to study the impact of cultural variables on leadership behaviors and organizational effectiveness."[21] GLOBE has evolved into a network of more than 160 scholars from 62 societies since the project was launched in Calgary, Canada, in 1994. Most of the researchers are native to the particular cultures they study, thus greatly enhancing the credibility of the project. During the first of two

Anthropologists employed by large companies have been researching how people use technology in Asia and the Pacific to learn more about values and habits in emerging markets. A result of this research is the telephone shown here. Targeted toward Muslim consumers, it has features such as the automatic listing and announcement of prayer times anywhere in the world, a compass showing the direction of prayer toward Mecca, and a complete transcription of the Koran in Arabic with accompanying English translation.

www.mcgrawhillconnect.com

Go to Connect for an interactive exercise to test your knowledge of the GLOBE project.

phases of the GLOBE project, a list of nine basic cultural dimensions or characteristics was identified and statistically validated. Translated questionnaires based on the nine dimensions were administered to thousands of managers in the banking, food, and telecommunications industries around the world. Results of studies using this database are published on a regular basis. And while achieving the goal stated above will take years to achieve, the nine common cultural dimensions and preliminary findings provide a comprehensive, valid, and up-to-date tool for better understanding cross-cultural similarities and differences.

The nine cultural dimensions from the GLOBE project are the following:

1. *Power distance*—How much unequal distribution of power should there be in organizations and society?

2. *Uncertainty avoidance*—How much should people rely on social norms and rules to avoid uncertainty and limit unpredictability?

3. *Institutional collectivism*—How much should leaders encourage and reward loyalty to the social unit, as opposed to the pursuit of individual goals?

4. *In-group collectivism*—How much pride and loyalty should individuals have for their family or organization?

5. *Gender egalitarianism*—How much effort should be put into minimizing gender discrimination and role inequalities?

6. *Assertiveness*—How confrontational and dominant should individuals be in social relationships?

7. *Future orientation*—How much should people delay gratification by planning and saving for the future?

8. *Performance orientation*—How much should individuals be rewarded for improvement and excellence?

9. *Humane orientation*—How much should society encourage and reward people for being kind, fair, friendly, and generous?[22]

GLOBE and the Hofstede Study

Before continuing our discussion of GLOBE it is appropriate to discuss the landmark work of Geert Hofstede. The GLOBE Project built on his work. Hofstede conducted a unique cross-cultural comparison of 116,000 IBM employees from 53 countries worldwide. The study identified four common cultural dimensions: (1) *power distance*—how much inequality does someone expect in social situations?; (2) *individualism-collectivism*—how loosely or closely is the person socially bonded?; (3) *masculinity-femininity*—does the person embrace stereotypically competitive, performance-oriented masculine traits or nurturing, relationship-oriented feminine traits?; and (4) *uncertainty avoidance*—how strongly does the person desire highly structured situations?[23]

As you can see, GLOBE not only includes Hofstede's four dimensions but also adds others. Perhaps the most important difference is that GLOBE assesses both values (what should be) and practices/norms (what is) for each dimension. (Think espoused and enacted values from Chapter 2.) It therefore allows for a richer if not more comprehensive account of group or country-level culture. Moreover, the general belief is that values and practices should be aligned, or put another way, effective practices are manifestations of their underlying values.[24]

Bringing the GLOBE Cultural Dimensions to Life   A fun and worthwhile exercise is to reflect on your own cultural roots, family traditions, and belief system and develop a personal cultural profile, using as many of the GLOBE dimensions as possible. As a case in point, which of the GLOBE cultural dimensions relates to the following biographical sketch?

> Christopher Jones, 24, [is] a UCLA grad who's a musician, playing with his rock band at clubs in Los Angeles. Like many his age, he has no money for rainy-day savings, let alone the long term. "At this point, my attitude of life is 'carpe diem.' If I have some money, take a trip, something like that," Jones said. "I understand that being a young person and saving money is the right thing to do. But finding happiness is more important to me than having a little money down the line."[25]

If you said "future orientation," you're right! Indeed, like too many Americans (of all ages), Christopher Jones scores low on future orientation and thus has inadequate savings for the future.

Country Profiles and Practical Implications   How do different countries score on the GLOBE cultural dimensions? Data from 18,000 managers yielded the profiles in Table 3–1. A quick overview shows a great deal of cultural diversity around

Countries Ranking Highest and Lowest on the GLOBE Cultural Dimensions   TABLE 3–1

Dimension	Highest	Lowest
Power distance	Morocco, Argentina, Thailand, Spain, Russia	Denmark, Netherlands, South Africa—black sample, Israel, Costa Rica
Uncertainty avoidance	Switzerland, Sweden, Germany—former West, Denmark, Austria	Russia, Hungary, Bolivia, Greece, Venezuela
Institutional collectivism	Sweden, South Korea, Japan, Singapore, Denmark	Greece, Hungary, Germany—former East, Argentina, Italy
In-group collectivism	Iran, India, Morocco, China, Egypt	Denmark, Sweden, New Zealand, Netherlands, Finland
Gender egalitarianism	Hungary, Poland, Slovenia, Denmark, Sweden	South Korea, Egypt, Morocco, India, China
Assertiveness	Germany—former East, Austria, Greece, United States, Spain	Sweden, New Zealand, Switzerland, Japan, Kuwait
Future orientation	Singapore, Switzerland, Netherlands, Canada—English speaking, Denmark	Russia, Argentina, Poland, Italy, Kuwait
Performance orientation	Singapore, Hong Kong, New Zealand, Taiwan, US	Russia, Argentina, Greece, Venezuela, Italy
Humane orientation	Philippines, Ireland, Malaysia, Egypt, Indonesia	Germany—former West, Spain, France, Singapore, Brazil

SOURCE: Adapted from M Javidan and R J House, "Cultural Acumen for the Global Manager: Lessons from Project GLOBE," *Organizational Dynamics*, Spring 2001, pp 289–305.

the world. But thanks to the nine GLOBE dimensions, we have more precise understanding of *how* cultures vary. Closer study reveals telling cultural patterns, or cultural fingerprints for nations. The U.S. managerial sample, for instance, scored high on assertiveness and performance orientation. Accordingly, Americans are widely perceived as pushy and hardworking. Switzerland's high scores on uncertainty avoidance and future orientation help explain its centuries of political neutrality and world-renowned banking industry. Singapore is known as a great place to do business because it is clean and safe and its people are well educated and hardworking. This is no surprise, considering Singapore's high scores on institutional collectivism, future orientation, and performance orientation.

These illustrations bring us to an important practical lesson: *Knowing the cultural tendencies of foreign business partners and competitors can give you a strategic competitive advantage.* For example, when managers need to discipline employees for shortcomings, they should keep in mind that employees in a collectivist culture are likely to feel they have let down their group. And in cultures with high power distance, employees are most likely to accept discipline when delivered by someone who is clearly of higher status—or to ignore it if the person does not obviously rank higher.[26]

Individualism versus Collectivism: A Closer Look

Have you ever been torn between what you personally wanted and what the group, organization, or society expected of you? If so, you have firsthand experience with a fundamental and important cultural distinction in both the GLOBE and Hofstede studies: individualism versus collectivism. Awareness of this distinction, as we will soon see, can spell the difference between success and failure in cross-cultural business dealings.

www.mcgrawhillconnect.com

Go to Connect for a video case to view Disney Imagineering and how they handle operating in divergent cultures.

Individualistic cultures, **characterized as "I" and "me" cultures, give priority to individual freedom and choice.** Senior citizens in individualistic US culture are more likely to see themselves as responsible for their own well-being, in contrast to Europeans, who more often expect help at this stage of their lives.[27] ***Collectivist cultures,*** **oppositely called "we" and "us" cultures, rank shared goals higher than individual desires and goals.** People in collectivist cultures are expected to subordinate their own wishes and goals to those of the relevant social unit. A worldwide survey of 30,000 managers by Trompenaars and Hampden-Turner, who prefer the term *communitarianism* to collectivism, found the highest degree of individualism in Israel, Romania, Nigeria, Canada, and the United States. Countries ranking lowest in individualism—thus qualifying as collectivist cultures—were Egypt, Nepal, Mexico, India, and Japan. Brazil, China, and France also ended up toward the collectivist end of the scale.[28]

A Business Success Factor   Of course, one can expect to encounter both individualists and collectivists in culturally diverse countries such as the United States. For example, imagine the frustration of Dave Murphy, a Boston-based mutual fund salesperson, when he recently tried to get Navajo Indians in Arizona interested in saving money for their retirement. After several fruitless meetings with groups of Navajo employees, he was given this cultural insight by a local official: "If you come to this environment, you have to understand that money is different. It's there to be spent. If you have some, you help your family."[29] To traditional Navajos, enculturated as collectivists, saving money is an unworthy act of selfishness. Subsequently, the sales pitch was tailored to emphasize the *family* benefits of individual retirement savings plans.

Allegiance to Whom?   The Navajo example brings up an important point about collectivist cultures. Specifically, which unit of society predominates? For the Navajos, family is the key reference group. But, as Trompenaars and Hampden-Turner observe, important differences exist among collectivist (or communitarian) cultures:

> For each single society, it is necessary to determine the group with which individuals have the closest identification. They could be keen to identify with their trade union, their family, their corporation, their religion, their profession, their nation, or the state apparatus. The French tend to identify with *la France, la famille, le cadre;* the Japanese with the corporation; the former eastern bloc with the Communist Party; and Ireland with the Roman Catholic Church. Communitarian goals may be good or bad for industry depending on the community concerned, its attitude and relevance to business development.[30]

High-Context and Low-Context Cultures   LO3.4

People from *high-context cultures*—**including China, Korea, Japan, Vietnam, Mexico, and Arab cultures—rely heavily on situational cues for meaning when perceiving and communicating with others.**[31] Nonverbal cues such as one's official position, status, or family connections convey messages more powerfully than do spoken words. Thus, we come to better understand the ritual of exchanging and reading business cards in China. Chinese culture is relatively high context compared to the U.S. culture. A business card, listing employer and official position, conveys vital silent messages about one's status to members of China's homogeneous society. Also, people from high-context cultures who are not especially talkative during a first encounter with a stranger are not necessarily being unfriendly; they are simply taking time to collect "contextual" information.

Shanghai, along with China more generally, has experienced tremendous growth in the past decade. This growth has provided many opportunities for workers from both China and abroad. Assume you are managing the construction workers in the foreground, or white collar employees in the skyscrapers in the back. What would you do to show you are aware of the high context Chinese culture?

Reading the Fine Print in Low-Context Cultures In *low-context cultures,* **written and spoken words carry the burden of shared meanings.** Low-context cultures include those found in Germany, Switzerland, Scandinavia, North America, and Great Britain. True to form, Germany has precise written rules for even the smallest details of daily life. In *high*-context cultures, agreements tend to be made on the basis of someone's word or a handshake, after a rather prolonged get-acquainted and trust-building period. Low-context Americans and Canadians, who have cultural roots in Northern Europe, see the handshake as a signal to get a signature on a detailed, lawyer-approved, iron-clad contract.

Avoiding Cultural Collisions Misunderstanding and miscommunication often are problems in international business dealings when the parties are from high- versus low-context cultures. A Mexican business professor noticed that over time and across cultures there are different opinions on what is expected from a business report. U.S. managers, for instance, take a pragmatic, get-to-the-point approach, and expect reports to be concise and action oriented. They don't have time to read long explanations. In contrast, Latin American managers will usually provide long explanations that go beyond the simple facts. This is captured in the example of a Latin America representative for a U.S. firm. His boss requested regular reports on sales activities. His reports are long and include detailed explanations on the context and possible interpretations. His boss regularly answers these reports with very brief messages, telling him to "cut the crap and get to the point!"[32]

Awkward situations such as this can be avoided when those on both sides of the context divide make good-faith attempts to understand and accommodate their counterparts. For instance, people from low-context cultures should make the effort to provide information about the history and personalities involved in a situation, and people from high-context cultures should ask questions when they aren't given information that will help them.

Cultural Perceptions of Time

In North American and Northern European cultures, time seems to be a simple matter. It is linear, relentlessly marching forward, never backward, in standardized chunks. To the American who received a watch for his or her third birthday, time is like money. It is spent, saved, or wasted.[33] Americans are taught to show up 10 minutes early for appointments. When working across cultures, however, time becomes a very complex matter. For example, consider that it took years for Kanawha Scales & Systems to complete its first deal to sell its coal-loading machines in China. The CEO, Jim Bradbury, made his first trip to China in 1986, spending a month in Beijing in a fruitless quest for an order. Six years later, the company finally landed its first deal, a $3 million contract to install coal load-out systems at a Chinese coal mine.[34] After Bradbury took the time to establish business relationships, however, his Poca, West Virginia, company began bringing in sales of more than $10 million a year from China.

The need for patience in this cross-cultural business deal can be explained in part by the distinction between monochronic time and polychronic time. *Monochronic time* **is revealed in the ordered, precise, schedule-driven use of public time that typifies and even caricatures efficient Northern Europeans and North Americans.** *Polychronic time* **is seen in the multiple and cyclical activities and concurrent involvement with different people in Mediterranean, Latin American, and especially Arab cultures.**[35]

A Matter of Degree   Monochronic and polychronic are relative rather than absolute concepts. Generally, the more things a person tends to do at once, the more polychronic that person is.[36] Thanks to computers and advanced telecommunications systems, highly polychronic managers and employees can engage in "multitasking." For instance, it is possible to talk on the telephone, read and respond to e-mail messages, print a report, check an instant phone message, and eat a stale sandwich all at the same time. Unfortunately, this extreme polychronic behavior too often is not as efficient as hoped and can be very stressful. (Multitasking and its implications for communications and performance are discussed in more detail in Chapter 12.) Monochronic people prefer to do one thing at a time. What is your attitude toward time?

Practical Implications   Low-context cultures, such as that of the United States, tend to run on monochronic time while high-context cultures, such as that of Mexico, tend to run on polychronic time. People in polychronic cultures view time as flexible, fluid, and multidimensional. The Germans and Swiss have made an exact science of monochronic time. In fact, a radio-controlled watch made by a German company, Junghans, is "guaranteed to lose no more than one second in 1 million years."[37] Many a visitor has been a minute late for a Swiss train, only to see its taillights leaving the station. Time is more elastic in polychronic cultures. During the Islamic holy month of Ramadan in Middle Eastern nations, for example, the faithful fast during daylight hours, and the general pace of things markedly slows. Managers need to reset their mental clocks when doing business across cultures.

Leadership Lessons from the GLOBE Project

LO3.5

In phase 2 of the GLOBE Project, researchers set out to discover which, if any, attributes of leadership were universally liked or disliked. They surveyed 17,000 middle managers working for 951 organizations across 62 countries. Their results, summarized in Table 3–2, have important implications for present and future global managers. Visionary and inspirational *charismatic leaders* who are good team builders generally do the best. On the other hand, *self-centered leaders* seen as loners or facesavers generally receive a poor reception worldwide. (See Chapter 14 for a comprehensive treatment of leadership.) Local and foreign managers who heed these results are still advised to use a contingency approach to leadership after using their cultural intelligence to read the local people and culture.[38] A fascinating example is provided by Reckitt Benckiser (RB), a leading international consumer products manufacturer of brands such as Air Wick, Calgon, Lysol, Mucinex, Vanish, and Woolite. RB, the result of a merger between a British and a Dutch company, takes being a global company to a new level. CEO Bart Becht described the goal of building a company without borders. It operates in more than 60 countries, and its 400 top managers have 53 different nationalities. An Italian runs the UK business, an American the German business, a Dutchman the U.S., an Indian in China, and a Frenchman runs Russia. This is by design, as the company purposefully avoids having managers in charge of their own countries and cultures. Becht clarifies, you can work in your home country, but at RB you have the opportunity to lead on the international stage. International assignments are not simply brief stops on the path to a "bigger job" at the corporate headquarters. Instead, many employees choose and have the opportunity to relocate and stay, or relocate again. The company even avoids declaring its country of origin.[39] If you desire a "deep dive," international opportunity versus simply an assignment, perhaps you should inquire at RB.

TABLE 3–2 Leadership Attributes Universally Liked and Disliked across 62 Nations

Universally Positive Leader Attributes	Universally Negative Leader Attributes
Trustworthy	Loner
Just	Asocial
Honest	Noncooperative
Foresighted	Irritable
Plans ahead	Nonexplicit
Encouraging	Egocentric
Positive	Ruthless
Dynamic	Dictatorial
Motive arouser	
Confidence builder	
Motivational	
Dependable	
Intelligent	
Decisive	
Effective bargainer	
Win–win problem solver	
Administratively skilled	
Communicative	
Informed	
Coordinator	
Team builder	
Excellence oriented	

SOURCE: Excerpted and adapted from P W Dorfman, P J Hanges, and F C Brodbeck, "Leadership and Cultural Variation: The Identification of Culturally Endorsed Leadership Profiles," in *Culture, Leadership, and Organizations: The GLOBE Study of 62 Societies,* eds R J House, P J Hanges, M Javidan, P W Dorfman, and V Gupta (Thousand Oaks, CA: Sage, 2004), Tables 21.2 and 21.3, pp 677–78.

Preparing for a Foreign Assignment

www.mcgrawhillconnect.com

Go to Connect for a self-assessment to assess your readiness for an international assignment.

As the reach of global companies continues to grow, so too do the opportunities for living and working in foreign countries. Not only do employers want to develop employees with global-business capabilities, but in some locations, the demand for local talent with necessary skills continues to outstrip the supply. In China, for example, fast-growing businesses are hard-pressed to find enough managers with leadership and teamwork skills. Companies therefore need talented people who are willing to work in China and help to develop the leaders of the future. More generally, global players need a vibrant and growing cadre of employees who are willing and able to do business across cultures. Thus, the purpose of this final section is to help you prepare yourself and others to work successfully in foreign countries. In fact, when *Fortune* listed "Five Ways to Ignite Your Career," the number-one suggestion was this: "Go global. International operations aren't a backwater—they're a way to prove you get it."[40] The Great Recession has forced global companies, such as

Siemens, Cemex, Walmart, and Samsung to get much more creative and flexible in their international assignments. They modified qualifications, duration, expectations, compensation, career stage, and repatriation.[41]

A Poor Track Record for Expatriates

As we use the term here, ***expatriate refers to anyone living and/or working outside their home country.*** Hence, they are said to be *expatriated* when transferred to another country and *repatriated* when transferred back

Many jobs require employees to travel and interact with people from other cultures. What would be your greatest challenges related to a two year foreign assignment?

home. US expatriate managers usually are characterized as culturally inept and prone to failure on international assignments. Sadly, research supports this view.

Studies show that as many as 40% of expatriates tended to leave their assignments early due to job dissatisfaction and problems adjusting to the culture of the host country.[42] Worse still, a Pricewaterhouse Coopers study revealed that over 25 percent of repatriated employees quit their jobs within one year of returning from an international assignment.[43] A review of research shows the following common types of expatriate performance failures:

1. Early return from assignment
2. Delayed productivity or project start time
3. Disruption of relationship between expatriate and host nationals
4. Damage to employer's image
5. Lost opportunities
6. Problematic repatriation (e.g., job dissatisfaction and voluntary turnover)[44]

These results suggest that multinational organizations clearly need to do a better job of preparing employees and their families for foreign assignments. This section presents suggested ways to accomplish this goal.

Avoiding OB Trouble Spots in the Foreign Assignment Cycle

Finding the right person (often along with a supportive and adventurous family) for a foreign position is a complex, time-consuming, and costly process.[45] For our purposes, it is sufficient to narrow the focus to common OB trouble spots in the foreign assignment cycle. As illustrated in Figure 3–2, the first and last stages of the cycle occur at home. The middle two stages occur in the foreign or host country. Each stage hides an OB-related trouble spot that needs to be anticipated and neutralized. Otherwise, the bill for another failed foreign assignment will grow. The Skills & Best Practices on page 75 provides some guidance as to which cross-cultural competencies can be beneficial and help you avoid trouble spots.

FIGURE 3-2   The Foreign Assignment Cycle (with OB Trouble Spots)

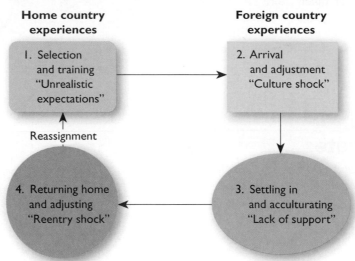

Avoiding Unrealistic Expectations with Cross-Cultural Training

Realistic job previews (RJPs) have proven effective at bringing people's unrealistic expectations about a pending job assignment down to earth by providing a realistic balance of good and bad news. People with realistic expectations tend to quit less often and be more satisfied than those with unrealistic expectations. RJPs are a must for future expatriates. Another way to set expatriates up to be successful is cross-cultural training.

Historically, *cross-cultural training (CCT)* **focused on preparing employees for international assignments.** Now, however, CCT has a broader meaning and includes any activities aimed at enhancing the cultural awareness of employees to enable them to work more effectively with people from different cultural backgrounds. As you can see, this means that CCT can be appropriate even for domestic employees who are not actually working internationally, but whose jobs require them to interact with people of diverse backgrounds.[46] Although costly, companies believe cross-cultural training is less expensive than failed foreign assignments. Programs vary widely in type and also in rigor. Of course, the greater the difficulty, the greater the time and expense.

CCT also differs in terms of timing. Predeparture training accounts for the largest proportion of training. Post-arrival training is more common for short assignments to reduce cost (time and money). Sequential training combines the first two and often is more effective if the home and host cultures differ greatly. Support for all three forms was found in a sample of 165 American expatriates assigned to China. Participants indicated a strong preference for some form of predeparture training, although they also expressed appreciation for postarrival training.[47]

As a general rule the more rigorous the cross-cultural training, the better. One study involving U.S. employees in South Korea led the researcher to recommend a *combination* of informational and experiential predeparture training.[48] Agilent Technologies, formerly a part of Hewlett-Packard (HP) and a global leader in industrial measurement systems, emphasizes selecting the right people and invests heavily in assessing candidate's multicultural awareness and ability to work across organizations (interorganizational

Key Cross-Cultural Competencies

Cross-Cultural Competency Cluster	Knowledge or Skill Required
Building relationships	Ability to gain access to and maintain relationships with members of host culture
Valuing people of different cultures	Empathy for difference; sensitivity to diversity
Listening and observation	Knows cultural history and reasons for certain cultural actions and customs
Coping with ambiguity	Recognizes and interprets implicit behavior, especially nonverbal cues
Translating complex information	Knowledge of local language, symbols or other forms of verbal language, and written language
Taking action and initiative	Understands intended and potentially unintended consequences of actions
Managing others	Ability to manage details of a job including maintaining cohesion in a group
Adaptability and flexibility	Views change from multiple perspectives
Managing stress	Understands own and others' mood, emotions, and personality

SOURCE: Excerpted from Y Yamazaki and D C Kayes, "An Experiential Approach to Cross-Cultural Learning: A Review and Integration of Competencies for Successful Expatriate Adaptation," *Academy of Management Learning and Education*, December 2004, Table 2, p 372.

competence). IBM also emphasizes selection and uses both aptitude tests and behavioral interviews designed specifically for working in a cross-cultural context.[49]

So, which approach is the best? Research to date does not offer a final answer. And despite the growing trend of globalization, a review of 25 years of CCT research found such training of any form is relatively underutilized.[50] Nevertheless, the nine competencies detailed in Skills & Best Practices above should be the core of any comprehensive CCT program.

Our personal experience with teaching OB to foreign students both in the United States and abroad reminds us that there really is no substitute for an intimate knowledge of the local culture, language, customs, and etiquette. Bill Roedy, President of MTV Networks International, used this advice to land an important deal in Saudi Arabia.

His job requires getting often risqué programming into as many countries as he can without offending local sensibilities. . . . Roedy was in town to persuade the mayor of Mecca to give his blessing to MTV Arabia, the network's biggest global launch, which had the potential to reach 2,000 million Arabs across the region. "Presidents and sheiks don't normally watch MTV, so we have to help them overcome stereotypical views they have," says Roedy. "Nobody was more important than the mayor of Mecca, the religious center of Islam. We had to get it right."

While there he attended recording sessions with the Arab rappers Jeddah Legends, where he learned that their lyrics tended to be about family and religion—themes that he would draw on during his meeting with the mayor of Mecca.[51]

A lesson here is that the success of your own international assignment may depend on personal initiative—as it did for Bill Roedy of MTV—rather than on formal, company-sponsored CCT. However, it is worth noting that 95% of the companies on Hay Group's 2010 List of Best Companies for Leadership provided programs to assist expatriates adjust to the local culture.[52]

Avoiding Culture Shock   Have you ever been in a totally unfamiliar situation and felt disoriented and perhaps a bit frightened? If so, you already know something about culture shock. According to anthropologists, *culture shock* **involves anxiety and doubt caused by an overload of unfamiliar expectations and social cues.** For Chinese people who come to the United States to work, one of the challenges they face is that their U.S. colleagues generally are far less interested in socializing and disclosing their personal lives. *Wall Street Journal* columnist Li Yuan, a Chinese native, explains, "In China, the office is both a work space and a social space. . . . It's quite common for co-workers to go out for dinner, karaoke and team sports after work a couple of times a week, and those who rarely participate in group activities are considered arrogant or lacking in social graces." Coworkers are eager to learn about one another's marital status, salary, housing costs, love life, and so on. To people coming from this culture, American workers seem cold and detached, and life in America seems lonely. For her part, Yuan has come to see Americans' reluctance to talk about certain subjects as a way to maintain harmony in a diverse culture. She has grown accustomed to the difference—but when she gets a raise, she shares the news with her friends in China.[53]

Despite classes, in which young students learn basic Chinese, managers in the United States are likely to lag behind those in China in their ability to understand and appreciate someone else's language and culture. Many experts worry that lack of foreign language skills goes hand in hand with a general lack of global awareness in the United States.

The best defense against culture shock is comprehensive cross-cultural training, including intensive language study. Once again, the only way to pick up subtle—yet important—social cues is via the local language. And as today's businesspeople are discovering, learning a language is a lot more than translating words from one language to another. At Computer Sciences Corporation, which has offices in 49 countries, a French employee was offended by a British colleague's dry humor. At Reuters Group, American programmers thought they were giving directions by saying when they would "like" work to be done, while their Thai colleagues saw the statement more literally as a description of their preferences. Responding to miscommunications such as these, language-training programs are beginning to broaden their curriculum to include strategies for avoiding cross-cultural misunderstandings.[54]

Building a Support Network During a Foreign Assignment   Especially during the first six months, when everything is so new to the expatriate, a support system needs to be in place. *Host-country sponsors,* assigned to individual managers or families, are recommended because they serve as "cultural seeing-eye dogs." In a foreign country, where even the smallest errand can turn into an utterly exhausting production, sponsors can get things done quickly because they know the cultural and geographical territory. Honda's Ohio employees, for example, enjoyed the help of family sponsors when training in Japan:

> Honda smoothed the way with Japanese wives who once lived in the U.S. They handled emergencies such as when Diana Jett's daughter Ashley needed stitches in her chin. When Task Force Senior Manager Kim Smalley's daughter, desperate to fit in at elementary school, had to have a precisely shaped bag for her harmonica, a Japanese volunteer stayed up late to make it.[55]

Recent research by a group of scholars at the University of Maryland acknowledged the critical importance of a support network in a host country. They recommended a five-stage process for developing a network of people to provide two valuable forms of support—*informational* and *emotional*. **Informational support includes knowledge to assist expatriates' functioning and problem solving in the host country. Emotional support helps expatriates feel better about themselves and their situation when adjustment is difficult or overwhelming.** The goal of such a support network is to help improve expatriate knowledge of the host country, reduce uncertainty, and improve adjustment.

Stage 1: First, if not also foremost, expatriates need to be motivated to seek support.

Stage 2: Next, potential sources of support need to be identified and approached.

Stage 3: And once identified, the support provider's willingness and ability to support needs to be determined and support needs to be utilized.

Stage 4: Support needs to be utilized.

Stage 5: Include support provider in the expatriate's network—if the support was helpful.[56]

BACK TO THE CHAPTER-OPENING CASE   Again assume you are responsible for training the many new employees at Tata Consultancy Services. Refer to Figure 3–2 and the text and then:

1. Describe how you would help *one new employee* avoid or overcome each of the OB trouble spots.

2. Describe how your recommendations might change given that you are responsible for hiring 25,000 employees.

Summary Suggestions for Successful Repatriation and Successful International Assignments Strange as it may seem, many otherwise successful expatriate managers encounter their first major difficulty only after their foreign assignment is over—reentry shock. Why? Returning to one's native culture is taken for granted because it seems so routine and ordinary. But having adjusted to another country's way of doing things for an extended period of time can put one's own culture and surroundings in a strange new light. Three areas for potential reentry shock are work, social activities, and general environment (e.g., politics, climate, transportation, food). Ira Caplan's return to New York City exemplifies reentry shock:

> During the past 12 years, living mostly in Japan, he and his wife had spent their vacations cruising the Nile or trekking in Nepal. They hadn't seen much of the U.S. They are getting an eyeful now . . . Prices astonish him. The obsession with crime unnerves him. What unsettles Mr. Caplan more, though, is how much of himself he has left behind. In a syndrome of return no less stressful than that of departure, he feels displaced, disregarded, and diminished. . . . In an Italian restaurant, crowded at lunchtime, the waiter sets a bowl of linguine in front of him. Mr Caplan stares at it. "In Asia, we have smaller portions and smaller people," he says.
>
> Asia is on his mind. He has spent years cultivating an expertise in a region of huge importance. So what? This is New York.[57]

Researchers and the authors of this textbook encourage you to consider the following three points to help you assure the ultimate success of your international opportunities.

1. Be sure that repatriation is an explicit part of your international assignment plan. A major reason for repatriate dissatisfaction and turnover is upon their return no positions were available for them. Their new skills and experiences were under appreciated and not utilized.

2. Identify, establish, and maintain communications with sources of ongoing support in your home country. Many repatriates complain that they became disconnected and out of the loop while away. They felt that their opportunities were limited once they returned because nobody was looking out for them while they were away (e.g., manager, mentor, or career coach).

3. Confirm that senior management openly and genuinely values international expertise. For instance, be certain that international expertise is considered and matters when identifying candidates for future opportunities.[58]

Utilize the knowledge and tools provided in this chapter to help take advantage of the immense opportunities available in the growing global economy.

key terms

collectivist culture 68	ethnocentrism 62	low-context cultures 70
cross-cultural training (CCT) 74	expatriate 73	monochronic time 70
cultural intelligence 65	high-context cultures 69	polychronic time 70
culture shock 76	individualistic culture 68	societal culture 59
emotional support 77	informational support 77	

chapter summary

- *Describe a global mind-set, and explain how to build its three component forms of capital.* A global mind-set is characterized by a broader awareness and openness to other cultural values and practices. It is composed of intellectual, psychological, and social capital. Intellectual capital can be built by educating oneself about the history and norms of other cultures. Psychological capital can be increased by being open to cultural diversity and a willingness to adapt one's behaviors accordingly. Social capital is expanded by connecting to people in other cultures and being empathetic and diplomatic about differences.

- *Identify and describe the nine cultural dimensions from the GLOBE project.* (1) *Power distance*—How equally should power be distributed? (2) *Uncertainty avoidance*—How much should social norms and rules reduce uncertainty and unpredictability? (3) *Institutional collectivism*—How much should loyalty to the social unit override individual interests? (4) *In-group collectivism*—How strong should one's loyalty be to family or organization? (5) *Gender egalitarianism*—How much should gender discrimination and role inequalities be minimized? (6) *Assertiveness*—How confrontational and dominant should one be in social relationships? (7) *Future orientation*—How much should one delay gratification by planning and saving for the future? (8) *Performance orientation*—How much should individuals be rewarded for improvement and excellence? (9) *Humane orientation*—How much should individuals be rewarded for being kind, fair, friendly, and generous?

- *Draw a distinction between individualistic cultures and collectivist cultures.* People in individualistic cultures think primarily in terms of "I" and "me" and place a high value on freedom and personal choice. Collectivist cultures teach people to be "we" and "us" oriented and to subordinate personal wishes and goals to the interests of the relevant social unit (such as family, group, organization, or society).

- *Demonstrate your knowledge of these two distinctions: high-context versus low-context cultures and monochronic versus polychronic cultures.* People in high-context cultures (such as China, Japan, and Mexico) derive great meaning from situational cues, above and beyond written and spoken words. Low-context cultures (including Germany, the United States, and Canada) derive key information from precise and brief written and spoken messages. In monochronic cultures (e.g., the United States), time is precise and rigidly measured. Polychronic cultures, such as those found in Latin America and the Middle East, view time as multidimensional, fluid, and flexible. Monochronic people prefer to do one thing at a time, while polychronic people like to tackle multiple tasks at the same time.

- *Explain what the GLOBE project has taught us about leadership.* Across 62 cultures, they identified leader attributes that are universally liked and universally disliked. The universally liked leader attributes—including trustworthy, dynamic, motive arouser, decisive, and intelligent—are associated with the charismatic/transformational leadership style that is widely applicable. Universally disliked leader attributes—such as noncooperative, irritable, egocentric, and dictatorial—should be avoided in all cultures.

- *Identify an OB trouble spot for each stage of the foreign assignment cycle.* The four stages of the foreign assignment cycle (and OB trouble spots) are (a) selection and training (unrealistic expectations), (b) arrival and adjustment (culture shock), (c) settling in and acculturating (lack of support), and (d) returning home and adjusting (reentry shock).

discussion questions

1. Based on reading this chapter, what recommendation do you have for Tata Consultancy Services (see the chapter-opening case) when hiring so many people globally?
2. How would you describe the prevailing culture in your country to a stranger from another land, in terms of the nine GLOBE project dimensions?
3. Why are people from high-context cultures such as China and Japan likely to be misunderstood by low-context Westerners?
4. How strong is your desire for a foreign assignment? Why? If it is strong, where would you like to work? Why? How prepared are you for a foreign assignment? What do you need to do to be better prepared?
5. What is your personal experience with culture shock?
6. Which of the OB trouble spots in Figure 3–2 do you believe is the greatest threat to expatriate employee success? Explain.

legal/ethical challenge

A Case of Morphing Legal Charges in China

The Rio Tinto company of Australia is one of the largest producers of iron ore in the world. It is a major supplier to China, which has the largest steel industry in the world. This relationship, however, has been strained over the past several years. The tension and complexity of this relationship was highlighted by the prosecution of Rio Tinto executives by the Chinese government. The executives were originally charged with espionage, accused of bribing Chinese steel industry officials for information that would enable the company to inflate iron ore prices. The executives were detained in China for nearly a year pending the trial. The case was "considered the most closely watched prosecution of executives from a foreign country." This was due to the potential implications for the many companies that currently and hope to do business in China.

However, when the executives arrived at trial the charges had been changed. Now the Rio Tinto executives were charged with *accepting* $12 million worth of bribes from Chinese steel industry officials. These officials presumably attempted to gain pricing information for iron ore to aid in their negotiations for allocations.

Chinese prosecutors (and officials) did not explain why the charges were switched, why they would charge foreign executives for *accepting* bribes, or why they have not yet charged or arrested anybody from steel companies that offered bribes.

"Chinese police and prosecutors have considerable leeway to arrest and even indict suspects for one offense and then change course and bring them to trial on different charges. [Such practices] prompted fears among mining company executives, foreign workers, and investors that they could be subject to legal penalties if they get into disputes with their local partners."[59]

What Would You Do?

Considering only the information above, answer the following questions.

Part A. Assume you are a high-potential, rising-star manager within Rio Tinto and are offered a position at a company facility in China. Because China is the company's biggest customer, an assignment there is likely to advance your career.

1. Would you take the position? If yes, then explain why. Also describe what you might do to prevent a situation similar to the one above.

2. If no, then explain why you made this choice. Also explain how you would communicate this decision to the manager who offered you the position.

   Part B. Assume you are the CEO of Rio Tinto.

3. Considering only the information above, what changes if any would you make to company policy related to doing business in China?

   Part C. Additional information came to light after the trial. Just before the executives were detained, the Chinese steel industry association complained about inflated iron ore prices and blamed Rio Tinto and others for a breakdown in iron ore contract talks. Additionally, "Rio Tinto scrapped plans to accept a $19.5 billion investment from Chinalco, one of China's biggest state-owned mining groups."[60]

4. Based on this new information, do your answers to questions 1, 2, and 3 change? Explain why or why not.

If you're looking for additional study materials, be sure to check out the Online Learning Center at

www.mhhe.com/kininckiob5e

for more information and interactivities that correspond to this chapter.

Managing Individual Level Factors

Understanding and managing **Individual Level Factors**

EXTERNAL CONTEXT

ORGANIZATIONAL CONTEXT

Understanding and managing **Individual Level Factors**

Y O U
Current Work-Related Beliefs, Attitudes, and Experiences

Understanding and managing **Group Level Factors**

Understanding and managing **Organization Level Factors**

Performance at Three Levels
1. Individual
2. Group
3. Organization

chapter 4

Understanding Social Perception and Managing Diversity

After reading the material in this chapter, you should be able to:

LO4.1 Describe perception in terms of the social information processing model.

LO4.2 Explain seven managerial implications of social perception.

LO4.3 Explain, according to Kelley's model, how external and internal causal attributions are formulated.

LO4.4 Demonstrate your familiarity with the demographic trends that are creating an increasingly diverse workforce.

LO4.5 Identify the barriers and challenges to managing diversity.

LO4.6 Discuss organizational practices used to manage diversity.

Why Did Navy Leaders Allow Offensive Videos to be Shown on the USS *Enterprise*?

The Navy moved quickly to pledge to investigate videos in which a senior officer used anti-gay slurs and mimics masturbation, while a prominent gay-rights group praised the military's condemnation of the video.

Capt. Owen Honors, who commands the USS *Enterprise,* based in Norfolk, Virginia, stars in the videos that were aired on the aircraft carrier's closed-circuit television system in 2006 and 2007 when he was the ship's second in command. The videos have made Honors an Internet sensation.

"What we see here is, unfortunately, a 49-year-old Navy captain acting like a 19-year-old fraternity boy," said Aubrey Sarvis, executive director of the Servicemembers Legal Defense Network, which has advocated for gay military members. "There is no place for that type of frat-house behavior."

Honors appeared in the videos while he was USS *Enterprise*'s executive officer. He took command of the ship, which is expected to deploy soon, in May. The man who captained the ship in 2006 and 2007 has been promoted to rear admiral.

It is not clear why the videos are surfacing now or whether the Navy investigated the videos earlier and decided to promote Honors to the USS *Enterprise*'s top job despite their content.

But once the videos surfaced on the Internet, the Navy moved quickly to condemn them.

"Production of videos, like the ones produced four or five years ago on the USS *Enterprise* and now being written about in the *Virginian-Pilot*, were not acceptable then and are not acceptable in today's Navy," said Cmdr. Chris Sims, a Navy spokesperson. "The Navy does not endorse or condone these kinds of actions. Those in command . . . are charged to lead by example and are held accountable for setting the proper tone and upholding the standards of honor, courage, and commitment that we expect sailors to exemplify."

Since the story broke, hundreds of current and past *Enterprise* crew members have created Facebook accounts to support Honors. Another site with far fewer "friends" condemns him and calls for his resignation. . . .

Ryan Adams, now a student at Virginia Tech, left the Navy in 2009 after serving in 2006 and 2007 on the *Enterprise*. "Everyone I know who

Owen Paul Honors, Jr., United States Navy

worked on the *Enterprise* is backing him 100 percent," Adams said.

Every sailor interviewed by the AP said they had heard no complaints onboard about Honors's skits.

It is unlikely the videos, which include several anti-gay slurs, will have any effect on the Pentagon's efforts to allow gay men and lesbians to serve openly. "Most of your service members are professionals," Sarvis said. "I don't see any implications to transitioning to openly gay service for gays and lesbians."[1]

▲ **THE CHAPTER-OPENING CASE HIGHLIGHTS** an important aspect of the perception process: People do not have the same perceptions about things we encounter on a daily basis. For example, many sailors on the *Enterprise* defended the captain on Facebook postings, saying that his antics were "simply providing a much-needed morale boost during long deployments at sea." In contrast, Navy officials concluded that "the videos were extreme and showed a disturbing lack of judgment."[2] What is your perception of Capt. Honors's behavior and the Navy's response?

Our perceptions and feelings are influenced by information we receive from newspapers, magazines, television, radio, family, and friends. You see, we all use information stored in our memories to interpret the world around us, and our interpretations, in turn, influence how we respond and interact with others. As human beings, we constantly strive to make sense of our surroundings. The resulting knowledge influences our behavior and helps us navigate our way through life. Think of the perceptual process that occurs when meeting someone for the first time. Your attention is drawn to the individual's physical appearance, mannerisms, actions, and reactions to what you say and do. You ultimately arrive at conclusions based on your perceptions of this social interaction. The brown-haired, green-eyed individual turns out to be friendly and fond of outdoor activities. You further conclude that you like this person and then ask him or her to go to a concert, calling the person by the name you stored in your memory.

The reciprocal process of perception, interpretation, and behavioral response also applies at work. Bernie Madoff, for example, used the perception process to help orchestrate a $50-billion Ponzi scheme against unsuspecting investors. Madoff, who was described as "entrepreneurial, rich, and charming," used the success of his company in the 1980s and 1990s to create an image of a can't-lose investment strategist. His offices "oozed success" and the trading room looked "very profitable—and totally legitimate." He was active in social circles and charitable organizations. All told, these perceptions helped Madoff to recruit wealthy investors and money managers and to maintain the perception that he was running one of the most exclusive and successful investment firms in the world. Unfortunately, it was a lie that continued to exist partly because of the perception process.[3]

Managing diversity is a sensitive, potentially volatile, and sometimes uncomfortable issue. Yet managers are required to deal with it in the name of organizational survival. Accordingly, the purpose of this chapter is to enhance your understanding of the perceptual process and how it influences the manner in which managers manage diversity. We begin by focusing on a social information processing model of perception and then discuss the perceptual outcome of causal attributions. Next, we define diversity and describe the organizational practices used to manage diversity effectively.

A Social Information Processing Model of Perception

Perception is a cognitive process that enables us to interpret and understand our surroundings. Recognition of objects is one of this process's major functions. For example, both people and animals recognize familiar objects in their environments. You would recognize a picture of your best friend; dogs and cats can recognize their food dishes or a favorite toy. Reading involves recognition of visual patterns representing letters in the alphabet. People must recognize objects to meaningfully interact with their environment. But since organizational behavior's (OB's) principal focus is on people, the following discussion emphasizes *social* perception rather than object perception.

Social perception involves a four-stage information processing sequence (hence, the label "social information processing"). Figure 4–1 illustrates a basic social information processing model. Three of the stages in this model—selective attention/

Social Perception: A Social Information Processing Model   FIGURE 4–1

Stage 1	Stage 2	Stage 3	Stage 4
Selective attention/ comprehension	Encoding and simplification	Storage and retention	Retrieval and response

Competing environmental stimuli
- People
- Events
- Objects

A
B
C
D
E
F

Interpretation and categorization

A
C
F

Memory

C

Judgments and decisions

SOURCE: R Kreitner and A Kinicki, *Organizational Behavior,* 9th ed (Burr Ridge, IL: McGraw-Hill), 2010, p. 185.

comprehension, encoding and simplification, and storage and retention—describe how specific social information is observed and stored in memory. The fourth and final stage, retrieval and response, involves turning mental representations into real-world judgments and decisions.

Keep the following everyday example in mind as we look at the four stages of social perception. Suppose you were thinking of taking a course in, say, personal finance. Three professors teach the same course, using different types of instruction and testing procedures. Through personal experience, you have come to prefer good professors who rely on the case method of instruction and essay tests. According to social perception theory, you would likely arrive at a decision regarding which professor to take following the steps outlined in the following sections.

LO4.1

Stage 1: Selective Attention/Comprehension

People are constantly bombarded by physical and social stimuli in the environment. Because they do not have the mental capacity to fully comprehend all this information, they selectively perceive subsets of environmental stimuli. This is where attention plays a role. ***Attention* is the process of becoming consciously aware of something or someone.** Attention can be focused on information either from the environment or from memory. Regarding the latter situation, if you sometimes find yourself thinking about totally unrelated events or people while reading a textbook, your memory is the focus of your attention. Research has shown that people tend to pay attention to salient stimuli.

Salient Stimuli   Something is *salient* when it stands out from its context. For example, a 250-pound man would certainly be salient in a women's aerobics class but not at a meeting of the National Football League Players' Association. One's needs and goals often dictate which stimuli are salient. For a driver whose gas gauge is on empty, an Exxon or Shell sign is more salient than a McDonald's or Burger King sign. Moreover, research shows that people have a tendency to pay more attention to negative than positive information. This leads to a negativity bias.[4] This bias helps explain the gawking factor that slows traffic to a crawl following a car accident, and it can affect employee behavior at work. Consider the case of Falcon Containers: At Austin-based Falcon Containers, CEO Stephen Shang suggested in 2009 that his sales team quit watching economic news for two weeks and spend more time connecting with customers. The result is that the company, which leases repurposed shipping containers as storage units, made a deal to create an Iraqi "village" out of the containers for an anti-IED effort by the U.S. Air Force. That led to more military business, thereby fostering a 20% sales increase.[5] Shang was able to increase revenue by getting his employees to stop paying attention to negative economic news and focus on spending more time with customers.

Back to Our Example   You begin your search for the "right" personal finance professor by asking friends who have taken classes from the three available professors. You also may interview the various professors who teach the class to gather still more relevant information. Returning to Figure 4–1, all the information you obtain represents competing environmental stimuli labeled A through F. Because you are concerned about the method of instruction (e.g., line A in Figure 4–1), testing procedures (e.g., line C), and past grade distributions (e.g., line F), information in those areas is particularly salient to you. Figure 4–1 shows that these three salient pieces of information thus are perceived, and you then progress to the second stage of information processing. Meanwhile, competing stimuli represented by lines B, D, and E in Figure 4–1 fail to get your attention and are discarded from further consideration.

Stage 2: Encoding and Simplification

Observed information is not stored in memory in its original form. Encoding is required; raw information is interpreted or translated into mental representations. To accomplish this, perceivers assign pieces of information to ***cognitive categories.*** **"By *category* we mean a number of objects that are considered equivalent.** Categories are generally designated by names, e.g., *dog, animal.*"[6] People, events, and objects are interpreted and evaluated by comparing their characteristics with information contained in schemata (or schema in singular form).

Schema   According to social information processing theory, a ***schema* represents a person's mental picture or summary of a particular event or type of stimulus.** For example, picture your image of a sports car. Does it contain a smaller vehicle with two doors? Is it red? If you answered yes, you would tend to classify all small, two-door, fire-engine-red vehicles as sports cars because this type of car possesses characteristics that are consistent with your sports car schema.

> **BACK TO THE CHAPTER-OPENING CASE**   Does Capt. Honors's behavior fit your schema for an effective leader? Explain.

Stereotypes Are Used During Encoding   People use stereotypes during encoding in order to organize and simplify social information. "A ***stereotype* is an individual's set of beliefs about the characteristics or attributes of a group."**[7] Stereotypes are not always negative. For example, the belief that engineers are good at math is certainly part of a stereotype. Stereotypes may or may not be accurate. Engineers may in fact be better at math than the general population. In general, stereotypic characteristics are used to differentiate a particular group of people from other groups.

Unfortunately, stereotypes can lead to poor decisions; can create barriers for women, older individuals, people of color, and people with disabilities; and can undermine loyalty and job satisfaction. A recent summary of research on gender stereotypes, for example, revealed that (1) people often prefer male bosses, (2) women have a harder time being perceived as an effective leader (e.g., women were seen as more effective than men only when the organization faced a crisis and turnaround), and (3) women of color are more negatively affected by sex-role stereotypes than white women or men in general.[8] Studies of race-based stereotypes also demonstrated that people of color experienced more perceived discrimination, racism-related stress, and less psychological support than whites.[9] Another example of an inaccurate stereotype is the belief that older workers are less motivated, not as committed, less productive than their younger coworkers, and more apt to be absent from work, a stereotype that may discourage younger workers from accepting older employees. Research has refuted all of these negative beliefs.[10]

Stereotyping is a four-step process. It begins by categorizing people into groups according to various criteria, such as gender, age, race, and occupation. Next, we infer that all people within a particular category possess the same traits or characteristics (e.g., all women are nurturing, older people have more job-related accidents, all African-Americans are good athletes, all professors are absentminded). Then, we form expectations of others and interpret their behavior according to our stereotypes. Finally, stereotypes are maintained by (1) overestimating the frequency of stereotypic behaviors exhibited by others, (2) incorrectly explaining expected and unexpected behaviors, and (3) differentiating minority individuals from oneself. Although these steps are self-reinforcing, there are ways to break the chain of stereotyping.

What is your impression of this person? Are you surprised to know that it is Dylan Lauren, owner of Dylan's Candy Bar, the largest candy store in the world? Does the photo make more sense now that you know her professional role? People tend to use stereotypes when making judgments without complete information about others.

Research shows that the use of stereotypes is influenced by the amount and type of information available to an individual and his or her motivation to accurately process information.[11] People are less apt to use stereotypes to judge others when they encounter salient information that is highly inconsistent with a stereotype. For instance, you are unlikely to assign stereotypic "professor" traits to a new professor you have this semester if he or she rides a Harley-Davidson, wears leather pants to class, and has a pierced nose. People also are less likely to rely on stereotypes when they are motivated to avoid using them. That is, accurate information processing requires mental effort. Stereotyping is generally viewed as a less effortful strategy of information processing.

Encoding Outcomes   We use the encoding process to interpret and evaluate our environment. Interestingly, this process can result in differing interpretations and evaluations of the same person or event. Table 4–1 describes five common perceptual errors that influence our judgments about others. Because these perceptual errors often distort the evaluation of job applicants and of employee performance, managers need to guard against them.

TABLE 4–1   Commonly Found Perceptual Errors

Perceptual Error	Description	Example	Recommended Solution
Halo	A rater forms an overall impression about an object and then uses that impression to bias ratings about the object.	Rating a professor high on the teaching dimensions of ability to motivate students, knowledge, and communication because we like him or her.	Remember that an employee's behavior tends to vary across different dimensions of performance. Keep a file or diary to record examples of positive and negative employee performance throughout the year.
Leniency	A personal characteristic that leads an individual to consistently evaluate other people or objects in an extremely positive fashion.	Rating a professor high on all dimensions of performance regardless of his or her actual performance. The rater who hates to say negative things about others.	It does not help employees when they are given positive feedback that is inaccurate. Try to be fair and realistic when evaluating others.
Central tendency	The tendency to avoid all extreme judgments and rate people and objects as average or neutral.	Rating a professor average on all dimensions of performance regardless of his or her actual performance.	It is normal to provide feedback that contains both positive and negative information. The use of a performance diary can help to remember examples of employee performance.
Recency effects	The tendency to remember recent information. If the recent information is negative, the person or object is evaluated negatively.	Although a professor has given good lectures for 12 to 15 weeks, he or she is evaluated negatively because lectures over the last 3 weeks were done poorly.	It is critical to accumulate examples of performance that span the entire rating period. Keep a file or diary to record examples of performance throughout the year.
Contrast effects	The tendency to evaluate people or objects by comparing them with characteristics of recently observed people or objects.	Rating a good professor as average because you compared his or her performance with three of the best professors you have ever had in college. You are currently taking courses from the three excellent professors.	It is important to evaluate employees against a standard rather than your memory of the best or worst person in a particular job.

Back to Our Example   Having collected relevant information about the three personal finance professors and their approaches, you compare this information with other details contained in schemata. This leads you to form an impression and evaluation of what it would be like to take a course from each professor. In turn, the relevant information contained on paths A, C, and F in Figure 4–1 are passed along to the third stage of information processing.

Nutrisystem and Unilever Use Everyday People Instead of Celebrities in Their Ads

Nutrisystem sent flip video cameras to customers in search of stories to use in its advertising. Here is what Charlotte Husser, 54, had to say.

> "What you're hearing from me has to come from the heart; there's no script," says Husser, who says she shed 32 pounds to become a size 6 after eating Nutrisystem's meals for 5 months.... Nutrisystem's CEO, Joe Redling, noted that "Nutrisystem wants to convey how they're helping people lose weight and how it's affecting lives of people that are noncelebrities." ...
>
> The Campaign for Real Beauty used by Unilever to promote its Dove soap is the classic case of using regular folk in ads.... Dove's marketing blitz, which began in 2004 and has featured women from age 20 to 95, aims to boost the self-esteem of girls by showcasing real people instead of models. Although the company won't provide numbers, Unilever spokesman David Perez says, "Response to our campaigns featuring real women has been overwhelmingly positive."

SOURCE: Excerpted from L Patton, "Nutrisystem Gets Real with Its Diet Ads," *Bloomberg BusinessWeek,* January 10, 2011, pp 19–20.

Stage 3: Storage and Retention

This phase involves storage of information in long-term memory. Long-term memory is like an apartment complex consisting of separate units connected to one another. Although different people live in each apartment, they sometimes interact. In addition, large apartment complexes have different wings (such as A, B, and C). Long-term memory similarly consists of separate but related categories. Like the individual apartments inhabited by unique residents, the connected categories contain different types of information. Information also passes among these categories. Finally, long-term memory is made up of three compartments (or wings) containing categories of information about events, semantic materials, and people.

Event Memory   This compartment is composed of categories containing information about both specific and general events. These memories describe appropriate sequences of events in well-known situations, such as going to a restaurant, going on a job interview, going to a food store, or going to a movie.

Semantic Memory   Semantic memory refers to general knowledge about the world. In so doing, it functions as a mental dictionary of concepts. Each concept contains a definition (e.g., a good leader) and associated traits (outgoing), emotional states (happy), physical characteristics (tall), and behaviors (works hard). Just as there are schemata for general events, concepts in semantic memory are stored as schemata. Given our previous discussion of international OB in Chapter 3, it should come as no surprise that there are cultural differences in the type of information stored in semantic memory.

Person Memory   Categories within this compartment contain information about a single individual (your professor) or groups of people (professors). You are more likely to remember information about a person, event, or an advertisement if it contains characteristics that are similar to something stored in the compartments of

www.mcgrawhillconnect.com

Go to Connect for a video case to view the Todd MacFarlane company and what role perception plays in its operation.

memory. For example, companies such as Nutrisystem and Unilever are increasingly using "regular" individuals rather than celebrities in their ads because people don't identify with celebrities (see the Skills & Best Practices on page 89).

Back to Our Example   As the time draws near for you to decide which personal finance professor to take, your schemata of them are stored in the three categories of long-term memory. These schemata are available for immediate comparison and/or retrieval.

Stage 4: Retrieval and Response

People retrieve information from memory when they make judgments and decisions. Our ultimate judgments and decisions are either based on the process of drawing on, interpreting, and integrating categorical information stored in long-term memory or on retrieving a summary judgment that was already made.

Concluding our example, it is registration day and you have to choose which professor to take for personal finance. After retrieving from memory your schemata-based impressions of the three professors, you select a good one who uses the case method and gives essay tests (line C in Figure 4–1). In contrast, you may choose your preferred professor by simply recalling the decision you made two weeks ago.

Managerial Implications

Social cognition is the window through which we all observe, interpret, and prepare our responses to people and events. A wide variety of managerial activities, organizational processes, and quality-of-life issues are thus affected by perception. Consider, for example, the following implications.

LO4.2

Hiring   Interviewers make hiring decisions based on their impression of how an applicant fits the perceived requirements of a job. Unfortunately, many of these decisions are made on the basis of implicit cognition. *Implicit cognition* **represents any thoughts or beliefs that are automatically activated from memory without our conscious awareness.** The existence of implicit cognition leads people to make biased decisions without an understanding that it is occurring.[12] This tendency has been used as an explanation of alleged discriminatory behavior at Walmart, FedEx, Johnson & Johnson, and Cargill. Experts recommend two solutions for reducing this problem.[13] First, managers can be trained to understand and reduce this type of hidden bias. Second, bias can be reduced by using structured as opposed to unstructured interviews, and by relying on evaluations from multiple interviewers rather than just one or two people.

Performance Appraisal   Faulty schemata about what constitutes good versus poor performance can lead to inaccurate performance appraisals, which erode work motivation, commitment, and loyalty. For example, a study of 166 production employees indicated that they had greater trust in management when they perceived that the performance appraisal process provided accurate evaluations of their performance.[14] Therefore, it is important for managers to accurately identify the behavioral characteristics and results indicative of good performance at the beginning of a performance review cycle. These characteristics then can serve as the benchmarks for evaluating employee performance. The importance of using objective rather than subjective measures of employee performance was highlighted in a meta-analysis involving

50 studies. Results revealed that objective and subjective measures of employee performance were only moderately related. The researchers concluded that objective and subjective measures of performance are not interchangeable.[15] Managers are thus advised to use more objectively based measures of performance as much as possible because subjective indicators are prone to bias and inaccuracy. In those cases where the job does not possess objective measures of performance, however, managers should still use subjective evaluations. Furthermore, because memory for specific instances of employee performance deteriorates over time, managers need a mechanism for accurately recalling employee behavior. Research reveals that individuals can be trained to be more accurate raters of performance.[16]

Perception colors our interpretation of management behaviors. An employee whose manager multitasks while talking to her is likely to believe that their conversation—and therefore the employee's work and even the employee herself—are not very important. Have you ever been treated this way?

Leadership   Research demonstrates that employees' evaluations of leader effectiveness are influenced strongly by their schemata of good and poor leaders. A leader will have a difficult time influencing employees when he or she exhibits behaviors contained in employees' schemata of poor leaders. A team of researchers investigated the behaviors contained in our schemata of good and poor leaders. Good leaders were perceived as exhibiting the following behaviors: (1) assigning specific tasks to group members, (2) telling others that they had done well, (3) setting specific goals for the group, (4) letting other group members make decisions, (5) trying to get the group to work as a team, and (6) maintaining definite standards of performance. Another recent study found that good leaders were perceived as those who consistently treated all members of a work unit in a fair manner.[17]

Communication and Interpersonal Influence   Managers must remember that social perception is a screening process that can distort communication, both coming and going. Because people interpret oral and written communications by using schemata developed through past experiences, your ability to influence others is affected by information contained in others' schemata regarding age, gender, ethnicity, appearance, speech, mannerisms, personality, and other personal characteristics. It is important to keep this in mind when trying to influence others or when trying to sell your ideas.

Counterproductive Work Behaviors   Past research showed that employees exhibited a variety of counterproductive work behaviors, which are discussed in Chapter 6, when they perceived that they were treated unfairly.[18] It is very important for managers to treat employees fairly, remembering that perceptions of fairness are in the eye of the beholder. Chapter 7 discusses how this can be done in greater detail.

Physical and Psychological Well-Being   The negativity bias can lead to both physical and psychological problems. Specifically, research shows that perceptions of fear, harm, and anxiety are associated with the onset of illnesses such as asthma and depression.[19] We should all attempt to avoid the tendency of giving negative thoughts too much attention. Try to let negative thoughts roll off yourself just like water off a duck.

Designing Web Pages   Researchers have recently begun to explore what catches viewers' attention on web pages by using sophisticated eye-tracking equipment. This research can help organizations to spend their money wisely when designing web pages. Kara Pernice Coyne, director of a research project studying web page design, praised the web pages of JetBlue Airways and Sears while noting problems with the one used by Agere Systems.[20]

Causal Attributions

Attribution theory is based on the premise that people attempt to infer causes for observed behavior. Rightly or wrongly, we constantly formulate cause-and-effect explanations for our own and others' behavior. Attributional statements such as the following are common: "Joe drinks too much because he has no willpower; but I need a couple of drinks after work because I'm under a lot of pressure." Formally defined, *causal attributions* **are suspected or inferred causes of behavior.** Even though our causal attributions tend to be self-serving and are often invalid, it is important to understand how people formulate attributions because they profoundly affect organizational behavior. For example, a supervisor who attributes an employee's poor performance to a lack of effort might reprimand that individual. However, training might be deemed necessary if the supervisor attributes the poor performance to a lack of ability.

www.mcgrawhillconnect.com

Go to Connect to take an interactive exercise to determine your understanding of causal attributions.

Generally speaking, people formulate causal attributions by considering the events preceding an observed behavior. This section introduces Harold Kelley's model of attribution and two important attributional tendencies.

Kelley's Model of Attribution

Current models of attribution, such as Kelley's, are based on the pioneering work of the late Fritz Heider. Heider, the founder of attribution theory, proposed that behavior can be attributed either to *internal factors* **within a person (such as ability)** or to *external factors* **within the environment (such as a difficult task).** Building on Heider's work, Kelley attempted to pinpoint major antecedents of internal and external attributions. Kelley hypothesized that people make causal attributions after gathering information about three dimensions of behavior: consensus, distinctiveness, and consistency.[21] These dimensions vary independently, thus forming various combinations and leading to differing attributions.

LO4.3

Figure 4–2 presents performance charts showing low versus high consensus, distinctiveness, and consistency. These charts are now used to help develop a working knowledge of all three dimensions in Kelley's model.

- *Consensus* involves a comparison of an individual's behavior with that of his or her peers. There is high consensus when one acts like the rest of the group and low consensus when one acts differently. As shown in Figure 4–2, high consensus is indicated when persons A, B, C, D, and E obtain similar levels of individual performance. In contrast, person C's performance is low in consensus because it significantly varies from the performance of persons A, B, D, and E.

- *Distinctiveness* is determined by comparing a person's behavior on one task with his or her behavior on other tasks. High distinctiveness means the individual has performed the task in question in a significantly different manner than he or she has performed other tasks. Low distinctiveness means stable performance or quality from one task to another. Figure 4–2 reveals that the employee's performance on task 4 is highly distinctive because it significantly varies from his or her performance on tasks 1, 2, 3, and 5.

- *Consistency* is determined by judging if the individual's performance on a given task is consistent over time. High consistency implies that a person performs a certain task the same way, time after time. Unstable performance of a given task over time would mean low consistency. The downward spike in performance depicted in the consistency graph of Figure 4–2 represents low consistency. In this case, the employee's performance on a given task varied over time.

It is important to remember that consensus relates to other *people,* distinctiveness relates to other *tasks,* and consistency relates to *time.* The question now is, How does information about these three dimensions of behavior lead to internal or external attributions?

Kelley hypothesized that people attribute behavior to *external* causes (environmental factors) when they perceive high consensus, high distinctiveness, and low consistency. *Internal* attributions (personal factors) tend to be made when observed behavior is characterized by low consensus, low distinctiveness, and high consistency. So, for example, when all employees are performing poorly (high consensus), when the poor performance occurs on only one of several tasks (high distinctiveness), and the poor performance occurs during only one time period (low consistency), a supervisor will probably attribute an employee's poor performance to an external source such as peer pressure or an overly difficult task. In contrast, performance will be attributed to an employee's personal characteristics (an internal attribution) when only the individual in question is performing poorly (low consensus), when the inferior performance is found across several tasks (low distinctiveness), and when the low performance has persisted over time (high consistency). Many studies supported this predicted pattern of attributions.[22] The attribution process also has been extended by marketing researchers to examine consumers' attributions about customer service, product characteristics, and advertising and by OB researchers to study employees' response to workplace aggression and sexual harassment.[23]

Performance Charts Showing Low and High Consensus, Distinctiveness, and Consistency Information   FIGURE 4–2

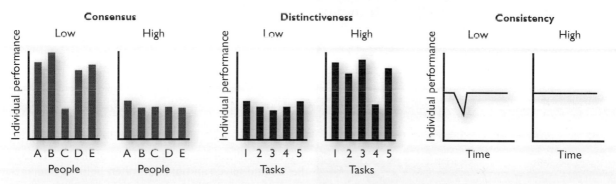

BACK TO THE CHAPTER-OPENING CASE   What attribution would you make about Capt. Honors's behavior? Do you think his behavior is due to external or internal causes?

Pat Murphy, former head coach of men's baseball at Arizona State University. His very successful career at the university came to an end when the program violated NCAA rules. Do you think it's natural to use the self-serving bias when faced with allegations of exhibiting inappropriate behavior or violating a formal policy?

Attributional Tendencies

Researchers have uncovered two attributional tendencies that distort one's interpretation of observed behavior—*fundamental attribution bias* and *self-serving bias.*

Fundamental Attribution Bias   The *fundamental attribution bias* reflects one's tendency to attribute another person's behavior to his or her personal characteristics, as opposed to situational factors.** This bias causes perceivers to ignore important environmental forces that often significantly affect behavior. For example, a woman was fired from her job on the night shift at a poultry plant for falling asleep. Although management may have thought that she was lazy, it turns out "that she paid for child care during the night while she was working, but she didn't earn enough to pay someone to watch her baby during the day. So, she would come home from the night shift and be greeted with a wide-awake kid."[24] A more likely attribution is that she fell asleep because of issues in her personal life and low wages paid by the poultry firm. A recent study of shareholders similarly showed that shareholders attributed the price of stocks more to CEO behavior and less to market fluctuations.[25]

Self-Serving Bias   The *self-serving bias* represents one's tendency to take more personal responsibility for success than for failure.** The self-serving bias suggests employees will attribute their success to internal factors (high ability or hard work) and their failures to uncontrollable external factors (tough job, bad luck, unproductive coworkers, or an unsympathetic boss). This tendency plays out in all aspects of life. For example, Bob Poznanovich was a vice president for sales and marketing for Zenith, now LG Electronics, before he was fired for using drugs. He admits to spending $1,000 per day getting high with other employees and customers, and that he was coming in late to work and missing days of work. Poznanovich blames the company for his continued use of drugs. He says he "would have run out and gotten help" if management had warned him about his bad behavior.[26] Pat Murphy, former head baseball coach at Arizona State University (ASU), similarly blames management for

Increase Personal Success through Planning and Accurate Attributions

- Set goals for what you want to accomplish. The goals should be SMART (see Chapter 6).
- Find a coach or sounding board. It helps to have someone you can talk to while trying to accomplish your goals. This person can help you to make accurate attributions and provide moral support.
- Develop milestones that must be accomplished in order to meet your goals. Each milestone should have an associated date in which the activity must be accomplished.
- Remember that people perceive the same events differently. Stay positive in the face of adversity and be careful not to fall prey to attributional biases.
- To avoid attributional biases, conduct research to determine the actual causes of performance. If possible, shift failure attributions away from ability and toward attributions of low effort or some other external cause (e.g., lack of resources).
- Do not overpromise as it could lead to an expectation that is impossible to achieve. This in turn can lead to negative attributions about your performance.

SOURCE: Based partly on R Courtney, "Believe You Can Succeed and It's Likely You Will." Retrieved January 11, 2011, from http://www.leadershippundit.com/2011/01/believe-you-can-succeed-and-its-likely-you-will/.

his department's violation of NCAA rules regarding phone calls with prospective student athletes. He believes that management did not properly instruct his staff on how to complete telephone logs. Management, on the other hand, blames Murphy for not making record keeping of phone calls a priority and concluded that "Murphy gave every impression of promoting a program of compliance while at the same time, unbeknownst to ASU, he was not following all of ASU's policies himself and was providing inaccurate telephone logs and representations to ASU's compliance staff.[27] The NCAA banned the baseball program from any postseason play in 2011.[28]

Managerial Application and Implications   Attribution models can be used to explain how managers handle poorly performing employees. For example, one study revealed that managers gave employees more immediate, frequent, and negative feedback when they attributed their performance to low effort. Another study indicates that managers tended to transfer employees whose poor performance was attributed to a lack of ability. These same managers also decided to take no immediate action when poor performance was attributed to external factors beyond an individual's control.[29]

   The preceding situations have several important implications for managers. First, managers tend to disproportionately attribute behavior to *internal* causes. This can result in inaccurate evaluations of performance, leading to reduced employee motivation. No one likes to be blamed because of factors they perceive to be beyond their control. Further, because managers' responses to employee performance vary according to their attributions, attributional biases may lead to inappropriate managerial actions, including promotions, transfers, layoffs, and so forth. This can dampen motivation and performance. Attributional training sessions for managers are in order. Basic attributional processes can be explained, and managers can be taught to detect and avoid attributional biases. Finally, an employee's attributions for his or her own performance have dramatic effects on subsequent motivation, performance, and personal attitudes such as self-esteem. For instance, people tend to give up, develop lower expectations for future success, and experience decreased self-esteem when they attribute failure to a lack of ability. In contrast, employees are more likely to display high performance and job satisfaction when they attribute success to internal factors such as ability and effort.[30] The Skills & Best Practices feature on page 95 outlines several steps you can take to increase success in your life through planning and positive attributions.

Defining and Managing Diversity

Diversity **represents the multitude of individual differences and similarities that exist among people.** This definition underscores a key issue about managing diversity. There are many different dimensions or components of diversity. This implies that diversity pertains to everybody. It is not an issue of age, race, or gender. It is not an issue of being heterosexual, gay, or lesbian or of being Catholic, Jewish, Protestant, or Muslim. Diversity also does not pit white males against all other groups of people. Diversity pertains to the host of individual differences that make all of us unique and different from others.

This section begins our journey into managing diversity by first reviewing the key dimensions of diversity. Because many people associate diversity with affirmative action, we then compare affirmative action with managing diversity. Next, we review the demographic trends that are creating an increasingly diverse workforce. This section concludes by describing the organizational practices used to effectively manage diversity.

Layers of Diversity

www.mcgrawhillconnect.com

Go to Connect for a self-assessment that will help to determine your appreciation and value of diversity.

Like seashells on a beach, people come in a variety of shapes, sizes, and colors. This variety represents the essence of diversity. Lee Gardenswartz and Anita Rowe, a team of diversity experts, identified four layers of diversity to help distinguish the important ways in which people differ (see Figure 4–3). Taken together, these layers define your personal identity and influence how each of us sees the world.

Figure 4–3 shows that personality is at the center of the diversity wheel. Personality is at the center because it represents a stable set of characteristics that is responsible for a person's identity: The dimensions of personality are discussed later in Chapter 5. The next layer of diversity consists of a set of internal dimensions that are referred to as the primary dimensions of diversity. These dimensions, for the most part, are not within our control, but strongly influence our attitudes and expectations and assumptions about others, which, in turn, influence our behavior. Take the encounter experienced by an African-American woman in middle management while vacationing at a resort:

> While she was sitting by the pool, "a large 50-ish white male approached me and demanded that I get him extra towels. I said, 'Excuse me?' He then said, 'Oh, you don't work here,' with no shred of embarrassment or apology in his voice."[31]

Stereotypes regarding one or more of the primary dimensions of diversity most likely influenced this man's behavior toward the woman.

Figure 4–3 reveals that the next layer of diversity is composed of external influences, which are referred to as secondary dimensions of diversity. They represent individual differences that we have a greater ability to influence or control. Examples include where you grew up and live today, your religious affiliation, whether you are

The Four Layers of Diversity   FIGURE 4–3

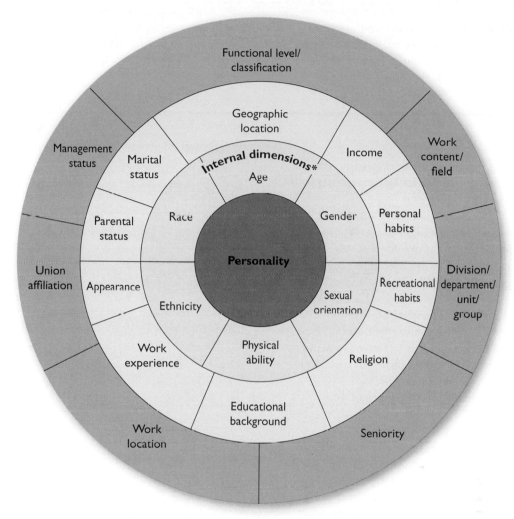

* Internal dimensions and external dimensions are adapted from Loden and Rosener, *Workforce America!* (Homewood, IL: Business One Irwin, 1991).
SOURCE: From L Gardenswartz and A Rowe, *Diverse Teams at Work: Capitalizing on the Power of Diversity,* published by the Society for Human Resource Management, 1994, 2003, p 33. Reprinted with permission.

married and have children, and your work experiences. These dimensions also exert a significant influence on our perceptions, behavior, and attitudes. The final layer of diversity includes organizational dimensions such as seniority, job title and function, and work location.

BACK TO THE CHAPTER-OPENING CASE   Which layers of diversity were involved with events on the USS *Enterprise?*

HANDS-ON EXERCISE

What Is Your Attitude Toward Diversity?

INSTRUCTIONS: Complete the following survey items by considering either your current job or one that you have held in the past. If you have never worked, identify a friend who is working and ask the individual to complete the questionnaire for his or her organization. Read each item and circle your response by using the rating scale shown below. Compute your total score by adding up your responses and compare it to the scoring norms.

	Strongly Disagree	Disagree	Neutral	Agree	Strongly Agree
1. The minorities in this organization do not have a greater difficulty getting along with others.	1	2	3	4	5
2. If one of my coworkers were racist, I would confront that person and let him or her know of my disapproval.	1	2	3	4	5
3. Workers who are prejudiced have no place in this organization.	1	2	3	4	5
4. I feel that women do not have a more difficult time handling positions of authority relative to men.	1	2	3	4	5
5. I would feel just as comfortable with a black or Hispanic supervisor as I do with a white supervisor.	1	2	3	4	5
6. It seems that most minorities in supervisory positions are just as effective relative to other supervisors.	1	2	3	4	5
7. I feel that diversity is good for this organization even if it means I will have a supervisor who is a minority.	1	2	3	4	5
8. Most of the minority supervisors in this organization possess the same leadership qualities as those supervisors who are white.	1	2	3	4	5
9. All employees are held to the same performance standards regardless of gender or race.	1	2	3	4	5
10. I believe that increasing the hiring of women and minorities can only help this organization.	1	2	3	4	5

SCORING NORMS

1–18 = Unfavorable attitudes
19–36 = Moderate attitudes
37–50 = Favorable attitudes

SOURCES: Adapted from M Montei, G Adams, and L Eggers, "Validity of Scores on the Attitudes Toward Diversity Scale," *Educational and Psychological Measurement,* April 1996, pp 298–99.

Now that you understand the layers of diversity, we would like you to assess your attitudes toward diversity. Take a moment to complete the survey shown in the hands-on exercise on page 98. There are no right or wrong answers. Circle the response that best represents your opinion or feelings about the survey item. How did you score? What does your score suggest about your approach to working with diverse people?

Affirmative Action and Managing Diversity

Effectively managing diversity requires organizations to adopt a new way of thinking about differences among people. Rather than pitting one group against another, managing diversity entails recognition of the unique contribution every employee can make. For example, Cisco, Whole Foods Market, Container Store, Adobe Systems, and Zappos focus on hiring and promoting diverse employees as part of a strategy to create and market products appealing to a broader and more diverse customer base.[32] This section highlights the differences between affirmative action and managing diversity.

Affirmative Action   Affirmative action is an outgrowth of equal employment opportunity (EEO) legislation. The goal of this legislation is to outlaw discrimination and to encourage organizations to proactively prevent discrimination. ***Discrimination occurs when employment decisions about an individual are due to reasons not associated with performance or are not related to the job.*** For example, organizations cannot discriminate on the basis of race, color, religion, national origin, sex, age, physical and mental disabilities, and pregnancy.

In contrast to the proactive perspective of EEO legislation, ***affirmative action is an artificial intervention aimed at giving management a chance to correct an imbalance, an injustice, a mistake, or outright discrimination that occurred in the past.*** Affirmative action does not legitimize quotas. Quotas are illegal. They can only be imposed by judges who conclude that a company has engaged in discriminatory practices. It also is important to note that under no circumstances does affirmative action require companies to hire unqualified people.

Although affirmative action created tremendous opportunities for women and minorities, it does not foster the type of thinking that is needed to manage diversity effectively. For example, a meta-analysis summarizing 35 years of research involving 29,000 people uncovered the following results: (1) affirmative action plans are perceived more negatively by white males than women and minorities because it is perceived to work against their own self-interests; (2) affirmative action plans are viewed more positively by people who are liberals and Democrats than conservatives and Republicans; and (3) affirmative action plans are not supported by people who possess racist or sexist attitudes.[33]

Achieving diversity remains a challenge for many organizations, including the New York City Fire Department, which, despite efforts to recruit more blacks, Hispanics, Asian Americans, and women, remains predominantly white and male. Fewer women and minorities apply than white men, and fewer still complete the five steps needed to reach the final hiring pool. One Brooklyn councilwoman applauded the department's diversity recruiting efforts but noted that "women have not necessarily been embraced once they've gotten on the force, notwithstanding their own intestinal fortitude."

Affirmative action programs also were found to negatively affect the women and minorities expected to benefit from them. Research demonstrates that women and minorities, supposedly hired on the basis of affirmative action, feel negatively stigmatized as unqualified or incompetent. They also experience lower job satisfaction and more stress than employees supposedly selected on the basis of merit.[34] Another study, however, shows that these negative consequences are reduced for women when a merit criterion is included in hiring decisions. In other words, women hired under affirmative action programs feel better about themselves and exhibit higher performance when they believe they were hired because of their competence rather than their gender.[35]

Managing Diversity   *Managing diversity* **enables people to perform up to their maximum potential.** It focuses on changing an organization's culture and infrastructure such that people provide the highest productivity possible. Sodexo, a firm in the hospitality industry with 380,000 employees in 80 countries, is a good example of a company that effectively manages diversity. Sodexo was rated by DiversityInc in 2010 as the very best company for diversity based on its annual 200-question survey of 449 firms (see the Skills & Best Practices feature on page 101).[36] Ann Morrison, a diversity expert, conducted a study of 16 organizations that successfully managed diversity. Her results uncovered three key strategies for success: education, enforcement, and exposure. She describes them as follows:

> The education component of the strategy has two thrusts: one is to prepare nontraditional managers for increasingly responsible posts, and the other is to help traditional managers overcome their prejudice in thinking about and interacting with people who are of a different sex or ethnicity. The second component of the strategy, enforcement, puts teeth in diversity goals and encourages behavior change. The third component, exposure to people with different backgrounds and characteristics, adds a more personal approach to diversity by helping managers get to know and respect others who are different.[37]

You can conclude from this description that Sodexo uses all of these diversity strategies.

In summary, both consultants and academics believe that organizations should strive to manage diversity rather than only valuing it or simply using affirmative action.

LO4.4

Increasing Diversity in the Workforce

This section explores the managerial implications of four demographic-based characteristics of the workforce: (1) women navigate a labyrinth after breaking the glass ceiling, (2) racial groups are encountering a glass ceiling and perceived discrimination, (3) there is a mismatch between workers' educational attainment and occupational requirements, and (4) generational differences in an aging workforce.

Women Navigate a Labyrinth After Breaking the Glass Ceiling

The term *glass ceiling* was coined in 1986. **It was used to represent an absolute barrier or solid roadblock that prevented women from advancing to higher-level positions.** There are a variety of statistics that support the existence of a glass ceiling.[38] That said, Alice Eagly and her colleague Linda Carli conducted a thorough investigation into the organizational life of women and concluded that women had finally broken through the glass ceiling.[39] We arrived at the following results after updating data reported in Eagly and Carli's book. There were many more female CEOs in 2010 (12 and 26 female CEOs within Fortune 500 and Fortune 1000 firms, respectively) and more women in managerial, professional, and related occupations (51% in 2009) than there were in the 1980s and 1990s.[40] Statistics further showed

Sodexo Ranked as Best Company for Managing Diversity

The deep leadership commitment to diversity is an integral part of Sodexo's moral fiber and strong ethics. Global CEO Michel Landel, U.S. President and CEO George Chavel, and Senior Vice President and Global Chief Diversity Officer Dr. Rohini Anand are constantly on the front lines of new and expanded diversity initiatives.

Sodexo has led every other company in its ability to implement, measure, and assess strong internal diversity initiatives. Its Spirit of Mentoring program is an example for all organizations of a focused, practical, and extremely comprehensive mentoring effort that includes advanced training and benchmarks at regular intervals to examine how mentoring pairs are relating to each other and accomplishing goals.

Sodexo is at the forefront of creative ways to examine the ROI of diversity initiatives. Recently, for example, the company undertook a comprehensive study of more than 1,700 members of employee-resource groups to understand their perceived benefits of group participation.

The company's diversity training, mandatory for its entire workforce, offers an example to others. Over the past five years, Sodexo has developed an integrated metrics tool that assesses behavior at all levels of the organization, including the C-suite. The company measures its progress with its Sodexo Diversity Index, an innovative scorecard that tracks both quantitative and qualitative results.

Sodexo also reaches out externally, holding forums and meetings with clients to improve their diversity initiatives and to help them understand how critical diversity is to everyone's success. Sodexo's strong reputation and proven success in diversity have led many of its clients to tell DiversityInc that is the reason they enhanced their business relationship with the food-service company.

SOURCE: Excerpted from "No. 1: Sodexo." Retrieved December 27, 2010, from http://www.diversityinc.com/article/7252/.

that women made great strides in terms of (1) educational attainment (women earned the majority of bachelor's, master's, professional, and PhD degrees from 2006 through 2010); (2) holding seats on boards of directors of Fortune 500 firms (a 6.1% increase between 1995 and 2010); (3) obtaining leadership positions in educational institutions (in 2010, women represented 18.7% of college presidents and 29.9% of board members); and (4) receiving federal court appointments (in 2010, 22% and 28% of federal district court judges and U.S. circuit court judges, respectively, were women).[41]

You can interpret the above statistics in one of two ways. On the one hand, you might believe that women are underpaid and underrepresented in leadership positions and that they are victims of discriminatory organizational practices. Alternatively, you can agree with Eagly and Carli's conclusion that "women have made substantial progress but still have quite far to go to achieve equal representation as leaders. . . . These statistics demonstrate considerable social change and show that women's careers have become far more successful than they were in the past. Men still have more authority and higher wages, but women have been catching up. Because some women have moved into the most elite leadership roles, absolute barriers are a thing of the past."[12] These authors believe that women are not victims. Rather, they propose that a woman's career follow a pattern more characteristic of traveling through a labyrinth. Eagly and Carli used the labyrinth metaphor because they believe that a woman's path to success is not direct or simple, but rather contains twists, turns, and obstructions, particularly for married women with children.

Andrea Jung, Chairman and CEO of Avon Products, Inc. successfully navigated the labyrinth of career success. In addition to her responsibilities at Avon, she serves on the board of directors for General Electric and Apple. Do you think Asian females have a harder time achieving this type of success than a white male? Why?

Racial Groups Are Encountering a Glass Ceiling and Perceived Discrimination

The United States will become increasingly diverse. For example, Asians and Hispanics are expected to have the largest growth in population between 2000 and 2050. The Asian population will triple to 33 million by 2050, and Hispanics will increase their ranks by 118% to 102.6 million. Hispanics will account for 25% of the population in 2050. All told, the so-called minority groups will constitute approximately 55% of the workforce in 2050, according to the Census Bureau.[43]

Unfortunately, three additional trends suggest that current-day minority groups are experiencing their own glass ceiling. First, minorities are advancing even less in the managerial and professional ranks than women. For example, whites, blacks, Asians, and Hispanics or Latinos held 38%, 29.21%, 48.8%, and 19.4% of all managerial, professional, and related occupations in the United States in 2009.[44] Second, the number of race-based charges of discrimination that were deemed to show reasonable cause by the U.S. Equal Employment Opportunity Commission increased from 294 in 1995 to 1,061 in 2008. Companies paid a total of $79.3 million to resolve these claims outside of litigation in 2008.[45] Third, minorities also tend to earn less personal income than whites. Median annual earnings in 2009 were $51,861, $32,584, $65,469, and $38,039 for whites, blacks, Asians, and Hispanics, respectively. Interestingly, Asians had the highest median income.[46]

Mismatch between Educational Attainment and Occupational Requirements

Approximately 28% of the labor force has a college degree, and college graduates typically earn substantially more than workers with less education.[47] At the same time, however, three trends suggest a mismatch between educational attainment and the knowledge and skills needed by employers. First, recent studies show that college graduates, while technically and functionally competent, are lacking in terms of teamwork skills, critical thinking, and analytic reasoning. Second, there is a shortage of college graduates in technical fields related to science, math, and engineering. Third, organizations are finding that high-school graduates working in entry-level positions do not possess the basic skills needed to perform effectively. This latter trend is partly due to a national high-school graduation rate of only 75% and the existence of about 32 million adults in the United States that are functionally illiterate.[48] Literacy is defined as "an individual's ability to read, write, and speak English, compute and solve problems at levels of proficiency necessary to function on the job and in society, to achieve one's goals, and develop one's knowledge and potential."[49] Illiteracy costs corporate America around $60 billion a year in lost productivity. These statistics are worrisome to both government officials and business leaders.

CVS Caremark Implements Programs to Retain and Transfer Knowledge of Older Employees

CVS identified a strategic need for older workers well over a decade ago, when 7% of its employees were past the half-century age. . . .

Part of CVS's success stems from providing flexible programs and benefits that particularly appeal to older workers. A prime example is its "Snowbird" program, which allows older workers to transfer to different CVS/pharmacy locations on a seasonal basis. . . . "The retention rate of the snowbirds is significantly higher than the industry average," says David L. Casey, vice president, diversity officer for CVS Caremark. The program enables CVS to manage the swell of business in warm-climate stores during the winter, and the snowbirds drive customer loyalty. . . .

Another program CVS is piloting in Chicago has older pharmacists—some still working, some retired—mentor pharmacy technicians and high school students. It has proven to be as much a learning experience for the mentors as the mentees.

SOURCE: Excerpted from J Mullich, "Coming of Age," *The Wall Street Journal*, October 7, 2010, p B6.

Generational Differences in an Aging Workforce America's population and workforce are getting older. In 2011, half of the U.S. workforce is over 50 years of age, and 80% will be over 50 by 2018.[50] Life expectancy is increasing as well. The number of people living into their 80s is increasing rapidly, and this group disproportionately suffers from chronic illness. The United States is not the only country with an aging population. The United Nations estimates that 33% of the population in developed countries will be over the age of 60 by 2050, and one in three people will be pensioners. These statistics led some experts to conclude that the global financial crises in 2009–2010 "will be nothing compared with the costs of an aging global population."[51]

An aging population in the United States underscores a potential skill gap in the future. As those employees in the baby-boom generation retire—the 78 million people born between 1946 and 1964—the U.S. workforce will lose the skills, knowledge, experience, and relationships possessed by the more than a quarter of all Americans. This situation will likely create skill shortages in fast-growing technical fields. Proactive companies like CVS Caremark have already implemented programs aimed at overcoming this knowledge transfer problem (see the Skills & Best Practices feature above).

In addition to the challenges associated with an aging workforce, the four generations of employees working together underscore the need for managers to deal effectively with generational differences in values, attitudes, and behaviors among the workforce: A fifth generation will enter the workforce around 2020. For example, companies such as IBM, Lockheed Martin, Ernst & Young LLP, and Aetna have addressed this issue by providing training workshops on generational diversity.

Table 4–2 presents a summary of generational differences that exist across commonly labeled groups of people: Traditionalists, Baby Boomers, Gen Xers, Millennials also known as Gen Ys, and the forthcoming Gen 2020 group. Before examining these proposed differences, it is important to note that these labels and distinctions are generalizations and are used for sake of discussion. There are always exceptions to the characterizations shown in Table 4–2 and all conclusions should be

www.mcgrawhillconnect.com

Go to Connect for an interactive exercise to test your knowledge of generational differences in the workplace.

TABLE 4–2   Generational Differences

	Traditionalists	Baby Boomers	Gen Xers	Millennials (Gen Ys)	Gen 2020
Birth Time Span	1925–1945	1946–1964	1965–1979	1980–2001	2002–
Current Population	38.6 million	78.3 million	62 million	92 million	23 million
Key Historical Events	Great Depression, World War II, Korean War, Cold War era, rise of suburbs	Vietnam War; Watergate; assassinations of John and Robert Kennedy and Martin Luther King Jr.; women's rights; Kent State killings; first man on the moon	MTV, AIDS epidemic, Gulf War, fall of Berlin Wall, Oklahoma City bombing, 1987 stock market crash, Bill Clinton-Monica Lewinsky scandal	September 11th terrorist attack, Google, Columbine High School shootings, Enron and other corporate scandals, wars in Iraq and Afghanistan, Hurricane Katrina, financial crisis of 2008 and high unemployment	Social media, election of Barack Obama, financial crisis of 2008 and high unemployment
Broad Traits	Patriotic, loyal, disciplined, conformist, high work ethic, respects authority	Workaholic, idealistic, work ethic, competitive, materialistic, seeks personal fulfillment	Self-reliant, seeks work–life balance, adaptable, cynical, distrusts authority, independent, technologically savvy	Entitled, civic minded, seeks close parental involvement, cyberliterate, appreciates diversity, multitasks, seeks work–life balance, technologically savvy	Multitasking, online life, cyberliteracy, communicate fast and online
Defining Invention	Fax machine	Personal computer	Mobile phone	Google and Facebook	Social media and iPhone apps

SOURCE: Adapted from J C Meister and K Willyerd, *The 2020 Workplace* (New York: Harper Collins, 2010), pp 54–55; and R Alsop, *The Trophy Kids Grow Up* (San Francisco: Jossey-Bass, 2008) p 5.

interpreted with caution.[52] Table 4–2 reveals that Millennials account for the largest block of employees in the workforce, followed by Baby Boomers. This is important because many Millennials are being managed by Boomers who possess a very different set of personal traits. Traits, which are discussed in Chapter 5, represent stable physical and mental characteristics that form an individual's identity. Conflicting traits are likely to create friction between people. For example, the workaholic and competitive nature of Boomers is likely to conflict with the entitled and work–life balance perspective of Millennials. As discussed in the next section, managers and employees alike will need to be sensitive to the generational differences highlighted in Table 4–2 in the pursuit of effectively managing diversity.

Managerial Implications of Demographic Diversity   It is important for organizations to draw the best talents and motivation from employees given the globally based and technologically connected nature of business. Organizations simply cannot afford to alienate segments of the workforce. Consider the issue of sexual orientation. A 2010 National Survey of Health and Behavior in the United States revealed that approximately 7% of women and 8% of men identified themselves as lesbian, gay, or bisexual. It also is currently legal in 30 states to fire employees who are lesbian or gay, and it is legal in 37 states to fire transgender individuals.[53] This situation is likely to create negative job attitudes and feelings of marginalization for lesbian, gay, bisexual, and transgender (LGBT) people.[54] Corporate law firm Bingham McCutchen and Adobe Systems have tried to overcome this problem by instituting programs such as additional benefits for transgender employees and same-sex partner benefits.[55]

Regardless of sexual orientation, gender, race, or age, all organizations need to hire, retain, and develop a diverse workforce that provides a deeper pool of talent and unique perspectives that help the organization identify and meet the needs of a diverse customer base. For example, a Citizens Union Bank branch in Louisville, Kentucky, designed and staffed the branch with the goal of attracting more Latino customers. The interior contains "bright, colorful walls of yellows and blues, large-scale photos of Latin American countries, comfortable couches, sit-down desks, a children's play area, a television tuned to Hispanic programming and even a vending area stocked with popular Latin American-brand soft drinks and snacks. Along with its interior design, this branch has a different name: 'Nuestro Banco,' Spanish for 'Our Bank.'"[56] Branch deposits are setting records, and the CEO is planning to use this same model in other locations. The point to remember is that companies need to adopt policies and procedures that meet the needs of all employees. As such, programs such as day care, elder care, flexible work schedules, and benefits such as paternal leaves, less-rigid relocation policies, concierge services, and mentoring programs are likely to become more popular.

Special effort is needed to help women navigate through the labyrinth of career success. Organizations can do this by providing women the developmental assignments that prepare them for promotional opportunities.[57] Andrea Jung, chair and CEO of Avon Products, recommends that women should find a company or industry that they love because "the hard work and sacrifices required are only possible if you are fully engaged in your company and enjoy what you do."[58]

Given the projected increase in the number of Hispanics entering the workforce over the next 25 years, managers should consider progressive methods to recruit, retain, and integrate this segment of the population into their organizations. For example, Miami Children's Hospital and Shaw Industries Inc. in Dalton, Georgia, attempted to improve employee productivity, satisfaction, and motivation by developing customized training programs to improve the communication skills of their Spanish-speaking employees.[59] Research further reveals that the retention and career progression of minorities can be significantly enhanced through effective mentoring.

Mismatches between the amount of education needed to perform current jobs and the amount of education possessed by members of the workforce will create a shortage of qualified people in technical fields. To combat this issue, both Lockheed Martin and Agilent Technologies offer some type of paid apprenticeship or internship to attract high-school students interested in the sciences.[60]

The following seven initiatives can help organizations to motivate and retain an aging workforce.[61]

1. Provide challenging work assignments that make a difference to the firm.

2. Give the employee considerable autonomy and latitude in completing a task.

3. Provide equal access to training and learning opportunities when it comes to new technology.

4. Provide frequent recognition for skills, experience, and wisdom gained over the years.

5. Provide mentoring opportunities whereby older workers can pass on accumulated knowledge to younger employees.

6. Ensure that older workers receive sensitive, high-quality supervision.

7. Design a work environment that is both stimulating and fun.

Generational differences outlined in Table 4–2 can affect employee motivation and productivity, thereby necessitating a need to educate employees about working with diverse employees. Traditional and Boomer managers are encouraged to consider their approach toward managing the technologically savvy Gen Xers and Gen Ys. Gen Xers and Ys, for instance, are more likely to visit social networking sites during the work day, often perceiving this activity as a "virtual coffee break." In contrast, Traditional and Boomer managers are more likely to view this as wasted time, thereby leading to policies that attempt to shut down such activity. Experts suggest that restricting access to social media will not work in the long run if an employer wants to motivate younger employees.[62]

Organizational Practices Used to Effectively Manage Diversity

Many organizations throughout the United States are unsure of what it takes to manage diversity effectively. In addition, the sensitive and potentially volatile nature of managing diversity has led to significant barriers when trying to move forward with diversity initiatives. This section reviews the barriers to managing diversity and discusses a framework for categorizing organizational diversity initiatives.

Barriers and Challenges to Managing Diversity

LO4.5

Organizations encounter a variety of barriers when attempting to implement diversity initiatives. It thus is important for present and future managers to consider these barriers before rolling out a diversity program. The following is a list of the most common barriers to implementing successful diversity programs.[63]

1. *Inaccurate stereotypes and prejudice.* This barrier manifests itself in the belief that differences are viewed as weaknesses. In turn, this promotes the view that diversity hiring will mean sacrificing competence and quality.

2. *Ethnocentrism.* The ethnocentrism barrier represents the feeling that one's cultural rules and norms are superior or more appropriate than the rules and norms of another culture.

3. *Poor career planning.* This barrier is associated with the lack of opportunities for diverse employees to get the type of work assignments that qualify them for senior management positions.

4. *An unsupportive and hostile working environment for diverse employees.* Sexual, racial, and age harassment are common examples of hostile work environments. Hostile environments are demeaning, unethical, and demotivating. Consider the situation between ESPN announcer Ron Franklin and Jeannine Edwards, a sideline reporter at the 2010 Fiesta Bowl. Franklin allegedly said the following to Edwards at a meeting: "Why don't you leave this to the boys, sweet baby?" When Edwards objected to the derogatory language, Franklin responded, "okay then, [expletive]." Franklin was pulled from covering the game and ultimately fired.[64]

5. *Lack of political savvy on the part of diverse employees.* Diverse employees may not get promoted because they do not know how to "play the game" of getting along and getting ahead in an organization. Research reveals that women and people of color are excluded from organizational networks.[65]

6. *Difficulty in balancing career and family issues.* Women still assume the majority of the responsibilities associated with raising children. This makes it harder for women to work evenings and weekends or to frequently travel once they have children. Even without children in the picture, household chores take more of a woman's time than a man's time.

7. *Fears of reverse discrimination.* Some employees believe that managing diversity is a smoke screen for reverse discrimination. This belief leads to very strong resistance because people feel that one person's gain is another's loss.

8. *Diversity is not seen as an organizational priority.* This leads to subtle resistance that shows up in the form of complaints and negative attitudes. Employees may complain about the time, energy, and resources devoted to diversity that could have been spent doing "real work."

9. *The need to revamp the organization's performance appraisal and reward system.* Performance appraisals and reward systems must reinforce the need to manage diversity effectively. This means that success will be based on a new set of criteria. Employees are likely to resist changes that adversely affect their promotions and financial rewards.

10. *Resistance to change.* Effectively managing diversity entails significant organizational and personal change. As discussed in Chapter 16, people resist change for many different reasons.

> **BACK TO THE CHAPTER-OPENING CASE** Which of these barriers occurred on the USS *Enterprise?*

Research suggests that organizations should take two key steps to overcome these obstacles. First, leaders are encouraged to explain to their employees why the organization values diversity. In a study of 184 college students, groups of students performed better if they had first received information supporting the value of diversity for group performance.[66] Second, it is important for managers to challenge stereotypical expectations that people have about others.[67]

R Roosevelt Thomas Jr's Generic Action Options

So what are organizations doing to effectively manage diversity? Answering this question requires that we provide a framework for categorizing organizational initiatives. Researchers and practitioners have developed relevant frameworks. One was developed by R Roosevelt Thomas Jr, a diversity expert. He identified eight generic action options that can be used to address any type of diversity issue. After describing each action option, we discuss relationships among them.[68]

LO4.6

Option 1: Include/Exclude   This choice is an outgrowth of affirmative-action programs. Its primary goal is to either increase or decrease the number of diverse people at all levels of the organization. Shoney's restaurant represents a good example of a company that attempted to include diverse employees after settling a discrimination lawsuit. The company subsequently hired African-Americans into positions of dining-room supervisors and vice presidents, added more franchises owned by African-Americans, and purchased more goods and services from minority-owned companies.[69]

Option 2: Deny   People using this option deny that differences exist. Denial may manifest itself in proclamations that all decisions are color, gender, and age blind and that success is solely determined by merit and performance. Consider State Farm Insurance, for example. "Although it was traditional for male agents and their regional managers to hire male relatives, State Farm Insurance avoided change and denied any alleged effects in a nine-year gender-bias suit that the company lost."[70]

Option 3: Assimilate   The basic premise behind this alternative is that all diverse people will learn to fit in or become like the dominant group. It only takes time and reinforcement for people to see the light. Organizations initially assimilate employees through their recruitment practices and the use of company-orientation programs. New hires generally are put through orientation programs that aim to provide employees with the organization's preferred values and a set of standard-operating procedures. Employees then are encouraged to refer to the policies and procedures manual when they are confused about what to do in a specific situation. These practices create homogeneity among employees.

Option 4: Suppress   Differences are squelched or discouraged when using this approach. This can be done by telling or reinforcing others to quit whining and complaining about issues. The old "you've got to pay your dues" line is another frequently used way to promote the status quo.

Option 5: Isolate   This option maintains the current way of doing things by setting the diverse person off to the side. In this way the individual is unable to influence organizational change. Managers can isolate people by putting them on special projects. Entire work groups or departments are isolated by creating functionally independent entities, frequently referred to as "silos." Shoney Inc's employees commented to a *Wall Street Journal* reporter about isolation practices formerly used by the company:

UnitedHealthcare Fosters Mutual Adaptation

Shortly after she'd [Lois Quam] had twins Will and Steve, Quam was offered another high-profile opportunity. Her boss wanted her to run UnitedHealthcare's public-sector services division. . . . "It was so overwhelming with twins. You can't pretend it doesn't make a difference. So I said, 'I'd really like to do this, but my primary focus for this period of my life is my sons.'" She remembers thinking, "This is going badly. It isn't strategic to be so blunt." But her boss surprised her. "He said, 'It's not a job that pays by the hour. You do it in a way that works for you, and if it doesn't work for me, I'll tell you.'"

Looking back, Quam describes her reaction as an "amazing gift" . . . because it affirmed her instincts about the best way to balance career and family.

SOURCE: A Beard, "Surviving Twin Challenges—At Home and Work," *Harvard Business Review*, January–February 2011, p 164.

White managers told of how Mr Danner [previous chairman of the company] told them to fire blacks if they became too numerous in restaurants in white neighborhoods; if they refused, they would lose their jobs, too. Some also said that when Mr Danner was expected to visit their restaurant, they scheduled black employees off that day or, in one case, hid them in the bathroom. Others said blacks' applications were coded and discarded.[71]

Option 6: Tolerate   Toleration entails acknowledging differences but not valuing or accepting them. It represents a live-and-let-live approach that superficially allows organizations to give lip service to the issue of managing diversity. Toleration is different from isolation in that it allows for the inclusion of diverse people. However, differences are not really valued or accepted when an organization uses this option.

Option 7: Build Relationships   This approach is based on the premise that good relationships can overcome differences. It addresses diversity by fostering quality relationships—characterized by acceptance and understanding—among diverse groups. Rockwell Collins, Inc, a producer of aviation electronics in Cedar Rapids, Iowa, is a good example of a company attempting to use this diversity option. Rockwell is motivated to pursue this option because it has a shortage of qualified employees in a state that is about 6% nonwhite. To attract minority candidates the company "is building closer relationships with schools that have strong engineering programs as well as sizable minority populations. It also is working more closely with minority-focused professional societies."[72] The city of Cedar Rapids is also getting involved in the effort by trying to offer more cultural activities and ethnic-food stores that cater to a more diverse population base.

Option 8: Foster Mutual Adaptation   In this option, people are willing to adapt or change their views for the sake of creating positive relationships with others. This implies that employees and management alike must be willing to accept differences, and most important, agree that everyone and everything is open for change. Lois Quam's experience at UnitedHealthcare is a good example of mutual adaptation (see the Skills & Best Practices feature above).[73]

> **BACK TO THE CHAPTER-OPENING CASE** Which of Thomas's action options were used by leaders on the USS *Enterprise*?

Conclusions about Action Options Although the action options can be used alone or in combination, some are clearly better than others. Exclusion, denial, assimilation, suppression, isolation, and toleration are among the least preferred options. Inclusion, building relationships, and mutual adaptation are the preferred strategies. That said, Thomas reminds us that mutual adaptation is the only approach that unquestionably endorses the philosophy behind managing diversity. In closing this discussion, it is important to note that choosing how to best manage diversity is a dynamic process that is determined by the context at hand. For instance, some organizations are not ready for mutual adaptation. The best one might hope for in this case is the inclusion of diverse people.

key terms

affirmative action 99
attention 85
causal attributions 92
cognitive categories 86
discrimination 99
diversity 96

external factors 92
fundamental attribution bias 94
glass ceiling 100
implicit cognition 90
internal factors 92
managing diversity 100

perception 84
schema 86
self-serving bias 94
stereotype 86

chapter summary

- *Describe* perception *in terms of the social information processing model.* Perception is a mental and cognitive process that enables us to interpret and understand our surroundings. Social perception, also known as social cognition and social information processing, is a four-stage process. The four stages are selective attention/comprehension, encoding and simplification, storage and retention, and retrieval and response. During social cognition, salient stimuli are matched with schemata, assigned to cognitive categories, and stored in long-term memory for events, semantic materials, or people.

- *Explain seven managerial implications of social perception.* Social perception affects hiring decisions, performance appraisals, leadership perceptions, communication and interpersonal influence, counterproductive work behaviors, physical and psychological well-being, and the design of web pages. Inaccurate schemata or racist and sexist schemata may be used to evaluate job applicants. Similarly, faulty schemata

about what constitutes good versus poor performance can lead to inaccurate performance appraisals. Invalid schemata need to be identified and replaced with appropriate schemata through coaching and training. Further, managers are advised to use objective rather than subjective measures of performance. With respect to leadership, a leader will have a difficult time influencing employees when he or she exhibits behaviors contained in employees' schemata of poor leaders. Because people interpret oral and written communications by using schemata developed through experiences, an individual's ability to influence others is affected by information contained in others' schemata regarding age, gender, ethnicity, appearance, speech, mannerisms, personality, and other personal characteristics.

Research reveals that employees exhibit counterproductive work behaviors when they perceive unfair treatment. There also is a connection between negative thinking and one's physical and psychological health. We should all attempt to avoid the tendency of giving negative thoughts too much attention. Finally, the extent to which a web page garners interests and generates sales is partly a function of perceptual processes. Organizations are encouraged to consider the characteristics of effective web page design.

- *Explain, according to Kelley's model, how external and internal causal attributions are formulated.* Attribution theory attempts to describe how people infer causes for observed behavior. According to Kelley's model of causal attribution, external attributions tend to be made when consensus and distinctiveness are high and consistency is low. Internal (personal responsibility) attributions tend to be made when consensus and distinctiveness are low and consistency is high.

- *Demonstrate your familiarity with the demographic trends that are creating an increasingly diverse workforce.* There are four key demographic trends: (a) women navigate a labyrinth after breaking the glass ceiling, (b) racial groups are encountering a glass ceiling and perceived discrimination, (c) a mismatch exists between workers' educational attainment and occupational requirements, and (d) generational differences in an aging workforce.

- *Identify the barriers and challenges to managing diversity.* There are 10 barriers to successfully implementing diversity initiatives: (a) inaccurate stereotypes and prejudice, (b) ethnocentrism, (c) poor career planning, (d) an unsupportive and hostile working environment for diverse employees, (e) lack of political savvy on the part of diverse employees, (f) difficulty in balancing career and family issues, (g) fears of reverse discrimination, (h) diversity is not seen as an organizational priority, (i) the need to revamp the organization's performance appraisal and reward system, and (j) resistance to change.

- *Discuss organizational practices used to manage diversity.* Organizations have eight options that they can use to address diversity issues: (a) include/exclude the number of diverse people at all levels of the organization, (b) deny that differences exist, (c) assimilate diverse people into the dominant group, (d) suppress differences, (e) isolate diverse members from the larger group, (f) tolerate differences among employees, (g) build relationships among diverse employees, and (h) foster mutual adaptation to create positive relationships.

discussion questions

1. Why is it important for managers to have a working knowledge of perception and attribution?
2. How would you formulate an attribution, according to Kelley's model, for the behavior of a classmate who starts arguing in class with your professor?
3. Does diversity suggest that managers should follow the rule, "Do unto others as you would have them do unto you"?
4. How can diversity initiatives be helpful in overcoming the barriers and challenges to managing diversity?
5. How does the perception process become linked with the manner in which companies manage diversity?

legal/ethical challenge

Should Joseph Casias Be Fired by Walmart?[74]

This case takes place in Michigan, a state that allows the use of medical marijuana.

Joseph Casias, a 30-year-old father of two, began work in 2004 as an entry-level grocery stocker at the Walmart in Battle Creek, Michigan. By 2008, he had progressed to inventory control manager and was recognized as Associate of the Year, an honor given to only 2 of 400 employees.

In November 2009, Casias twisted his knee at work; because Walmart policy requires drug testing after a workplace injury,

he underwent a urine test. Before the test, he showed the testing staff a registry card stating that he was a medical marijuana patient under Michigan law. He explained that he had been diagnosed with inoperable brain cancer at age 17, and the marijuana, prescribed by his oncologist, helped alleviate daily pain.

When the drug test revealed marijuana metabolites in Casias's system, the store manager told him that Walmart would not honor his registry card—and Casias was terminated.

What Would You Do if You Were an Executive at Walmart?

1. Give Casias his job back. He is a great employee and is not violating state law about using marijuana for medical conditions.
2. Zero tolerance should be applied, and he should be fired. Regardless of what state law says, it is illegal under federal law to use marijuana. Standards for marijuana should be the same as any other drug.
3. He should be fired because he presents a safety hazard to himself and others. The company must protect all employees from people who use drugs.
4. Invent other options. Discuss.

If you're looking for additional study materials, be sure to check out the Online Learning Center at

www.mhhe.com/kinickiob5e

for more information and interactivities that correspond to this chapter.

chapter 5

Appreciating Individual Differences: Intelligence, Ability, Personality, Core Self-Evaluations, Attitudes, and Emotions

After reading the material in this chapter, you should be able to:

LO5.1 Identify at least five of Gardner's eight multiple intelligences, and explain "practical intelligence."

LO5.2 Identify and describe the Big Five personality dimensions, specify which one is correlated most strongly with job performance, and describe proactive personality.

LO5.3 Explain the four components of core self-evaluations.

LO5.4 Distinguish between self-esteem and self-efficacy.

LO5.5 Explain the difference between an internal and external locus of control.

LO5.6 Identify the three components of attitudes and discuss cognitive dissonance.

LO5.7 Explain the concepts of emotional intelligence, emotional contagion, and emotional labor.

LEARNING OBJECTIVES

The Man Behind Facebook

Mark Zuckerberg, the founder of Facebook, was born in 1984. He is the son of a dentist and has three sisters. His father described him as a very strong-minded and persistent child. He wouldn't accept simple answers. And if you told him "no," then you had better make a compelling argument backed up with data and logic. Today, he is not physically commanding at only 5'8" tall and average build. He also is now legendarily casually dressed, like Steve Jobs, the iconic Apple Computer founder, CEO, and wunderkind of an earlier generation. Zuckerberg is most often clad in jeans, t-shirt, and a hoodie sweatshirt. Definitely casual for a CEO whose net worth is estimated to top $6 billion!

As for his personality, in the movie *The Social Network* he was portrayed as socially awkward, disinterested, or even inept. But many that either know or have spent time with him say that's inaccurate. Such informed people instead say that conversation is an information exchange for Zuckerberg, one in which he stares and listens first, and if what you have to offer is neither stimulating nor interesting then he quickly tunes out or turns away. According to Andrew Bosworth, director of engineering at Facebook: "He's not trying to be rude. He's just like, 'Okay, you're not the best use of this time anymore.' He's going to find a better use of his time, even if you're sitting right there." Those that know Mark claim he has a warm presence, not a cold one. He likes people, and they are drawn to him—his smile, confidence, and dry humor. (He was seldom without a girlfriend during college.) He is calm in social settings, rather than withdrawn or anxious. This maybe attributable to the fact that his entire life has been spent in the company of strong, supportive sociable groups, such as his family, his roommates and friends at Harvard, and now colleagues at Facebook.

Some of his closest friends are employees.

Not only does Zuckerberg like people, but he also understands them. In college he was both a computer science and psychology major. Zuckerberg explains that he has always been interested in how the two interact. "For me, computers were always just a way to build good stuff, not like an end in itself." This is part of Zuckerberg's edge. Others can write code better, although not many, but he also understands people. "He has great EQ," says Naomi Gleit, Facebook's product manager for growth and internationalization. Mark's understanding and interest in people pervade all of his projects up to and

including Facebook. This is evidenced by how he runs the company and treats employees—free meals, snacks, and dry cleaning. However, the most compelling attraction is Zuckerberg and his vision. Many new employees allegedly share the same recruiting and hiring experience. Candidates-turned-employees describe their conversions: "I'm not interested. My current job is important and stimulating." But according to Chris Cox, Facebook's vice president of product, who was doing a masters in artificial intelligence at Stanford at the time, "The interview completely changed my mind. I saw the vision. I came in, and I saw it on the whiteboard."[1]

THE CHAPTER-OPENING CASE ILLUSTRATES many fascinating organizational behavior (OB) concepts and individual characteristics of Facebook's wunderkind founder. The case suggests that some people appreciate and like Mark's interpersonal style while others may not. This underscores the notion that there is not one type of person that is universally successful. More generally, the vast array of individual differences possessed by employees makes modern organizations rich and interesting places to work. However, these individual differences make a manager's job endlessly challenging. Growing workforce diversity, detailed in Chapter 4, compels managers to view individual differences (IDs) in a fresh new way. Rather than limiting diversity, as in the past, today's managers need to better understand and accommodate employee diversity and individual differences. We organized this chapter to help you in this pursuit.

The chapter begins by reviewing an OB model for studying individual differences because it provides a broad structure for integrating the various individual differences discussed. We then explore a subset of individual differences found to be particularly important in the work context and supported by research: (1) intelligence and cognitive abilities, (2) personality dynamics, (3) core self-evaluations, (4) attitudes, and (5) emotions.

A Model for Studying Individual Differences

A model for studying individual differences is shown in Figure 5–1. The many IDs shown are especially important because they affect the individual-level outcomes listed at the far right: job performance, job satisfaction, turnover, organizational citizenship behaviors, and counterproductive work behaviors (all discussed in Chapter 6). Be sure to note that individual differences affect work outcomes within the organizational context. As discussed in Chapter 1, all behavior occurs in and is affected by contextual factors, such as organizational culture (Chapter 2) and societal culture (Chapter 3).

Returning to Figure 5–1, note that the individual differences are arranged on a continuum from top to bottom. At the top are intelligence and ability which are relatively fixed—stable over time and across situations—and difficult to change. At the bottom are attitudes and emotions which are relatively flexible—they change over time, from situation to situation, and can be altered more easily. The distinction between relatively fixed and flexible individual differences has great practical value for managers. Because managers have little impact on fixed IDs, it is more important to select employees based on positive job relevant IDs that are relatively stable. This enables managers to capitalize on the personal strengths that someone brings to a job because these stable strengths affect behavior and performance in most every work situation.[2] Intelligence and analytical abilities, for example, are likely to be beneficial in front of customers, in teams with coworkers, and working alone on a project. In contrast, managers have more influence on relatively flexible IDs that influence individual-level work outcomes. This implies that managers are more likely to influence individual-level work outcomes, like performance and job satisfaction, by implementing different policies and practices that positively impact employee attitudes and emotions. Chapters 6 and 7 will review a number of OB theories and models that you can use for this purpose.

Figure 5–1 can be applied for your personal benefit as well. Considered as an integrated package, the factors in Figure 5–1 provide a foundation for better understanding yourself and why you behave the way you do in various situations. For example, knowledge of your personality and attitudes helps explain how you can enhance your

An OB Model for Studying Individual Differences   FIGURE 5–1

ability to influence others: Influence tactics and leadership styles are discussed in detail in Chapters 13 and 14, respectively. It also can help you identify jobs that are a good fit with your personality. The concept of person-environment fit (PE fit) is discussed in Chapter 6.

Intelligence and Cognitive Abilities

Although experts do not agree on a specific definition, *intelligence* **represents an individual's capacity for constructive thinking, reasoning, and problem solving.**[3] Historically, intelligence was believed to be an innate capacity, passed genetically from one generation to the next. Research since has shown, however, that intelligence (IQ) (like personality) also is a function of environmental influences.[4] The study of intelligence is important because meta-analytic studies show that it is correlated with performance.[5] This section provides a brief overview of research on intelligence and mental abilities, and then highlights practical implications associated with this work.

Key Mental Abilities

Researchers have identified key mental abilities by using an empirical approach that examines relationships between measures of mental abilities and behavior. Using this empirical procedure, pioneering psychologist Charles Spearman proposed in 1927 that all cognitive performance is determined by two types of abilities. The first can be characterized as a general mental ability needed for *all* cognitive tasks. He labeled this "G" for general mental ability. The second is unique to the task at hand. For example, an individual's ability to complete crossword puzzles is a function of his or her broad mental abilities as well as the specific ability to perceive patterns in partially completed words.

The empirical approach to studying mental abilities has uncovered three important insights. The first is associated with a unique five-year study that demonstrated an individual's tendency to "gravitate into jobs commensurate with their abilities."[6] It appears that people are happier and more productive when their work matches their cognitive abilities. The second relates to the steady and significant rise in average intelligence among those in developed countries that has been observed over the last 70 years. Why? Experts at an American Psychological Association conference concluded, "Some combination of better schooling, improved socioeconomic status, healthier nutrition, and a more technologically complex society might account for the gains in IQ scores."[7] So if you think you're smarter than your parents and your teachers, you're probably right!

 LO5.1

The final insight pertains to the question of whether or not people possess multiple intelligences. Howard Gardner, a professor at Harvard's Graduate School of Education, investigated this issue for years and summarized his findings in his 1983 book *Frames of Mind: The Theory of Multiple Intelligences.*[8] He identified eight different intelligences that vastly broaden the long-standing concept of Spearman's "G." Gardner's concept of multiple intelligences (MIs) includes not only cognitive abilities but social and physical abilities and skills as well:

1. *Linguistic intelligence:* potential to learn and use spoken and written languages.
2. *Logical-mathematical intelligence:* potential for deductive reasoning, problem analysis, and mathematical calculation.
3. *Musical intelligence:* potential to appreciate, compose, and perform music.
4. *Bodily-kinesthetic intelligence:* potential to use mind and body to coordinate physical movement.
5. *Spatial intelligence:* potential to recognize and use patterns.
6. *Interpersonal intelligence:* potential to understand, connect with, and effectively work with others.
7. *Intrapersonal intelligence:* potential to understand and regulate oneself.
8. *Naturalist intelligence:* potential to live in harmony with one's environment.[9]

Practical Implications

Many educators and parents have embraced MI because it helps explain how a child could score poorly on a standard IQ test yet be obviously gifted in one or more ways (e.g., music, sports, relationship building). Moreover, they believe the concept of MI underscores the need to help each child develop in his or her own unique way and at his or her own pace. They say standard IQ tests deal only with the first two intelligences on Gardner's list: These two are most closely aligned with Spearman's "G." Meanwhile, most academic psychologists and intelligence specialists continue to criticize Gardner's model as too subjective and poorly integrated. They prefer the traditional model of intelligence as a unified variable measured by a single test.

While the academic debate continues, we can draw additional practical benefits from Gardner's notion of MI. For instance, Yale's Robert J Sternberg recently applied

Gardner's "naturalist intelligence" to the domain of leadership under the heading *practical intelligence.* He explains,

> Practical intelligence is the ability to solve everyday problems by utilizing knowledge gained from experience in order to purposefully adapt to, shape, and select environments. It thus involves changing oneself to suit the environment (adaptation), changing the environment to suit oneself (shaping), or finding a new environment within which to work (selection). One uses these skills to (*a*) manage oneself, (*b*) manage others, and (*c*) manage tasks.[10]

Others believe MI has important implications for employee selection, training, and peformance.[11] One-size-fits-all training programs fall short when MI diversity is taken into consideration. Near the end of this chapter, you will encounter the concept of *emotional intelligence,* which can be used for selection and other purposes. We look forward to breakthroughs in this area as MI attracts OB researchers and practicing managers.

Personality Dynamics

Individuals have their own way of thinking and acting, their own unique style or *personality.* **Personality is defined as the combination of stable physical and mental characteristics that give the individual his or her identity.** These characteristics or traits—including how one looks, thinks, acts, and feels—are the product of interacting genetic and environmental influences and are stable over time and across cultures.[12] In this section, we introduce the Big Five personality dimensions, proactive personality, and managerial implications associated with personality dynamics.

The Big Five Personality Dimensions

 LO5.2

Long and confusing lists of personality dimensions have been distilled in recent years to the Big Five.[13] They are extraversion, agreeableness, conscientiousness, emotional stability, and openness to experience (see Table 5–1 for descriptions). Standardized personality tests determine how positively or negatively a person scores on each of the Big Five. For example, someone scoring negatively on extraversion would be an introverted

The Big Five Personality Dimensions   **TABLE 5–1**

Personality Dimension	Characteristics of a Person Scoring Positively on the Dimension
1. Extraversion	Outgoing, talkative, sociable, assertive
2. Agreeableness	Trusting, good-natured, cooperative, softhearted
3. Conscientiousness	Dependable, responsible, achievement oriented, persistent
4. Emotional stability	Relaxed, secure, unworried
5. Openness to experience	Intellectual, imaginative, curious, broad-minded

SOURCE: Adapted from M R Barrick and M K Mount, "Autonomy as a Moderator of the Relationships between the Big Five Personality Dimensions and Job Performance," *Journal of Applied Psychology,* February 1993, pp 111–18.

person prone to shy and withdrawn behavior.[14] Someone scoring negatively on emotional stability would be nervous, tense, angry, and worried. A person's scores on the Big Five reveal a personality profile as unique as his or her fingerprints. We would like you to take a couple of minutes to complete the assessment of your standing on the Big Five—see the Hands-On Exercise on page 121. Are you surprised by the results?

BACK TO THE CHAPTER-OPENING CASE   Profile Mark Zuckerberg using the Big Five.

1. Which dimensions do you think are highest?
2. Which dimensions are lowest?
3. Explain the potential implications for him and Facebook.

But one important question lingers: Are personality models ethnocentric and unique to the culture in which they were developed? At least as far as the Big Five model goes, cross-cultural research evidence points in the direction of "no." Specifically, the Big Five personality structure held up very well in a study of women and men from Russia, Canada, Hong Kong, Poland, Germany, and Finland.[15] A recent comprehensive analysis of Big Five studies led the researchers to this conclusion: "To date, there is no compelling evidence that culture affects personality structure."[16]

Terri Kelly, CEO of W L Gore & Associates, understands the importance of self-awareness in managers. In fact, in a company famous for its lack of hierarchy, Kelly has an acute perception about her own role. "The idea of me as CEO managing the company is a misperception," she says. "My goal is to provide the overall direction. I spend a lot of time making sure we have the right people in the right roles."

Proactive Personality

As suggested by the preceding discussion, someone who scores high on the Big Five dimension of conscientiousness is probably a *better* and *safer* worker. Thomas Bateman and J Michael Crant took this important linkage an additional step by formulating the concept of the proactive personality. They define and characterize ***proactive personality*** **in these terms: "someone who is relatively unconstrained by situational forces and who effects environmental change. Proactive people identify opportunities and act on them, show initiative, take action, and persevere until meaningful change occurs."**[17] In short, people with proactive personalities are "hardwired" to change the status quo. Research also supports other positive relationships between this personality trait and the work outcomes shown in Figure 5–1. For example, a recent meta-analysis involving 3,096 people found proactivity to be positively associated with performance, satisfaction, affective organizational commitment (genuine desire to remain a member of an organization), and social networking.[18]

Successful entrepreneurs exemplify the proactive personality. Consider Joaquin Galan, founder of Galypso International, an export company with $13 million in revenues. Following the death of his father when Galan was just

HANDS-ON EXERCISE

Your Own Big Five Profile

INSTRUCTIONS: Using the scale below, indicate to what extent each of the following statements describes you.

		1 Not at all like me	2 A little bit like me	3 Somewhat like me	4 Like me	5 Very much like me
1.	I talk to many different people at parties.	1	2	3	4	5
2.	I don't mind being the center of attention.	1	2	3	4	5
3.	I sympathize with other people's feelings.	1	2	3	4	5
4.	I take time out for others.	1	2	3	4	5
5.	I am always prepared.	1	2	3	4	5
6.	I pay attention to details.	1	2	3	4	5
7.	I am relaxed most of the time.	1	2	3	4	5
8.	I am not easily bothered by things.	1	2	3	4	5
9.	I enjoy hearing new ideas.	1	2	3	4	5
10.	I enjoy thinking about things.	1	2	3	4	5

SCORING KEY: Add Q1 and Q2 = _____ Extraversion Score
Add Q3 and Q4 = _____ Agreeableness Score
Add Q5 and Q6 = _____ Conscientiousness Score
Add Q7 and Q8 = _____ Emotional Stability Score
Add Q9 and Q10 = _____ Openness to Experience Score

INTERPRETATION: A score greater than 8 indicates a high level of that particular personality factor. A score between 6 and 8 indicates a moderate level on that factor, and a score less than 6 indicates a low level on that factor.

SOURCE: L R Goldberg, J A Johnson, H W Eber, R Hogan, M C Ashton, C R Cloninger, & H C Gough "The International Personality Item Pool and the Future of Public-domain Personality Measures," *Journal of Research in Personality* 40 (2006), pp 84–96.

15, he worked hard to help support his family, took a sales job with a company that would help pay for classes toward a master's degree in business administration, and launched a furniture business that failed and left him with tremendous debt. Undaunted, Galan started Galypso with his last $1,000 and a small line of credit. With similar resilience, Rachel Coleman founded Two Little Hands Productions, which produces DVDs that teach American Sign Language to children, after discovering that her baby daughter was severely hearing impaired. When Coleman learned of her daughter's disability, she abandoned her career as singer/songwriter, taught herself to sign, and began teaching children at local preschools. She and her sister made their first video just to teach others, but when *The Today Show* inquired, Coleman saw an opportunity and started building a business.[19]

People with proactive personalities truly are valuable *human capital*, as defined in Chapter 1. Those wanting to get ahead would do well to cultivate the initiative, drive, and perseverance of someone with a proactive personality.

www.mcgrawhillconnect.com

Go to Connect for a video case to view Andre Thornton, the CEO of GPI Procurement Services and how personality affects his success in the marketplace.

Research and Managerial Implications

Everybody assumes that personality matters at work. But we know that assumptions can be dangerous. You thus are well served to ask and answer: Does personality affect performance? If yes, then which characteristics and to what extent? Under what conditions? A knowledge of OB helps you answer these questions and guides the application of this knowledge.

Personality and Job Performance   Those interested in OB want to know the connection between the Big Five and job performance. Ideally, Big Five personality dimensions that correlate positively and strongly with job performance would be helpful in the selection, training, and appraisal of employees. A meta-analysis of 117 studies involving 23,994 subjects from many professions offers guidance.[20] Among the Big Five, *conscientiousness* had the strongest positive correlation with job performance and training performance. According to the researchers, "[T]hose individuals who exhibit traits associated with a strong sense of purpose, obligation, and persistence generally perform better than those who do not."[21] Conscientiousness or a sixth personality measure, honesty-humility, also has been associated with high scores on integrity tests and less counterproductive behavior.[22] So it comes as no surprise that British researchers recently found that people scoring *low* on conscientiousness tended to have significantly more accidents both on and off the job.[23]

Another expected finding: Extraversion (an outgoing personality) was associated with success for managers and salespeople. Also, extraversion was a stronger predictor of job performance than agreeableness, across all professions. The researchers concluded, "It appears that being courteous, trusting, straightforward, and softhearted has a smaller impact on job performance than being talkative, active, and assertive."[24] Not surprisingly, another study found a strong linkage between conscientiousness and performance among those with polished social skills.[25] As an added bonus for extraverts, a recent positive psychology study led to this conclusion: "All you have to do is act extraverted and you can get a happiness boost."[26] So the next time you are on the job, go initiate a conversation with someone and be more productive *and* happier!

Personality Testing in the Workplace   Personality testing as a tool for making decisions about hiring, training, and promotion is commonplace. A recent study by the Aberdeen Group, a human capital market research firm, found 53% of companies use some form of pre- and post-hiring assessments. Many of these are personality-type tests. According to the same study, 86% of "best in class" companies used assessments in the prehire stage.[27] However, despite their widespread use, a panel of industrial-organizational psychologists concluded that the typical personality test is not a valid predictor of job performance.[28] One reason might be that many test-takers don't describe themselves accurately but instead try to guess what answers the employer is looking for. And while personality actually is related to performance, managers need a better way to measure personality than the current tests if they want to select employees based on personality traits. Another reason for dismal results is that such tests are typically bought off the shelf, given indiscriminately, often by people who aren't trained or qualified.[29] Managers are therefore wise to learn about personality and tools used to measure it before investing in and/or utilizing the data from such tests. Table 5–2 on page 123 provides some insights.

There Is No "Ideal Employee" Personality   A word of caution is in order here. The Big Five personality dimensions of conscientiousness and extraversion and

Advice and Words of Caution about Personality Testing in the Workplace   TABLE 5–2

Researchers, test developers, and organizations that administer personality assessments offer the following suggestions for getting started or for evaluating whether tests already in use are appropriate for forecasting job performance:

- Determine what you hope to accomplish. If you are looking to find the best fit of job and applicant, analyze the aspects of the position that are most critical for it.
- Look for outside help to determine if a test exists or can be developed to screen applicants for the traits that best fit the position. Industrial psychologists, professional organizations, and a number of Internet sites provide resources.
- Insist that any test recommended by a consultant or vendor be validated scientifically for the specific purpose that you have defined. Vendors should be able to cite some independent, credible research supporting a test's correlation with job performance.
- Ask the test provider to document the legal basis for any assessment: Is it fair? Is it job-related? Is it biased against any racial or ethnic group? Does it violate an applicant's right to privacy under state or federal laws? Vendors should provide a lawyer's statement that a test does not adversely affect any protected class, and employers may want to get their own lawyer's opinion, as well.
- Make sure that every staff member who will be administering tests or analyzing results is educated about how to do so properly and keeps results confidential. Use the scores on personality tests in tandem with other factors that you believe are essential to the job—such as skills and experience—to create a comprehensive evaluation of the merits of each candidate, and apply those criteria identically to each applicant.

SOURCE: From S. Bates, "Personality Counts," *HR Magazine,* February 2002, p. 34. Reprinted with permission of the Society for Human Resource Management (www.shrm.org), Alexandria, VA, publisher of HR Magazine. © SHRM.

the proactive personality are generally desirable in the workplace, but they are not panaceas. Given the complexity of today's work environments, the diversity of today's workforce, and recent research evidence, the quest for an ideal employee personality profile is sheer folly. Just as one shoe does not fit all people, one personality profile does not fit all job situations. Good management involves taking the time to get to know *each employee's unique combination* of personality traits, abilities, and potential and then creating a productive and satisfying person-job fit. In other words, a contingency approach to managing people is best (recall the discussion in Chapter 1).

Core Self-Evaluations

Our discussion of intelligence and mental abilities began with a definition of Spearman's "G," which is a high-level, general concept representing overall intelligence. This broad view evolved into a more detailed and fine-grained explanation of multiple intelligences and multiple dimensions of personality. Researchers have debated the relative benefits of broad versus narrow concepts to describe individuals and predict behavior. The argument is similar to testing the axiom of whether "the whole is greater than the sum of the parts." Those who argue in favor of narrow concepts—musical intelligence versus "G," and extraversion versus one's general personality—claim that they enable you to more specifically *describe* people.

For example, a narrow concepts approach would conclude that it is more insightful to say Steve Vai, a phenomenal progressive rock guitarist (a favorite of one of your authors), has incredible musical intelligence than to say that he is intelligent. In contrast, those who argue in favor of broader or more general concepts claim that doing so enables you to better *predict* behavior—"the whole is greater than the sum of the parts." The rationale is that broader concepts provide a more comprehensive and practical account of an individual.[30] Part of Vai's guitar-playing prowess likely is due to other factors beyond his musical intelligence. While there is no clear answer regarding the validity of these two approaches, researchers have identified a broad individual difference concept that has significant relationships with a host of individual-level work outcomes. It is called core self-evaluations (CSEs).

LO5.3

Core self-evaluations **represent a broad personality trait comprised of four narrower individual personality traits: (1) self-esteem, (2) generalized self-efficacy, (3) locus of control, and (4) emotional stability.**[31] This section discusses these component traits and highlights research and managerial implication for each separately. This is done because it is necessary to understand the component traits to comprehend CSEs and to fully appreciate the practical value. We conclude by comparing what we know about these individual traits with what research reveals about combining them into the broad concept of CSE and implications for various individual-level outcomes.

Self-Esteem

Self-esteem **is a belief about one's own self-worth based on an overall self-evaluation.** Self-esteem is measured by having survey respondents indicate their agreement or disagreement with both positive and negative statements. An example of a positive statement is, "I feel I am a person of worth, the equal of other people." An example of a negative statement is, "I feel I do not have much to be proud of." Those who agree with the positive statements and disagree with the negative statements have high self-esteem. They see themselves as worthwhile, capable, and acceptable. People with low self-esteem view themselves in negative terms. They do not feel good about themselves and are hampered by self-doubts.[32]

Go to Connect for a self-assessment to assess your core self evaluations.

Cross-Cultural, Life-Span, and Gender Perspectives   What are the cross-cultural implications for self-esteem, a concept that has been called uniquely Western? In a survey of 13,118 students from 31 countries worldwide, a moderate positive correlation was found between self-esteem and life satisfaction. But the relationship was stronger in individualistic cultures (e.g., United States, Canada, New Zealand, Netherlands) than in collectivist cultures (e.g., Korea, Kenya, Japan). The researchers concluded that individualistic cultures socialize people to focus more on themselves, while people in collectivist cultures "are socialized to fit into the community and to do their duty. Thus, how a collectivist feels about him- or herself is less relevant to . . . life satisfaction."[33] Global managers need to remember to deemphasize self-esteem when doing business in collectivist ("we") cultures, as opposed to emphasizing it in individualistic ("me") cultures.[34]

A recent meta-analysis of 80,433 people showed that self-esteem is stable over the course of one's life. The biggest changes happened in the first 10 years of adulthood with little significant change after age 30. A particularly interesting result was that self-esteem did not change much during adolescence, and the differences between men and women were small at best.[35] While this suggests that self-esteem is consistent over time, it begs the question: Can it be improved?

Can General Self-Esteem Be Improved?   The short answer is yes. More detailed answers come from research. In one study, youth-league baseball coaches who were trained in supportive teaching techniques had a positive effect on the self-esteem of young boys. A control group of untrained coaches had no such positive effect.[36] Another study led to this conclusion: "Low self-esteem can be raised more by having the person think of *desirable* characteristics *possessed* rather than of undesirable characteristics from which he or she is free."[37] Research also showed that supportive clinical mentors improved medical residents' self-esteem.[38]

Yet another comprehensive study threw cold water on the popular view that high self-esteem is the key to better performance. The conclusion:

> [S]elf-esteem and school or job performance are correlated. But long overdue scientific scrutiny points out the foolishness of supposing that people's opinion of themselves can be the *cause* of achievement. Rather, high-esteem is the *result* of good performance.[39]

Bottom line: Research is mixed on the relationship between self-esteem and performance. However, research continues. A recent study showed that self-esteem positively affected performance when the task at hand was relevant to one's self-esteem. In other words, if getting an A in your OB course is part of your evaluation of your self-worth, then you will be motivated to work harder and presumably perform better.[40]

The next topic, self-efficacy, sheds more light on the issue of performance.

Self-Efficacy ("I Can Do That.")

Have you noticed how those who are confident about their ability tend to succeed, while those who are preoccupied with failing tend to fail? Perhaps that explains the

comparative golfing performance of the authors of this book! One consistently stays in the fairways and hits the greens. The other spends the day thrashing through the underbrush, wading in water hazards, and blasting out of sand traps. At the heart of this performance mismatch is a specific dimension of self-esteem called self-efficacy. **Self-efficacy is a person's belief about his or her chances of successfully accomplishing a specific task.** According to one OB writer, "Self-efficacy arises from the gradual acquisition of complex cognitive, social, linguistic, and/or physical skills through experience."[41]

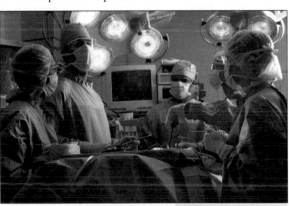

Many individual factors influence performance. Of those discussed so far in this chapter, which do you think are most important for surgeons?

Helpful nudges in the right direction from parents, role models, and mentors are central to the development of high self-efficacy. Consider the medical resident study mentioned above. Mentor guidance and social support improved the resident's clinical self-efficacy.[42] Now consider, which would you prefer—a surgeon who is confident (high self-esteem) or one that is good (high self-efficacy)? Self-efficacy also can be enhanced via training. See the Skills & Best Practices on page 126 for an example.

The relationship between self-efficacy and performance is a cyclical one. Efficacy → performance cycles can spiral upward toward success or downward toward failure.[43] Researchers have documented a strong linkage between high self-efficacy expectations and success in widely varied physical and mental tasks, anxiety reduction, addiction control, pain tolerance, and illness recovery.[44] Oppositely, those with

Investments in Self-Efficacy Training = Investments in Success

Vanguard, a leading financial services company, revamped and revitalized its employee training during the financial crisis in 2009. Leaders of the firm realized that the devastating losses and intensely negative market conditions required employees to have very different conversations with their clients—conversations few were equipped to have. The firm's past training programs did not adequately prepare employees to effectively deal with client's concerns. Part of the answer was training. New training content and methods were rolled out across the company. Vanguard "pulled out all the stops, and made sure all (employees) had strong confidence in their ability to help clients with their investment decisions," said Vanguard University Principal Bridget Olesiewicz.

Kathy Gubanich, Vanguard's human resources managing director, explained that the financial crisis forced the firm to get creative with allocating resources (money and people) and training. She said, "investing in the long term' applies not only to the advice it gives to clients, but to how it invests in its people. Our talent philosophy is one where we don't hire people just for a job; we hire them for a career." Not only was this clear acknowledgement of the importance of human capital (discussed in Chapter 1), but it also illustrated the belief that confident and efficacious employees are better able to perform at a high level.

SOURCE: Excerpted and adapted from M Weinstein, "Investing in Success," *Training*, February 2010, pp 40–44.

www.mcgrawhillconnect.com

Go to Connect for an interactive exercise to test your understanding of the mechanisms of self-efficacy.

low self-efficacy expectations tend to have low success rates. Chronically low self-efficacy is associated with a condition called **_learned helplessness,_ the severely debilitating belief that one has no control over one's environment.**[45] Although self-efficacy sounds like some sort of mental magic, it operates in a very straightforward manner, as the model discussed below will show.

Mechanisms of Self-Efficacy A basic model of self-efficacy is displayed in Figure 5–2. It draws on the work of Stanford psychologist Albert Bandura.[46] Let us explore this model with a simple illustrative task. Imagine you have been told to prepare and deliver a 10-minute talk to an OB class of 50 students on the workings of the self-efficacy model in Figure 5–2. Your self-efficacy calculation would involve cognitive appraisal of the interaction between your perceived capability and situational opportunities and obstacles.

As you begin to prepare for your presentation, the four sources of self-efficacy beliefs would come into play. Because prior experience is the most potent source, according to Bandura, it is listed first and connected to self-efficacy beliefs with a solid line.[47] Past success in public speaking would boost your self-efficacy. But bad experiences with delivering speeches would foster low self-efficacy. Regarding behavior models as a source of self-efficacy beliefs, you would be influenced by the success or failure of your classmates in delivering similar talks. Their successes would tend to bolster you (or perhaps their failure would if you were very competitive and had high self-esteem). Likewise, any supportive persuasion from your classmates that you will do a good job would enhance your self-efficacy. Physical and emotional factors also might affect your self-confidence. A sudden case of laryngitis or a bout of stage fright could cause your self-efficacy expectations to plunge. Your cognitive evaluation of the situation then would yield a self-efficacy belief—ranging from high to low expectations for success. Importantly, self-efficacy beliefs are not merely

Self-Efficacy Beliefs Pave the Way for Success or Failure   FIGURE 5–2

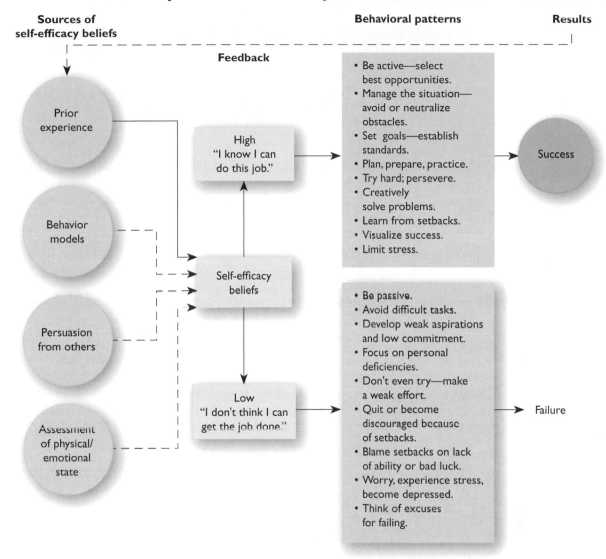

SOURCES: Adapted from discussion in A Bandura, "Regulation of Cognitive Processes through Perceived Self-Efficacy," *Developmental Psychology,* September 1989, pp 729–35; and R Wood and A Bandura, "Social Cognitive Theory of Organizational Management," *Academy of Management Review,* July 1989, pp 361–84.

boastful statements based on bravado; they are deep convictions supported by experience.

Moving to the *behavioral patterns* portion of Figure 5–2, we see how self-efficacy beliefs are acted out. In short, if you have high self-efficacy about giving your 10-minute speech you will work harder, more creatively, and longer when preparing for your talk than will your low-self-efficacy classmates. The results would then take shape accordingly. People program themselves for success or failure by enacting their self-efficacy expectations. Positive or negative results subsequently become feedback for one's base of personal experience. Bob Schmonsees, a software entrepreneur, is an inspiring example of the success pathway through Figure 5–2:

> A contender in mixed-doubles tennis and a former football star, Mr. Schmonsees was standing near a ski lift when an out-of-control skier rammed him. His legs were paralyzed. He would spend the rest of his life in a wheelchair.
>
> Fortunately, he discovered a formula for his different world: Figure out the new rules for any activity, then take as many small steps as necessary to master those rules. After learning the physics of a tennis swing on wheels and the geometry of playing a second bounce (standard rules), he became the world's top wheelchair player over age 40.[48]

Managerial Implications   On-the-job research evidence encourages managers to nurture self-efficacy, both in themselves and in others. In fact, two different meta-analyses including over 20,000 subjects found a significant positive correlation between self-efficacy and job performance and self-efficacy and job satisfaction.[49] Self-efficacy requires constructive action in each of the following managerial areas:

1. *Recruiting/selection/job assignments.* Interview questions can be designed to probe job applicants' general self-efficacy as a basis for determining orientation and training needs. Pencil-and-paper tests for self-efficacy are not in an advanced stage of development and validation. Care needs to be taken not to hire solely on the basis of self-efficacy because studies have detected below-average self-esteem and self-efficacy among women and protected minorities.[50]

2. *Job design.* Complex, challenging, and autonomous jobs tend to enhance perceived self-efficacy.[51] Boring, tedious jobs generally do the opposite.

3. *Training and development.* Employees' self-efficacy expectations for key tasks can be improved through guided experiences, mentoring, and role modeling.[52]

4. *Self-management.* Systematic self-management training involves enhancement of self-efficacy expectations.[53]

5. *Goal setting and quality improvement.* Goal difficulty needs to match the individual's perceived self-efficacy.[54] As self-efficacy and performance improve, goals and quality standards can be made more challenging.

6. *Creativity.* Supportive managerial actions can enhance the strong linkage between self-efficacy beliefs and workplace creativity.[55]

7. *Coaching.* Those with low self-efficacy and employees victimized by learned helplessness need lots of constructive pointers and positive feedback.[56]

8. *Leadership.* Needed leadership talent surfaces when top management gives high self-efficacy managers a chance to prove themselves under pressure.

9. *Rewards.* Small successes need to be rewarded as stepping-stones to a stronger self-image and greater achievements.

Locus of Control: Self or Environment?

Individuals vary in terms of how much personal responsibility they take for their behavior and its consequences. Julian Rotter, a personality researcher, identified a dimension of personality he labeled *locus of control* to explain these differences. He proposed that people tend to attribute the causes of their behavior primarily to either themselves or environmental factors.[57] This personality trait produces distinctly different behavior patterns.

Thomas Mathes Fights the Financial Crisis with Service and Style

Thomas Mathes, a 34-year-old from Memphis, fell in love with hotels and the hotel business as a boy. After high school he began working in a Kimpton hotel in Chicago and never looked back. He worked at multiple locations for Kimpton, always moving to positions of greater responsibility, and eventually landing in New York City. In 2009 he took on the challenge of general manager and was responsible for opening the Eventi property in Manhattan. The timing was terrible. The $600 million property was planned to open during a period when hotel occupancy and rates were at all-time lows. All of the major chains (e.g., Marriott and Starwood) were losing money, and the situation was even worse for high-end hotels in prime, highly competitive markets such as New York.

But Mathes was undeterred. He worked from Starbucks because his office had no heat. He maintained deadlines even though windows for the facility were delayed. He and his marketing assistant even scouted competing hotels, "disguised" as representatives for a fragrance company, to get ideas and to identify their competitors' major business customers.

Mathes left nothing to chance. He oversaw every detail of the hotel's construction. He even personally sat in every single chair in the facility. He thought this was necessary, as the Eventi positioned itself as an upscale boutique hotel with unique decor. He also interviewed each and every candidate for every job.

For the opening in May 2010, Mathes arranged for the hotel's first guest to be picked up in a sports car, personally escorted him to his room, and provided the guest with two tickets to a U2 concert that night. (Mathes had gathered information about the guest and learned that U2 was his favorite band.)

Mathes left nothing to chance. He took charge and delivered!

SOURCE: Based on D Leonard, "The Eventi: Kimpton's Hotel Long Shot," *Bloomberg Businessweek*, December 9, 2010.

LO5.5

People who believe they control the events and consequences that affect their lives are said to possess an *internal locus of control*. For example, such a person tends to attribute positive outcomes, such as getting a passing grade on an exam, to her or his own abilities. Similarly, an "internal" tends to blame negative events, such as failing an exam, on personal shortcomings—not studying hard enough, or perhaps just not being good at math. Many entrepreneurs eventually succeed because their *internal locus of control* helps them overcome setbacks and disappointments.[58] They see themselves as masters of their own fate and not as simply lucky. Likewise, when people with an internal locus of control must shoulder a heavy workload, they look for solutions, such as the example presented in the Skills & Best Practices on page 131.

On the other side of this personality dimension are **those who believe their performance is the product of circumstances beyond their immediate control. These individuals are said to possess an** *external locus of control* and tend to attribute outcomes to environmental causes, such as luck or fate. Unlike someone with an internal locus of control, an "external" would attribute a passing grade on an exam to something external (an easy test or a good day) and attribute a failing grade to an unfair test or problems at home.

Research Lessons Researchers have found important behavioral differences between internals and externals:

- Internals display greater work motivation.
- Internals have stronger expectations that effort leads to performance.

- Internals exhibit higher performance on tasks involving learning or problem solving, when performance leads to valued rewards.
- There is a stronger relationship between job satisfaction and performance for internals than for externals.
- Internals obtain higher salaries and greater salary increases than externals.
- Externals tend to be more anxious than internals.[59]

Emotional Stability

As described in our discussion of the Big 5 and in Table 5–1, **individuals with high levels of *emotional stability* tend to be relaxed, secure, unworried, and less likely to experience negative emotions under pressure.**[60] In contrast, those with low levels are prone to anxiety and tend to view the world negatively. How is this knowledge useful at work? One example was provided by researchers who found beneficial relationships between emotional stability and three individual-level outcomes illustrated in Figure 5–1: job performance, organizational citizenship behaviors (OCBs—going above and beyond one's job responsibilities), and counterproductive work behaviors (CWBs—undermining your own or other's work). (Both OCBs and CWBs are discussed in Chapter 6.) The researchers found curvilinear, or inverted-U, relationships. This means that as the emotional stability of participants (602 public service workers) increased so too did their job performance and OCBs, but only to a point. As emotional stability continued to increase, the beneficial effects declined. The reasoning was that as emotional stability increased, participants focused their attention on the task at hand, including their coworkers. However, at a certain level emotional stability became problematic, too much of a good thing, and participants began to obsess over details and lost sight of the larger objectives and those with whom they worked. A similar result and explanation was found for CWBs. Emotional stability buffered or protected participants against stressors at work (e.g., trouble with their supervisors, unfair policies, and too much work), such that they were less bothered and thus less likely to act out (commit CWBs). But there was a tipping point when the stress became too much, and emotional stability could not prevent employees from committing CWBs.[61] A study of 412 trauma surgeons also showed that emotional stability (and extraversion) were the only Big Five personality dimensions related to greater job satisfaction.[62] Another excellent example is provided in the Skills & Best Practices on page 131. What is the lesson to take away? Emotional stability is an asset for many types of jobs, but it will only take you so far.

The Whole Is Greater Than the Sum of the Parts: CSEs, Its Component Traits, and Outcomes

As shown in Figure 5–1, core self-evaluations are composed of self-esteem, self-efficacy, locus of control, and emotional stability. To clarify the value of CSEs as a whole versus its component traits, think of basketball as a metaphor. Clearly a team outperforms any individual playing alone. Even the greatest player ever would have no chance against an entire team. The five greatest players ever, playing individually, still have no chance against an entire team. Individually they would never score! Thus the sum of their individual efforts would be zero. However, if you assembled a team of the

A Female Wall Street Financial Chief Avoids the Pitfall That Stymied Others

Ruth Porat is the current chief financial officer of Morgan Stanley and one of the most powerful women on Wall Street. She is not an accountant and has never worked in a finance department. However, she has effectively leveraged her Stanford economics degree and Wharton MBA. More impressive than this is that she has overcome many adversities during her rise to the C-suite. She started in finance in 1987 at Morgan Stanley, just before the market crashed. She survived and a few years later moved on to Smith Barney, a move she immediately regretted and feared ruined her career. Obviously it didn't. In 1996 she made her way back to Morgan Stanley and eventually became a technology banker during the tech boom, and bust, of the late 1990s.

Porat then transformed herself into a financial services banker and rode out the financial crisis of 2008–2010 and was named CFO of Morgan Stanley. Many of her colleagues on the Street cautioned her about her new role. They noted that the last two female CFOs for Wall Street firms—Erin Callan of Lehman and Sally Krawcheck of Citigroup—were casualties of the crisis. Worse still, Zoe Cruz, formerly a co-president at Morgan, also was kicked off the island.

But once again Porat was undaunted. Despite also weathering two bouts of breast cancer in the 2000s, she stayed the career course. Her colleagues recognize her as one of the smartest, hardest working, and unshakeable people with whom they have worked. She even made client calls in the delivery room during the birth of her first child. She also insisted on finishing a business presentation while lying on a conference room table, after throwing her back out!

Ruth Porat epitomizes emotional stability—relaxed, secure, and unworried!

SOURCE: Adapted from S Craig, "DealBook: A Female Wall Street Financial Chief Avoids Pitfalls That Stymied Others," *The New York Times,* November 9, 2010.

five greatest players (you can debate this with a classmate—the authors have their own picks) they would likely perform very well. We don't want to overemphasize the team concept that is addressed in detail in Chapter 9, but the combination of (talented) players in a team enables individual players to do things they couldn't otherwise do on their own. Moreover, history tells us that teams with the best individual players ("all-star teams") don't win every game. The fact that such teams lose shows that indeed the whole is greater than the sum of the parts—for their competitors! The sum of the all-stars is less than the sum of their lesser competitors, at least sometimes. CSEs and its component traits are much the same. Core self-evaluation is the team and the traits are the individual players—the whole is greater than the sum of the parts.

But what effect do CSEs have on the important individual-level outcomes illustrated in Figure 5–1? The answer to this question reveals the practical value of the concept for OB. The work of Tim Judge, a noted OB scholar, and others show that CSEs more effectively describe individual behavior than its component traits. For instance, CSEs have been associated with increased job performance, job and life satisfaction, motivation, organizational citizenship behaviors, and better adjustment to international assignments. They also were linked to lower stress and reduced conflict. CSEs predicted all of these, while often the identical studies showed relationships between the individual component traits and these same outcome to be highly mixed—sometimes individual traits were related to outcomes and other times they were not.[63] CSEs also have been studied in the C-suite. A study of 129 CEOs and top management teams showed that CEOs with high core self-evaluations had a positive influence on their organization's drive to take risks, innovate, and seek new opportunities. This effect was especially strong in dynamic business environments.[64]

How can CSEs be used by managers? First, CSEs can be used in employee selection. It is more efficient to select using this one, broad personality characteristic rather than its four component traits. Doing so also enables managers and employers to take advantage of the many beneficial outcomes described above. Second, the component traits of CSEs can be targets for training. Think again of basketball—individual players are coached and practice their respective shooting skills. Although unlike a basketball team, the training potential of CSEs and its component traits is limited. Self-efficacy is relatively more flexible than the other three components and thus can be enhanced as explained above. (Figure 5–2 is an excellent "how to" guide.) However, self-esteem, locus of control, and emotional stability are relatively stable over time and across situations. Therefore these are not valuable targets for manager influence or training. This shortcoming is addressed in the next section of this chapter when we address attitudes, which are much more easily changed compared to CSEs and the other individual differences discussed thus far.

BACK TO THE CHAPTER-OPENING CASE

1. Profile Mark Zuckerberg using the four elements of core self-evaluations. Indicate whether he is high, medium, or low on each.

2. Then describe the implications for his effectiveness as the CEO of Facebook in terms of each CSE element.

Attitudes

Hardly a day goes by without the popular media reporting the results of another attitude survey. The idea is to take the pulse of public opinion. What do we think about President Obama, terrorism, the war on drugs, gun control, or taxes? In the workplace, meanwhile, managers conduct attitude surveys to monitor such things as job satisfaction and employee engagement (both are discussed in detail in Chapter 6). All this attention to attitudes is based on the realization that our attitudes influence our behavior. For example, research demonstrated that seniors with a positive attitude about aging had better memory, had better hearing, and lived longer than those with negative attitudes.[65] In a work setting, meta-analytic studies revealed that job attitudes were positively related to performance and negatively associated with indicators of withdrawal—lateness, absenteeism, and turnover.[66] In this section, we discuss the components of attitudes and examine the connection between attitudes and behavior.

The Nature of Attitudes

An *attitude* **is defined as "a learned predisposition to respond in a consistently favorable or unfavorable manner with respect to a given object."**[67] Consider your attitude toward chocolate ice cream. You are more likely to purchase a chocolate ice cream cone if you have a positive attitude toward chocolate ice cream. In contrast, you are more likely to purchase some other flavor, say vanilla caramel swirl, if you have a positive attitude toward vanilla and a neutral or negative attitude toward chocolate ice cream. Let us consider a work example. If you have a positive attitude about your job (i.e., you like what you are doing), then you would be more willing to extend yourself at work by working longer and harder. These examples illustrate that attitudes propel us to act in a specific way in a specific context. Moreover, attitudes affect behavior at a different level than do values. While values represent global beliefs that influence behavior across *all* situations, attitudes relate only to behavior directed toward *specific* objects, persons, or situations. Values and attitudes generally, but not always, are in harmony. A manager who strongly values helpful behavior may have a negative attitude toward helping an unethical coworker. The difference between attitudes and values is clarified by considering the three components of attitudes: affective, cognitive, and behavioral. It is important to note that your overall attitude toward someone or something is a function of the combined influence of all three components.

LO5.6

- **Affective Component** The *affective component* **of an attitude contains the feelings or emotions one has about a given object or situation.** For example, how do you *feel* about people who talk on cell phones in restaurants? If you feel annoyed or angry with such people, you are expressing negative affect or feelings toward people who talk on cell phones in restaurants. In contrast, the affective component of your attitude is neutral if you are indifferent about people talking on cell phones in restaurants.

- **Cognitive Component** What do you *think* about people who talk on cell phones in restaurants? Do you believe this behavior is inconsiderate, productive, completely acceptable, or rude? Your answer represents the cognitive component of your attitude toward people talking on cell phones in restaurants. The *cognitive component* **of an attitude reflects the evaluation or belief one has about an object or situation.**

- **Behavioral Component** The *behavioral component* **refers to how one intends or expects to act toward someone or something.** For example, how would you intend to respond to someone talking on a cell phone sitting in close proximity to you and your guest at a restaurant? Attitude theory suggests that your ultimate behavior in this situation is a function of all three attitudinal components. You are unlikely to say anything to someone using a cell phone in a restaurant if you are not irritated by this behavior (affective), if you believe cell phone use helps people to manage their lives (cognitive), and you have no intention of confronting this individual (behavioral).[68]

When Attitudes and Reality Collide: Cognitive Dissonance

What happens when a strongly held attitude is contradicted by reality? Suppose you are extremely concerned about getting AIDS, which you believe is transferred from contact with body fluids, including blood. Then you find yourself in a life-threatening accident in a foreign country and need surgery and blood transfusions—including transfusions of blood (possibly AIDS-infected) from a blood bank with unknown quality control. Would you reject the blood to remain consistent with your concern about getting AIDS? According to social psychologist Leon Festinger, this situation would create cognitive dissonance.

Cognitive dissonance **represents the psychological discomfort a person experiences when his or her attitudes or beliefs are incompatible with his or her behavior.**[69] Festinger proposed that people are motivated to maintain consistency between their attitudes and beliefs and their behavior. He therefore theorized that people will seek to reduce the "dissonance," or psychological tension, through one of three main methods:

1. *Change your attitude or behavior, or both.* This is the simplest solution when confronted with cognitive dissonance. Returning to our example about needing a blood transfusion, this would amount to either (1) telling yourself that you can't get AIDS through blood and take the transfusion or (2) simply refusing to take the transfusion.

2. *Belittle the importance of the inconsistent behavior.* This happens all the time. In our example, you could belittle the belief that you can get AIDS from the foreign blood bank. (The doctor said she regularly uses blood from that blood bank.)

3. *Find consonant elements that outweigh dissonant ones.* This approach entails rationalizing away the dissonance. You can tell yourself that you are taking the transfusion because you have no other options. After all, you could die if you don't get the required surgery.

Recent research counters previous beliefs that attitudes are stable throughout adulthood. For example, how has your attitude towards school changed over time? How has your attitude towards politics changed? How do you expect your attitude towards work to change in the next 10 years?

How Stable Are Attitudes?

In one landmark study, researchers found the *job* attitudes of 5,000 middle-aged male employees to be very stable over a five-year period. Positive job attitudes remained positive; negative ones remained negative. Even those who changed jobs or occupations tended to maintain their prior job attitudes.[70] More recent research suggests the foregoing study may have overstated the stability of attitudes because it was restricted to a middle-aged sample. This time, researchers asked, What happens to attitudes over the entire span of adulthood? *General* attitudes were found to be more susceptible to change during early and late adulthood than during middle adulthood. Three factors accounted for middle-age attitude stability: (1) greater personal certainty, (2) perceived abundance of knowledge, and (3) a need for strong attitudes. Thus, the conventional notion that general attitudes become less likely to change as the person ages was rejected. Elderly people, along with young adults, can and do change their general attitudes because they are more open and less self-assured.[71]

Because our cultural backgrounds and experiences vary, our attitudes and behavior vary. Attitudes are translated into behavior via behavioral intentions. Let us examine an established model of this important process.

Attitudes Affect Behavior via Intentions

Building on Leon Festinger's work on cognitive dissonance, Icek Ajzen and Martin Fishbein further delved into understanding the reason for discrepancies between individuals' attitudes and behavior. Ajzen ultimately developed and refined a model focusing on intentions as the key link between attitudes and planned behavior. His theory of planned behavior in Figure 5–3 shows three separate but interacting determinants of one's intention (a person's readiness to perform a given behavior) to exhibit a specific behavior.

Ajzen's Theory of Planned Behavior   FIGURE 5–3

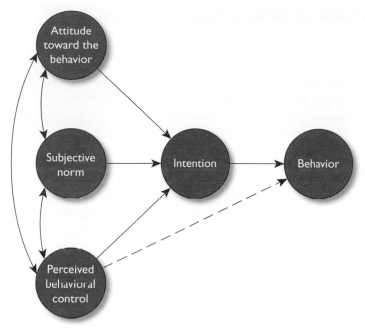

SOURCE: Reprinted from *Organizational Behavior and Human Decision Processes,* Vol. 50, No. 2, Icek Ajzen, "The Theory of Planned Behavior, pp. 179-211, Copyright © 1991, with permission from Elsevier.

Importantly, this model only predicts behavior under an individual's control, not behavior due to circumstances beyond one's control. For example, this model can predict the likelihood that Egyptian citizens would protest against President Hosni Mubarak in 2011. But it would be a poor model for predicting whether or not a specific individual would arrive at a specific protesting site at a designated time and date because uncontrolled circumstances such as traffic delays or the amount of military blocking the route to the site.[72]

Determinants of Intention

Ajzen has explained the nature and roles of the three determinants of intention as follows:

> The first is the *attitude toward the behavior* and refers to the degree to which a person has a favorable or unfavorable evaluation or appraisal of the behavior in question. The second predictor is a social factor termed *subjective norm;* it refers to the perceived social pressure to perform or not to perform the behavior. The third antecedent of intention is the degree of *perceived behavior control,* which . . . refers to the perceived ease or difficulty of performing the behavior and it is assumed to reflect past experience as well as anticipated impediments and obstacles.[73]

To bring these three determinants of intention to life, let us consider the example of a current (or past) college roommate who often stays in bed rather than go to class. His attitude toward class is that it is boring, and why should he bother doing anything that isn't exciting or fun? He perceives the subjective norm is favorable because he knows many of his fellow classmates also routinely skip classes. As for perceived control, he has complete control to act on his intention and skip class. So he turns off the alarm and goes back to sleep. Sweet dreams!

Intentions and Behavior Research—Lessons and Implications

According to the model of planned behavior, someone's intention to engage in a given behavior is a strong predictor of that behavior. For example, the quickest and possibly most accurate way of determining whether an individual will quit his or her job is to have an objective third party ask if he or she intends to quit. A meta-analysis of 34 studies of employee turnover involving more than 83,000 employees validated this direct approach. The researchers found stated behavioral intentions to be a better predictor of employee turnover than job satisfaction, satisfaction with the work itself, or organizational commitment.[74] Another study took these findings one step further by considering whether or not job applicants' intention to quit a job before they were hired would predict voluntary turnover six months after being hired. Results demonstrated that intentions to quit significantly predicted turnover.[75]

Research has demonstrated that Ajzen's model accurately predicted intentions to buy consumer products, to search for a new job, to have children, to vote for specific political candidates, to recycle, and to hire older workers. Attitudes and behaviors regarding affirmative-action programs, weight-loss intentions and behavior, using Internet services to facilitate the shipping of products, and nurses' willingness to work with older patients have also been predicted successfully by the model.[76] From a practical standpoint, the theory of planned behavior has important managerial implications. Managers are encouraged to use prescriptions derived from the model to implement interventions aimed at changing employees' behavior.

According to this model, changing behavior starts with the recognition that behavior is modified through intentions, which in turn are influenced by three different determinants (see Figure 5–3). Managers can thus influence behavioral change by doing or saying things that affect the three determinants of employees' intentions to exhibit a specific behavior: attitude toward the behavior, subjective norms, and perceived behavioral control.[77]

It is important to remember that employee beliefs can be influenced through the information management provides on a day-by-day basis, the organization's culture, the content of training programs, the behavior of key employees, and the rewards that are targeted to reinforce certain beliefs. Consider how H C Jackson, founder of Jackson's Hardware in San Rafael, California, used these ideas to change employees' beliefs about taking over ownership of the company.

> As part of creating an ownership culture, Jackson's spends ample time teaching employees about the benefits of ownership. . . . The company has a committee whose role is to educate employees about stock ownership and how their work is directly related to the success of the business—and thus their own financial well-being. Jackson's also puts out an annual ownership plan newsletter and selects an "Employee Owner for the Month" who receives a gas card and $600 toward a weekend getaway and dinner or store purchases.[78]

On a personal level, you also can use this model to influence your own behavior. If you want to increase the amount of time you spend studying, for example, you might begin by trying to influence your attitude toward studying. You could tell yourself that more studying leads to better grades, which in turn can help you find a rewarding job after graduation. You also can reward yourself for reaching a target score on the next exam. Subjective norms to study can be influenced by arranging to study with other students who are doing well in the class or by talking with your parents about what is going on in the class. Finally, it is important to remember that the amount of time you have for studying might be somewhat outside of your control. Our advice: control what you can and plan for contingencies.

OB Gets Emotional

In the ideal world of management theory, employees pursue organizational goals in a logical and rational manner. Emotional behavior seldom is factored into the equation. Yet day-to-day organizational life shows us how prevalent and powerful emotions can be. Anger and jealousy, both potent emotions, often push aside logic and rationality in the workplace. Managers use fear and other emotions to both motivate and intimidate. For example, Eliot Spitzer, former governor of New York who resigned after a sex scandal in 2008, was known for his emotional outbursts. Here is what the former CEO of General Electric, Jack Welch, told a reporter from *Fortune* about an interaction he had with Spitzer about Ken Langone. Langone was a former director at both GE and the New York Stock Exchange.

> "We were having an amiable chat," Welch recalled. "Then—boom—he flipped his lid. He snapped. He started sticking his finger in my chest and said, 'You can tell your friend Langone that I'm gonna put a stake through his heart!'"[79]

A combination of curiosity and fear is said to drive Barry Diller, one of the media world's legendary dealmakers. Says Diller, "I and my friends succeeded because we were scared to death of failing."[80] These admired corporate leaders would not have achieved what they have without the ability to be logical and rational decision makers *and* be emotionally charged. Too much emotion, however, could have spelled career and organizational disaster for either one of them.

In this final section, our examination of individual differences turns to defining emotions, reviewing a typology of 10 positive and negative emotions, and discussing the topics of emotional contagion, emotional labor, and emotional intelligence.

U.S. House of Representatives Speaker, John Boehner, is well known for shedding tears in public (e.g., during interviews and speeches). How do you think such displays of emotions help or hurt his effectiveness? More generally, how can showing emotions help or hurt you at work?

Positive and Negative Emotions

Emotions **are complex, relatively brief responses to particular information or experiences that change psychological and/or physiological states.**[81] Importantly, researchers draw a distinction between *felt* and *displayed* emotions.[82] For example, when a boss makes repeated demands that sound impossible, you might feel angry or frightened (felt emotion); you might keep your feelings to yourself or begin to cry (either response is the displayed emotion). The boss might feel alarmed by your tears (felt emotion) but could react constructively (displayed emotion) by asking if you'd like to talk about the situation when you feel calmer.[83] Emotions play roles in both causing and adapting to stress and its associated biological and psychological problems.[84] The destructive effect of emotional behavior on social relationships is all too obvious in daily life.

The definition of emotions centers on a person's goals.[85] Accordingly, a distinction between positive and negative emotions is goal oriented. *Negative* emotions are triggered by frustration and failure when pursuing one's goals. They are said to be goal incongruent. For example, which of the six negative emotions in Figure 5–4 are you likely to experience if you fail the final exam in a required course? Failing the exam would be incongruent with your goal of graduating on time. On the other hand, which of the four *positive* emotions in Figure 5–4 would you probably experience if you

FIGURE 5–4 Positive and Negative Emotions

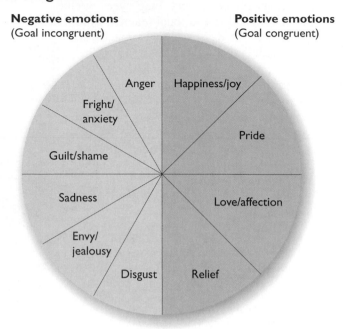

SOURCE: Adapted from discussion in R S Lazarus, *Emotion and Adaptation* (New York: Oxford University Press, 1991), Chs 6, 7.

www.mcgrawhillconnect.com

Go to Connect for an interactive exercise to help you better understand emotional intelligence.

graduated on time and with honors? The emotions you would experience in this situation are positive because they are congruent (or consistent) with an important lifetime goal. The individual's goals, it is important to note, may or may not be socially acceptable. Thus, a positive emotion, such as love/affection, may be undesirable if associated with sexual harassment. Oppositely, slight pangs of guilt, anxiety, and envy can motivate extra effort. On balance, the constructive or destructive nature of a particular emotion must be judged in terms of both its intensity and the person's relevant goal.

LO5.7 # Developing Emotional Intelligence

People cope with their own and others' emotions in lots of different ways. For a long time many people simply considered this maturity. However, since the mid-1990s an increasingly popular way in research, consulting, and management circles to describe emotional maturity is with the phrase *emotional intelligence.* In 1995, Daniel Goleman, a psychologist turned journalist, created a stir in education and management circles with the publication of his book *Emotional Intelligence.* Hence, an obscure topic among positive psychologists became mainstream. According to Goleman, traditional models of intelligence (IQ) are too narrow, failing to consider interpersonal competence. Besides, IQ tends to plateau about age 17 while EQ continues to develop and grow past 50.[86] EQ is therefore more flexible than IQ and can be developed throughout your working life. Goleman's broader agenda includes "abilities such as being able to motivate oneself and persist in the face of frustrations; to control impulse and delay gratification; to regulate one's moods and keep distress from swamping the ability to think; to empathize and to hope."[87] Thus, *emotional intelligence* **is the ability to manage oneself and one's relationships in mature and constructive ways.** Referred to by some as EI and others as EQ, emotional intelligence is said to have four key components:

Developing Emotional Intelligence

Personal Competence: These capabilities determine how we manage ourselves.

Self-Awareness

- *Emotional self-awareness:* Reading one's own emotions and recognizing their impact; using "gut sense" to guide decisions.
- *Accurate self-assessment:* Knowing one's strengths and limits.
- *Self-confidence:* A sound sense of one's self-worth and capabilities.

Self-Management

- *Emotional self-control:* Keeping disruptive emotions and impulses under control.
- *Transparency:* Displaying honesty and integrity; trustworthiness.
- *Adaptability:* Flexibility in adapting to changing situations or overcoming obstacles.
- *Achievement:* The drive to improve performance to meet inner standards of excellence.
- *Initiative:* Readiness to act and seize opportunities.
- *Optimism:* Seeing the upside in events.

Social Competence: These capabilities determine how we manage relationships.

Social Awareness

- *Empathy:* Sensing others' emotions, understanding their perspective, and taking active interest in their concerns.
- *Organizational awareness:* Reading the currents, decision networks, and politics at the organizational level.
- *Service:* Recognizing and meeting follower, client, or customer needs.

Relationship Management

- *Inspirational leadership:* Guiding and motivating with a compelling vision.
- *Influence:* Wielding a range of tactics for persuasion.
- *Developing others:* Bolstering others' abilities through feedback and guidance.
- *Change catalyst:* Initiating, managing, and leading in a new direction.
- *Conflict management:* Resolving disagreements.
- *Building bonds:* Cultivating and maintaining a web of relationships.
- *Teamwork and collaboration:* Cooperation and team building.

self-awareness, self-management, social awareness, and relationship management.[88] The first two constitute *personal competence;* the second two feed into *social competence* (see Skills & Best Practices above). Recall the earlier discussion of inter- and intrapersonal intelligences described by Gardner. (EI builds on this earlier work, although scholars and consultants don't always acknowledge this history or similarity.)

Research has linked EI to many outcomes. One review showed that EI generally predicted better social relationships, well-being, and satisfaction across contexts and ages. These findings also applied to relationships at work, where those with higher EI were perceived more positively by coworkers and more effective as sellers (but not buyers) in negotiations. EI's ability to predict job performance was mixed, however. [89] One study found that EI was related to higher sales and greater customer retention for both real estate and insurance sales representatives.[90] Meta-analysis results showed EI boosted performance in jobs that required high levels of emotional labor, discussed next, but decreased performance in jobs that required low emotional labor.[91] A study of Australian public service executives showed that *how* those with high EI produced results was rated positively by subordinates, but the actual results themselves were not related to EI.[92] A review of EI and leadership similarly showed mixed results. EI was positively related to leadership emergence, behavior, and effectiveness (all discussed in detail in Chapter 14). But the relationships between EI and a host of job performance, satisfaction, and other outcomes were mixed. Researchers suggested that the inconsistent results were due to methodological issues (e.g., how EI is measured) and more complex relationships between EI and other factors that have yet to be identified.[93]

Taken together, recent research regarding EI concludes that it is an important predictor of many OB behaviors and outcomes. However, because many relationships and methodological issues need further attention, we encourage you to identify and develop your own EI to utilize the clear interpersonal benefits. We do caution the use of EI as a predictor of job performance and other important OB outcomes: Use discretion.

BACK TO THE CHAPTER-OPENING CASE

1. Describe Mark Zuckerberg's emotional intelligence using the information provided in the Skills & Best Practices feature on page 139.

2. Which aspects do you think are relatively strong versus relatively less developed?

3. Describe the potential implications (benefits and challenges) of his EI in his role as CEO of Facebook.

Practical Research Insights about Emotional Contagion and Emotional Labor

Two streams of OB research on emotions provide additional, interesting, and instructive insights:

- *Emotional contagion.* Have you ever had someone's bad mood sour your mood? That person could have been a parent, supervisor, coworker, friend, or someone serving you in a store or restaurant. Appropriately, researchers call this *emotional contagion.* We, quite literally, can catch another person's mood or displayed emotions—positive or negative. This effect was documented in a recent study of 131 bank tellers (92% female) and 220 exit interviews with their customers. Tellers who expressed positive emotions tended to have more satisfied customers.[94] Two field studies with nurses and accountants as subjects found a strong linkage between both work group's collective mood and each individual's mood.[95] Both foul moods and good moods turned out to be contagious. Management professor Sigal Barsade says you cannot necessarily change your coworkers' bad moods, but you can inoculate yourself against them. For example, you can decide ahead of time not to let a negative person bother you or take up your attention. One manager started each day by passing the desk of an employee who was grumpy in the morning. The manager simply found a different route through the office and thus avoided this negative start to the day.[96]

- *Emotional labor.* Although they did not have the benefit of a catchy label or a body of sophisticated research, generations of managers have known about the power of emotional contagion in the marketplace. "Smile, look happy for the customers," employees are told over and over. But what if the employee is having a rotten day? What if he or she has to mask his or her true feelings and emotions? What if the employee has to fake it? Researchers have begun studying the dynamics of what they call *emotional labor.* A pair of authors, one from Australia, the other from the United States, recently summarized research lessons:

  Emotional labor can be particularly detrimental to the employee performing the labor and can take its toll both psychologically and physically. Employees . . . may bottle up feelings of frustration, resentment, and anger, which are not appropriate to express. These feelings result, in part, from the constant requirement to monitor one's negative emotions and express positive ones. If not given a healthy expressive outlet, this emotional repression can lead to a syndrome of emotional exhaustion and burnout.[97]

A recent review of the literature finds that emotional labor may cause less stress and burnout if the employees work on actually feeling the emotions they express—for example, by trying to empathize with why a difficult customer may be acting that way and then expressing sympathy with the customer's plight.[98] Like these results, recent research demonstrated that emotional labor (e.g., faking emotions) does affect individual and organizational well-being and performance.[99] For instance, one study showed that uncivil customers increased emotional exhaustion for bank tellers and also decreased customer service ratings. No surprise. However, the interesting finding was that emotional labor was the link or suspected cause of the exhaustion. In other words, it wasn't the customer's horrible behavior that was exhausting, but instead it was the fact that the tellers faked positive emotions in response. Furthermore, faking positive emotions did not improve customer service ratings.[100] What do these results suggest? One alternative is simply to tell rude customers how you feel! According to this study you're not going to improve your customer ratings anyway, and you'll avoid emotional exhaustion. Obviously, these results and their practical implications need to be considered carefully.

In summary, emotions research has major practical implications for employee behaviors and a host of important OB outcomes. Managers need to be particularly aware of workplace anger, aggression, and violence, which are discussed in Chapter 6. To do this managers need to be attuned to (and responsive to) the emotional states and needs of their people. This requires emotional intelligence.

key terms

chapter summary

- *Identify at least five of Gardner's eight multiple intelligences, and explain "practical intelligence."* Harvard's Howard Gardner broadens the traditional cognitive abilities model of intelligence to include social and physical abilities. His eight multiple intelligences include: linguistic, logical-mathematical, musical, bodily-kinesthetic, spatial, interpersonal, intrapersonal, and naturalist. Someone with practical intelligence, according to Sternberg, is good at solving everyday problems and learning from experience by adapting to the environment, reshaping their environment, and selecting new environments in which to work.

- *Identify and describe the Big Five personality dimensions; specify which one is correlated most strongly with job performance; and describe the proactive personality.* The Big Five personality dimensions are extraversion (social and talkative), agreeableness (trusting and cooperative), conscientiousness (responsible and persistent), emotional stability (relaxed and unworried), and openness to experience (intellectual and curious). Conscientiousness is the best predictor of job performance. A person with a proactive personality shows initiative, takes action, and perseveres until a desired change occurs.

- *Explain the four components of core self-evaluations.* Organizational and management researchers have developed an aggregated and broad individual difference concept over the past 10 years—core self-evaluations (CSEs). CSEs represent an individual's evaluations of him- or herself and are composed of four individual personality traits: self-esteem, self-efficacy, locus of control, and emotional stability. Together, these personality traits are stronger predictors of performance than any of the traits individually. CSEs can be improved by enhancing one or more of the particular traits.

- *Distinguish between self-esteem and self-efficacy.* Self-esteem is an overall evaluation of oneself—one's perceived self-worth. Self-efficacy is the belief in one's ability to successfully perform a task.

- *Explain the difference between an internal and external locus of control.* People with an *internal* locus of control, such as entrepreneurs, believe they are masters of their own fate. Those with an *external* locus of control attribute their behavior and its results to situational forces.

- *Identify the three components of attitudes and discuss cognitive dissonance.* The three components of attitudes are affective, cognitive, and behavioral. The affective component represents the feelings or emotions one has about a given object or situation. The cognitive component reflects the beliefs or ideas one has about an object or situation. The behavioral component refers to how one intends or expects to act toward someone or something. Cognitive dissonance represents the psychological discomfort an individual experiences when his or her attitudes or beliefs are incompatible with his or her behavior.

- *Explain the concepts of emotional intelligence, emotional contagion, and emotional labor.* Four key components of emotional intelligence are self-awareness and self-management (for personal competence) and social awareness and relationship management (for social competence). Emotions are indeed contagious, with good and bad moods "infecting" others. Emotional labor occurs when people need to repress their felt emotions and display others. Resentment, frustration, and even anger can result when a worker "puts on a happy face" for customers and others.

discussion questions

1. Describe how you might use your knowledge of intelligences at work.
2. Describe three things you can do to build your self-efficacy for your OB course.
3. Using your Big Five personality profile (Hands-On Exercise on page 121), describe the suitability of your profile for your present (or chosen) line of work?
4. Assume you are the chief financial officer of a bank. You have one vice president of finance position to fill and three candidates to consider. Explain how you could use the core self-evaluation profiles of these three candidates to help inform your choice.
5. Based on the three components underlying attitudes, what is your attitude toward the president of the United States?
6. Which of the four key components of emotional intelligence is (or are) your strong suit? Which is (or are) your weakest? What are the everyday implications of your EI profile?

legal/ethical challenge

Companies Shift Smoking Bans to *Smoker* Ban[101]

An increasing number of companies are using smoking as a reason to turn away job applicants. Employers argue that such policies increase worker productivity, reduce health care costs, and encourage healthier lifestyles. These policies up the ante on previous, less-effective efforts, such as no-smoking work environments, cessation programs, and higher health care premiums for smokers.

"Tobacco-free hiring" often requires applicants to submit to a urine test for nicotine, and if hired, violations are cause for termination. The shift from "smoke-free" to "smoker-free" workplaces has prompted sharp debate about employers intruding into employee's private lives and regulating legal behaviors.

Some state courts have upheld the legality of refusing to employ smokers. For example, hospitals in Florida, Georgia, Massachusetts, Missouri, Ohio, Pennsylvania, Tennessee, and Texas, among others, stopped hiring smokers in the past year. Some justified the new policies as ways to reduce health care costs and to advance their institutional missions of promoting personal well-being.

Supporters of these policies note that smoking continues to be the leading cause of preventable death. About 20% of Americans still smoke, and smokers cost approximately $3,391 per year in lost productivity and additional health care expenses. Opponents argue that such policies are a slippery slope. Successful non-smoker policies may lead to limits on other legal employee behaviors, like drinking alcohol, eating fast food, and participating in dangerous sports.

Many companies add their own wrinkle to the smoking ban and even forbid nicotine patches. And while most companies apply the rules only to new employees, a few eventually mandated that existing employees must quit smoking or lose their jobs.

How Should Employers Deal with the Smoking Problem?

1. Today's discrimination against smokers is equivalent to now illegal racial and gender discrimination years ago. Do you agree or disagree? Explain.

2. Assume you are the VP of HR and a member of the executive board of your company. Also assume you plan to propose implementing a smoker ban for your company. Explain how you would make the case.

3. Now, assume you are the employee representative on the executive board at your company. You know the VP of HR plans to propose a smoker ban to begin June 1 for all new hires and the following January for all existing employees. Describe what you will you say (i.e., your position).

4. More generally, under what circumstances do companies have the right to consider and ban legal employee behaviors during the hiring process? Explain.

5. What is your position regarding policy changes (e.g., smoker ban) and applying them to existing employees that were hired under different guidelines? Explain your position.

If you're looking for additional study materials, be sure to check out the Online Learning Center at

www.mhhe.com/kinickiob5e

for more information and interactivities that correspond to this chapter.

chapter 6

Motivation I: Needs, Job Design, and Satisfaction

What Is Your Dream Job?

Asked what job they would take if they could have their choice of any, people unleash their imaginations and dream of exotic places, powerful positions, or work that involves alcohol and a paycheck at the same time.

Or so you'd think.

None of that appeals to Lori Miller who, as a lead word processor, has to do things that don't seem so dreamy, including proofreading, spell checking, and formatting. But she loves it.

"I like and respect nearly all my coworkers, and most of them feel the same way about me," she says. "Just a few things would make it a little better," she says, including a shorter commute and the return of some great people who used to work there. And one more thing:

She'd appreciate it if everyone would put their dishes in the dishwasher.

It's not a lot to ask for and, it turns out a surprising number of people who dream up their ideal job don't ask for much. One could attribute it to lack of imagination, setting the bar low, or "anchoring," the term referring to the place people start and never move far from. One could chalk it up to rationalizing your plight.

But maybe people simply like what they do and aren't, as some management would have you believe, asking for too much—just the elimination of a small but disproportionately powerful amount of office inanity.

That may be one reason why two-thirds of Americans would take the same job over again "without hesitation" and why 90% of Americans are at least somewhat satisfied with their jobs, according to a Gallup poll.

So money doesn't interest Elizabeth Gray as much as a level playing field. "I like what I do," says the city project manager, who once witnessed former colleagues award a contractor, paid for work he never completed, with the title of "Contractor of the Year."

Thus: "My dream job would be one free of politics," she says. "All advancement would be based on merit. The people who really did the work would be the ones who received the credit."

Frank Gastner has a similar ideal: "VP in charge of destroying inane policies." Over the years, he's had to hassle with the simplest of design flaws that would cost virtually nothing to fix were it not for the

One person's idea of a dream job is as simple as a place where coworkers would put their dishes in the dishwasher. What is your idea of a dream job?

bureaucracies that entrenched them. So the retired manufacturer's representative says he would address product and process problems with the attitude, "It's not right; let's fix it now without a committee meeting."

Monique Huston actually has her dream job—and many tell her it's theirs, too. She's general manager of a pub in Omaha, the Dundee Dell, which boasts 650 single-malt scotches on its menu. She visits bars, country clubs, people's homes, and Scotland for whiskey tastings. "I stumbled on my passion in life," she says.

Still, some nights she doesn't feel like drinking—or smiling. "Your face hurts," she complains. And when you have your dream job you wonder what in the world you'll do next.[1]

EFFECTIVE EMPLOYEE MOTIVATION has long been one of management's most difficult and important duties. Success in this endeavor is becoming more important in light of global competition to produce higher quality products at lower prices and the need to manage a more diverse workforce. As revealed in the opening case, managers should not attempt to motivate employees with one general approach. Rather, employee motivation and satisfaction are based on considering the individual differences discussed in Chapter 5. The purpose of this chapter, as well as the next, is to provide you with a foundation for understanding the complexities of employee motivation.

After discussing the fundamentals of employee motivation, this chapter focuses on (1) an overview of job design methods used to motivate employees, (2) the process of enhancing employee engagement, (3) the causes and consequences of job satisfaction, and (4) the motivational challenges of preventing counterproductive work behaviors. Coverage of employee motivation extends to Chapter 7.

The Fundamentals of Employee Motivation

LO6.1

The term *motivation* derives from the Latin word *movere,* meaning "to move." In the present context, **motivation represents "those psychological processes that cause the arousal, direction, and persistence of voluntary actions that are goal directed."**[2] Managers need to understand these psychological processes if they are to successfully guide employees toward accomplishing organizational objectives. This section thus provides an integrated model of motivation and examines key need theories of motivation.

An Integrated Model of Motivation

Figure 6–1 presents an integrated model of motivation. It provides a framework for understanding the material reviewed in this chapter and illustrates how several variables discussed in previous and subsequent chapters affect employee motivation. Figure 6–1 shows that personal factors and contextual factors are the two key categories of variables that influence motivation and employee engagement. As discussed in Chapter 5, employees bring personality, ability, core self-evaluations, emotions, and attitudes to the work setting. This chapter explains how employees' needs also impact employee motivation and engagement. Contextual factors include organizational culture (recall Chapter 2), cross-cultural values (see Chapter 3), job design and the physical environment (discussed in this chapter), rewards and reinforcement (see Chapter 8), group norms (reviewed in Chapter 9), communication technology such as e-mail and social media (see Chapter 12), leader behavior (discussed in Chapter 14), and organizational design (see Chapter 15). These two categories of factors influence each other as well as an employee's level of motivation and engagement at work. In turn, motivation and employee engagement impact a host of motivated behaviors and outcomes.[3]

Consider how American Express increased customer service and profitability by using the components of Figure 6–1.

American Express has always prided itself on its customer service; CEO Ken Chenault lists delivering superior service as one of AmEx's top three priorities for 2010 (the other two: growth and efficiency). So last year when it gave its global customer service division a makeover, it decided to focus on making life better for its 26,000 call-center employees. The theory: Happier employees mean happier customers. "We've learned the importance of the attitude of the employee," says Jim Bush, EVP of world service. AmEx started by asking customer service employees what

An Integrated Model of Motivation   FIGURE 6–1

Personal factors

•Personality
•Ability
•Core self-evaluations
•Emotions
•Attitudes
•Needs

Contextual factors

•Organizational culture
•Cross-cultural values
•Job design
•Physical environment
•Rewards and reinforcement
•Group norms
•Communication technology
•Leader behavior
•Organizational design

Motivation and employee engagement

Motivated	Behaviors and outcomes	
	Positive	**Negative**
•**Individual level**	•organizational citizenship	•Counterproductive work behavior
	•job satisfaction	•Turnover
	•performance	
•**Group level**	•information sharing	•Politics
	•collaboration	•Social loafing
•**Organizational level**	•information sharing	•Poor service
	•financial performance	•Poor quality

they wanted to see—and then delivered better pay, flexible schedules, and more career development. It also switched from a directive to keep calls short and transaction oriented to engaging customers in longer conversations. Collectively, the moves have boosted service margins by 10%.[4]

Can you identify which of the personal and contextual factors were changed by AmEx?

As you read the remainder of this chapter, try to link the various models and theories discussed to Figure 6–1. This should help you develop a richer understanding about motivating others. We now consider need theories of motivation.

> **BACK TO THE CHAPTER-OPENING CASE**   Which of the personal and contextual factors influenced Lori Miller, Elizabeth Gray, Frank Gastner, and Monique Huston's choice of a dream job?

Need Theories of Motivation

Needs **are physiological or psychological deficiencies that arouse behavior.** They can be strong or weak and are influenced by environmental factors. Human needs thus vary over time and place and represent a key personal factor (see Figure 6–1) that influences motivation. Two popular need theories are discussed in this section: Maslow's need hierarchy theory and McClelland's need theory.

 LO6.2

Maslow's Need Hierarchy Theory   In 1943, psychologist Abraham Maslow published his now-famous need hierarchy theory of motivation. Although the theory was based on his clinical observation of a few neurotic individuals, it has subsequently been used to explain the entire spectrum of human behavior. Maslow proposed that motivation is a function of five basic needs—physiological, safety, love, esteem, and self-actualization.

Maslow said these five need categories are arranged in a prepotent hierarchy. In other words, he believed human needs generally emerge in a predictable stair-step fashion. Accordingly, when one's physiological needs are relatively satisfied, one's safety needs emerge, and so on up the need hierarchy, one step at a time. Once a need is satisfied it activates the next higher need in the hierarchy. This process continues until the need for self-actualization is activated.[5]

Although research does not clearly support this theory of motivation, there is one key managerial implication of Maslow's theory worth noting. That is, a satisfied need may lose its motivational potential. Therefore, managers are advised to motivate employees by devising programs or practices aimed at satisfying emerging or unmet needs. Many companies have responded to this recommendation by offering employees targeted benefits that meet their specific needs. Consider Joie de Vivre, a hotel chain in California's Bay Area. Management uses Maslow's principles to verify that the company is building employee satisfaction and loyalty in a variety of ways. For example, Joie de Vivre managers provide recognition with formal processes to identify and comment on occasions when employees have provided exceptional service. They try to help housekeepers derive meaning from their jobs by bringing them together to talk about what the guests' experience would be like if the housekeepers weren't making their stay more comfortable.[6] Managers also can use customized surveys in order to assess the specific needs of their employees. In conclusion, managers are more likely to fuel employee motivation by offering benefits and rewards that meet individual needs.

Sir James Dyson, founder of Dyson and inventor of the Dual Cyclone bagless vacuum cleaner, believes that the death of his father at an early age contributed to his achievement motivation. Do you think that this is possible? Why?

McClelland's Need Theory   David McClelland, a well-known psychologist, has been studying the relationship between needs and behavior since the late 1940s. Although he is most recognized for his research on the need for achievement, he also investigated the needs for affiliation and power. Let us consider each of these needs:

- The *need for achievement* is defined by the following desires: **To accomplish something difficult.** To master, manipulate, or organize physical objects, human beings, or ideas. To do this as rapidly and as independently as possible. To overcome obstacles and attain a high standard. To excel one's self. To rival and surpass others. To increase self-regard by the successful exercise of talent.[7]

Achievement-motivated people share three common characteristics: (1) a preference for working on tasks of moderate difficulty; (2) a preference for situations in which performance is due to their efforts rather than other factors, such as luck; and (3) they desire more feedback on their successes and failures than do low achievers. A review of research on the entrepreneurial personality showed that entrepreneurs were found to have a higher need for achievement than nonentrepreneurs.[8] James Dyson, inventor and manufacturer of the Dyson Dual Cyclone bagless vacuum cleaner is a good example. He went through 5,127 different prototypes of the vacuum's design before finding the model that would dominate the market. Dyson told an interviewer that the death of his father when he was nine was instrumental in his achievement orientation. "Not having a father, particularly at that time, was very unusual. I felt different. I was on my own. I can't quite explain it, but I think subconsciously I felt a need to prove myself."[9]

- People with a high ***need for affiliation*** **prefer to spend more time maintaining social relationships, joining groups, and wanting to be loved.** Individuals high in this need are not the most effective managers or leaders because they have a hard time making difficult decisions without worrying about being disliked.

- The ***need for power*** **reflects an individual's desire to influence, coach, teach, or encourage others to achieve.** People with a high need for power like to work and are concerned with discipline and self-respect. There is a positive and negative side to this need. The negative face of power is characterized by an "if I win, you lose" mentality. In contrast, people with a positive orientation to power focus on accomplishing group goals and helping employees to feel competent. More is said about the two faces of power in Chapter 13. Because effective managers must positively influence others, McClelland proposes that top managers should have a high need for power coupled with a low need for affiliation.

www.mcgrawhillconnect.com

Go to Connect for a video case to view Hot Topic and how they handle employee motivation.

There are three managerial implications associated with McClelland's need theory. First, given that adults can be trained to increase their achievement motivation, and achievement motivation is correlated with performance, organizations should consider the benefits of providing achievement training for employees.[10] Second, achievement, affiliation, and power needs can be considered during the selection process, for better placement. For example, a study revealed that people with a high need for achievement were more attracted to companies that had a pay-for-performance environment than those with a low-achievement motivation.[11] Finally, it is important to balance the above recommendations with the downside of high achievement. McClelland noted that people with high achievement might be more prone to "cheat and cut corners and to leave people out of the loop." Byrraju Ramalinga Raju, founder and former chairman of Satyam Computers, is a good example. Raju was known as a highly driven executive who had a grand vision for using technology to help develop rural India. He also was highly involved with several foundations in India. Unfortunately, Raju apparently also took some illegal shortcuts to meet Satyam's short-term financial goals (see Skills & Best Practices below).[12]

 SKILLS & BEST PRACTICES

High-Achievement Needs Can Lead to Negative Outcomes

"Ramalinga Raju founded Satyam Computers in 1987 and was its chairman until January 7, 2009 when he resigned from the Satyam board after admitting to cheating six million shareholders. . . . In his letter of resignation, Raju described how an initial cover-up for a poor quarterly performance escalated: 'It was like riding a tiger, not knowing how to get off without being eaten.'" . . . "Raju had also used dummy accounts to trade in Satyam's shares, violating the insider trading norm. It has now not been alleged that these accounts may have been the means of siphoning off the missing funds. Raju has admitted to overstating the company's case reserves by USD $1.5 billion."

Raju was released on bail in August 2010, but was recently remanded back to prison.

SOURCE: Excerpted from "Byrraju Ramalinga Raju," Wikipedia, last updated January 27, 2011, http://en.wikipedia.org.

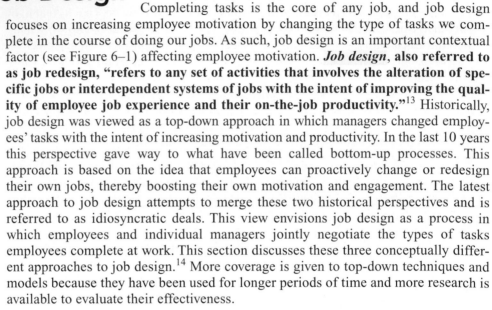

BACK TO THE CHAPTER-OPENING CASE   What needs are motivating Lori Miller, Elizabeth Gray, Frank Gastner, and Monique Huston?

Motivating Employees through Job Design

LO6.3

Completing tasks is the core of any job, and job design focuses on increasing employee motivation by changing the type of tasks we complete in the course of doing our jobs. As such, job design is an important contextual factor (see Figure 6–1) affecting employee motivation. ***Job design*, also referred to as job redesign, "refers to any set of activities that involves the alteration of specific jobs or interdependent systems of jobs with the intent of improving the quality of employee job experience and their on-the-job productivity."**[13] Historically, job design was viewed as a top-down approach in which managers changed employees' tasks with the intent of increasing motivation and productivity. In the last 10 years this perspective gave way to what have been called bottom-up processes. This approach is based on the idea that employees can proactively change or redesign their own jobs, thereby boosting their own motivation and engagement. The latest approach to job design attempts to merge these two historical perspectives and is referred to as idiosyncratic deals. This view envisions job design as a process in which employees and individual managers jointly negotiate the types of tasks employees complete at work. This section discusses these three conceptually different approaches to job design.[14] More coverage is given to top-down techniques and models because they have been used for longer periods of time and more research is available to evaluate their effectiveness.

connect

www.mcgrawhillconnect.com

Go to Connect for an interactive exercise to test your knowledge of motivating employees through job design.

Top-Down Approaches

The fundamental premise of top-down approaches is that management is responsible for creating efficient and meaningful combinations of work tasks for employees. We now consider the five principal top-down approaches to job design: scientific management, job enlargement, job rotation, job enrichment, and the job characteristics model.

Scientific Management   Scientific management draws from research in industrial engineering and is most heavily influenced by the work of Frederick Taylor. Taylor, a mechanical engineer, developed the principles of scientific management based on research and experimentation to determine the most efficient way to perform jobs. ***Scientific management* is "that kind of management which conducts a business or affairs by *standards* established by facts or truths gained through *systematic* observation, experiment, or reasoning."**[15]

Designing jobs according to the principles of scientific management has both positive and negative consequences. On the positive side, employee efficiency and productivity are increased. On the other hand, research reveals that simplified, repetitive jobs also lead to job dissatisfaction, poor mental health, higher levels of stress, and a low sense of accomplishment and personal growth.[16] These negative consequences pave the way for the next four top-down approaches.

Job Enlargement   This technique was first used in the late 1940s in response to complaints about tedious and overspecialized jobs. ***Job enlargement* involves putting more variety into a worker's job by combining specialized tasks of comparable difficulty.** Some call this *horizontally loading* the job. Researchers recommend using job enlargement as part of a broader approach that uses multiple motivational methods because it does not have a significant and lasting positive effect on job performance by itself.[17]

Job Rotation   As with job enlargement, the purpose of job rotation is to give employees greater variety in their work. ***Job rotation* calls for moving employees from one specialized job to another.** Rather than performing only one job, workers are trained and given the opportunity to perform two or more separate jobs on a rotating basis. By rotating employees from job to job, managers believe they can stimulate interest and motivation while providing employees with a broader perspective of the organization. India-based Tata Consultancy Services (TCS) uses job rotation to develop its Indian employees. Employees rotate throughout offices in the 42 countries in which the company operates in order to learn best practices being used by others and to develop their technical skills. The goal of the program is for employees to bring best practices gained from international experience back to the home office.[18] Despite positive experiences from companies like Tata, it is not possible to draw firm conclusions about the value of job rotation programs because they have not been adequately researched.

Tata Consultancy Services, which is part of the Tata group, one of India's largest conglomerates, employs 198,500 consultants in 42 countries to deliver IT services. Why is job rotation a good idea for the company and its employees?

Job Enrichment   Job enrichment is the practical application of Frederick Herzberg's motivator–hygiene theory of job satisfaction. Herzberg's theory is based on a landmark study in which he interviewed 203 accountants and engineers.[19] These interviews sought to determine the factors responsible for job satisfaction and dissatisfaction. Herzberg found separate and distinct clusters of factors associated with job satisfaction and dissatisfaction. Job satisfaction was more frequently associated with achievement, recognition, characteristics of the work, responsibility, and advancement. These factors were all related to outcomes associated with the *content* of the task being performed. Herzberg labeled these factors ***motivators* because each was associated with strong effort and good performance.** He hypothesized that motivators cause a person to move from a state of no satisfaction to satisfaction (see Figure 6–2). Therefore, Herzberg's theory predicts managers can motivate individuals by incorporating "motivators" into an individual's job.

Herzberg found job *dissatisfaction* to be associated primarily with factors in the work *context* or environment. Specifically, company policy and administration, technical supervision, salary, interpersonal relations with one's supervisor, and working conditions were most frequently mentioned by employees expressing job dissatisfaction. Herzberg labeled this second cluster of factors ***hygiene factors*.** He further proposed that they were not motivational. At best, according to Herzberg's interpretation, an individual will experience no job dissatisfaction when he or she has no grievances about hygiene factors (refer to Figure 6–2).

FIGURE 6–2   Herzberg's Motivator–Hygiene Model

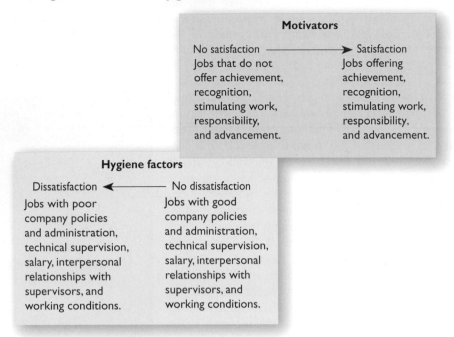

SOURCE: Adapted in part from D A Whitsett and E K Winslow, "An Analysis of Studies Critical of the Motivator–Hygiene Theory," *Personnel Psychology,* Winter 1967, pp 391–415.

Electronic Arts, an international developer, publisher, and distributor of video games, does not agree with this aspect of Herzberg's theory. Management is attempting to increase employees' job satisfaction and reduce turnover by creating positive hygiene factors. These initiatives include the following: (1) allowing employees to bring pets to work, (2) creating workday intramural sporting events like basketball, soccer, and beach volleyball, (3) creating arcades where employees can play Ping-Pong, pool, and video games, (4) establishing an information resource center in which employees can borrow the latest video games, movies, books, and magazines for free, and (5) providing a gym with group fitness classes.[20]

The key to adequately understanding Herzberg's motivator–hygiene theory is recognizing that he believes that satisfaction is not the opposite of dissatisfaction. Herzberg concludes that "the opposite of job satisfaction is not job dissatisfaction, but rather no job satisfaction; and similarly, the opposite of job dissatisfaction is not job satisfaction, but no dissatisfaction."[21] Herzberg thus asserts that the dissatisfaction–satisfaction continuum contains a zero midpoint at which dissatisfaction and satisfaction are absent. Conceivably, an organization member who has good supervision, pay, and working conditions but a tedious and unchallenging task with little chance of advancement would be at the zero midpoint. That person would have no dissatisfaction (because of good hygiene factors) and no satisfaction (because of a lack of motivators).

Herzberg's theory generated a great deal of research and controversy. Although research does not support the two-factor aspect of his theory, it does support many of the theory's implications for job design.[22] Job enrichment is based on the application of Herzberg's ideas. Specifically, ***job enrichment*** **entails modifying a job**

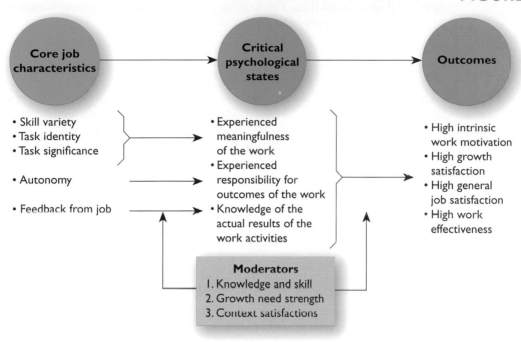

The Job Characteristics Model   FIGURE 6–3

SOURCE: *From J Richard Hackman and Greg R Oldham, Work Redesign, 1st, Copyright ©1980. Printed and electronically reproduced by permission of Pearson Education, Inc., Upper Saddle River, New Jersey.*

such that an employee has the opportunity to experience achievement, recognition, stimulating work, responsibility, and advancement. These characteristics are incorporated into a job through vertical loading. Rather than giving employees additional tasks of similar difficulty (horizontal loading), *vertical loading* consists of giving workers more autonomy and responsibility. Intuit, for example, attempts to do this by "encouraging workers to take four hours a week of 'unstructured time' for their own projects and hosting 'idea jams,' where teams present new concepts for prizes."[23]

The Job Characteristics Model   Two OB researchers, J Richard Hackman and Greg Oldham, played a central role in developing the job characteristics approach. These researchers tried to determine how work can be structured so that employees are internally or intrinsically motivated. *Intrinsic motivation* occurs when an individual is "turned on to one's work because of the positive internal feelings that are generated by doing well, rather than being dependent on external factors (such as incentive pay or compliments from the boss) for the motivation to work effectively."[24] Intrinsic motivation is closely aligned with the concept of employee engagement, which is discussed later in this chapter. These positive feelings power a self-perpetuating cycle of motivation. As shown in Figure 6–3, internal work motivation is determined by three psychological states. In turn, these psychological states are fostered by the presence of five core job characteristics. As you can see in Figure 6–3, the object of this approach is to promote high intrinsic motivation by designing jobs that possess the five core job characteristics shown in Figure 6–3. Let us examine the core job characteristics.

In general terms, ***core job characteristics* are common characteristics found to a varying degree in all jobs.** Three of the job characteristics shown in Figure 6–3 combine to determine experienced meaningfulness of work:

- *Skill variety.* The extent to which the job requires an individual to perform a variety of tasks that require him or her to use different skills and abilities.
- *Task identity.* The extent to which the job requires an individual to perform a whole or completely identifiable piece of work. In other words, task identity is high when a person works on a product or project from beginning to end and sees a tangible result.
- *Task significance.* The extent to which the job affects the lives of other people within or outside the organization.

Experienced responsibility is elicited by the job characteristic of autonomy, defined as follows:

- *Autonomy.* The extent to which the job enables an individual to experience freedom, independence, and discretion in both scheduling and determining the procedures used in completing the job.

Finally, knowledge of results is fostered by the job characteristic of feedback, defined as follows:

- *Feedback.* The extent to which an individual receives direct and clear information about how effectively he or she is performing the job.[25]

Hackman and Oldham recognized that not everyone wants a job containing high amounts of the five core job characteristics. They incorporated this conclusion into their model by identifying three attributes that affect how individuals respond to job enrichment. These attributes are concerned with the individual's knowledge and skill, growth need strength (representing the desire to grow and develop as an individual), and context satisfactions (see the box labeled Moderators in Figure 6–3). Context satisfactions represent the extent to which employees are satisfied with various aspects of their job, such as satisfaction with pay, coworkers, and supervision.

Research underscores three practical implications of the job characteristics model. First, managers may want to use this model to also increase employee job satisfaction. A meta-analysis involving over 75,000 people demonstrated a moderately strong relationship between job characteristics and satisfaction.[26] Second, this same large-scale meta-analysis showed that managers can enhance employees' intrinsic motivation, job involvement, and performance, while reducing absenteeism and stress by increasing the core job characteristics. Consistent with this finding, Nugget Market, rated as the eighth best place to work by *Fortune* in 2011, uses a creative recognition program to enhance motivation and performance. "Employee rallies are an everyday event at this nine-store supermarket chain, where a big flat-screen monitor in each store delivers awards and pumps up the troops. Workers who watch diligently can get $20 − $1,500 bonuses."[27] Finally, managers are likely to find noticeable increases in the quality of performance after a job redesign program. Results from 21 experimental studies revealed that job redesign resulted in a median increase of 28% in the quality of performance.[28]

Bottom-Up Approaches

As the term *bottom-up* suggests, this approach to job design is driven by employees rather than managers and is referred to as job crafting. ***Job crafting* is defined as "the physical and cognitive changes individuals make in the task or relational boundaries of**

Forms of Job Crafting   TABLE 6–1

Form	Example	Effect on Meaning of Work
Changing number, scope, and type of job tasks	Design engineers engaging in relational tasks that move a project to completion	Work is completed in a more timely fashion; engineers change the meaning of their jobs to be guardians or movers of projects.
Changing quality and/or amount of interaction with others encountered in a job	Hospital cleaners actively caring for patients and families, integrating themselves into the workflow of their floor units	Cleaners change the meaning of their jobs to be helpers of the sick; see the work of the floor unit as an integrated whole of which they are a vital part.
Changing cognitive task boundaries	Nurses taking responsibility for all information and "insignificant" tasks that may help them to care more appropriately for a patient	Nurses change the way they see the work to be more about patient advocacy, as well as high-quality technical care.

SOURCE: *From A Wrzesniewski and J E Dutton, "Crafting a Job: Revisioning Employees As Active Crafters of Their Work," Academy of Management Review, April 2001, p. 195. Copyright © 2001 with permission of Academy of Management via Copyright Clearance Center.*

their work."[29] Employees are viewed as "job crafters" according to this model because they are expected to define and create their own job boundaries. As such, this approach to job design represents proactive and adaptive employee behavior aimed at changing tasks, relationships, and cognitions associated with one's job. Table 6–1 defines and illustrates the three key forms of job crafting.

The first form of job crafting involves changing one's task boundaries. You can do this by altering the scope or nature of tasks you complete at work or you can take on fewer or more tasks. This is illustrated by the example of engineers taking on more relationship-oriented activities in order to complete projects. The second form of job crafting shown in Table 6–1 entails changing the relational nature of one's job. Specifically, you can alter the quantity or quality of interactions you have with others at work or you can establish new relationships. An example would be a hospital janitorial employee interacting with patients, ultimately making this employee feels like he or she can impact patient care. Cognitive crafting is the final form of job crafting. It encompasses a change in how you perceive or think about the tasks and relationships associated with your job. For example, a nurse can view accurate record keeping as a key component of providing high-quality health care as opposed to a chore that detracts from helping patients.

The final column in Table 6–1 outlines the potential impact of job crafting on employee motivation and performance. You can see that job crafting is expected to change how employees perceive their jobs. Job crafting is expected to result in more positive attitudes about one's job, which, in turn, is expected to increase employee motivation, engagement, and performance. Preliminary research supports this proposition.[30]

Idiosyncratic Deals (I-Deals)

This last approach to job design represents a middle ground between top-down and bottom-up methods and attempts to overcome their limitations.

LeBron James's "i-deal" with the Miami Heat caused quite a stir among basketball fans, particularly those from Cleveland. He left the Cleveland Cavaliers for Miami because he thought the Heat had a much better chance of winning an NBA title. Do you think i-deals are a good thing for organizations? Why or why not?

For example, top-down approaches are constrained by the fact that managers cannot always create changes in task characteristics that are optimum for everyone. Similarly, job crafting is limited by the amount of latitude people have in changing their own jobs. ***Idiosyncratic deals (i-deals)* represent "employment terms individuals negotiate for themselves, taking myriad forms from flexible schedules to career development."**[31] Although "star performers" have long negotiated special employment contracts or deals, demographic trends and the changing nature of work have created increased opportunities for more employees to negotiate i-deals.

I-deals tend to involve personal flexibility, developmental needs, and task-related content. The goal of such deals is to increase employee motivation and productivity by allowing employees the flexibility to negotiate employment relationships that meet their needs and values. RSM McGladrey Inc. is a great example. The company promotes and encourages the creation of i-deals among its 8,000 employees. The focus of RSM McGladrey's program is to create innovative and flexible ways of working. The company believes that this approach to job design fuels employee engagement, satisfaction, productivity, and customer satisfaction while reducing employee turnover. This belief seems to be true based on the many awards the company has received in the last few years. It was named to *Working Mother*'s Top 100 Companies list for the third time in 2009, ranked fifth by *Accounting Today* in its list of Top 100 firms in 2010, and one of the Best Places to Launch a Career by *BusinessWeek* in 2009.[32] The Skills & Best Practices on page 157 explains how these i-deals are negotiated.

Although this approach to job design is too new to have generated much research, preliminary evidence is positive. A recent study of hospitals in both the United States and Germany showed that i-deals were associated with less stress and more opportunities to perform meaningful work, which in turn led to higher levels of employee engagement.[33] Future research is needed to determine the generalizability of these encouraging results.

Cultivating Employee Engagement

The Gallup Organization has been studying employee engagement around the world for many years. A 2009 survey of 42,000 randomly selected adults in the United States revealed that 49 and 18 percent were actively engaged (i.e., loyal, productive, and satisfied) and actively disengaged (i.e., "checked out" and disenchanted with their workplace), respectively. Gallup estimated that employee disengagement in the United States costs roughly $350 billion a year.[34] This cost is staggering, and you will learn that managers can do something about it.

Employee engagement is a relatively new concept to the field of organizational behavior (OB). It was defined in 1990 by William Kahn on the basis of two qualitative studies of people at work. Based on his observations of workers at a summer camp and architecture firm, Kahn defined ***employee engagement* as "the harnessing of organization members' selves to their work roles; in engagement, people employ and express themselves physically, cognitively, and emotionally during role performance."**[35] The essence of this definition is the idea that engaged employees "give it their all" at work. Further study of this attitudinal variable reveals that it contains four components: (1) feelings of urgency, (2) feelings of being focused, (3) feelings of intensity, and (4) feelings of enthusiasm.[36] Researchers believe that motivation and employee engagement are strongly related, but represent conceptually different concepts.

RSM McGladrey Encourages I-Deals

[The program allows] employees across the nation to take a portion of the year off, while working full-time or part-time the remainder of the year and receiving a prorated paycheck and full benefits all year. . . .

McGladrey employees have been taking advantage of FlexYear schedules for years. . . . The design is simple and focuses on business impact. It makes sense for the company, employees, and clients.

First, an interested employee who has been with the firm a minimum of three months and has a performance rating of "achieving expectations" or better initiates a request for one of the firm's seven flexible work options by completing an eight-question business proposal that requires him or her to assess the impact of the request on the firm, its clients, and his or her co-workers—and to propose solutions to issues that could arise as a result.

Second, managers evaluate proposals based on the impact on the business. Employees' personal reasons for pursuing the flexible work option are not considered. . . . Typically, employees take about two months off during the summer, but the duration and time of year may vary.

Third, if a proposal will create a neutral or positive impact, managers are encouraged to approve the request, at least on a pilot basis, to keep the employee on board. If there is a negative impact on the business, managers are encouraged to decline the request—even if that means having a difficult conversation with an employee.

Finally, once approved, flexible work options are continually monitored to ensure that they still work for the employee, firm, and our clients. They can be modified or ended by the firm or the employee at any time, based on individual and business needs.

By making FlexYear part of this business-based approach to flexibility, we were able to position it as a strategic tool that helps leaders manage the cyclical nature of our business while responding to the diverse needs of employees. . . .

Michelle Hickox, a partner in our Dallas office, has been on a FlexYear schedule for eight years and has seen firsthand the positive impact on her family and the firm. Through FlexYear, Hickox has enjoyed taking June and July off each year to make invaluable memories with her girls. This option also allows her to develop deep relationships with her clients through open conversations about her schedule. And, FlexYear provides stretch opportunities for employees on Hickox's team who work with her clients while she is out.

SOURCE: *Excerpted from T Hopke, "Go Ahead, Take a Few Months Off," HR Magazine, September 2010, pp. 72, 74. Reprinted with permission of the Society for Human Resource Management (www.shrm.org), Alexandria, VA, publisher of HR Magazine. © SHRM.*

Have you ever felt engaged at work or school? You can complete the Hands-On Exercise on page 158 to measure your level of engagement with your studies. Do you feel engaged? If yes, then you understand why academics, consultants, and managers want to understand how they can harness the power of employee engagement. We now unravel the performance enhancing potential of employee engagement by considering its causes and consequences.

What Contributes to Employee Engagement?

Figure 6–1 reveals that employee engagement is caused by a host of variables that can be separated into personal and contextual factors. Personal characteristics found or thought to influence employee engagement include positive or optimistic personalities, proactive personality, conscientiousness, person-environment fit (PE Fit), and

HANDS-ON EXERCISE

Are You Engaged in Your Studies?

INSTRUCTIONS: The following survey was designed to assess the extent to which you are engaged in your studies. There are no right or wrong answers to the statements. Circle your answer by using the rating scale provided. After evaluating each of the survey statements, complete the scoring guide.

	Strongly Disagree	Disagree	Neither Agree nor Disagree	Agree	Strongly Agree
1. When I get up in the morning, I feel like going to class.	1	2	3	4	5
2. When I'm doing my work as a student, I feel bursting with energy.	1	2	3	4	5
3. I can continue studying for very long periods of time.	1	2	3	4	5
4. My study inspires me.	1	2	3	4	5
5. I am enthusiastic about my studies.	1	2	3	4	5
6. I am proud of my studies.	1	2	3	4	5
7. Time flies when I am studying.	1	2	3	4	5
8. I am immersed in my studies.	1	2	3	4	5
9. I feel happy when I am studying intensely.	1	2	3	4	5

SCORING NORMS
9–18 points = Low engagement _____
19–35 points = Moderate engagement _____
36–45 points = High engagement _____

SOURCE: Items derived from W B Schaufeli, M Salanova, V González-Romá, and A Baker, "The Measurement of Engagement and Burnout: A Two Sample Confirmatory Factor Analytic Approach," *Journal of Happiness Studies* 3, March 2002, pp 88–89.

being present or mindful.[37] ***PE Fit* is defined "as the compatibility between an individual and a work environment that occurs when their characteristics are well matched."**[38] Results from a meta-analysis of more than 40,000 workers demonstrated that people have higher job satisfaction and commitment to their organizations and lower intentions to quit when their personal characteristics (e.g., skills, abilities, and personalities) and values (e.g., integrity) match or fit the job requirements, organizational values, and the values of the workgroup.[39] Mindfulness represents the extent to which someone is focused on a moment in time and what is happening rather than daydreaming about something or somewhere else.

There is a broad set of contextual factors that potentially impacts employee engagement. One clearly involves organizational culture. For example, employees are more likely to be engaged when an organization has a clan culture (see Chapter 2) that promotes employee development, recognition, and trust between management and employees.[40] For example, Scripps Health, ranked by *Fortune* as the 37th best place to work in the United States in 2011, provides all employees with at least one training class per year. The company spent $30 million in training and development programs in 2010.[41]

OB researcher Ken Thomas proposed a model of intrinsic motivation that contains four key contextual factors we need to consider. He developed his model by integrating research on empowerment, which is discussed in Chapter 13, with two previous models of intrinsic motivation.[42] Thomas specifically linked components of the job characteristics model of job design discussed in the last section with Edward Deci and Richard Ryan's cognitive evaluation theory. Deci and Ryan proposed people must satisfy their needs for autonomy and competence when completing a task for it to be engaging.[43] Thomas recommended that managers design jobs in order to create the following psychological states:

- *Sense of meaningfulness*   Gives employees important and meaningful tasks to complete.

- *Sense of choice*   Allows employees to use judgment and freedom when completing tasks.

- *Sense of competence*   Provides feedback and recognition to instill feelings of accomplishing high-quality work.

- *Sense of progress*   Uses feedback and communication to create the feeling of making progress toward accomplishing something important.

Job security and feelings of psychological safety are contextual factors that also propel employee engagement. Psychological safety occurs when people feel safe to display engagement. In other words, employees must be free of any fears associated with trying new, innovative ideas or behaviors at work.[44] Leader behavior is another key contextual variable, particularly transformational leadership.[45] (Transformational leadership is discussed in Chapter 16.) Finally, employee engagement is higher when people feel that they are being supported by both their direct supervisor and the company as a whole and when they have a line of sight with the organization's vision, strategies, and goals. Line of sight represents the extent to which employees understand how their jobs influence the achievement of broader strategic goals.[46] Consider how AtlantiCare creates line of sight.

> New hires at AtlantiCare receive a strategy map showing how specific corporate goals such as building customer loyalty, increasing patient volume, and maintaining a favorable bond rating related to corporate values that include safety, team spirit, and treating others with respect. "All employees are urged to review the map frequently and to jot down ways they can personally contribute to performance excellence."[47]

UnitedHealth Group is a good example of a company using several contextual factors to increase employee engagement (see Skills & Best Practices feature on page 160).

BACK TO THE CHAPTER-OPENING CASE   Which of the personal and contextual factors that contribute to employee engagement affected the choice of dream jobs by Lori Miller, Elizabeth Gray, Frank Gastner, and Monique Huston?

What Are the Consequences of Employee Engagement?

Consulting firms such as Gallup, Hewitt Associates LLC, and Watson Wyatt have been in the forefront of collecting proprietary data supporting the practical value of employee engagement. For example, Gallup researchers conducted a meta-analysis involving 198,514 individuals from 7,930 business units and found that employee engagement was significantly associated with organizational-level customer satisfaction/loyalty, profitability, productivity, turnover, and safety outcomes.[48] Gallup estimates that organizations can achieve 12% higher customer satisfaction/loyalty, 18%

UnitedHealth Group Focuses on Improving Employee Engagement

Lori Sweere, executive vice president of human capital at the Minneapolis-based headquarters, was given the charge of developing a strategy to boost employee engagement. She began the effort by studying results from an employee engagement survey and conducting focus groups with managers and employees. She decided to implement the following initiatives based on this input.

"Manager's performance, communication, and understanding of how each employee's job contributes to the business strategy were identified as areas for improvement that could enhance employee engagement. Now, 'I have personal and monthly communications with our 6,000 managers about how to engage employees, such as how to talk to employees about personal and business challenges in the economic downturn,'" according to Sweere.

"Another way UnitedHealth Group drives engagement is by using a Facebook-style tool called U-Link to help people connect. Employees form groups, and Sweere writes a blog and answers questions. 'People become engaged by promoting their brands and having access to people they never had access to before,' Sweere says. 'We have 15,000 telecommuters who need this technology to connect with others. We list name, title, where they work. People can volunteer to add more to their profiles. And people can search for expertise.'"

UnitedHealth Group serves over 75 million people worldwide.

The above initiatives were successful. Employee engagement scores from the survey increased over time, employee turnover decreased, customer satisfaction increased, and revenues were higher.

SOURCE: Excerpted from A Fox, "Raising Engagement," *HR Magazine,* May 2010, p. 38

more productivity, and 12% greater profitability when their employees are highly engaged.[49] Other recent scientific studies similarly showed a positive relationship between employee engagement and employees' performance and physical and psychological well-being, and corporate-level financial performance and customer satisfaction.[50]

Practical Takeaways

There are four practical recommendations. The first entails budgeting resources to measure, track, and respond to surveys of employee engagement. The Ritz-Carlton, for instance, was able to significantly lower employee turnover (18% versus an industry average of 158%) and increase both customer satisfaction and customer spending by following this recommendation.[51] Second, it is important to consider assessing the individual traits associated with employee engagement during the hiring process. Remember, traits are unlikely to change over time and you get what you get when hiring people. Behavior-based questions or personality tests might be used for this purpose.

Third, top-down approaches to job design can be used to redesign jobs so that they contain the four psychological states highlighted by Ken Thomas. For example, managers can foster a sense of *meaningfulness* by inspiring their employees and modeling desired behaviors. This can be done by helping employees identify their passions at work and creating an exciting organizational vision that employees are motivated to pursue. As Starbucks recently sought to rekindle excitement for its brand, it brought employees together to retrain and recommit them to "the soul of the past." They watched a videotape of the company's founder say, "This is about the love and compassion and commitment that we all need to have for the customer."[52] Managers can lead for *choice* by empowering employees and delegating meaningful assignments and tasks. Managers can enhance a sense of *competence* by supporting and coaching their employees. At its employee retraining sessions, Starbucks strengthened choice and competence by emphasizing the barista's role in crafting drinks by, for example, pouring espresso into shot glasses to examine its color rather than relying on automation to get the product just right. Employees practiced their technique and discussed ways to improve the quality of their drinks. Finally, managers can increase employees' sense of *progress* by monitoring and rewarding them. For example, American Family Assurance conducts a "Bonus Day" festival in which all employees receive a bonus based on corporate performance. The company distributed $14.4 million in 2010. On-the-spot incentives represent another useful way to reward a broader-based group of employees. Google, for example, extended this idea to all employees. Google employees can "award one another $175 peer spot bonuses—last year [2010] more than two-thirds of them did so."[53]

The final recommendation is one that both authors have used in our careers. Specifically, we increased our engagement levels by relying on job crafting to create the psychological states recommended by Thomas. This recommendation requires you to take ownership in creating your own level of engagement. Try it; it worked for us.

LO6.4

Job Satisfaction

***Job satisfaction* is an affective or emotional response toward various facets of one's job.** This definition means job satisfaction is not a unitary concept. Rather, a person can be relatively satisfied with one aspect of his or her job and dissatisfied with one or more other aspects. For example, a recent survey of 11,000 people indicated that Gen Ys were more satisfied with their managers than Gen Xers or Baby Boomers. In contrast, overall job satisfaction was higher for Boomers than it was for Gen Ys and Gen Xers.[54]

Researchers at Cornell University developed the Job Descriptive Index (JDI) to assess one's satisfaction with the following job dimensions: work, pay, promotions, coworkers, and supervision. Researchers at the University of Minnesota concluded there are 20 different dimensions underlying job satisfaction.[55] Although researchers do not have consensus about the exact number of dimensions that constitute job satisfaction, they do agree that it has five predominant causes. Let us consider these causes.

The Causes of Job Satisfaction

Five predominant models of job satisfaction specify its causes. They are need fulfillment, discrepancy, value attainment, equity, and dispositional/genetic components. A brief review of these models will provide insight into the complexity of this seemingly simple concept.

LO6.5

Need Fulfillment   These models propose that satisfaction is determined by the extent to which the characteristics of a job allow an individual to fulfill his or her needs. For example, a survey by the Society for Human Resource Management asked employees to choose the aspects of their job that were very important to their job satisfaction. Their top four choices were compensation, benefits, job security, and work/life balance—all directly related to employees' ability to meet a variety of basic needs.[56] Although these models generated a great degree of controversy, it is generally accepted that need fulfillment is correlated with job satisfaction.

Methodist Hospital System instituted a program for employees to volunteer their time to spend with terminal patients. How would this program help to achieve a sense of value attainment within the hospital?

Discrepancies   These models propose that satisfaction is a result of met expectations. *Met expectations* **represent the difference between what an individual expects to receive from a job, such as good pay and promotional opportunities, and what he or she actually receives.** When expectations are greater than what is received, a person will be dissatisfied. In contrast, this model predicts the individual will be satisfied when he or she attains outcomes above and beyond expectations. A meta-analysis that included 17,241 people demonstrated that met expectations were significantly related to job satisfaction.[57] Many companies use employee attitude or opinion surveys and focus groups to assess employees' expectations and concerns. To that end, a recent study revealed that employees of all income levels were less likely to express their honest opinions when they felt "that speaking up would be futile."[58] This underscores the recommendation that management should report the results of employee surveys or focus groups back to employees. Employees simply want to see a response to their requested input.[59]

connect
www.mcgrawhillconnect.com

Go to Connect to take a self-assessment to determine how satisfied you are with your present job.

Value Attainment   The idea underlying *value attainment* **is that satisfaction results from the perception that a job allows for fulfillment of an individual's important work values.** In general, research consistently supports the prediction that value fulfillment is positively related to job satisfaction. Managers can thus enhance employee satisfaction by structuring the work environment and its associated rewards and recognition to reinforce employees' values.

Equity   In this model, satisfaction is a function of how "fairly" an individual is treated at work. Satisfaction results from one's perception that work outcomes, relative to inputs, compare favorably with a significant other's outcomes/inputs. A meta-analysis involving 64,757 people supported this model. Employees' perceptions of being treated fairly at work were highly related to overall job satisfaction.[60] Managers thus are encouraged to monitor employees' fairness perceptions and to interact with employees in such a way that they feel equitably treated. Chapter 7 explores this promising model in more detail.

Dispositional/Genetic Components   Have you ever noticed that some of your coworkers or friends appear to be satisfied across a variety of job circumstances, whereas others always seem dissatisfied? This model of satisfaction attempts to explain this pattern. Specifically, the dispositional/genetic model is based on the belief that job satisfaction is partly a function of both personal traits and genetic factors. As such, this model implies that stable individual differences are just as important in explaining job satisfaction as are characteristics of the work environment. Although there are a limited number of studies that tested these propositions, a recent meta-analysis revealed that dispositional factors were not significantly associated with all aspects of job satisfaction. Dispositions had stronger relationships with intrinsic aspects of a job (e.g., having autonomy) than with extrinsic aspects of work (e.g., receipt of rewards).[61] Genetic factors also were found to significantly predict life satisfaction, well-being, and general job satisfaction.[62] Overall, researchers estimate that 30% of an individual's job satisfaction is associated with dispositional and genetic components.[63]

Connect
www.mcgrawhillconnect.com

Go to Connect for an interactive exercise to test your knowledge of the causes of job satisfaction.

> **BACK TO THE CHAPTER-OPENING CASE**   Which of the five models of job satisfaction best explain the job satisfaction of Lori Miller and Elizabeth Gray?

Major Correlates and Consequences of Job Satisfaction

This area has significant managerial implications because thousands of studies have examined the relationship between job satisfaction and other organizational variables. Because it is impossible to examine them all, we will consider a subset of the more important variables from the standpoint of managerial relevance.

Table 6–2 summarizes the pattern of results. The relationship between job satisfaction and these other variables is either positive or negative. The strength of the relationship ranges from weak (very little relationship) to strong. Strong relationships imply that managers can significantly influence the variable of interest by increasing job satisfaction. Let us now consider several of the key correlates of job satisfaction.

Motivation   A meta-analysis of nine studies and 1,739 workers revealed a significant positive relationship between motivation and job satisfaction. Because satisfaction with supervision also was significantly correlated with motivation, managers are advised to consider how their behavior affects employee satisfaction.[64] Managers can potentially enhance employees' motivation through various attempts to increase job satisfaction.

Job Involvement   Job involvement, which is a component of employee engagement, represents the extent to which an individual is personally involved with his or her work role. A meta-analysis involving 27,925 individuals demonstrated that job involvement was moderately related with job satisfaction.[65] Managers are thus encouraged to foster satisfying work environments in order to fuel employees' job involvement.

Organizational Commitment   Organizational commitment reflects the extent to which an individual identifies with an organization and is committed to its goals. A meta-analysis of results from 490,624 individuals uncovered a significant and moderate relationship between organizational commitment and satisfaction.[66] Managers are advised to increase job satisfaction in order to elicit higher levels of commitment. In turn, higher commitment can facilitate higher productivity.

Organizational Citizenship Behavior   *Organizational citizenship behaviors (OCBs)* consist of employee behaviors that are beyond the call of duty.

TABLE 6–2 Correlates of Job Satisfaction

Variables Related with Satisfaction	Direction of Relationship	Strength of Relationship
Motivation	positive	moderate
Job involvement	positive	moderate
Organizational commitment	positive	moderate
Organizational citizenship behavior	positive	moderate
Withdrawal cognitions	negative	strong
Turnover	negative	moderate
Heart disease	negative	moderate
Perceived stress	negative	strong
Pro-union voting	negative	moderate
Job performance	positive	moderate
Life satisfaction	positive	moderate
Mental health	positive	moderate
Customer satisfaction	**positive**	**moderate**

Examples include "such gestures as constructive statements about the department, expression of personal interest in the work of others, suggestions for improvement, training new people, respect for the spirit as well as the letter of housekeeping rules, care for organizational property, and punctuality and attendance well beyond standard or enforceable levels."[67] Managers certainly would like employees to exhibit these behaviors. A meta-analysis involving 21 separate studies revealed a significant and moderately positive correlation between organizational citizenship behaviors and job satisfaction.[68] Moreover, two recent, and more extensive meta-analytic studies indicated that OCBs were significantly related to both individual-level consequences (e.g., performance appraisal ratings, intentions to quit, absenteeism, and turnover) and organizational-level outcomes (e.g., productivity, efficiency, lower costs, customer satisfaction, and unit-level satisfaction and turnover).[69] These results are important for two reasons. First, exhibiting OCBs is likely to create positive impressions about you among your colleagues and manager. In turn, these impressions affect your ability to work with others, your manager's evaluation of your performance, and ultimately your promotability. Second, the aggregate amount of employees' OCBs affects important organizational outcomes. Thus, it is important for managers to foster an environment that promotes OCBs. Managers are encouraged to make and implement employee-related decisions in an equitable fashion in order to foster OCBs. More is said about this in Chapter 7.

Withdrawal Cognitions Although some people quit their jobs impulsively or in a fit of anger, most go through a process of thinking about whether or not they should quit. *Withdrawal cognitions* **encapsulate this thought process by representing an individual's overall thoughts and feelings about quitting.** What causes an individual to think about quitting his or her job? Job satisfaction is believed to be one of the most significant contributors. For example, a study of managers, salespersons, and auto mechanics from a national automotive retail store chain demonstrated that job dissatisfaction caused employees to begin the process of thinking about quitting. In turn, withdrawal cognitions had a greater impact on employee turnover than job satisfaction in this sample.[70] Results from this study imply that managers can indirectly help to reduce employee turnover by enhancing employee job satisfaction.

Turnover   Let us consider the pros and cons of turnover before discussing the relationship between job satisfaction and turnover. Yes, turnover can be a good thing when a low-performing person like George Costanza from the Seinfeld show quits or is fired. This situation enables managers to replace the Georges of the world with better or more diverse individuals or to realign the budget. In contrast, losing a good employee is bad because the organization loses valuable human and social capital (recall our discussion in Chapter 1) and it can be costly.[71] Costs of turnover fall into two categories: separation costs and replacement costs.

> Separation costs may include severance pay, costs associated with an exit interview, outplacement fees, and possible litigation costs, particularly for involuntary separation. Replacement costs are the well-known costs of a hire, including sourcing expenses, HR processing costs for screening and assessing candidates, the time spent by hiring managers interviewing candidates, travel and relocation expenses, signing bonuses, if applicable, and orientation and training costs.[72]

Experts estimate that the cost of turnover for an hourly employee is roughly 30% of annual salary, whereas the cost can range up to 150% of yearly salary for professional employees.[73]

Although there are various things a manager can do to reduce employee turnover, many of them revolve around attempts to improve employees' job satisfaction. This trend is supported by results from a meta-analysis covering 24,556 people. Job satisfaction obtained a moderate negative relationship with employee turnover.[74] Given the strength of this relationship, managers are advised to try to reduce employee turnover by increasing employee job satisfaction. This recommendation is even more important for high performers.[75] For example, a recent survey of 20,000 employees with a high potential indicated that 27% plan to find another job within a year.[76] Google seems to be aware of this issue in light of its decision to give all employees a 10% raise in 2010 despite a poor economy. Google obviously wanted to reduce defections of its talented workforce.[77]

Dual career ladders represent a specific program that can be used to jointly increase job satisfaction and reduce turnover. A ***dual career ladder*** **"is a career development plan that allows upward mobility for employees without requiring that they move to supervisory or managerial positions."**[78] This program is most useful for technically oriented employees who want to advance without having to take on managerial responsibilities. Dual career ladders are more common in scientific, medical, engineering, software, and technology oriented fields. The Skills & Best Practices feature on page 166 outlines the steps that should be considered when implementing a dual career ladder program.

Perceived Stress   Stress can have very negative effects on organizational behavior and an individual's health. Stress is positively related to absenteeism, turnover, coronary heart disease, and viral infections. Based on a meta-analysis covering 11,063 individuals, Table 6–2 reveals that perceived stress has a strong, negative relationship with job satisfaction. Perceived stress also was found to be negatively associated with employee engagement. We recommend that managers attempt to reduce the negative

Steps for Implementing a Dual Career Ladder

1. Determine the knowledge, skills, abilities, and other personal factors (KSAOs) needed to perform jobs in the dual career ladder. Determine the amount of ability needed for each factor.
2. Determine the extent to which positions in the ladder require each of the KSAOs.
3. Develop job descriptions for each position in the ladder and identify the steps needed to advance to each successive level.
4. Use internal and external salary data to develop salary ranges for each job in the ladder.
5. Ensure that equity exists between people in traditional managerial jobs and those in the program.
6. Communicate details about how the program works. Be sure to allow flexibility in moving between managerial jobs and those in the dual career ladder.

SOURCE: Adapted from M Fiester, "What Is Meant by the Term 'Dual Career Ladder'?" *HR Magazine*, November 2010, p 21.

effects of stress by improving job satisfaction and encouraging employees to detach from work during off-job time (i.e., stop thinking about work).[79]

Job Performance   One of the biggest controversies within OB research centers on the relationship between job satisfaction and job performance. Although researchers have identified seven different ways in which these variables are related, the dominant beliefs are either that satisfaction causes performance or performance causes satisfaction. A team of researchers recently attempted to resolve this controversy through a meta-analysis of data from 54,417 individuals.[80] There were two key findings from this study. First, job satisfaction and performance were moderately related. This is an important finding because it supports the belief that employee job satisfaction is a key work attitude managers should consider when attempting to increase employees' job performance. Second, the relationship between job satisfaction and performance was much more complex than originally thought. It is not as simple as satisfaction causing performance or performance causing satisfaction. Rather, researchers now believe both variables indirectly influence each other through a host of individual differences and work-environment characteristics. There is one additional consideration to keep in mind regarding the relationship between job satisfaction and job performance.

Researchers believe the relationship between satisfaction and performance is understated due to incomplete measures of individual-level performance. For example, if performance ratings used in past research did not reflect the actual interactions and interdependencies at work, inaccurate measures of performance served to lower the reported correlations between satisfaction and performance. Examining the relationship between *aggregate* measures of job satisfaction and organizational performance is one solution to correct this problem. In support of these ideas, a team of researchers conducted a recent meta-analysis of over 5,000 business units. Results uncovered significant positive relationships between business-unit-level employee satisfaction and business-unit outcomes of productivity, turnover, absenteeism, and customer satisfaction.[81] It thus appears managers can positively affect a variety of important organizational outcomes such as performance and customer satisfaction by increasing employee job satisfaction.

Counterproductive Work Behavior

Figure 6–1 shows that low motivation or low employee engagement may be associated with a variety of negative behaviors and outcomes. Counterproductive work behavior is a prime example. *Counterproductive work behaviors (CWBs)* **represent types of behavior that harm employees, the organization as a whole, or organizational stakeholders such as customers and shareholders.** Examples of CWBs include theft, gossiping, back-stabbing, drug and alcohol abuse, destroying organizational property, violence, purposely doing bad or incorrect work, surfing the net for personal use, excessive socializing, tardiness, sabotage, and sexual harassment.[82] Consider the following three examples:

> Recently, a Maryland man swiped 32 laptops from his nonprofit health-care employer and put them on eBay. A chief financial officer changed the color of the type on some spreadsheet data from black to white so as to render the fake numbers invisible while juicing the totals—and his bonus. One regional vice-president for sales billed his corporate card $4,000 for Victoria's Secret lingerie—and not for his wife, either.[83]

Experts expect incidents like this to increase during recessionary times. Let us now consider two common categories of CWB and the causes and prevention of CWB.

Mistreatment of Others

Most forms of CWBs involve mistreatment of coworkers, subordinates, or even customers. For example, employees engage in harassment, bullying, or blatant unfairness. Unfortunately, a recent Zogby poll indicated that more than 50% of American adults had been bullied or had witnessed bullying at work. Another poll of 12,000 people from 24 countries indicated that about 10% were harassed either sexually or physically at work.[84] Abuse by supervisors is especially toxic because employees report that when they feel they have been intimidated, humiliated, or undermined by an abusive supervisor, they are more likely to retaliate with counterproductive behavior aimed at the supervisor or their coworkers.[85] This type of response is especially likely when the organization does not provide channels through which employees can complain and find a resolution to the problem of mistreatment.

Mistreatment can also involve animals. Michael Vick is a very talented quarterback for the Philadelphia Eagles. Sadly, he served only 21 months in prison for his involvement in an illegal interstate dog fighting ring. Why would a wealthy person like Vick get involved with dog fighting?

Violence at Work

Terrifying images of the shootings at Virginia Tech and that of U.S. Representative Gabby Giffords and innocent bystanders in Tucson, Arizona, have brought home the urgency of protecting people in organizations from sudden acts of violence committed by insiders or outsiders. Often, coworkers are first to notice that an employee explodes in anger or seems depressed or troubled. Psychiatrist and consultant Roger Brunswick says, "Violence rarely begins with someone walking in and shooting others. Violence usually builds slowly and starts with bullying, intimidation, and threats."[86] A first line of defense should be for the organization to set up and publicize how employees can report troubling behavior to their supervisor or human resource department. Pitney Bowes set up a hotline that employees can call anonymously to report any concerns, and it has trained managers in identifying signs that something is wrong with an employee.[87]

 LO6.6

Causes and Prevention of CWBs

Employers obviously want to prevent CWBs, so they need to know the causes of such behavior. A study that followed the work behaviors of more than 900 young adults for 23 years found that a diagnosis of conduct disorder in adolescence was associated with CWBs, but criminal convictions before entering the workforce were not associated with CWBs.[88] Personality traits and job conditions also could make CWBs more likely.[89] For example, young adults who scored higher on compulsion to adhere to norms, control their impulses, and avoid hostility tended not to use CWBs. They also were less likely to engage in CWBs if they had satisfying jobs that offered autonomy—and more likely to engage in CWBs if they had more resource power (such as more people to supervise). Intelligence may play a role, too. A study of applicants for law enforcement jobs found that higher scores for cognitive ability were associated with fewer reports of CWBs such as violence and destruction of property after candidates were hired.[90]

These findings suggest the following implications for management:

- Organizations can limit CWBs by hiring individuals who are less prone to engage in this type of behavior. Cognitive ability is associated with many measures of success, so it is a logical quality to screen for in hiring decisions. Personality tests also may be relevant.

- Organizations should ensure they are motivating desired behaviors and not CWBs, for example, by designing jobs that promote satisfaction and by preventing abusive supervision. A study of 265 restaurants found that CWBs were greater in restaurants where employees reported abuse by supervisors and where managers had more employees to supervise.[91] CWBs in these restaurants were associated with lower profits and lower levels of customer satisfaction, so adequate staffing and management development could not only make employees' lives more pleasant but also improve the bottom line.

- If an employee does engage in CWBs, the organization should respond quickly and appropriately, defining the specific behaviors that are unacceptable and the requirements for acceptable behavior. Chapter 8 describes guidelines for effective feedback.

key terms

chapter summary

- *Discuss the integrated model of motivation.* Personal factors and contextual factors are the two key categories of variables that influence employee motivation and employee engagement. In turn, motivation and engagement impact a host of motivated behaviors and outcomes.

- *Contrast Maslow's and McClelland's need theories.* Two well-known need theories of motivation are Maslow's need hierarchy and McClelland's need theory. Maslow's notion of a prepotent or stair-step hierarchy of five levels of needs has not stood up well under research. McClelland believes that motivation and performance vary according to the strength of an individual's need for achievement. High achievers prefer moderate risks and situations where they can control their own destiny. Top managers should have a high need for power coupled with a low need for affiliation.

- *Describe the three conceptually different approaches to job design.* The premise of top-down approaches is that management is responsible for creating efficient and meaningful combinations of work tasks for employees. There are five principal top-down approaches: scientific management, job enlargement, job enrichment, job rotation, and a contingency approach called the job characteristics model. Bottom-up approaches, which are referred to as job crafting, are driven by employees rather than managers. Employees are viewed as job crafters who define and create their own job boundaries. Idiosyncratic deals (i-deals) view job design as a process in which employees and managers jointly negotiate the types of tasks employees complete at work.

- *Review the personal and contextual factors that contribute to employee engagement and its consequences.* Employee engagement occurs when employees give it their all at work. It contains feelings of urgency, feelings of being focused, feelings of intensity, and feelings of enthusiasm. Employee engagement is influenced by a host of personal and contextual factors, and it is positively associated with individual-level outcomes such as performance, satisfaction, and well-being. It also is related to the organizational-level outcomes of customer satisfaction and financial performance.

- *Discuss the causes and consequences of job satisfaction.* Job satisfaction is an affective or emotional response toward various facets of one's job. Five models of job satisfaction specify its causes. They are need fulfillment, discrepancy, value attainment, equity, and trait/genetic components. Job satisfaction has been correlated with hundreds of consequences. Table 6–2 summarizes the pattern of results found for a subset of the more important variables.

- *Identify the causes of counterproductive work behavior and measures to prevent it.* Counterproductive work behaviors (CWBs) may result from personal characteristics coupled with a lack of autonomy and job satisfaction. CWBs are more likely in situations where supervisors are abusive and responsible for many employees. Organizations can limit CWBs by hiring individuals with appropriate cognitive skills and personality traits. They can design jobs to promote satisfaction. They can develop managers to supervise effectively without abuse and should deliver immediate feedback and discipline if anyone engages in CWBs.

discussion questions

1. Think of a time when you observed negative behavior by one of your colleagues at work or a fellow student in a team project. Now use Figure 6–1 to diagnose the causes of this behavior. What could a manager or project team leader have done to correct this behavior?

2. Which of the three conceptually different types of job design is most likely to be used in the future? Explain your rationale.

3. To what extent is your behavior as a student a function of engagement? Explain.

4. Have you ever observed someone exhibiting counterproductive work behavior? What were the cause and consequence of this behavior?

5. What are the three most valuable lessons about employee motivation that you have learned from this chapter?

legal/ethical challenge

How Would You Handle a Confrontation between an Employee and a Customer?

Mala Amarsingh, a JetBlue Airways Corp. attendant, was standing in the Las Vegas airport in June, waiting to hitch a ride to New York to start her shift. An intoxicated female passenger approached her, started cursing, threatened to beat her up, and then spit in her face. The flight attendant says she lost her cool, cursed back at the passenger, and later was terminated by the airline for "inappropriate behavior." JetBlue won't comment about personnel matters, but said, "Customers traveling today are more frustrated by delays and perceived service lapses."

Amarsingh thinks "uniformed flight attendants are walking targets for passenger frustrations," which "absolutely" have gotten worse in her more than six years in the job.[92]

Assume That You Are a Vice President of JetBlue and That You Just Became Aware of the

Situation Involving Ms Amarsingh. What Would You Do?

1. Nothing. Amarsingh's behavior violated corporate policy about the treatment of customers, so she deserved to be fired. Changing the decision would set a bad precedent for other employees.

2. Acknowledge that the employee's behavior violates corporate policy, but hire her back given the extenuating circumstances. Provide Amarsingh with back pay for any lost time.

3. Hire Amarsingh back and use company resources to sue the customer. The customer committed assault and battery by purposely spitting in her face. Rehiring Amarsingh would send a clear message that you care about your employees and that JetBlue managers will not allow their employees to be assaulted.

4. Invent other options.

If you're looking for additional study materials, be sure to check out the Online Learning Center at

www.mhhe.com/kinickiob5e

for more information and interactivities that correspond to this chapter.

chapter 7

Motivation II: Equity, Expectancy, and Goal Setting

After reading the material in this chapter, you should be able to:

LO7.1 Discuss the role of perceived inequity in employee motivation.

LO7.2 Describe the practical lessons derived from equity theory.

LO7.3 Explain Vroom's expectancy theory.

LO7.4 Describe the practical implications of expectancy theory.

LO7.5 Identify five practical lessons to be learned from goal-setting research.

LO7.6 Specify issues that should be addressed before implementing a motivational program.

Should Teacher Pay Be Tied to Student Achievement?

Michelle Rhee, former chancellor of Washington, D.C. schools, attempted to implement components of several motivation theories in order to increase teacher performance. She was driven to create change because past practice revealed that 95% of the school system's teachers were evaluated as excellent and nobody was fired for poor performance. At the same time, student test scores were among the lowest in the nation. In 2010 she fired 241 teachers, which amounted to roughly 6% of all teachers in the system. She also informed 737 additional teachers that they could lose their jobs if they didn't improve over the next year.

"The district has been at the forefront of a national effort to rid classrooms of low-performing teachers. Of the 241 teachers fired, 165 were let go because of poor performance; the remainder didn't have proper teaching credentials."

Rhee made these changes after creating a new teacher evaluation system and negotiating a new compensation agreement with the Washington Teachers Union (WTU).

The evaluation system is regarded as one of the most rigorous in the United States.

It requires numerous classroom observations of teacher performance and measures teachers against student achievement. . . . Teachers are evaluated five times a year by school administrators and master teachers on such things as creating coherent lesson plans and engaging students. After an initial observation, teachers receive a plan detailing weaknesses and are offered coaching for improvement. . . . Teachers are ranked into four categories. This year, 16% reached the highest ranking, compared with 45% in past years. Some 20% landed in the bottom rating, compared with 4% in years past.

The new compensation system stipulated that "good teachers would get more money (including a 21.6% pay increase through 2012 and opportunities for merit pay). In exchange, bad teachers could be shown the door."

George Parker, president of the WTU, was unhappy about the firings and indicated that the union would appeal the dismissals. He also

Michelle Rhee, former Chancellor of Washington, D.C. public schools

threatened to file an unfair labor charge against the school district. He believes that the teacher evaluation system is unfair.

"Jeanne Allen, president of the Center for Education Reform, a national voice for charter and school choice, says the responses from union leaders show they are not used to dealing with a chancellor willing to call their bluff. 'The union has been given so much credit for coming to the table,' she says. 'But if you really believe what you signed, you don't then announce to the local paper you are filing a grievance when the other side tries to make good on that contract.'"

Richard Whitmire, author of *The Bee Eater: Michelle Rhee Takes on the Nation's Worst School District*, studied Rhee's reforms. He noted that during her 3½ year tenure a third of the principals turned over and she fired about 400 teachers for poor performance. All told, he thought her approach was a bit harsh but acknowledged that Rhee needed to take a tough stance toward motivating teachers because "only about a third of D.C. teachers were capable of carrying out" high-quality instruction.[1] Time will tell whether or not other school systems use the motivational techniques implemented by Michelle Rhee.

▲ **AS YOU WILL LEARN LATER** in this chapter, expectancy theory is based on the principle that an individual's pay should be tied to his or her performance. The fundamental concept underlying this theory is that employee motivation is higher when people are rewarded with rewards they value, such as higher pay. Contrary to this theory, however, the chapter-opening case illustrates that the teachers' union was fighting Michelle Rhee's attempt to use expectancy theory. Why? Because there are many factors that influence employee motivation that go beyond the receipt of rewards.

The last chapter identified two of these factors: individual needs and job design. This chapter extends this discussion by focusing on three cognitive theories of work motivation: equity, expectancy, and goal setting. Each theory is based on the premise that employees' cognitions are the key to understanding their motivation. To help you apply what you have learned about employee motivation, we conclude this chapter by discussing some practical issues to consider when trying to motivate others.

Adams's Equity Theory of Motivation

Defined generally, *equity theory* **is a model of motivation that explains how people strive for** *fairness* **and** *justice* **in social exchanges or give-and-take relationships.** Equity theory is based on cognitive dissonance theory, developed by social psychologist Leon Festinger in the 1950s.[2]

According to Festinger's theory, people are motivated to maintain consistency between their cognitive beliefs and their behavior. Perceived inconsistencies create cognitive dissonance (or psychological discomfort), which, in turn, motivates corrective action. For example, a cigarette smoker who sees a heavy-smoking relative die of lung cancer probably would be motivated to quit smoking if he or she attributes the death to smoking. Accordingly, when victimized by unfair social exchanges, our resulting cognitive dissonance prompts us to correct the situation. Corrective action may range from a slight change in attitude or behavior to sabotage to the extreme case of trying to harm someone. For example, supporters of WikiLeaks conducted cyberattacks against MasterCard and Visa because they thought that these companies were unfairly trying to stifle WikiLeak's dissemination of secret US diplomatic communications. Both MasterCard and Visa systems were temporarily down as a result of these attacks.[3]

Psychologist J Stacy Adams pioneered application of the equity principle to the workplace. Central to understanding Adams's equity theory of motivation is an awareness of key components of the individual–organization exchange relationship. This relationship is pivotal in the formation of employees' perceptions of equity and inequity.

The Individual–Organization Exchange Relationship

Adams points out that two primary components are involved in the employee–employer exchange, *inputs* and *outcomes*. An employee's inputs, for which he or she expects a just return, include education/training, skills, creativity, seniority, age, personality traits, effort expended, and personal appearance. On the outcome side of the exchange, the organization provides such things as pay/bonuses, medical benefits, challenging assignments, job security, promotions, status symbols, recognition, and participation in important decisions. These outcomes vary widely, depending on one's organization and rank.

Negative and Positive Inequity

On the job, feelings of inequity revolve around a person's evaluation of whether he or she receives adequate rewards to compensate for his or her contributive inputs. People perform these evaluations by comparing the perceived fairness of their employment exchange to that of relevant others. This comparative process, which is based on an equity norm, was found to generalize across personalities and countries.[4] People tend to compare themselves to other individuals with whom they have close interpersonal ties—such as friends—and/or to similar others—such as people performing the same job or individuals of the same gender or educational level—rather than dissimilar others. For example, we do not compare our salaries to that of the head football coach at Arizona State University. But we do consider our pay relative to other college business professors. This brings up an interesting trend within the legal profession. Big law firms have taken to paying "outsize salaries to star attorneys, in some cases 10 times what they give other partners, in a strategy that is stretching compensation gaps and testing morale at firms. . . . While there has always been a pay gap at big firms, in the past partners with ownership stakes were paid relatively similar amounts to encourage a team approach and to ward off possible resentment."[5] Do you think that this practice will negatively affect people's work attitudes and levels of engagement?

Three different equity relationships are illustrated in Figure 7-1: equity, negative inequity, and positive inequity. Assume the two people in each of the equity relationships in Figure 7-1 have equivalent backgrounds (equal education, seniority, and so forth) and perform identical tasks. Only their hourly pay rates differ. Equity exists for an individual when his or her ratio of perceived outcomes to inputs is equal to the ratio of outcomes to inputs for a relevant coworker (see part A in Figure 7-1). Because equity is based on comparing *ratios* of outcomes to inputs, inequity will not necessarily be perceived just because someone else receives greater rewards. If the other person's additional outcomes are due to his or her greater inputs, a sense of equity may still exist. However, if the comparison person enjoys greater outcomes for similar inputs, ***negative inequity*** will be perceived (see part B in Figure 7-1). On the other hand, a person will experience ***positive inequity*** when his or her outcome to input ratio is greater than that of a relevant coworker (see part C in Figure 7-1).

Dynamics of Perceived Inequity

Managers can derive practical benefits from Adams's equity theory by recognizing that (1) people have varying sensitivities to perceived equity and inequity and (2) inequity can be reduced in a variety of ways.

Thresholds of Equity and Inequity   Have you ever noticed that some people become very upset over the slightest inequity whereas others are not bothered at all? Research has shown that people respond differently to the same level of inequity due to an individual difference called equity sensitivity. ***Equity sensitivity* reflects an individual's "different preferences for, tolerances for, and reactions to the level of equity associated with any given situation."**[6] Equity sensitivity spans a continuum ranging from benevolents to sensitives to entitled.

Benevolents are people who have a higher tolerance for negative inequity. They are altruistic in the sense that they prefer their outcome/input ratio to be lower than ratios from comparison with others. In contrast, equity *sensitives* are described as individuals who adhere to a strict norm of reciprocity and are quickly motivated to resolve both

FIGURE 7–1 Negative and Positive Inequity

A. An equitable situation

B. Negative inequity

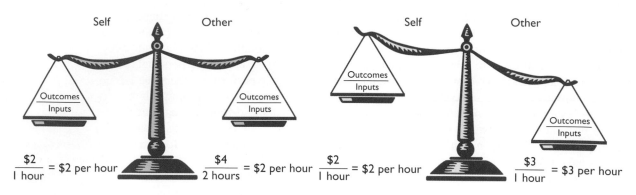

$$\frac{\$2}{1 \text{ hour}} = \$2 \text{ per hour}$$

$$\frac{\$4}{2 \text{ hours}} = \$2 \text{ per hour}$$

$$\frac{\$2}{1 \text{ hour}} = \$2 \text{ per hour}$$

$$\frac{\$3}{1 \text{ hour}} = \$3 \text{ per hour}$$

C. Positive inequity

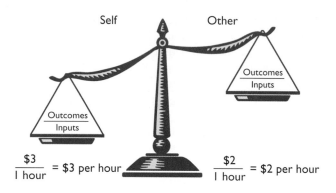

$$\frac{\$3}{1 \text{ hour}} = \$3 \text{ per hour}$$

$$\frac{\$2}{1 \text{ hour}} = \$2 \text{ per hour}$$

negative and positive inequity. Finally, *entitleds* have no tolerance for negative inequity. They actually expect to obtain greater output/input ratios than comparison with others and become upset when this is not the case.[7]

Reducing Inequity Equity ratios can be changed by attempting to alter one's outcomes or adjusting one's inputs. For example, negative inequity might be resolved by asking for a raise or a promotion (i.e., raising outputs) or by reducing inputs (i.e., working fewer hours or exerting less effort). It also is important to note that equity can be restored by altering one's equity ratios behaviorally and/or cognitively. A cognitive strategy entails psychologically distorting perceptions of one's own or a comparison person's outcomes and inputs (e.g., conclude that comparison other has more experience or works harder).

It is important to note that people also seek equity in a consumer context. The Skills & Best Practices feature on page 177 illustrates how companies can use a "HERO Compact" to overcome image problems created by consumers who use social media to complain about perceptions of inequity. Such complaints can become viral, ultimately resulting in negative views of a company's brand. In addition to HERO Compacts, organizations monitor and respond to items that are posted online in order to combat this trend.[8]

Feelings of Consumer Inequity Can Go Viral

Maybe you've heard about the musician Dave Carroll and his experience as a United Airlines customer. He was so incensed that the company rejected his damage claim after its baggage handlers broke his guitar that he made a catchy YouTube video, "United Breaks Guitars." Eight million people have already viewed this decidedly negative take on the United brand.

Carroll's reaction is hardly unique. The popular mommy blogger Heather Armstrong was so upset over the failure of her Maytag washer and the company's ensuing service missteps that, using her mobile phone, she told her million-plus followers on Twitter they should never buy a Maytag. Greenpeace supporters barraged Nestlé's Facebook page with complaints about how the company's sourcing policies led to environmental damage.

A team from Forrester Research, a technology and market research firm, recommended that managers can overcome this problem by using the same technologies and social media used by disgruntled consumers. They proposed that the "key is to let employees experiment with technology, make high-profile decisions on the fly, build systems that customers can see, and publicly speak for the organization. Managers and IT leaders need to give these HEROes ('highly empowered and resourceful operatives') guidance, help, and limits."

A crucial part of the solution is the HERO Compact—a three-way agreement for managing technological innovation. In the compact, HEROes agree to innovate within a safe framework, managers agree to encourage innovation and manage risk, and IT agrees to support and scale up HERO projects.

SOURCE: *Reprinted by permission of Harvard Business Review. Excerpt from "Empowered," by J. Bernoff and T. Schadler, August 2010. Copyright 2010 by the Harvard Business School Publishing Corporation; all rights reserved.*

Expanding the Concept of Equity: Organizational Justice

Beginning in the later 1970s, researchers began to expand the role of equity theory in explaining employee attitudes and behavior. This led to a domain of research called *organizational justice.* Organizational justice reflects the extent to which people perceive that they are treated fairly at work. This, in turn, led to the identification of three different components of organizational justice: distributive, procedural, and interactional.[9] **Distributive justice reflects the perceived fairness of how resources and rewards are distributed or allocated. Procedural justice is defined as the perceived fairness of the process and procedures used to make allocation decisions.** Research shows that positive perceptions of distributive and procedural justice are enhanced by giving employees a "voice" in decisions that affect them. Voice represents the extent to which employees who are affected by a decision can present relevant information about the decision to others. Voice is analogous to asking employees for their input into the decision-making process.

Whole Foods Market has more than 300 stores in North America and the United Kingdom. The company's CEO, John Mackey (fourth from the left), has implemented a pay program that encourages equity among employees. He implemented a salary cap that limits the pay of top executives to 19 times the average full-time employee, and even reduced his own salary to $1. How do you think his decisions to cut his pay and cap executive salaries affect employee motivation?

The last justice component, *interactional justice,* **relates to the "quality of the interpersonal treatment people receive when procedures are implemented."[10]** This form of justice does not pertain to the outcomes or procedures associated with decision making, but rather it focuses on whether or not people believe they are treated fairly when decisions are implemented. Fair interpersonal treatment necessitates that managers communicate truthfully and treat people with courtesy and respect. Consider the role of interactional justice in how a manager of information-management systems responded to being laid off by a New Jersey chemical company. The man gained access to the company's computer systems from home by using another executive's password and deleted critical inventory and personnel files. The sabotage ultimately caused $20 million in damage and postponed a public stock offering that had been in the works. Why would a former employee do something like this?

> An anonymous note that he wrote to the company president sheds light on his motive. "I have been loyal to the company in good and bad times for over 30 years," he wrote. "I was expecting a member of top management to come down from his ivory tower to face us with the layoff announcement, rather than sending the kitchen supervisor with guards to escort us off the premises like criminals. You will pay for your senseless behavior."[11]

This employee's direct retaliation against the company was caused by the insensitive manner—interactional justice—in which employees were notified about the layoffs.

Practical Lessons from Equity Theory

LO7.2

Equity theory has at least six important practical implications. First, research on equity theory emphasizes the need for managers to pay attention to employees' perceptions of what is fair and equitable.[12] No matter how fair management thinks the organization's policies, procedures, and reward system are, each employee's *perception* of the equity of those factors is what counts. For example, a nationwide study of 3,000 U.S. workers revealed that 39% felt underpaid and only 37% reported feeling valued by their employer.[13] Managers thus are encouraged to make hiring decisions on merit-based, job-related information, and to make more attempts at providing positive recognition about employee behavior and performance.

Second, managers benefit by allowing employees to participate in making decisions about important work outcomes. In general, employees' perceptions of procedural justice are enhanced when they have a voice in the decision-making process. Managers are encouraged to seek employee input on organizational changes that are likely to impact the workforce. For instance, managers at Shell Refining decided to ask top-performing supervisors at its Port Arthur, Texas, refinery for input on how to improve plant performance. The result of this action was higher employee morale and a 30% reduction in unplanned maintenance repairs.[14]

Third, employees should be given the opportunity to appeal decisions that affect their welfare. Being able to appeal a decision fosters perceptions of distributive and procedural justice. Fourth, managers can promote cooperation and teamwork among group members by treating them equitably. This can be done by sharing power among group members, sharing resources with other teams, being careful to avoid linguistic triggers that cause feelings of envy (i.e., subtle cues that suggest certain skills and successes are more important than other skills and successes), and evenly delegating tasks/projects across the team.[15] This recommendation is supported by research revealing that people are just as concerned with fairness in group settings as they are with their own personal interests.[16] Fifth, employees' perceptions of justice are strongly influenced by the leadership behavior exhibited by their managers (leadership is discussed in Chapter 16). Thus it is important for managers to consider the justice-related implications of their decisions, actions, and public communications. Consider the lawsuit being filed by the Equal Employment Opportunity Commission (EEOC) on behalf of three women who worked for FedEx.

> Federal officials filed a discrimination lawsuit on behalf of three women who say that FedEx Freight, Inc. gave a human-resources job at its Phoenix facility to a less-qualified male candidate.
>
> All three women had prior human-resources experience and were recommended for the position. . . . Two of the women had earned bachelor's degrees, and one had a degree in human-resource management.
>
> FedEx officials hired a male dock worker to be a human-resources field representative. The man did not have a bachelor's degree, the EEOC said.[17]

The three women were clearly motivated to file a lawsuit based on their feelings of inequity regarding FedEx's hiring decision.

Finally, managers need to pay attention to the organization's climate for justice. For example, an organization's climate for justice was found to significantly influence employees' organizational commitment and job satisfaction.[18] Researchers also believe a climate of justice can significantly influence the type of customer service provided by employees. In turn, this level of service is likely to influence customers' perceptions of "fair service" and their subsequent loyalty and satisfaction.

Managers can attempt to follow these practical implications by monitoring equity and justice perceptions through informal conversations, interviews, or attitude surveys. For example, researchers have developed and validated a host of surveys that can be used for this purpose. Take a moment now to complete the Hands-On Exercise on page 180. It contains part of a survey that was developed to measure employees' perceptions of fair interpersonal treatment. If you perceive your work organization as interpersonally unfair, you are probably dissatisfied and have contemplated quitting. In contrast, your organizational loyalty and attachment are likely greater if you believe you are treated fairly at work.

www.mcgrawhillconnect.com

Go to Connect for a self-assessment to determine how fairly you perceive you are treated at work.

> **BACK TO THE CHAPTER-OPENING CASE** To what extent are Michelle Rhee's changes consistent with the practical lessons derived from equity theory?

Expectancy Theory of Motivation

Expectancy theory holds that **people are motivated to behave in ways that produce desired combinations of expected outcomes.** Perception plays a central role in expectancy theory because it emphasizes cognitive ability to anticipate likely consequences of behavior. Embedded in expectancy theory is the principle of hedonism. Hedonistic people strive to maximize their pleasure and minimize their pain. Generally, expectancy theory can be used to predict behavior in any situation in which a choice between two or more alternatives must be made. For instance, it can be used to predict whether to quit or stay at a job; whether to exert substantial or minimal effort at a task, and whether to major in management, computer science, accounting, marketing, psychology, or communication.

This section explores Victor Vroom's version of expectancy theory. Understanding the cognitive processes underlying this theory can help managers develop organizational policies and practices that enhance employee motivation.

LO7.3

HANDS-ON EXERCISE

Measuring Perceived Fair Interpersonal Treatment

INSTRUCTIONS: The following survey was designed to assess the extent to which you are treated fairly at your current job: If you are not working, use a past job or your role as a student to complete the survey. There is no right or wrong answer to the statements. Circle your answers by using the rating scale provided. After evaluating each of the survey statements, complete a total score and compare your total to the arbitrary norms.

		Strongly Disagree	Disagree	Neither	Agree	Strongly Agree
1.	Employees are praised for good work.	1	2	3	4	5
2.	Supervisors do not yell at employees.	1	2	3	4	5
3.	Employees are trusted.	1	2	3	4	5
4.	Employees' complaints are dealt with effectively.	1	2	3	4	5
5.	Employees are treated with respect.	1	2	3	4	5
6.	Employees' questions and problems are responded to quickly.	1	2	3	4	5
7.	Employees are treated fairly.	1	2	3	4	5
8.	Employees' hard work is appreciated.	1	2	3	4	5
9.	Employees' suggestions are used.	1	2	3	4	5
10.	Employees are told the truth.	1	2	3	4	5
	Total score =					

ARBITRARY NORMS   Very fair organization = 38–50
Moderately fair organization = 24–37
Unfair organization = 10–23

SOURCE: Adapted in part from M A Donovan, F Drasgow, and L J Munson, "The Perceptions of Fair Interpersonal Treatment Scale Development and Validation of a Measure of Interpersonal Treatment in the Workplace," *Journal of Applied Psychology*, October 1998, pp 683–92.

Vroom's Expectancy Theory

Victor Vroom formulated a mathematical model of expectancy theory in his 1964 book *Work and Motivation*. Vroom's theory has been summarized as follows:

connect
www.mcgrawhillconnect.com

Go to Connect for an interactive exercise to test your knowledge of Vroom's Expectancy Theory.

> The strength of a tendency to act in a certain way depends on the strength of an expectancy that the act will be followed by a given consequence (or outcome) and on the value or attractiveness of that consequence (or outcome) to the actor.[19]

Motivation, according to Vroom, boils down to the decision of how much effort to exert in a specific task situation. This choice is based on a two-stage sequence of expectations (effort → performance and performance → outcome). First, motivation is affected by an individual's expectation that a certain level of effort will produce the intended performance goal. For example, if you do not believe increasing the amount of time you spend studying will significantly raise your grade on an exam, you probably will not study any harder than usual. Motivation also is influenced by the employee's perceived chances of getting various outcomes as a result of accomplishing his or her performance goal. Finally, individuals are motivated to the extent that they value the outcomes received.

Vroom used a mathematical equation to integrate these concepts into a predictive model of motivational force or strength. For our purposes, however, it is sufficient to define and explain the three key concepts within Vroom's model: *expectancy, instrumentality,* and *valence.*

Expectancy   An *expectancy,* **according to Vroom's terminology, represents an individual's belief that a particular degree of effort will be followed by a particular level of performance.** In other words, it is an effort → performance expectation. Expectancies take the form of subjective probabilities. As you may recall from a course in statistics, probabilities range from zero to one. An expectancy of zero indicates effort has no anticipated impact on performance.

For example, suppose you do not know how to type on a keyboard. No matter how much effort you exert, your perceived probability of typing 30 error-free words per minute likely would be zero. An expectancy of one suggests that performance is totally dependent on effort. If you decided to take a typing course as well as practice a couple of hours a day for a few weeks (high effort), you should be able to type 30 words per minute without any errors. In contrast, if you do not take a typing course and only practice an hour or two per week (low effort), there is a very low probability (say, a 20% chance) of being able to type 30 words per minute without any errors.

The following factors influence an employee's expectancy perceptions:

- Self-esteem.
- Self-efficacy.
- Previous success at the task.
- Help received from others.
- Information necessary to complete the task.
- Good materials and equipment to work with.[20]

Venus Williams, winner of 21 Grand Slam titles and three Olympic gold medals, surely has a high expectancy for winning. What factors most strongly affect her expectations?

Instrumentality   An *instrumentality* **is a performance → outcome perception.** It represents a person's belief that a particular outcome is contingent on accomplishing a specific level of performance. Performance is instrumental when it leads to something else. For example, passing exams is instrumental to graduating from college.

Instrumentalities range from −1.0 to 1.0. An instrumentality of 1.0 indicates attainment of a particular outcome is totally dependent on task performance. An instrumentality of zero indicates there is no relationship between performance and receiving an outcome. For example, most companies link the number of vacation days to seniority, not job performance. Finally, an instrumentality of −1.0 reveals that high performance reduces the chance of obtaining an outcome while low performance increases the chance. For example, the more time you spend studying to get an A on an exam (high performance), the less time you will have for enjoying leisure activities. Similarly, as you lower the amount of time spent studying (low performance), you increase the amount of time that may be devoted to leisure activities.

The concept of instrumentality is illustrated by the pay practices being used at household cleaning products company Reckitt Benckiser. The pay plan has three parts: base salary and both short- and long-term bonuses/incentives.

Base salaries are set near the median for competitors' pay. The real benefit comes in the form of bonuses. A manager who meets all targets will typically receive 40% of his or her base salary as a bonus that year. A manager who blows the targets out of the water (usually that means doubling the target numbers) can earn a bonus of up to 144%. Long-term compensation, in the form of options and performance-related restricted stock, depends on meeting three-year corporate growth targets for earnings per share. New long-term goals are put into place each year.[21]

Reckitt Benckiser clearly makes bonuses contingent on performance.

Valence   As Vroom used the term, ***valence* refers to the positive or negative value people place on outcomes.** Valence mirrors our personal preferences. For example, most employees have a positive valence for receiving additional money or recognition. In contrast, being laid off or being ridiculed for making a suggestion would likely be negatively valent for most individuals. In Vroom's expectancy model, *outcomes* refer to different consequences that are contingent on performance, such as pay, promotions, or recognition. An outcome's valence depends on an individual's needs and can be measured for research purposes with scales ranging from a negative value to a positive value. For example, an individual's valence toward more recognition can be assessed on a scale ranging from -2 (very undesirable) to 0 (neutral) to $+2$ (very desirable).

Vroom's Expectancy Theory in Action   Vroom's expectancy model of motivation can be used to analyze a real-life motivation program. Consider the following performance problem described by Frederick W Smith, founder and chief executive officer of Federal Express Corporation:

> [W]e were having a helluva problem keeping things running on time. The airplanes would come in, and everything would get backed up. We tried every kind of control mechanism that you could think of, and none of them worked. Finally, it became obvious that the underlying problem was that it was in the interest of the employees at the cargo terminal—they were college kids, mostly—to run late, because it meant that they made more money. So what we did was give them all a minimum guarantee and say, "Look, if you get through before a certain time, just go home, and you will have beat the system." Well, it was unbelievable. I mean, in the space of about 45 days, the place was way ahead of schedule. And I don't even think it was a conscious thing on their part.[22]

How did Federal Express get its college-age cargo handlers to switch from low effort to high effort? According to Vroom's model, the student workers originally exerted low effort because they were paid on the basis of time, not output. It was in their best interest to work slowly and accumulate as many hours as possible. By offering to let the student workers *go home early if and when they completed their assigned duties,* Federal Express prompted high effort. This new arrangement created two positively valued outcomes: guaranteed pay plus the opportunity to leave early. The motivation to exert high effort became greater than the motivation to exert low effort.

LO7.4   Research on Expectancy Theory and Managerial Implications

Many researchers have tested expectancy theory. In support of the theory, a meta-analysis of 77 studies indicated that expectancy theory significantly predicted performance, effort, intentions, preferences, and choice.[23] All told, there is widespread agreement that behavior and attitudes are influenced when organizations link rewards to targeted behaviors.[24]

Managerial and Organizational Implications   TABLE 7–1
of Expectancy Theory

Implications for Managers	Implications for Organizations
Determine the outcomes employees value	Reward people for desired performance, and do not keep pay decisions secret
Identify good performance so appropriate behaviors can be rewarded	Design challenging jobs
Make sure employees can achieve targeted performance levels	Tie some rewards to group accomplishments to build teamwork and encourage cooperation
Link desired outcomes to targeted levels of performance	Reward managers for creating, monitoring, and maintaining expectancies, instrumentalities, and outcomes that lead to high effort and goal attainment
Make sure changes in outcomes are large enough to motivate high effort	Monitor employee motivation through interviews or anonymous questionnaires
Monitor the reward system for inequities	Accommodate individual differences by building flexibility into the motivation program

Nonetheless, expectancy theory has been criticized for a variety of reasons. For example, the theory is difficult to test, and the measures used to assess expectancy, instrumentality, and valence have questionable validity. In the final analysis, however, expectancy theory has important practical implications for individual managers and organizations as a whole (see Table 7-1).

Managers are advised to enhance effort → performance expectancies by helping employees accomplish their performance goals. Managers can do this by engaging in what is called performance management leadership. This type of leadership is discussed in Chapter 8 and includes behaviors associated with goal setting, communication, feedback, coaching, providing consequences, and establishing/monitoring performance expectations.[25]

It also is important for managers to influence employees' instrumentalities and to monitor valences for various rewards. This conclusion raises two important issues. This first involves employees' perception about the link between performance and pay. It is essential that employees believe that there is clear link between performance and pay. A recent Hay Group survey of 1,300 companies from 80 countries revealed that this recommendation is being followed by more companies. Thirty-nine percent of the responding firms indicate that they plan to increase the amount of pay tied to specific financial goals.[26] The second issue pertains to whether organizations should use monetary rewards as the primary method to reinforce performance. Although money is certainly positively valent for most people, there are three additional considerations regarding the relative balance between monetary and nonmonetary rewards.

First, research shows that some workers value interesting work and recognition more than money.[27] Second, extrinsic rewards can lose their motivating properties over

One way to link rewards to performance is to pay employees on the selling floor commissions on the products they sell. Sears has expanded its policy so that employees earn commissions in all departments of the store, not just in specialized areas like appliances or tools.

time and may undermine intrinsic motivation.[28] This conclusion, however, must be balanced by results from a meta-analysis of 39 studies. Findings showed that financial incentives were positively related to performance quantity but not to performance quality.[29] Third, monetary rewards must be large enough to generate motivation. For example, Robert Heneman, professor of management at Ohio State University, estimates that monetary awards must be at least 7% above employees' base pay to truly motivate people.[30] This recommendation does not bode well for employee motivation given organizational practices over the last few years. A nationwide survey by Hewitt Associates revealed that base salaries for salaried workers increased 2.4 percent in 2010 and are expected to rise an additional 2.9 percent in 2011.[31] This situation implies that organizations will need to rely on nonfinancial rewards to motivate employees. DPR Construction, for example, attempts to overcome this problem by engaging in a lot of celebrating. The Redwood City, California, firm celebrates birthdays, baby showers, anniversaries, engagements, and supports TGIF parties.[32]

In summary, there is no one best type of reward. For example, a recent survey of 1,047 employees from a variety of industries revealed that nonfinancial incentives such as praise, attention from leaders, and opportunity to lead projects were more effective at motivating respondents than financial incentives.[33] Is this true for you? We suspect that some people prefer nonfinancial rewards while others want money. The point is that managers should focus on linking employee performance to valued rewards regardless of the type of reward used to enhance motivation. The Skills & Best Practices feature below illustrates how General Motors is trying to implement this recommendation. Hourly workers at GM historically received pay raises based on seniority and job descriptions. The new approach is designed to directly link pay with performance. GM executives are hoping this new incentive system will lead to higher levels of productivity and profitability. It seems the plan may be working, as GM earned $4.7 billion in 2010, its first year of profit since 2004, and it paid out $200 million in profit sharing to unionized workers in the United States. This is the largest payout in GM history.[34]

SKILLS & BEST PRACTICES

GM's Incentive System Is Consistent with Expectancy Theory

General Motors Co. wants pay for union-represented workers tied to employees' work performance and the company's financial health—much like the way its salaried workers are paid. . . .

GM wants more flexible pay levels for workers as a way to encourage better performance and avoid locking the company into handing out big raises when the company isn't performing well, the company executives say.

"They are trying to give hourly workers the same metrics as salaried workers," GM Vice Chairman Stephen Girsky said Tuesday at the Detroit auto show. "There is a big pay-for-performance element going through the company and there is going to be more of it."

In addition to the performance-based pay, the union and U.S. automakers are exploring the idea of a profit-sharing formula as a way for workers to cash in on the industry's improving fortunes.

The profit-sharing agreement led to a $200 million quarterly payment to the company's 45,000 U.S. union employees. The average profit-sharing payment was $4,200 per worker.

SOURCE: Excerpted from S Terlep, "GM Rethinks Pay for Unionized Workers," *The Wall Street Journal,* January 12, 2011, p B6; and S Terlep, "GM Rebounds with Best Year Since 1999," *The Wall Street Journal,* February 25, 2011, pp B1, B2.

BACK TO THE CHAPTER-OPENING CASE To what extent is Michelle Rhee's motivation program consistent with the managerial and organizational implications of expectancy theory? Explain.

Motivation through Goal Setting

Regardless of the nature of their specific achievements, successful people tend to have one thing in common. Their lives are goal-oriented. This is as true for politicians seeking votes as it is for world-class athletes. Within the context of employee motivation, this section explores the theory, research, and practice of goal setting.

Goals: Definition and Background

Edwin Locke, a leading authority on goal setting, and his colleagues define a *goal* **as "what an individual is trying to accomplish; it is the object or aim of an action."**[35] The motivational effect of performance goals and goal based reward plans has been recognized for a long time. At the turn of the century, Frederick Taylor attempted to scientifically establish how much work of a specified quality an individual should be assigned each day. He proposed that bonuses be based on accomplishing those output standards. More recently, goal setting has been promoted through a widely used management technique called management by objectives (MBOs).

Management by objectives **is a management system that incorporates participation in decision making, goal setting, and objective feedback.** A meta-analysis of MBO programs showed productivity gains in 68 of 70 different organizations using the system. Specifically, results uncovered an average gain in productivity of 56% when top management commitment was high. The average gain was only 6% when commitment was low. A second meta-analysis of 18 studies further demonstrated that employees' job satisfaction was significantly related to top management's commitment to an MBO implementation.[36] These impressive results highlight the positive benefits of implementing MBO and setting goals. To further understand how MBO programs can increase both productivity and satisfaction, let us examine the process by which goal setting works.

How Does Goal Setting Work?

Despite abundant goal-setting research and practice, goal-setting theories are surprisingly scarce. An instructive model was formulated by Locke and his associates. According to Locke's model, goal setting has four motivational mechanisms.[37]

Goals Direct Attention Goals direct one's attention and effort toward goal-relevant activities and away from goal-irrelevant activities. If, for example, you have a term project due in a few days, your thoughts and actions tend to revolve around completing that project. American Fidelity Assurance focuses employees on goal accomplishment by giving each employee a wallet-size card that "spells out the company's beliefs and goals."[38] As true for American Fidelity employees, however, we often work on multiple goals at once. This highlights the importance of prioritizing your goals so that you effectively allocate your efforts over time.[39]

Goals Regulate Effort   Not only do goals make us selectively perceptive, they also motivate us to act. The instructor's deadline for turning in your term project would prompt you to complete it, as opposed to going out with friends, watching television, or studying for another course. Generally, the level of effort expended is proportionate to the difficulty of the goal.

Siemens, a German engineering conglomerate with over 400,000 employees in 190 countries, has businesses in three sectors—industry, energy, and healthcare. The company's approach to goal setting has contributed to its success.

Goals Increase Persistence   Within the context of goal setting, persistence represents the effort expended on a task over an extended period of time: It takes effort to run 100 meters; it takes persistence to run a 26-mile marathon. Persistent people tend to see obstacles as challenges to be overcome rather than as reasons to fail. A difficult goal that is important to an individual is a constant reminder to keep exerting effort in the appropriate direction. Peter Löscher, CEO of Siemens, wanted to build on the power of persistence by setting goals associated with "green consciousness" and increased wind-energy sales. To do this he hired Peter Solmssen from GE because "the one thing GE does better than anybody is execution," said Solmssen. "They set a target, and they achieve it. That's it." With Solmssen's help, Löscher's new goal-driven approach led to increased wind-energy sales and a 48 percent increase in stock price.[40]

Go to Connect for a video case to view Hot Topic and how goal setting helps employees stay motivated.

www.mcgrawhillconnect.com

Goals Foster the Development and Application of Task Strategies and Action Plans   If you are here and your goal is out there somewhere, you face the problem of getting from here to there. For example, think about the challenge of starting a business. Do you want to earn profits, grow larger, or make the world a better place? To get there, you have to make a tremendous number of decisions and complete a myriad of tasks. Goals can help because they encourage people to develop strategies and action plans that enable them to achieve their goals. A series of studies conducted in South Africa, Zimbabwe, and Namibia found that small businesses were more likely to grow and succeed if their owners engaged in "elaborate and proactive planning."[41] The power of action plans also was used by Chris Liddell, Chief Financial Officer for General Motors, when he successfully executed the company's IPO in 2010 (see the Skills & Best Practices feature on page 187).

LO7.5

Insights from Goal-Setting Research

Research consistently has supported goal setting as a motivational technique. Setting performance goals increases individual, group, and organizational performance. Further, the positive effects of goal setting were found in six other countries or regions: Australia, Canada, the Caribbean, England, West Germany, and Japan. Goal setting works in different cultures. Reviews of the many goal-setting studies conducted over the past few decades have given managers five practical insights:

1. *Specific high goals lead to greater performance.* **Goal specificity** pertains to the quantifiability of a goal. For example, a goal of selling nine cars a month is more specific than telling a salesperson to do his or her best. Results from more than 1,000 studies entailing over 88 different tasks and

Chris Liddell Executed Detailed Plans to Complete GM's IPO

General Motors Co.'s historic IPO was a trial by fire for Chief Financial Officer Chris Liddell. The 52-year-old had to please the automaker's largest shareholder—the U.S. government—while managing a $23.1 billion offering that spanned three continents, 35 underwriting banks and 90 promotional meetings. Mr. Liddell, a top-flight rugby player in his native New Zealand, started planning the initial offering in March [2010]. "One of the disciplines he learned as a rugby player was the level of preparation that you need to accomplish something great," says James B. Lee, Jr., vice chairman of underwriter, J.P. Morgan Chase & Co.

Mr. Liddell told a *Wall Street Journal* reporter that "this thing was planned like a military campaign. Nine months of preparation went into those last two weeks. We knew exactly what we were going to say, how we were going to run the whole demand, book-building process. It was incredibly well executed."

SOURCE: Excerpted from D K Berman and S Terlep, "GM's IPO Point Man: Planning Is All," *The Wall Street Journal,* **December 4–5, 2010, pp B1, B2.**

40,000 people demonstrated that performance was greater when people had specific high goals.[42] It is important to remember what you learned about self-efficacy in Chapter 5 when setting goals for yourself and others. People are more likely to accomplish goals that are perceived as attainable. This means that we should set goals that are challenging, but not impossible.

2. *Feedback enhances the effect of specific, difficult goals.* Feedback plays a key role in all of our lives. For example, consider the role of feedback in bowling. Imagine going to the bowling lanes only to find that someone had hung a sheet from the ceiling to the floor in front of the pins. How likely is it that you would reach your goal score or typical bowling average? Not likely, given your inability to see the pins. Regardless of your goal, you would have to guess where to throw your second ball if you did not get a strike on your first shot. The same principles apply at work.

   Feedback lets people know if they are headed toward their goals or if they are off course and need to redirect their efforts. Goals plus feedback is the recommended approach. Goals inform people about performance standards and expectations so that they can channel their energies accordingly. In turn, feedback provides the information needed to adjust direction, effort, and strategies for goal accomplishment.

3. *Participative goals, assigned goals, and self-set goals are equally effective.* Both managers and researchers are interested in identifying the best way to set goals. Should goals be participatively set, assigned, or set by the employee him- or herself? A summary of goal-setting research indicated that no single approach was consistently more effective than others in increasing performance.[43]

   Managers are advised to use a contingency approach by picking a method that seems best suited for the individual and situation at hand. For example, employees' preferences for participation should be considered. Some employees desire to participate in the process of setting goals, whereas others do not. Employees are also more likely to respond positively to the opportunity to participate in goal setting when they have greater task information, higher levels of experience and training, and greater levels of task involvement. Finally, a participative approach stimulates information exchange, which in turn results in the development of more effective task strategies and higher self-efficacy.[44]

4. *Action planning facilitates goal accomplishment.* An ***action plan* outlines the activities or tasks that need to be accomplished in order to obtain a goal.** They can also include dates associated with completing each task, resources needed, and obstacles that must be overcome. Managers can use action plans as a vehicle to have performance discussions with employees, and employees can use them to monitor progress toward goal achievement. An action plan also serves as a cue to remind us of what we should be working on, which in turn was found to lead to goal-relevant behavior and success. As a case in point, research shows that goal setting and action planning helped college students increase their academic performance.[45] Finally, managers are encouraged to allow employees to develop their own action plans because this autonomy fuels higher goal commitment and a sense of doing meaningful work.[46]

5. *Goal commitment and monetary incentives affect goal-setting outcomes.* ***Goal commitment* is the extent to which an individual is personally committed to achieving a goal.** In general, an individual is expected to persist in attempts to accomplish a goal when he or she is committed to it. Researchers believe that goal commitment moderates the relationship between the difficulty of a goal and performance. That is, difficult goals lead to higher performance only when employees are committed to their goals. Conversely, difficult goals are hypothesized to lead to lower performance when people are not committed to their goals. A meta-analysis of 21 studies supported these predictions.[47] It also is important to note that people are more likely to commit to difficult goals when they have high self-efficacy about successfully accomplishing their goals.

   Like goal setting, the use of monetary incentives to motivate employees is seldom questioned. Unfortunately, research uncovered some negative consequences when goal achievement is linked to individual incentives. Case studies, for example, reveal that pay should not be linked to goal achievement unless (a) performance goals are under the employees' control; (b) goals are quantitative and measurable; and (c) frequent payments are made for performance achievement.[48] Goal-based incentive systems are more likely to produce undesirable effects if these three conditions are not satisfied.

   Moreover, empirical studies demonstrated that goal-based bonus incentives produced higher commitment to easy goals and lower commitment to difficult goals. People were reluctant to commit to difficult goals that were tied to monetary incentives. People with high goal commitment also offered less help to their coworkers when they received goal-based bonus incentives to accomplish difficult individual goals. Individuals also neglected aspects of the job that were not covered in the performance goals.[49] Finally, a recent survey of 227 executives from multiple industries revealed that 51 percent "bent the rules" in order to accomplish goals.[50] These results suggest that blind pursuit of goal accomplishment can foster unethical behavior.

The above discussion underscores some of the dangers of using goal-based incentives, particularly for employees in complex, interdependent jobs requiring cooperation. Managers need to consider the advantages, disadvantages, and dilemmas of goal-based incentives prior to implementation.

Practical Application of Goal Setting

There are three general steps to follow when implementing a goal-setting program. Serious deficiencies in one step cannot make up for strength in the other two. The three steps need to be implemented in a systematic fashion.

Step 1: Set Goals   Amazingly, this common sense first step is not always followed according to two field surveys. A survey of 1,900 managers revealed that nearly 46% of their project teams were not given specific, attainable goals. Another nationwide survey of 6,489 people focused on assessing the quality of the performance appraisal process. Almost 40% said the performance reviews failed to help them do their jobs, and 25 percent indicated that the review did not include setting future performance goals.[51] Let us consider how managers can set goals with their employees or project teams.

Guitar Center is one of the fastest-growing retailers in the United States. At its 218 stores, service as a core value translates into a specific goal—salespeople are expected to answer the phone before the fourth ring. Company executives place calls periodically to make sure the goal is being met. Do you like this approach to monitoring employee performance?

A number of sources can be used as input during this goal-setting stage. Time and motion studies are one source. Goals also may be based on the average past performance of job holders. Third, the employee and his or her manager may set the goal participatively, through give-and-take negotiation. Fourth, goals can be set by conducting external or internal benchmarking. Benchmarking is used when an organization wants to compare its performance or internal work processes to those of other organizations (external benchmarking) or to other internal units, branches, departments, or divisions within the organization (internal benchmarking). For example, a company might set a goal to surpass the customer service levels or profit of a benchmarked competitor. Finally, the overall strategy of a company (e.g., become the lowest-cost producer) may affect the goals set by employees at various levels in the organization.

In accordance with available research evidence, goals should be "SMART," an acronym that stands for specific, measurable, attainable, results oriented, and time bound. Table 7-2 contains a set of guidelines for writing SMART goals. There are two additional recommendations to consider when setting goals. First, for complex tasks, managers should train employees in problem-solving techniques and encourage them to develop a performance action plan.

Second, because of individual differences (recall our discussion in Chapter 5), it may be necessary to establish different goals for employees performing the same job. For example, a study of 103 undergraduate business students revealed that individuals high in conscientiousness had higher motivation, had greater goal commitment, and obtained higher grades than students low in conscientiousness.[52] An individual's goal orientation is another important individual difference to consider when setting goals. Three types of goal orientations are a learning goal orientation, a performance-prove goal orientation and a performance-avoid goal orientation. A team of researchers described the differences and implications for goal setting in the following way:

> People with a high learning goal orientation view skills as malleable. They make efforts not only to achieve current tasks but also to develop the ability to accomplish future tasks. People with a high performance–prove goal orientation tend to focus on performance and try to demonstrate their ability by looking better than others. People with a high performance–avoid goal orientation also focus on performance, but this focus is grounded in trying to avoid negative outcomes.[53]

Although some studies showed that people set higher goals, exerted more effort, had higher self-efficacy, and achieved higher performance when they possessed a learning goal orientation as opposed to either a performance–prove or performance–avoid goal orientation, other research demonstrated a more complex series of relationships.[54] The best we can conclude is that an individual's goal orientation influences the actions that

connect

www.mcgrawhillconnect.com

Go to Connect for an interactive exercise to test your knowledge of how to set effective goals.

TABLE 7–2   Guidelines for Writing SMART Goals

Specific	Goals should be stated in precise rather than vague terms. For example, a goal that provides for 20 hours of technical training for each employee is more specific than stating that a manager should send as many people as possible to training classes. Goals should be quantified when possible.
Measurable	A measurement device is needed to assess the extent to which a goal is accomplished. Goals thus need to be measurable. It also is critical to consider the quality aspect of the goal when establishing measurement criteria. For example, if the goal is to complete a managerial study of methods to increase productivity, one must consider how to measure the quality of this effort. Goals should not be set without considering the interplay between quantity and quality of output.
Attainable	Goals should be realistic, challenging, and attainable. Impossible goals reduce motivation because people do not like to fail. Remember, people have different levels of ability and skill.
Results oriented	Corporate goals should focus on desired end results that support the organization's vision. In turn, an individual's goals should directly support the accomplishment of corporate goals. Activities support the achievement of goals and are outlined in action plans. To focus goals on desired end results, goals should start with the word "to," followed by verbs such as complete, acquire, produce, increase, and decrease. Verbs such as develop, conduct, implement, or monitor imply activities and should not be used in a goal statement.
Time bound	Goals specify target dates for completion.

SOURCE: A J Kinicki, *Performance Management Systems* (Superstition Mt., AZ: Kinicki and Associates, 1992), pp 2–9. Reprinted with permission; all rights reserved.

he or she takes in the pursuit of accomplishing goals in specific situations. In conclusion, managers are encouraged to consider individual differences when setting goals.

Step 2: Promote Goal Commitment   Obtaining goal commitment is important because employees are more motivated to pursue goals they view as reasonable, obtainable, and fair. We recommend involving employees in the goal setting and action planning process in order to foster goal commitment. Why? Because employees are more likely to set personally meaningful goals during this process, and personally meaningful goals foster higher levels of employee engagement in the pursuit of achieving the goals.[55] During the goal setting process it also is important for managers to explain the rationale behind higher level goals (e.g., corporate strategic goals) and to help employees understand how their goals contribute to higher level goals. This creates a line of sight that can boost employee engagement.[56]

Step 3: Provide Support and Feedback   Step 3 calls for providing employees with the necessary support elements or resources to get the job done. This includes ensuring that each employee has the necessary abilities, training, technology/equipment, and information needed to achieve his or her goals. At Verizon Wireless, for example, all training must be explicitly linked to business goals. Not only does this focus ensure that training equips employees to meet goals, but it also provides a basis for measuring whether the training itself is meeting objectives.[57] Finally, as we discuss in detail in Chapter 8, employees should be provided with timely, specific feedback (knowledge of results) on how they are doing.

> **BACK TO THE CHAPTER-OPENING CASE** Assume you were hired by Michelle Rhee to incorporate goal setting into her motivational program. How could goal setting be used to motivate teachers to provide a higher quality learning experience for students? Describe what you would do.

Putting Motivational Theories to Work

Successfully designing and implementing motivational programs is not easy. Managers cannot simply take one of the theories discussed in this book and apply it word for word. Dynamics within organizations interfere with applying motivation theories in "pure" form. According to management scholar Terence Mitchell,

LO7.6

> There are situations and settings that make it exceptionally difficult for a motivational system to work. These circumstances may involve the kinds of jobs or people present, the technology, the presence of a union, and so on. The factors that hinder the application of motivational theory have not been articulated either frequently or systematically.[58]

With Mitchell's cautionary statement in mind, this section uses Figure 6–1 (see page 147 in Chapter 6) to raise issues that need to be addressed before implementing a motivational program. Our intent is not to discuss all relevant considerations but rather to highlight a few important ones.

Assuming a motivational program is being considered to improve productivity, quality, or customer satisfaction, the first issue revolves around the difference between motivation and performance. As shown in Figure 6–1, motivation and performance are not one and the same. Motivation is only one of several factors that influence performance. For example, poor performance may be more a function of outdated or inefficient materials and machinery, not having goals to direct one's attention, a monotonous job, feelings of inequity, a negative work environment characterized by political behavior and conflict, poor supervisory support and coaching, or poor work flow. Motivation cannot completely overcome deficient contextual factors (see Figure 6–1). Managers, therefore, need to carefully consider the causes of poor performance and employee misbehavior. Employee surveys can be used to help determine the contextual causes of low motivation.

Importantly, managers should not ignore the individual inputs identified in Figure 6–1. As discussed in this chapter as well as Chapters 5 and 6, individual differences are an important input that influence motivation and motivated behavior. Managers are advised to develop employees so that they have the ability and job knowledge to effectively perform their jobs. In addition, attempts should be made to nurture positive employee characteristics, such as self-esteem, self-efficacy, positive emotions, need for achievement, and a learning goal orientation.

AIG Implements New Motivation System

American International Group (AIG) is rolling out a plan to revamp how it doles out annual incentive pay to its employees, as the government-controlled insurance giant moves away from retention bonuses that have proved controversial over the past year.

The new initiative, called a "forced distribution" system, is being pushed by Chief Executive Robert Benmosche. Under the plan, thousands of AIG employees will be ranked on a scale of 1 to 4 based on their performance relative to their peers, and their annual variable compensation, which may include bonuses, will be determined by their rank. Individuals ranked in the top 10% will get far more relative to their peers. . . .

Under the plan, only 10% of the ranked employees will get the top "1" ranking and stand to receive much more year-end incentive pay, which could comprise variable salary and bonuses, then those with lower rankings.

About 20% of employees on the scale would be ranked "2," and 50% would be ranked "3." Individuals in these two categories would generally be considered to have performed well or within expectations and would get meaningful incentive pay commensurate with their rankings. A bottom group of 20% would be ranked "4" and receive lower variable pay.

SOURCE: *Excerpted from S Ng and J S Lubin, "AIG Pay Plan: Rank and Rile," The Wall Street Journal, February 11, 2010, pp. C1, C4. Copyright © 2010. Reproduced with permission of Dow Jones & Company, Inc. via Copyright Clearance Center.*

Because motivation is goal directed, the process of developing and setting goals should be consistent with our previous discussion. Moreover, the method used to evaluate performance also needs to be considered. Without a valid performance appraisal system, it is difficult, if not impossible, to accurately distinguish good and poor performers. Managers need to keep in mind that both equity and expectancy theory suggest that employee motivation is squelched by inaccurate performance ratings. Further, it is important for organizations to train their managers to properly assess people. Consider the appraisal and incentive system being implemented by American International Group Inc. (see the Skills & Best Practices feature above).[59] Would you like to be rated on this system? Is it consistent with equity and expectancy theories?

Finally, we end this chapter by noting two key challenges faced by managers as they try to devise motivation programs. First, many managers are stretched in their job duties. They feel pulled in multiple directions and spend far too much time fighting fires instead of proactively focusing on employees' needs. This situation is frustrating and can lead to lower engagement, motivation, and job satisfaction for managers. It still is imperative, however, for managers to find the time, and a positive attitude, to apply to the task of employee motivation. Jack and Suzy Welch commented on this issue and concluded that "no boss is doing his job properly if he's not letting each of his people know where they stand in constructive detail" and delivering "outsize rewards for outsize performance."[60] Second, managers may not know how to motivate people beyond the simple use of monetary rewards. It is important for managers to use a broader or more integrated approach when trying to motivate employees. This approach should consider the various theories and models discussed in this chapter as well as concepts covered in previous chapters. Organizations can help managers by providing them with training and coaching that focuses on how they can improve their ability to "motivate others."

key terms

action plan   188

distributive justice   177

equity sensitivity   175

equity theory   174

expectancy   181

expectancy theory   179

goal   185

goal commitment   188

goal specificity   186

instrumentality   181

interactional justice   177

management by objectives (MBO)   185

negative inequity   175

positive inequity   175

procedural justice   177

valence   182

chapter summary

- *Discuss the role of perceived inequity in employee motivation.* Equity theory is a model of motivation that explains how people strive for fairness and justice in social exchanges. On the job, feelings of inequity revolve around a person's evaluation of whether he or she receives adequate rewards to compensate for his or her contributive inputs. People perform these evaluations by comparing the perceived fairness of their employment exchange with that of relevant others. Perceived inequity creates motivation to restore equity.

- *Describe the practical lessons derived from equity theory.* Equity theory has at least six practical implications. First, managers should pay attention to employees' *perceptions* of what is fair and equitable. It is the employee's view of reality that counts when trying to motivate someone, according to equity theory. Second, managers benefit by allowing employees to participate in making decisions about important work outcomes. Third, employees should be given the opportunity to appeal decisions that affect their welfare. Fourth, managers can promote cooperation and teamwork among group members by treating them equitably. Fifth, employees' perceptions of justice are influenced by the leadership behavior exhibited by their manager. Sixth, managers need to pay attention to the organization's climate for justice because it influences employee attitudes and behavior.

- *Explain Vroom's expectancy theory.* Expectancy theory assumes motivation is determined by one's perceived chances of achieving valued outcomes. Vroom's expectancy model of motivation reveals how effort → performance expectancies and performance → outcome instrumentalities influence the degree of effort expended to achieve desired (positively valent) outcomes.

- *Describe the practical implications of expectancy theory.* Managers are advised to enhance effort → performance expectancies by helping employees accomplish their performance goals. With respect to instrumentalities and valences, managers should attempt to link employee performance and valued rewards. It is important to remember that people do not always value the same rewards.

- *Identify five practical lessons to be learned from goal-setting research.* Specific high goals lead to greater performance. Second, feedback enhances the effect of specific, difficult goals. Third, participative goals, assigned goals, and self-set goals are equally effective. Fourth, action planning facilitates goal accomplishment. Fifth, goal commitment and monetary incentives affect goal-setting outcomes.

- *Specify issues that should be addressed before implementing a motivational program.* Managers need to consider the variety of causes of poor performance and employee misbehavior. Undesirable employee performance and behavior may be due to a host of individual factors (e.g., personality, ability, attitudes) and contextual factors (e.g., organizational culture, job design, and leader behavior). Goals should be SMART. The method used to evaluate performance as well as the link between performance and rewards must be examined and rewards should be equitably distributed. Managers need to find the time and energy to focus on motivating others. It is important to use both financial and nonfinancial rewards.

discussion questions

1. Are there some people who simply can't be motivated at work? Discuss.
2. Could a manager's attempt to treat his or her employees equally lead to perceptions of inequity? Explain.
3. If someone who reported to you at work had a low expectancy for successful performance, what could you do to increase this person's expectancy?
4. Goal-setting research suggests that people should be given difficult goals. How does this prescription mesh with expectancy theory? Explain.
5. How could a professor use equity, expectancy, and goal-setting theory to motivate students?

legal/ethical challenge

A High School Teacher Must Deal with Plagiarizing Students[61]

High school teacher Christine Pelton wasted no time after discovering that nearly a fifth of her biology students had plagiarized their semester projects from the Internet.

She had received her rural Kansas district's backing before when she accused students of cheating, and she expected it again this time after failing the 28 sophomores.

Her principal and superintendent agreed: It was plagiarism, and the students should get a zero for the assignment.

But after parents complained, the Piper School Board ordered her to go easier on the guilty. . . . The board ordered her to give the students partial credit and to decrease the project's value from 50% of the final course grade to 30%.

One of the complaining parents, Theresa Woolley, told the *Kansas City Star* that her daughter did not plagiarize but was not sure how much she needed to rewrite research material.

But Pelton said the course syllabus, which she required students to sign, warned of the consequences of cheating and plagiarism. . . .

What is worse, McCabe said [Donald McCabe is a professor of management at Rutgers University], is that toler-

ance of dishonesty disheartens other students, who have to compete with the cheaters to get into college.

"If they see teachers looking the other way, students feel compelled to participate even though it makes them uncomfortable," McCabe said.

What Would You Do If You Were Christine Pelton?

1. Resign your position in protest over the school board's lack of support. Explain your rationale.
2. Do what the school board ordered. Discuss the impact of this choice on the students who plagiarized and those who did not.
3. Ignore the school board's order and give the failing grades. Explain your rationale.
4. Invent other options. Discuss.

If you're looking for additional study materials, be sure to check out the Online Learning Center at

www.mhhe.com/kinickiob5e

for more information and interactivities that correspond to this chapter.

chapter 8

Improving Performance with Feedback, Rewards, and Positive Reinforcement

After reading the material in this chapter, you should be able to:

LO8.1 Specify the two basic functions of feedback and three sources of feedback.

LO8.2 Define upward feedback and 360-degree feedback, and summarize the general tips for effectively providing and receiving feedback.

LO8.3 Distinguish between extrinsic and intrinsic rewards, and give a job-related example of each.

LO8.4 Summarize the research lessons about pay for performance, and explain why rewards often fail to motivate employees.

LO8.5 State Thorndike's "law of effect" and explain Skinner's distinction between respondent and operant behavior.

LO8.6 Demonstrate your knowledge of positive reinforcement, negative reinforcement, punishment, and extinction, and explain behavior shaping.

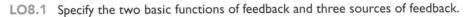

Aligning Performance Management with Strategic Objectives at Sprint

The clarity of Sprint's compensation strategy was dialed up a notch when Chief Executive Officer Dan Hesse took the reins in late 2007. "He did not want any question in our employees' minds about what's important and what we are focused on as a company," explains Stan Sword, vice president of total rewards.

Hesse laid out three pillars for Sprint's strategy: improve the customer experience, strengthen the brand, generate cash and increase profits. The incentive compensation program is designed to support these objectives. Everyone has some pay at risk, ranging from 5% for entry-level employees to roughly 50% and higher

at the vice president level and above. "We have a very strong pay for performance philosophy," Sword asserts. The new twist is the way executives support the incentive program with performance management. In the past year, HR staff has streamlined performance management and trained managers to invest more time coaching employees. "Coaching is what truly moves the performance needle," says Ann Rhoads, vice president of talent management.

Bureaucracy was reduced from the performance management processes by replacing ratings measured on a scale of 1 to 5 with pass–fail ratings of 3 to 5 criteria. Each links to a strategic objective or pillar.

The shift was supported by simplified documentation within a performance management tool. Sprint uses the tool to track metrics, such as what percentage of employees receive coaching as part of their ongoing performance appraisals (the target is 100%). In Sprint's call centers and retail stores—where the majority of roughly 40,000 employees work—performance management technology allows employees to go online and see continual updates of their individual performance objectives and their progress toward those goals. "The move also helped drive home the point that managers need to supply employees with frequent and meaningful feedback on performance through daily interaction and ongoing coaching."

While Sprint's strategic objectives remained constant during the recession, its financial forecasts and targets fluctuated in response to the volatile economy. To ensure that bonus links to performance

remained viable and fair, Sprint abbreviated the performance period from 12 to 6 months. Employees still receive bonus payouts once per year, but bonus is determined based on their achievements during two distinct six-month periods. "The change allows us to be more agile," Sword notes. "If our forecast changes dramatically, as it did during 2008, then we can adjust our performance targets during the second half of the year."

For example, Sprint was the first to introduce a countrywide 4G network, at which time the company tied 10% of bonus pay to 4G subscriber growth in the first half of 2010, before manufacturers of 4G-compatible phones released most of their products. Once competitors'

Dan Hesse, CEO of Sprint, is a firm believer in performance management. Employee pay is clearly linked to strategic objectives and sales of particular phones and products.

4G cell phones hit the market in June, Sprint increased the 4G subscriber growth objective weighting to 20% for the second half of last year. "Weightings may change, and we may calibrate in other ways to increase effectiveness," Sword adds, "but we always work to consistently tie incentive pay to the key pillars of corporate strategy."[1]

THIS FINAL CHAPTER OF PART 2 SERVES as a practical capstone for what we have learned so far in Parts 1 and 2. Our focus here is on improving individual job performance. We need to put to work what we have learned about cultural and individual differences, perception, and motivation. Some organizations apply these principles effectively, as illustrated in the opening case regarding Sprint. Unfortunately, a longitudinal study of more than 500 managers found that hardly any of them provided their employees with daily information about performance requirements, measurable goals, feedback on their work performance, and rewards for achievement.[2]

The popular term these days for doing things the right way is performance management. **Performance management is an organization wide system whereby managers integrate the activities of goal setting, monitoring and evaluating; providing feedback and coaching; and rewarding employees on a continuous basis.**[3] Performance management systems are now utilized around the world. Wayne Cascio, a noted human resource scholar, surveyed 278 companies across 15 countries. He found that approximately 91% of organizations studied implemented a formal performance management system. But despite their popularity, many workers do not perceive the intended benefits of such systems. Only 30% of workers reported that their company's system helped them improve their performance and less than 40% said their systems provided clear goals or generated honest feedback.[4] Performance management systems contrast with the haphazard tradition of annual performance appraisals, a largely unsatisfying experience for everyone involved. In fact, 58% of 576 HR executives surveyed graded their company's performance management systems as a C or worse.[5] OB can shed valuable light on key aspects of performance management: goal setting (discussed in Chapter 7), feedback and coaching, and rewards and positive reinforcement.

As indicated in Figure 8–1, the performance management process needs a life-support system. Like an astronaut drifting in space without the protection and support of a space suit, job performance will not thrive without a support system. First, people with the requisite abilities, skills, and job knowledge need to be hired. Next, training is required to correct any job knowledge shortfalls. The organization's culture (discussed in Chapter 2), job design (discussed in Chapter 6), and supervisory practices also can facilitate or hinder job performance. At the heart of the model in Figure 8–1 are the key aspects of the performance improvement cycle. First, as we saw in Chapter 7, effective goals show employees where to direct their efforts. Next, as we will discuss in this chapter, feedback shows employees when they are succeeding and where they need to improve, while rewards and positive reinforcement give them reasons to continue their efforts.

Providing Effective Feedback

Mike Duke, the CEO of Walmart, is a firm believer in candid feedback. He routinely visits stores and asks employees at all levels for feedback.

Numerous surveys tell us employees have a hearty appetite for feedback. So also do achievement-oriented students. Following a difficult exam, for instance, students want to know two things: how they did and how their peers did. By letting students know how their work measures up to grading and competitive standards, an instructor's feedback permits the students to adjust their study habits so they can reach their goals.[6] Likewise, managers in well-run organizations follow up goal setting with a feedback program to provide a rational basis for adjustment and improvement. For example, notice the importance Mike Duke, the CEO of Walmart, places on goals and feedback when outlining his philosophy of leadership:

Improving Individual Job Performance: A Continuous Process   FIGURE 8–1

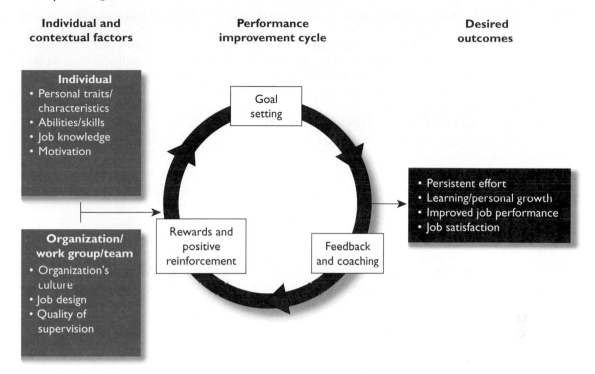

Leadership is about . . . listening and getting feedback from a broad array of constituents. . . . It's about setting aggressive goals and not being afraid to go after very aggressive goals and targets. I think it's even better for a leader to set an aggressive goal and come up a little short than it would be to set a soft goal and to exceed it. . . . Hard feedback is in some environments viewed in a very threatening way, and people don't want to hear feedback. In our environment, I think there is a desire to hear candid feedback. When we leave a meeting, before we'll even drive away, I'll ask, "Well, give me feedback." I think a leader asking for feedback sets a good tone.[7]

www.mcgrawhillconnect.com

Go to Connect for an interactive exercise to test your knowledge on giving effective feedback.

Feedback too often gets shortchanged. In a survey by Watson Wyatt Worldwide, 43% of employees said they "feel they don't get enough guidance to improve their performance." This is reinforced by a survey of 3,611 employees from 291 companies across the United States and Canada. It revealed that 67% of employees felt they received too little positive feedback in general, and 51% too little constructive criticism from their bosses. Worse still, those that said they did not receive enough feedback were 43% less likely to recommend their employer to others![8]

As the term is used here, ***feedback* is information about individual or collective performance shared with those in a position to improve the situation.** Do not confuse feedback as information with the evaluation of performance. Feedback is only information, not an evaluation. Subjective assessments such as, "You're lazy" or "You have a bad attitude" do not qualify as effective feedback. But hard data such as units sold, days absent, dollars saved, projects completed, customers satisfied, and quality rejects are all candidates for effective feedback programs. Christopher D Lee, author of *Performance Conversations: An Alternative to Appraisals,* clarifies the concept of feedback by contrasting it with performance appraisals:

Feedback is the exchange of information about the status and quality of work products. It provides a road map to success. It is used to motivate, support, direct, correct and regulate work efforts and outcomes. Feedback ensures that the manager and employees are in sync and agree on the standards and expectations of the work to be performed. Traditional appraisals, on the other hand, discourage two-way communication and treat employee involvement as a bad thing. Employees are discouraged from participating in a performance review, and when they do, their responses are often considered "rebuttals."[9]

Two Functions of Feedback

Experts say feedback serves two functions for those who receive it: one is *instructional* and the other *motivational*.[10] Feedback instructs when it clarifies roles or teaches new behavior. For example, an assistant accountant might be advised to handle a certain entry as a capital item rather than as an expense item. Feedback motivates when it serves as a reward or promises a reward. Hearing the boss say, "Take the rest of the day off," is a pleasant reward for hard work, but many employees also appreciate the attention and interest expressed by the very act of providing feedback, whatever its content.

Chapter 7 documented the motivational function of feedback by concluding that "feedback enhances the effect of specific, difficult goals."[11] A laboratory study with college students divided into superior-subordinate pairs demonstrated not only the positive impact of helpful feedback on performance, but a dampening effect on perceived organizational politics as well.[12] As discussed in Chapter 13, organizational politics are often dysfunctional.

LO8.1 Three Sources of Feedback: Others, Task, and Self

It almost goes without saying that employees receive objective feedback from *others* such as peers, supervisors, lower-level employees, and outsiders. Perhaps less obvious is the fact that the *task* itself is a ready source of objective feedback.[13] Skilled tasks such as computer programming, landing a jet airplane, or driving a golf ball provide a steady stream of feedback about how well or poorly one is doing. A third source of feedback is *oneself,* but self-serving bias and other perceptual problems can contaminate this source (discussed in Chapter 4). Those high in self-confidence tend to rely on personal feedback more than those with low self-confidence. This challenge increases as one moves up the organizational hierarchy because it is more difficult to get useful feedback from others. Nobody likes to give the boss negative feedback. This problem is compounded by the fact that task feedback is less feasible for senior managers because their day-to-day activities are more abstract than frontline employees (e.g., formulating strategy versus closing a sale).

So what can an executive or (high-level) manager do? John Baldoni, a leadership development consultant and author of *Lead Your Boss: The Subtle Art of Managing Up,* has the following suggestions. First, they can seek feedback from others by creating an environment in which employees feel they can be honest and open. Second, separating feedback from the performance review process also helps, especially for executives who typically are not reviewed formally if at all. Third is to create a mechanism to collect feedback anonymously. This is useful if the source of the feedback is not particularly important. For example, a CEO based at headquarters in Phoenix is curious how she is perceived by the design team in Shanghai. In this instance she doesn't need to know the views of any specific employee, just the views of employees from that location.[14]

HANDS-ON EXERCISE

Measuring Your Desire for Performance Feedback

INSTRUCTIONS: Circle one number indicating the strength of your agreement or disagreement with each statement. Total your responses, and compare your score with the arbitrary norms listed below.

		Disagree				Agree
1.	As long as I think that I have done something well, I am not too concerned about how other people think I have done.	5	4	3	2	1
2.	How other people view my work is not as important as how I view my own work.	5	4	3	2	1
3.	It is usually better not to put much faith in what others say about your work, regardless of whether it is complimentary or not.	5	4	3	2	1
4.	If I have done something well, I know it without other people telling me so.	5	4	3	2	1
5.	I usually have a clear idea of what I am trying to do and how well I am proceeding toward my goal.	5	4	3	2	1
6	I find that I am usually a pretty good judge of my own performance.	5	4	3	2	1
7.	It is very important to me to know what people think of my work.	1	2	3	4	5
8.	It is a good idea to get someone to check on your work before it's too late to make changes.	1	2	3	4	5
9.	Even though I may think I have done a good job, I feel a lot more confident of it after someone else tells me so.	1	2	3	4	5
10.	Since I cannot be objective about my own performance, it is best to listen to the feedback provided by others.	1	2	3	4	5

Total score = _____

ARBITRARY NORMS

10–23 = Low desire for feedback
24–36 = Moderate desire for feedback
37–50 = High desire for feedback

SOURCE: Excerpted and adapted from D M Herold, C K Parsons, and R B Rensvold, "Individual Differences in the Generation and Processing of Performance Feedback," *Educational and Psychological Measurement*, February 1996, Table 1, p. 9, Copyright © 1996. Reproduced with permission of Sage Publications, Inc. via Copyright Clearance Center.

Although circumstances vary, an employee can be bombarded by feedback from all three sources simultaneously. This is where the gate-keeping functions of perception and cognitive evaluation are needed to help sort things out.

The Recipient's Perception of Feedback

The need for feedback is variable, across both individuals and situations (see Hands-On Exercise to assess your desire for feedback). Remember, feedback itself is simply information, neither positive nor negative. It only becomes positive or negative when it is compared to a goal, standard, or expectation. This comparison provides the basis for improvement. Generally, people tend to perceive and recall positive feedback more accurately than they do negative feedback.[15] But negative feedback (e.g., being told your performance is below average) can have a *positive* motivational effect. In fact, in one study, those who were told they were below average on a creativity test subsequently outperformed those who were led to believe their results were above average. The subjects apparently took the negative feedback as a challenge and set and pursued higher goals. Those receiving positive feedback apparently were less motivated to do better.[16] Nonetheless, feedback with a negative message or threatening content needs to be administered carefully to avoid creating insecurity and defensiveness. Self-efficacy also can be damaged by negative feedback, as discovered in a pair of experiments with business students. The researchers concluded, "To facilitate the development of strong efficacy beliefs, managers should be careful about the provision of negative feedback. Destructive criticism by managers which attributes the cause of poor performance to internal factors reduces both the beliefs of self-efficacy and the self-set goals of recipients." One therefore needs to be careful when delivering feedback, due to the effect feedback on self-efficacy and goals.[17]

Upon receiving feedback, people cognitively evaluate factors such as its accuracy, the credibility of the source, the fairness of the system (e.g., performance appraisal system), their performance-reward expectancies, and the reasonableness of the standards. Any feedback that fails to clear one or more of these cognitive hurdles will be rejected or downplayed. Personal experience largely dictates how these factors are weighed. For example, a review of research on disciplinary practices found that people have different perceptions of a disciplinary act based on the sex of the person delivering the discipline, the cultural characteristics of the people involved, and the supervisor's use of apologies and explanations.[18] Given these differences in perception, we recommend that the supervisor utilize two-way communication, follow up with the employee to make sure the discipline was understood, use apologies or empathy to lessen the employee's anger, and focus on an objective of helping the employee in the long run.

Behavioral Outcomes of Feedback

In Chapter 7, we discussed how goal setting gives behavior direction, increases effort, and fosters persistence. Because feedback is intimately related to the goal-setting process, it involves the same behavioral outcomes: direction, effort, and persistence. However, while the fourth outcome of goal setting involves formulating goal-attainment strategies, the fourth possible outcome of feedback is *resistance* (resistance is discussed in detail in Chapter 13). Feedback schemes that smack of manipulation or fail one or more of the perceptual and cognitive evaluation tests mentioned previously breed resistance.[19] Evaluative feedback also tends to create defensiveness and resistance because it is perceived as an attack. Feedback is more likely to be accepted when it is positive, specific, timely, and given by a credible source.[20]

LO8.2   Upward and 360-Degree Feedback

Traditional top-down feedback programs have given way to some interesting variations in recent years. Two newer approaches, discussed in this section, are upward feedback and 360-degree feedback. Aside from breaking away from a strict superior-to-subordinate feedback approach, these newer approaches are different because they

SKILLS & BEST PRACTICES

Responding to a Bad Performance Review

Performance reviews include a reviewer and a reviewee. Both roles are important. However, if you're the reviewee you typically have little control over the content of the message or how it is delivered. But you can control how you respond. And how you respond can make a world of difference in both the short and long run. The following advice should help:

1. *Don't get defensive.* Resist the urge! Keep an open mind and listen to the points that are highlighted in the review. It also is helpful to note the positives instead of fixating only on the negatives.

2. *Don't discuss the review with coworkers.* Don't vent to your coworkers. The news of a bad performance for review often travels like wildfire through the organization. And as you learned in Chapter 4, the message can and often does morph as it travels. Accurate, negative information can be painful enough, and nobody needs the additional pain of accurate or distorted negative information.

3. *Develop an action plan.* Instead of wallowing in misery, make a plan of how to respond and improve. You may also want to set a follow-up appointment with your boss and enlist his or her help in formulating your plan. Then, follow up to be sure you are on track and making progress.

4. *Make sure you understand the review.* Be sure to clarify, especially if the bad news is a surprise. Misunderstandings and miscommunication are common. It thus is important to remedy these disconnects so that both parties are clear.

5. *Don't take it personally.* Much easier said than done! Regardless of how the feedback is delivered, you can reframe it in terms of your performance rather than you as a person. After all, your action plan will focus on behaviors, not your personality or other fixed traits.

SOURCE: Adapted from J A Johnson, "Bad Performance Review? Don't Lose Your Cool," *Arizona Republic*, August 22, 2010.

typically involve *multiple sources* of feedback.[21] Instead of getting feedback from one boss, often during an annual performance appraisal, more and more managers are getting structured feedback from superiors, lower-level employees, peers, and even outsiders such as customers. Nontraditional feedback is growing in popularity for at least six reasons:

1. Traditional performance appraisal systems have created widespread dissatisfaction. This was clearly evident in a survey of 96 human resource managers: Sixty one percent said managers have not been trained on how to properly assess people; 40 percent say the competencies managers are using to assess their employees do not accurately reflect the job, and 28 percent report that managers play favorites.[22]

2. Team-based organization structures are replacing traditional hierarchies. This trend requires managers to have good interpersonal skills that are best evaluated by team members.

3. Multiple-rater systems are said to make feedback more valid than single-source feedback.[23]

4. Advanced computer network technology (the Internet and company intranets) greatly facilitates multiple-rater systems.[24]

5. Bottom-up feedback meshes nicely with the trend toward participative management and employee empowerment.

6. Coworkers and lower-level employees are said to know more about a manager's strengths and limitations than the boss.[25]

Together, these factors make a compelling case for looking at better ways to give and receive performance feedback. See the Skills & Best Practices feature on page 203 for suggestions on how to respond to negative feedback or a poor review.

Upward Feedback   *Upward feedback* **stands the traditional approach on its head by having lower-level employees provide feedback on a manager's style and performance.** This type of feedback is generally anonymous. Most students are familiar with upward feedback programs from years of filling out anonymous teacher evaluation surveys. In the workplace, however, managers often resist upward feedback programs because they believe it erodes their authority. Other critics say anonymous upward feedback can become little more than a personality contest or, worse, be manipulated by managers who make promises or threats. What does the research literature tell us about upward feedback?

Studies with diverse samples have given us these useful insights:

- The question of whether upward feedback should be *anonymous* was addressed by a study at a large U.S. insurance company. All told, 183 employees rated the skills and effectiveness of 38 managers. Managers who received anonymous upward feedback received *lower* ratings and liked the process *less* than did those receiving feedback from identifiable employees. This finding confirmed the criticism that employees will tend to go easier on their boss when not protected by confidentiality.[26]

- A large-scale study at the U.S. Naval Academy, where student leaders and followers live together day and night, discovered a positive impact of upward feedback on leader behavior.[27]

- In a field study of 238 corporate managers, upward feedback had a positive impact on the performance of low-to-moderate performers.[28]

See the Skills & Best Practices feature on page 205 for guidance on providing upward feedback.

360-Degree Feedback   **Letting individuals compare their own perceived performance with behaviorally specific (and usually anonymous) performance information from their manager, subordinates, and peers is known as** *360-degree feedback.* Even outsiders may be involved in what is sometimes called full-circle feedback. The idea is to let individuals know how their behavior affects others, with the goal of guiding and motivating change. For example, HCL Technologies, one of India's three largest IT services companies, implements a 360-feedback program for the CEO, Vineet Nayar, and 3,800 managers. The CEO's reviews are transparent, posted on the company's internal Web for all 50,000 employees to see. The managers' results are posted too, so raters can see others' views. Mr Nayar describes this as "reverse accountability," wherein managers are accountable to employees, opposite of the business norm.[29]

Top-management support and an organizational climate of openness can help 360-degree feedback programs succeed. A good example was provided by Bob Brennan, the CEO of Iron Mountain, an information management company. Here is what he said to an interviewer from *The New York Times:*

How Can I Know if You Don't Tell Me?

Managers and leaders who simply rely on the chain of command are unlikely to receive honest and useful feedback. A subordinate's input is essential to help managers understand how they are perceived by others and to make adjustments if needed. This matters because such perceptions can either facilitate or impede his or her ability to influence others (i.e., lead). However, delivering upward feedback needs to be done with care. The following suggestions can help.

- *Nature of the relationship.* If your relationship is positive and you know your boss is open to your input, then it is in everybody's best interests to share your insights. Be developmental, but straight and accurate. However, if you have a rocky relationship or you know your boss is close-minded to input, then don't bother. Your input will likely cause only pain without any gain.

- *An invitation helps.* It is obviously best if your boss solicits feedback. Unfortunately, this is relatively rare. You thus are often in the position of having to solicit an invitation to provide feedback. You can simply ask, "Would you like some feedback?" Or, you can look for opportunities where you introduce your boss to a new client or start a new project. In these scenarios you can open with: "Given my relationship with this client, it is probably best for everybody if I provide you some feedback or guidance before this meeting. Are you interested?" Or, "Given my involvement with this project, would you like some feedback about how it is going?" Again, be developmental versus critical. Don't sugarcoat but don't use vinegar, either.

- *Speak from your shoes—not your boss's shoes.* Simply describe what you observe and hear from others, rather than telling your boss what you would do if you had her job. You *don't* have her job and oftentimes are unaware of pertinent information and demands.

- *Don't get bit.* It is common for people to get defensive when receiving negative feedback. Your boss is no different. It therefore is important that you frame your feedback in a developmental fashion. It also can help to frame it in terms of his or her goals. You can say, "I'm sharing this to help you meet your personal goals of being an effective manager and the goals of the team/department."

- *When in doubt, keep quiet.* Your boss typically has a boss, and hopefully that person will do his or her job and provide the necessary feedback. Alternatively, time may present an opportunity that is more appropriate. Don't force feedback on your boss.

    Obviously, many of these suggestions apply to most any feedback: up, down, or sideways.

    SOURCE: Adapted from A Gallo, "How to Give Your Boss Feedback," *Harvard Business Review*, March 24, 2010.

It's important for us to establish a framework that says, "Here's how we want to behave." For instance, you need to seek constructive feedback on your performance from the people who report to you. We're not talking about 360 reviews once a year. It should be a constant dialogue and one-on-ones about 'How can I improve my game?' If I'm not seeking that feedback, I'm creating an unsafe environment for you." (Interviewer: Unsafe? That's a strong word.) "It is, in fact, unsafe, if I'm reviewing your work, but I'm not asking you to collaborate with me in review[ing] mine. That would presume that I'm fine with the way I'm performing, yet I've been sitting here offering constructive or destructive feedback on your performance. There is no symmetry to the conversation. Does that feel safe to you? I don't think that's safe."[30]

www.mcgrawhillconnect.com

Go to Connect for a self-assessment to determine how strong your desire for performance feedback is.

Practical Recommendations Research evidence on upward and 360-degree feedback leads us to *favor* anonymity and *discourage* use for pay and promotion decisions.

Otherwise, managerial resistance and self-serving manipulation might prevail.[31] We enthusiastically endorse the use of upward and/or 360-degree feedback for management development and training purposes.

Feedback Do's and Don'ts

According to Annie Stevens and Greg Gostanian, managing partners at ClearRock, an outplacement and executive coaching firm, "Giving feedback to employees—and receiving feedback yourself—is one of the most misunderstood and poorly executed human resource processes."[32] Experts have identified the following set of do's and don'ts for giving feedback.

Do not:

1. Use feedback to punish, embarrass, or put down employees.
2. Provide feedback that is irrelevant to the person's work.
3. Provide feedback that is too late to do any good.
4. Provide feedback about something that is beyond the individual's control.
5. Provide feedback that is overly complex or difficult to understand.[33]

Do:

1. Keep feedback relevant by relating it to existing goals.
2. Deliver feedback as soon as possible to the time the behavior was displayed.
3. Provide specific and descriptive feedback. For example, it is better to say, "Gupta, your report had 10 spelling errors and was submitted two days late," than to say "Gupta, your work was terrible."
4. Focus the feedback on things employees can control.
5. Be honest, developmental, and constructive. Remember, people like to succeed at work and negative information can be deflating.
6. Facilitate two-way communication—give the other person the opportunity to clarify and respond.[34]

> **BACK TO THE CHAPTER-OPENING CASE**   Sprint's performance management system emphasizes management feedback. Assume you work for a consulting company hired to train Sprint's managers on how to provide effective feedback. Describe the content and methods of the training.

Organizational Reward Systems

As illustrated in Figure 8–1, rewards are a critical component of a performance improvement cycle. And just as any particular motivational approach affects people differently (as you learned in Chapters 6 and 7), so do rewards. Some employees see their job as the source of a paycheck and little else. Others derive great pleasure from their job and association with coworkers. Even volunteers who donate

Key Factors in Organizational Reward Systems   FIGURE 8–2

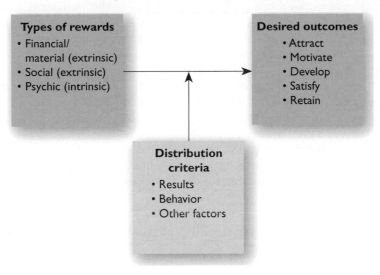

www.mcgrawhillconnect.com

Go to Connect for an interactive exercise to test your knowledge of effective reward systems.

their time to charitable organizations, such as the Red Cross, walk away with rewards in the form of social recognition and the pride of having given unselfishly of their time. Hence, the subject of organizational rewards includes, but goes far beyond, monetary compensation. This section examines key components of organizational reward systems.

Despite the fact that reward systems vary widely, it is possible to identify and interrelate some common components. The model in Figure 8–2 focuses on three important components: (1) types of rewards, (2) distribution criteria, and (3) desired outcomes. Let us examine these components and then discuss pay for performance.

Types of Rewards

LO8.3

Including the usual paycheck, the variety and magnitude of organizational rewards has evolved into a mind-boggling array—from subsidized day care to college tuition reimbursement to stock grants and options.[35] In fact, today it is common for non-wage benefits to be 50% or more of total compensation. A recent report by the Society for Human Resource Management describes the current and broader perspective on rewards. The phrase "compensation and benefits" has given way to "total rewards." ***Total rewards* encompass not only compensation and benefits, but also personal and professional growth opportunities and a motivating work environment that includes recognition, job design (Chapter 6), and work–life balance.** A total rewards perspective therefore includes:

- Compensation—base pay, merit pay, incentives, promotions, and pay increases
- Benefits   health and welfare, paid time off, and retirement
- Personal growth—training, career development, and performance management[36]

This broader view of rewards is due in part to stiffer competition and challenging economic conditions, which have made it difficult for cost-conscious organizations to offer higher wages and more benefits each year. Employers have had to find alternative forms of rewards that cost less but still motivate employees to excel.

Total rewards are a powerful means for aligning organizational goals with employees' personal and work-related goals. Using rewards in this manner is a method for developing human capital (recall our discussion in Chapter 1) and creating a competitive advantage for talent and profits. Total rewards are therefore an integral part of an effective performance management system. It is one that requires leaders and managers to explicitly consider and actively engage in performance management leadership and employee development. As reviewed in Chapter 7, the effective use of rewards is a critical component to enhancing employee motivation. Let us now consider the types of rewards managers have at their disposal.

Extrinsic and Intrinsic Rewards   Another way to classify and understand rewards is the distinction between extrinsic and intrinsic forms. **Financial, material, and social rewards qualify as *extrinsic rewards* because they come from the environment. Psychic rewards, however, are *intrinsic rewards* because they are self-granted.** An employee who works to obtain extrinsic rewards, such as money or praise, is said to be extrinsically motivated. As we discussed in Chapter 6, one who derives pleasure from the task itself, feels their work is meaningful, or has a sense of responsibility will likely become engaged with his or her work: Employee engagement is fueled by intrinsic motivation. The relative importance of extrinsic and intrinsic rewards is a matter of culture, personal preferences, and pressing circumstances.

The developed economies of the world have a long, deeply entrenched cultural emphasis on extrinsic rewards, most notably money and promotions. This is despite the common knowledge that people work and derive satisfaction from many things besides money and titles. For example, a review of 25 studies showed that compensation and benefits were associated with nurse retention rates in Europe, Australia, and the United States. However, the same review showed that intrinsic elements were also critically important, such as feeling valued by their managers, increased autonomy (covered in Chapter 6), and opportunities for continued learning and development.[37] And although it might seem hard to find intrinsic benefits in running a retailer during an economic slowdown, Carol Tomé, chief financial officer of the Home Depot, told a reporter that she has gained satisfaction from working to turn around that company because she is "passionate about finding out what we can be best at."[38]

Alternatives to Money and Promotions   The recent Great Recession has had extreme effects on (extrinsic) rewards: salary freezes, reduced or eliminated bonuses, suspended 401k contributions, and even salary and benefit cuts. Many feared that such cuts would have negative effects on employee motivation and engagement. This predicament forced managers and companies to get more creative and consider the concept of "total rewards." The recent WorldatWork survey revealed some interesting if not encouraging findings:

- Base pay and benefits had a weaker relationship with the organization's ability to foster high levels of employee engagement and motivation compared to nonfinancial incentives, intangible rewards, and quality of leadership.

- "Quality of work, career development, organization climate and work–life balance all have a greater perceived impact on employee engagement than financial rewards such as base salaries, benefits and monetary incentives," said Tom McMullen, North American practice leader for the Hay Group consulting firm, a partner in the study.

- "Quality of leadership has a profound impact on employee engagement motivation," added Paul Rowson, managing director at WorldatWork. "Organizations must think in terms of total rewards and not just financial rewards if they are to enhance employee involvement, commitment, job satisfaction—and performance."[39]

Another recent study involving 320 organizations across the United States and Canada, conducted by Mercer, a large international human resources consulting company, supported the use of total rewards. It showed that companies dramatically increased their use of noncash rewards, such as communicating the value of total rewards to employees, implementing work–life programs, detailing formalized career paths, and providing special project opportunities.[40]

Results from the WorldatWork and Mercer surveys are helpful. These studies also revealed the importance of employee involvement and voice in reward systems. Recall our discussion of motivation and procedural justice in Chapter 7. Involving employees in the design, selection, and assessment of rewards programs increases the chance that the rewards provided will be perceived as fair and valuable. (Valuable rewards are valent outcomes in expectancy theory from Chapter 7.) Involvement also fosters employee engagement—discussed in Chapter 6—as it makes them feel valued. The WorldatWork survey further showed that only 11% of respondents said their companies involved employees in the design of reward programs,[41] which means that 89% of companies do not involve employees. This may present you and your current or future employers with an opportunity: Involving employees is one way to get ahead of the competition. Doing so may provide managers and employers a bigger bang for their reward bucks!

Distribution Criteria

According to one expert on organizational reward systems, three general criteria for the distribution of rewards are as follows:

- *Performance: results.* Tangible outcomes such as individual, group, or organizational performance; quantity; and quality.
- *Performance: actions and behaviors.* Such as teamwork, cooperation, risk taking, and creativity.
- *Nonperformance considerations.* Customary or contractual, where the type of job, nature of the work, equity, tenure, level in hierarchy, etc., are rewarded.[42]

The trend today is toward *performance* criteria and away from nonperformance criteria. We turn our attention to pay for performance after completing our discussion of the reward systems model in Figure 8–2.

Desired Outcomes

As listed in Figure 8–2, a good reward system should attract talented people and motivate and satisfy them once they have joined the organization.[43] Further, it should foster personal growth and development and keep talented people from leaving. Let us consider how pay for performance programs accomplish these objectives.

For Urban Outfitters, the trendy clothing chain, everyone is expected to help with trend spotting, and they're well rewarded. Employees from managers to interns who bring back news of hot trends and styles to the buyers and design teams receive free concert tickets and evenings out, courtesy of the company. The chain won't give away exactly who it's spying on.

LO8.4

Making Pay for Performance Work

A study by Sibson Consulting that included interviews in 27 organizations and surveys of another 138 revealed that those with the best pay for performance results:

- Paid top performers substantially higher than the other employees
- Reduced "gaming" of the system by increasing transparency
- Utilized multiple measures of performance
- Calibrated performance measures to assure accuracy and consistency

Jim Kochanski, senior vice president at Sibson, also noted that besides a well-designed pay for performance system, a company culture must be supportive of such practices. And leadership support is considered the most important contributor to such a culture. Organizations with ineffective pay for performance programs tend to blame limited compensation budgets as the cause. This is often an excuse by managers who want to avoid confronting mediocre performers with low salary increases. "Though they may also have limited compensation dollars due to budget constraints or market trends, the best pay for performance organizations often carve out funds for extra rewards to high performers and tend to see fewer employees whose performance is rated as high," added Myrna Hellerman, another senior vice president at Sibson.

SOURCE: Excerpted and adapted from S Miller, "Study: Keys to Effective Performance Pay," *Society for Human Resource Management,* December 15, 2010.

Pay for Performance

Pay for performance **is the popular term for monetary incentives linking at least some portion of the paycheck directly to results or accomplishments.** It is compensation above and beyond basic wages and salary, and its use is consistent with recommendations derived from the expectancy theory of motivation discussed in the previous chapter. Many refer to it simply as *incentive or variable pay.* The general idea behind pay-for-performance schemes—including but not limited to merit pay, bonuses, and profit sharing—is to give employees an incentive for working harder or smarter. Proponents of incentive compensation say something extra is needed, because hourly wages and fixed salaries do little more than motivate people to show up at work and put in the required hours.[44] The most basic form of pay for performance is the traditional piece-rate plan, whereby the employee is paid a specified amount of money for each unit of work. Sales commissions, whereby a salesperson receives a specified amount of money for each unit sold, are another long-standing example of pay for performance.

Nutrisystem, the weight loss program, provides a skillful and creative example of how to meet multiple organizational objectives via pay-for-performance. The company's plan aims to increase sales, staff particular working hours, and expand the customer base. Its call-center sales associates are paid the greater of either an hourly rate ($10 an hour for the first 40 hours per week, $15 an hour for any additional hours), or a flat rate payment based on sales. Unlike conventional commissions, the flat-rate is not tied to the sales price of the product. Instead, the payments vary depending on the shift during which the sale occurs and whether the sale resulted from an incoming or outgoing call. Higher payments are made for outgoing calls and for sales during off-peak times. This system incentivizes employees to work less desirable hours and to make outgoing calls. It also allows the company to avoid overtime payments while at the same time rewarding the desired employee behaviors.[45] This example underscores the evolution and increasingly common practice of using performance versus nonperformance criteria in reward systems.

It is worth noting that the trend toward using specific *performance* criteria was well underway when the recent financial crisis occurred. This trend has grown as companies, regulators, and legislators consider distribution criteria and pay for performance even more carefully than before. Much of this attention is an attempt to avoid excessive risk taking by senior leaders, which was a central cause of the financial meltdown. The problem was that executives and other employees (e.g., traders) were paid based only on short-term gains. They had no consequences (risk) for the mid- and long-term performance of the financial product (e.g., a mortgage or mortgage backed security) or their company's stock. In effect, performance didn't matter. If the mortgage ultimately defaulted or the stock tanked everybody had already been paid. Now, however, changes are being made to tie portions of compensation (bonuses and stock) to performance over time.[46] (The Ethical Challenge at the end of this chapter provides additional insights into this problem.)

Research results show mixed outcomes from pay for performance. In an experiment with college students, paying for performance resulted in greater productivity than paying a fixed amount for completing the task.[47] Not only did the subjects put forth more effort under the pay-for-performance scheme, but higher-performing individuals also tended to opt for performance-based pay. These results suggest that companies can improve productivity by offering pay for performance, which should help them attract workers with the best skills. However, in another study, incentive pay had a *negative* effect on the performance of 150,000 managers from 500 financially distressed companies.[48] A meta-analysis of 39 studies found only a modest positive correlation between financial incentives and performance *quantity* and no impact on performance *quality*.[49] Other researchers have found only a weak statistical link between large executive bonuses paid out in good years and subsequent improvement in corporate profitability.[50] Clearly, the pay-for-performance area is still very much up in the air. However more recent research offers some helpful insights. See the Skills & Best Practices feature on page 212.

Why Rewards Often Fail to Motivate

Despite huge investments of time and money for organizational reward systems, the desired motivational effect often is not achieved. A management consultant/writer recently offered these eight reasons:

1. Too much emphasis on monetary rewards.

2. Rewards lack an "appreciation effect."

3. Extensive benefits become entitlements.

4. Types of counterproductive behavior discussed in Chapter 6 are rewarded. For example: In one case, city officials in Albuquerque, New Mexico, decided to pay trash truck crews for eight hours of work, no matter how long it actually took them to finish their routes. They wanted this move to encourage workers to finish the job quickly and thus lower the city's overtime expenses. Instead, the crews began to cut corners. They missed pickups, resulting in numerous complaints from customers. Some drove too fast and caused accidents. Others incurred fines for driving to the dump with overloaded trucks.[51]

5. Too long a delay between performance and rewards.

6. Too many one-size-fits-all rewards.

7. Use of one-shot rewards with a short-lived motivational impact.

Best Practices for Recognition and Rewards

Companies that deliver superior financial results, not coincidentally, are also top performers in the area of employee engagement. Rewards and recognition are key components of employee engagement. The best practices followed by companies that place a premium on rewards and recognition can be boiled down to the five Cs:

- *Consistency.* Program objectives are measurable, attainable, and aligned with the company's core values. Recognition opportunities and processes are consistent and fair across the organization.
- *Control.* The organization knows who was recognized, why they were recognized, and how much they earned. A systematic tracking and reporting system is in place.
- *Communication.* Expectations are clear, and employees receive timely, personal feedback and reinforcement. Managers understand why and how to recognize.
- *Choice.* Employees receive meaningful recognition and awards that they want, plus flexibility to satisfy near-term desires or invest in long-term goals.
- *Commitment.* Management "walks the talk" by making employee reward and recognition a priority, and by providing adequate funding.

SOURCE: Excerpted from T Gentry and K Glotzbach, "Incentives without Borders," *HR Magazine*, 2007 Special Advertising Supplement, pp 77–82.

8. Continued use of demotivating practices such as layoffs, across-the-board raises and cuts, and excessive executive compensation.[52]

Clearly, effective reward and compensation practices are major and consequential challenges. The research and recommendations provided here should help you both understand and manage these challenges better. The Skills & Best Practices feature above provides additional insights.

> **BACK TO THE CHAPTER-OPENING CASE** Again, assume you work for a consulting company hired by Sprint. But in addition to feedback training, you are asked to revamp their rewards system. Using Figure 8–2 describe your recommendations. Be sure to include types of rewards, distribution criteria, and outcomes.

Principles of Reinforcement

Figure 8–1 shows that the use of rewards and positive reinforcement is the last stage of the performance management process. Unfortunately, many managers can't seem to get it right. Consider these scenarios:

- A young programmer stops emailing creative suggestions to his boss because she never responds.
- The office politician gets a great promotion while her more skilled coworkers scratch their heads and gossip about the injustice.

In the first instance, a productive behavior faded away for lack of encouragement. In the second situation, unproductive behavior was unwittingly rewarded. Feedback and rewards need to be handled more precisely. Fortunately, the field of behavioral psychology can help. Thanks to the pioneering work of Edward L Thorndike, B F Skinner, and many others, behavior modification and *reinforcement* techniques help managers achieve needed discipline and desired effect when providing feedback and granting rewards.[53]

Thorndike's Law of Effect

LO8.5

During the early 1900s, psychologist Edward L Thorndike observed in his lab that a cat would behave randomly and wildly when placed in a small box with a secret trip lever that opened a door. However, once the cat accidentally tripped the lever and escaped, the animal would go straight to the lever when placed back in the box. Hence, Thorndike formulated his famous *law of effect*, **which says** *behavior with favorable consequences tends to be repeated, while behavior with unfavorable consequences tends to disappear.*[54] This was a dramatic departure from the prevailing notion a century ago that behavior was the product of inborn instincts.

Skinner's Operant Conditioning Model

Skinner refined Thorndike's conclusion that behavior is controlled by its consequences. Skinner's work became known as *behaviorism* because he dealt strictly with observable behavior.[55] As a behaviorist, Skinner believed it was pointless to explain behavior in terms of unobservable inner states such as needs, drives, attitudes, or thought processes.[56] He similarly put little stock in the idea of self-determination.

In his 1938 classic, *The Behavior of Organisms,* Skinner drew an important distinction between two types of behavior: respondent and operant behavior.[57] **He labeled unlearned reflexes or stimulus–response (S–R) connections** *respondent behavior*. This category of behavior was said to describe a very small proportion of adult human behavior, such as shedding tears while peeling onions and reflexively withdrawing one's hand from a hot stove.[58] **Skinner attached the label** *operant behavior* **to behavior that is learned when one "operates on" the environment to produce desired consequences.** Some call this the response–stimulus (R–S) model. Years of controlled experiments with pigeons in "Skinner boxes" helped Skinner develop a sophisticated technology of behavior control, or operant conditioning. For example, he taught pigeons how to pace figure eights and how to bowl by reinforcing the underweight (and thus hungry) birds with food whenever they more closely approximated target behaviors. Skinner's work has significant implications for OB because the vast majority of organizational behavior falls into the operant category.[59]

CRAIG SWANSON © WWW.PERSPICUITY.COM

When clearly linked, consequences powerfully affect the behavior of both humans and animals.

Contingent Consequences

Contingent consequences, according to Skinner's operant theory, control behavior in four ways: positive reinforcement, negative reinforcement, punishment, and extinction.[60] The term *contingent* means there is a systematic if-then linkage between the target behavior and the consequence. This represents an instrumentality according to expectancy theory. It therefore is helpful to first think of the target behavior, and then think of the consequence you will provide when applying contingent consequences (see Figure 8–3).

LO8.6

Increase Desired Behaviors with Positive and Negative Reinforcement
Positive reinforcement **is the process of strengthening a behavior by contingently presenting something pleasing.** (Importantly, a behavior is strengthened when it increases in frequency and weakened when it decreases in frequency.) For instance, in the wake of the BP oil spill in 2010, newly appointed CEO Bob Dudley made 100% of variable pay (bonuses) based on safety for the fourth quarter of 2010.[61]

Negative reinforcement **also strengthens a desired behavior by contingently withdrawing something displeasing.** For example, an army sergeant who stops yelling when a recruit jumps out of bed has negatively reinforced that particular behavior. The desired behavior is getting up on time. The displeasing consequence removed is yelling. Similarly, many probationary periods for new hires are applications of negative reinforcement. During probation periods (often your first 30, 60, or 90 days on the job) you need to have weekly meetings with your boss or have somebody sign-off on your work. Once you've demonstrated your skill these requirements are removed.

Unfortunately, the vast majority of people confuse negative reinforcement with negative feedback, which is a form of punishment. They are indeed different and have opposite effects on behavior. Negative reinforcement, as the word *reinforcement* indicates, strengthens a behavior because it provides relief from something undesirable (e.g., paperwork, meetings, and yelling).

Weaken Behavior with Punishment and Extinction   *Punishment* **is the process of weakening behavior through either the contingent presentation of something displeasing or the contingent withdrawal of something positive.** For

FIGURE 8–3   Contingent Consequences in Operant Conditioning

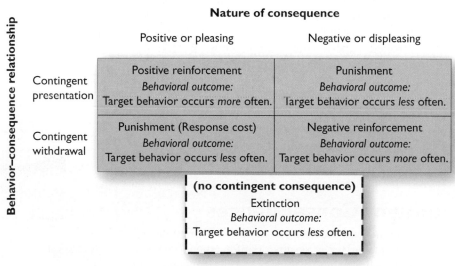

Nature of consequence

	Positive or pleasing	Negative or displeasing
Contingent presentation	Positive reinforcement *Behavioral outcome:* Target behavior occurs *more* often.	Punishment *Behavioral outcome:* Target behavior occurs *less* often.
Contingent withdrawal	Punishment (Response cost) *Behavioral outcome:* Target behavior occurs *less* often.	Negative reinforcement *Behavioral outcome:* Target behavior occurs *more* often.

(Behavior–consequence relationship)

(no contingent consequence)
Extinction
Behavioral outcome:
Target behavior occurs *less* often.

example, the U.S. Department of Transportation now fines airlines up to $27,500 per passenger for planes left on the tarmac for more than three hours. This reduced the reported cases to 12 from 535 for the same period in 2010 versus 2009.[62] Other examples of withdrawing something positive include docking a tardy employee's pay or forbidding the use of the Internet in the classroom or at work.

Weakening a behavior by ignoring it or making sure it is not *reinforced* **is referred to as** *extinction*. Getting rid of a former boyfriend or girlfriend by refusing to return their phone calls or unfriending them on Facebook are extinction strategies. These will reduce not only communications with this person but also the heartache. A good analogy for extinction is to imagine what would happen to your houseplants if you stopped watering them. Like a plant without water, a behavior without occasional reinforcement eventually dies. Although very different processes, both punishment and extinction have the same weakening effect on behavior.

At Granite Construction in Watsonville, California, 20% of every manager's bonus depends on the person's "people skills." For most of its 80 years, a call from the boss's office meant bad news. "Employees were only contacted when something went wrong," says division manager Bruce McGowan, a 20-year veteran who oversees a staff of 700. Now the emphasis is on positive reinforcement.

Knowing the difference between these various forms of contingent consequences provides you with a number of powerful tools with which to manage yourself and others.

Schedules of Reinforcement

While contingent consequences are important determinants of behavior, the timing of consequences can be even more important. Based on years of tedious laboratory experiments with pigeons in highly controlled environments, Skinner and his colleagues discovered distinct patterns of responding for various schedules of reinforcement.[63] Although some of their conclusions can be generalized to negative reinforcement, punishment, and extinction, it is best to think only of positive reinforcement when discussing schedules.

Continuous Reinforcement   **As indicated in Table 8–1, every instance of a target behavior is reinforced when a** *continuous reinforcement* **(CRF) schedule is in effect.** For instance, when your personal computer is operating properly, you are reinforced when it successfully boots up every time you turn it on (a CRF schedule). But, as with any CRF schedule of reinforcement, the behavior of turning on your personal computer will undergo rapid extinction if it breaks.

Intermittent Reinforcement   **Unlike CRF schedules,** *intermittent reinforcement* **involves reinforcement of some but not all instances of a target behavior.** Four subcategories of intermittent schedules, described in Table 8–1, are fixed and variable ratio schedules and fixed and variable interval schedules. Some common examples of the four types of intermittent reinforcement are as follows:

- *Fixed ratio.* Piece-rate pay; bonuses tied to the sale of a fixed number of units
- *Variable ratio.* Slot machines that pay off after a variable number of lever pulls; lotteries that pay off after the purchase of a variable number of tickets.

connect™

www.mcgrawhillconnect.com

Go to Connect for an interactive exercise to test your knowledge of the schedules of reinforcement.

TABLE 8–1   Reinforcement Schedules

Schedule	Description	Probable Effects on Responding
Continuous (CRF)	Reinforcer follows every response	Steady high rate of performance as long as reinforcement continues to follow every response.
		High frequency of reinforcement may lead to early satiation.
		Behavior weakens rapidly (undergoes extinction) when reinforcers are withheld.
		Appropriate for newly emitted, unstable, or low-frequency responses.
Intermittent	Reinforcer does not follow every response	Capable of producing high frequencies of responding.
		Low frequency of reinforcement precludes early satiation.
		Appropriate for stable or high-frequency responses.
Fixed ratio (FR)	A fixed number of responses must be emitted before reinforcement occurs	A fixed ratio of 1:1 (reinforcement occurs after every response) is the same as a continuous schedule.
		Tends to produce a high rate of response, which is vigorous and steady.
Variable ratio (VR)	A varying or random number of responses must be emitted before reinforcement occurs.	Capable of producing a high rate of response, which is vigorous, steady, and resistant to extinction.
Fixed interval (FI)	The first response after a specific period of time has elapsed is reinforced.	Produces an uneven response pattern varying from a very slow, unenergetic response immediately following reinforcement to a very fast, vigorous response immediately preceding reinforcement.
Variable interval (VI)	The first response after varying or random periods of time have elapsed is reinforced	Tends to produce a high rate of response, which is vigorous, steady, and resistant to extinction.

SOURCE: F Luthans and R Kreitner, *Organizational Behavior Modification and Beyond: An Operant and Social Learning Approach* (Glenview, IL: Scott, Foresman, 1985), p. 59. Used with permission of the authors.

- *Fixed interval.* Paychecks (once every two weeks or once a month); annual bonus.
- *Variable interval.* Random supervisory praise and pats on the back for employees who have been doing a good job.

Proper Scheduling Is Important   The schedule of reinforcement can more powerfully influence behavior than the magnitude of reinforcement. Although this proposition grew out of experiments with pigeons, subsequent on-the-job research confirmed it. Consider, for example, a field study of 12 unionized beaver trappers employed by a lumber company to keep the large rodents from eating newly planted tree seedlings.[64]

The beaver trappers were randomly divided into two groups that alternated weekly between two different bonus plans. Under the first schedule, each trapper earned his regular $7 per hour wage plus $1 for each beaver caught. Technically, this bonus was paid on a CRF schedule. The second bonus plan involved the regular $7 per hour wage plus a one-in-four chance (as determined by rolling the dice) of receiving $4 for each beaver trapped. This second bonus plan qualified as a variable ratio (VR-4) schedule. In the long run, both incentive schemes averaged out to a $1-per-beaver bonus. Surprisingly, however, when the trappers were under the VR-4 schedule, they were 58% more productive than under the CRF schedule, despite the fact that the net amount of pay averaged out the same for the two groups during the 12-week trapping season.

Work Organizations Typically Rely on the Weakest Schedule
Generally, variable ratio and variable interval schedules of reinforcement produce the strongest behavior that is most resistant to extinction. As gamblers will attest, variable schedules hold the promise of reinforcement after the next target response. In contrast, fixed and continuous schedules are the least likely to have the desired effects over time. For instance, Google's employees provide spot, peer rewards of $175. In 2010 two-thirds of employees doled out such intermittent (variable interval) rewards.[65] Despite the trend toward pay-for-performance, time-based pay schemes such as hourly wages and yearly salaries that rely on the weakest schedule of reinforcement (fixed interval) are still the rule in today's workplaces. Figure 8–4 provides an excellent example. It illustrates "window dressing," which is the practice banks use to reduce the amount of debt on their books at the end of each quarter. As you can see, the 18 big banks represented by this data reduced the amount of debt on their books by an average of 42% at the end of each quarter.[66] In other words, they "dressed up" their debt numbers at the end of each quarter to have the lowest levels of debt at the time that matters most—the end of the quarter. This coincides with when banks need to report their quarterly performance numbers (debt is one of them), and this also coincides with banker's quarterly performance numbers and rewards . Therefore, the fixed interval (every quarter) predicts when debt is lowest, which is when banks (and bankers) need to report their debt numbers and when they are rewarded. Is this a coincidence? Of course not! It is exactly the outcome the performance management system and (fixed interval) reinforcement is designed to produce. The better question, perhaps: Is window dressing desirable?

> **BACK TO THE CHAPTER-OPENING CASE**   In your consulting role, describe how knowledge of reinforcement schedules could be used to boost the effectiveness of the rewards you proposed in the previous Back to the Chapter-Opening Case exercise on page 212.

FIGURE 8–4 Reinforcement Schedules and Performance

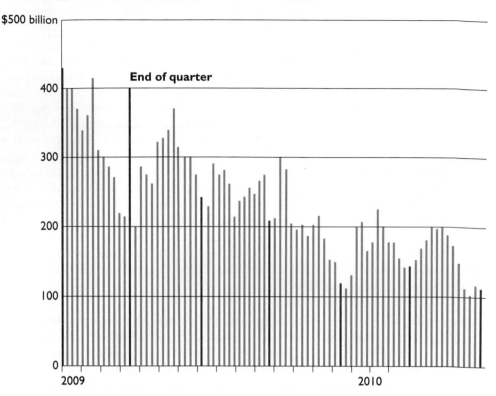

SOURCE: Data from M Rapoport, "Regulators to Target 'Window Dressing,'" *The Wall Street Journal,* September 16, 2010.

Shaping Behavior with Positive Reinforcement

Have you ever wondered how trainers at aquarium parks manage to get bottle-nosed dolphins to do flips, killer whales to carry people on their backs, and seals to juggle balls? The results are seemingly magical. Actually, a mundane learning process called shaping is responsible for the animals' antics. Two-ton killer whales, for example, have big appetites and for agreement in number find buckets of fish very reinforcing. So if the trainer wants to ride a killer whale, he or she reinforces very basic behaviors that will eventually lead to the whale being ridden. The killer whale is contingently reinforced with a few fish for coming near the trainer, then for being touched, then for putting its nose in a harness, then for being straddled, and eventually for swimming with the trainer on its back. In effect, the trainer systematically raises the behavioral requirement for reinforcement. **Thus, *shaping* is defined as the process of reinforcing closer and closer approximations to a target behavior.**

Shaping works very well with people, too, especially in training and quality programs involving continuous improvement. Praise, recognition, and instructive and credible feedback cost managers little more than moments of their time.[67] Yet, when used in conjunction with a behavior-shaping program, these consequences can efficiently foster significant improvements in job performance.[68] The key to successful behavior shaping lies in reducing a complex target behavior to easily learned steps and then faithfully (and patiently) reinforcing any improvement. John Mackey, founder and CEO of Whole Foods Markets, uses behavior shaping to improve the health of his employees. The desired behavior is healthy employee habits, which he defines and measures using body mass index (BMI), cholesterol, and blood pressure. Employees labeled platinum—BMI below 24, cholesterol below 150, and blood pressure of 110/70—receive a 30% discount on their health premiums. Bronze rated employees receive a 22% discount, and silver and gold are in-between.[69] Employee rewards (discounts) increase as they get closer to the platinum level. This example of shaping also parallels our discussion of goal setting in Chapter 7: Break a larger goal into smaller goals, and reward achievement of each of these goals as a means for motivating and shaping behavior. Mackey's reasoning is that health and healthy lifestyles reflect company values (remember our discussion in Chapter 2). He further believes that rewards are effective means for aligning employee behavior with the company's values and culture. Indeed they are!

key terms

chapter summary

- *Specify the two basic functions of feedback and three sources of feedback.* Feedback, in the form of objective information about performance, both instructs and motivates. Individuals receive feedback from others, the task, and from themselves.

- *Define upward feedback and 360-degree feedback, and summarize the general tips for effectively providing and receiving feedback.* Lower-level employees provide upward feedback (usually anonymous) to their managers. A focal person receives 360-degree feedback from subordinates, the manager, peers, and selected others such as customers or suppliers. Good feedback is tied to performance *goals* and clear *expectations*, linked with *specific* behavior and/or results, reserved for *key result areas*, given as soon as possible, provided for *improvement* as well as for final results, focused on *performance* rather than on personalities, and based on *accurate* and *credible* information. As for receiving feedback, don't get defensive—just listen. Do not discuss your review with coworkers, which will only spread the news unnecessarily. News of good and bad reviews gets around fast enough. Make sure you *understand* the content of the review and *develop an action plan* for responding. Although difficult, *don't take it personally.*

- *Distinguish between extrinsic and intrinsic rewards, and give a job-related example of each.* Extrinsic rewards, which are granted by others, include pay and benefits, recognition and praise, and favorable assignments and schedules. Intrinsic rewards are experienced internally or, in a sense, self-granted. Common intrinsic rewards include feelings of satisfaction, pride, and a sense of accomplishment.

- *Summarize the research lessons about pay for performance, and explain why rewards often fail to motivate employees.* Research on pay for performance has yielded mixed results, with no clear pattern of effectiveness. Reward systems can fail to motivate employees for these reasons: overemphasis on money, no appreciation effect, benefits become entitlements, wrong behavior is rewarded, rewards are delayed too long, use of one-size-fits-all rewards, one-shot rewards with temporary effect, and demotivating practices such as layoffs.

- *State Thorndike's "law of effect," and explain Skinner's distinction between respondent and operant behavior.* According to Edward L Thorndike's law of effect, behavior with favorable consequences tends to be repeated, while behavior with unfavorable consequences tends to disappear. B F Skinner called unlearned stimulus–response reflexes *respondent behavior.*

He applied the term *operant behavior* to all behavior learned through experience with environmental consequences.

- *Demonstrate your knowledge of positive reinforcement, negative reinforcement, punishment, and extinction, and explain behavior shaping.* Positive and negative reinforcement are consequence management strategies that strengthen behavior, whereas punishment and extinction weaken behavior. These strategies need to be defined objectively in terms of their actual impact on behavior frequency, not subjectively on the basis of intended impact. Behavior shaping occurs when closer and closer approximations of a target behavior are reinforced. In effect, the standard for reinforcement is made more difficult as the individual learns. The process begins with continuous reinforcement, which gives way to intermittent reinforcement when the target behavior becomes strong and habitual.

discussion questions

1. Returning to the chapter-opening case, what recommendations or principles discussed in this chapter are being used by Dan Hesse?
2. Provide a personal example for feedback you received that was instructional and another example of feedback that was motivational.
3. How would you summarize the practical benefits and drawbacks of 360-degree feedback?
4. How would you respond to a manager who said, "Employees cannot be motivated with money"?
5. Describe personal examples of positive reinforcement, negative reinforcement, punishment, and extinction. Also explain why each example was either effective or ineffective.

legal/ethical challenge

Hedging Undermines New Compensation Regulations for Bankers[70]

Spurred by the recent financial crisis, legislators and regulators have urged Wall Street to modify its compensation practices. Many firms responded by shifting a greater portion of executive compensation to stock. The argument is that doing so better aligns executives' interests and behaviors with those of the company and reduces excessive risk taking. While in theory this makes sense, the common practice of hedging allows executives to undermine the intended benefits of these changes.

Executives and other investors can hedge holdings of a stock by purchasing options to protect them against price declines. Doing so enables an investor either to limit losses or increase gains. Hedging therefore provides distinct advantages over more common "buy and sell" practices and is very common among executives. For instance, more than a quarter of Goldman Sachs's 475 partners used hedging strategies from July 2007 through November 2010—the peak of the crisis. Hedges were intended to protect executives' personal portfolios when their firm's stocks were highly volatile. To put this in perspective, one prominent Goldman investment banker avoided more than $7 million in losses in a four-month period.

Legislators and regulators are now debating whether Wall Street executives should be allowed to hedge their own company's stock. The argument is that such practices obscure or even break the link between compensation and company performance. Hedges help guard against falling share prices, which may cause an executive's interests to run counter to the company's.

More broadly, critics argue that hedging is yet another way in which the financial industry is weakening reform and leaving the system vulnerable to future crises. "Wall Street is saying it is reforming itself by granting stock to executives and exposing them to the long-term risk of that investment," said Wayne Turner, a former Securities and Exchange Commission chief accountant. "Hedging the risk can substantially undo that reform."

Many public companies, including investment banks, have policies that ban the practice for certain employees, but such policies vary greatly. For example, Bank of America bans all employees from hedging company stock, while J P Morgan Chase, Morgan Stanley, and Goldman Sachs prohibit only their highest-ranking executives from such transactions.

Which Argument Do You Agree with Most?

1. Regulators *should not* prohibit executives from hedging their company's stock. Explain your argument for this position.

2. Regulators *should* prohibit executives from hedging their company's stock. Explain your argument for this position.

3. Regulated or not, executives should not hedge their company's stock. Explain your argument.

4. Companies should be those who determine whether executives (and other employees) can or cannot hedge the company's stock. Explain your argument.

5. Think of another alternative/argument and explain.

If you're looking for additional study materials, be sure to check out the Online Learning Center at

www.mhhe.com/kinickiob5e

for more information and interactivities that correspond to this chapter.

part 3

Managing Group Level Factors and Social Processes

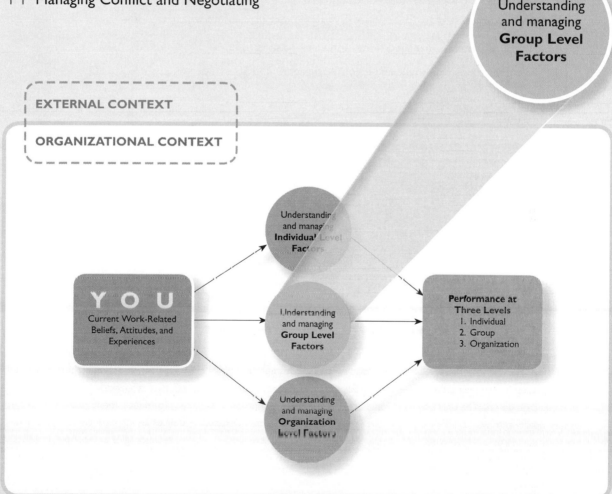

EXTERNAL CONTEXT

ORGANIZATIONAL CONTEXT

Understanding and managing **Group Level Factors**

Understanding and managing **Individual Level Factors**

YOU
Current Work-Related Beliefs, Attitudes, and Experiences

Understanding and managing **Group Level Factors**

Understanding and managing **Organization Level Factors**

Performance at Three Levels
1. Individual
2. Group
3. Organization

Effective Groups and Teams

After reading the material in this chapter, you should be able to:

LO9.1 Describe the five stages of Tuckman's theory of group development.

LO9.2 Contrast roles and norms, and specify four reasons why norms are enforced in organizations.

LO9.3 Describe four attributes of a team player.

LO9.4 Explain three ways to build trust and three ways to repair trust.

LO9.5 Describe self-managed teams and virtual teams.

LO9.6 Describe groupthink, and identify at least four of its symptoms.

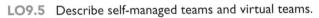

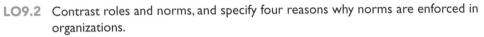

What's the Cure for Health Care in America? Effective Teamwork!

Historically, physicians in America were told to go to the hospital before dawn, stay until their patients were stable, focus on the needs of each patient before their own, and not worry about costs. They were taught to review every test result with their own eyes—to depend on no one. The only way to ensure quality care was to adopt high personal standards and then meet them. Such norms were reinforced by organization and industry-level factors. Medicine has been organized around what doctors do rather than what patients need. Hospitals, for example, often have separate units for cardiology, cardiac surgery, cardiac anesthesiology, and radiology; each includes doctors and other clinicians who contribute to the care of patients with heart disease. Every unit also has a physician leader, keeps an administrative staff, and submits its own bills. Inefficiencies abound in this health care model, and it is no wonder that delivering quality care and controlling costs are ever-present challenges. An alternative model is needed, one that involves effective teamwork.

To meet patient needs, health care utilizes an increasingly complex array of technologies and people. Patients often see a variety of physicians and other personnel spread across time and locations. This reality requires effective teamwork to deliver quality care and control costs. The fundamental problem with this reality, however, is that a team approach "collides with the image of the all-knowing, heroic lone healer"—the doctor. "We've celebrated cowboys, but what we need is more pit crews," says Atul Gawande, a surgeon and author of *The Checklist Manifesto*.

If we agree that teamwork is part of the solution, then how do we persuade physicians and others that a team approach is superior to the existing model? Dr. Gawande provides two answers, both derived from fundamental benefits of teams. First, the complexity of many patients' needs means that no single person can achieve the desired clinical outcome—quality care—alone. It requires many working in concert: administrators, physicians and other clinicians, and insurers. The quality of care is only as good as the weakest link in this chain. Second, the political and economic environment requires physicians to focus on value, which means quality care at a reasonable cost. Coordinated team efforts are a means for both, boosting efficiencies in care delivery and in reducing redundant or unnecessary costs.

An example of a new team-based model exists at Geisinger Health System of Pennsylvania, one of the largest rural providers in the country. As evidence, it cut hospital readmissions by half using an effective team approach. This is significant given that 20% of Medicare patients discharged from hospitals across the United States are readmitted within 30 days. These "bounce backs" should be

seen for what they are—failures of the delivery system to meet patients' needs. A key to Geisinger's success is placing nurses ("care coordinators") in the offices of patients' primary care physicians. They coordinate care in the hospital and beyond, figuring out which patients need to see which physicians and when.

As is the case at Geisinger, a critical component in this model is a culture in which care coordinators can actually coordinate care. It requires physicians to be both team leaders and team players. Not long ago, in the strict hierarchy of medicine, nurses were largely regarded as technicians whose job was to follow orders. No decision was made without a physician's knowledge and consent. The notion of a nurse as a critical contributor and independent decision maker on a clinical team would have seemed absurd. Thankfully, this is changing in many places. Providers that deliver care in the traditional way simply can't match the performance of Geisinger and other organizations where physicians work in teams with care coordinators. In these organizations the coordinator's role

is something like that of a point guard in basketball, with the physician acting as a combined general manager and player-coach. Leading these teams requires physicians to hand off considerable responsibility to nurses. The payoff is improved performance on the metrics that matter most to them and their patients—quality care and reduced costs.

Teambuilding therefore is a critical competency for physician groups, their leaders, and their larger health system employers. The fortunes of physician groups and others in all areas of medicine will depend on leaders who can improve performance by inspiring or requiring teamwork. Because insurers are now refusing to cover expenses above and beyond particular rates, most patients are not allowed to see any physician they choose. And from the physician's perspective, if the patients don't come, the income goes away, and so does the group and thus their livelihood.

The bottom line is that the ability to build high-performance teams is a source of competitive advantage and is essential to solve the challenges plaguing health care.[1]

BOTH DAILY EXPERIENCE and research reveal the importance of social skills for individual and organizational success. Research has uncovered a number of flaws that tend to derail executive careers. A derailed executive "is one who, having reached the general manager level, finds that there is little chance of future advancement due to a misfit between job requirements and personal skills."[2] What do you think are the traits or behaviors that lead to derailment? A recent study of more than 450 Fortune 500 executives and another including 11,000 leaders across companies and industries sheds light on this question. The derailers included:

1. Lack of energy and enthusiasm
2. Accept their own mediocre performance
3. Lack clear vision and direction
4. Have poor judgment
5. Don't collaborate
6. Don't walk the talk
7. Resist new ideas
8. Don't learn from mistakes
9. Lack interpersonal skills
10. Fail to develop others.[3]

Notice how many of these traits or behaviors point to an inability to get along and work effectively with others. Without question, teamwork and influencing others are important tools for effective managers, and this chapter will help you to develop these skills.

The purpose of this chapter is to shift the focus from individual behavior to collective behavior. As illustrated in the chapter-opening case, the collective effort put forth by teams can significantly contribute to organizational success. It thus is important to understand the dynamics of teamwork and the roles team members play in creating an environment that supports teamwork. This chapter will help you to understand these issues. We explore groups and teams, key features of organizational life, and discuss how to make them effective while avoiding common pitfalls. Among the interesting variety of topics in this chapter are group development, trust, self-managed teams, virtual teams, and groupthink.

Fundamentals of Group Behavior

McGraw Hill **connect**
www.mcgrawhillconnect.com

Go to Connect for a video case to view Pike Place Fish Market and how it manages group behavior in the workplace.

Drawing from the field of sociology, we define a **group** as two or more freely interacting individuals who share collective norms and goals and have a common identity.[4] Organizational psychologist Edgar Schein shed additional light on this concept by drawing instructive distinctions between a group, a crowd, and an organization:

> The size of a group is thus limited by the possibilities of mutual interaction and mutual awareness. Mere aggregates of people do not fit this definition because they do not interact and do not perceive themselves to be a group even if they are aware of each other as, for instance, a crowd on a street corner watching some event. A total department, a union, or a whole organization would not be a group in spite of thinking of themselves as "we," because they generally do not all interact and are not all aware of each other. However, work teams, committees, subparts of departments, cliques, and various other informal associations among organizational members would fit this definition of a group.[5]

Take a moment now to think of various groups of which you are a member. Does each of your "groups" satisfy the four criteria in our definition?

Formal and Informal Groups

Individuals join groups, or are assigned to groups, to accomplish various purposes. **If the group is formed by a manager to help the organization accomplish its goals, then it qualifies as a *formal group.*** Formal groups typically wear such labels as work group, team, committee, or task force. An ***informal group* exists when the members' overriding purpose of getting together is friendship.**[6] Formal and informal groups often overlap, such as when a team of corporate auditors heads for the tennis courts after work. Friendships forged on the job can be so strong as to outlive the job itself in an era of job hopping, reorganizations, and mass layoffs. For example, membership in organized corporate "alumni" groups is increasingly in vogue.

There are now alumni groups for hundreds of companies, including Hewlett-Packard, Ernst & Young, and Texas Instruments. Some groups are started by former employees, while others are formally sanctioned by employers as a way to stay in touch, creating a potential pool of boomerang workers that employers can draw from when hiring picks up.[7] A quick Google search in early 2011 revealed 8,510 "ex-employee groups," many of which are facilitated by Facebook.

However, the desirability of overlapping formal and informal groups is debatable.[8] Some managers firmly believe personal friendship fosters productive teamwork on the job whereas others view such relationships as a serious threat to productivity. Both situations are common, and it is the manager's job to strike a workable balance, based on the maturity and goals of the people involved. A recent survey of 1,000 U.S. adults revealed that 61% consider their bosses to be friends. Although, approximately a third of those who are connected with their boss on a social networking site wish they weren't![9]

Teams serve many purposes at Whole Foods Market, where all employees belong to teams. Team members share equally in any savings they achieve for the company and vote on whether newcomers will be permanently hired. Would you like to work in this environment? Why?

Functions of Formal Groups

Researchers point out that formal groups fulfill two basic functions: *organizational* and *individual.*[10] The various functions are listed in Table 9–1. Complex combinations of these functions can be found in formal groups at any given time.

Consider, for example, the law firm of Baker Donelson. The firm highly values community service and has doubled the number of pro bono hours each year since 2008. To formalize their commitment to such work, they appointed Lisa Borden as pro bono shareholder and created a pro bono committee.[11] Not only does this show the alignment of cultural values and norms discussed in Chapter 2, but it also illustrates both the organizational and individual functions of formal groups. Specifically, the committee helps coordinate pro bono work across the many offices and practice areas of the firm (organizational function). And free services support Baker Donelson's organizational values and goals of being a good citizen in their communities and increasing attorney satisfaction (organizational functions). In addition, providing pro bono work most likely fulfills individual functions, such as confirming an attorney's sense of identity (as kind, caring individuals), building strong work relationships, and living according to their values.

www.mcgrawhillconnect.com

Go to Connect for an interactive exercise to test your knowledge of formal groups.

TABLE 9–1   Formal Groups Fulfill Organizational and Individual Functions

Organizational Functions	Individual Functions
1. Accomplish complex, interdependent tasks that are beyond the capabilities of individuals.	1. Satisfy the individual's need for affiliation.
2. Generate new or creative ideas and solutions.	2. Develop, enhance, and confirm the individual's self-esteem and sense of identity.
3. Coordinate interdepartmental efforts.	3. Give individuals an opportunity to test and share their perceptions of social reality.
4. Provide a problem-solving mechanism for complex problems requiring varied information and assessments.	4. Reduce the individual's anxieties and feelings of insecurity and powerlessness.
5. Implement complex decisions.	5. Provide a problem-solving mechanism for personal and interpersonal problems.
6. Socialize and train newcomers.	

SOURCE: Adapted from E H Schein, *Organizational Psychology*, 3rd ed (Englewood Cliffs. NJ: Prentice-Hall, 1980), pp 149–51.

The Group Development Process

LO9.1

Groups and teams in the workplace go through a maturation process, such as one would find in any life-cycle situation (e.g., humans, organizations, products). While there is general agreement among theorists that the group development process occurs in identifiable stages, they disagree about the exact number, sequence, length, and nature of those stages.[12] One oft-cited model is the one proposed in 1965 by educational psychologist Bruce W Tuckman. His original model involved only four stages (forming, storming, norming, and performing). The five-stage model in Figure 9–1 evolved when Tuckman and a doctoral student added "adjourning" in 1977.[13] A word of caution is in order. Similar to Maslow's need hierarchy theory, Tuckman's theory has not withstood rigorous empirical testing. Results are mixed or nonsignificant. Nevertheless, many researchers and practitioners like Tuckman's five-stage model of group development because of its easy-to-remember labels and commonsense appeal.

Let us briefly examine each of the five stages in Tuckman's model. Notice in Figure 9–1 how individuals give up a measure of their independence when they join and participate in a group.[14] Also, the various stages are not necessarily of the same duration or intensity. For instance, the storming stage may be practically nonexistent or painfully long, depending on the goal clarity and the commitment and maturity of the members. You can make this process come to life by relating the various stages to your own experiences with work groups, committees, athletic teams, fraternities/sororities, religious groups, or class project teams. Some group experiences that surprised you when they occurred may now make sense or strike you as inevitable when seen as part of a natural development process.

Stage 1: Forming   During this "ice-breaking" stage, group members tend to be uncertain and anxious about such things as their roles, the people in charge, and the

Tuckman's Five-Stage Theory of Group Development   FIGURE 9–1

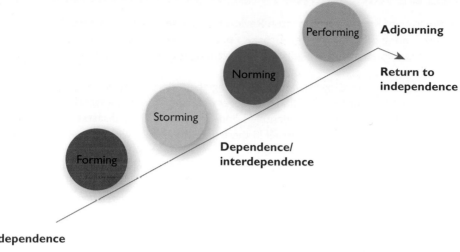

Individual issues	"How do I fit in?"	"What's my role here?"	"What do the others expect me to do?"	"How can I best perform my role?"	"What's next?"
Group issues	"Why are we here?"	"Why are we fighting over who is in charge and who does what?"	"Can we agree on roles and work as a team?"	"Can we do the job properly?"	"Can we help members transition out?"

group's goals. Mutual trust is low, and there is a good deal of holding back to see who takes charge and how. Interestingly, research showed that this is just the time in a group's development where some conflict among group members is beneficial. A study of 71 technology project teams revealed that conflict in the early stages of the group development process increased creativity.[15] However, the results can be quite different in other situations. For example, in life-and-death situations sometimes faced by surgical teams and airline cockpit crews, the uncertainty inherent in the early stages of development (e.g., forming and storming) can be dangerous. According to the National Transportation Safety Board, "73% of commercial airline pilots' serious mistakes happen on crews' first day together."[16] If the formal leader (e.g., a supervisor) does not assert his or her authority, an emergent leader will eventually step in to fulfill the group's need for leadership and direction (the details of leadership are discussed in Chapter 14).

Stage 2: Storming   This is a time of testing. Individuals test the leader's policies and assumptions as they try to determine how they fit into the power structure. Subgroups take shape, and subtle forms of rebellion, such as procrastination, occur. For an example of a small company that successfully navigated the storming and norming phases, see the Skills & Best Practices on page 230. Many groups stall in stage 2 because power and politics erupt into open rebellion.

Tragedy Halted Development . . . Or Was It an Accelerator?

Grockit competes with the likes of Kaplan and Princeton Review to provide test prep services for the SAT, ACT, GMAT, GRE, and LSAT, among others. However, Grockit's product takes a different approach from its competitors. It utilizes social networks, adaptive algorithms, and gaming mechanics to the process of learning and education.

In the spring of 2009 the company's employees were mostly engineers devoted to developing the product, while Farbood Nivi, the founder and CEO, fulfilled most every leadership and managerial role. Other roles, responsibilities, and people were yet to be identified and developed. Then disaster struck. Nivi's scooter was hit by a minivan, and the CEO found himself in the emergency room with a severely damaged kidney. He underwent surgery and was out of the office for about six weeks. Shortly after his return he learned that he needed a second operation, which was followed by another long recovery period. While Nivi spent time recovering, his company grew increasingly ill. Three of the 15 employees quit, and even though a beta version of their product existed, the company had no revenues and was burning through its seed money quickly.

While recovering, and to keep the company alive, he and the remaining employees needed to accelerate the development of its people, its product, and Nivi's larger dream. To do this, he hired a chief marketing officer, a chief business development and strategy officer, and a veteran Google manager as CEO. (Today, Nivi serves as president and chief product officer.)

Whether by wisdom or luck, Farbood Nivi's actions kept the young company from sliding further backward in its development or ceasing altogether. He instead spurred it forward to higher performance. The company now has more than 20 employees, a product, and revenues. By bringing in new people from the outside, he effectively accelerated Grockit's development and growth.

SOURCE: Excerpted and adapted from D McGinn, "How a CEO's Injury Helped Him Revitalize His Young Firm," *Harvard Business Review*, March 1, 2011.

Stage 3: Norming   Groups that make it through stage 2 generally do so because a respected member, other than the leader, challenges the group to resolve its power struggles so something can be accomplished. Questions about authority and power are best resolved through unemotional, matter-of-fact group discussion. A feeling of team spirit is experienced because members believe they have found their proper roles. **Group cohesiveness, defined as the "we feeling" that binds members of a group together, is the principal by-product of stage 3.**[17]

connect™
www.mcgrawhillconnect.com

Go to Connect for an interactive exercise to test your knowledge of the group development process.

Stage 4: Performing   Activity during this vital stage is focused on solving task problems. As members of a mature group, contributors get their work done without hampering others. There is a climate of open communication, strong cooperation, and lots of helping behavior. Conflicts and job boundary disputes are handled constructively and efficiently. Cohesiveness and personal commitment to group goals help the group achieve more than could any one individual acting alone.

Stage 5: Adjourning   The work is done; it is time to move on to other things. Having worked so hard to get along and get something done, many members feel a compelling sense of loss. The return to independence can be eased by rituals celebrating "the end" and "new beginnings." Parties, award ceremonies, graduations, or mock funerals can provide the needed punctuation at the end of a significant group project. Leaders need to emphasize valuable lessons learned in group dynamics to prepare everyone for future group and team efforts.

BACK TO THE CHAPTER-OPENING CASE   Assume you are the director of a large group of orthopedic surgeons at Geisinger Health System. You thus are responsible for transitioning the group to a team-based approach to patient care. Describe three things you would do to help the group manage the forming and storming stages of its transition and development to team-based care.

Group Member Roles

A *role* **is a set of expected behaviors for a particular position, and a group role is a set of expected behaviors for members of the group as a whole.**[18] Therefore each role you play is defined in part by the expectations of that role. As a student, you are expected to be motivated to learn, conscientious, participative, and attentive. Professors are expected to be knowledgeable, prepared, and genuinely interested in student learning. Sociologists view roles and their associated expectations as a fundamental basis of human interaction and experience. In the many arenas of life (e.g., work, family, school), people often play multiple roles. At work, for example, employees frequently play roles that go beyond duties in a job description, such as helping coworkers and suggesting improvements.[19] Moreover, employees regularly are members of multiple groups and may play one or more roles within each group. Two types of roles are particularly important—*task* and *maintenance.* Effective groups ensure that both roles are fulfilled (see Table 9–2).[20]

Task versus Maintenance Roles   *Task roles* **enable the work group to define, clarify, and pursue a common purpose.** Meanwhile, *maintenance roles* **foster supportive and constructive interpersonal relationships.** In short, task roles keep the group *on track* while maintenance roles keep the group *together.* A project team member is performing a task function when he or she says at an update meeting, "What is the real issue here? We don't seem to be getting anywhere." Another individual who says, "Let's hear from those who oppose this plan," is performing a maintenance function. Importantly, each of the various task and maintenance roles may be played in varying combinations and sequences by either the group's leader or any of its members.[21]

Checklist for Managers   The task and maintenance roles listed in Table 9–2 on page 232 can serve as a handy checklist for managers and group leaders who wish to ensure proper group development. Roles that are not always performed when needed, such as those of coordinator, evaluator, and gatekeeper, can be performed in a timely manner by the formal leader or assigned to other members. Leaders can further ensure that roles are fulfilled by clarifying specifically what is expected of employees in the group. Sallie Krawcheck of Bank of America, who was 24th on *Fortune's* 2010 List of Most Powerful Women in Business, provided an excellent example. When she took over as the president of the Global Wealth and Investment Management (GWIM)

Danica Patrick, one of the only female race car drivers, as well as all other professional race car drivers rely on their teams to develop strategies to win races. How do the stages of team development apply to race car teams?

TABLE 9–2 Task and Maintenance Roles

Task Roles	Description
Initiator	Suggests new goals or ideas
Information seeker/giver	Clarifies key issues
Opinion seeker/giver	Clarifies pertinent values
Elaborator	Promotes greater understanding through examples or exploration of implications
Coordinator	Pulls together ideas and suggestions
Orienter	Keeps group headed toward its stated goal(s)
Evaluator	Tests group's accomplishments with various criteria such as logic and practicality
Energizer	Prods group to move along or to accomplish more
Procedural technician	Performs routine duties (e.g., handing out materials or rearranging seats)
Recorder	Performs a "group memory" function by documenting discussion and outcomes

Maintenance Roles	Description
Encourager	Fosters group solidarity by accepting and praising various points of view
Harmonizer	Mediates conflict through reconciliation or humor
Compromiser	Helps resolve conflict by meeting others "halfway"
Gatekeeper	Encourages all group members to participate
Standard setter	Evaluates the quality of group processes
Commentator	Records and comments on group processes/dynamics
Follower	Serves as a passive audience

SOURCE: Adapted from discussion in K D Benne and P Sheats, "Functional Roles of Group Members," *Journal of Social Issues,* Spring 1948, pp 41–49.

group in 2008, she was quick to fulfill both task and maintenance roles. At the embattled bank she quickly tended to task roles and appointed eight executives to oversee various operations within the group, such as heads of the U.S. brokerage force and private wealth management. New goals were set; she also worked diligently to integrate and harmonize the cultures (maintenance roles) of B of A and Merrill Lynch, which it acquired at the height of the financial crisis.[22] A study of more than 20,000 US workers found that they were most likely to agree on their roles when job requirements were defined in terms of specific tasks. They had less agreement about their role as defined in terms of general responsibilities and least consensus for requirements defined by the traits the employee should possess.[23]

The task roles of initiator, orienter, and energizer are especially important because they are *goal-directed* roles. Research studies on group goal setting confirm the motivational power of challenging goals. As with individual goal setting (in Chapter 7), difficult but achievable goals are associated with better group results.[24] Also in line with individual goal-setting theory and research, group goals are more effective if group members clearly understand them and are both individually and collectively committed to achieving them. Initiators, orienters, and energizers can be very helpful in this regard. Moreover, international managers need to be sensitive to cultural differences regarding the relative importance of task and maintenance roles. For example, Asian cultures often value maintenance roles more than groups from the West.

Norms

Norms are more encompassing than roles. While roles involve behavioral expectations for specific positions, norms help organizational members determine right from wrong and good from bad. According to one respected team of management consultants: **"A *norm* is an attitude, opinion, feeling, or action—shared by two or more people—that guides their behavior."**[25] Although norms are typically unwritten and seldom discussed openly, they have a powerful influence on group and organizational behavior. Recall our discussion of organizational culture in Chapter 2 and societal culture in Chapter 3. In both instances culture shaped individual behavior via the shared nature of expectations and norms. The same applies at the group level. Norms help guide behavior for groups and their members. For example, the 3M Company has a norm wherein employees devote 15% of their time to think big, pursue new ideas, or further develop something spawned from their other work. The "15 percent time" program, as it is called, was started in 1948 and supports the culture of innovation 3M is known for. Google implements a similar program and allows employees to allocate 20% of their time to ideas and projects beyond their own jobs. It is alleged, but not confirmed, that projects developed during this time were Gmail and Google Earth.[26]

Group members positively reinforce those who adhere to current norms with friendship and acceptance. On the other hand, nonconformists experience criticism and even ostracism or rejection by group members. Anyone who has experienced the "silent treatment" from a group of friends knows what a potent social weapon ostracism can be.[27] The usefulness of norms is enhanced by understanding how they develop and why they are enforced.

> **BACK TO THE CHAPTER-OPENING CASE** Again, assume you are the director of a large group of orthopedic surgeons at Geisinger Health System. Describe how you would fulfill two task roles and two maintenance roles during the transition to team-based care.

How Norms Are Developed   Experts say norms evolve in an informal manner as the group or organization determines what it takes to be effective. Generally speaking, norms develop in various combinations of the following four ways:

1. *Explicit statements by supervisors or coworkers.* For instance, your professor might explicitly set norms against texting and surfing the Web during class.

2. *Critical events in the group's history.* Commercial jet manufacturer Airbus—a consortium among France, Germany, Great Britain, and Spain—had a norm that groups drawn from each nation worked independently from the others. However, the approach caused so much inefficiency and poor communication

that it threatened the launch of its superjumbo A380 aircraft. After continued delays management required German engineers to travel to France, where their French colleagues would help them use newer, more efficient design software than they had in Germany. Eventually, successes began to reinforce the new norm of information sharing.[28]

3. *Primacy.* The first behavior pattern that emerges in a group often sets group expectations. For example, differences and fierce arguments occurred when the 10 representatives of the Commonwealth Health Insurance Connector began deliberating how to implement universal health coverage in Massachusetts. But on the first tough decision, which involved whether to charge low-income citizens a premium for participating, one influential member (Celia Wcislo) decided to compromise for the sake of unity and a chance to move forward. Ultimately, according to an analysis of the group's work, Wcislo's cooperative behavior established a norm that other group members followed on other issues.[29]

4. *Carryover behaviors from past situations.* Carryover of individual behaviors from past situations can increase the predictability of group members' behaviors in new settings and facilitate task accomplishment. For instance, students and professors carry fairly constant sets of expectations from class to class.[30]

Why Norms Are Enforced   Norms tend to be enforced by group members when they

- Help the group or organization survive.
- Clarify or simplify behavioral expectations.
- Help individuals avoid embarrassing situations.
- Clarify the group's or organization's central values and/or unique identity.[31]

Teams, Trust, and Teamwork

The team approach has many significant implications for both individuals and organizations. Teams are a cornerstone of progressive management for the foreseeable future. General Electric's CEO, Jeffrey Immelt, offers this blunt overview: "You lead today by building teams and placing others first. It's not about you." [32] This means virtually all employees will need to polish their team skills. While Immelt's position is accepted by many CEOs across industries, some also are quick to emphasize the important roles of individual team members. For instance, JP Morgan's CEO, Jamie Dimon stated, "While teamwork is important and often code for getting along, equally important is an individual's ability to have the courage to stand alone and do the right thing."[33] Research reported in the *Corporate Finance Review* supports these views. Executives from 300 companies indicated that teamwork was the single most desirable soft skill (64% of executives). Interpersonal, social, and managerial skills were also noted.[34]

In this team-focused environment, organizations need leaders who are adept at teamwork themselves and can cultivate the level of trust necessary to foster constructive teamwork. In a recent survey by consulting firm Development Dimensions International, the top three traits of a boss admired by employees were trust in employees, honesty/authenticity, and great team-building skills.[35] In this section, we define the term *team,* look at teamwork competencies and team building, discuss trust as a key to effective teamwork, and explore two evolving forms of teamwork—self-managed teams and virtual teams.

A Team Is More Than Just a Group

Jon R Katzenbach and Douglas K Smith, management consultants at McKinsey & Company, say it is a mistake to use the terms *group* and *team* interchangeably. After studying many different kinds of teams—from athletic to corporate to military—they concluded that successful teams tend to take on a life of their own. Katzenbach and Smith define a **team** as "**a small number of people with complementary skills who are committed to a common purpose, performance goals, and approach for which they hold themselves mutually accountable.**"[36]

Thus, a group becomes a team when the following criteria are met:

1. *Leadership* becomes a shared activity.
2. *Accountability* shifts from strictly individual to both individual and collective.
3. The group develops its own *purpose* or mission.
4. *Problem solving* becomes a way of life, not a part-time activity.
5. *Effectiveness* is measured by the group's collective outcomes and products.[37]

Bob Lane, the former CEO of Deere & Company, emphasizes the purpose and effectiveness of teams when he talks about his company being a team, not a family. A reporter summarized his words this way: "While family members who don't pull their weight may not be welcome at the Thanksgiving dinner table, they remain members of the family. But if you're not pulling your weight here, I'm sorry, you're not part of the team."[38]

Relative to Tuckman's theory of group development covered earlier—forming, storming, norming, performing, and adjourning—teams are task groups that have matured to the *performing* stage. Because of conflicts due to power, authority, and unstable interpersonal relations, many work groups never qualify as a real team. Katzenbach and Smith clarified the distinction this way: "The essence of a team is common commitment. Without it, groups perform as individuals; with it, they become a powerful unit of collective performance."[39] This underscores two other important distinctions between teams and groups: Teams assemble to accomplish a common task and require collaboration.[40]

When Katzenbach and Smith refer to "a small number of people" in their definition, they mean between 2 and 25 team members. They found effective teams to typically have fewer than 10 members. This conclusion was echoed in a survey of 400 workplace team members in the United States and Canada: "The average North American team consists of 10 members. Eight is the most common size."[41] These findings are consistent with more recent recommendations by Richard Hackman, a noted organizational psychologist and author of *Leading Teams*. He suggested that teams be limited to nine or fewer people. Coordinating any more becomes too difficult, if not counterproductive.[42] More practically, however, we all are well advised not to fixate on any particular team size. Instead, team size should be determined by the requirements of the task at hand. "As projects get larger in size, thus may also the need to add personnel. Similarly, as the task is complex and uncertain, team members with diverse skill sets and knowledge bases must be included in the team to address task complexity, and the team must collaborate closely to integrate this knowledge."[43]

Eight Characteristics of Effective Team Players

1. Are open to new ideas and different ways of working
2. Share information, experience, and specialized knowledge
3. Seek opportunities for improvement
4. Develop working relationships with people from different functions
5. Look for win-win solutions to build trust and sustain relationships
6. Join only those teams whose goals they highly value, which fosters personal commitment
7. Are reliable—they do what they say, when they say it, and are prompt and respectful
8. Are results oriented

Notice that all of these characteristics are action oriented. Being a team player is more than a state of mind: it is about action!

SOURCE: Excerpted and adapted from *Harvard Business Essentials: Creating Teams with an Edge,* Chapter 8. February 19, 2004.

 LO9.3

Developing Teamwork Competencies and Being a Team Player

Forming workplace teams and urging employees to be team players are good starting points on the road to creating effective teams. But they are not enough today. Teamwork skills and competencies need to be role modeled and taught. These include group problem solving, mentoring, conflict management skills, and emotional intelligence. Research has found that teams collaborate most effectively when companies develop and encourage teamwork skills. Teamwork competencies should be rewarded, too.

So, what does it mean to be a team player? While each of us has our own ideas, it is likely that our views share the 3 Cs of team players:

1. *Committed*
2. *Collaborative*
3. *Competent*[44]

To make the point, think of a team scenario and it would be difficult to consider any individual member a team player if he or she didn't possess and exhibit all three. Effective team players therefore don't just *feel* the 3 Cs; they *display* them. Think of a team of which you are a member. Now, think of somebody on that team who clearly displays the 3 Cs and somebody who does not. What is the difference to you? The team? Additional and more detailed characteristics of team players are found in the Skills & Best Practices above.

Team Building

***Team building* is a catchall term for a host of techniques aimed at improving the internal functioning of work groups.** Whether conducted by company trainers or hired consultants (and done on-site or off-site), team-building workshops strive for greater cooperation, better communication, and less dysfunctional conflict. Rote memorization and lectures or discussions are discouraged by team builders who prefer *active* versus passive learning. Greater emphasis is placed on *how* work groups get the job done than on the task itself. Experiential learning techniques such as interpersonal trust exercises, conflict role-play sessions, and competitive games are common if not expected.

Does Team Building Work?   It's hard to say if team building works. While many businesspeople are confident that development efforts yield results, cost conscious executives increasingly insist on determining the return on investment (ROI) for team building and other talent-development investments. One estimate is that fewer than 20% of companies that invest in development actually calculate ROI.[45] Part of the problem is that many if not most organizations do not set clear objectives for team building (or training more generally). Three fundamental elements are recommended for those interested in establishing the ROI for team building:

Clear objectives. This is the starting point for ROI estimates. Many outcomes are possible, but it is important to identify which are most relevant for a particular team, such as increased sales, increased customer satisfaction, timeliness, or quality.

Validation. Not to be confused with the objectives, validation involves confirming that team-building efforts actually link to the desired changes in behavior and attitudes. For example, a positive attitude toward customers likely affects the quality of work produced by the team.

Performance information. What data are needed to track the previous two elements and how will they be obtained?[46] Attitudes toward customers can be measured with employee surveys, quality can be gauged by the number of reworked products, and customer satisfaction can be determined with surveys or interviews.

ROI aside, and assuming objectives are clearly defined, pre- and post-exercise activities (preparation and follow-up) are critical for realizing the benefits of team building. For example, if the objective is simply to get team members to know each other and have fun, then an engaging exercise itself is enough. If instead the objective is to translate the training into action on the job, then it is recommended to use reminders and follow-up activities. However, if genuine trust and collaboration on the job are desired outcomes, then it is beneficial to have the exercise itself mirror the same challenges faced by the team on the job, including contextual factors, and to have extensive follow-up as a team.[47]

Full-time employees of the Container Store receive 263 hours of training their first year. Communication and transparency also are highly valued. CEO Kip Tindell believes that all information and data (except salaries) should be shared with employees. Such practices foster trust, teamwork, and organizational effectiveness at the company. Besides trust, what are the benefits of transparency and investments in training?

Practical Applications   Team building is frequently used given the prevalence of teams in today's organizations. It thus is important to implement it effectively. Jerry Garfield and Ken Stanton provide six tools that managers can use in this pursuit.

1. *Share personal histories.* Doing so reveals competencies and generates respect.

2. *Ask what has worked for you in the past.* This signals that past experiences are valued and may make contributions to the current team and objectives.

3. *Describe how the team will work together.* Clearly state the team's purpose and plan, and each member's role.

4. *Optimize members' strengths.* Align assignments with the abilities and experiences of various team members.

5. *Establish norms for making decisions.* Clarify which decisions can be made individually and which need to be given to the leader and/or made by the team.

6. *Establish processes for giving and receiving feedback.* This is important to assure information is shared appropriately and timely—in all directions.[48]

BACK TO THE CHAPTER-OPENING CASE   You (still) are the director of a large group of orthopedic surgeons at Geisinger Health System. Describe three things you would do to build teamwork among your physicians, nurses, and insurers in the new team-based model. Be sure to include not only *what* but also *how* you would do each of the three things you choose.

Trust: A Key Ingredient of Teamwork

The importance of trust in organizational life cannot be overstated. Trust is the interpersonal lubricant for relationships within and between all organizational levels—individual, group, and organizational—and drives many important team outcomes (e.g., cooperation, communication, performance, and innovation). Yet, these have not been good times for trust in the corporate world. Years of mergers, layoffs, bloated executive bonuses, and corporate criminal proceedings have left many of us justly cynical about trusting management and our employers. Public opinion polls show the resulting damage. A Harris Interactive survey in 2010 showed that only 18% of Americans think that the reputation of big business is good. While this number is pathetic, it is actually the first rise in four years—in 2009 it was 12%![49]

While challenging readers of the *Harvard Business Review* to do a better job of investing in social capital, experts offered this constructive advice:

> No one can manufacture trust or mandate it into existence. When someone says, "You can trust me," we usually don't, and rightly so. But leaders can make deliberate investments in trust. They can give people reasons to trust one another instead of reasons to watch their backs. They can refuse to reward successes that are built on untrusting behavior. And they can display trust and trustworthiness in their own actions, both personally and on behalf of the company.[50]

These efforts are important for creating an ethical climate (discussed in Chapter 1). And on a practical note, recent research found that people are more likely to be cooperative in situations where they believe the person in authority is procedurally fair (discussed in Chapter 7) and trustworthy.[51]

Reciprocity and Three Forms of Trust   Trust is defined in many different ways. One that is particularly useful for organizational behavior (OB): *Trust* **is a reciprocal faith that the intentions and behaviors of another will consider the implications for you.** The reciprocal (give-and-take) aspect of trust means that when we feel or observe that others trust us, then we are more inclined to trust them, and the converse also is true.[52]

For our purposes in OB, we discuss three particular forms of trust:

1. *Contractual trust.* Trust of character. Do people do what they say they are going to do? Do managers and employees make clear what they expect of one another?

2. *Communication trust.* Trust of disclosure. How well do people share information and tell the truth?

3. *Competence trust.* Trust of capability. How well do people carry out their responsibilities and acknowledge other people's skills and abilities?[53]

Answering these questions provides both a good assessment of trustworthiness and a guide for building trust.

Building and Repairing Trust   According to our definition of trust we tend to give what we get: Trust begets trust; distrust begets distrust. Therefore the practical application of this knowledge is to act in ways that demonstrate each of the aforementioned forms of trust. Doing so builds trust. Beyond this, you can benefit by following the six guidelines offered by management professor and consultant Fernando Bartolomé for building and maintaining trust: **LO9.4**

1. *Communication.* Keep team members and employees informed by explaining policies and decisions and providing accurate feedback. Be candid about one's own problems and limitations. Tell the truth.[54]

2. *Support.* Be available and approachable. Provide help, advice, coaching, and support for team members' ideas.

3. *Respect.* Delegation, in the form of real decision-making authority, is the most important expression of managerial respect. Delegating meaningful responsibilities to somebody shows trust in them. Actively listening to the ideas of others is a close second.

4. *Fairness.* Be quick to give credit and recognition to those who deserve it. Make sure all performance appraisals and evaluations are objective and impartial.

5. *Predictability.* Be consistent and predictable in your daily affairs. Keep both expressed and implied promises.

6. *Competence.* Enhance your credibility by demonstrating good business sense, technical ability, and professionalism.[55]

Just as trust can be built, it can be eroded. Violating, or even the perception of violating, another's trust can diminish trust and lead to *distrust.* As you know from personal experience, trust is violated in many different ways—sometimes unknowingly and other times seemingly purposefully. In either case, it is important to repair trust when it is damaged. Dennis and Michelle Reina developed a popular approach to trust and trust repair. See the Skills & Best Practices on page 240 for their suggested protocol on rebuilding trust.

Self-Managed Teams

 LO9.5

Have you ever thought you could do a better job than your boss? Well, if the trend toward self-managed work teams continues to grow, you just may get your chance. More than 75% of the top 1,000 U.S. companies currently use some form of self-managed team.[56] For example, teams at Google have wide latitude to evaluate and launch projects. One team, whose business responsibility is encouraging programmers outside the company to develop more open-source software, decided to do this by

Reina's Seven-Step Model for Rebuilding Trust

Regardless of who is responsible for eroding or damaging trust, both parties need to be involved in the repair of trust. The following seven-step process can help, whether you are the perpetrator or victim.

1. Acknowledge what caused trust to be compromised.
2. Allow feelings and emotions to be discussed, constructively.
3. Get and give support to others in the process.
4. Reframe the experience and shift from being a victim to taking a look at options and choices. How you respond to what happens matters.
5. Take responsibility. Ask, "What did I do or not do that caused this to happen?"
6. Forgive yourself and others.
7. Let go and move on.

SOURCE: Excerpted and adapted from R Hastings, "Broken Trust Is Bad for Business," *Society of Human Resource Management,* March 7, 2011.

recruiting students. Without the need to go through an extensive process to get management approval, they launched the program, quickly expanding it "from 400 paid interns to 900 in 90 countries."[57] Typically, self-managed teams schedule work and assign duties, with managers present to serve as trainers and facilitators. However, self-managed teams—variously referred to as semiautonomous work groups, autonomous work groups, and superteams—come in every conceivable format today, some more autonomous than others (see the Hands-On Exercise on page 241 to assess one of your own team's autonomy).

Self-managed teams **are defined as groups of workers who are given administrative oversight for their task domains.** Administrative oversight involves delegated activities such as planning, scheduling, monitoring, and staffing. These are "chores" normally performed by managers. In short, employees in these unique work groups act as their own supervisor. Accountability is maintained *indirectly* by outside managers and leaders.

Managerial Resistance   Something much more complex is involved than this apparently simple label suggests. The term *self-managed* does not mean simply turning workers loose to do their own thing. Indeed, an organization embracing self- managed teams should be prepared to undergo revolutionary changes in management philosophy, structure, staffing and training practices, and reward systems. The traditional notions of managerial authority (discussed in detail in Chapter 13) and control are turned on their heads. Not surprisingly, many managers strongly resist giving up the reins of power to people they view as subordinates. They see self-managed teams as a threat to their job security.

Cross-Functionalism   **A common feature of self-managed teams, particularly among those above the shop-floor or clerical level, is *cross-functionalism*.**[58] In other words, specialists from different areas are put on the same team. New product development is a popular area in which organizations utilize cross-functional teams. An example was provided by Brian Walker, the CEO of furniture maker Herman Miller. In an interview with FastCompany, Mr. Walker described how the company makes use of self-management and cross-functional teams to utilize the talents of employees more fully in product development and boost company performance:

HANDS-ON EXERCISE

How Autonomous Is Your Work Group?

INSTRUCTIONS: Think of your current (or past) job and work group. Characterize the group's situation by selecting one number on the following scale for each statement. Add your responses for a total score:

Strongly Disagree | | | | | | **Strongly Agree**
1   2   3   4   5   6   7

Work Method Autonomy

1. My work group decides how to get the job done. _____
2. My work group determines what procedures to use. _____
3. My work group is free to choose its own methods when carrying out its work. _____

Work Scheduling Autonomy

4. My work group controls the scheduling of its work. _____
5. My work group determines how its work is sequenced. _____

6. My work group decides when to do certain activities. _____

Work Criteria Autonomy

7. My work group is allowed to modify the normal way it is evaluated so some of our activities are emphasized and some deemphasized. _____
8. My work group is able to modify its objectives (what it is supposed to accomplish). _____
9. My work group has some control over what it is supposed to accomplish. _____

Total score = _____

SCORING NORMS

9–26 = Low autonomy
27–45 = Moderate autonomy
46–63 = High autonomy

SOURCE: Adapted from an individual autonomy scale in J A Breaugh, "The Work Autonomy Scales: Additional Validity Evidence," *Human Relations,* November 1989, pp 1033–56.

We strive to realize the potential of all our employees and allow them to enjoy what they do. This often involves moving people beyond their current jobs and areas of expertise. If I can have 5,000 or 6,000 people who are passionate about what they do, using every bit of their capabilities in solving problems and finding solutions to our customers' problems, I'm going to be much better off than if I leave that to 10 percent of that population who tell the other people what to do. . .

[To do this] we're big believers in putting teams together . . . we're very willing to move folks around between departments. In our design process, for example, we deliberately create tension by putting together a cross-functional team that includes people from manufacturing, finance, research, ergonomists, marketing and sales. The manufacturing guys want something they know they can make easily and fits their processes. The salespeople want what their customers have been asking for. The tension comes from finding the right balance, being willing to follow those creative leaps to the new place, and convincing the organization it's worth the risk.[59]

Are Self-Managed Teams Effective? Research from the 1990s and 2000s showed mixed results. Self-managed teams have been shown to improve work–life quality, customer service, and productivity. However, other studies reported low or no improvement in these same outcomes.[60] A review of three meta-analyses covering 70 individual studies concluded that self-managed teams had a positive effect on productivity and on specific attitudes relating to self-management (e.g., responsibility and control). But self-managed teams had no significant effect on general attitudes (e.g., job satisfaction and organizational commitment) and no significant effect on absenteeism or turnover.[61]

Although encouraging, these results do not qualify as a sweeping endorsement of self-managed teams. Nonetheless, experts say the trend toward self-managed work teams will continue upward in North America because of a strong cultural bias in favor of direct participation. Managers need to be prepared for the resulting shift in organizational administration.

Virtual Teams

A *virtual team* is a physically dispersed task group that conducts its business through information communication technology (ICT). Virtual teams are a product of evolving information technologies discussed in Chapter 12, such as webcasts, Skype, teleconferencing, Telepresence, email, instant messaging, texting, and GoTo-Meeting, among others. Traditional team meetings, for example, are location-specific. Team members are either physically present or absent. Virtual teams, in contrast, convene electronically with members reporting in from different locations, different organizations, and even different time zones. In other words, the workforce is *distributed*. Distributed workers often have no permanent office at their companies, preferring to work in home offices, cafés, airports, high-school stadium bleachers, client conference rooms, the beach, or other places. They are members of teams and projects connected by the Web. Advocates say virtual teams are very flexible and efficient because they are driven by information and skills, not by time and location.[62] People with needed information and/or skills can be team members, regardless of where or when they actually do their work. Today it seems that most people are connected to work remotely at least some of the time. One estimate is that nearly 1 billion people will work remotely via the Internet in 2011.[63] And more than 60% of companies with more than 5,000 employees utilize virtual teams.[64]

Technology not only allows people to communicate with whom, where, and when they wish, but it also allows many people (and organizations) to work without offices. For you personally, what would be/are the advantages and disadvantages of telecommuting and virtual work?

Research Insights—Benefits and Challenges   Virtual teams and distributed workers present many potential benefits: reduced real estate costs (limited or no office space); ability to leverage diverse knowledge, skills, and experience across geography (e.g., one doesn't have to have an SAP expert in every office); and ability to share knowledge of diverse markets. The flexibility often afforded by virtual teams also can reduce work-life conflicts for employees (discussed in Chapter 11).[65] However, virtual teams have challenges, too. A 2010 survey by an intercultural consulting company provided many interesting insights into virtual teams in multinational companies. The survey included 1,592 employees from 77 countries and showed that differing times zones was the number-one challenge (noted by 81% of participants), followed by language difficulties (64%), and then holidays, local laws, and customs (59%). Interpersonally, members of virtual teams also reported the inability to observe nonverbal cues, a lack of collegiality, and difficulties establishing trust.[66] Different time zones and the inability to observe nonverbals are challenges that easily generalize to virtual teams more generally, not only those that cross national borders.

Practical Considerations   David Clemons and Michael Kroth, authors of *Managing the Mobile Workforce,* offer several recommendations to help team members and teams as a whole to overcome the above challenges.

- *Be strategic about communications.* Be sure you talk to the right people, at the right times, about the right topics. Don't just blanket everybody via email—focus the message, target the audience, and choose the appropriate communication medium (more on this in Chapter 12). Accommodate the differing time zones in a fair and consistent manner.
- *Develop productive relationships with key people on the team.* This may require extra attention, communication, and travel, but do what it takes. Key people are the ones you can lean on and the ones that will make or break the team assignment.
- *Partner.* It is common that members of virtual teams are not direct employees of your employer (e.g., contractors). Nevertheless, your success and that of your team depend on them. Treat them like true partners and not hired help. You need them and presumably they need you.
- *Pace.* Because of different time zones, some projects can receive attention around the clock, as they are handed off from one zone to the next. Doing this effectively requires that both senders and receivers clearly specify what they have completed and what they need in each transfer.
- *Focus.* Keeping individuals and the team on task requires clear priorities and consistent updates. Clearly defining roles and responsibilities also helps. The importance of this increases as the size and geographic dispersion of the team grows.[67]

Researchers and consultants are consistent about one aspect of virtual teams—*there is no substitute for face-to-face contact.* Members need to put faces to names and work. Meeting in person is especially beneficial early in virtual team development,[68] and team leaders are encouraged to meet even more frequently with key members.[69] Furthermore, virtual teams cannot succeed without some additional and old-fashioned factors, such as effective decision making, trust, communication, training, a clear mission and specific objectives, effective leadership, schedules, and deadlines.[70] Additional recommendations for managing virtual teams and meetings are provided in the Skills & Best Practices on page 244.

Threats and Facilitators of Group and Team Effectiveness

No matter how carefully managers staff and organize task groups and teams, group dynamics can still go haywire. Forehand knowledge of two major threats to group effectiveness—groupthink and social loafing—can help managers and team members alike take necessary preventive steps. Likewise, it is appropriate to conclude our discussion of groups and teams by addressing some key means for enhancing their effectiveness.

Tips for Effectively Managing Virtual Teams and Meetings

- Prepare and distribute agendas in advance.
- Initiate meetings with "roll call" of all participants; review agenda, meeting objectives, and time frame.
- Identify the key roles of facilitator and scribe.
- Position participants in locations free of distractions or background noise.
- Promote a climate of collaboration and inclusion; encourage every attendee to participate and express his or her view.
- Encourage participants to use available technology effectively.
- Conduct a meeting evaluation at the close of the session.
- Establish expectations for distribution of the meeting minutes.
- Establish "next steps" and make follow-up assignments.

SOURCE: N Lockwood, "Successfully Transitioning to a Virtual Organization: Challenges, Impact, and Technology," *Society of Human Resource Management—Research Quarterly*, First Quarter 2010.

Threats to Effectiveness

LO9.6

Groupthink   Systematic analysis of the decision-making processes underlying the war in Vietnam and other U.S. foreign policy fiascoes prompted Yale University's Irving Janis to coin the term *groupthink*.[71] Modern managers can all too easily become victims of groupthink, just like professional politicians, if they passively ignore the danger. **Janis defines *groupthink* as "a mode of thinking that people engage in when they are deeply involved in a cohesive in-group, when members' strivings for unanimity override their motivation to realistically appraise alternative courses of action."**[72] He adds, "Groupthink refers to a deterioration of mental efficiency, reality testing, and moral judgment that results from in-group pressures."[73] Members of groups victimized by groupthink tend to be friendly and tightly knit.

According to Janis's model, there are eight classic symptoms of groupthink. The greater the number of symptoms, the higher the probability of groupthink:

1. *Invulnerability.* An illusion that breeds excessive optimism and risk taking.
2. *Inherent morality.* A belief that encourages the group to ignore ethical implications.
3. *Rationalization.* Protects personal or "pet" assumptions.
4. *Stereotyped views of opposition.* Cause group to underestimate opponents.
5. *Self-censorship.* Stifles critical debate.
6. *Illusion of unanimity.* Silence interpreted to mean consent.
7. *Peer pressure.* Loyalty of dissenters is questioned.
8. *Mindguards.* Self-appointed protectors against adverse information.[74]

These conditions often create a climate of fear in participants, described by Duke Business professor Richard Larrick as: "the fear that everyone else knows more, so I'll just go along . . . [and] the fear that the boss has already really decided, so why bother to stick my neck out?"[75]

Janis believes that prevention is better than cure when dealing with groupthink (see Skills & Best Practices on page 245 for his preventive measures).[76] Researchers at

How to Prevent Groupthink

1. Each member of the group should be assigned the role of critical evaluator. This role involves actively voicing objections and doubts.
2. Top-level executives should not use policy committees to rubber-stamp decisions that have already been made.
3. Different groups with different leaders should explore the same policy questions.
4. Subgroup debates and outside experts should be used to introduce fresh perspectives.
5. Someone should be given the role of devil's advocate when discussing major alternatives. This person tries to uncover every conceivable negative factor.
6. Once a consensus has been reached, everyone should be encouraged to rethink their position to check for flaws.

SOURCE: Adapted from discussion in I L Janis, *Groupthink,* 2nd ed (Boston: Houghton Mifflin, 1982), chap 11.

Wharton Business School provided other preventative suggestions. They recommended that teams charged with creativity or developing new ideas (e.g., new products, cost savings, or novel marketing plans) should first brainstorm individually. Members can then come together and critique alternatives as a group. Their research showed that groups using this practice performed better than those that simply brainstormed together. (A more thorough discussion of decision-making techniques follows in Chapter 10.)[77]

At pharmaceutical company Alkermes, chief financial officer Jim Frates applies these principles when groups assemble to make major decisions. He avoids revealing his own opinion, questions assumptions, and speaks in favor of ideas not getting much attention, to see if there is quiet support. For example, when Frates and others were interviewing candidates for a senior finance job, group members were eager to extend an offer to one individual. To proceed carefully and ensure that all views were being aired, Frates asked the group to state negatives as well as positives about the candidate they were rushing to hire. It quickly became clear that they had hoped for someone with more management experience, so the group backed away from its first choice and continued recruiting until they found the right person for this key job.[78]

Social Loafing   Is group performance less than, equal to, or greater than the sum of its parts? Can three people working together, for example, accomplish less than, the same as, or more than they would working separately? An interesting study conducted more than a half century ago by a French agricultural engineer named Ringelmann found the answer to be "less than."[79] In a rope-pulling exercise ("tug-of-war"), Ringelmann reportedly found that three people pulling together could achieve only two and a half times the average individual rate. Eight pullers achieved less than four times the individual rate. **This tendency for individual effort to decline as group size increases has come to be called** *social loafing.*[80] Let us briefly analyze this threat to group effectiveness and synergy with an eye toward avoiding it.

Social Loafing Theory and Research   Generally, social loafing or "free-riding" increases as group size increases and work is more widely dispersed.[81] A number of reasons explain this phenomenon, such as: (1) equity of effort ("Everyone else is goofing off, so why shouldn't I?"), (2) loss of personal accountability ("I'm lost in the crowd, so who cares?"), (3) motivational loss due to the sharing of rewards ("Why should I work harder than the others when everyone gets the same reward?"), and (4) coordination loss as more people perform the task ("We're getting in each other's way.").

However, recent laboratory research with 90 four-member teams showed that hybrid rewards—those that include team and individual components—reduced social loafing and improved information sharing. Hybrid rewards held members accountable both as individuals and as a team.[82] Research further suggests that self-reliant "individualists" are more prone to social loafing than are group-oriented "collectivists." Individualists also can be made more cooperative by keeping the group small and holding each member personally accountable for results.[83]

Facilitators of Effectiveness

We conclude this chapter with some practical suggestions to enhance group and team effectiveness. While there are many, the following encompass many of the topics covered in this chapter and are supported by research and practice. We first present research based on a nationwide survey that asked respondents, "What is a high-performance team?" Participants were also asked to describe their peak experiences in teams. The following eight attributes of high-performance teams emerged:

1. *Participative leadership.* Creating an interdependency by empowering, freeing up, and serving others.

2. *Shared responsibility.* Establishing an environment in which all team members feel as responsible as the manager for the performance of the work unit.

3. *Aligned on purpose.* Having a sense of common purpose about why the team exists and the function it serves.

4. *High communication.* Creating a climate of trust and open, honest communication.

5. *Future focused.* Seeing change as an opportunity for growth.

6. *Focused on task.* Keeping meetings focused on results.

7. *Creative talents.* Applying individual talents and creativity.

8. *Rapid response.* Identifying and acting on opportunities.[84]

More recent research provides three additional and important factors to consider when building effective teams.

- *Team charters and performance strategies.* Both researchers and practitioners urge groups and teams to plan before tackling their tasks, early in the group development process (e.g., storming stage). These plans should include **team charters that describe how the team will operate, such as processes for sharing information and decision making (teamwork).** Teams should also create and implement **team performance strategies, which are deliberate plans that outline what exactly the team is to do, such as defining particular tasks and member responsibilities.**[85]

- *Team composition.* **Team composition is a term that describes the collection of jobs, personalities, knowledge, skills, abilities, and experience of its members.** It is important that team member characteristics fit the responsibilities of the team for it to be effective. Fit facilitates team effectiveness and misfit impedes it—you need the right people on your team. It therefore is best if the objectives of the team are known, at least preliminarily, and that careful consideration is then given to team composition. While best if done early in the development process, the composition may need to change as the team clarifies its charter and strategies, moves through the development process, and external demands change.

- *Team adaptive capacity.* Research shows that **team adaptive capacity (i.e., adaptability) is important to meet changing demands and to effectively transition members in and out.** It is fostered by individuals who are motivated both to achieve an accurate view of the world (versus an ethnocentric or self-centered view) and to work effectively with others to achieve outcomes.[86]

These elements combined should provide you with many tools with which to analyze and manage teams and groups more effectively.

key terms

cross-functionalism 240	norm 233	team building 236
formal group 227	role 231	team charters 246
group 226	self-managed teams 240	team composition 246
group cohesiveness 230	social loafing 245	team performance strategies 216
groupthink 244	task roles 231	trust 238
informal group 227	team 235	virtual team 242
maintenance roles 231	team adaptive capacity 247	

chapter summary

- *Describe the five stages of Tuckman's theory of group development.* The five stages in Tuckman's theory are *forming* (the group comes together), *storming* (members test the limits and each other), *norming* (questions about authority and power are resolved as the group becomes more cohesive), *performing* (effective communication and cooperation help the group get things done), and *adjourning* (group members go their own way).

- *Contrast roles and norms, and specify four reasons why norms are enforced in organizations.* While roles are specific to the person's position, norms are shared attitudes that differentiate appropriate from inappropriate behavior in a variety of situations. Norms evolve informally and are enforced because they help the group or organization survive, clarify behavioral expectations, help people avoid embarrassing situations, and clarify the group's or organization's central values.

- *Describe four attributes of a team player.* Team players do more than "just get along." They are committed, collaborative, and competent. Their attitudes and actions exhibit (1) openness to new ideas and different ways of working;

(2) sharing of information, experience, and specialized knowledge; (3) seek opportunities for improvement; (4) develop working relationships with people from different functions; (5) look for win-win solutions to build trust and sustain relationships; (6) only join teams whose goals they highly value which fosters personal commitment; (7) reliable—do what you say, when you say it, are prompt and respectful; and are (8) results oriented.

- *Explain three ways to build trust and three ways to repair trust.* Six recommended ways to build trust are through communication, support, respect (especially delegation), fairness, predictability, and competence. Besides tending to each of these means for building trust, trust can be *repaired* using the following process: Acknowledge what caused trust to be compromised; allow feelings and emotions to be discussed constructively; get and give support to others in the process; reframe the experience and shift from being a victim to taking a look at options and choices; how you respond to what happens matters; take responsibility and ask, "What did I do or not do that caused this to happen?"; forgive yourself and others; and finally—let go and move on.

- *Describe self-managed teams and virtual teams.* Self-managed teams are groups of workers who are given administrative oversight for various chores normally performed by managers—such as planning, scheduling, monitoring, and staffing. They are typically cross-functional, meaning they are staffed with a mix of specialists from different areas. Self-managed teams vary widely in the autonomy or freedom they enjoy. A virtual team is a physically dispersed task group that conducts its business through modern information technology such as the Internet. Periodic and meaningful face-to-face contact seems to be crucial for virtual team members, especially during the early stages of group development.

- *Describe groupthink, and identify at least four of its symptoms.* Groupthink plagues cohesive in-groups that shortchange moral judgment while putting too much emphasis on unanimity. Symptoms of groupthink include invulnerability, inherent morality, rationalization, stereotyped views of opposition, self-censorship, illusion of unanimity, peer pressure, and mindguards. Critical evaluators, outside expertise, and devil's advocates are among the preventive measures recommended by Irving Janis, who coined the term *groupthink*.

discussion questions

1. Describe the importance of trust in the smooth functioning of teams.
2. What is your opinion about managers being friends with the people they supervise (in other words, overlapping formal and informal groups)?
3. Think of a situation at work (or school) where somebody violated your trust. What was the impact on your work? If this trust was later repaired, then explain what was done and why it worked.
4. Are virtual teams likely to be a passing fad? Why or why not?
5. Have you ever witnessed groupthink or social loafing first-hand? Explain the circumstances and how things played out. Looking back, what could have been done to prevent or remedy the situation?

legal/ethical challenge

When an A Is Not an A—Who's Responsible?

It is well known that the financial meltdown and recent recession were intimately tied to the mortgage market. At the heart of this was the pursuit of greater and greater returns. Financial institutions of all sorts (e.g., mortgage lenders, banks, investment banks, and insurance companies) got increasingly "creative" with their mortgage-related products and qualifications. This creativity enabled financial institutions to sell more homes, more mortgages, more mortgage-backed securities, and more insurance than they could otherwise. This also enabled millions of Americans to purchase homes that they otherwise could not qualify for or afford. Then the bubble popped! Home values dropped, credit dried up, returns fell, and so on. Now millions of homeowners are in foreclosure or are underwater on their homes (i.e., obligated to pay more than market value). Countless, mostly smaller, financial institutions went out of business while the largest were acquired or bailed out.

One important character in this story is missing, however: Ratings agencies! S&P, Moody's, and Fitch are the three biggest in the United States. They assign grades much like school—As, Bs, and Cs—to the securities created by pooling many mortgages into packages (e.g., bonds and other mortgage-backed securities). These grades were (and still are) fundamentally important to the entire market, as they determined to whom and at what terms these securities were sold. For example, many institutions (e.g., pension funds) can only purchase A-graded securities. It also is important to note that the agencies were and are paid for their "grading services" by the firms whose products they grade. Citigroup, for instance, pooled many mortgages it bought into packages—bonds. They then took these bonds to S&P to be graded, grades for which they paid. (A-rated bonds have more buyers than Bs, which have more than Cs.) It is no surprise then that those financial institutions shopped around for higher grades.

As it is now well known, the agencies' grades were often inaccurate. Like a professor assigning grades to papers without looking at them, they assigned A's to many securities that weren't worthy. If this isn't problem enough, under current law, the agencies are not legally responsible for their ratings or grades. (It's like the professor randomly assigning A's to everybody in the class with no consequences to the professor.) The agencies have long contended that their conclusions are simply "opinions" and are protected by the First Amendment.[87] While pending legislation intends to hold agencies accountable and liable, as it stands today they are not responsible for the grades they assign.

As a Regulator, What Should Be Done about Ratings Agencies?

1. Ratings agencies should be liable for their ratings. If financial institutions that create and sell fraudulent securities (e.g., those they expect to fail) can be prosecuted, then so too should the agencies that rated them as secure and sellable (e.g., an A rating).

2. Ratings agencies cannot be expected to fully understand the increasingly complex financial products presented to them. It is unreasonable for them to be held accountable.

3. Neither answer 1 nor 2 matters. The entire situation would take care of itself if the financial institutions were not the ones paying agencies for their ratings. An alternative payment arrangement would remedy the situation.

4. Invent another alternative and explain.

If you're looking for additional study materials, be sure to check out the Online Learning Center at

www.mhhe.com/kinickiob5e

for more information and interactivities that correspond to this chapter.

Making Decisions

Was Poor Decision Making a Cause of the Deepwater Horizon Disaster?

Federal authorities investigating BP's oil spill in the Gulf of Mexico are zeroing in on bad decisions, missed warnings, and worker disagreements in the hours before the April 20, 2010, inferno aboard the *Deepwater Horizon* that spawned one of the worst environmental disasters in U.S. history.

In particular, the panel is examining why rig workers missed telltale signs that the well was close to an uncontrollable blowout, according to an internal document assembled by the investigators and reviewed by *The Wall Street Journal*. The document lists more than 20 "anomalies" in the well's behavior

and the crew's response that particularly interest the investigators.

Investigators are also turning attention to decisions made by employees of Transocean Ltd, the rig's owner, in addition to those made by BP that day. In particular, the document suggests investigators are looking at whether better coordination between the two companies might have prevented the disaster. The document includes several instances of unexpected pressure increases, which triggered disagreements between workers from the two firms.

The list of 20 anomalies includes several irregularities in the well's behavior, some of which were already known. The list also includes instances where common well-control protocols weren't followed.

Aboard a rig, any single problem by itself might not be cause for alarm, according to industry officials with experience in deep-water drilling. But the cascade of problems on the *Deepwater Horizon* in the hours before it exploded should have been a warning to workers to try to shut the well or take other precautions to avoid potential disaster.

Eleven people died aboard the rig as it burned in April and sank.

In this week's planned testimony, the investigative panel is likely to ask rig workers why none of the signs led to a halt in work. Instead, workers from BP and Transocean kept taking steps to complete the well, including removing heavy fluid, known as drilling "mud," that is used to tamp down pressure within a well, according to documents previously released to congressional investigators.

It isn't clear if the crew noticed in the hours before the explosion that more fluid was leaving the well than workers were putting into it—a potential sign of a serious imbalance deep within a well that can lead to a catastrophe. These signs continued for several hours, until the well exploded shortly before 10 p.m.

At noon on April 20, some 10 hours before the blowout occurred, more fluid left the pipe than was expected during routine test. And around 4 p.m., pressure on the drill pipe was higher than expected, the panel notes. Both are indications that workers were losing control.

Workers were having a tough time determining exactly how much fluid was entering and leaving the well because simultaneous operations were underway. The panel was critical of this. "Hard to track fluid volumes in the wellbore when you are pumping mud to boat . . . and also [pumping] saltwater into the hole," the list notes.

Shortly before 5 p.m., pressure built up unexpectedly on the section of pipe suspended in the well. Managers from BP and Transocean disagreed on the significance of this. "Some employees recalled a disagreement between Transocean and BP on the rig floor about the negative test and pressure on the work string," the list notes.

At 7:10 p.m., BP's two top officials on the rig met near the spot where the pipe comes out of the water and through the rig's floor. They discussed the high pressure, according to the investigative panel, which has been gathering evidence for two months. Transocean rig workers offered an explanation that didn't raise an alarm.

That employees of Transocean, the rig's owner, might not have realized the seriousness of the situation—and may have misunderstood the data from the well—could shift some scrutiny onto that company. But most of the spotlight so far has fallen on BP, which owned the well and hired Transocean to drill it. BP has emerged as a target of criticism for, among other things, choosing a well design that was less costly to build than alternative designs, but which came with additional risks. The investigative panel's list of anomalies underscores how easy it can be to overlook signs that a deepwater well is in trouble and could turn deadly.[1]

THE CHAPTER-OPENING CASE reinforces the importance of managerial decision making. Decisions made by BP and Transocean led to the deaths of 11 men, 4.9 million barrels of oil being leaked into the Gulf, and hundreds of lawsuits filed for damages to the environment and for lost livelihoods. Experts estimate that these companies could be liable for billions.[2]

Individually, we all make decisions on a daily basis. From deciding what clothes to wear to whom we want to marry, our decisions impact our lives in many ways. Sometimes our choices are good and other times they are bad. At work, however, decision making is one of the primary responsibilities of being a manager, and the quality of one's decisions can have serious consequences. Consider the case of Ronald Shaich, chairman and CEO of Panera Bread Company. Despite objections from others around him, Shaich relied on his own judgment and intuition and sold off Au Bon Pain in 1998 in order to grow Panera Bread Company. He said it was a "bet-the-job kind of choice." At the time, Panera had 135 stores, but the sale resulted in $73 million to invest in Panera, and the rest is history. Panera now operates 1,500 cafés around the country.[3]

Decision making **entails identifying and choosing alternative solutions that lead to a desired state of affairs.** The process begins with a problem and ends when a solution has been chosen. To gain an understanding of how managers can make better decisions, this chapter focuses on (1) models of decision making, (2) decision-making biases, (3) evidence-based decision making, (4) the dynamics of decision making, and (5) group decision making.

Models of Decision Making

LO10.1

You can use two broad approaches to make decisions. You can follow a *rational model* or various *nonrational models*. Let us consider how each of these approaches works.

The Rational Model

The *rational model* **proposes that managers use a rational, four-step sequence when making decisions** (see Figure 10–1). According to this model, managers are completely objective and possess complete information to make a decision. Despite criticism for being unrealistic, the rational model is instructive because it analytically breaks down the decision-making process and serves as a conceptual anchor for newer models.[4] Let us now consider each of these four steps.

Stage 1: Identify the Problem or Opportunity—Determining the Actual versus the Desirable
A *problem* **exists when an actual situation and a desired situation differ.** As a manager, you will have no shortage of problems: customer complaints, employee turnover, new competitive products, production problems. Consider the problems faced by Mattel's CEO, Bob Eckert. He realized that his company had a problem when two of his top managers came to his office to tell him lead had been discovered in one of the company's toys. Around the same time, newspapers were publishing reports that magnets were becoming dislodged from other Mattel toys: If a small child swallowed them, they could cause serious damage by attaching themselves together in the child's intestines. Eckert had to decide whether his company had a publicity problem, a design problem, or a production problem—and if it were a production problem, where that problem was occurring and why.[5]

The Four Stages in Rational Decision Making   FIGURE 10–1

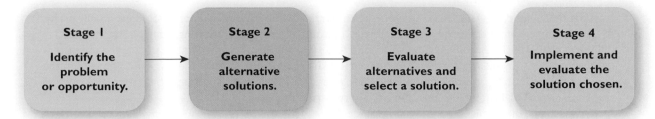

Stage 1	Stage 2	Stage 3	Stage 4
Identify the problem or opportunity.	**Generate alternative solutions.**	**Evaluate alternatives and select a solution.**	**Implement and evaluate the solution chosen.**

However, managers also have to make decisions regarding opportunities. An *opportunity* **represents a situation in which there are possibilities to do things that lead to results that exceed goals and expectations.** For example, Reed Hastings, founder, chairman, and CEO of Netflix, saw great opportunities in transforming his DVD-by-mail company into a streaming-video company (see Skills & Best Practices on page 254). Financial results suggest that Reed clearly capitalized on opportunity: Netflix was the stock of the year in 2010, increasing 200% since January, as compared to the S&P 500's 7% gain.[6]

Whether you face a problem or an opportunity, the goal is always the same: to make improvements that change conditions from their current state to more desirable ones. This requires you to diagnose the causes of the problem.

Stage 2: Generate Alternative Solutions—Both the Obvious and the Creative   After identifying a problem and its causes, the next logical step is generating

alternative solutions. Unfortunately, a research study of 400 strategic decisions revealed that managers struggled during this stage because of three key decision-making blunders. These blunders were (1) rushing to judgment, (2) selecting readily available ideas or solutions, and (3) making poor allocation of resources to study alternative solutions. Decision makers thus are encouraged to slow down when making decisions, to evaluate a broader set of alternatives, and to invest in studying a greater number of potential solutions.[7]

Stage 3: Evaluate Alternatives and Select a Solution—Ethics, Feasibility, and Effectiveness   In this stage, you need to evaluate alternatives in terms of several criteria. Not only are costs and quality important, but you should consider the following questions: (1) Is the potential solution ethical? (If not, don't consider it.) Returning to the earlier example of Mattel's problems, CEO Eckert said, "How you achieve success is just as important as success itself."[8] He announced a recall

Managers at Mattel had some serious decisions to make when they learned that toys on store shelves were contaminated with lead paint and magnets that could come loose. Do you think they made the right decision to recall several million toys?

of 18.2 million toys, the largest recall in Mattel's history. The company also announced that its magnet toys had been redesigned to make them safer and that it had investigated the Chinese contractor that had used the paint containing lead. (2) Is it feasible? (If time is an issue, costs are high, resources are limited, technology is needed, or

Reed Hastings Seizes Opportunities to Grow Netflix

Hastings anticipated, virtually from the moment he started Netflix, that consumers would eventually prefer to get movies instantly delivered via the Internet. (Hastings's foresight is amazing, considering that back in 2000, less than 7% of U.S. homes had broadband.) And so rather than let any number of current and potential competitors—including premium cable channels like HBO … and some of the biggest companies in the tech world—swoop in and deliver a lethal blow, Hastings is now retooling Netflix as a streaming-video company, disrupting his own business before it gets disrupted.

For Hastings, the decline of AOL is a reminder of what happens to companies unwilling to take risks. AOL, the dominant dial-up online service, struggled as broadband service proliferated. It had good e-mail and some unique content, but those services didn't buy AOL loyalty or make it synonymous with broadband, and ultimately AOL lost customers.

The opportunity faced by Hastings involved deciding how to get Netflix's 10 million subscribers to switch from DVD to streaming. He ultimately decided to give streaming away for free.

SOURCE: Excerpted from M V Copeland, "Reed Hastings: Leader of the Pack," *Fortune,* **December 6, 2010, p 123.**

---

customers are resistant, for instance, then the alternative is not feasible.) (3) Will it remove the causes and solve the problem?

Stage 4: Implement and Evaluate the Solution Chosen Once a solution is chosen, it needs to be implemented. After a solution is implemented, the evaluation phase is used to assess its effectiveness. If the solution is effective, it should reduce the difference between the actual and desired states that created the problem. If the gap is not closed, the implementation was not successful, and one of the following is true: Either the problem was incorrectly identified, or the solution was inappropriate. In the first case, the decision maker should return to the beginning of the process and redefine the problem. In the second case, the decision maker should try to generate more solutions and select a different solution to implement.

www.mcgrawhillconnect.com

Go to Connect for an interactive exercise to test your knowledge of the rational decision making model.

Summarizing the Rational Model The rational model is based on the premise that managers optimize when they make decisions. ***Optimizing* involves solving problems by producing the best possible solution.** As noted by Herbert Simon, a decision theorist who in 1978 earned the Nobel Prize for his work on decision making, "The assumptions of perfect rationality are contrary to fact. It is not a question of approximation; they do not even remotely describe the processes that human beings use for making decisions in complex situations."[9]

That said, there are three benefits of trying to follow a rational process as much as realistically possible.

1. The quality of decisions may be enhanced, in the sense that they follow more logically from all available knowledge and expertise.

2. It makes the reasoning behind a decision transparent and available to scrutiny.

3. If made public, it discourages the decider from acting on suspect considerations (such as personal advancement or avoiding bureaucratic embarrassment).[10]

Nonrational Models of Decision Making

In contrast to the rational model's focus on how decisions should be made, ***nonrational models* attempt to explain how decisions actually are made.** They are based on the assumption that decision making is uncertain, that decision makers do not possess complete information, and that it is difficult for managers to make optimal decisions. Two nonrational models are Herbert Simon's *normative* model and the *garbage can model*.

Simon's Normative Model   Herbert Simon proposed this model to describe the process that managers actually use when making decisions. The process is guided by a decision maker's bounded rationality. ***Bounded rationality* represents the notion that decision makers are "bounded" or restricted by a variety of constraints when making decisions.** These constraints include any personal characteristics or internal and external resources that reduce rational decision making. Personal characteristics include the limited capacity of the human mind, personality (a meta-analysis of 150 studies showed that males displayed more risk taking than females),[11] and time constraints. Examples of internal resources are the organization's human and social capital, financial resources, technology, plant and equipment, and internal processes and systems. External resources include things the organization cannot directly control such as employment levels in the community, capital availability, and government policies.[12]

Ultimately, these limitations result in the tendency to acquire manageable rather than optimal amounts of information. In turn, this practice makes it difficult for managers to identify all possible alternative solutions. In the long run, the constraints of bounded rationality cause decision makers to fail to evaluate all potential alternatives, thereby causing them to satisfice.

***Satisficing* consists of choosing a solution that meets some minimum qualifications, one that is "good enough."** Satisficing resolves problems by producing solutions that are satisfactory, as opposed to optimal. Finding a radio station to listen to in your car is a good example of satisficing. You cannot optimize because it is impossible to listen to all stations at the same time. You thus stop searching for a station when you find one playing a song you like or do not mind hearing.

A recent national survey by the Business Performance Management Forum underscores the existence of satisficing: only 26% of respondents indicated that their companies had formal, well-understood decision-making processes. Respondents noted that the most frequent causes of poor decision making included:

- Poorly defined processes and practices.
- Unclear company vision, mission, and goals.
- Unwillingness of leaders to take responsibility.
- A lack of reliable, timely information.[13]

The Garbage Can Model   Another response to the rational model's inability to explain how decisions are actually made assumes that organizational decision making is a sloppy and haphazard process. According to the ***garbage can model*, decisions result from a complex interaction between four independent streams of events: problems, solutions, participants, and choice opportunities.**[14] The interaction of these events creates "a collection of choices looking for problems, issues and feelings looking for decision situations in which they might be aired, solutions looking for issues to which they might be the answer, and decision makers looking for work."[15]

A similar type of process occurs in your kitchen garbage basket. We randomly discard our trash, and it gets mashed together based on chance interactions and timing. Just like the process of mixing garbage in a trash container, the garbage can model of decision making assumes that decision making does not follow an orderly series of steps. Rather, attractive solutions can get matched up with whatever handy problems exist at a given point in time, or people get assigned to projects because their work load is low at that moment. This model of decision making thus attempts to explain how problems, solutions, participants, and choice opportunities interact and lead to a decision.

The garbage can model has four practical implications. First, this model of decision making is more pronounced in industries that rely on science-based innovations such as pharmaceutical companies.[16] Managers in these industries thus need to be more alert for the potential of haphazard decision making. Second, many decisions are made by oversight or by the presence of a salient opportunity. For example, the Campbell Soup Company needed to find a way to motivate supermarkets to give them more space on the shelves. They thus decided to create a new shelving system that automatically slides soup cans to the front when a shopper picks up a can. The decision was a success. Customers bought more soup, increasing the revenue for both Campbell and the supermarkets, and the supermarkets reduced their restocking costs.[17]

Third, political motives frequently guide the process by which participants make decisions. It thus is important for you to consider the political ramifications of your decisions. Organizational politics are discussed in Chapter 13. Finally, important problems are more likely to be solved than unimportant ones because they are more salient to organizational participants.[18]

Integrating Rational and Nonrational Models

Applying the idea that decisions are shaped by characteristics of problems and decision makers, consultants David Snowden and Mary Boone have come up with their own approach that is not as haphazard as the garbage can model but acknowledges the challenges facing today's organizations. They identify four kinds of decision environments and an effective method of decision making for each.[19]

1. A *simple* context is stable, and clear cause-and-effect relationships can be discerned, so the best answer can be agreed on. This context calls for the rational model, where the decision maker gathers information, categorizes it, and responds in an established way.

2. In a *complicated* context, there is a clear relationship between cause and effect, but some people may not see it, and more than one solution may be effective. Here, too, the rational model applies, but it requires the investigation of options, along with analysis of them.

3. In a *complex* context, there is one right answer, but there are so many unknowns that decision makers don't understand cause-and-effect relationships. Decision makers therefore need to start out by experimenting, testing options, and probing to see what might happen as they look for a creative solution.

4. In a *chaotic* context, cause-and-effect relationships are changing so fast that no pattern emerges. In this context, decision makers have to act first to establish order and then find areas where it is possible to identify patterns so that aspects of the problem can be managed. The use of intuition and evidence-based decision making, both of which are discussed later in this chapter, may be helpful in this situation.[20]

> **BACK TO THE CHAPTER-OPENING CASE**   What type of model of decision making best exemplifies what happened on the *Deepwater Horizon* rig?

Decision-Making Biases

People make a variety of systematic mistakes when making decisions. These mistakes are generally associated with a host of biases that occur when we use judgmental heuristics. ***Judgmental heuristics* represent rules of thumb or shortcuts that people use to reduce information-processing demands.**[21] We automatically use them without conscious awareness. The use of heuristics helps decision makers reduce the uncertainty inherent within the decision-making process. Because these shortcuts represent knowledge gained from experience, they can help decision makers evaluate current problems. But they also can lead to systematic errors that erode the quality of decisions. For example, a recent study of medical malpractice claims showed that diagnostic errors, which are partly a function of judgmental heuristics, accounted for about 40% of such cases. Diagnostic errors kill 40,000 to 80,000 people a year in the United States. Experts suggest that we need to become more involved with our health care and follow up on lab results to help reduce such mistakes.[22]

 LO10.2

More specifically, eight biases may affect decision making:

1. **Availability heuristic.** The availability heuristic represents a decision maker's tendency to base decisions on information that is readily available in memory. Information is more accessible in memory when it involves an event that recently occurred, when it is salient (e.g., a plane crash), and when it evokes strong emotions (e.g., a college student shooting other students). This heuristic is likely to cause people to overestimate the occurrence of unlikely events such as a plane crash or a college shooting. This bias also is partially responsible for the recency effect discussed in Chapter 4. For example, a manager is more likely to give an employee a positive performance evaluation if the employee exhibited excellent performance over the last few months.

2. **Representativeness heuristic.** The representativeness heuristic is used when people estimate the probability of an event occurring. It reflects the tendency to assess the likelihood of an event occurring based on one's impressions about similar occurrences. A manager, for example, may hire a graduate from a particular university because the past three people hired from this university turned out to be good performers. In this case, the "school attended" criterion is used to facilitate complex information processing associated with employment interviews. Unfortunately, this shortcut can result in a biased decision. Similarly, an individual may believe that he or she can master a new software package in a short period of time because a different type of software was easy to learn. This estimate may or may not be accurate. For example, it may take the individual much longer to learn the new software because it involves learning a new programming language.

3. **Confirmation bias.** The confirmation bias has two components. The first is to subconsciously decide something before investigating why it is the right decision. This directly leads to the second component, which is to seek information that supports our point of view and to discount information that does not.

Go to Connect for an interactive exercise to test your knowledge of decision making biases.

4. **Anchoring bias.** How would you answer the following two questions? Is the population of Iraq greater than 40 million? What's your best guess about the population of Iraq? Was your answer to the second question influenced by the number *40 million* suggested by the first question? If yes, you were affected by the anchoring bias. The anchoring bias occurs when decision makers are influenced by the first information received about a decision, even if it is irrelevant. This bias happens because initial information, impressions, data, feedback, or stereotypes anchor our subsequent judgments and decisions.

5. **Overconfidence bias.** The overconfidence bias relates to our tendency to be overconfident about estimates or forecasts. This bias is particularly strong when you are asked moderate to extremely difficult questions rather than easy ones. Research shows that overoptimism significantly influences entrepreneurs' decisions to start and sustain new ventures.[23] Imagine the challenges this bias might create for managers in difficult and dangerous situations. To what extent do you think this bias affected the *Deepwater Horizon* oil rig explosion featured in the chapter-opening case? A presidential oil-spill commission concluded that technological arrogance, hubris, and the overconfidence bias played major roles (see Skills & Best Practices on page 259).[24]

6. **Hindsight bias.** Imagine yourself in the following scenario: You are taking an organizational behavior (OB) course that meets Tuesday and Thursday, and your professor gives unannounced quizzes each week. It's the Monday before a class, and you are deciding whether to study for a potential quiz or to watch Monday night football. Two of your classmates have decided to watch the game rather than study because they don't think there will be a quiz the next day. The next morning you walk into class and the professor says, "Take out a sheet of paper for the quiz." You turn to your friends and say, "I knew we were going to have a quiz; why did I listen to you?" The hindsight bias occurs when knowledge of an outcome influences our belief about the probability that we could have predicted the outcome earlier. We are affected by this bias when we look back on a decision and try to reconstruct why we decided to do something.

7. **Framing bias.** This bias relates to the manner in which a question is posed. Consider the following scenario: Imagine that the United States is preparing for the outbreak of an unusual Asian disease that is expected to kill 600 people. Two alternative programs to combat the disease have been proposed. Assume that the exact scientific estimates of the consequences of the programs are as follows:

   Program A: If Program A is adopted, 200 people will be saved.

   Program B: If Program B is adopted, there is a one-third probability that 600 people will be saved and a two-thirds probability that no one will be saved. Which of the two programs would you recommend?[25]

   Research shows that most people chose Program A even though the two programs produce the same results. This result is due to the framing bias. The framing bias is the tendency to consider risks about gains—saving lives—differently than risks pertaining to losses—losing lives. You are encouraged to frame decision questions in alternative ways in order to avoid this bias.

8. **Escalation of commitment bias.** The escalation of commitment bias refers to the tendency to stick to an ineffective course of action when it is unlikely that the bad situation can be reversed. Personal examples include investing more

Overconfidence Bias Partly to Blame for Oil-Rig Disaster

According to Bob Bea, an engineering professor at the University of California, Berkeley, "Technological disasters, like the BP oil spill, follow a well-worn 'trail of tears.'" Bea has investigated 630 different types of disasters and is an expert on offshore drilling.

"Bea categorizes disasters into four groups. One such group is when an organization simply ignores warning signs through overconfidence and incompetence. He thinks the BP spill falls into that category. Bea pointed to congressional testimony that BP ignored problems with a dead battery, leaky cement job, and loose hydraulic fittings."

"Disasters don't happen because of 'an evil empire,' Bea said. 'It's hubris, arrogance and indolence.'"

The *Deepwater Horizon* drilling rig

"Cutting-edge technology often works flawlessly. At first, everyone worries about risk. Then people get lulled into complacency by success, and they forget that they are operating on the edge, say experts who study disasters. Corners get cut, problems ignored. Then boom."

Charles Perrow, a professor at Yale University, concluded that "there's nothing safe out there. We like to pretend there is and argue afterward, 'That's why we took the risks, because it hadn't failed before.'"

SOURCE: Excerpted from S Borenstein, "Disasters Often Stem from Hubris," *The Arizona Republic,* **July 12, 2010, p A4.**

money into an old or broken car, waiting an extremely long time for a bus to take you somewhere when you could have walked just as easily, or trying to save a disruptive personal relationship that has already lasted 10 years. A business example pertains to Blockbuster "asking creditors to put up more money to help it exit bankruptcy protection, prompting a debate among bondholders about whether to invest further in the struggling video chain or put it up for sale."[26] Would you invest in Blockbuster? Researchers recommend the following actions to reduce the escalation of commitment:

- Set minimum targets for performance, and have decision makers compare their performance against these targets.
- Regularly rotate managers in key positions throughout a project.
- Encourage decision makers to become less ego-involved with a project.
- Make decision makers aware of the costs of persistence.[27]

BACK TO THE CHAPTER-OPENING CASE Which of the decision-making biases played a potential role in the disaster?

Evidence-Based Decision Making

LO10.3

Interest in the concept of evidence-based decision making stems from two sources. The first is the desire to avoid the decision-making biases discussed in the previous section, and the second is research done on evidence-based medicine. Dr David Sackett defines evidence-based medicine as "the conscientious, explicit, and judicious use of current best evidence in making decisions about the care of individual patients." Researchers and practitioners are studying evidence-based medicine because research suggests that physicians only make 15% of their decisions based on evidence, and this approach helps determine the most efficient use of health care resources.[28] OB researchers have taken this framework and applied it to the context of managerial decision making.

Quite simply, *evidence-based decision making (EBDM)* **represents a process of conscientiously using the best available data and evidence when making managerial decisions.** We explore this new approach to decision making by beginning with a model of EBDM and then reviewing a set of implementation principles that can help companies to implement this model of decision making. We conclude by examining the reasons why it is hard to implement EBDM. Understanding this material will help you reduce the susceptibility to decision-making biases.

A Model of Evidence-Based Decision Making (EBDM)

Figure 10–2 illustrates a five-step model of EBDM.[29] You can see that the process begins by gathering internal and external data and evidence about a problem at hand. This information is then integrated with views from stakeholders (e.g., employees, shareholders, customers) and ethical considerations to make a final decision. All told, the process shown in Figure 10–2 helps managers to face hard facts and avoid their personal biases when making decisions. EBDM's use of relevant and reliable data from different sources is clearly intended to make any decision-making context more explicit, critical, systematic, and fact-based.

It is important to consider that evidence is used in three different ways within the process depicted in Figure 10–2: to make a decision, to inform a decision, and to support a decision.[30] "Evidence is used to *make* a decision whenever the decision follows

FIGURE 10–2   Evidence-Based Decision-Making Model

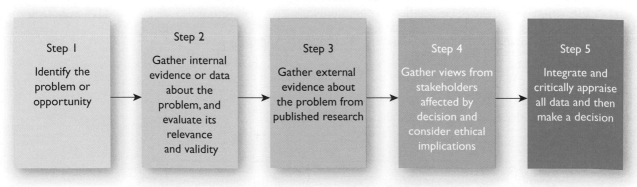

Step 1	Step 2	Step 3	Step 4	Step 5
Identify the problem or opportunity	Gather internal evidence or data about the problem, and evaluate its relevance and validity	Gather external evidence about the problem from published research	Gather views from stakeholders affected by decision and consider ethical implications	Integrate and critically appraise all data and then make a decision

SOURCE: Derived from R B Briner, D Denyer, and D M Rousseau, "Evidence-Based Management: Concept Cleanup Time?" *Academy of Management Perspectives,* November 2009, pp 19–32.

directly from the evidence." For example, if you wanted to purchase a particular used car (e.g., Toyota Prius) based on price and color (e.g., red), you would obtain data from the Internet and classified ads and then choose the seller offering the lowest-priced red Prius. "Evidence is used to inform a decision whenever the decision process combines hard, objective facts with qualitative inputs, such as intuition or bargaining with stakeholders." For instance, in hiring new college graduates, objective data about applicants' past experience, education, and participation in student organizations would be relevant input to making a hiring decision. Nonetheless, subjective impressions garnered from interviews and references would typically be combined with the objective data to make a final decision. These two uses of evidence are clearly positive and should be encouraged. The same cannot be said about using evidence to support a decision.

"Evidence is used to *support* a decision whenever the evidence is gathered or modified for the sole purpose of lending legitimacy to a decision that has already been made." This application of evidence has both positive and negative effects. On the positive side, manufactured evidence can be used to convince an external audience that the organization is following a sound course of action in response to a complex and ambiguous decision context. This can lead to confidence and goodwill about how a company is responding to environmental events. On the negative side, this practice can stifle employee involvement and input because people will come to believe that management is going to ignore evidence and just do what it wants. There are two takeaways about using evidence to support a decision. First, this practice should not always be avoided. Second, because this practice has both pros and cons, management needs to carefully consider when it "might" be appropriate to ignore disconfirming evidence and push its own agenda or decisions.

Seven Implementation Principles

Stanford professors Jeffrey Pfeffer and Robert Sutton have been studying evidence-based management for quite some time. Based on this experience, they offer seven implementation principles to help companies integrate EBDM into an organization's culture.[31]

1. **Treat your organization as an unfinished prototype.** The thrust of this principle involves creating a mindset that the organization is an unfinished prototype that may be broken and in need of repair, thus avoiding the hubris and arrogance of concluding that nothing needs to be changed in the organization. For example, the products QCV sells were chosen through a process of experimentation in which EBDM is used to understand why some products sell and others don't. The use of experiments, as done at QVC, is one recommendation for making this happen. The Skills & Best Practices on page 262 illustrates how one retailer uses experimentation to determine the best type of promotions.[32]

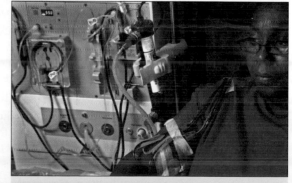

2. **No brag, just facts.** This slogan is used by DaVita, a company that operates 600 dialysis centers, to reinforce a culture that supports EBDM. The company measures, monitors, and rewards the effectiveness of its dialysis centers and patient well-being on a regular basis. In contrast, Hewlett Packard's former CEO, Carly Fiorina, bragged to the press about the company's merger

DaVita's dialysis centers attempt to provide better customer service to patients like this by using EBDM. Why would EBDM help to provide better service in this context?

A Retailer Experiments with Discount Promotions

The retailer designed six experimental conditions—a control and five discount levels that ranged from zero to 35% for the private-label items. The retailer divided its stores into six groups, and the treatments were randomized across the groups. This meant each store had a mixture of the experimental conditions distributed across the different products in the study. For example, in Store A, label sugar was discounted 20% and private-label mascara was full price, whereas in Store B mascara was discounted, but sugar was not. This experimental design allowed the retailer to control for variations in sales that occurred because the store groups were not identical.

The test revealed that matching the national-brand promotions with moderate discounts on the private-label products generated 10% more profits than not promoting the private-label items. As a result, the retailer now automatically discounts private-label items when the competing national brands are under promotion.

SOURCE: Excerpted from E T Anderson and D Simester, "Every Company Can Profit from Testing Customers' Reactions to Changes. Here's How to Get Started," *Harvard Business Review*, March 2011, p 103.

with Compaq but failed to do any research on consumers' opinions about Compaq products prior to the merger. These products were viewed as among the worst in the industry.

3. **See yourself and your organization as outsiders do.** Many managers are filled with optimism and inflated views of their talents and chances for success. This leads them to downplay risks and to commit an escalation of commitment bias. "Having a blunt friend, mentor, or counselor," Pfeffer and Sutton suggest, "can help you see and act on better evidence."

4. **Evidence-based management is not just for senior executives.** Research shows that the best organizations are those in which all employees, not just top managers, are committed to EBDM.[33] Pfeffer and Sutton encourage managers to "treat employees as if a big part of their job is to invent, find, test, and implement the best ideas." This implies that employees must be given the training and resources needed to engage in EBDM.

5. **Like everything else, you still need to sell it.** "Unfortunately, new and exciting ideas grab attention even when they are vastly inferior to old ideas," say Pfeffer and Sutton. "Vivid, juicy stories and case studies sell better than detailed, rigorous, and admittedly dull data—no matter how wrong the stories or how right the data." This means that you will need to similarly use vivid stories and case studies, such as the DaVita example used earlier, to sell the value of EBDM. You can also hire gurus to help sell the value of evidence-based practices.

6. **If all else fails, slow the spread of bad practice.** Because employees may face pressures to do things that are known to be ineffective, it may be necessary to engage in what Pfeffer and Sutton call "evidence-based misbehavior." This can include ignoring requests and delaying action. Be cautious if you use this principle.

7. **The best diagnostic question: what happens when people fail?** "Failure hurts, it is embarrassing, and we would rather live without it," say the Stanford professors. "Yet there is no learning without failure. . . . If you look at how the most effective systems in the world are managed, a hallmark is that when

something goes wrong, people face the hard facts, learn what happened and why, and keep using those facts to make the system better." The U.S. civil aviation system is a good example. It has created the safest system in world through its accident and incident reporting system. Ford's CEO Alan Mulally is another example. He meets with his top 15 executives every Thursday morning at 7 a.m. for 2½ hours to conduct a business plan review. "He requires his direct reports to post more than 300 charts, each of them color-coded red, yellow, or green to indicate problems, caution, or progress. . . . Afterward, the adjoining Tauras and Continental rooms are papered with these charts so Mulally can study them. As the CEO likes to say, 'You can't manage a secret. When you do this every week, you can't hide."[34]

Why Is It Hard to be Evidence Based?

Despite the known value of using EBDM, there are seven reasons why it is hard for anyone to bring the best evidence to bear when making decisions. They are: (1) There's too much evidence. (2) There's not enough good evidence. (3) The evidence doesn't quite apply. (4) People are trying to mislead you. (5) You are trying to mislead you. (6) The side effects outweigh the cure. (7) Stories are more persuasive anyway.[35] Your ability to use EBDM in your current and future jobs will depend on your ability to overcome these obstacles.

Dynamics of Decision Making

This section examines four dynamics of decision making: decision-making styles, intuition, a decision tree for making ethical decisions, and creativity. An understanding of these dynamics can help you make better decisions.

General Decision-Making Styles

This section focuses on how an individual's decision-making style affects his or her approach to decision making. A ***decision-making style* reflects the combination of how an individual perceives and comprehends stimuli and the general manner in which he or she chooses to respond to such information.**[36] A team of researchers developed a model of decision-making styles that is based on the idea that styles vary along two different dimensions: value orientation and tolerance for ambiguity.[37] *Value orientation* reflects the extent to which an individual focuses on either task and technical concerns or people and social concerns when making decisions. The second dimension pertains to a person's *tolerance for ambiguity*. This individual difference indicates the extent to which a person has a high need for structure or control in his or her life. When the dimensions of value orientation and tolerance for ambiguity are combined, they form four styles of decision making (see Figure 10–3): directive, analytical, conceptual, and behavioral.

Directive   People with a directive style have a low tolerance for ambiguity and are oriented toward task and technical concerns when making decisions. They are efficient, logical, practical, and systematic in their approach to solving problems. People with this style are action oriented and decisive and like to focus on facts. In their

⬥LO10.4

FIGURE 10–3   Decision-Making Styles

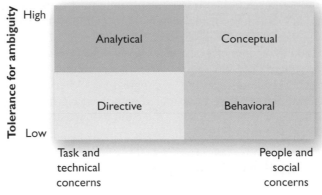

SOURCE: Based on discussion contained in A J Rowe and R O Mason, *Managing with Style: A Guide to Understanding, Assessing, and Improving Decision Making* (San Francisco: Jossey-Bass, 1987), pp 1–17.

pursuit of speed and results, however, these individuals tend to be autocratic, exercise power and control, and focus on the short run. Interestingly, a directive style seems well-suited for an air-traffic controller. Here is what Paul Rinaldi had to say about his decision-making style to a reporter from *Fortune*.

> It's not so much analytical as it is making a decision quickly and sticking with it. You have to do that knowing that some of the decisions you're going to make are going to be wrong, but you're going to make that decision be right. You can't back out. You've constantly got to be taking into account the speed of the airplane, its characteristics, the climb rate, and how fast it's going to react to your instructions. You're taking all that in and processing it in a split second, hoping that it'll all work together. If it doesn't, then you go to plan B. . . . The percentage of us that makes it to retirement is not real high. It takes a toll on you. We can't make mistakes.[38]

Air-traffic controller Paul Rinaldi uses a directive style to make quick decisions at Dulles International Airport. Would you like to work in this role?

Analytical   This style has a much higher tolerance for ambiguity and is characterized by the tendency to overanalyze a situation. People with this style like to consider more information and alternatives than do directives. Analytic individuals are careful decision makers who take longer to make decisions but who also respond well to new or uncertain situations. They can often be autocratic.

Zhang Guangming is a good example of someone with an analytical style. "Zhang Guangming's car-buying synapses have been in overdrive for months. He has spent hours poring over Chinese car buff magazines, surfing Web sites to mine data on various models, and trekking out to a dozen dealerships across Beijing. Finally, Zhang settled on either a Volkswagen Bora or a Hyundai Sonata sedan. But with cutthroat competition forcing dealers to slash prices, he's not sure whether to buy now or wait."[39]

Conceptual   People with a conceptual style have a high tolerance for ambiguity and tend to focus on the people or social aspects of a work situation. They take a broad perspective to problem solving and like to consider many options and future possibilities. Conceptual types adopt a long-term perspective and rely on intuition and discussions with others to acquire information. They also are willing to take risks and are good at finding creative solutions to problems. On the downside, however, a conceptual style can foster an idealistic and indecisive approach to decision making. Howard Stringer, Sony Corporation's first non-Japanese CEO, possesses characteristics of a conceptual style.

> Mr Stringer . . . says he recognizes the risk of falling behind amid breakneck changes in electronics. But he says there's an equal risk of moving too aggressively. "I don't want to change Sony's culture to the point where it's unrecognizable from the founder's vision," he says. . . . He tried gently persuading managers to cooperate with one another and urged them to think about developing products in a new way.[40]

Behavioral   People with a behavioral style work well with others and enjoy social interactions in which opinions are openly exchanged. Behavioral types are supportive, receptive to suggestions, show warmth, and prefer verbal to written information. Although they like to hold meetings, people with this style have a tendency to avoid conflict and to be too concerned about others. This can lead behavioral types to adopt a "wishy-washy" approach to decision making, to have a hard time saying no to others, and to have a hard time making difficult decisions.

Research and Practical Implications   Take a moment to complete the Hands-On Exercise on page 266. It assesses your decision-making style. How do your scores compare with the following norms: directive (75), analytical (90), conceptual (80), and behavioral (55)?[41] What do the differences between your scores and the survey norms suggest about your decision-making style?

Research shows that very few people have only one dominant decision-making style. Rather, most managers have characteristics that fall into two or three styles. Studies also show that decision-making styles vary across occupations, personality, gender, and countries.[42] You can use knowledge of decision-making styles in three ways. First, knowledge of styles helps you to understand yourself. Awareness of your style assists you in identifying your strengths and weaknesses as a decision maker and facilitates the potential for self-improvement. Second, you can increase your ability to influence others by being aware of styles. For example, if you are dealing with an analytical person, you should provide as much information as possible to support your ideas. This same approach is more likely to frustrate a directive type. Finally, knowledge of styles gives you an awareness of how people can take the same information and yet arrive at different decisions by using a variety of decision-making strategies. It is important to conclude with the caveat that there is not a best decision-making style that applies in all situations. We should all strive to capitalize on the strengths of the various decision-making styles while trying to achieve a "state of clarity" when making decisions.

Intuition in Decision Making

If you have ever had a hunch or gut feeling about something, you have experienced the effects of intuition. ***Intuition* represents judgments, insights, or decisions that "come to mind on their own, without explicit awareness of the evoking cues and of course without explicit evaluation of the validity of these cues."**[43] Research reveals that anyone can be intuitive, and its use is unrelated to gender.[44] In many decisions, it

HANDS-ON EXERCISE

What Is Your Decision-Making Style?

INSTRUCTIONS: This survey consists of 20 questions, each with four responses. You must consider each possible response for a question and then rank it according to how much you prefer each response. Because many of the questions are anchored to how individuals make decisions at work, you can use your student role as a frame of reference to answer the questions. For each question, use the space on the survey to rank the four responses with either a 1, 2, 4, or 8. Use the number 8 for the responses that are *most* like you, a 4 for those that are *moderately* like you, a 2 for those that are *slightly* like you, and a 1 for the responses that are *least* like you. For example, a question could be answered [8], [4], [2], [1]. Do not repeat any number when answering a question, and place the numbers in the boxes next to each of the answers. Once all of the responses for the 20 questions have been ranked, total the scores in each of the four columns. The total score for column 1 represents your directive style, column 2 your analytical style, column 3 your conceptual style, and column 4 your behavioral style.

	Directive style	Analytical style	Conceptual style	Behavioral style
1. My prime objective in life is to:	have a position with status	be the best in whatever I do	be recognized for my work	feel secure in my job
2. I enjoy work that:	is clear and well defined	is varied and challenging	lets me act independently	involves people
3. I expect people to be:	productive	capable	committed	responsive
4. My work lets me:	get things done	find workable approaches	apply new ideas	be truly satisfied
5. I communicate best by:	talking with others	putting things in writing	being open with others	having a group meeting
6. My planning focuses on:	current problems	how best to meet goals	future opportunities	needs of people in the organization
7. I prefer to solve problems by:	applying rules	using careful analysis	being creative	relying on my feelings

is as important as rational analysis. Ray Kroc, for example, recalls that intuition drove his decision to buy the McDonald's brand: "I'm not a gambler, and I didn't have that kind of money, but my funny bone instinct kept urging me on."[45]

Unfortunately, the use of intuition does not always lead to blockbuster decisions such as Ray Kroc's. To enhance your understanding of intuition's role in decision making, this section presents a model of intuition and discusses the pros and cons of using intuition to make decisions.

A Model of Intuition Figure 10–4 presents a model of intuition. Starting at the far right, the model shows two types of intuition:

1. A *holistic hunch* represents a judgment that is based on a subconscious integration of information stored in memory. People using this form of intuition may

(concluded)

8. I prefer information:	that is simple and direct	that is complete	that is broad and informative	that is easily understood
9. When I'm not sure what to do:	I rely on my intuition	I search for alternatives	I try to find a compromise	I avoid making a decision
10. Whenever possible, I avoid:	long debates	incomplete work	technical problems	conflict with others
11. I am really good at:	remembering details	finding answers	seeing many options	working with people
12. When time is important, I:	decide and act quickly	apply proven approaches	look for what will work	refuse to be pressured
13. In social settings, I:	speak with many people	observe what others are doing	contribute to the conversation	want to be part of the discussion
14. I always remember:	people's names	places I have been	people's faces	people's personalities
15. I prefer jobs where I:	receive high rewards	have challenging assignments	can reach my personal goals	am accepted by the group
16. I work best with people who:	are energetic and ambitious	are very competent	are open minded	are polite and understanding
17. When I am under stress, I:	speak quickly	try to concentrate on the problem	become frustrated	worry about what I should do
18. Others consider me:	aggressive	disciplined	imaginative	supportive
19. My decisions are generally:	realistic and direct	systematic and logical	broad and flexible	sensitive to the other's needs
20. I dislike:	losing control	boring work	following rules	being rejected
Total score				

SOURCE: © Dr Alan J Rowe, Distinguished Emeritus Professor. Revised 12/18/98. Reprinted with permission.

not be able to explain why they want to make a certain decision, except that the choice "feels right."

2. *Automated experiences* represent a choice that is based on a familiar situation and a partially subconscious application of previously learned information related to that situation. For example, when you have years of experience driving a car, you react to a variety of situations without conscious analysis.

Returning to Figure 10–4, intuition is represented by two distinct processes. One is automatic, involuntary, and mostly effortless. The second is quite the opposite in that it is controlled, voluntary, and effortful. Research reveals that these two processes can operate separately or jointly to influence intuition.[46] These intuitive processes are influenced by two sources: expertise and feelings (see Figure 10–4). *Expertise* represents an individual's combined explicit knowledge (i.e., information that can easily be put into

FIGURE 10–4   A Dual Model of Intuition

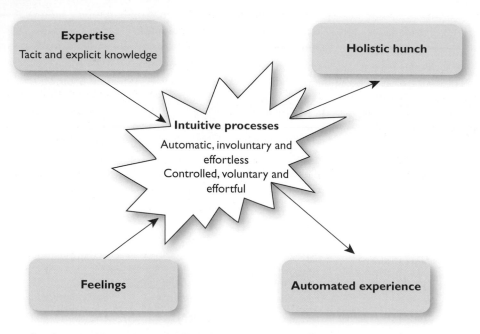

SOURCE: Based in part on D Kahneman and G Klein, "Conditions for Intuitive Expertise," *American Psychologist,* September 2009, pp 515–26; E Sadler-Smith and E Shefy, "The Intuitive Executive: Understanding and Applying 'Gut Feel' in Decision-Making," *Academy of Management Executive,* November 2004, pp 76–91; and C C Miller and R D Ireland, "Intuition in Strategic Decision Making: Friend or Foe in the Fast-Paced 21st Century," *Academy of Management Executive,* February 2005, pp 19–30.

words) and tacit knowledge (i.e., information gained through experience that is difficult to express and formalize) regarding an object, person, situation, or decision opportunity. This source of intuition increases with age and experience. The *feelings* component reflects the automatic, underlying effect one experiences in response to an object, person, situation, or decision opportunity. An intuitive response is based on the interaction between one's expertise and feelings in a given situation.

Pros and Cons of Using Intuition   On the positive side, intuition can speed up the decision-making process.[47] Intuition thus can be valuable in our complex and ever-changing world. Intuition may be a practical approach when resources are limited and deadlines are tight. On the downside, intuition is subject to the same types of biases associated with rational decision making. It is particularly susceptible to the availability and representativeness heuristics, as well as the anchoring, overconfidence, and hindsight biases.[48] In addition, the decision maker may have difficulty convincing others that the intuitive decision makes sense, so a good idea may be ignored.

Where does that leave us with respect to using intuition? We believe that intuition and rationality are complementary and that managers should attempt to use both when making decisions. We thus encourage you to use intuition when making decisions.

> **BACK TO THE CHAPTER-OPENING CASE**   Was intuition used too much during this case? Explain.

Creativity

This section is a natural extension to the previous one because both intuition and creativity can help organizations to stimulate innovation. Although many definitions have been proposed, ***creativity* is defined here as the process of using intelligence, imagination, and skill to develop a new or novel product, object, process, or thought.**[49] It can be as simple as locating a new place to hang your car keys or as complex as developing a pocket-size microcomputer. Creativity can also be applied to the context of cutting costs. For example, President Barack Obama and members of Congress are currently looking for creative ways to cut costs in the federal budget.[50] This definition highlights three broad types of creativity. One can create something new (creation), one can combine or synthesize things (synthesis), or one can improve or change things (modification).

Researchers are not absolutely certain how creativity takes place. Nonetheless, we do know that creativity involves "making remote associations" between unconnected events, ideas, information stored in memory (recall our discussion in Chapter 4), or physical objects. Consider how Dr William Foege, then working for the US Centers for Disease Control and Prevention, led the effort to eradicate smallpox in Nigeria. Foege realized that his supply of vaccine was insufficient for the whole population. But he observed how people congregated to shop in markets, so he targeted his campaign to vaccinate the people in those crowded areas, even if they were merely visitors. In so doing, Foege (now a senior fellow with the Carter Center and the Bill and Melinda Gates Foundation) created a model for future vaccination campaigns that efficiently interrupt the paths by which a virus spreads.[51] The idea of "remote associations" describes thinking such as Foege's connection of shopping behavior and a virus's spread. But it doesn't explain how Foege was able to make this creative link. This led researchers to study the stages of the creative process.

The Creativity Stages   Researchers, however, have identified five stages underlying the creative process: preparation, concentration, incubation, illumination, and verification. The *preparation* stage reflects the notion that creativity starts from a base of knowledge. Experts suggest that creativity involves a convergence between tacit and explicit knowledge. Renowned choreographer Twyla Tharp emphasizes the significance of preparation in the creative process: "I think everyone can be creative, but you have to prepare for it with routine."[52] Tharp's creativity-feeding habits include reading literature, keeping physically active (which stimulates the brain as well as the rest of the body), and choosing new projects that are very different from whatever she has just completed. Even an activity as simple as looking up a word in the dictionary offers an opportunity for preparation: Tharp looks at the word before and after, too, just to see if it gives her an idea.

During the *concentration* stage, an individual focuses on the problem at hand. Creative ideas at work are often triggered by work-related problems, incongruities, or failures. That said, research shows that when you focus too much on trying to come up with creative solutions it can actually block creativity. For example, daydreaming has been linked with creativity. Other research demonstrated that "Internet leisure browsing" increased creativity.[53] Allow yourself time to be distracted when searching for creative solutions as it can enhance the next stage of creativity—the incubation stage. We find that creative ideas sometimes come when we quit trying to be creative.

Incubation is done unconsciously. During this stage, people engage in daily activities while their minds simultaneously mull over information and make remote associations. Martha Beck, author of six books, uses a technique she calls the "kitchen sink" during this stage. The Skills & Best Practices on page 271 illustrate its application when she was trying to write an article on how to better use the creative side of our brains. Associations generated in this stage ultimately come to life in the *illumination* stage. Finally, *verification* entails going through the entire process to verify, modify, or try out the new idea.

Practical Recommendations for Increasing Creativity While some consultants recommend hypnotism as a good way to increase employees' creativity, we prefer suggestions derived from research and three executives leading creative or innovative companies: Jeffrey Katzenberg, CEO of Dreamworks Animation; Ed Catmull, cofounder of Pixar; and David Kelley, founder of IDEO. Both research and practical experience underscore the conclusion that creativity can be enhanced by effectively managing the stages of creativity and by fostering a positive and supportive work environment. To that end, managers are encouraged to establish an organizational culture that emphasizes innovation, to establish innovation goals (e.g., develop five new patents), and to allocate rewards and resources to innovative activities. At a minimum, individuals need the time and space to reflect and think about whatever issues or problems need creative solutions.

All three executives further recommend that management should create a "safe" work environment that encourages risk taking, autonomy, collaboration, and trusting relationships among employees.[54] These executives suggest that it is important to develop a "peer environment" in which people are more concerned about working for the greater good then their own personal success. This norm can be nurtured through the use of transformational leadership, which is discussed in Chapter 16.[55] The willingness to give and accept ongoing feedback in a nondefensive manner is another critical component of a culture dedicated to creativity. For example, Pixar uses daily reviews or "dailies" as a process of giving and receiving constant feedback. This will be most effective if organizations train managers in the process of providing effective feedback. Catmull and Kelley also emphasize the importance of hiring great people who possess a breadth of experience. This can be done by asking job applicants "for a story, example or insight that reveals thinking, judgment and problem-solving skills." For example, you might ask an individual to describe a situation in which he or she improvised or how he or she handled a complex problem in a previous job.[56] Finally, these executives also suggest that management should stay connected with innovations taking place in the academic community. For example, Dreamworks invites academics to deliver lectures and Pixar encourages technical artists to publish and attend academic conferences. In summary, creativity is a process that can be managed, and it is built around the philosophy of hiring and retaining great people to work in a positive and supportive work environment.

Road Map to Ethical Decision Making: A Decision Tree

In Chapter 1 we discussed the importance of ethics and the growing concern about the lack of ethical behavior among business leaders. Unfortunately, research shows that many types of unethical behavior go unreported and unethical behavior is negatively associated with employee engagement.[57] While these trends partially explain the passage of laws to regulate ethical behavior in corporate America, we believe that ethical acts ultimately involve individual or group decisions. It thus is important to consider the issue of ethical decision making. Harvard Business School professor Constance Bagley suggests that a decision tree can help managers to make more ethical decisions.[58]

Martha Beck's "Kitchen Sink" Technique Increases Creativity

This morning I sat down to write about how we can all learn to better use the right hemispheres of our brains. For 30 minutes, I tapped restlessly at a laptop. Nothing much happened, idea-wise. Flat beer.

Finally I resorted to a strategy I call the Kitchen Sink. I read bits of eight books: four accounts of brain research, one novel about India, one study of bat behavior, one biography of Theodore Roosevelt, and one memoir of motherhood. Next, I drove to my favorite Rollerblading location, listening en route to a stand-up comic, a mystery novel, and an Eckhart Tolle lecture. I yanked on my Rollerblades and skated around, squinting slack-jawed into the middle distance. After a while, a tiny lightbulb went on. Well, I thought, I could write about this.

Duh.

The Kitchen Sink, you see, is one way to activate your brain's creative right hemisphere.

SOURCE: M Beck, "Half a Mind Is a Terrible Thing to Waste," *The Oprah Magazine*, November 2009, p 57.

Author Martha Beck

A *decision tree* is a graphical representation of the process underlying decisions and it shows the resulting consequences of making various choices. Decision trees are used as an aid in decision making. Ethical decision making frequently involves trade-offs, and a decision tree helps managers navigate through them. The decision tree shown in Figure 10–5 can be applied to any type of decision or action that an individual manager or corporation is contemplating. Looking at the tree, the first question to ask is whether or not the proposed action is legal. If the action is illegal, do not do it. If the action is legal, then consider the impact of the action on shareholder value. A decision maximizes shareholder value when it results in a more favorable financial position (e.g., increased profits) for an organization. Whether or not an action maximizes shareholder value, the decision tree shows that managers still need to consider the ethical implications of the decision or action. For example, if an action maximizes shareholder value, the next question to consider is whether or not the action is ethical. The answer to this question is based on considering the positive effect of the action on an organization's other key constituents (i.e., customers, employees, the community, the environment, and suppliers) against the benefit to the shareholders. According to the decision tree framework, managers should make the decision to engage in an action if the benefits to the shareholders exceed the benefits to the other key constituents. Managers should not engage in the action if the other key constituents would benefit more from the action than shareholders.

Figure 10–5 illustrates that managers use a slightly different perspective when their initial conclusion is that an action does not maximize shareholder value. In this case, the question becomes, Would it be ethical not to take action? This question necessitates that a manager consider the *harm* or *cost* of an action to shareholders against the *costs* or *benefits* to other key constituents. If the costs to shareholders from a

FIGURE 10–5   An Ethical Decision Tree

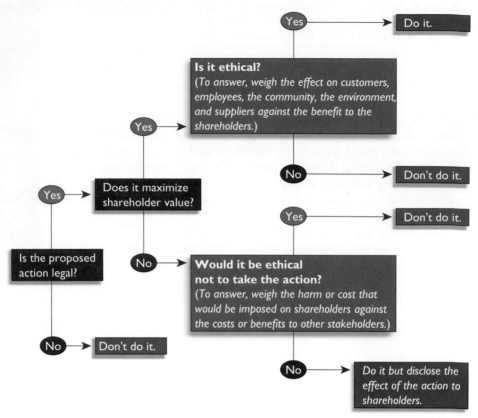

managerial decision exceed the costs or benefits to other constituents, the manager or company should not engage in the action. Conversely, the manager or company should take action when the perceived costs or benefits to the other constituents are greater than the costs to shareholders. Let us apply this decision tree to IBM's decision to raise the amount of money it required retirees to contribute to their health benefits.[59] The company made this decision in order to save money.

Is it legal for a company to decrease its contribution to retiree health care benefits while simultaneously raising retirees' contributions? The answer is yes. Does an organization maximize shareholder value by decreasing its retiree health care expenses? Again, the answer is yes. We now have to consider the overall benefits to shareholders against the overall benefits to other key constituents. The answer to this question is more complex than it appears and is contingent on an organization's corporate values. Consider the following two examples. In company one, the organization is losing money and it needs cash in order to invest in new product development. Management believes that new products will fuel the company's economic growth and ultimate survival. This company's statement of corporate values also reveals that the organization values profits and shareholder return more than employee loyalty. In this case, the company should make the decision to increase retirees' health care contributions. Company two, in contrast, is profitable and has been experiencing increased market share with its products.

This company's statement of corporate values also indicates that employees are the most important constituent it has, even more than shareholders: Southwest Airlines is a good example of a company with these corporate values. In this case, the company should not make the decision to decrease its contribution to retirees' benefits.

It is important to keep in mind that the decision tree cannot provide a quick formula that managers and organizations can use to evaluate every ethical question. Ethical decision making is not always clear-cut and it is affected by cross-cultural differences. That said, the decision tree does provide a framework for considering the trade-offs between managerial and corporate actions and managerial and corporate ethics. Try using this decision tree the next time you are faced with a significant ethical question or problem.

> **BACK TO THE CHAPTER-OPENING CASE** Use Figure 10–5 to assess whether it was an ethical decision to continue to work on completing the oil well.

Group Decision Making

This section explores issues associated with group decision making. Specifically, we discuss (1) group involvement in decision making, (2) advantages and disadvantages of group decision making, and (3) group problem-solving techniques.

Group Involvement in Decision Making

Whether groups assemble in face-to-face meetings or rely on other technologically based methods to communicate, they can contribute to each stage of the decision-making process. In order to maximize the value of group decision making, however, it is important to create an environment in which group members feel free to participate and express their opinions. A study sheds light on how managers can create such an environment.

A team of researchers conducted two studies to determine whether a group's innovativeness was related to *minority dissent,* defined as the extent to which group members feel comfortable disagreeing with other group members, and a group's level of participation in decision making. Results showed that the most innovative groups possessed high levels of both minority dissent and participation in decision making.[60] How can you apply these results to your own group meetings at school or work? One way is to foster more discussion among group members during meetings. Research also confirms a side benefit to this recommendation. Group members' job satisfaction and performance are increased through group discussion.[61] Another suggestion is to seek divergent views from group members during decision making, and do not ridicule or punish people who disagree with the majority opinion.

Take a moment now to complete the Hands-On Exercise on page 274. It assesses the amount of minority dissent and participation in group decision making for a group project you have completed or are currently working on in school or on the job. Is your satisfaction with the group related to minority dissent and participation in decision making? If not, what might explain this surprising result?

LO10.5

www.mcgrawhillconnect.com

Go to Connect for a self-assessment to assess your participation in group decision making.

Assessing Participation in Group Decision Making

INSTRUCTIONS: The following survey measures minority dissent, participation in group decision making, and satisfaction with a group. For each of the items, use the rating scale shown below to circle the answer that best represents your feelings based on a group project you were or currently are involved in. Next, use the scoring key to compute scores for the levels of minority dissent, participation in decision making, and satisfaction with the group.

1 = Strongly disagree
2 = Disagree
3 = Neither agree nor disagree
4 = Agree
5 = Strongly agree

	1	2	3	4	5
1. Within my team, individuals disagree with one another.	1	2	3	4	5
2. Within my team, individuals do not go along with the majority opinion.	1	2	3	4	5
3. Within my team, individuals voice their disagreement with the majority opinion.	1	2	3	4	5
4. Within my team, I am comfortable voicing my disagreement of the majority opinion.	1	2	3	4	5
5. Within my team, individuals do not immediately agree with one another.	1	2	3	4	5
6. As a team member, I have a real say in how work is carried out.	1	2	3	4	5
7. Within my team, most members have a chance to participate in decisions.	1	2	3	4	5
8. My team is designed so that everyone has the opportunity to participate in decisions.	1	2	3	4	5
9. I am satisfied with my group.	1	2	3	4	5
10. I would like to work with this group on another project.	1	2	3	4	5

SCORING KEY

Minority dissent (add scores for items 1, 2, 3, 4, 5): _____
Participation in decision making (add scores for items 6, 7, 8): _____
Satisfaction (add scores for items 9, 10): _____

ARBITRARY NORMS

Low minority dissent = 5–15
High minority dissent = 16–25
Low participation in decision making = 3–8
High participation in decision making = 9–15
Low satisfaction = 2–5
High satisfaction = 6–10

SOURCES: The items in the survey were developed from C K W De Dreu and M A West, "Minority Dissent and Team Innovation: The Importance of Participation in Decision Making," *Journal of Applied Psychology*, December 2001, pp 119–201.

The previously discussed study about minority dissent reinforces the notion that the quality of group decision making varies across groups. This, in turn, raises the issue of how to best assess a group's decision-making effectiveness. Although experts do not agree on the one "best" criterion, there is agreement that groups need to work through various aspects of decision making in order to be effective. One expert proposed that decision-making effectiveness in a group is dependent on successfully accomplishing the following:[62]

1. Developing a clear understanding of the decision situation.
2. Developing a clear understanding of the requirements for an effective choice.
3. Thoroughly and accurately assessing the positive qualities of alternative solutions.
4. Thoroughly and accurately assessing the negative qualities of alternative solutions.

To increase the probability of groups making high-quality decisions, managers, team leaders, and individual group members are encouraged to focus on satisfying these four requirements.

Mc Graw Hill **connect**
www.mcgrawhillconnect.com

Go to Connect for a video case to view New Belgium Brewery and how decision making is managed there.

Advantages and Disadvantages of Group Decision Making

Including groups in the decision-making process has both pros and cons (see Table 10-1). On the positive side, groups contain a greater pool of knowledge, provide

Advantages and Disadvantages of Group-Aided Decision Making   **TABLE 10–1**

Advantages	Disadvantages
1. *Greater pool of knowledge.* A group can bring much more information and experience to bear on a decision or problem than can an individual acting alone.	1. *Social pressure.* Unwillingness to "rock the boat" and pressure to conform may combine to stifle the creativity of individual contributors.
2. *Different perspectives.* Individuals with varied experience and interests help the group see decision situations and problems from different angles.	2. *Domination by a vocal few.* Sometimes the quality of group action is reduced when the group gives in to those who talk the loudest and longest.
3. *Greater comprehension.* Those who personally experience the give-and-take of group discussion about alternative courses of action tend to understand the rationale behind the final decision.	3. *Logrolling.* Political wheeling and dealing can displace sound thinking when an individual's pet project or vested interest is at stake.
4. *Increased acceptance.* Those who play an active role in group decision making and problem solving tend to view the outcome as "ours" rather than "theirs."	4. *Goal displacement.* Sometimes secondary considerations such as winning an argument, making a point, or getting back at a rival displace the primary task of making a sound decision or solving a problem.
5. *Training ground.* Less experienced participants in group action learn how to cope with group dynamics by actually being involved.	5. *"Groupthink."* Sometimes cohesive "in-groups" let the desire for unanimity override sound judgment when generating and evaluating alternative courses of action. (Groupthink is discussed in Chapter 9.)

SOURCE: From R Kreitner, *Management,* 10E. Copyright © 2007 South-Western, a part of Cengage Learning, Inc. Reproduced by permission. *www.cengage.com/permissions.*

John Mackey, CEO of Whole Foods Market, Believes in Consensual Decision Making

Here is what Mackey had to say to an interviewer from *Harvard Business Review* about his emphasis on consensual decision making.

> I found that when you make decisions by consensus, and you let all the disagreements get expressed, you make better decisions. If you don't do that, there is a natural human tendency on the part of whoever didn't get their way to want to be proved right. It's like "See, I told you that wasn't going to work."

Mr. Mackey also was asked if gaining consensus takes a long time. He responded that "It can. Generally, if you're making decisions that really are going to impact the business, it's good to talk them over. It's a little bit like Japanese manage-

CEO John Mackey walking an aisle in one of his stores.

ment decision-making—they spend a lot more time trying to develop consensus in the decision group. The virtue of it is that although it takes longer to make the decision, implementation goes a lot faster, because there isn't resistance or sabotage that works its way through the organization."

SOURCE: Excerpted from "What Is It That Only I Can Do?" *Harvard Business Review,* **January–February 2011, pp 119–20.**

more varied perspectives, create more comprehension of decisions, increase decision acceptance, and create a training ground for inexperienced employees. John Mackey, CEO of Whole Foods Market, reinforced some of these positive characteristics during an interview for the *Harvard Business* Review (see the Skills & Best Practices above). These advantages must be balanced, however, with the disadvantages listed in Table 10-1. In doing so, managers need to determine the extent to which the advantages and disadvantages apply to the decision situation. The following three guidelines may then be applied to help decide whether groups should be included in the decision-making process:

1. If additional information would increase the quality of the decision, managers should involve those people who can provide the needed information.

2. If acceptance is important, managers need to involve those individuals whose acceptance and commitment are important.

3. If people can be developed through their participation, managers may want to involve those whose development is most important.[63]

Group versus Individual Performance   Before recommending that managers involve groups in decision making, it is important to examine whether groups perform better or worse than individuals. After reviewing 61 years of relevant research, a decision-making expert concluded that "Group performance was generally qualitatively and quantitatively superior to the performance of the average individual."[64] Although subsequent research of small-group decision making generally supported this conclusion, additional research suggests that managers should use a contingency approach when determining whether to include others in the decision-making process. Let us now consider these contingency recommendations.

Practical Contingency Recommendations   If the decision occurs frequently, such as deciding on promotions or who qualifies for a loan, use groups because they tend to produce more consistent decisions than do individuals. Given time constraints, let the most competent individual, rather than a group, make the decision. In the face of environmental threats such as time pressure and the potentially serious effects of a decision, groups use less information and fewer communication channels. This increases the probability of a bad decision.[65] This conclusion underscores a general recommendation that managers should keep in mind: Because the quality of communication strongly affects a group's productivity, on complex tasks it is essential to devise mechanisms to enhance communication effectiveness.

BACK TO THE CHAPTER-OPENING CASE   Why weren't the benefits of group decision making realized in this case?

Group Problem-Solving Techniques

Using groups to make decisions generally requires that they reach a consensus. According to a decision-making expert, a *consensus* **"is reached when all members can say they either agree with the decision or have had their 'day in court' and were unable to convince the others of their viewpoint. In the final analysis, everyone agrees to support the outcome."**[66] This definition indicates that consensus does not require unanimous agreement because group members may still disagree with the final decision but are willing to work toward its success.

LO10.6

Groups can experience roadblocks when trying to arrive at a consensus decision. For one, groups may not generate all relevant alternatives to a problem because an individual dominates or intimidates other group members. This is both overt and/or subtle. For instance, group members who possess power and authority, such as a CEO, can be intimidating, regardless of interpersonal style, simply by being present in the room. Moreover, shyness inhibits the generation of alternatives. Shy or socially anxious individuals may withhold their input for fear of embarrassment or lack of confidence. Satisficing is another hurdle to effective group decision making. As previously noted, groups satisfice due to limited time, information, or ability to handle large amounts of information.

A management expert offered the following "do's" and "don'ts" for successfully achieving consensus: Groups should use active listening skills, involve as many members as possible, seek out the reasons behind arguments, and dig for the facts. At the same time, groups should not horse trade (I'll support you on this decision because you supported me on the last one), vote, or agree just to avoid "rocking the boat."[67] Voting works against consensus by splitting the group into winners and losers, but in some situations, speedy arrival at a decision is the greater priority.

Decision-making experts have developed three group problem-solving techniques—brainstorming, the nominal group technique, and the Delphi technique—to reduce the above roadblocks. Knowledge of these techniques can help you to more effectively use groups in the decision-making process. Further, the advent of computer-aided decision making enables managers to use these techniques to solve complex problems with large groups of people.

Brainstorming   Brainstorming was developed by A F Osborn, an advertising executive, to increase creativity.[68] ***Brainstorming* is used to help groups generate multiple ideas and alternatives for solving problems.** For example, "Jim Albaugh, chief executive of Boeing's commercial airplanes business, tapped eight retired Boeing executives last fall to form a senior advisory group."[69] The group's goal was to brainstorm with current engineers and project managers about how best to get the 787 Dreamliner program on track. Production of the plane experienced a series of setbacks and is currently more than three years behind its original delivery date.

When brainstorming, a group such as Boeing's senior advisory group is convened, and the problem at hand is reviewed. Individual members then are asked to silently generate ideas/alternatives for solving the problem. Silent idea generation is recommended over the practice of having group members randomly shout out their ideas because it leads to a greater number of unique ideas. Groups tend to focus on a more limited number of ideas and get fixated on one idea when they don't conduct silent brainstorming before sharing in a group setting.[70] Next, these ideas/alternatives are solicited and shared in writing. Research findings suggest that managers or team leaders may want to collect the brainstormed ideas anonymously because more controversial and nonredundant ideas were generated by anonymous than nonanonymous brainstorming groups.[71] Finally, a second session is used to critique and evaluate the alternatives. Managers are advised to follow the seven rules for brainstorming used by IDEO.[72]

1. *Defer judgment.* Don't criticize during the initial stage of idea generation. Phrases such as "we've never done it that way," "it won't work," "it's too expensive," and "our manager will never agree" should not be used.

2. *Build on the ideas of others.* Encourage participants to extend others' ideas by avoiding "buts" and using "ands."

3. *Encourage wild ideas.* Encourage out-of-the-box thinking. The wilder and more outrageous the ideas, the better.

4. *Go for quantity over quality.* Participants should try to generate and write down as many new ideas as possible. Focusing on quantity encourages people to think beyond their favorite ideas.

5. *Be visual.* Use different colored pens (e.g., red, purple, blue) to write on big sheets of flip chart paper, white boards, or poster board that are put on the wall.

6. *Stay focused on the topic.* A facilitator should be used to keep the discussion on target.

7. *One conversation at a time.* The ground rules are that no one interrupts another person, no dismissing of someone's ideas, no disrespect, and no rudeness.

Brainstorming is an effective technique for generating new ideas or alternatives. It is not appropriate for evaluating alternatives or selecting solutions.

The Nominal Group Technique   The ***nominal group technique (NGT)* helps groups generate ideas and evaluate and select solutions.** NGT is a structured group meeting that follows this format:[73] A group is convened to discuss a particular problem or issue. After the problem is understood, individuals silently generate ideas in writing. Each individual, in round-robin fashion, then offers one idea from his or her list. Ideas are recorded on a blackboard or flip chart; they are not discussed at this stage of the process. Once all ideas are elicited, the group discusses them. Anyone may criticize or defend any item. During this step, clarification is provided as well as general agreement or disagreement with the idea. The "30-second soap box" technique, which entails giving each participant a maximum of 30 seconds to argue for or against any of the ideas under consideration, can be used to facilitate this discussion. Alternatively, groups can create an effort/benefit matrix to facilitate this discussion. This is done by identifying the amount of effort and the costs required to implement each idea and comparing these to the potential benefits associated with each idea. Finally, group members anonymously vote for their top choices. The group leader then adds the votes to determine the group's choice. Prior to making a final decision, the group may decide to discuss the top-ranked items and conduct a second round of voting.

The nominal group technique reduces the roadblocks to group decision making by (1) separating brainstorming from evaluation, (2) promoting balanced participation among group members, and (3) incorporating mathematical voting techniques in order to reach consensus. NGT has been successfully used in many different decision-making situations, and has been found to generate more ideas than a standard brainstorming session.[74]

The Delphi Technique   This problem-solving method was originally developed by the Rand Corporation for technological forecasting.[75] It now is used as a multipurpose planning tool. The *Delphi technique* **is a group process that anonymously generates ideas or judgments from physically dispersed experts.** Unlike the NGT, experts' ideas are obtained from questionnaires or via the Internet as opposed to face-to-face group discussions.

A manager begins the Delphi process by identifying the issue(s) he or she wants to investigate. For example, a manager might want to inquire about customer demand, customers' future preferences, or the effect of locating a plant in a certain region of the country. Next, participants are identified and a questionnaire is developed. The questionnaire is sent to participants and returned to the manager. In today's computer-networked environments, this often means that the questionnaires are e-mailed to participants. The manager then summarizes the responses and sends feedback to the participants. At this stage, participants are asked to (1) review the feedback, (2) prioritize the issues being considered, and (3) return the survey within a specified time period. This cycle repeats until the manager obtains the necessary information.

The Delphi technique is useful when face-to-face discussions are impractical, when disagreements and conflict are likely to impair communication, when certain individuals might severely dominate group discussion, and when groupthink is a probable outcome of the group process.[76]

Computer-Aided Decision Making   The purpose of computer-aided decision making is to reduce consensus roadblocks while collecting more information in a shorter period of time. There are two types of computer-aided decision-making systems: chauffeur driven and group driven.[77] Chauffeur-driven systems ask participants to answer predetermined questions on electronic keypads or dials. Live television audiences on shows are frequently polled with this system. The computer system tabulates participants' responses in a matter of seconds.

Group-driven electronic meetings are conducted in one of two major ways. First, managers can use e-mail systems or the Internet to collect information or brainstorm about a decision that must be made. For example, Miami Children's Hospital uses a combination of the Internet and a conferencing software technology to make decisions about the design of its training programs. Here is what Loubna Noureddin, director of staff and community education, had to say about the organization's computer-aided decision making:

> "What I truly like about it is my connection to other hospitals," Noureddin says. "I'm able to understand what other hospitals are doing about specific things. I put my question out, and people can respond, and I can answer back." She explains, for instance, that using the system, she and her colleagues have received guidance from other corporate educators, and even subject matter experts, on how to best train workers in such fields as critical care. "You get many other hospitals logging into the system, and telling us what they do," she says.[78]

Noureddin claims that the system has saved the company time and money.

The second method of computer-aided, group-driven meetings are conducted in special facilities equipped with individual workstations that are networked to each other. Instead of talking, participants type their input, ideas, comments, reactions, or evaluations on their keyboards. The input simultaneously appears on a large projector screen at the front of the room, thereby enabling all participants to see all input. This computer-driven process reduces consensus roadblocks because input is anonymous, everyone gets a chance to contribute, and no one can dominate the process. Research demonstrated that computer-aided decision making produced greater quality and quantity of ideas than either traditional brainstorming or the nominal group technique for both small and large groups of people.[79]

In conclusion, we expect the use of computer-aided decision making to increase in the future. These systems are well suited for modern organizational life and for the large number of Millennials or Gen Ys entering the workforce.

key terms

chapter summary

- *Compare and contrast the rational model of decision making, Simon's normative model, and the garbage can model.* The rational decision-making model consists of identifying the problem or opportunity, generating alternative solutions, evaluating and selecting a solution, and implementing and evaluating the solution. Research indicates that decision makers do not follow the series of steps outlined in the rational model.

Simon's normative model is guided by a decision maker's bounded rationality. Bounded rationality means that decision makers are bounded or restricted by a variety of constraints when making decisions. The normative model suggests that decision making is characterized by (a) limited information processing, (b) the use of judgmental heuristics, and (c) satisficing.

The garbage can model holds that decision making in practice is sloppy and haphazard, resulting from a complex interaction of problems, solutions, participants, and choice opportunities. Thus, many decisions are the result of oversight or a salient opportunity, often guided by political motives. Specific problems are less likely to be solved as the total number of problems increases, and important problems are more likely to be solved than unimportant ones.

- *Review the eight decision-making biases.* When people use judgmental heuristics, they tend to make systematic mistakes. The availability heuristic is a tendency to base decisions on information that is readily recalled. The representativeness heuristic is the tendency to assess an event's likelihood based on impressions about similar occurrences. Confirmation bias consists of (1) subconsciously deciding something before investigating the alternative's value and (2) seeking information that supports this preconceived opinion and discounting information that does not. The anchoring bias occurs when decision makers are influenced by the first information they receive about a decision, whether or not it is relevant. The overconfidence bias is a tendency to be overconfident about estimates or forecasts. The hindsight bias occurs when knowledge of an outcome causes the decision maker to overestimate the probability he or she could have predicted that outcome. Framing bias is the tendency to evaluate risks about gains differently from risks about losses. And escalation of commitment is the tendency to stick to an ineffective course of action on the (illogical) basis that an investment has already been made in that decision.

- *Discuss the thrust of evidence-based decision making and its implementation principles.* The goal of evidence-based decision making is to conscientiously use the best data when making decisions. Seven implementation principles help companies to integrate this process into an organization's culture: (1) treat your organization as an unfinished prototype, (2) no brag, just facts, (3) see yourself and your organization as outsiders do, (4) evidence-based management is not just for senior executives, (5) like everything else, you still need to sell it, (6) if all else fails, slow the spread of bad practices, and (7) the best diagnostic question: what happens when people fail?

- *Describe the model of decision-making styles, the role of intuition in decision making, the stages of the creative process, and a decision tree for making ethical decisions.* The model of decision-making styles is based on the idea that styles vary along two different dimensions: value orientation and tolerance for ambiguity. When these two dimensions are combined, they form four styles of decision making: directive, analytical, conceptual, and behavioral. People with a directive style have a low tolerance for ambiguity and are oriented toward task and technical concerns. Analytics have a higher tolerance for ambiguity and are characterized by a tendency to overanalyze a situation. People with a conceptual style have a high threshold for ambiguity and tend to focus on people or social aspects of a work situation. The behavioral style is the most people oriented of the four styles.

Intuition is a capacity for getting direct knowledge or understanding without consciously applying logic or thought. It results from a combination of expertise and feelings and is expressed as a holistic hunch or automated experience. Intuition can speed up decision making but is subject to biases. It can be used as a complementary tool with rationality, where one is used as a check on the other.

Creativity is defined as the process of using intelligence, imagination, and skill to develop a new or novel product, object, process, or thought. There are five stages of the creative process: preparation, concentration, incubation, illumination, and verification.

The ethical decision tree presents a structured approach for making ethical decisions. Managers work through the tree by answering a series of questions and the process leads to a recommended decision.

- *Summarize the pros and cons of involving groups in the decision-making process.* There are both pros and cons to involving groups in the decision-making process (see Table 10-1). Although research shows that groups typically outperform the average individual, managers need to use a contingency approach when determining whether to include others in the decision-making process.

- *Contrast brainstorming, the nominal group technique, the Delphi technique, and computer-aided decision making.* Group problem-solving techniques facilitate better decision making within groups. Brainstorming is used to help groups generate multiple ideas and alternatives for solving problems. The nominal group technique assists groups both to generate ideas and to evaluate and select solutions. The Delphi technique is a group process that anonymously generates ideas or judgments from physically dispersed experts. The purpose of computer-aided decision making is to reduce consensus roadblocks while collecting more information in a shorter period of time.

discussion questions

1. In general, what model of decision making do you think is used by the president of the United States? Explain.
2. Describe a situation in which you exhibited escalation of commitment. Why did you escalate a losing situation?
3. Do you believe in the value of evidence-based decision making? Why isn't it used more often by managers and politicians?
4. Can you recall a time in which you used intuition to make a decision? Describe the situation and your intuitive moment.
5. Given the time it takes to get a group to reach consensus in decision making and the potential for conflict, are groups worth the effort?

legal/ethical challenge

Is It Okay to Walk Away from a Mortgage When You Can Afford to Pay?[80]

This ethical challenge deals with a situation facing many homeowners, and focuses on the case of Chris Hanson. Hanson runs a real-estate investment firm, and he purchased a luxury condominium in Arizona for $875,000. He had no problem paying the down payment of $90,000 or the monthly payment of $5,000. That said, he decided to miss his first monthly payment and to walk away from the property because the condominium is now worth about 50 percent of what he initially paid. He believes that it will take 10 years for the property to recover its value.

He plans to let the lender foreclose on the home and he will rent an even nicer unit in either the same complex or one nearby, which he figures will cost less than half of his monthly mortgage payment.

Hanson's case illustrates the growing risk that borrowers in hard-hit housing markets will "strategically" default, even when they can afford to stay in the homes. . . .

Hanson said that he felt little moral obligation to make his payments because he felt banks' shoddy lending practices were primarily responsible for fueling the housing boom and bust.

Should We Allow People to Walk Away from Mortgages When They Have Enough Income to Pay?

1. Absolutely not! Chris Hanson signed a contract and he should uphold his end of the deal. After all, he still makes enough money to pay the bill. Further, Chris obviously understands the housing market and he simply is avoiding his responsibility and shirking the debt to financial institutions. Financial institutions will ultimately try to recover these losses, which in turn will affect consumers at large.

2. Yes. Why should someone continue to pay a mortgage when a home is worth substantially less than the original purchase price? The banks should refinance the original loan based on the current value of the property.

3. It depends. If the person can afford the mortgage, such as Chris Hanson, then he should not be allowed to walk away and stiff others with his debt. If the person cannot afford the mortgage, then he or she should be allowed to walk away.

If you're looking for additional study materials, be sure to check out the Online Learning Center at

www.mhhe.com/kininckiob5e

for more information and interactivities that correspond to this chapter.

chapter 11

Managing Conflict and Negotiating

After reading the material in this chapter, you should be able to:

LO11.1 Define the term *conflict*, distinguish between functional and dysfunctional conflict, and identify three desired outcomes of conflict.

LO11.2 Define *personality conflicts*, and explain how they should be managed.

LO11.3 Discuss the role of in-group thinking in intergroup conflict, and explain what can be done to avoid cross-cultural conflict.

LO11.4 Define work–family conflict and describe what can be done to manage it.

LO11.5 Explain how managers can program functional conflict, and identify the five conflict-handling styles.

LO11.6 Identify and describe at least four alternative dispute resolution (ADR) techniques.

LO11.7 Draw a distinction between distributive and integrative negotiation, and explain the concept of added-value negotiation.

LEARNING OBJECTIVES

Who's Going to Manage the Lawyers?

The last few years have been difficult for the corporate world and its lawyers. Executives are insisting that business units cut expenses, stretch budgets, and manage more efficiently—corporate law departments included. Legal departments have responded by becoming increasingly businesslike and hiring or appointing professional administrators. While some are attorneys, others are not. In either case, they play the role of professional managers and are responsible for negotiating fees with law firms that provide outside counsel, managing conflicts between business and legal units, and running a productive legal department.

The importance and influence of professional managers in legal departments increased along with the use of technology. Specifically, in the early 2000s technology facilitated electronic billing, which enabled companies to track and manage their legal expenses more precisely. This, along with increased competitive pressures more generally, motivated both corporate legal departments and law firms to operate more like conventional businesses.

Susan Hackett, general counsel of the Association of Corporate Counsel, said, "These are people who are not necessarily heard or seen outside of the legal department, but they wield a tremendous amount of power. . . . They are business people for the legal department. They are the organizational glue." And while their role is important, it is by no means easy. Whether they have law degrees or MBAs, the managers themselves will tell you that they are not readily accepted—their jobs are wrought with conflict. Non-lawyers that fill the role aren't always embraced by in-house counsel with open arms or open minds. "Lawyers can be a little snobby at times," observes Suzanne Hawkins, who is in-house counsel for GE. And lawyers that fill the managing counsel role often lack the necessary business acumen. After all, they were trained in law and not business. This can lead to challenges from attorneys and business-types alike.

DuPont Co. has fully embraced the role of professional manager in the legal department. Evelyn Brantley, an attorney, took the job in 2010 and is the seventh person in 20 years to fulfill this role at the company. She primarily oversees relationships with the company's 40 outside law firms that provide litigation support. Her administrator role has a two to three year term limit, and each new person to the position is purposefully chosen to be significantly different from the previous individual. "It's helpful that the new person coming in has a different background or different experience," she says.

According to DuPont's general counsel Tom Sager, who is ultimately in charge of all things legal at the company, "The managing counsel job is tough." Managing conflict is a central part of the job and requires excellent communication skills to be effective. Personality conflicts, for example, sometimes require high-level

Evelyn Brantley and Tom Sager are the managing and general counsels, respectively, for DuPont Co.

attorneys (e.g., managing partners) to be removed from handling DuPont's cases. Other times vendor firms have conflicts with each other. "You have to be very direct, yet tactful," says Sager, and nip problems early before they damage relationships.[1]

THE CHAPTER-OPENING CASE illustrates that managing conflict productively is essential to individual, departmental, and organizational effectiveness. It also shows that conflict is an unavoidable, if not essential, aspect of modern life. Five major trends conspire to make organizational conflict inevitable:

- Constant change
- Greater employee diversity
- More teams (virtual and self-managed)
- Less face-to-face communication (more electronic interaction)
- A global economy with increased cross-cultural dealings

Paul Spector, an OB expert on conflict, concluded that conflict "is part of the human condition. It occurs at all levels of social interaction from married couples to nations, ranging from simple arguments to all-out war. In organizations conflict occurs at all levels, both within workgroups and between workgroups. A considerable effort on the part of management is devoted to dealing with conflict and its aftermath."[2]

Researchers and practitioners believe that conflict has both positive and negative consequences. For example, we learned earlier in Chapter 4 that diversity within workgroups can create conflict, but that training can be used to help diverse groups to achieve higher levels of performance. The goal of this chapter is to help you understand how to avoid the negative side of conflict while also gaining from its positive outcomes. We begin by providing a foundation for understanding conflict and then discuss the major forms of conflict. We next review methods and tools for managing conflict and conclude by exploring the skill of negotiation.

A Modern View of Conflict

A comprehensive review of the conflict literature yielded this consensus definition: "***Conflict* is a process in which one party perceives that its interests are being opposed or negatively affected by another party.**"[3] The word *perceives* reminds us that sources of conflict and issues can be real or imagined. The resulting conflict is the same. Conflict can escalate (strengthen) or de-escalate (weaken) over time. "The conflict process unfolds in a context, and whenever conflict, escalated or not, occurs the disputants or third parties can attempt to manage it in some manner."[4] Consequently, current and future managers need to understand the dynamics of conflict and know how to handle it effectively (both as disputants and as third parties).

A Conflict Continuum

 LO11.1

Ideas about managing conflict underwent an interesting evolution during the 20th century. Initially, scientific management experts such as Frederick W Taylor believed all conflict ultimately threatened management's authority and thus had to be avoided or quickly resolved.[5] Later, human relationists recognized the inevitability of conflict and advised managers to learn to live with it. Emphasis remained on resolving conflict whenever possible, however. Beginning in the 1970s, OB specialists realized conflict had both positive and negative outcomes, depending on its nature and intensity. This perspective introduced the revolutionary idea that organizations could suffer from *too little* conflict.

Work groups, departments, or organizations experiencing too little conflict tend to be plagued by apathy, lack of creativity, indecision, and missed deadlines. Excessive conflict, on the other hand, can erode organizational performance because of political infighting, dissatisfaction, lack of teamwork, and turnover. Workplace aggression and violence can be manifestations of excessive conflict.[6] Appropriate types and levels of conflict energize people in constructive directions.[7]

Functional versus Dysfunctional Conflict

The distinction between *functional conflict* and *dysfunctional conflict* pivots on whether the organization's interests are served. ***Functional conflict* is commonly referred to in management circles as constructive or cooperative conflict and is characterized by consultative interactions, a focus on the issues, mutual respect, and useful give and take.** In such situations people often feel comfortable disagreeing and presenting opposing views. Positive outcomes frequently result. Each of these elements is lacking or even opposite in cases of ***dysfunctional conflict,* which threatens an organization's interests.**[8]

Management actions obviously affect whether a conflict is functional or dysfunctional. Consider the conflicts confronting Trevor David, manager of a small security company in the midwestern United States. The recent recession hit that part of the country especially hard and caused many auto suppliers and dealerships to close, some of whom had been Trevor's largest customers. When business is lost the payroll needs to be cut to align with reduced income. Historically, David simply laid off employees who worked for the customer accounts they lost. On the one hand this approach was functional—he reduced the payroll to align with reduced revenues—but it also had dysfunctional side effects. He lost some of his best and most loyal employees simply because they worked for customers who left. The same employees felt unappreciated and resentful, which made it difficult to rehire them when new accounts were added or past customers returned. The remaining employees commonly politicked to work on the accounts they perceived to be more stable to mitigate the likelihood of being laid off in the future (politics are discussed in detail in Chapter 13). Making matters worse, some employees quit when they heard that the account on which they worked was struggling or laying off its own employees.

These experiences caused David to do things differently when a customer recently closed its Michigan operations. This time he involved employees in the decision-making process (recall the discussion of procedural justice in Chapter 7 and participative decision making in Chapter 10). He shared the number of hours that needed to be reduced and then asked employees to generate solutions for closing the gap. To his surprise and delight, employees willingly accepted fewer hours to avoid layoffs, accepted shifts they didn't normally work, and considered employee seniority and performance factors in their decisions. Although the business environment is still difficult for David's company, he has more committed employees and a stronger financial position because he transformed dysfunctional into functional conflict.

Layoff survivors typically complain about being overworked, thus paving the way for stress and conflict. What can managers do to help employees cope with the stress associated with surviving a large layoff?

Antecedents of Conflict

Certain situations produce more conflict than others. By knowing the antecedents of conflict, managers are better able to anticipate conflict and take steps to resolve it if it becomes dysfunctional. Table 11–1 lists many of the situations that tend to produce either functional or dysfunctional conflict.[9]

TABLE 11–1   Situations That Produce Functional or Dysfunctional Conflict

• Incompatible personalities or value systems	• Inadequate communication
• Overlapping or unclear job boundaries	• Interdepartment/intergroup competition
• Competition for limited resources	• Unreasonable deadlines or extreme time pressure
• Unreasonable or unclear policies, standards, or rules	• Decision making by consensus (dissenters may feel coerced)
• Organizational complexity (conflict tends to increase as the number of hierarchical layers and specialized tasks increase)	• Collective decision making (the greater the number of people participating in a decision, the greater the potential for conflict)
• Interdependent tasks (e.g., one person cannot complete his or her assignment until others have completed their work)	• Unmet expectations (employees who have unrealistic expectations about job assignments, pay, or promotions are more prone to conflict)

Proactive managers carefully read these early warnings and take appropriate action. For example, group conflict sometimes can be reduced by making decisions on the basis of majority approval rather than striving for a consensus, as was the case with Trevor David.

BACK TO THE CHAPTER-OPENING CASE

1. Describe antecedents of conflict most likely to confront Evelyn Brantley in her role as managing counsel at DuPont.
2. If you had her job, describe three things you might do to prevent conflict.

Why People Avoid Conflict

Are you uncomfortable in conflict situations? Do you go out of your way to avoid conflict? If so, you're not alone. Many of us avoid conflict for a variety of both good and bad reasons. Tim Ursiny, in his entertaining and instructive book *The Coward's Guide to Conflict* contends that we avoid conflict because we fear various combinations of harm, rejection, loss of relationship, anger, being seen as selfish, saying the wrong thing, failing, hurting someone else, getting what you want, and intimacy.[10] This list is self-explanatory, except for the fear of "getting what you want." By this, Ursiny is referring to those who, for personal reasons, feel undeserving and/or fear the consequences of success so they tend to sabotage themselves. Of course, avoiding conflict doesn't make it go away. The same situation is likely to continue or even escalate. What is the alternative? See the Skills & Best Practices on page 289 for suggestions. For our present purposes, it is sufficient to become consciously aware of our fears and practice overcoming them. Reading, understanding, and acting on the material in this chapter are steps in a positive direction.

Avoiding Conflict is Like Ignoring Cancer—It Grows!

Karen Duncum, owner of Star Performance Consulting, is against avoiding conflict and instead recommends the following:

1. *Stop ignoring a conflict.* Ignoring or working around a conflict won't make it go away and may cause further escalation. Instead, she recommends bringing both sides together.
2. *Act decisively to improve the outcome.* Delay only causes the problem, real or perceived, to fester. Addressing a conflict in short order can help unveil misunderstandings or simple oversights before they grow into something more or spread.
3. *Make the path to resolution open and honest.* Involve all relevant parties, collect information, and determine a desired outcome. Doing so helps resolve misunderstandings and focuses everybody on the end state instead of wallowing in the (alleged) offenses.
4. *Use descriptive language instead of evaluative.* Beware of accusations and judgmental language. Both put people on the defensive and impede progress. Instead, focus on the problem (behaviors, feelings, implications) and solution rather than the perpetrator.
5. *Make the process a team-building opportunity.* If the problem affects the team, then it may be beneficial to approach the conflict and its solution as a team. Such resolutions may improve relationships in such a way that the team functions even better than it did before the conflict.
6. *Keep the upside in mind.* Effective conflict resolution creates "success momentum." In other words, conflicts are signs along the road to the final and desired destination. Don't get bogged down and lose sight of the ultimate goal or bigger picture.

SOURCE: Excerpted and adapted from K Duncum, "Turning Conflict into Cooperation," *Bloomberg Businessweek,* October 15, 2010.

Desired Outcomes of Conflict

Conflict management is more than simply a quest for agreement. If progress is to be made and dysfunctional conflict minimized, a broader agenda is in order. Dean Tjosvold's cooperative conflict model includes three desired outcomes:

1. *Agreement.* But at what cost? Equitable and fair agreements are best. An agreement that leaves one party feeling exploited or defeated will tend to breed resentment and subsequent conflict.
2. *Stronger relationships.* Good agreements enable conflicting parties to build bridges of goodwill and trust for future use. Moreover, conflicting parties who trust each other are more likely to keep their end of the bargain.
3. *Learning.* Functional conflict can promote greater self-awareness and creative problem solving. Like the practice of management itself, successful conflict handling is learned primarily by doing. Knowledge of the concepts and techniques in this chapter is a necessary first step, but there is no substitute for hands-on practice. In a contentious world, there are plenty of opportunities to practice conflict management.[11]

Major Forms of Conflict

Certain antecedents of conflict deserve a closer look. This section explores the nature and organizational implications of four common forms of conflict: personality conflict, intergroup conflict, cross-cultural conflict, and work–family conflict. Our discussion of each form of conflict includes some practical tips.

Personality Conflicts

LO11.2

As discussed in Chapter 5, your *personality* is the package of stable traits and characteristics creating your unique identity. Given the many possible combinations of personality traits, it is clear why personality conflicts are inevitable. We define a *personality conflict* as **interpersonal opposition based on personal dislike and/or disagreement.** This is an important topic, as evidenced by a survey of 173 managers in the United States. When the managers were asked what makes them most uncomfortable, an overwhelming 73% said, "Building relationships with people I dislike." "Asking for a raise" (25%) and "speaking to large audiences" (24%) were the distant second and third responses.[12]

Pictured here is Joseph Tucci, CEO of EMC, a leading data storage cloud computing company. His personality has been described as low key and unruffled, while prone to making decisions and taking action quickly. Direct and easy to talk to, "He is not the imperial CEO," says his company's chief financial officer. These qualities help people trust and believe in him, and he has succeeded in leading more than one company out of a steep decline.

Workplace Incivility: The Seeds of Personality Conflict *Workplace incivility* is a form of counterproductive work behavior (recall the discussion from Chapter 6). It is defined as low-intensity deviant behavior intended to harm the target person in ways that violate norms of mutual respect. Generally speaking, incivility is rudeness or a lack of regard for another person. A survey provides evidence for its many forms and prevalence in the U.S. workplace: 42% heard a *sexually inappropriate comment* (up 8% from the year before); 35% heard a *racial slur;* 33% heard an *ethnic slur;* 27% heard *age-related ridicule;* and 23% heard *ridicule about sexual orientation.*[13] Researchers view incivility as a vicious cycle, like daily hassles, that creates workplace stress and can even end in violence[14] (see the Hands-On Exercise on page 291 to gauge your personal level of incivility).

Similar results were found for abusive behavior by supervisors in a survey of more than 1,000 U.S. workers conducted by the Employment Law Alliance:

- 44% said they have worked for a supervisor or employer they considered abusive.

- More than half have witnessed supervisors making sarcastic jokes or teasing remarks, criticizing, giving dirty looks, or ignoring subordinates (acting as if they don't exist).

- Employees in the Northeast (56%) were more likely than those in the Midwest (48%) or South (34%) to say they have experienced an abusive boss.

- 64% said they should have the right to sue and recover damages for such offenses.[15]

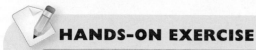
Workplace Incivility: Are *You* Part of the Problem?

How often have you engaged in these workplace behaviors during the past year?

	Never				Often
1. Paid little attention to a statement made by someone or showed little interest in their opinion.	1	2	3	4	5
2. Made demeaning, rude, or derogatory remarks about someone.	1	2	3	4	5
3. Made unwanted attempts to draw someone into a discussion of personal matters.	1	2	3	4	5
4. Made fun of someone at work.	1	2	3	4	5
5. Made an ethnic, religious, or racial remark or joke at work.	1	2	3	4	5
6. Cursed at someone at work.	1	2	3	4	5
7. Publicly embarrassed someone at work.	1	2	3	4	5
8. Played a mean prank on someone at work.	1	2	3	4	5

Total score = _____

WHAT-GOES-AROUND-COMES-AROUND SCALE

8–16 = Good organizational citizen

17–31 = Careful, your mean streak is showing

32–40 = A real social porcupine

SOURCE: Eight survey items excerpted from **G Blau and L Andersson, "Testing a Measure of Instigated Workplace Incivility,"** *Journal of Occupational and Organizational Psychology,* **December 2005, Table 1, pp 595–614.**

Clearly, such behavior creates very negative dynamics among employees. But research also shows that the effects extend beyond uncivil employees to customers who witness such behavior. Customers who saw employee-to-employee incivility generalized the same negative behavior to others who work for the organization and the organization as a whole. Worse still, participants indicated they then generalized negative expectations for future encounters with the organization—they expected poor treatment for themselves![16]

Dealing with Personality Conflicts   Given the results of research, it is clear that the vicious cycles of incivility need to be avoided or broken early. Early action can prevent a single irritating behavior from precipitating into a full-blown personality conflict (or worse). Another way to reduce conflict and its negative effects is with an organizational culture that places a high value on respect for coworkers. This requires managers and leaders to act as caring and courteous role models and provide constructive feedback. Research supports these suggestions. For example, collectivist cultures (recall our discussion of Hofstede in Chapter 3) were found to dampen or even eliminate incivility in a study involving U.S. and Taiwanese executive MBAs.[17] Diversity training and penalties for misconduct also would help.

Traditionally, managers dealt with personality conflicts by either ignoring them or transferring one party.[18] The Skills & Best Practices on page 293 presents practical tips for both nonmanagers and managers who are involved in or affected by personality conflicts. Our later discussions of handling dysfunctional conflict and alternative dispute resolution techniques also apply. Whatever the case, recent research clearly recommends not ignoring or avoiding such conflicts![19]

Intergroup Conflict

LO11.3

Conflict among work groups, teams, and departments is a common threat to organizational competitiveness. For example, the American Airlines pilots' union has an ongoing and nasty contract dispute with the company. They have made more than 300 demands! For their part, the company says that many of these demands are unreasonable and would bankrupt the already struggling company.[20] Each group wants to protect its own interests, and the groups see their interests as being in conflict. Managers who understand the mechanics of intergroup conflict are better equipped to face this sort of challenge.

In-Group Thinking: The Seeds of Intergroup Conflict   As we discussed in Chapter 9, *cohesiveness*—a "we feeling" binding group members together—can be a good or bad thing. A certain amount of cohesiveness can turn a group of individuals into a smooth-running team. Too much cohesiveness, however, can breed groupthink because a desire to get along pushes aside critical thinking. The study of in-groups by small group researchers has revealed a whole package of challenges associated with increased group cohesiveness. Specifically,

- Members of in-groups view themselves as a collection of unique individuals, while they stereotype members of other groups as being "all alike."
- In-group members see themselves positively and as morally correct, while they view members of other groups negatively and as immoral.
- In-groups view outsiders as a threat.
- In-group members exaggerate the differences between their group and other groups. This typically involves a distorted perception of reality.[21]

Such patterns of thought and behavior represent a form of ethnocentrism, discussed as a cross-cultural barrier in Chapter 3, and virtually guarantee conflict. Managers cannot eliminate in-group thinking, but they certainly should not ignore it when handling intergroup conflicts.

Research Lessons for Handling Intergroup Conflict   Sociologists have long recommended the contact hypothesis for reducing intergroup conflict. According to the *contact hypothesis,* the more the members of different groups interact, the less intergroup conflict they will experience. Those interested in improving race, international, and union–management relations typically encourage cross-group interaction. The hope is that *any* type of interaction, short of actual conflict, will reduce stereotyping and combat in-group thinking. But research has shown this approach to be naive and limited. For example, a study of over 1,600 ethnic majority (in-group) and ethnic minority (out-group) students from Germany, Belgium, and England revealed that contact did in fact reduce prejudice. Specifically, contact over time resulted in a lower desire for social distance and fewer negative emotions related to the out-group. The quality of contacts mattered, especially regarding equal status, cooperation, and closeness.

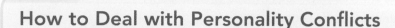

SKILLS & BEST PRACTICES

How to Deal with Personality Conflicts

Tips for Employees Having a Personality Conflict	Tips for Third-Party Observers of a Personality Conflict	Tips for Managers Whose Employees Are Having a Personality Conflict
• All employees need to be familiar with and *follow* company policies for diversity, antidiscrimination, and sexual harassment.		
• Communicate directly with the other person to resolve the perceived conflict (emphasize problem solving and common objectives, not personalities).	• Do not take sides in someone else's personality conflict.	• Investigate and document conflict.
• Avoid dragging coworkers into the conflict.	• Suggest the parties work things out themselves in a constructive and positive way.	• If appropriate, take corrective action (e.g., feedback or behavior modification).
• If dysfunctional conflict persists, seek help from direct supervisors or human resource specialists.	• If dysfunctional conflict persists, refer the problem to the parties' direct supervisors.	• If necessary, attempt informal dispute resolution.
		• Refer difficult conflicts to human resource specialists or hired counselors for formal resolution attempts and other interventions.

It wasn't enough simply to encounter members of the out-group (e.g., just an introduction). However, *prejudice also reduced contact.* Those in the out-group were more reluctant to engage or contact the in-group. Moreover, contact had no effect on reducing prejudice of the minority out-group on the majority in-group.[22] One interpretation of these results is that contact matters, quality contact matters more, but both matter most from the in-group's perspective.

Nevertheless, intergroup friendships are still desirable, as is documented in many studies,[23] but they are readily overpowered by negative intergroup interactions. Thus, the top priority for managers faced with intergroup conflict is to identify and root out specific negative linkages between (or among) groups. Managers are therefore wise to note negative interactions between members and groups and determine if influential third parties are gossiping negatively about another member or group. If either of these is discovered, then several alternative actions are recommended, such as the following:

- Work to eliminate specific negative interactions (obvious enough).
- Conduct team building to reduce intragroup conflict and prepare for cross-functional teamwork (discussed in Chapter 9).
- Encourage and facilitate friendships via social events (e.g., happy hours, sports leagues, book clubs).

- Foster positive attitudes (e.g., empathy and compassion).
- Avoid or neutralize negative gossip.
- Practice the above—be a role model.[24]

BACK TO THE CHAPTER-OPENING CASE   Evelyn Brantley undoubtedly experiences and must manage intergroup conflict in her role as managing counsel at DuPont.

1. Describe three groups with which she is most likely to have such conflicts.
2. Explain why each is likely to occur.
3. Describe how you might deal with each.

Cross-Cultural Conflict: Why It Happens and How to Overcome It

LO11.4

Doing business with people from different cultures is commonplace in our global economy where cross-border mergers, joint ventures, outsourcing, and alliances are the order of the day. Because of differing assumptions about how to think and act, the potential for cross-cultural conflict is both immediate and huge. Success or failure when conducting business across cultures often hinges on avoiding and minimizing actual or perceived conflict. It also is important to realize that such conflicts are *not* a matter of who is right and who is wrong; rather, it is a matter of accommodating cultural differences for a successful business transaction. Awareness of the cross-cultural differences we discussed in Chapter 3 is an important first step. Beyond that, cross-cultural conflict can be minimized by using international consultants and building cross-cultural relationships.

Some cultural conflicts have resulted from the outsourcing of many jobs overseas to areas where labor is much cheaper than the US. What is your opinion of outsourcing and offshoring jobs?

Overcoming or preventing cross-cultural conflict is critically important at the individual, group, and organizational levels. Rosalie L Tung's study of 409 expatriates from U.S. and Canadian multinational firms is very instructive.[25] Her survey sought to pinpoint success factors for the expatriates (14% female) who were working in 51 different countries worldwide. Nine specific ways to facilitate interaction with host-country nationals, as ranked from most useful to least useful by the respondents, are listed in the Skills & Best Practices on page 295. Good listening skills topped the list, followed by sensitivity to others and cooperativeness rather than competitiveness. Interestingly, U.S. managers often are culturally characterized as just the opposite: poor listeners, blunt to the point of insensitivity, and excessively competitive. Some managers need to add self-management to the list of ways to minimize cross-cultural conflict.

How to Build Cross-Cultural Relationships

Behavior	Rank
Be a good listener.	1
Be sensitive to needs of others.	2 ⎫
Be cooperative, rather than overly competitive.	2 ⎭ Tie
Advocate inclusive (participative) leadership.	3
Compromise rather than dominate.	4
Build rapport through conversations.	5
Be compassionate and understanding.	6
Avoid conflict by emphasizing harmony.	7
Nurture others (develop and mentor).	8

SOURCE: Adapted from R L Tung, "American Expatriates Abroad: From Neophytes to Cosmopolitans," *Journal of World Business*, Summer 1998, Table 6, p 136.

Work–Family Conflict

A complex web of demographic and economic factors makes the balancing act between our work and family lives very challenging for many of us. ***Work–family conflict* occurs when the demands of one's work role conflict with those of the family role.** This is particularly true during a recessionary period of higher unemployment. "Work–family conflict can take two distinct forms: work interference with family and family interference with work."[26] For example, suppose two managers in the same department have daughters playing on the same soccer team. One manager misses the big soccer game to attend a last-minute department meeting; the other manager skips the meeting to attend the game. Both may experience work–family conflict, but for different reasons.[27]

Practical Research Insights about Work–Family Conflict   This is a new but very active area of OB research. A recent meta-analysis involving more than 32,000 people demonstrated that an individual's personal life spills over into his or her work life and vice versa. As a result, employees' job satisfaction, organizational commitment, and intentions to quit are significantly related to the amount of work–family conflict that exists in their lives.[28] Research provides a number of other interesting conclusions:

• *Work–family balance begins at home.* Case studies of successful executives reveal that family and spousal support is critical for reaching senior-level positions.[29] This in turn suggests that both men and women need help with domestic responsibilities if there is any chance of achieving work–family balance.

• *An employer's family-supportive philosophy is more important than specific programs.* This means that the organizational culture must support the use of family-friendly programs for employees to use them. For instance, it's not enough to provide child care; employees must also feel supported and comfortable using it.

The same goes for leaving early to attend a child's soccer game or recital. Policy can allow it, but do managers and coworkers support it?

- *Informal flexibility in work hours and in allowing people to work at home is essential to promoting work–family balance.* Quite simply, flexibility allows people to cope more effectively with competing demands across their personal and work lives. This conclusion was supported by a recent study of 511 HR professionals. Ninety-one percent of respondents indicated that flexible work arrangements positively influenced morale, and 58% said that work–family balance "is the most effective tactic for attracting, rewarding and retaining top employees."[30]

- *Supportive bosses and colleagues can help.* Research demonstrated that work–family conflict was lower when employees had good relationships with their direct supervisor and work colleagues.[31] It is important that you proactively discuss potential work–family conflicts with your boss and colleagues prior to their occurrence.

- *The importance of work–family balance varies across generations.* A recent longitudinal study of work values across 16,000 people from different generational groups suggests that organizations should consider implementing work policies that are targeted toward different generational groups.[32] For example, flextime and compressed work programs can be used to attract and retain both Gen Ys and Gen Xers while job enrichment discussed in Chapter 8, may be used to motivate Baby Boomers.

Organizational Response to Work–Family Issues   Organizations have implemented a variety of family-friendly programs and services aimed at helping employees to balance the interplay between their work and personal lives. For example, General Mills increased the size of its infant-care center at corporate headquarters by 43% and subsidizes 25% of the cost. Intuit provides a $650 match of funds for dependent care accounts and makes a $65 contribution for in-home care when a child is sick.[33] Although these programs are positively received by employees, experts now believe that such efforts are partially misguided because they focus on balancing work–family issues rather than on integrating them. Balance is needed for opposites, and work and family are not opposites. Rather, our work and personal lives should be a well-integrated whole. The idea of work–life integration is discussed further in Chapter 12.

Managing Conflict

As we have seen, conflict has many faces and is a constant challenge for managers who are responsible for reaching organizational goals. Our attention now turns to the active management of both functional and dysfunctional conflict. We discuss how to stimulate functional conflict, how to handle dysfunctional conflict, and how third parties can deal effectively with conflict.

Programming Functional Conflict

LO11.5

Sometimes committees and decision-making groups become so bogged down in details and procedures that nothing substantive is accomplished. Carefully monitored functional conflict can help get the creative juices flowing once again. Managers essentially have two options. They can fan the fires of naturally occurring conflict—although this approach can be unreliable and slow. Alternatively, managers can resort to programmed conflict. Experts in the field define ***programmed conflict*** as **"conflict that raises different opinions regardless of the personal feelings of the managers."**[34] The challenge is to get contributors to either defend or criticize ideas based on relevant facts rather than on the basis of personal preference or political interests. This requires disciplined role-playing and effective leadership. Two programmed conflict techniques with proven track records are devil's advocacy and the dialectic method. Let us explore these two ways of stimulating functional conflict.

Devil's Advocacy

This technique gets its name from a traditional practice within the Roman Catholic Church. When someone's name comes before the College of Cardinals for elevation to sainthood, it is absolutely essential to ensure that he or she had a spotless record. Consequently, one individual is assigned the role of *devil's advocate* to uncover and air all possible objections to the person's canonization. In accordance with this practice, ***devil's advocacy*** in today's organizations **involves assigning someone the role of critic.**[35] Recall from Chapter 9 that Irving Janis recommended the devil's advocate role for preventing groupthink. Research supports this claim. Experiments involving 119 students showed that the use of devil's advocacy reduced escalation of commitment across multiple decisions and team compositions.[36] Escalation of commitment was discussed in Chapter 10.

In the left half of Figure 11–1, note how devil's advocacy alters the usual decision-making process in steps 2 and 3. This approach to programmed conflict is intended to generate critical thinking and reality testing. It is a good idea to rotate the job of devil's advocate so no one person or group develops a strictly negative reputation. Moreover, periodic devil's advocacy role-playing is good training for developing analytical and communication skills and emotional intelligence.

The Dialectic Method

Like devil's advocacy, the dialectic method is a time-honored practice. This particular approach to programmed conflict traces back to the dialectic school of philosophy in ancient Greece. Plato and his followers attempted to synthesize truths by exploring opposite positions (called *thesis* and *antithesis*). Court systems in the United States and elsewhere rely on directly opposing points of view for determining guilt or innocence. Accordingly, today's ***dialectic method*** **calls for managers to foster a structured debate of opposing viewpoints prior to making a decision.**[37] Steps 3 and 4 in the right half of Figure 11–1 set the dialectic approach apart from the normal decision-making process.

A major drawback of the dialectic method is that "winning the debate" may overshadow the issue at hand. Also, the dialectic method requires more skill training than does devil's advocacy. Research on the relative effectiveness of the two methods ended in a tie, although both methods were more effective than consensus decision making.[38] However, a laboratory study showed that devil's advocacy produced more potential solutions and made better recommendations for a case problem than did groups using the dialectic method.[39]

In light of this mixed evidence, managers have some latitude in using either devil's advocacy or the dialectic method for pumping creative life back into stalled deliberations. Personal preference and the role players' experience may well be the deciding factors in choosing one approach over the other. The important thing is to actively stimulate functional conflict when necessary, such as when the risk of blind conformity or groupthink is high.

connect
www.mcgrawhillconnect.com

Go to Connect for an interactive exercise to test your knowledge of the Devil's Advocacy approach to decision making.

FIGURE 11–1   Techniques for Stimulating Functional Conflict:
Devil's Advocacy and the Dialectic Method

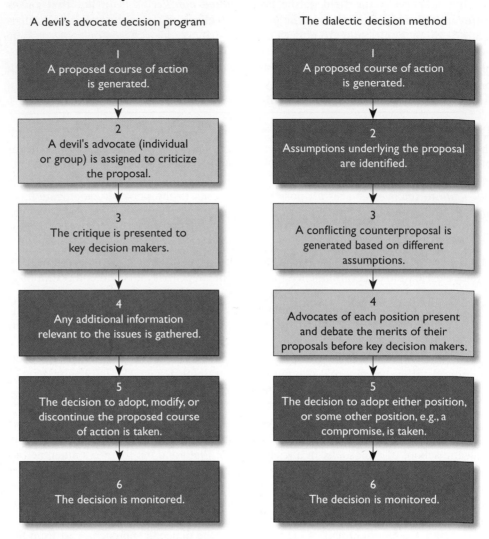

SOURCE: From R A Casler and R C Schwenk, "Agreement and Thinking Alike: Ingredients for Poor Decisions," *Academy of Management Executive*, February 1990, pp. 72–73. Copyright © 1990 with permission of Academy of Management via Copyright Clearance Center.

Alternative Styles for Handling Dysfunctional Conflict

People tend to handle negative conflict in patterned ways referred to as *styles*. Several conflict styles have been categorized over the years. According to conflict specialist Afzalur Rahim's model, five different conflict-handling styles can be plotted on a 2 × 2 grid. High to low concern for *self* is found on the horizontal axis of the grid while low to high concern for *others* forms the vertical axis (see Figure 11–2). Various combinations of these variables produce the five different conflict-handling styles: integrating, obliging, dominating, avoiding, and compromising.[40]

Five Conflict-Handling Styles   FIGURE 11–2

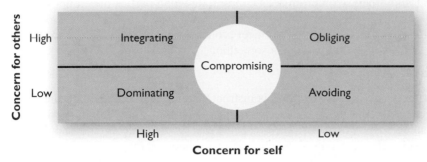

SOURCE: From M A Rahim, "A Strategy for Managing Conflict in Complex Organizations," *Human Relations*, Vol. 38. No. 1, p 84. Copyright © 1985 by Sage Publications, Inc. Reprinted by permission of Sage.

Integrating (Problem Solving)   In this style, interested parties confront the issue and cooperatively identify the problem, generate and weigh alternatives, and select a solution. Integrating is appropriate for complex issues plagued by misunderstanding. However, it is inappropriate for resolving conflicts rooted in opposing value systems. Its primary strength is its longer-lasting impact because it deals with the underlying problem rather than merely with symptoms. The primary weakness of this style is that it is very time consuming.

Obliging (Smoothing)   An obliging person shows low concern for self and a great concern for others. Such people tend to minimize differences and highlight similarities to please the other party.[41] Obliging may be an appropriate conflict-handling strategy when it is possible to eventually get something in return. But it is inappropriate for complex or worsening problems. Its primary strength is that it encourages cooperation. Its main weakness is that it's a temporary fix that fails to confront the underlying problem.

Lloyd Blankfein, CEO of Goldman Sachs, has dealt with numerous conflicts related to the financial crisis. His ability to handle conflicts influences his effectiveness as CEO, fines charged to the firm, and Goldman's reputation.

Dominating (Forcing)   High concern for self and low concern for others encourages "I win, you lose" tactics. The other party's needs are largely ignored. This style is often called forcing because it relies on formal authority to force compliance. Dominating is appropriate when an unpopular solution must be implemented, the issue is minor, or a deadline is near. It is inappropriate in an open and participative climate. Speed is its primary strength. The primary weakness of this domineering style is that it often breeds resentment.[42]

Avoiding   This tactic may involve either passive withdrawal from the problem or active suppression of the issue. Avoidance is appropriate for trivial issues or when the costs of confrontation outweigh the benefits of resolving the conflict. It is inappropriate for difficult and worsening problems. The main strength of this style is that it buys time in unfolding or ambiguous situations. The primary weakness is that the tactic provides a temporary fix that sidesteps the underlying problem.

www.mcgrawhillconnect.com

Go to Connect for a self-assessment to determine your conflict handling style.

Compromising   This is a give-and-take approach involving moderate concern for both self and others. Compromise is appropriate when parties have opposite goals or possess equal power. But compromise is inappropriate when overuse would lead to inconclusive action (e.g., failure to meet production deadlines). The primary strength of this tactic is that everyone gets something, but it's a temporary fix that can stifle creative problem solving.

Research Findings   Research is instructive on the effectiveness of the aforementioned styles. For instance, cooperative styles (integrating and obliging) improved new product development (NPD) performance between 193 buyers and suppliers across several industries in Hong Kong. In contrast, uncooperative styles (dominating and avoiding) increased numerous types of conflicts and hampered NPD performance. Compromising had no effect on performance.[43] NPD relationships are increasingly important in the global economy; it therefore is wise to give careful consideration to the styles used when working with such partners. The Rahim scale also was found to accurately describe the conflict-handling styles of owner-managers of small Indian businesses.[44] This finding, along with the previous study, demonstrates the cross-cultural usefulness or and potential generalizability of this tool.

Particularly noteworthy is the considerable research attention given to conflict in the nursing occupation. For instance, emotional intelligence (covered in Chapter 5) was positively related to collaborative and negatively related to accommodating conflict-handling styles in a sample of nurses.[45] Given the intense shortage of nurses in many parts of the (Western) world, turnover is a critical and top of the mind issue for nursing managers and health care administrators alike. Therefore, reducing conflict (e.g., bullying) is an important and effective means for reducing turnover.

Collectively, research suggests that no one style is best for every situation. Employees and managers are both well served to apply a contingency approach (see our Chapter 1 discussion) to conflict-handling styles.

Third-Party Interventions: Alternative Dispute Resolution

Disputes between employees, between employees and their employer, and between companies too often end up in lengthy and costly court battles. According to one estimate, U.S. businesses spent $254.7 billion on *direct legal costs* in 2008 or $836 per citizen. This estimate is dwarfed when compared to *indirect legal costs,* such as opportunities not pursued due to litigation concerns, disclaimers, and extra testing. All such costs are ultimately passed on to consumers in the form of higher prices.[46] It therefore is no wonder that a more constructive, less expensive approach called alternative dispute resolution has seen enthusiastic growth in recent years. The intent of **alternative dispute resolution (ADR), according to a pair of Canadian labor lawyers, is that it "uses faster, more user-friendly methods of dispute resolution, instead of traditional, adversarial approaches (such as unilateral decision making or litigation)."**[47] For example, Georgia Pacific, a paper, pulp, and packaging company, has embraced ADR with impressive results. The company's ADR program saved approximately $42 million from 1997 through 2006. This is remarkable even for a company with annual revenues in the billions.[48] See the Skills & Best Practices feature on page 301 for suggestions on how to implement an ADR system similar to Georgia Pacific's.

LO11.6   The following ADR techniques represent a progression of steps third parties can take to resolve organizational conflicts.[49] They are ranked from easiest and least expensive to

Implementing ADR at Your Company

The legal team at Georgia Pacific (GP) has implemented an effective alternative dispute resolution system since the 1990s. Aided by top management support, the company's ADR program is a deeply embedded alternative dispute resolution tool. The leaders at GP recommend the following for companies that seek to realize similar benefits:

- *Get top management support.* Show economic benefits of early case resolution versus winning at all costs.
- *Start training.* While attorneys often are familiar with ADR, they need training on using it effectively.
- *Start small.* Don't attempt a wholesale change of processes and procedures. Choose areas/cases that are best suited for ADR and try those first.
- *Incorporate ADR.* Build ADR into contracts and other agreements and practices.
- *Grant authority.* Devote a person or persons with authority to handle ADR.
- *Begin immediately.* Speed is an advantage of ADR; use it. To do this, set up a process for quickly screening cases and identify those that qualify for ADR.
- *Build and collect ADR resources.* Like other forms of institutional knowledge, build "libraries" or repositories of ADR cases and information.
- *Don't be afraid to litigate.* Not all cases are appropriate for ADR.
- *Measure results.* Measuring actual and potential costs is both art and science. Get uncomfortable and devise a means to capture the appropriate outcomes (e.g., time, money, and relationships).
- *Be patient.* Effective ADR programs evolve over time.

SOURCE: Excerpted and adapted from P M Armstrong, P J Hall, and E A Infante, "Anatomy of a Successful Mediation," Association of Corporate Counsel, 2006. Retrieved March 24, 2011, from: http://www.acc.com/vl/public/ProgramMaterial/loader.cfm

most difficult and costly. A growing number of organizations have formal ADR policies involving an established sequence of various combinations of these techniques:

- *Facilitation.* A third party, usually a manager, informally urges disputing parties to deal directly with each other in a positive and constructive manner.

- *Conciliation.* A neutral third party informally acts as a communication conduit between disputing parties. This is appropriate when conflicting parties refuse to meet face to face. The immediate goal is to establish direct communication, with the broader aim of finding common ground and a constructive solution.

- *Peer review.* A panel of trustworthy coworkers, selected for their ability to remain objective, hears both sides of a dispute in an informal and confidential meeting. Any decision by the review panel may or may not be binding, depending on the company's ADR policy. Membership on the peer review panel often is rotated among employees.[50]

- *Ombudsman.* Someone who works for the organization, and is widely respected and trusted by his or her coworkers, hears grievances on a confidential basis and attempts to arrange a solution. This approach, more common in Europe than North America, permits someone to get help from above without relying on the formal hierarchy chain.

- *Mediation.* "The mediator—a trained, third-party neutral—actively guides the disputing parties in exploring innovative solutions to the conflict. Although some companies have in-house mediators who have received ADR training, most also use external mediators who have no ties to the company."[51] Unlike an arbitrator, a mediator does *not* render a decision. It is up to the disputants to reach a mutually acceptable decision.

- *Arbitration.* Disputing parties agree ahead of time to accept the decision of a neutral arbitrator in a formal courtlike setting, often complete with evidence and witnesses. Statements are confidential. Decisions are based on legal merits. Trained arbitrators, typically from outside agencies such as the American Arbitration Association, are versed in relevant laws and case precedents. In many instances, employee arbitration is mandatory for resolving disputes. Heated debate has occurred, however, over the past several years regarding mandatory versus voluntary arbitration. On the one hand, many employers have not realized the time and cost savings promised by arbitration and now prefer to litigate. On the other, many employees feel that arbitration unfairly benefits employers who have skilled arbitrators whose job it is to handle such disputes (recall the issues of equity and justice covered in Chapter 7).[52]

Negotiating

Formally defined, **negotiation** **is a give-and-take decision-making process involving interdependent parties with different preferences.**[53] Common examples include labor-management negotiations over wages, hours, and working conditions and negotiations between supply chain specialists and vendors involving price, delivery schedules, and credit terms. Self-managed work teams with overlapping task boundaries also need to rely on negotiated agreements. Negotiating skills are more important than ever today.

Two Basic Types of Negotiation

🔥**LO11.7**

Negotiation experts distinguish between two types of negotiation—*distributive* and *integrative.* Understanding the difference has great practical implications.

A *distributive* negotiation usually involves a single issue—a "fixed-pie"—in which one person gains at the expense of the other. For example, haggling over the price of a rug in a bazaar is a distributive negotiation. In most conflicts, however, more than one issue is at stake, and each party values the issues differently. The outcomes available are no longer a fixed-pie divided among all parties. An agreement can be found that is better for both parties than what they would have reached through distributive negotiation. This is an *integrative* negotiation.

> However, parties in a negotiation often don't find these beneficial trade-offs because each *assumes* its interests *directly* conflict with those of the other party. "What is good for the other side must be bad for us" is a common and unfortunate perspective that most people have. This is the mind-set we call the *mythical* "fixed-pie."[54]

Distributive negotiation involves traditional win–lose thinking. Integrative negotiation calls for a progressive win–win strategy.[55] For example, as president of the Environmental Defense Fund, Fred Krupp helps the nonprofit organization achieve more of its objectives by seeking win–win negotiations with businesses. The Environmental Defense Fund opened a Bentonville, Arkansas, office near Walmart's headquarters to help that company achieve goals for energy efficiency and packaging reduction, and when other environmental groups wanted to combat acid rain with strict limits on sulfur dioxide emissions, the Environmental Defense Fund partnered with utilities to push for a cap-and-trade system that offers business greater flexibility while still reducing emissions. Regarding the latter effort, William Reilly, the Environmental Protection Agency's leader at the time, says Krupp's willingness to take a business-friendly stance "helped us in Congress and in the eyes of the public" to get the new regulations enacted.[56] Finding areas of common ground can be difficult; successful negotiators are able to weigh multiple issues affecting a problem and gather information about which issues are most important to the other parties and why.[57]

Added-Value Negotiation

One practical application of the integrative approach is **added-value negotiation (AVN). During AVN, the negotiating parties cooperatively develop multiple deal packages while building a productive long-term relationship.** AVN consists of these five steps:

www.mcgrawhillconnect.com

Go to Connect for a video case to view Starbuck's and how they manage conflict and negotiations.

1. *Clarify interests.* After each party identifies its tangible and intangible needs, the two parties meet to discuss their respective needs and find common ground for negotiation.

2. *Identify options.* A marketplace of value is created when the negotiating parties discuss desired elements of value (such as property, money, behavior, rights, and risk reduction).

3. *Design alternative deal packages.* While aiming for multiple deals, each party mixes and matches elements of value from both parties in workable combinations.

4. *Select a deal.* Each party analyzes deal packages proposed by the other party. Jointly, the parties discuss and select from feasible deal packages, with a spirit of creative agreement.

5. *Perfect the deal.* Together the parties discuss unresolved issues, develop a written agreement, and build relationships for future negotiations.[58]

> **BACK TO THE CHAPTER-OPENING CASE**   Assume you are Evelyn Brantley, the managing counsel at DuPont. Also assume that you are negotiating fees with the managing partner of an outside law firm you want to hire. The managing partner insists on a $400 per hour rate. Describe how you would negotiate with the partner using AVN. Keep in mind that one of your own key performance expectations is to reduce costs in the legal department.

Recent Research Findings and Implications

A recent study conducted by researchers at MIT and the University of California at Berkeley provided several interesting insights. They followed MBA students' job offer negotiations, as well as their job and compensation satisfaction and intentions to quit a year later. Among the interesting findings were the following:

- *Concessions.* Job negotiators achieved concessions on 15 different items — signing bonus, salary, relocation (moving expenses, housing, cost-of-living assistance), start date, performance bonus, stock options, vacation time, benefits

Negotiating Your Salary

Experts offer this advice for getting the best compensation you can.

- *Know the market rate.* Research what companies are paying for other employees with similar jobs in the same area.
- *Consider the economy.* When the economy is slowing or in recession, don't expect big raises. For example, if you're a recent graduate, salaries won't be bigger than the previous year's. In tough times, show that you understand the business's challenges.
- *Know your own value.* Can you justify making more than the market rate? Be ready to offer specific examples of your experience and accomplishments; tell how you benefited your past and present employers.
- *Be honest.* Don't exaggerate your pay or accomplishments.
- *Don't go first.* Try to wait for the other person to name a number. You might say you want to be paid the going rate for someone with your qualifications. If you have to give an answer, give a range, not a specific dollar figure.
- *Consider benefits, too.* Some of the most valuable parts of your compensation package may be insurance and retirement savings. Retirement may seem like eons away, but an employer match of 5% to your 401(k) plan is like an extra 5% of pay—without an immediate tax bite.
- *Look at the long term.* If you can't get a big pay package, consider whether you can ask for something else that will help your long-term career, for example, a chance to work on an important assignment.

SOURCE: Based on B Brophy, "Bargaining for Bigger Bucks: A Step-by-Step Guide to Negotiating Your Salary," *Business 2.0,* May 2004, p 107; S Curran, "Compensation Advice for New Grads," *BusinessWeek,* April 30, 2007, www.businessweek.com; and F Di Meglio, "Job Searchers Face a New Reality," *BusinessWeek,* April 3, 2008, www.businessweek.com.

(health insurance), debt refinancing, additional training, geographic location, visa assistance, calendar for considering promotion, time to decide on an offer, and the level of position.

- *Subjective value versus economic value.* They studied not only the **economic value (EV) of the negotiations (i.e., how much salary and bonus)** but also the **subjective value (SV)** of negotiations. **SV captures the social and psychological consequences of negotiations, such as the emotions and perceptions of the process, people, and outcomes.** This is a more comprehensive view of negotiations, and when combined with the many concession items, enables both sides to apply integrative negotiation strategies.

- *Satisfaction and intentions to quit one year later.* If the above findings don't move you, and you would rather just focus on the money, then perhaps you should consider their other findings. Notably, the study showed that SV and not EV predicted compensation satisfaction, job satisfaction, and intentions to quit a year later. In other words, their work suggests that while money matters, the social and psychological elements matter more.[59] For additional insights and guidance on negotiating your salary see the Skills & Best Practices above.

key terms

added-value negotiation (AVN)   303

alternative dispute resolution (ADR)   300

conflict   286

devil's advocacy   297

dialectic method   297

dysfunctional conflict   287

economic value (EV)   304

functional conflict   287

negotiation   302

personality conflict   290

programmed conflict   297

subjective value (SV)   304

work–family conflict   295

chapter summary

- *Define conflict, distinguish between functional and dysfunctional conflict, and identify three desired outcomes of conflict.* Conflict is a process in which one party perceives that its interests are being opposed or negatively affected by another party. It is inevitable and not necessarily destructive. Too little conflict, as evidenced by apathy or lack of creativity, can be as great a problem as too much conflict. Functional conflict enhances organizational interests while dysfunctional conflict is counterproductive. Three desired conflict outcomes are agreement, stronger relationships, and learning.

- *Define personality conflicts, and explain how they should be managed.* Personality conflicts involve interpersonal opposition based on personal dislike and/or disagreement (or as an outgrowth of workplace incivility). Care needs to be taken with personality conflicts in the workplace because of the legal implications of diversity, discrimination, and sexual harassment. Managers should investigate and document personality conflicts, take corrective actions such as feedback or behavior modification if appropriate, or attempt informal dispute resolution. Difficult or persistent personality conflicts need to be referred to human resource specialists or counselors.

- *Discuss the role of in-group thinking in intergroup conflict, and explain what can be done to avoid cross-cultural conflict.* Members of in-groups tend to see themselves as unique individuals who are more moral than outsiders, whom they view as a threat and stereotypically as all alike. In-group thinking is associated with ethnocentric behavior. International consultants can prepare people from different cultures to work effectively together. Cross-cultural conflict can be minimized by having expatriates build strong cross-cultural relationships with their hosts (primarily by being good listeners, being sensitive to others, and being more cooperative than competitive).

- *Define work–family conflict and describe what can be done to manage it.* Work–family conflict occurs when the demands of one's work role conflicts with those of the family role. Two forms of work–family conflict can occur: work interference with family and family interference with work. Such conflicts can be reduced in several ways. Supportive spouses and family members are key, but support needs to be mutual. Employers who adopt and practice family-friendly policies (e.g., flextime and telecommuting) can make a big impact. Understanding and supportive relationships with bosses and coworkers are helpful. Finally, the importance of work–family balance differs across generations. Employers and managers are well served to be aware of and address these differences.

- *Explain how managers can program functional conflict, and identify the five conflict-handling styles.* Functional conflict can be stimulated by permitting antecedents of conflict to persist or programming conflict during decision making with devil's advocates or the dialectic method. The five conflict-handling styles are integrating (problem solving), obliging (smoothing), dominating (forcing), avoiding, and compromising. There is no single best style.

- *Identify and describe at least four alternative dispute resolution (ADR) techniques.* Alternative dispute resolution (ADR) involves avoiding costly court battles with more informal and user-friendly techniques such as facilitation, conciliation, peer review, ombudsman, mediation, and arbitration.

- *Draw a distinction between distributive and integrative negotiation, and explain the concept of added-value negotiation.* Distributive negotiation involves fixed-pie and win–lose thinking. Integrative negotiation is a win–win approach to better results for both parties. The five steps in added-value negotiation are as follows: Step 1, clarify interests; Step 2, identify options; Step 3, design alternative deal packages; Step 4, select a deal; and Step 5, perfect the deal. Elements of value, multiple deals, and creative agreement are central to this approach.

discussion questions

1. Based on reading this chapter, how might you handle a conflict with a classmate on a team project for this class? Explain.
2. What examples of functional and dysfunctional conflict have you observed in organizations lately? What were the outcomes? What caused the dysfunctional conflict?
3. Which of the five conflict-handling styles is your strongest? Your weakest? How can you improve your ability to handle conflict?
4. Which of the six ADR techniques appeals the most to you? Why?
5. How could added-value negotiation make your life a bit easier? Explain in terms of a specific problem, conflict, or deadlock.

legal/ethical dilemma

Financial Fraud Case Pits Arbitration versus Class Action

Mr Groetsch has an issue with his stockbroker from Securities America. Despite Mr Groetsch's diagnosis of Alzheimer's disease and his family's formal request for Securities America to not do any business with him, Securities America broker Ron Carazo sold Groetsch a Medical Capital Holdings bond worth $500,000. Groetsch's health issues aside, the sale was made despite internal memos at Securities America questioning the legitimacy of Medical Capital. These concerns were disseminated to brokers across the company, yet Securities America continued to sell these bonds for years. Medical Capital was eventually exposed as a fraud, and now Groetsch is trying to recoup his losses. Does this seem straightforward? It's not.

Groetsch is pursuing an arbitration claim, which is often the preferred route for investors. Arbitration can be shorter, cheaper, less complex, and profitable. But Groetsch's conflict is compounded by the fact that numerous other defrauded clients are seeking remedies via litigation in the form of class action lawsuits. For example, authorities in Montana and Massachusetts have brought separate class action suits against Securities America, claiming that the firm described the investments as conservative, even though an internal committee raised red flags about the risks. This scenario pits arbitration versus litigation. Many people may not see a problem here—all claims will eventually be settled

and the plaintiffs paid. Although logical, this may not happen. A judge has put the brakes on Groetsch's arbitration, due to concerns that the awards he may be granted will deplete the funds available for pending class action lawsuits. More specifically, the fear is that enough funds will not be left to pay the many, many plaintiffs in the class action suits. The class action attorneys argue that they may be able to collect only 10 cents on the dollar of funds lost by the defrauded investors they represent.[60]

What Should the Judge Do?

1. Let the arbitration proceed. Mr Groetsch has his right to be compensated for his losses. If nothing is left for the others, then that is unfortunate but irrelevant. Explain your reasoning.

2. Delay the arbitration and wait for the outcome of the class action suits. Once settled, then allow the arbitration to proceed to its end. Explain your reasoning.

3. Suggest to, although you cannot force, Mr Groetsch to drop his arbitration and fold him into one of the class action suits (if possible). Explain your reasoning.

4. Create and explain other alternatives.

 If you're looking for additional study materials, be sure to check out the Online Learning Center at

www.mhhe.com/kinickiob5e

for more information and interactivities that correspond to this chapter.

chapter 12

Communicating in the Digital Age

After reading the material in this chapter, you should be able to:

LO12.1 Describe the perceptual process model of communication.

LO12.2 Describe the process, personal, physical, and semantic barriers to effective communication.

LO12.3 Contrast the communication styles of assertiveness, aggressiveness, and nonassertiveness.

LO12.4 Discuss the primary sources of nonverbal communication.

LO12.5 Review the five dominant listening styles and 10 keys to effective listening.

LO12.6 Discuss the impact of information communication technologies (ICT) on productivity.

LO12.7 Describe the challenges of managing teleworkers, and the advantages and concerns associated with social media at work.

Social Media—A Blessing and a Curse

I was on an overseas business trip when my phone began ringing at 4 a.m. The first person to reach me was Best Buy's VP of operations. The crisis related to my Twitter account. I tweet on a variety of subjects—experiences in our stores and my kids. But this morning my coworkers back in the United States—and my 5,000 Twitter followers—read an unusual tweet from me: "I'VE BEEN HAVING A LOT OF GREAT SEX LATELY, AND HERE'S WHY." I'd been hacked.

I'm a heavy user of Twitter and Facebook and learn a lot from interacting directly with customers and employees. I see trends and news I otherwise might miss. Ultimately, I believe that Best Buy's message has to be where the people are. Today, that means being on social media networks. Many CEOs disagree. You'd be amazed at the number of people I talk to—people who run big businesses around the world—who think social networking is just a fad or simply clutter. If a company, or even its chief executive, doesn't have a presence on social networks today, the company risks not being in the conversation at all. Over time, I believe, that can be fatal to a business.

When I first joined these sites I was surprised at how many employees friended me. I quickly learned it was an effective way of connecting with our employees, given the company's demographics, although I'm still astonished by the things people reveal about themselves. For instance, one of these friends posted a status update that he couldn't believe how much he drank the previous night, and hoped not to do it again—at least not until the coming weekend. This is what you want to say about yourself in public? Still, it's fascinating.

Twitter took longer to get used to. I've read so many banal tweets about everyday activities—"I'm having a taco"—that no one cares about. I had to learn that Twitter is a way to let people know what's on my mind, that tweeting could be an extension of my thinking. When I tweet, I know I'm communicating with my employees. I pass along good things that I see in a store or hear about a customer's experience, and people are thrilled to know that I'm hearing good things about them. Best Buy also has Twelpforce on Twitter. Customers can post their tech problems, and Best Buy associates—or other Twitter users—can suggest solutions. By monitoring the feed, we're able to learn what our customers are doing and help them in real time. People are going to shop with the companies they think really care

Best Buy CEO, Brain Dunn, has personally experienced the advantages and disadvantages of social media at work.

about them. Twitter demonstrates we are one of those companies.

I like the immediacy and sharing of my interests—baseball, basketball, and my kids—as it allows us all to be humanized a little bit. Sometimes people ask me if I have an intern or staff member handle my Twitter account. I don't. I do get help in writing posts for my Best Buy blog, but on Facebook and Twitter it's all me.

There are downsides however. An employee created and posted an animated video on YouTube. While it didn't mention Best Buy directly, it was obvious enough for anybody viewing it. The video depicted an associate–customer interaction that made the customer look stupid. By the time I learned of this video it had been viewed 1.5 million times. Today it has been viewed more than 9 million times. The Twitter link to YouTube indirectly alerted me to a problem. I soon learned that the

same employee posted several other videos in which Best Buy was specifically mentioned—in ways that weren't flattering to our customers. Those videos were taken down, but the issue quickly became a big blogosphere drama about whether Best Buy was going to terminate the employee. He was suspended while we investigated the details. We ultimately invited him back to work, but he decided to pursue a career in filmmaking. What you can do is try to educate employees about what's appropriate to post and what's not, what's intellectual property and what's not. Last year we created a social media policy that applies to all employees. They must disclose that they are employees when discussing the company online, and must keep nonpublic financial or operational data private. "Basically," it says, "if you find yourself wondering if you can talk about something you learned at work—don't."[1]

THE CHAPTER-OPENING CASE illustrates effective communication with those internal and external to the organization can be critical to success at all levels—individual, group, and organizational. The case also shows the explosive use and dramatic effects information communication technologies (ICT) have had on organizational communication and organizational behavior (OB). Despite the prevalence today, many people would not have guessed that companies would use blogs to communicate with customers and to obtain input during internal strategic planning meetings. Managers need more than good interpersonal skills to effectively communicate in today's workplace. They also need to understand the pros and cons of different types of communication media and information technology.

It is important to note that while the significance of communication skills is widely acknowledged by businesspeople, consultants, and the general public, OB researchers have given relatively little attention to the topic. Nevertheless, this chapter will help you to better understand how managers can both improve their communication skills and design more effective communication programs. We discuss (1) basic dimensions of the communication processes, focusing on a perceptual process model and barriers to effective communication; (2) interpersonal communication; and (3) the implications of ICT for OB.

Basic Dimensions of the Communication Process

Communication is defined as **"the exchange of information between a sender and a receiver, and the inference (perception) of meaning between the individuals involved."**[2] Managers who understand this process can analyze their own communication patterns as well as design communication programs that fit organizational needs. This section reviews a perceptual process model of communication and discusses the barriers to effective communication.

A Perceptual Process Model of Communication

LO12.1

As we all know, communicating is not that simple or clear-cut. Communication is fraught with miscommunication. Researchers recognize this and have begun to examine communication as a form of social information processing (recall the discussion in Chapter 4) in which receivers interpret messages by cognitively processing information. This view led to development of a perceptual model of communication that depicts communication as a process in which receivers create meaning in their own minds. Let us consider the parts of this process and then integrate them with an example.

Sender, Message, and Receiver   The sender is the person wanting to communicate information—the message. The receiver is the person, group, or organization for whom the message is intended.

Encoding   Communication begins when a sender encodes an idea or thought. Encoding entails translating thoughts into a code or language that can be understood by others. This forms the foundation of the message. For example, if a professor wants to communicate to you about an assignment, he or she must first think about what information he or she wants to communicate. Once the professor resolves this issue in his or her mind (encoding), he or she can select a medium with which to communicate.

Selecting a Medium   Managers can communicate through a variety of media. Potential media include face-to-face conversations and meetings, telephone calls, charts and graphs, and the many digital forms (e.g., e-mail, texting, voice mail, videoconferencing, Twitter, Facebook, Blackboard, etc.). Choosing the appropriate media depends on many factors, including the nature of the message, its intended purpose, the type of audience, proximity to the audience, time horizon for disseminating the message, and personal preferences.[3] Janice Fields, the current president of McDonald's USA, used to spend 85% of her time as chief operating officer traveling for face-to-face meetings with franchise owners.[4] No doubt, Fields's personal preferences as a manager shaped this preference for communicating in person, but the medium also is suitable for the complex task of motivating franchisees and identifying problems and opportunities.

All media have advantages and disadvantages. Face-to-face conversations, for example, are useful for communicating about sensitive or important issues that require feedback and intensive interaction.[5] Radio Shack, for instance, was made infamous for notifying 400 employees via e-mail that their jobs were eliminated.[6] In contrast, telephones are convenient, fast, and private, but lack nonverbal information. Although writing memos or letters is time consuming, it is a good medium when it is difficult to meet with the other person, when formality and a written record are important, and when face-to-face interaction is not necessary to enhance understanding. An extreme and interesting example was provided by NBC president Jeff Zucker. He put handwritten invitations in the rooms of the 1,600 attendees of the Association of National Advertisers 2010 annual meeting. While many events occurred during the meeting, recipients of the invitations said that

Although managers can communicate through a variety of media, face-to-face communication is useful for delivering sensitive or important issues that require feedback, intensive interaction, or nonverbal cues.

the handwritten nature of NBC's Zucker stood out.[7] Electronic communication, which is discussed later in this chapter, can be used to communicate with a large number of dispersed people and is potentially a very fast, efficient medium. Electronic communications also tend to save money compared with paper-based alternatives, but experts disagree over whether paper or electronic messages are more secure.[8]

Decoding and Creating Meaning   Decoding occurs when receivers receive a message. It is the process of interpreting and making sense of a message. Returning to our example of a professor communicating about an assignment, decoding would occur among students when they receive the message from the professor.

In contrast to the conduit model's assumption that meaning is directly transferred from sender to receiver, the perceptual model is based on the belief that a receiver creates the meaning of a message in his or her mind. This means that the same message can be interpreted differently by different people. Consider the following example that occurred to a reporter from *The Wall Street Journal* when he was on assignment in China.

> I was riding the elevator a few weeks ago with a Chinese colleague here in the *Journal*'s Asian headquarters. I smiled and said, "Hi." She responded, "You've gained weight." I might have been appalled, but at least three other Chinese co-workers also have told me I'm fat. I probably should cut back on the pork dumplings. In China, such an intimate observation from a colleague isn't necessarily an insult. It's probably just friendliness.[9]

This example highlights that decoding and creating the meaning of a message are influenced by cultural norms and values (recall our discussion in Chapter 2).

Feedback   Have you ever been on your cell phone and thought that you lost your connection with the person you were talking to? If yes, something like the following probably occurred. "Hello, Donna are you there?" "Donna, can you hear me?" The other person may say back, "Yes, I can hear you, but your voice is cutting in and out." This is an example of feedback—the receiver expresses a reaction to the sender's message.

Noise   *Noise* **represents anything that interferes with the transmission and understanding of a message.** It affects all linkages of the communication process. Noise includes factors such as the all-too-common unreliable or slow networks ("Can you hear me now?" or AT&T Wireless's unreliable connections associated with iPhone use). But there are many other sources of noise: speech impairment, illegible handwriting, inaccurate statistics, poor hearing and eyesight, environmental noises, people talking, and physical distance between sender and receiver. Our many communication devices can introduce noise literally, as when your smartphone makes your desktop's speakers buzz, or figuratively, as when a person is trying to listen to someone while also checking a text message. Nonverbal communication, discussed later in this chapter, also is a source of noise, as are cross-cultural differences between senders and receivers (recall our discussion in Chapter 3).

Noise and the other elements of the communication process all play a role in the example in Figure 12–1. Notice that the communication process is sequential. From a practical view, it is wise to consider all of these elements, as any one of them can influence outcomes. The Skills & Best Practices on page 313 provides communication suggestions when searching for a job.

Barriers to Effective Communication

 LO12.2   For communication to be effective, senders must accurately communicate their intended message, and receivers must perceive and interpret the message accurately. Anything that gets in the way of the accurate transmission and reception of a message

FIGURE 12–1   Communication Process in Action

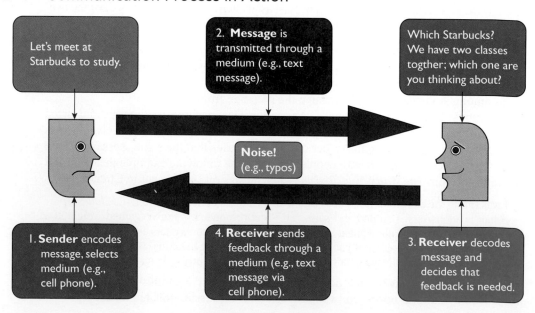

Communication Counts in Landing a Job

As a job seeker, it is your responsibility to prove that you're the one best candidate for the job. Effective communication skills enable you to sell yourself and to calm your nerves. Performing well during an interview depends on both what you say and how you say it!

What You Say

- *Direct the conversation.* Many people simply wait to be asked questions. Small talk can get things started, but whatever you choose be sure it is short and noncontroversial.
- *Pick your selling points.* Identify and focus on your top two or three selling points. If you have little experience, then perhaps focus on personal qualities. If you have experience, then highlight significant achievements.
- *Substantiate.* Provide evidence (e.g., stories and/or data) to illustrate your selling points.
- *What's in it for them?* Ask not what the job will do for you, but what you can do on the job. Explain why you're a good match and what you bring to the party.
- *Don't forget to do your homework.* Be sure to thoroughly research the company, using the Web and other resources. Look for information relevant to past, current, and future company events and initiatives. Use this knowledge when talking or asking questions about the company.
- *Anticipate challenging questions.* Know that you will be asked, "What are your weaknesses?" The key here is to identify a challenge briefly, then discuss how you solved the problem.

How You Say It

- *Show them that you'll "bring it."* Express your enthusiasm and willingness to do anything, not just the most interesting stuff.
- *Smile.* It's one of the easiest ways to win people over.
- *Take your time.* Nerves often make us rush through an answer—just to get it over with. Slow yourself down and speak in a normal conversational tone.
- *Eye contact.* Don't stare in the other person's eyes, but don't stare at the floor or out the window either.
- *Dress how they dress.* Regardless of your own style or wardrobe, your choices need to match what is common at the company. The rule: "anything that distracts, detracts."
- *Close with a handshake.* End the interview with a "thank you" and a firm handshake.
- *Follow-up.* At the end of the interview ask when the interviewer would like you to follow up. Then drop your interviewer a note of thanks.

Fighting Nerves

- Prepare.
- Breathe.
- Pause before answering.
- Never say you're nervous.
- Use positive self-talk and visualization.

SOURCE: Adapted from M Civiello, "Communication Counts in Landing a Job," *Training & Development,* **February 2009, pp 82–83.**

is a barrier to effective communication. You should understand these barriers so that you can be aware of their existence and try to reduce their impact.

Some barriers are actually part of the communication process itself (see Table 12–1). The communication process will fail if any step in the process is blocked. From a practical point of view, however, three types of barriers are likely to influence communication's effectiveness: (1) personal barriers, (2) physical barriers, and (3) semantic barriers.

TABLE 12–1   Communication Barriers within the Communication Process

- **Sender barrier—no message gets sent.** Have you ever had an idea but were afraid to voice it because you feared criticism? Then obviously no message got sent. Technology often poses sender barriers too. Perhaps you were not copied on an e-mail and thus didn't receive the message. Or, you didn't actually receive the multiple memos regarding "TPS reports" (e.g., the movie *Office Space*).

- **Encoding barrier—the message is not expressed correctly.** No doubt you've sometimes had difficulty trying to think of the correct word to express how you feel about something. Or, you choose the right words but use the wrong tone. Technology often exacerbates encoding barriers because the message is reduced only to words or texting-shorthand.

- **Medium barrier—the communication channel is blocked.** You never get through to someone because his or her phone always has a busy signal. The computer network is down and the e-mail message you sent doesn't go through. These are instances of the communication medium being blocked.

- **Decoding barrier—the recipient doesn't understand the message.** Your boss tells you to "lighten up" or "buckle down," but because English is not your first language, you don't understand what the messages mean. Or perhaps you're afraid to show your ignorance when someone is throwing computer or financial jargon at you and says that your computer connection has "a bandwidth problem" or this relates to "structured finance."

- **Receiver barrier—no message gets received.** Because you were busy multitasking, you didn't "catch the message" from your supervisor about today's work assignments. You therefore needed to ask her to repeat the announcement.

- **Feedback barrier—the recipient doesn't respond enough.** No doubt you've had the experience of giving someone street directions, but since they only nod their heads and don't repeat the directions back to you, you don't really know whether you were understood. The same thing can happen in many workplace circumstances.

SOURCE: Excerpted and adapted from A Kinicki and B Williams, *Management: A Practical Introduction,* 3rd ed (Burr Ridge, IL: McGraw-Hill, 2008), p 493.

BACK TO THE CHAPTER-OPENING CASE

1. Which of the communication barriers do you think are most likely to affect Brian Dunn when communicating via social media with Best Buy employees?
2. Which barriers do you think are most likely when communicating with Best Buy customers?

Personal Barriers   Have you ever communicated with someone and felt totally confused? This may have led you to wonder: is it them or is it me? Personal barriers represent any individual attributes that hinder communication. Let's examine nine common personal barriers that contribute to miscommunication.

 1. *Variable skills in communicating effectively.* Some people are simply better communicators than others. They have the speaking and listening skills, the ability to use gestures for dramatic effect, the vocabulary to alter the message to fit the audience, the writing skills to convey concepts in simple and concise terms, and the social skills to make others feel comfortable.[10]

2. *Variations in how information is processed and interpreted.* Did you grow up in the country, in the suburbs, or in a city? Did you attend private or public school? Are you from a loving home or one marred with fighting, yelling, and lack of structure? Answers to these questions are relevant because they make up the different frames of references and experiences people use to interpret the world around them. As you may recall from Chapter 4, people selectively attend to various stimuli based on their unique frames of reference. This means that these differences affect our interpretations of what we see and hear.

3. *Variations in interpersonal trust.* Chapter 9 discussed the manner in which trust affects interpersonal relationships. Communication is more likely to be distorted when people do not trust each other. Rather than focusing on the message, a lack of trust is likely to cause people to be defensive and question the accuracy of what is being communicated.

4. *Stereotypes and prejudices.* We noted in Chapter 4 that stereotypes are oversimplified beliefs about specific groups of people. They potentially distort communication because their use causes people to misperceive and recall distorted information. It is important for all of us to be aware of our potential stereotypes and to recognize that they may subconsciously affect the interpretation of a message. At the same time, people often worry that well-intentioned words will be interpreted as "politically incorrect" slurs against members of one group or another.

www.mcgrawhillconnect.com

Go to Connect for a video case to view 1154 Lil Studios and how they handle communication.

5. *Big egos.* Our egos, whether due to pride, self-esteem, superior ability, or arrogance, are a communication barrier. Egos can cause political battles, turf wars, and pursuit of power, credit, and resources. Egos influence how we treat others as well as our receptiveness to being influenced by others. Have you ever had someone put you down in public? Then you know how ego feelings can influence communication.

6. *Poor listening skills.* How many times have you been in class when one student asks the same question that was asked minutes earlier? How about going to a party and meeting someone who only talks about him- or herself and never asks questions about you? This experience certainly doesn't make one feel important or memorable. It's hard to communicate effectively when one of the parties is not listening. We discuss listening skills in a later section of this chapter.

7. *Natural tendency to evaluate others' messages.* What do you say to someone after watching the latest movie in a theater? What did you think of the movie? He or she might say, "It was great; best movie I've seen all year." You then may say "I agree," or alternatively, "I disagree, that movie stunk." The point is that we all have a natural tendency, according to renowned psychologist Carl Rogers, to evaluate messages from our own point of view or frame of reference, particularly when we have strong feelings about the issue.[11]

8. *Inability to listen with understanding.* Listening with understanding occurs when a receiver can "see the expressed idea and attitude from the other person's point of view, to sense how it feels to him, to achieve his frame of reference in regard to the thing he is talking about."[12] Try to listen with understanding; it will make you less defensive and can improve your accuracy in perceiving messages.

9. *Nonverbal communication.* Communication accuracy is enhanced when one's facial expression and gestures are consistent with the intent of a message. Interestingly, people may not even be aware of this issue. More is said about this important aspect of communication later in this chapter.

Physical Barriers: Sound, Time, Space, and More   Have you ever been talking to someone on a cell phone while standing in a busy area with traffic noise and people talking next to you? You know what physical barriers are. Other such barriers include time-zone differences, telephone-line static, a weak signal (few or no bars), distance from others, and crashed computers. Office design is another physical barrier, which is why more organizations are hiring experts to design facilities that promote open interactions, yet provide space for private meetings.[13]

Some managers tell employees they have an open-door policy to invite communication, but in fact, erect physical barriers by literally closing their door. Of course, managers need uninterrupted periods of time. David Mammano, CEO of Next Step Publishing, acknowledges both needs. He and Next Step's other employees each have a foot-shaped loofah they can hang on their door or outside their cubicle for an hour each day. While the foot is displayed, they are not to be disturbed; the rest of the time, the door really is open for communication.[14]

Semantic Barriers: When Words Matter   When your boss tells you, "We need to complete this project right away," what does it mean? Does "we" mean just you? You and your coworkers? Or you, your coworkers, and the boss? Does "right away" mean today, tomorrow, or next week? These are examples of semantic barriers. **Semantics is the study of words.** And of course words matter, as they are how you, the sender, communicate your intended message (thoughts) to others. Moreover, our selection of words influences whether our message is interpreted as intended by the receiver.[15]

Semantic barriers are more likely in today's multicultural workforce. Their frequency also is fueled by the common practice of outsourcing customer service operations to foreign countries (e.g., India). Unfortunately, some Americans are incensed over having to communicate with customer-service employees working in such call centers. Consider the message that Mitul Pandley, a specialist working in a call center located in India, received from a customer living in Mt. Pleasant, Pennsylvania. "I wish not to have anyone from India or any foreign country or anyone with an Indian accent or foreign accent continue handling my case."[16] Exchanges like this prompted Wipro BPO, Pandley's employer, to institute training programs aimed at reducing semantic barriers.

Jargon is another key semantic barrier and represents language or terminology that is specific to a particular profession, group, or company. The use of jargon has increased as our society becomes more technologically oriented. (For example, "The CIO wants the RFP to go out ASAP" means "The chief information officer wants the request for proposal to go out as soon as possible.") It is important to remember that words that are ordinary to you may be mysterious to outsiders. If we want to be understood more clearly, it is important to choose our language more carefully.

www.mcgrawhillconnect.com

Go to Connect for a self-assessment to assess your business etiquette.

Interpersonal Communication

The quality of interpersonal communication within an organization is very important. People with good communication skills help groups to make more innovative decisions and are promoted more frequently than individuals with less developed skills.[17] Although there is no universally accepted definition of **communication competence, it is a performance-based index of an individual's abilities to effectively use communication behaviors in a given context.**[18] Business etiquette, for example, is one component of communication competence. At this time we would like you to complete the business etiquette test in the Hands-On Exercise.

HANDS-ON EXERCISE

What Is Your Business Etiquette?

INSTRUCTIONS: Business etiquette is one component of communication competence. Test your business etiquette by answering the following questions. After circling your response for each item, calculate your score by reviewing the correct answers listed in note 19 in the Endnotes section of the book.[19] Next, use the norms at the end of the test to interpret your results.

1. The following is an example of a proper introduction: "Ms Boss, I'd like you to meet our client, Mr Smith."
   True   False

2. If someone forgets to introduce you, you shouldn't introduce yourself, you should just let the conversation continue.
   True   False

3. If you forget someone's name, you should keep talking and hope no one will notice. This way you don't embarrass yourself or the person to whom you are talking.
   True   False

4. When shaking hands, a man should wait for a woman to extend her hand.
   True   False

5. Who goes through a revolving door first?
   a. Host   *b.* Visitor

6. It is all right to hold private conversations, either in person or on a cell phone, in office bathrooms, elevators, and other public spaces.
   True   False

7. When two U.S. businesspeople are talking to one another, the space between them should be approximately
   a. 1.5 feet   *b.* 3 feet   *c.* 7 feet

8. Business casual attire requires socks for men and hose for women.
   True   False

9. To signal that you do not want a glass of wine, you should turn your wine glass upside down.
   True   False

10. If a call is disconnected, it's the caller's responsibility to redial.
    True   False

11. When using a speakerphone, you should tell the caller if there is anyone else in the room.
    True   False

12. You should change your voice mail message if you are going to be out of the office.
    True   False

ARBITRARY NORMS

Low business etiquette (0–4 correct): Consider buying an etiquette book or hiring a coach to help you polish your professional image.

Moderate business etiquette (5–8 correct): Look for a role model or mentor, and look for ways you can improve your business etiquette.

High business etiquette (9–12 correct): Good for you. You should continue to practice good etiquette and look for ways to maintain your professional image.

SOURCE: Test was adapted from material contained in M Brody, "Test Your Etiquette," *Training & Development*, February 2002, pp. 64–66. Reproduced with permission of American Society for Training and Development via Copyright Clearance Center.

Howard Schultz, CEO of Starbucks, has some definite ideas about interpersonal communication, which both starts and fills his day. He likes to keep it personal. "In the early morning I focus on Europe. I'll call Greece or Spain or whatever, either at home or on the drive into work, to talk about challenges ... or to congratulate them. These personal conversations are very important. ... I'm not a big e-mailer, though; it's a crutch that hinders person-to-person communication."

Communication competence is determined by three components: communication abilities and traits, situational factors, and the individuals involved in the interaction (see Figure 12–2). Cross-cultural awareness, for instance, is an important communication ability or trait. Individuals involved in an interaction also affect communication competence. People are likely to withhold information and react emotionally or defensively when interacting with someone they dislike or do not trust. You can improve your communication competence through five communication styles/skills/traits under your control: assertiveness, aggressiveness, nonassertiveness, nonverbal communication, and active listening. We explain these next and then conclude this section with a discussion of gender and generational differences in communication.

FIGURE 12–2   Communication Competence Affects Upward Mobility

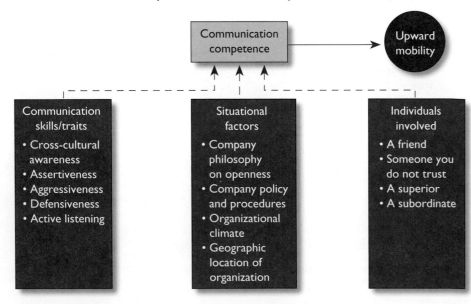

Assertiveness, Aggressiveness, and Nonassertiveness

The saying "You can attract more flies with honey than with vinegar" captures the difference between using an assertive communication style and an aggressive style. Studies indicate that assertiveness is more effective than aggressiveness in both work-related and consumer contexts.[20] An **assertive style is expressive and self-enhancing and is based on the "ethical notion that it is not right or good to violate our own or others' basic human rights, such as the right to self-expression or the right to be treated with dignity and respect."**[21] In contrast, an **aggressive style is expressive and self-enhancing and strives to take unfair advantage of others.** A **nonassertive style is characterized by timid and self-denying behavior.** Nonassertiveness is ineffective because it gives the other person an unfair advantage.

Managers can improve their communication competence by trying to be more assertive and less aggressive or nonassertive. This can be achieved by using the appropriate nonverbal and verbal behaviors listed in Table 12–2. For instance, managers should attempt to use the nonverbal behaviors: good eye contact; a strong and

LO12.3

Communication Styles   TABLE 12–2

Communication Style	Description	Nonverbal Behavior Pattern	Verbal Behavior Pattern
Assertive	Pushing hard without attacking; permits others to influence outcome; expressive and self-enhancing without intruding on others	Good eye contact Comfortable but firm posture Strong, steady, and audible voice Facial expressions matched to message Appropriately serious tone Selective interruptions to ensure understanding	Direct and unambiguous language No attributions or evaluations of others' behavior Use of "I" statements and cooperative "we" statements
Aggressive	Taking advantage of others; expressive and self-enhancing at others' expense	Glaring eye contact Moving or leaning too close Threatening gestures (pointed finger; clenched fist) Loud voice Frequent interruptions	Swear words and abusive language Attributions and evaluations of others' behavior Sexist or racist terms Explicit threats or put-downs
Nonassertive	Encouraging others to take advantage of us; inhibited; self-denying	Little eye contact Downward glances Slumped posture Constantly shifting weight Wringing hands Weak or whiny voice	Qualifiers ("maybe"; "kind of") Fillers ("uh," "you know," "well") Negaters ("It's not really that important", "I'm not sure")

SOURCE: Adapted in part from J A Waters, "Managerial Assertiveness," *Business Horizons*, September–October 1982, pp 24–29.

audible voice, and selective interruptions. They should avoid nonverbal behaviors such as glaring or little eye contact, threatening gestures, slumped posture, and a weak or whiny voice. Appropriate verbal behaviors include direct and unambiguous language and the use of "I" messages instead of "you" statements. For example, when you say, "Mike, I was disappointed with your report because it contained typographical errors," rather than "Mike, your report was poorly done," you reduce defensiveness. "I" statements describe your feelings about someone's performance or behavior instead of laying blame on the person. Research supports these suggestions. In a study of 279 Dutch government agency employees, aggressive leader communication styles were associated with lower satisfaction with the leader and perceptions of lower performance.[22] Another study of physicians in the state of Massachusetts concluded that communication styles were likely a stronger predictor of malpractice claims than performance![23] Leadership styles are discussed in detail in Chapter 14.

As discussed in Chapter 11, conflicts are a part of organizational life. Communication styles are one potential cause. Taking an "active approach by being aware of others' communication styles and then adapting your style to find that balance" is a means for avoiding or reducing conflict.[24] We urge you to apply this knowledge.

Sources of Nonverbal Communication

 LO12.4

Nonverbal communication **is "[a]ny message, sent or received independent of the written or spoken word. . . . [I]t includes such factors as use of time and space, distance between persons when conversing, use of color, dress, walking behavior, standing, positioning, seating arrangement, office locations and furnishings."[25]**

Experts estimate that 65% to 95% of every conversation is interpreted through nonverbal communication. "Managers who rely solely on verbal cues to communicate with employees are missing the majority of what their employees are saying."[26] It thus is important to ensure that your nonverbal signals are consistent with your intended verbal messages. Because of the prevalence of nonverbal communication and its significant effect on organizational behavior—including, but not limited to, perceptions of others, hiring decisions, work attitudes, turnover, and the acceptance of one's ideas in a presentation—it is important that managers become consciously aware of the sources of nonverbal communication. For instance, a recent meta-analysis of nonverbal expressions of emotions found that those who more effectively demonstrated their own emotions, and perceived the emotional cues of others, performed better across a range of situations. (This research is closely related to our discussion of emotional intelligence in Chapter 5.)[27]

The importance of nonverbal communication is highlighted in this quote from a physician, Jordan Grumet:

> At varying stages in my medical career I have learned to acquire information in different ways. As a beginning medical student, I concentrated on case studies. As a resident, my focus changed to taking histories and physical exams. Now as an attending physician, I have learned to use both body language and my own emotional reactions to enhance patient care.[28]

Body Movements and Gestures   Body movements (e.g., leaning forward or backward) and gestures (e.g., pointing) provide additional nonverbal information that can either enhance or detract from the communication process. Open body positions, such as leaning backward or gesturing with palms facing up communicate *immediacy,* a term used to represent openness, warmth, closeness, and availability for communication. *Defensiveness* is communicated by gestures such as folding arms, crossing hands, and crossing one's legs. Although it is both easy and fun to interpret body movements and gestures, it is important to remember that body-language analysis is subjective, easily misinterpreted, and highly dependent on the context and cross-cultural differences.[29] Thus, managers need to be careful when trying to interpret body movements. Inaccurate interpretations can create additional "noise" in the communication process.

Touch   Touching is another powerful nonverbal cue. People tend to touch those they like. A meta-analysis of gender differences in touching indicated that women do more touching during conversations than men.[30] Touching conveys an impression of warmth and caring and can be used to create a personal bond between people. Hugs, for example, have replaced the handshake according to some. Nearly 50% of respondents to a Greenlight Community survey said they routinely hug at work instead of shaking hands.[31] Be careful about touching people from diverse cultures, however, as norms for touching vary significantly around the world.[32]

Facial Expressions   Facial expressions convey a wealth of information. Smiling, for instance, typically represents warmth, happiness, or friendship, whereas frowning conveys dissatisfaction or anger. Do you think these interpretations apply to different cross-cultural groups? A summary of relevant research revealed that the association between facial expressions and emotions varies across cultures.[33] A smile, for example, does not convey the same emotion in different countries. One study showed that people from the United States and Japan were able to accurately associate facial expressions with personality traits for politicians from both countries. They also were able to predict electoral success of these same candidates, but only for those from their own cultures.[34] Therefore, managers need to be careful when interpreting facial expressions among diverse groups of employees.

www.mcgrawhillconnect.com

Go to Connect for an interactive exercise to test your knowledge of non-verbal communication.

Eye Contact   Eye contact is a strong nonverbal cue that varies across cultures. Westerners are taught at an early age to look at their parents when spoken to. In contrast, Asians are taught to avoid eye contact with a parent or superior in order to show obedience and subservience.[35] Once again, managers should be sensitive to different orientations toward maintaining eye contact with diverse employees.

Practical Tips   It is important to have good nonverbal communication skills in light of the fact that they are related to the development of positive interpersonal relationships. The Skills & Best Practices on page 322 offers insights into improving your nonverbal communication skills. Practice these tips by turning the sound off while watching television and then trying to interpret emotions and interactions. Honest feedback from your friends about your nonverbal communication style also may help.

Active Listening

Some communication experts contend that listening is the keystone communication skill for employees involved in sales, customer service, or management. In support of this conclusion, listening effectiveness was positively associated with customer satisfaction and negatively associated with employee intentions to quit. Poor communication between employees and management also was cited as a primary cause of employee discontent and turnover.[36] Moreover, John Beeson, an executive coach and succession planning

Advice to Improve Nonverbal Communication Skills

Positive nonverbal actions include the following:

- Maintain eye contact.
- Nod your head to convey that you are listening or that you agree.
- Smile and show interest.
- Lean forward to show the speaker you are interested.
- Use a tone of voice that matches your message.

Negative nonverbal behaviors include the following:

- Avoiding eye contact and looking away from the speaker.
- Closing your eyes or tensing your facial muscles.
- Excessive yawning.
- Using body language that conveys indecisiveness or lack of confidence (e.g., slumped shoulders, head down, flat tones, inaudible voice).
- Speaking too fast or too slow.

consultant, noted that weak interpersonal communication skills, including listening, are major reasons managers are passed over for promotions to executive positions.[37]

Active listening can be improved through training. For example, Kevin Higgins, managing partner of a sales training company in Toronto, explains: "when salespeople engage in active listening—complete with note-taking and frequent paraphrasing—they're more likely to gain the client's confidence. This, too, can be rehearsed in a sales meeting. 'I'll talk for five minutes about any topic. The reps know I'm going to ask them to summarize what I've said in two or three sentences. That trains them to really turn off all the distraction in their minds.'"[38] Listening skills are particularly important for all of us because we spend a great deal of time listening to others. They also are critical when we give feedback to others.

LO12.5

Listening involves much more than hearing a message. Hearing is merely the physical component of listening. **Listening is the process of *actively* decoding and interpreting verbal messages.** Listening requires cognitive attention and information processing; hearing does not. With these distinctions in mind, we examine listening styles and offer some practical advice for becoming a more effective listener.

Listening Styles Communication experts believe that people listen with a preferred listening style. While people may possess a dominant listening style, we tend to use a combination of two or three. There are five dominant listening styles: appreciative, empathetic, comprehensive, discerning, and evaluative.[39] Let us consider each style.

An *appreciative* listener listens in a relaxed manner, preferring to listen for pleasure, entertainment, or inspiration. He or she tends to tune out speakers who provide no amusement or humor in their communications. *Empathetic* listeners interpret messages by focusing on the emotions and body language being displayed by the speaker as well as the presentation media. They also tend to listen without judging. A *comprehensive* listener makes sense of a message by first organizing specific thoughts and actions and then integrating this information by focusing on relationships among ideas. These listeners prefer logical presentations without interruptions. *Discerning* listeners attempt to understand the main message and determine important points. They like to take notes and prefer logical presentations. Finally, *evaluative* listeners listen analytically and continually formulate arguments and challenges to what is being said. They tend to accept or reject messages based on personal beliefs, ask a lot of questions, and can become interruptive.

Becoming a More Effective Listener   Effective listening is a learned skill that requires effort and motivation. That's right, it takes energy and desire to really listen to others. Unfortunately, it may seem like there are no rewards for listening, but there are negative consequences when we don't. Think of a time, for example, when someone did not pay attention to you by looking at his or her watch or doing some other activity, such as checking his or her phone or texting. How did you feel? You may have felt put down, unimportant, or offended. In turn, such feelings can erode the quality of interpersonal relationships as well as fuel job dissatisfaction and lower productivity. Listening is an important skill that can be improved by avoiding the 10 habits of bad listeners while cultivating the 10 habits of good listeners (see Table 12–3).

The Keys to Effective Listening   **TABLE 12–3**

Keys to Effective Listening	The Bad Listener	The Good Listener
1. Capitalize on thought speed	Tends to daydream	Stays with the speaker, mentally summarizes what is being said, weighs evidence, and listens between the lines
2. Listen for ideas	Listens for facts	Listens for central or overall ideas
3. Find an area of interest	Tunes out dry speakers or subjects	Listens for any useful information
4. Judge content, not delivery	Tunes out dry or monotone speakers	Assesses content by listening to entire message before making judgments
5. Hold your fire	Gets too emotional or worked up by something said by the speaker and enters into an argument	Withholds judgment until comprehension is complete
6. Work at listening	Does not expend energy on listening	Gives the speaker full attention
7. Resist distractions	Is easily distracted	Fights distractions and concentrates on the speaker
8. Hear what is said	Shuts out or denies unfavorable information	Listens to both favorable and unfavorable information
9. Challenge yourself	Resists listening to presentations of difficult subject matter	Treats complex presentations as exercise for the mind
10. Use handouts, overheads, or other visual aids	Does not take notes or pay attention to visual aids	Takes notes as required and uses visual aids to enhance understanding of the presentation

SOURCES: Derived from N Skinner, "Communication Skills," *Selling Power*, July–August 1999, pp 32–34; and G Manning, K Curtis, and S McMillen, *Building the Human Side of Work Community* (Cincinnati, OH: Thomson Executive Press, 1996), pp 127–54.

In addition, a communication expert suggests that we can all improve our listening skills by adhering to the following three fundamental recommendations:[40]

1. Attending closely to what's being said, not to what you want to say next.

2. Allowing others to finish speaking before taking our turn.

3. Repeating back what you've heard to give the speaker the opportunity to clarify the message.

> **BACK TO THE CHAPTER-OPENING CASE**   How effective of a listener is Brian Dunn? Use Table 12–3 and the text to support your answer.

Gender, Generations, and Communication

Women and men have communicated differently since the dawn of time. And now, with four generations in the workplace, many managers claim that communication challenges are compounded by age differences. Differences in communication are partly caused by the array of linguistic styles people use. Deborah Tannen, a communication expert, defines *linguistic style* as follows:

> **Linguistic style refers to a person's characteristic speaking pattern.** It includes such features as directness or indirectness, pacing and pausing, word choice, and the use of such elements as jokes, figures of speech, stories, questions, and apologies. In other words, linguistic style is a set of culturally learned signals by which we not only communicate what we mean but also interpret others' meaning and evaluate one another as people.[41]

Linguistic style not only helps explain communication differences between women and men and across generations, but it also influences our perceptions of others' confidence, competence, and abilities. For example, the similarity of 324 group members' linguistic styles predicted group cohesiveness and performance on a search task for 70 groups. The results were the same whether the task was done face to face or remotely (via Internet technology).[42] Linguistic styles also have been used to more efficiently deal with the customer complaints made via e-mail. Coding and adding linguistic style information to the text (words themselves), enabled companies to more effectively address customer concerns and achieve satisfaction via an automated complaint management system.[43] These results suggest that linguistic styles matter both in person and over the Internet. Therefore, increased awareness of linguistic styles can thus improve communication accuracy and communication competence. This section strives to increase your understanding of interpersonal communication between women and men and across generations. To do this, we discuss alternative explanations

Research reveals that men and women possess different communication styles. For example, men are more boastful about their accomplishments whereas women are more modest. How might differences in male and female communication patterns affect how men and women are perceived during group problem-solving meetings?

for differences in linguistic styles, various communication differences between groups (e.g., genders and generational), and recommendations for improving communication between them.

Communication Differences between Women and Men   Although researchers do not completely agree on the cause of communication differences between women and men, there are two competing explanations that involve the well-worn debate between *nature* and *nurture.* Some researchers believe that interpersonal differences between women and men are due to inherited biological differences between the sexes. This perspective, which also is called the "evolutionary psychology" or "Darwinian perspective," attributes gender differences in communication to drives, needs, and conflicts associated with reproductive strategies used by women and men. For example, proponents would say that males communicate more aggressively, interrupt others more than women, and hide their emotions because they have an inherent desire to possess features attractive to females. Although males are certainly not competing for mate selection during a business meeting, evolutionary psychologists propose that men cannot turn off the biologically based determinants of their behavior.[44]

In contrast, "social role theory" is based on the idea that females and males learn ways of speaking while growing up. Research shows that girls learn conversational skills and habits that focus on rapport and relationships, whereas boys learn skills and habits that focus on status and hierarchies. Accordingly, women come to view communication as a network of connections in which conversations are negotiations for closeness. This orientation leads women to seek and give confirmation and support more so than men. Men, on the other hand, see conversations as negotiations in which people try to achieve and maintain the upper hand. It thus is important for males to protect themselves from others' attempts to put them down or push them around. This perspective increases a male's need to maintain independence and avoid failure.[45]

Research demonstrates that women and men communicate differently in a number of ways.[46] Women, for example, are more likely to share credit for success, to ask questions for clarification, to tactfully give feedback by mitigating criticism with praise, and to indirectly tell others what to do. A study found that management teams with a higher proportion of women monitored feedback and employee development more closely. The same teams also tended to promote more interpersonal communication and employee involvement in decision making.[47] In contrast, men are more likely to boast about themselves, to bluntly give feedback, and to withhold compliments, and are less likely to ask questions and to admit fault or weaknesses.

Generational Differences in Communication   As discussed in Chapter 4, today's workplace often involves people from four different generations—Traditionalists, Baby Boomers, Gen Xers, and Millennials (Gen Ys). (Refer to Table 4–2 for additional details and characteristics.) Among the challenges in this scenario is the fact that Millennials are the largest cohort in the workforce, and they are most likely to be managed by Boomers. A consultant on the issue described the scenario this way: "Gen Y workers might have excellent technology skills but many need to improve their business writing and interpersonal communication skills."[48] Whether or not you agree with this statement, or see it simply as another stereotype, it is true that Millennials "don't remember a world without computers, and in many cases they have honed their communication skills via e-mails, instant messages, and text messages rather than by talking on the phone or in person, or by writing letters, memos, and reports."[49] Many, but certainly not all, Gen Xers were introduced to communication technologies at work, and their careers have paralleled the evolution of communication technologies and practices. The opposite assumption can be made for Traditionalists. Some people in this generation either resist technology altogether if their employers allow them to, or do only what is necessary. Digital technology got traction and widespread use in the later stages of their careers. Many Boomers, however, began their careers in a very different world, with analog and manual labor, and are now surrounded by and must adapt and integrate the old with the new digital workplace.[50] The following section provides recommendations on how to apply this knowledge.

Improving Communications between the Sexes and Generations

There are two important issues to keep in mind about the differences between men, women, and generations. First, the trends identified cannot be generalized to include all members of any group. Some men, for instance, are less likely to boast about their achievements while some women are less likely to share the credit. Some Traditionalists embrace technology and "younger" communication practices, while not all members of Gen Y are technological whizzes. The point is that there are always exceptions to the rule. Second, your linguistic style and communication practices influence perceptions about your confidence, competence, and authority. These judgments may, in turn, affect your future job assignments and subsequent promotability.

To realize the benefits of workers across generations, managers and employers more generally are urged to clearly define (written) communication do's and don'ts for all technology and employees:[51]

- Do use complete sentences.
- Don't use abbreviations.
- Do use proper capitalization and punctuation.
- Do spell words correctly.
- Don't begin an e-mail with "hey."

It may also be helpful to pair poor writers with good writers, especially across generations. The better writer can edit and guide the other as a sort of "communications mentor" (recall the mentoring discussion from Chapter 2).

Interpersonal do's and don'ts are of additional benefit:[52]

- Don't text, e-mail, or surf during meetings.
- Do listen without interrupting.
- Do watch your language.
- Do say "hello" and "good-bye."

The most powerful way to embed these practices is to have managers and leaders model these behaviors (role modeling is discussed with leadership in Chapter 14). Doing so sends a strong and consistent message of what is expected, regardless of gender or age.

We conclude this section with the following advice for managers: Utilize the similarities between genders and between generations, before trying to understand or deal with differences. Doing so is not only practical, but it also is consistent with current trends in positive organizational behavior.

Information Communication Technology and OB

We extend our Chapter 1 discussion of the OB implications of information communication technology (ICT) in this section. ICT, notably mobile Internet devices and social media, is dramatically affecting many aspects of organizational behavior. According to ComScore, a leading digital world measurement service:[53]

 LO12.6

- 234 million Americans over age 13 used mobile devices as of February 2011 (70 million of these are smartphones).

- Google (Android), RIM (BlackBerry), and Apple (iPhone) had 33%, 29%, and 25% of the smartphone market, respectively.

- Samsung and LG each had more than 20% of the handset market (Apple less than 7%).

- 69% of U.S. mobile subscribers used text messaging, browsers were used by 38%, and downloaded apps 37%.

- Social networking and blogs were used by 27% and playing games 25%.

Moreover, the average American spent 32 hours *per month* of their personal time online in 2010.[54] For comparison, the average American spent nearly 38 hours *per week* watching television.[55] The 45–54 age group had the highest Internet usage at 39 hours each month, 12–17 years of age the lowest at 22 hours, and the 18–24 group had 32 hours. The global nature of this phenomenon is evident in the use of social networking (Facebook and Twitter) in the United Kingdom, where 25% of users are 15–24 year olds, followed closely by 25–34 year olds at 24%. LinkedIn has an older demographic. Only 10% of its users worldwide are under 25.[56] Among the implications of these statistics is that the common stereotype that older people don't like or don't use ICT is inaccurate. The reason may be that ICT has become a necessity at work and is now a tool that is embraced in other areas of their lives.

Of course these statistics will be out of date before this book is even printed. But they nevertheless illustrate the pervasiveness of ICT and provide the context for its importance in OB. According to Meister and Willyerd, authors of *Workplace 2020:*

> [W]ork is becoming a place to collaborate, exchange ideas, and communicate with colleagues and customers. Your value as an employee will be determined not only by how well you perform your job but also by how much you contribute your knowledge and ideas back to the organization. The ways in which companies develop this culture of collaboration will become a significant competitive factor in attracting and engaging top talent in the twenty-first century.[57]

With the above as background, this section explores the impact of technology on communication and organizational behavior. We do this by discussing the impact of ICT on productivity, managing teleworkers, and the advantages and challenges associated with social media at work.

ICT and Productivity

A fundamental driving force behind technology (of all forms) at work is to boost productivity. The same is true for ICT. The 24/7 everywhere, anytime connectivity has forever changed the world of work. The key for employees, managers, and employers is to harness the potential and enhance performance at the individual, group, and organizational levels. Research shows that at the individual level employee benefits include increased job satisfaction and better work–life balance.[58] Reports from

McKinsey support these findings and show that networked organizations tend to out-compete their rivals. Response from 3,249 executives across industries showed that ICT improved access to valuable market and customer information, increased marketing effectiveness, reduced communication costs, and enhanced supplier and strategic partner satisfaction. All of these factors were related to market share gains and higher operating margins.[59] Additional benefits for employers are reduced employee turnover and reduced costs (e.g., fewer office leases due to telecommuters). On the surface these benefits are impressive. But what about the costs?

The luster of these benefits is greatly diminished by research on *multitasking.* Many people claim that doing several things at once is a necessity—that their jobs and lives require it. Other people simply prefer to multitask. In either case, researchers and consultants overwhelmingly agree that multitasking decreases productivity. They argue that two particular myths on the subject are widespread. First, people think they are actually doing more than one thing at a time. They are not. Instead they are actually shifting back-and-forth between tasks—dividing their time rather than multiplying their outcomes. Second, people believe they are more efficient or productive doing more than one thing at a time. Again, false. Research shows that "for all types of tasks, subjects lost time when they had to switch from one task to another . . . (and time lost) was even greater when the complexity and unfamiliarity of the task increased . . . not being able to concentrate for even ten minutes at a time could cost as much as 20–40 percent in terms of potential efficiency lost."[60] For instance, a study of 100 students by a Stanford researcher found that multitasking diminished performance, such that the more tasks that were added the more performance declined.[61] Those that focused on one task at a time outperformed the multitaskers in every measure of performance. This therefore suggests that no "optimal" amount of multitasking exists. Put another way, there is no "sweet spot" or optimum number of tasks—say three tasks versus four. Those who focus on a single task do better. For those of you who must or choose to multitask, see the Skills & Best Practices feature on page 329 for suggestions on managing multiple demands and your performance more effectively.

Working people have many and often competing demands. People often multitask in an attempt to manage multiple demands simultaneously. Counter to what many employees claim, research shows that multitasking actually divides attention and reduces productivity. For example, how does surfing the Web or texting during class negatively affect your performance in class?

We give particular attention to e-mail in this section on productivity. In our many years of teaching and consulting with employees across organizational levels and industries, we continually hear that e-mail is an ever-present challenge and often an enormous time drain. To be clear, most acknowledge that e-mail is necessary if not essential. But handling e-mail effectively can make it your friend instead of your foe. See Table 12–4 for the benefits, drawbacks, and tips on managing e-mail.

Managing Teleworkers

LO12.7   *Teleworkers*, **also known as telecommuters and distributed workers, are people who fulfill some portion of typically office-based job responsibilities outside the office via ICT.** Working remotely is increasingly common and is expected to exceed 1 billion workers in 2011.[62] A meta-analysis involving 12,883 employees uncovered the following benefits of teleworking: (1) increased autonomy, job satisfaction, and

Optimize versus Maximize Your Time

- *Prioritize and allocate based on value, not volume.* For a given block of time, optimizing is using it best and maximizing is doing the most. To translate this into practice, focus on providing the most value for a given block of time rather than doing the largest number of tasks. You could, for example, answer 20 e-mails from friends or update your Facebook page in the next 45 minutes, or you could read and prepare for tomorrow's class.
- *Rely on voice mail.* Because the phone rings doesn't mean you have to answer it. The same goes for your e-mail inbox. Set reasonable expectations for different groups (customers, colleagues, and friends) for when you will respond, such as within two hours or by the end of the day.
- *Manage meetings.* Set a specific start and stop time and stick to it. Also consider shortening the scheduled length of meetings. For instance, if you're inclined to schedule an hour-long meeting for your team case analysis, then instead schedule it for 40 minutes. Sending agendas and assigning roles and responsibilities in advance helps, too. As we learned in Chapter 7, setting specific, attainable, and time-bound goals increases the likelihood they will be achieved.
- *Use technology.* Not to multitask but to prioritize and plan. Outlook and customer relationship management (CRM) software allow for the efficient organization and allocation of your time.
- *Remove distractions.* You can turn off your phone, e-mail, and other alerts. Designate particular blocks of time for e-mail, meetings, and even chatting.

SOURCES: Excerpted and adapted from L Grensing-Pophal, "Efficiency Boosters: Making the Most of Your Time Resources," *Society of Human Resource Management Consultants Forum,* 2011; also R Ashkenas, "Multitasking Effectively," *Harvard Business Online,* September 11, 2009.

performance and (2) reduced work–family conflict, intentions to quit, and role stress. Further, results also indicated that the quality of relationships between teleworkers and their managers remained positive. This suggests that teleworkers' careers are not necessarily derailed because they do not have the same amount of face time as other workers.[63]

Although telecommuting represents an attempt to accommodate employee needs and desires, it requires adjustments and is not for everybody. Many people thoroughly enjoy the social camaraderie that exists within an office setting. These individuals probably would not like to telecommute. Others lack the self-discipline needed to work at home. This raises special challenges for managers. Managers of teleworkers are responsible for:[64]

- *Gatekeeping.* Determining who should be allowed to telecommute and why. Not every person or every job benefits.
- *Monitoring.* It is important to track work—schedules, volume, and quality—from afar. Traditional or existing methods typically are inadequate.
- *Social integration.* It is beneficial to make remote workers feel part of the larger organization and guard against feelings of being disconnected, unvalued islands.
- *Work–life boundary management.* Dealing with the boundaries is important to realize the potential benefits.
- *Work group culture.* Communicating and embedding the culture despite the lack of face-to-face contact can be particularly challenging.

TABLE 12–4   E-Mail: Benefits, Drawbacks, and Suggestions for Managing It

Benefits

- *Reduced costs of distributing information.* E-mail allows information to be sent electronically, thereby reducing the costs of sending information to employees and customers.
- *Increased teamwork.* Users can send messages to colleagues anywhere in the world and receive immediate feedback.
- *Reduced paper costs.* An expert estimates these savings at $9,000 per employee.
- *Increased flexibility.* Employees with laptops, cell phones, and handheld devices can access e-mail from anywhere.

Drawbacks

- *Wasted time and effort.* E-mail can distract people from completing their work responsibilities. People spend too much time searching.
- *Information overload.* The average corporate employee receives 171 messages a day, and 10 to 40% of these messages are unimportant.
- *Increased costs to organize, store, and monitor.* Systems are needed to protect privacy. The Federal Rules of Civil Procedures require organizations to keep tabs on e-mail and produce them in case of litigation.
- *Neglect of other media.* People unsuccessfully attempt to solve complex problems with e-mail. E-mail reduces the amount of face-to-face communication.

Managing E-Mail

- *Do not assume e-mail is confidential.* Employers are increasingly monitoring all e-mail. Assume your messages can be read by anyone.
- *Be professional and courteous.* Recommendations include: delete trailing messages, don't send chain letters and jokes, don't type in all caps—it's equivalent to shouting, don't respond immediately to a nasty e-mail, refrain from using colored text and background, don't expose your contact list to strangers, and be patient about receiving replies.
- *Avoid sloppiness.* Use a spell checker or reread the message before sending.
- *Don't use e-mail for volatile or complex issues.* Use a medium that is appropriate for the situation at hand.
- *Keep messages brief and clear.* Use accurate subject headings and let the reader know what you want right up front.
- *Save people time.* Type "no reply necessary" in the subject line or at the top of your message if appropriate.
- *Be careful with attachments.* Large attachments can crash someone's systems and use up valuable time downloading. Send only what is necessary, and get permission to send multiple attachments.

SOURCES: C Graham, "In-Box Overload," *The Arizona Republic*, March 16, 2007, p A14; M Totty, "Rethinking the Inbox," *The Wall Street Journal*, March 26, 2007, p R8; A Smith, "Federal Rules Define Duty to Preserve Work E-Mails," *HR Magazine*, January 2007, pp 27, 36; M Totty, "Letter of the Law," *The Wall Street Journal*, March 26, 2007, p R10; and "The Top 10 E-Mail Courtesy Suggestions," *Coachville Coach Training*, March 22, 2000, http://topten.org.content/tt.BN122.htm.

www.mcgrawhillconnect.com

Go to Connect for an interactive exercise to test your knowledge of effective e-mail usage in the organization.

Let's not forget those who do not telecommute. Telecommuters typically do so only part of the time (e.g., 3 days per week), and other employees always work in the office. This results in a "blended-workforce"—full- and partial-time office dwellers. The implication is that the managers of these employees also need a *blend* of appropriate skills.[65] It is not enough to effectively manage one group and not the other. Factors discussed throughout this book, such as human capital (Chapter 1), mentoring (Chapter 2), individual differences (Chapter 5), motivation (Chapters 6 and 7), performance management (Chapter 8), virtual teams (Chapter 9), and leadership (Chapter 14), among others, are important considerations in the selection, training, and development of managers of distributed and blended workforces.

Social Media at Work—Pros and Cons

We conclude this chapter by discussing *social media.* As you know, **social media uses Internet-based and mobile technologies to generate interactive dialogue with members of a network.** Because social media affects so many subjects covered in this book, it highlights the importance of communication as an OB topic. A Pew Research study of 24,790 people in 22 countries found the United States is leading the way with 46% of participants using social networking sites, followed by 43% in Poland, 43% in the United Kingdom, 40% in South Korea, 23% in Mexico, and 12% in India.[66] Recent research involving 2,471 Canadian college students concluded that people had five basic motives that affect participation in social networking: *community member-ship* (benefits of belonging to a group); *friendship connections* (efficiently interacting with friends); *information value* (access to the knowledge and experience of others); *participation confidence* (fear of looking bad to a large number of people); and *participation concerns* (privacy and being scammed). The first three are associated with social capital (see Chapter 1). The last two motives are common reasons people limit or choose not to participate in social media.[67] Which motives apply to you? In the remainder of this section, we discuss benefits, concerns, and recommendations for social media at work.

Benefits of Social Media   Given the pervasiveness and impact of this global phenomenon, it is no surprise that social media has now "come to work." Examples of its many forms and uses:

- Intuit, a Mountain View, California-based software firm, uses a blog and video-conferencing to keep employees informed and connected to the officers' semian-nual meeting.[68]
- The U.S. Geological Service (USGS) is exploring using Twitter as a supplement to its seismic monitors to alert the agency and others of earthquake activity.[69]
- Backus Hospital, in Norwich, Connecticut, uses a YouTube video for patients before surgery—"Prepare for Surgery, Heal Faster." The video is less than three minutes and shows patients how to prepare for surgery in ways that will speed recovery time.[70]

Savvy businesspeople realize that "social media is not just a new technology tool, but a revolution in the role technology plays in our lives and in the way we think both about technology and the world around us."[71] The essence is connectivity. If deployed effectively, social media enables businesses to connect in real time and over distances with many key stakeholders, such as employees, customers (past, current, and future), communities, suppliers, prospective talent, former employees (sources of future talent), and many others. As explained in the Chapter 9 discussion of virtual teams, social media has the potential to connect sources of knowledge across the organization, offices, and time zones. Linking knowledge in these ways is a means to realizing the potential of employee diversity (covered in Chapter 4) and enhancing productivity. Social networks also have the potential to become the "circulatory system" of a learn-ing organization, which is discussed in Chapter 16.

A particularly interesting and important aspect of social media at work is its ability to redefine conventional organizational boundaries and structure (covered in Chapter 15). GE's Ecomagination Challenge, for instance, asked people outside of the company for ideas to create the next-generation, smart power grid. PepsiCo has a similar ongoing program that solicits advertising ideas from outside the company. The winner receives

$1 million. One of these programs generated more than 5,600 entries for their Super Bowl spot. Both of these are examples of what is called "crowdsourcing." Companies invite nonemployees to contribute to particular goals and manage the process via the Internet.[72] Connections with people inside and outside the organization greatly expand a company's human and social capital. A more subtle yet more common example of crowdsourcing is seeking recommendations for a restaurant, a new car, or a professor on sites such as Facebook, Twitter, and RateMyProfessor.

Social Media Concerns   While the potential benefits to employers are numerous and clear, a number of downsides also exist. Employer concerns typically fall into five general categories: *productivity, time management, appropriate communication styles, confidentiality,* and *privacy.*[73] Plenty of evidence exists to put companies on the defensive. Consider Matt Blalock, an entrepreneur with 13 employees. He noticed the productivity of a talented staff member plummeting. A simple investigation revealed that the staffer was spending 85% of his work day surfing the Web, visiting social networking sites in particular. At the organizational level, Domino's Pizza took a serious hit when a YouTube video of two employees "abusing the food" went viral. Experts argue that the financial damage of Toyota's recall of 2.2 million vehicles from 2009 to 2011—estimated to be greater than $32 billion in stock value and legal expenses—increased due to the company's lack of awareness of social media warning signs. Specifically, the recall fervor built via social media complaints long before it gained critical mass and hit traditional media outlets. Experts say that had the company monitored these channels it could have gotten ahead of the news. Instead, the company's PR response was limited to traditional channels and means (press releases in print media and rebuttals by talking heads on television).[74] The list goes on.

The lesson here is that consequences can be enormous for ignoring or not effectively managing social media. Personal and organizational reputations (e.g., brands) hang in the balance. So what can be done? At the extreme, companies can and have the right to ban outside connectivity and social media. VW, Porsche, and other leading German firms banned all social networking sites from the workplace. They hope that doing so will improve employee productivity and reduce the chance they will share trade secrets.[75] Technological solutions, such as URL filters to block gambling and porn sites, can help but don't encompass employees' many personal and portable devices.

Legal and HR experts therefore recommend a cohesive *social media strategy* that includes technology, policy, and training. Policies are best if they explicitly state who is permitted to use which social media, for which purposes, where, and when. For instance, personal matters (e.g., checking and updating Facebook) can be limited to lunch breaks. Clear and consistent consequences for violations help embed the policy and clarify enforcement. And, as with most employee policies, training and a signed acknowledgment of receipt and understanding is advisable.[76] Joanne Deschenaux, an attorney and legal editor for the Society of Human Resource Management, suggests the following minimum requirements for companies:

1. *Establish a No Privacy Policy.* Tell employees not to expect communications to be private. Phones, computers, virtual private networks, and any other company-issued or managed devices or networks can be monitored, and this is what employees should expect.

2. *Maintain Boundaries between Personal and Professional.* Specify the expected communication styles (formal versus informal) and acceptable content. As a general rule, employees should be directed not to discuss professional matters

where they can be viewed by members outside the company (or designated partners—such as customers, suppliers, prospects, etc.). Conversely, personal matters should not be in view of members of your professional sphere. For instance, managers are advised not to friend their coworkers and vice versa. Some things you do not want shared.[77]

3. *Monitor the Internet.* Many services are available. Just be sure to tune into what customers, competitors, and employees are saying. Awareness is the first step for both identifying desirable opportunities and managing the message in the event of something undesirable.[78]

> **BACK TO THE CHAPTER-OPENING CASE** Assume you are Brian Dunn. Describe the elements of a social media policy you would put in place at Best Buy. Include an explanation of consequences for violations of the policy.

What can you do as an individual to protect your personal brand (reputation)? Follow the aforementioned recommendations for starters. Assume no privacy, and keep your worlds separate. Stephanie Marchesi of the marketing firm Fleishman-Hillard in New York heeds this advice. She maintains four devices to segment her professional and personal worlds: an iPhone and iPad for family and social uses and a Black-Berry and laptop for work. She also has separate e-mail accounts and calendars, so that members of one world cannot "see" the other.[79] Establishing and maintaining multiple accounts, and using discretion about what you post, can be a challenge or even impossible. But think of the potential implications—your reputation or job!

Individuals and organizations can use services, such as SocialMention.com and Google Alerts, to monitor comments in the public space.[80] Because of the popularity of Facebook, suggestions for using it for professional purposes are provided in the Skills & Best Practices feature on page 333. One final suggestion: do not expect others to keep your information private. The ongoing and significant privacy challenges for Facebook, Google, and others provide plenty of reason to be cautious. Companies can and do occasionally add new features, provide new apps, and/or change policies that blur or erase the lines of who can see specific material. And if most of us have heard stories of somebody being fired for a comment or a post, think of how many have suffered other consequences unknowingly![81]

Facebook is now an important communication and marketing tool for many organizations the world over. However, along with the benefits come challenges. Mark Zuckerberg, the company's founder, has had to address persistent issues related to privacy. What challenges do companies that use Facebook face? Describe other challenges that may confront companies that use Facebook?

We close the chapter with a quote from Best Buy CEO Brain Dunn. He summarizes the reality of technology, communication, and social media quite well. He explains that for all of the challenges and bad experiences: "Mostly, though, I focus on the positive aspects of social networking. I get asked all the time, 'How are you going to monetize this?' I think that's the wrong question. The right question is 'How am I going to deepen my relationship with customers and employees and deepen the conversation that goes on where they are?'"[82]

Using Facebook in Your Professional Life

- Abide by service norms for your organization and follow overall brand engagement framework.
- Brand the product or organizational profile—but go light on sales messages.
- Take sensitive customer issues into a private sphere—on- or off-line.
- Remember all wall posts (Facebook) are public—don't write anything that is not intended for wide consumption.
- All updates should be relevant.
- Manage the volume of updates—too many or too few is problematic.
- Use language relevant to the particular audience.
- Show appreciation and communicate with, not at, the target audience.
- Do ask questions on the wall posts, but follow up and respond to any feedback received.

SOURCE: Excerpted and adapted from M Ramsay, "Social Media Etiquette: A Guide and Checklist to the Benefits and Perils of Social Marketing," *Database Marketing & Customer Strategy Management*, 2010, pp 257–61.

key terms

chapter summary

- *Describe the perceptual process model of communication.* Communication is a process of consecutively linked elements. This model of communication depicts receivers as information processors who create the meaning of messages in their own mind. Because receivers' interpretations of messages often differ from those intended by senders, miscommunication is a common occurrence.

- *Describe the process, personal, physical, and semantic barriers to effective communication.* Every element of the perceptual model of communication is a potential process barrier. Eight personal barriers commonly influence communication: (a) the ability to effectively communicate, (b) the way people process and interpret information, (c) the level of interpersonal trust between people, (d) the existence of stereotypes and prejudices, (e) the egos of the people communicating, (f) the ability to listen, (g) the natural tendency to evaluate or judge a sender's message, and (h) the inability to listen with understanding. Physical barriers pertain to distance, physical objects, time, and work and office noise. Semantic barriers show up as encoding and decoding errors because these phases of communication involve transmitting and receiving words and symbols. Cultural diversity is a key contributor to semantic barriers.

- *Contrast the communication styles of assertiveness, aggressiveness, and nonassertiveness.* An assertive style is expressive and self-enhancing but does not violate others' basic human rights. In contrast, an aggressive style is expressive and self-enhancing but takes unfair advantage of others. A nonassertive style is characterized by timid and self-denying behavior. An assertive communication style is more effective than either an aggressive or nonassertive style.

- *Discuss the primary sources of nonverbal communication.* There are several identifiable sources of nonverbal communication effectiveness. Body movements and gestures, touch, facial expressions, and eye contact are important nonverbal cues. The interpretation of these nonverbal cues significantly varies across cultures.

- *Review the five dominant listening styles and 10 keys to effective listening.* The five dominant listening styles are appreciative, empathetic, comprehensive, discerning, and evaluative. Good listeners use the following 10 listening habits: (1) capitalize on thought speed by staying with the speaker and listening between the lines, (2) listen for ideas rather than facts, (3) identify areas of interest between the speaker and listener, (4) judge content and not delivery, (5) do not judge until the speaker has completed his or her message, (6) put energy and effort into listening, (7) resist distractions, (8) listen to both favorable and unfavorable information, (9) read or listen to complex material to exercise the mind, and (10) take notes when necessary and use visual aids to enhance understanding.

- *Discuss the impact of ICT on productivity.* Information communication technologies are pervasive and impact OB in many ways. The ability to communicate, collaborate, and exchange ideas with people both inside and outside virtual and real organizational boundaries are critical success factors within and between individual, group, and organizational levels. Individual-level employee benefits include increased job satisfaction and better work–life balance. At the organizational level, effectively networked companies tend to out-compete their rivals due to improved access to valuable market and customer information, increased marketing effectiveness, reduced communication costs, and enhanced supplier and strategic partner satisfaction. Additional benefits for employers are reduced employee turnover and reduced costs (e.g., fewer office leases due to telecommuters). These benefits come with costs, notably *multitasking*. Research overwhelmingly shows that multitasking decreases productivity.

- *Describe the challenges of managing teleworkers, and the advantages and concerns associated with social media at work.* Social media is an extension of ICT and provides many of the same benefits. If deployed effectively, social media enables businesses to connect in real time and over distances with many key stakeholders, such as employees, customers (past, current, and future), communities, suppliers, prospective talent, former employees (sources of future talent), and many others. Social media also has the potential to connect sources of knowledge across the organization, offices, and time zones. Linking knowledge in these ways is a means to realizing the potential of employee diversity, enhancing productivity, and fostering organizational learning. However, legal challenges also are growing, particularly around issues of privacy and what employers can and cannot do with information gathered from social media. Experts therefore recommend establishing clear social media policies that are supported with training.

discussion questions

1. Use the perceptual model (Figure 12–1) and barriers of communication (Table 12–1) to identify the most common barriers to communication between you and your boss or you and the professor of this class. What can you do to improve this communication? Do the same for communications between you and your professor.

2. What are some sources of noise that interfere with communication during a class lecture?

3. Which of the keys to effective listening are most difficult to follow when listening to a class lecture? Explain.

4. Which barrier to effective communication is most difficult to reduce? Explain.

5. What are the pros and cons of using social media at work? Discuss.

6. Describe the social media policy you would recommend for your employer or your class.

legal/ethical challenge

Employers Tread a Minefield

More than drunken college students suffer the consequences of Facebook gaffes these days. As social media invades the workplace, employers are tripping over legal potholes when dealing with social media. For instance, in 2011 a National Labor Relations Board judge considered whether a medical-transportation company illegally fired a worker after she criticized her boss on Facebook. This is the first complaint linked to social media heard by the board. In another case, workers sued a restaurant company when they were dismissed after managers accessed a private MySpace page that employees set up to chat about work. Even laid-off workers are not immune. A laid-off banker in the United Kingdom was denied her severance package after posting comments about the package.[83]

The issue is whether employers have the right to take action (e.g., discipline or termination) against employees based on information they post on social networking sites. Job seekers and employers have long been warned that risqué revelations on Facebook can jeopardize career prospects. But now companies are facing their own challenges for alleged blunders in dealing with social media.[84]

What Is Your Opinion about Criticizing Your Manager or Employer in Social Media?

1. The US Constitution allows free speech, and people should be allowed to say whatever they want. Very little of what people say is verifiable fact; most is simply opinion. Besides, it is normal for people to have different opinions about others, including their managers, coworkers, and employers. It therefore does not seem fair to prosecute an employee for expressing a negative opinion of somebody at work, or their employer, whether it is verifiable fact or not. Sharing it face to face or online via social media is the same—free speech. Moreover, the social media site that posts comments has no fault either.

2. Reputations of people and companies can be damaged by comments posted in social media. The targets of comments often have little recourse, whether the comments are true or false. It's one thing to complain to a friend in a private conversation, but it is different if comments are posted where others can see them and the consequences are potentially greater. It thus is appropriate to punish or even terminate employees for posting negative statements. Social media companies, however, should not be prosecuted, as many have millions of subscribers and policing the content and accuracy of all postings is unreasonable if not impossible.

3. Both the individuals making malicious or negative statements and the site posting them should be punished. One "committed the crime" and the other helped.

4. Individuals can say whatever they want about employees and employers as long as it is true. If what they say is untrue, then their employers should be allowed to punish or even terminate them. However, the social media company has no fault because it cannot possibly verify the truth of posted comments.

5. Invent other options.

If you're looking for additional study materials, be sure to check out the Online Learning Center at

www.mhhe.com/kinickiob5e

for more information and interactivities that correspond to this chapter.

chapter 13

Influence, Power, and Politics: An Organizational Survival Kit

After reading the material in this chapter, you should be able to:

LO13.1. Name five "soft" and four "hard" influence tactics, and summarize Cialdini's principles of influence and persuasion.

LO13.2. Identify and briefly describe French and Raven's five bases of power.

LO13.3. Define the term *empowerment*, and explain how to make it succeed.

LO13.4. Define *organizational politics*, explain what triggers political behavior, and specify the three levels of political action in organizations.

LO13.5. Distinguish between favorable and unfavorable impression management tactics.

LO13.6. Explain how to manage organizational politics.

How Do You Pull off a Major Acquisition during the Great Recession?

If you are Raj Gupta, the former CEO of Rohm and Haas (R&H), the answer is: Power, influence, politics, and luck. One of the largest shareholders of this specialty chemical company, the Haas family trust, asked Gupta to sell its entire stake. This request was a tremendous surprise to Gupta. The company was a consistently strong performer, and he was personally committed to the company and its employees. Moreover, he was only the sixth CEO in the company's 100-year history. Selling the company was particularly challenging given that only three companies in the world would or could consider such a purchase—Dow Chemical, BASF, and DuPont. Fortunately, Gupta had invested considerable time and effort in developing and maintaining close relationships with the CEOs of all three, which made it easier for him to ask. Ultimately, Gupta and Dow's CEO Andrew Liveris agreed on an $18 billion cash ($74 per share) offer. The relationship between the two men and the stellar reputations of their companies facilitated the largest friendly deal in the industry's history.

Regulatory approval was proceeding nicely and everything was in place to close the deal.

But then the Wall Street crisis hit and banks stopped lending money. A $9 billion payment Dow was due to receive from a joint venture with another company was canceled. Obviously a problem for Liveris, but Gupta also was in a tough spot. Not only was he responsible for closing the deal, but his reputation was on the line, too. Shareholders, employees, and customers were all depending on him to deliver. To his advantage, the contract was not contingent, meaning Dow had already signed and could not back out. They needed to close the deal and pay Rohm and Haas $18 billion.

Just before the deadline Liveris called his friend Gupta to tell him that Dow just couldn't close the deal. The company no longer had the resources it expected, and if they managed to do the deal in that environment the ratings agencies would cut Dow's credit rating to junk status. Gupta said, "I understand what you're dealing with, but you have to put yourself in my situation. I need something to take to my board. I'd like to tell them that you fully intend to close the deal but you need more time. Give me a deadline ..." Liveris couldn't and didn't. Dow therefore did not fulfill the terms of the contract or close the deal on time.

Rohm and Haas filed suit in federal court to force Dow to close the deal, even if it required them to sell assets to raise the money. This lawsuit was potentially very consequential. A ruling in favor of Rohm and Haas would essentially mean that *all* companies would

Raj Gupta, then CEO of Rohm and Haas, utilized numerous forms of influence to close the sale of his company to Dow Chemical.

have to honor each and every deal, regardless of the economic conditions and consequences.

Gupta then spent considerable time trying to console R&H employees and customers that the deal was a good idea and would close. Two days before the court date Liveris emailed Gupta and asked, "Raj, should we give this one last try?" The two met and found a way to finance the deal without Dow incurring piles of debt and in a way that preserved the company's credit rating. This involved creative financing arrangements with other

Rohm and Haas shareholders. Gupta and Liveris also jointly participated in meetings with the ratings agencies to assure them of the financial soundness of the deal.

All of this required more time—their day in court was near. Liveris asked Gupta if he would ask the judge to grant them more time. He agreed. The judge gladly granted more time, financing came through, and the deal closed for $78 per share. Gupta retired and Rohm and Haas assets soon accounted for nearly two-thirds of Dow's profits in what they refer to as performance businesses.[1]

THE CHAPTER-OPENING CASE illustrates how important it is to develop and utilize a variety of means for influencing individuals and groups. Raj Gupta skillfully utilized his relationships with competitors, his reputation, and the legal process to achieve a mutually beneficial outcome for himself, for R&H employees, and for shareholders from both R&H and Dow.

In a perfect world, individual and collective interests would be closely aligned and everyone would move forward as one. Instead, we typically find a rather messy situation in which self-interests often override the collective mission, which can be complicated even further by external factors (e.g., the economy or regulatory changes). Personal hidden agendas are pursued, political coalitions are formed, false impressions are made, and people end up working at cross purposes. Managers need to be able to guide diverse individuals, who are often powerfully motivated to put their own self-interests first, to pursue common objectives. At stake in this tug-of-war between individual and collective interests is no less than the ultimate survival of the organization.

The purpose of this chapter is to give you a survival kit for the rough-and-tumble side of organizational life. We do so by exploring the interrelated topics of organizational influence and persuasion, social power, employee empowerment, organizational politics, and impression management.

Influencing and Persuading Others

LO13.1

How do you get others to carry out your wishes? Do you simply tell them what to do? Or do you prefer a less direct approach, such as promising to return the favor? Whatever approach you use, the crux of the issue is *social influence*. A large measure of interpersonal interaction involves attempts to influence others, including parents, bosses, coworkers, spouses, teachers, friends, and children. Let's start sharpening your influence skills with a familiarity of the following research insights: influence tactics, influence outcomes, and persuading others.

Nine Generic Influence Tactics

A particularly fruitful stream of research, initiated by David Kipnis and his colleagues in 1980, reveals how people influence each other in organizations. The Kipnis methodology involved asking employees how they managed to get their bosses, coworkers, and subordinates to do what they wanted them to do.[2] Statistical refinements and replications by other researchers eventually yielded nine influence tactics. The nine tactics, ranked in diminishing order of use in the workplace are:

1. *Rational persuasion.* Trying to convince someone with reason, logic, or facts.

2. *Inspirational appeals.* Trying to build enthusiasm by appealing to others' emotions, ideals, or values.

3. *Consultation.* Getting others to participate in planning, making decisions, and changes.

4. *Ingratiation.* Getting someone in a good mood prior to making a request; being friendly, helpful, and using praise, flattery, or humor.

5. *Personal appeals.* Referring to friendship and loyalty when making a request.

6. *Exchange.* Making explicit or implied promises and trading favors.

7. *Coalition tactics.* Getting others to support your efforts to persuade someone.

8. *Pressure.* Demanding compliance or using intimidation or threats.

9. *Legitimating tactics.* Basing a request on one's authority or right, organizational rules or policies, or explicit or implied support from superiors.

www.mcgrawhillconnect.com

Go to Connect for an interactive exercise to test your knowledge of the nine generic influence tactics.

These approaches can be considered *generic* influence tactics because they characterize social influence in all directions. Researchers have found this ranking to be fairly consistent regardless of whether the direction of influence is downward, upward, or lateral.[3]

Some call the first five influence tactics—rational persuasion, inspirational appeals, consultation, ingratiation, and personal appeals—"soft" tactics because they are friendlier and not as coercive as the last four tactics. Exchange, coalition, pressure, and legitimating tactics accordingly are called "hard" tactics because they involve more overt pressure.

Three Influence Outcomes

According to researchers, an influence attempt has three possible outcomes:

1. *Commitment:* Substantial agreement followed by initiative and persistence in pursuit of common goals.
2. *Compliance:* Reluctant or insincere agreement requiring subsequent prodding to satisfy minimum requirements.
3. *Resistance:* Stalling, unproductive arguing, or outright rejection.[4]

Highly respected former Procter & Gamble CEO, A G Lafley, used persuasive power to win commitment to company goals.

BACK TO THE CHAPTER-OPENING CASE

1. Describe three influence tactics Raj Gupta used to close the deal with Andrew Liveris and Dow Chemical.
2. Explain how each of the three influence outcomes was evident during the deal between Dow and Rohm and Haas.

Commitment is the best outcome in the workplace because the target person's intrinsic motivation will energize good performance.[5] A G Lafley, the highly respected former CEO of 100,000-employee Procter & Gamble, made commitment the cornerstone of his growth plan after taking charge in 2000:

> I always talk about this hierarchy of commitment. On the high end its disciples— people who really believe in what you're doing and in you. And on the low end its saboteurs. And there's everything in between. So I had to make sure that we got rid of the saboteurs, built a strong cadre of disciples, and moved all fence sitters to the positive side.[6]

The fence sitters required Lafley's best powers of influence and persuasion during a hectic schedule of face-to-face meetings with P&G employees worldwide. Too often in today's hurried workplaces managers must settle for compliance or face resistance because they do not invest themselves in the situation, as Lafley did.

Practical Research Insights

Laboratory and field studies have taught us useful lessons about the relative effectiveness of influence tactics along with other instructive insights:

- Core influence tactics—rational persuasion, consultation, collaboration, and inspirational appeals—are most effective at building commitment.[7] Do not rely on pressure and coalition tactics.[8] Interestingly, in one study, managers were not very effective at downward influence. They relied most heavily on inspiration (an effective tactic), ingratiation (a moderately effective tactic), and pressure (an ineffective tactic).[9]

- Commitment is more likely when the influence attempt involves something important and enjoyable and is based on a friendly relationship.[10]

- Credible (believable and trustworthy) people tend to be the most persuasive.[11]

- In a survey of 101 employees from two different organizations, employees were more likely to resist change when managers used a legitimating tactic and were more apt to accept change when managers relied on a consultative strategy.[12]

- Ingratiation improved short-term but reduced long-term sales goal achievement in a study of 241 sales people.[13] Schmoozing can help today's sales but not tomorrow's.

- Subtle flattery and agreeing with the other person's opinion (both forms of ingratiation) were shown to increase the likelihood of executives being recommended to sit on boards of directors.[14]

- Research involving corporate managers of a supermarket chain showed that influence tactics can be taught. Managers who received 360-degree feedback on two occasions regarding their influence tactics showed an increased use of core influence tactics.[15]

The bottom line: The influence tactics listed above can be learned and improved to move resisters to compliance, and those that are compliant to committed. The Skills & Best Practices feature on page 343 provides additional suggestions on increasing your influence. Use this knowledge to achieve better outcomes for you, your team, and your organization.

How to Do a Better Job of Influencing and Persuading Others

Practical, research-based advice has been offered by Robert B Cialdini, a respected expert at Arizona State University. Based on many years of research—his own and others—Cialdini (pronounced Chal-*dee*-knee) derived the following six principles of influence and persuasion:[16]

1. *Liking.* People tend to like those who like them. Learning about another person's likes and dislikes through informal conversations builds friendship bonds. So do sincere and timely praise, empathy, and recognition.

2. *Reciprocity.* The belief that both good and bad deeds should be repaid in kind is virtually universal. Managers who act unethically and treat employees with contempt can expect the same in return. Worse still, those same employees, are likely to treat each other and their customers unethically and with contempt. Managers need to be positive and constructive role models and fair-minded to benefit from the principle of reciprocity.

Increasing Your Influence

1. *Know what you want and believe you can get it.* State your (influence) goals in a positive way. For example, say, "I would like to be part of the decision-making process," instead of "I don't think anybody will take me seriously." Put another way, *don't tell people what you don't want.*

2. *Credibility.* People are more likely to listen to those with credibility. Highlight yours by emphasizing your expertise, reputation, and/or track record.

3. *Trustworthiness.* It is difficult to influence if you don't have trust. To build and maintain trust, be authentic, deliver on what you promise, consider the interests of others, and don't do anything to diminish your trustworthiness.

4. *Empathy.* It often is best to assume somebody else's position before your own. People are more easily influenced when they feel others understand their situation.

5. *Strong communication capability.* All other personal characteristics aside, the ability to effectively communicate your ideas and listen to others bolsters one's influence.

6. *Being inspirational.* Enthusiasm is contagious. If you're excited, others are more likely to be excited and to follow.

7. *Open-mindedness.* Truly influential people are not afraid of being influenced themselves.

SOURCE: Excerpted and adapted from "Increasing Your Influence—The Seven Traits of Influential People," *Manager,* Winter 2010.

---

3. *Social proof.* People tend to follow the lead of those most like themselves. Role models and peer pressure are powerful cultural forces in social settings. Managers are advised to build support for workplace changes by first gaining the enthusiastic support of informal leaders who will influence their peers.

4. *Consistency.* People tend to do what they are personally committed to do. A manager who can elicit a verbal commitment from an employee has taken an important step toward influence and persuasion.

5. *Authority.* People tend to defer to and respect credible experts. According to Cialdini, too many managers and professionals take their expertise for granted, as in the case of a hospital where he consulted. The physical therapy staff was frustrated by the lack of follow-through by patients. No matter how much they emphasized the importance of continuing therapy, many stopped once they returned home. An investigation of the causes revealed that patients were unaware of the professional/clinical qualifications of their therapists. Once they were informed and their many diplomas and certifications were hung on the walls in the clinic, patient compliance was remarkable. Compliance increased 34%![17]

6. *Scarcity.* People want items, information, and opportunities that have limited availability. Special opportunities and privileged information are influence-builders for managers.

Importantly, Cialdini recommends using these six principles in combination, rather than separately, for maximum impact. Because of potential ethical implications, one's goals need to be worthy and actions need to be sincere and genuine when using these six principles.

By demonstrating the rich texture of social influence, the foregoing research evidence and practical advice whet our appetites for learning more about how today's managers reconcile individual and organizational interests. Let us focus on social power next.

Social Power and Empowerment

The term *power* evokes mixed and often passionate reactions. To skeptics, Lord Acton's time-honored declaration that "power corrupts and absolute power corrupts absolutely" is truer than ever. However, organizational behavior (OB) specialists remind us that, like it or not, power is a fact of life in modern organizations. According to one management writer:

> Power must be used because managers must influence those they depend on. Power also is crucial in the development of managers' self-confidence and willingness to support subordinates. From this perspective, power should be accepted as a natural part of any organization. Managers should recognize and develop their own power to coordinate and support the work of subordinates; it is powerlessness, not power, that undermines organizational effectiveness.[18]

Thus, power is a necessary and generally positive force in organizations. As the term is used here, ***social power* is defined as "the ability to marshal the human, informational, and material resources to get something done."**[19] To this end, we discuss common bases of power, employee empowerment, participative management, and empowering leadership. Each of these is an example of social power in organizations.

It is important to note that the use of power is not only top-down. Employees can and do exercise power upward and laterally. Their power also can affect people in other organizations—an increasingly important consideration as today's companies often collaborate across organizational boundaries.

LO13.2

Five Bases of Power

A popular classification scheme for social power traces back to the landmark work of John French and Bertram Raven. They proposed that power arises from five different bases: reward power, coercive power, legitimate power, expert power, and referent power.[20] Each involves a different approach to influencing others. Each has advantages and drawbacks.

Reward Power   Managers have ***reward power* if they can obtain compliance by promising or granting rewards.** Pay-for-performance plans and positive reinforcement practices attempt to exploit reward power.

www.mcgrawhillconnect.com

Go to Connect for an interactive exercise to test your knowledge of French and Raven's bases of power.

Coercive Power   **Threats of punishment and actual punishment give an individual *coercive power*.** For instance, the Federal Trade Commission filed suit against Roll International, the owner of popular beverages Fiji Water and Pom Wonderful. The FTC charged that the company made false health claims about the pomegranates in its Pom Wonderful juice. If found guilty, Roll will have to pay millions in fines and make corrections to its claims.[21]

Legitimate Power   This base of power is what most people think of as authority and is anchored to one's formal position. Thus, managers who obtain compliance primarily because of their formal authority to make decisions have ***legitimate power*. Legitimate power may be expressed either positively or negatively.** Positive legitimate power focuses constructively on job performance. For instance, the HP board ousted CEO Mark Hurd for inappropriately using company funds and sexually harassing a contractor with whom he had an affair.[22] Negative legitimate power, in contrast, tends to be threatening and demeaning to those being influenced. Its main purpose is to build the power holder's ego. Many U.S. politicians, for example, have used their legislative position power to name various "monuments" after themselves: the Charles Rangel Center for Public Service (a representative from New York), the Frank R Lautenberg Turnpike in New Jersey, and Ted Stevens Airport in Anchorage, Alaska. The late Robert Byrd from West Virginia had more than 30 monuments named after him. Worse still, others used taxpayer money to enshrine their names, such as the Harkin Wellness Grants courtesy of Senator Tom Harkin of Iowa and the Mitch McConnell Conservation Fund (a senator from Kentucky).[23]

Expert Power   **Valued knowledge or information gives an individual** *expert power* **over those who need such knowledge or information.** The power of supervisors is enhanced because they know about work assignments and schedules before their employees do. Marc Andreessen epitomizes expert power in Silicon

Marc Andreesen, founder of Netscape (an early Web browser bought by Microsoft), has gone on to start a number of other companies. His venture capital firm invests in promising technology start-ups. He also sits on the boards of Facebook, eBay, and HP. Describe the bases of power and how they are likely used by Andreesen.

Valley. He is the 39-year-old founder of Web browser Netscape, which when it went public in 1995 started the Internet era. He went on to start two other successful technology companies—Opsware (sold to Hewlett-Packard) and Ning (social networking). Andreessen also sits on the boards of eBay, Facebook, Hewlett-Packard, Skype, and Stanford Hospital. But now he is regarded as one of the hottest venture capitalists in technology. His knowledge, social capital, and success enabled him to raise nearly $1 billion and make big investments in Foursquare, Skype, and a number of other young tech companies.[24] Knowledge *is* power in today's workplaces. To make this more personal, just think of how powerful your IT support people are when you have a problem with your computer!

BACK TO THE CHAPTER-OPENING CASE

1. Provide examples of three different bases of power used by Raj Gupta in his dealings with Andrew Liveris and Dow Chemical.
2. Explain why each of these may have worked.

Referent Power   *Referent power* **comes into play when one's personal characteristics become the reason for compliance.** Charisma is commonly associated with referent power, but one does not need to be the life of the party to possess referent power. In Asian cultures, for instance, characteristics such as age, gender, or family name are sources of social status and power. Role models also have referent power over those who identify closely with them. And, of course, one's reputation is a form of power. Many companies hire new CEOs, in part, to reap the benefits of the executive's reputation. Ford Motor Company, for example, hired Alan Mulally as CEO because of his stellar reputation and success at Boeing.[25]

To further your understanding of these five bases of power, take a moment to complete the questionnaire in the Hands-On Exercise. What is your power profile? Which forms of power can you develop further?

HANDS-ON EXERCISE

How Much Power Do You Have?

INSTRUCTIONS: Score your various bases of power for your current (or former) job, using the following scale:

1 = Strongly disagree   4 = Agree
2 = Disagree   5 = Strongly agree
3 = Slightly agree

Reward Power Score = _____

1. I can reward persons at lower levels. _____
2. My review actions affect the rewards gained at lower levels. _____
3. Based on my decisions, lower-level personnel may receive a bonus. _____

Coercive Power Score = _____

1. I can punish employees at lower levels. _____
2. My work is a check on lower-level employees. _____
3. My diligence reduces error. _____

Legitimate Power Score = _____

1. My position gives me a great deal of authority. _____
2. The decisions made at my level are of critical importance. _____
3. Employees look to me for guidance. _____

Expert Power Score = _____

1. I am an expert in this job. _____
2. My ability gives me an advantage in this job. _____
3. Given some time, I could improve the methods used on this job. _____

Referent Power Score = _____

1. I attempt to set a good example for other employees. _____
2. My personality allows me to work well in this job. _____
3. My fellow employees look to me as their informal leader. _____

Arbitrary norms for each of the five bases of power are:

3–6 = Weak power base
7–11 = Moderate power base
12–15 = Strong power base

SOURCE: Adapted and excerpted in part from D L Dieterly and B Schneider, "The Effect of Organizational Environment on Perceived Power and Climate: A Laboratory Study." *Organizational Behavior and Human Performance,* June 1974, pp 316–37.

Practical Lessons from Research

Researchers have identified the following relationships between power bases and work outcomes such as job performance, job satisfaction, and turnover:

- Expert and referent power had a generally positive effect.
- Reward and legitimate power had a slightly positive effect.
- Coercive power had a slightly negative effect.[26]

A follow-up study involving 251 employed business school seniors looked at the relationship between influence styles and bases of power. This was a bottom-up study. In other words, employee perceptions of managerial influence and power were examined. Rational persuasion was found to be a highly acceptable managerial influence tactic. Why? Because employees perceived it to be associated with the three bases of power they viewed positively: legitimate, expert, and referent.[27]

National culture also influences the types of power people use at work. For example, a sample of French and Chinese mid-level managers showed that the French used

From Teammate to Manager: Taking Charge

If you've been promoted to lead your group, you suddenly have more legitimate power. But to be an effective leader, you need to exercise that power carefully in a way that doesn't alienate but motivates your former coworkers:

- *Don't show off.* It might be tempting to strengthen your leadership role with an aggressive, dominating style, overseeing every detail. But that approach stirs resentment.
- *Do accept responsibility.* Trying to stay buddies with group members will undermine your ability to get the job done and will erode respect for you and your ability to handle the position. Collaborate when it's the best way to accomplish goals, not to save a friendship.
- *Do your homework.* Work with your new supervisor to define goals for yourself and your team. Strengthen your network of mentors to improve your management skills. Meet with your staff to go over your vision and expectations. Setting a direction for the team enhances your credibility (expert power).
- *Pay attention to team members' concerns.* Show them how meeting the group's goals will put them on track toward meeting their own needs.

SOURCE: Based on E Garone, "Managing Your Former Peers Takes Extra Effort," *The Wall Street Journal,* March 10, 2008, http://online.wsj.com.

legitimate most often, followed by expert and then referent. The Chinese used expert, referent, and legitimate, respectively. Moreover, the Chinese managers relied on expert power to fulfill operational and strategic decision-making responsibilities, while the French utilized legitimate for operations and a mixture of legitimate and expert for strategic decision making.[28] These results suggest that the Chinese value expert power and the French legitimate. Awareness of these facts can guide your own uses of power and influence when doing business with people from either of these cultures.

Expert and referent power appear to get the best *combination* of results and favorable reactions from lower-level employees. See the Skills & Best Practices feature above for some practical advice on putting these lessons into practice. The usefulness of expert and referent power was supported by research involving students and professors. A sample of 559 U.S. business school students indicated that referent and expert power (soft tactics) were associated with increased student satisfaction, while reward, coercive, and legitimate had no effect.[29] The venture capital firm Kleiner Perkins presumably will enjoy benefits of expert and referent power from their new advisor Meg Whitman, the former eBay CEO and executive of Disney and P&G. Her new position lacks the legitimate power (authority) she had as CEO, but her expertise and reputation for effectively leading a marquee Internet company should help the firm assess and attract new business. Kleiner Perkins also no doubt expects Whitman to utilize her substantial network (social capital discussed in Chapter 1).[30] Both Whitman and the firm should benefit from her expert and referent power.

www.mcgrawhillconnect.com

Go to Connect for a video case on the use of power and influence in the aftermath of Hurricane Katrina.

Employee Empowerment

♠LO13.3

An exciting trend in today's organizations centers on giving employees a greater say in the workplace. This trend wears various labels, including "participative management" and "open-book management."[31] Regardless of the label one prefers, it is all about empowerment. Management consultant and writer W Alan Rudolph offers this definition of *empowerment:* **"recognizing and releasing into the organization the power that people already have in their wealth of useful knowledge, experience, and internal motivation."**[32]

A recent study used 45 in-depth interviews to determine the meaning of empowerment from an employee point of view. Interestingly, employees interpreted empowerment in terms of how much personal responsibility and control over their work they experienced. Results also showed that employees varied in terms of how much empowerment they desired. Some employees liked to have responsibility and freedom, and others did not.[33] Another study involving more than 1,000 employees and 1,772 customers of 91 bank branches showed that employees who felt empowered provided higher quality service than those who did not feel empowered.[34]

The concept of empowerment requires some adjustment in traditional thinking. First and foremost, power is *not* a zero-sum situation where one person's gain is another's loss. Social power is unlimited. This requires win–win thinking. Frances Hesselbein, the woman credited with modernizing the Girl Scouts of the USA, put it this way: "The more power you give away, the more you have."[35] Hesselbein's view was highlighted in a study of 113 global customer teams from six multinational companies. Teams who felt empowered—possessed decision-making authority and the necessary resources to meet their job responsibilities—more effectively communicated and collaborated with customers and each other, resolved internal conflicts efficiently, and were more proactive in meeting customer needs.[36] Authoritarian managers, in contrast, who view employee empowerment as a threat to their personal power presumably miss the point because of their win–lose thinking.[37]

The second adjustment to traditional thinking involves seeing empowerment as a matter of degree, not as an either–or proposition. Figure 13–1 illustrates how power can be shifted to the hands of nonmanagers step by step. The overriding goal is to increase productivity and competitiveness in leaner organizations. Each step in this evolution increases the power of organizational contributors who traditionally were told what, when, and how to do things. For example, at the level of consultation (influence sharing), Norman Regional Health System implements hundreds of employee suggestions each year, sending explanations to employees whose ideas are not accepted, so that everyone can see management's response. Pool Covers is a good example of the participation level. The company suffered dramatic revenue losses (greater than 49%) during the Great Recession that started in 2008. But rather than make the cuts themselves, management shared the financials with the employees, and seven installers voluntarily took layoffs. One of these, Christopher Darling, said, "If everybody stayed, we would all have felt the crunch." But he has no kids or mortgage, so he instead decided, "You don't want to be part of the problem. You want to be part of the solution."[38] At the delegation level (power distribution), coffee and tea trader Equal Exchange lives out its "fair trade" mission by organizing as a democracy; each employee has one vote on decisions including what to sell and where to operate.[39]

Participative Management

Confusion exists about the exact meaning of participative management (PM). Management experts have clarified this situation by defining *participative management* **as the process whereby employees play a direct role in (1) setting goals, (2) making decisions, (3) solving problems, and (4) making changes in the organization.** Participative management includes, but goes beyond, simply asking employees for their ideas or opinions.

The Evolution of Power: From Domination to Delegation   FIGURE 13–1

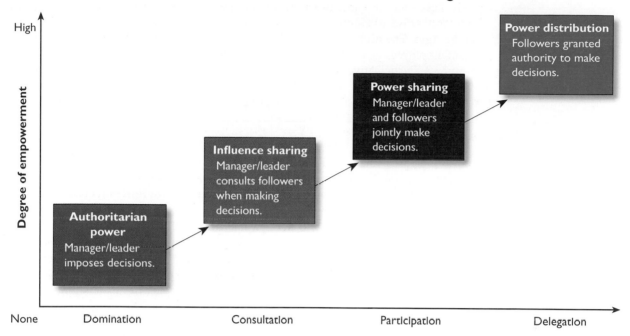

Advocates of PM claim employee participation increases employee satisfaction, commitment, and performance. For example, a study of teachers found that participative management—inclusion in developing policies, resolving learning problems, setting school goals, hiring staff, allocating budget, and evaluating students—was positively related to their performance and job satisfaction.[40] Consistent with both Maslow's needs theory and the job characteristics model of job design (see Chapter 6), participative management is predicted to increase motivation because it helps employees fulfill three basic needs: (1) autonomy, (2) meaningfulness of work, and (3) interpersonal contact. Satisfaction of these needs enhances feelings of acceptance and commitment, security, challenge, and satisfaction. In turn, these positive feelings supposedly lead to increased innovation and performance.[41]

Bosch, a Germany-based industrial manufacturer and technological services provider, uses a participative management approach to leadership development. Klaus Peter Fouquet, president of Bosch's UK operations, says the company develops leaders via a "learning by doing" program. "You have to be more a leader than a technical manager. . . . Bosch prefers a participative style of leadership. Our leadership style is not a very tough one. You need intelligent and good people and you should deal with them as though they are intelligent and good human beings." Employees often hold many different jobs, are involved in decision making, and have significant responsibilities throughout their careers. The company attributes part of its successful rebound from the recession to its participative approach to management and development. Fouquet also explains that employee participation at all levels is critical for innovation and competitiveness in the global marketplace.[42]

Participative management, however, does not work in all situations. The design of work, the level of trust between management and employees, and the employees' competence and readiness to participate represent three factors that influence the effectiveness of PM. With respect to the design of work, individual participation is counterproductive when employees are highly interdependent on each other, as on an assembly line. The problem with individual participation in this case is that interdependent employees generally do not have a broad understanding of the entire production process. Participative management also is less likely to succeed when employees do not trust management. Finally, PM is more effective when employees are competent, prepared, and interested in participating.

Empowering Leadership

Empowering leadership essentially marries employee empowerment to participative management. ***Empowering leadership* involves sharing power with employees by communicating the significance of employee jobs, providing decision-making autonomy, expressing confidence in employee performance capabilities, and removing barriers to performance.**[43] Leaders who share power in such ways communicate to followers that they are valued, their jobs are meaningful, and they are competent. Empowering leadership expresses trust in followers, which in turn often builds their trust in the leader. Just like giving trust is a means for building trust, sharing influence is a means for building influence. As we will discuss in Chapter 14, leadership is fundamentally about influence. Empowering others is thus a means for building one's own social power and leadership potential. It signals to followers that the leader believes in their abilities and builds the intrinsic motivational states discussed in Chapter 7. These same conclusions apply to leading teams and across cultures. Empowering team leadership was shown to influence team member motivation, empowerment, and organizational commitment in both U.S. and Chinese students who participated in a laboratory study.[44]

Making Empowerment Work

Empowerment has its fair share of critics and suffers from unrealistic expectations. But a recent meta-analysis of 142 articles provides some practical guidance. It shows that both the work environment (managerial practices, social and political support, leadership, and work design) and individual (self-evaluations, human capital, gender) characteristics are related to empowerment, and that empowered employees reported lower intentions to quit and higher levels of job satisfaction, organizational commitment, and performance.[45] Organizations can foster empowerment by:

- Providing employee training and development.
- Openly sharing information.
- Utilizing participative decision making (Chapter 10).
- Using contingent pay practices (discussed in Chapter 8).
- Modifying the five job characteristics discussed in Chapter 6.
- Selecting employees based on their positive core self-evaluations (see Chapter 5).

Finally, this same meta-analysis revealed that all of the relationships for empowerment found at the individual level applied to teams (Chapter 9).[46] It therefore is clear that a broad knowledge of OB equips managers to effectively empower employees and reap the associated benefits.

Organizational Politics and Impression Management

Organizational politics are typically regarded in terms of negative behaviors that include manipulation, control of information, and intimidation. This is an overly narrow and inaccurate view of organizational politics because politics also entail positive behaviors, such as persuading others to accept one's point of view and aligning people to efficiently execute strategic objectives.[47] Regardless of your point of view about organizational politics, they are an ever-present and sometimes annoying feature of modern work life. For example, a recent meta-analysis of 82 different studies revealed perceptions of organizational politics were associated with differences at three levels—organizational, job/work environment, and individual. Specifically, organizational justice (Chapter 7) was the strongest organizational influence on politics. Trust in coworkers (Chapter 9) and negative affect (negative emotions—Chapter 5) were the strongest work environment and individual difference predictors, respectively.[48] We explore this important and interesting area by (1) defining the term *organizational politics,* (2) identifying three levels of political action, (3) discussing eight specific political tactics, (4) considering a related area called *impression management,* and (5) discussing how to curb the negative effects of organizational politics.

LO13.4

Donald Trump is known for being both political and influential. Fans of *The Apprentice* have seen Trump and the contestants on the show prove this to be true. How has he used his power and influence to his advantage?

Definition and Domain of Organizational Politics

Organizational politics **are intentional acts of influence to enhance or protect the self-interest of individuals or groups that are not endorsed by the organization.**[49] An emphasis on *self-interest* distinguishes this form of social influence. Managers are endlessly challenged to achieve a workable balance between employees' self-interests and organizational interests, as discussed at the beginning of this chapter. When a proper balance exists, the pursuit of self-interest may serve the organization's interests. In contrast, when political activities are out of balance and conflict with the organization's interests they are considered negative and not sanctioned by the organization. This means that they are not an integral part of an employee's job role and not approved.

Political Behavior Is Triggered by Uncertainty   Political maneuvering is triggered primarily by *uncertainty.* Five common sources of uncertainty within organizations are:

1. Unclear objectives.
2. Vague performance measures.
3. Ill-defined decision processes.
4. Strong individual or group competition.[50]
5. Any type of change.

Closely related to the second factor—vague performance measures—is the problem of *unclear performance–reward linkages* (recall our discussion of expectancy motivation theory in Chapter 7). This is a significant problem, according to the results of a survey of 10,000 employees. Regarding the statement "Employees who do a better job get paid more," 48% of the responding managers agreed, whereas only 31% of the nonmanagers agreed.[51] Employees tend to resort to "politicking" when they are unsure about what it takes to get ahead. Relative to the fifth factor—any type of change—organization development specialist Anthony Raia noted, "Whatever we attempt to change, the political subsystem becomes active. Vested interests are almost always at stake and the distribution of power is challenged."[52] Tools for combating resistance to change are discussed in Chapter 16.

Because employees generally experience greater uncertainty during the earlier stages of their careers, are junior employees more political than more senior ones? The answer is yes, according to a survey of 243 employed adults in upstate New York. In fact, one senior employee nearing retirement told the researcher: "I used to play political games when I was younger. Now I just do my job."[53]

www.mcgrawhillconnect.com

Go to Connect for a self-assessment to determine how political you are.

Three Levels of Political Action   Although much political maneuvering occurs at the individual level, it also can involve group or collective action. Figure 13–2 illustrates three different levels of political action: the individual level, the coalition level, and the network level.[54] Each level has its distinguishing characteristics. At the individual level, personal self-interests are pursued by the individual. The political aspects of coalitions and networks are not so obvious, however.

People with a common interest can become a political coalition by fitting the following definition. In an organizational context, a **coalition is an informal group bound together by the *active* pursuit of a *single* issue.** Coalitions may or may not coincide with formal group membership. When the target issue is resolved (a sexually harassing supervisor is fired, for example), the coalition disbands. Experts note that political coalitions have "fuzzy boundaries," meaning they are fluid in membership, flexible in structure, and temporary in duration.[55]

Coalitions are a potent political force in organizations. For instance, a coalition representing farmers and airlines persuaded the Commodity Futures Trading Commission (CFTC) to exempt these industries from new legislation that requires companies that trade futures contracts, in commodities such as grain and jet fuel, to put up greater amounts of collateral.[56] Microsoft, in coalition with several small European Internet

FIGURE 13–2   Levels of Political Action in Organizations

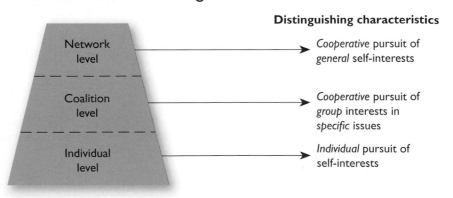

companies, has lobbied European Union regulators to take action against Google. They claim that the company unfairly dominates search in Europe.[57] Coalitions on the corporate boards of directors also assert their influence. This was the case when the CEOs of BP and Hewlett-Packard were ousted. This also happens when investors (e.g., private equity firms) use their seats on boards to further their strategic agendas. Fairholme Capital, for example, voted to remove the CEO and three other executives at St. Joe, a Florida-based residential real estate company. Fairholme wanted to take St. Joe in a different direction.[58]

A third level of political action involves networks. Unlike coalitions, which pivot on specific issues, networks are loose associations of individuals seeking social support for their general self-interests. Politically, networks are people-oriented, while coalitions are issue-oriented. Networks have broader and longer-term agendas than do coalitions. For instance, many former Goldman Sachs executives (e.g., Hank Paulson, Stephen Friedman, Josh Bolten, and Robert Rubin) went on to high-level government jobs. Many people have alleged that this large and powerful network has protected the interests of Wall Street firms generally and those of Goldman Sachs in particular.[59]

TABLE 13–1 Most Commonly Used Political Tactics

1. Building a network of useful contacts.
2. Using "key players" to support initiatives.
3. Making friends with power brokers.
4. Bending the rules to fit the situation.
5. Self-promotion.
6. Creating a favorable image. (Also known as *impression management*.)
7. Praising others (ingratiation).
8. Attacking or blaming others.
9. Using information as a political tool.

Frequently Used Political Tactics   Anyone who has worked in an organization has firsthand knowledge of blatant politicking. Although researchers have proposed many different categories of political tactics, two studies put these ideas to the test by asking samples of 87 U.S. and 250 British managers to identify the types of political behaviors they had experienced. Top-, middle-, and low-level managers were included in the samples. Table 13–1 contains the tactics noted as happening most frequently.[60]

The researchers distinguished between reactive and proactive political tactics. Some of the tactics, such as scapegoating, were reactive because the intent was to defend one's self-interest. Bank of America provided an excellent example after WikiLeaks founder, Julian Assange, hinted that he possessed files that would unveil widespread corruption and take down the bank. Bank of America reacted by devoting a team of 15 to 20 top officials to "scouring thousands of documents in the event that they become public, reviewing every case where a computer has gone missing and hunting for any sign that its systems might have been compromised."[61] Although nothing has yet been released by WikiLeaks, the bank wanted to be sure it was prepared to respond. Other tactics, such as building a network of useful contacts, were proactive because they sought to promote the individual's self-interest. Noted OB scholar and Stanford professor Jeffrey Pfeffer encourages all people in business to build, maintain, and use networks both internal and external to one's employer.[62]

> **BACK TO THE CHAPTER-OPENING CASE**   Describe how Raj Gupta used three different political tactics to close the sale of Rohm and Haas.

You may notice from the list above that politicking often occurs when things don't work out—in situations of underperformance. How one responds to underperformance (failure) is very important. Research involving several hundred thousand managers from every industry sector in the United States shows that 70% of the population tends to assign blame for failures in one of the following three ways: (1) blame others, (2) blame oneself, or (3) deny blame.[63] These tendencies are stable, just like personality and many of the other individual differences discussed in Chapter 5. And like other individual differences, one's "blaming style" likely fits some situations well and is problematic in others. It is helpful to assess your own tendencies, as well as those of your coworkers and people you must influence at work.

LO13.5   Impression Management

Impression management **is defined as any attempt to control or manipulate the images related to a person, organization, or ideas.**[64] This encompasses speech, behavior, and appearance. Most impression management attempts are directed at making a good impression on relevant others, although there are exceptions, as we will see. It is important to remember that anyone can be the intended target of impression management. Parents, teachers, peers, employees, and customers are all fair game when it comes to managing the impressions of others.

Good Impressions   Research conducted in the context of job interviews shows that impressions are formed very quickly and often subtly. Interviewers gather information on job candidates based on their handshake, smile, and manner of dress. All of this information is communicated before any questions are asked! More importantly, it was shown that these same factors were related to ultimate job offers.[65] There are questionable ways to create a good impression, as well. For instance, Stewart Friedman, director of the University of Pennsylvania's Leadership Program, offered this gem:

Craig's List founder Craig Newmark and CEO Jim Buckmaster seemingly pay little attention to impression management. Their office is in a small storefront, Buckmaster takes public transportation to work while Newmark drives himself in a modest car. Buckmaster says that neither of them is interested in being wildly wealthy and dealing with the associated challenges. Stopping short and avoiding the hassles is just fine for them.

Last year, I was doing some work with a large bank. The people there told me a story that astounded me: After 7 p.m., people would open the door to their office, drape a spare jacket on the back of their chair, lay a set of glasses down on some reading material on their desk—and then go home for the night. The point of this elaborate gesture was to create the illusion that they were just out grabbing dinner and would be returning to burn the midnight oil.[66]

Impression management often strays into questionable, if not unethical, territory. Recent research reports that CEOs often engage in impression management with Wall Street analysts. This is to be expected, and in and of itself is not a problem. However, a study of more than 600 CEOs of companies with more than $100 million in revenues showed that unfavorable analyst comments prompted CEOs to verbally communicate that their companies do indeed have policies and practices that are in shareholders' best interests. Related research showed that CEOs also routinely communicated that their own compensation plan was aligned with shareholder interests, although, in both instances, it was found that CEOs regularly misrepresented these issues.[67] For example, their companies often made job and R&D cuts that undermined the long-term health of the company (counter to shareholder interests). And their personal compensation often was increased even when the share price of their company plummeted.

A statistical analysis of the influence attempts reported by a sample of 84 bank employees (including 74 women) identified three categories of favorable upward impression management tactics.[68] Favorable upward impression management tactics can be job-focused (manipulating information about one's job performance), supervisor-focused (praising and doing favors for one's supervisor), and self-focused (presenting oneself as a polite and nice person). A moderate amount of upward impression management is a necessity for the average employee today. For example, a review of 69 studies suggests ingratiation can slightly improve your performance appraisal results and make your boss like you significantly more.[69] Too little impression management, and busy managers are liable to overlook some of your valuable contributions when they make job assignment, pay, and promotion decisions. Too much, and you run the risk of being branded a "schmoozer," a "phony," and other unflattering things by your coworkers.[70] Noticeable flattery and ingratiation can backfire by embarrassing the target person and damaging your credibility.[71] Also, the risk of unintended insult is very high when impression management tactics cross gender, racial, ethnic, and cultural lines.[72]

Bad Impressions   Remarkably, some people actually try to make a bad impression.[73] But because these people are relatively rare, we instead focus on common, if not subtle, ways people make bad impressions at work. In addition to the many obvious faux pas—don't cheat, don't lie, don't steal—many employees often make bad impressions without knowing it. Some common ways this happens and how to overcome them are:

- *Doing only the minimum.* Many employees aren't aware that not making the often simple extra effort to fulfill a coworker's request can be costly. Going the extra mile to check the status of a report, for instance, can go a long way toward conveying a positive impression.

- *Having a negative mind-set.* Most people consider themselves positive, but sometimes others have a different view. When presented with a new initiative, do you immediately think of and point out the potential pitfalls or complain? If so, then it is possible that others see you as negative. And managers prefer people who are supportive, not necessarily "yes men and women," but those who are constructive versus eternal naysayers.

- *Overcommitting.* Initiative is often good, but biting off more than you can chew means you might choke! The inability to deliver on-time or quality work is a sure way to make a bad impression. Prioritize and deliver, which requires saying no sometimes.

- *Taking no initiative.* The opposite of overcommitting—failing to take action when something needs to get done—can also make you look bad. If coworkers (including your boss) frequently come to you with the same questions or challenges, then step up and try to proactively solve the issue.

- *Waiting until the last minute to deliver bad news.* Of course you shouldn't report to or consult with your boss on every little hiccup in your work. But worse still is to inform her or him just before a deadline that you are having difficulties. This puts them in a bad spot too. Be smart, put yourself in the other person's shoes and consider if and when you would want to know the information you have.[74]

As CEO of BP during the massive Deepwater Horizon oil spill in 2010, Tony Hayward was criticized for being evasive and blaming others. By not handling the incident effectively, he damaged the reputation of the company and lost his job. How would you have handled the situation if you were CEO of BP?

Other ways to avoid employees making bad impressions can be found throughout this book. They include more challenging work, greater autonomy, better feedback, supportive leadership, clear and reasonable goals, and a less stressful work setting.

One final point is that much of impression management involves "spinning" a bad situation into something better, if not good. Public relations (PR), for instance, is impression management at the organizational level and often involves "managing the message," such as reducing the damage of bad press associated with a scandal. The massive BP oil spill is a prime example. The company downplayed the estimates of how much oil was leaking—first 1,000 barrels per day, then 5,000, and then nearly 50,000! It was later learned that the company knowingly underestimated the extent of the leak. Doing so dramatically undermined the credibility of a company that billed itself as: "BP—Beyond Petroleum—a paragon of environmental sustainability."[75]

The company also attempted to deflect blame for the spill onto contractors and downplayed the environmental impact. This made the company appear insensitive and led people to believe they were simply trying to avoid legal liabilities. Months after the spill began the company unleashed a barrage of television spots featuring BP employees from the Gulf, highlighting its commitment to the cleanup. According to one PR expert:

> It was one of the worst PR approaches that I've seen in my 56 years in the business. . . . They tried to be opaque. They had every excuse in the book. Right away they should have accepted responsibility and recognized what a disaster they faced. They basically thought they could spin their way out of catastrophe. It doesn't work that way.[76]

A communications professor summed it up this way: "BP could apologize everyday. . . [but] until the oil stopped, there was nothing that could be done to make it better, but there was plenty that could be said to make it worse."[77]

So how can organizations best handle crises? Howard Rubenstein, a highly regarded PR executive who represents the New York Yankees and News Corp, suggests that all organizations should create a crisis plan that includes how information is to be gathered, how to formulate a response, who will deliver the message, and via which media channels (recall our discussion of the importance of social media in Chapter 12). He also recommends that organizations be careful not to minimize a given problem, as no matter how small it is in the company's eyes, it is a big deal to somebody else. Be understanding and empathetic. Then, get on with doing business—whatever the organization does well (e.g., finding and creating petroleum products).[78]

Apologies   One way to remedy or at least reduce the impact of bad impressions, negative uses of power, or poor performance is with an apology. Apologies are a form of trust repair (discussed in Chapter 9) where one acknowledges an offense and often offers to make amends. It is a widely held norm in the United States and other cultures (e.g., Japan) to apologize when one's actions (or lack of action) cause harm to another, whether intentional or not. And much like our discussion of equity in Chapter 7, harm can be perceived or actual, but in either case it is real to the offended. Apologies are

Purposes for Leader Apologies and Their Desired Outcomes   **TABLE 13–2**

Purpose of Apology	Motive or Desired Outcome
Individual—Leader offended other	Encourage followers to forgive and forget
Institutional—Follower offended another organizational member	Restore functioning within the group or organization when one member offends another member(s)
Intergroup—Follower offended external party	Repair relations with an external group that perceived harm by a member of the leader's group
Moral—Genuine regret for wrongdoing	Request for forgiveness and redemption for regrettable (in)action

SOURCE: Based on B Kellerman, "When Should a Leader Apologize—And When Not?," *Harvard Business Review,* April 1, 2006.

important and are considered effective to the extent they restore trust and positively affect your ability to influence the offended party in the future.[79]

We know from life that not all people apologize, and when they do, the effects differ. But in business perhaps the better questions are when to apologize and how. (See Table 13–2 for the primary reasons leaders should apologize along with their associated motives.) Barbara Kellerman has written extensively on the subject and offers these suggestions. Apologize in the following situations:

- Doing so will serve an important purpose (see Table 13–2).
- The offense is of serious consequence.
- It's appropriate for the leader to assume responsibility for the offense.
- No one else can get the job done.
- The cost of saying something is likely to be lower than the cost of staying silent.[80]

Whether the apology is from a leader or not, Kellerman says that all effective apologies have the following four characteristics: (1) acknowledgment of wrongdoing, (2) acceptance of responsibility, (3) expression of regret, and (4) promise that offense will not be repeated.[81] It also is helpful to consider that a failure to apologize, or to do so in a timely manner, can turn a bad situation worse.[82]

Keeping Organizational Politics in Check

A meta-analysis involving 25,059 people revealed that perceptions of organizational politics were negatively associated with job satisfaction and organizational commitment, and positively related to job stress and intentions to quit.[83] Do these results suggest that managers should attempt to stop people from being political? Good luck. Organizational politics cannot be eliminated. A manager would be naive to expect such an outcome. But political maneuvering can and should be managed to keep it constructive and within reasonable bounds. Harvard's Abraham Zaleznik put the issue this way: "People can focus their attention on only so many things. The more it lands on politics, the less energy—emotional and intellectual—is available to attend to the problems that fall under the heading of real work."[84]

LO13.6

Make Politics Work for You

To build support for your ideas, consider the following:

1. Create a simple slogan that captures your idea.
2. Get your idea on the agenda. Describe how it addresses an important need or objective, and look for ways to make it a priority.
3. Score small wins early and broadcast them widely. Results build momentum and make it easier for other people to commit.
4. Form alliances with people who have the power to decide, fund, and implement.
5. Persist and continue to build support. It is a process, not an event.
6. Respond and adjust. Be flexible and accepting of other people's input; the more names on it, the more likely you are to succeed.
7. Lock it in. Anchor the idea into the organization through budgets, job descriptions, incentives, and other operating procedures.
8. Secure and allocate credit. You don't want your idea to be hijacked, nor do you want to blow your own horn. You need others to sing your praises to assure you get the credit you deserve.

SOURCE: Excerpted and adapted from "Best Practices for Managing Organizational Politics," *Nonprofit World*, July–August 2010.

An individual's degree of politicalness is a matter of personal values, ethics, and temperament. People who are either strictly nonpolitical or highly political generally pay a price for their behavior. The former may experience slow promotions and feel left out, while the latter may run the risk of being called self-serving and lose their credibility. People at both ends of the political spectrum may be considered poor team players. A moderate amount of prudent political behavior generally is considered a survival tool in complex organizations. Experts remind us that "Political behavior has earned a bad name only because of its association with politicians. On its own, the use of power and other resources to obtain your objectives is not inherently unethical. It all depends on what the preferred objectives are."[85]

With this perspective in mind, the practical steps in Skills & Best Practices feature above are recommended. Notice the importance of reducing uncertainty through clear performance–reward linkages. Measurable objectives are management's first line of defense against negative expressions of organizational politics.

key terms

chapter summary

- *Name five "soft" and four "hard" influence tactics, and summarize Cialdini's principles of influence and persuasion.* Five soft influence tactics are rational persuasion, inspirational appeals, consultation, ingratiation, and personal appeals. They are friendlier and less coercive than the four hard influence tactics: exchange, coalition tactics, pressure, and legitimating tactics. According to research, soft tactics are better for generating commitment and are perceived as fairer than hard tactics. Cialdini's six principles of influence and persuasion are liking (favoring friends), reciprocity (belief that one good or bad turn deserves to be repaid in kind), social proof (following those similar to oneself), consistency (following through on personal commitments), authority (deferring to credible and respected experts), and scarcity (seeking things of limited availability).

- *Identify and briefly describe French and Raven's five bases of power.* French and Raven's five bases of power are reward power (rewarding compliance), coercive power (punishing noncompliance), legitimate power (relying on formal authority), expert power (providing needed information), and referent power (relying on personal attraction).

- *Define the term* empowerment, *and explain how to make it succeed.* Empowerment involves sharing varying degrees of power and decision-making authority with lower-level employees to better serve the customer. According to Randolph's model, empowerment requires active sharing of key information, structure that encourages autonomy, transfer of control from managers to teams, and persistence. Trust and training also are very important.

- *Define* organizational politics, *explain what triggers it, and specify the three levels of political action in organizations.* Organizational politics is defined as intentional acts of influence to enhance or protect the self-interests of individuals or groups. Uncertainty triggers most politicking in organizations. Political action occurs at individual, coalition, and network levels. Coalitions are informal, temporary, and single-issue alliances.

- *Distinguish between favorable and unfavorable impression management tactics.* Favorable upward impression management can be job-focused (manipulating information about one's job performance), supervisor-focused (praising or doing favors for the boss), or self-focused (being polite and nice). Unfavorable upward impression management tactics include decreasing performance, not working to potential, withdrawing, displaying a bad attitude, and broadcasting one's limitations. Common behaviors that sometimes unknowingly cause a bad impression are: doing only the minimum, having a negative mind-set, over commitment, taking no initiative, and waiting until the last minute to deliver bad news. While avoiding each of these can help limit bad impressions, doing the opposite can help build positive impressions.

- *Explain how to manage organizational politics.* Although organizational politics cannot be eliminated, managers can keep it within reasonable bounds. Measurable objectives for personal accountability are key. Participative management also helps, especially in the form of open-book management. Formal conflict resolution and grievance programs are helpful. Overly political people should not be hired, and employees who get results without playing political games should be publicly recognized and rewarded. The "how-would-it-look-on-TV" ethics test can limit political maneuvering.

discussion questions

1. Choose one of your current work or school goals. Then identify somebody that can help you achieve that goal. Which bases of power and influence tactics can you use to influence that person to help you achieve your goal? Explain not only which bases of power and influence tactics you could use, but also how you would actually implement each.

2. Before reading this chapter, did the term *power* have a negative connotation for you? Do you view it differently now? Explain.

3. Describe a personal experience, or a situation you read about in the news, in which too much empowerment was used.

4. Why do you think organizational politics is triggered primarily by uncertainty?

5. How much impression management do you see in your classroom or workplace today? Citing specific examples, are those tactics effective?

6. Think of a situation at work or school where somebody clearly used politics in a negative way. What could have been done to prevent this from happening?

legal/ethical challenge

Secret Banking Elite Rules Trading in Derivatives

Nine people have a standing meeting in Manhattan one Wednesday each month. This is a highly secretive group of powerful people across Wall Street, known by critics as the "derivatives dealers club." The membership and discussions are strictly confidential. The focus: Protect the interests of the largest firms on Wall Street that serve as dealers in the highly lucrative derivatives market. Derivatives (swaps and options) are financial products used like insurance to hedge financial risk. Because derivatives do not trade on formal exchanges like stocks on the New York Stock Exchange (NYSE) and are largely unregulated by agencies such as the Securities and Exchange Commission (SEC), their creation and trading is largely self-managed by the firms themselves. This secretive group helps oversee and control this multitrillion-dollar market.

The dealers' club has attempted to block the efforts of other banks to enter the market and compete with select few member firms. It also has blocked many efforts by regulators and others to get full and free disclosure of dealer prices and fees. The situation is similar to a real estate agent selling a house and the buyer only knowing what he or she paid, the seller only knowing what he or she received, and the agent pocketing the rest in fees. These fees would not be known to either the buyer or the seller.

This lack of disclosure has implications far beyond the biggest banks. Pension funds, states, cities, airlines, food companies, and some small businesses use derivatives to offset and manage risk. These parties argue that without transparency they cannot determine if they receive a fair price. What is known, however, is that Wall Street's largest firms collect billions of dollars in undisclosed fees each year from trading these derivatives—fees that certainly would be smaller if there was more transparency and competition. These concerns have spurred investigation of anticompetitive practices by the Department of Justice and threats by some legislators. The firms, however, have powerful allies—the many politicians in Washington to whom they've made substantial campaign contributions.

Derivatives dealers' defense is that derivative prices are complex. Unlike shares of NetFlix stock, which are all equivalent—one share has the same price as all the rest—terms of oil derivatives can vary greatly. The complexity therefore requires customization, and greater transparency is impractical if not impossible.[86]

What Is Your Position on Derivatives Trading?

1. Regulators should assert influence over the derivatives market, like they do with stocks, and require derivatives to be traded on an open exchange where buyers and sellers disclose prices and fees.

2. Nothing should be done to change how derivatives are bought and sold. If buyers and sellers don't like the lack of dealer transparency then they can choose not to trade derivatives.

3. The derivatives market should be modified only slightly to allow other players (e.g., banks) to provide derivatives. If they then choose to disclose prices and fees, that is their choice, just as it is the choice of others to buy derivatives.

4. Invent other alternatives and explain.

If you're looking for additional study materials, be sure to check out the Online Learning Center at

www.mhhe.com/kinickiob5e

for more information and interactivities that correspond to this chapter.

Managing for Organizational Effectiveness

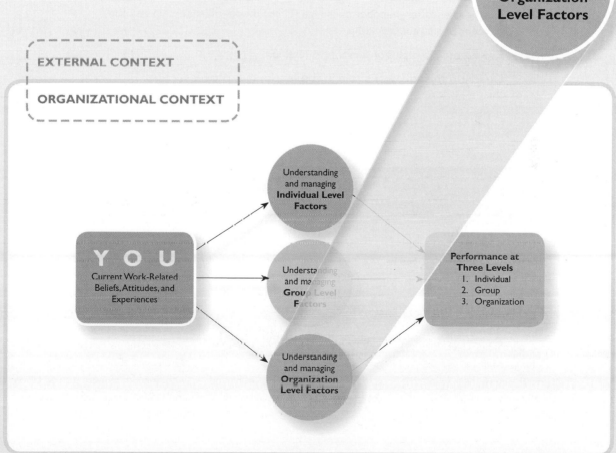

EXTERNAL CONTEXT

ORGANIZATIONAL CONTEXT

Understanding and managing **Organization Level Factors**

Understanding and managing **Individual Level Factors**

YOU
Current Work-Related Beliefs, Attitudes, and Experiences

Understanding and managing **Group Level Factors**

Understanding and managing **Organization Level Factors**

Performance at Three Levels
1. Individual
2. Group
3. Organization

chapter 14

Leadership

After reading the material in this chapter, you should be able to:

LO14.1 Review trait theory research, and discuss the takeaways from both the trait and behavioral styles theories of leadership.

LO14.2 Explain, according to Fiedler's contingency model, how leadership style interacts with situational control, and discuss the takeaways from this model.

LO14.3 Discuss House's revised path–goal theory and its practical takeaways.

LO14.4 Describe the difference between transactional and transformational leadership and discuss how transformational leadership transforms followers and work groups.

LO14.5 Explain the leader–member exchange (LMX) model of leadership and the concept of shared leadership.

LO14.6 Review the principles of servant-leadership.

LO14.7 Describe the follower's role in the leadership process.

LEARNING OBJECTIVES

Would You Like to Work for Lynn Tilton?

Earlier this year, private-equity chief Lynn Tilton flew to Detroit to try to improve sales at one of her auto-parts companies. She got a cool reception from Ford Motor Company's purchasing chief, Tony Brown, who asked if she was like other private-equity chiefs who "strip and flip" their companies.

"You must be mistaken," she shot back. "It's only men that I strip and flip. My companies I hold long and close to my heart."

With her platinum blonde hair, tight leather skirts, and penchant for racy remarks, Tilton has a talent for getting people's attention. Yet behind the glam facade is a sophisticated

distressed-debt investor and manufacturing tycoon who has quickly become one of the richest self-made women in America.

Through her New York–based holding company Patriarch Partners, Tilton owns all or part of 74 companies with revenues of more than $8 billion and 120,000 employees. By most measures, Patriarch is now the largest woman-owned business in America.

Ms Tilton, 52 years old, built her fortune from an unlikely corner of the economy: down-and-out industrial firms. Her strategy is to buy manufacturers headed for the scrap heap and bring them back to life with new management teams and products. In the process, she has become an unlikely crusader for America's rust belt. "The key to America's future is manufacturing," she says. "We simply have to become a country that can make things again."

Tilton also has made her share of mistakes. After buying American LaFrance, the fire truck maker, she drove down revenue by more than 50% in an effort to improve profits. Four years later, she still is trying to turn the company around. "That was a purchase I made more with my heart than my head," she said.

Tilton has the added distraction of her personality. Her office uniform usually includes five-inch stilettos, an eight-carat diamond necklace, and the occasional black leather jumpsuit. Her office walls are filled with whips and handcuffs sent to her by friends, Hashemite daggers given to her by Middle Eastern royals, New Age paintings, and a portrait of her stretched across the hood of a black Mercedes. Tilton makes no apologies for her unconventional look. "I am all woman," she says. "Sometimes it makes men uncomfortable, sure. But in business and in life, I have to remain faithful to my inner truth. In the end, I'd hope people judge me on my accomplishments and intelligence."

Lynn Tilton

Tilton started on Wall Street as a single mother, working 15-hour days and putting herself through Columbia's business school. She graduated from Yale as a nationally ranked college tennis player and aspiring poet, and married her college sweetheart. Soon after starting work on Wall Street, she got divorced and plunged into her work.

In 2000, she founded Patriarch, named after her late father. Her plan was to trade debt with her own money. Yet after buying two giant portfolios of distressed debt, she realized the only way to succeed was to take control of the companies in the portfolio. Suddenly, Tilton had gone from a debt investor to the accidental chief executive of dozens of failed companies. Her turnarounds were so profitable that she went on to buy more companies.

She sleeps only a few hours a night and sips a homemade concoction of clay, salt, and chlorophyll. She often stays up

late reading science fiction on her Kindle.

Walking down the manufacturing line at her MD helicopter plant in Arizona on a recent afternoon, Tilton looked out of place in her shimmering dress and heels. Yet she quickly bonded with workers with her earthy jokes and detailed knowledge of metal alloys and machine tools. "Workers really take to Lynn," said Duane Lugdon, a United Steelworkers union staffer who led tense negotiations with Tilton at the Maine paper plant. "She's just human and honest with people. I don't say that about many CEOs."

Her personal involvement in each company—she's still CEO of MD—is a blessing and a curse, former employees say. They say employee turnover at Patriarch is high because of Ms Tilton's tough personality. "I'm a benevolent dictator," Ms Tilton says. "I like to control things. What we do, the distressed area, is not for the faint of heart."[1]

THE **CHAPTER-OPENING CASE** highlights a lesson we discussed in Chapter 1. Specifically, a contingency approach toward management is more likely to produce positive results for individuals and organizations: A contingency approach calls for using management tools and leadership styles in a situationally appropriate manner instead of relying on "one best way" or "one size fits all." Lynn Tilton demonstrated this approach by changing the way she interacted with Ford's purchasing chief and employees at her paper plant in Maine. Tilton's unique leadership style clearly helped her to build the largest woman-owned business in America.

The overall goal of this chapter is to help you improve your leadership skills. After formally defining the term *leadership,* we focus on the following areas: (1) trait and behavioral approaches to leadership, (2) alternative situational theories of leadership, (3) the full range model of leadership, and (4) additional perspectives on leadership. Because there are many different leadership theories within each of these areas, it is impossible to discuss them all. This chapter reviews those theories with the most research support.

What Does Leadership Involve?

Disagreement about the definition of leadership stems from the fact that it involves a complex interaction among the leader, the followers, and the situation. For example, some researchers define leadership in terms of personality and physical traits, while others believe leadership is represented by a set of prescribed behaviors. In contrast, other researchers believe that leadership is a temporary role that can be filled by anyone. There is a common thread, however, among the different definitions of leadership. The common thread is social influence.

www.mcgrawhillconnect.com

Go to Connect for a self-assessment to determine how ready you are to assume a leadership role.

As the term is used in this chapter, ***leadership* is defined as "a social influence process in which the leader seeks the voluntary participation of subordinates in an effort to reach organizational goals."**[2] This definition implies that leadership involves more than wielding power and exercising authority and is exhibited at different levels. At the individual level, for example, leadership involves mentoring, coaching, inspiring, and motivating. Leaders build teams, create cohesion, and resolve conflict at the group level. Finally, leaders build culture and create change at the organizational level.[3]

There are two components of leadership missing from the above definition: the moral and follower perspectives. Leadership is not a moral concept. History is filled with examples of effective leaders who were killers, corrupt, and morally bankrupt. Barbara Kellerman, a leadership expert, commented on this notion by concluding: "Leaders are like the rest of us: trustworthy and deceitful, cowardly and brave, greedy and generous. To assume that all good leaders are good people is to be willfully blind to the reality of the human condition, and it more severely limits our scope for becoming more effective at leadership."[4] The point is that good leaders develop a keen sense of their strengths and weaknesses and build on their positive attributes.

Moreover, research on leadership has only recently begun to recognize that the expectations, attitudes, and behavior of followers also affect how well the presumed leader can lead. "Followership" is discussed in the last section of this chapter.

Trait and Behavioral Theories of Leadership

This section examines the two earliest approaches used to explain leadership. Trait theories focused on identifying the personal traits that differentiated leaders from followers. Behavioral theorists examined leadership from a different perspective. They tried to uncover the different kinds of leader behaviors that resulted in higher work-group performance. Both approaches to leadership can teach current and future managers valuable lessons about leading.

Trait Theory

Trait theory is the successor to what was called the "great man" theory of leadership. This approach was based on the assumption that leaders such as Abraham Lincoln, Martin Luther King Jr, or Mark Zuckerberg were born with some inborn ability to lead. In contrast, trait theorists believed that leadership traits were not innate, but could be developed through experience and learning. A *leader trait* **is a physical or personality characteristic that can be used to differentiate leaders from followers.**

Before World War II, hundreds of studies were conducted to pinpoint the traits of successful leaders. Dozens of leadership traits were identified. During the postwar period, however, enthusiasm was replaced by widespread criticism. Researchers simply were unable to uncover a consistent set of traits that accurately predicted which individuals became leaders in organizations.

What Traits Are Possessed by Effective Leaders? Early research demonstrated that five traits tended to differentiate leaders from average followers: (1) intelligence, (2) dominance, (3) self-confidence, (4) level of energy and activity, and (5) task-relevant knowledge.[5] More recent research on implicit leadership theory identified some additional traits. *Implicit leadership theory* **is based on the idea that people have beliefs about how leaders should behave and what they should do for their followers.** These beliefs are summarized in what is called a *leadership prototype.*[6] A *leadership prototype* **is a mental representation of the traits and behaviors that people believe are possessed by leaders.** It is important to understand the content of leadership prototypes because we tend to perceive that someone is a leader when he or she exhibits traits or behaviors that are consistent with our prototypes (recall our discussion of encoding and simplification in Chapter 4). Although past research demonstrated that people were perceived as leaders when they exhibited masculine-oriented traits and behaviors associated with masculinity, and dominance,[7] more recent studies showed an emphasis on more feminine traits and styles that emphasize empowerment, fairness, and supportiveness.[8] This change in prototypes bodes well for reducing bias and discrimination against women in leadership roles.

Two meta-analyses completed by Timothy Judge and his colleagues shed additional light on the question of traits. The first examined the relationship among the Big Five personality traits (see Table 5–1 for a review of these traits) and leadership emergence and effectiveness in 94 studies. Results revealed that extraversion was most consistently and positively related to both leadership emergence and effectiveness. Conscientiousness and openness to experience also were positively correlated with leadership effectiveness.[9] Judge's second meta-analysis involved 151 samples and demonstrated that intelligence was modestly related to leadership effectiveness. Judge concluded that personality is more important than intelligence when selecting leaders.[10]

If Judge's conclusion is accurate, then emotional intelligence should be associated with leadership effectiveness. Recall that *emotional intelligence,* which was discussed in Chapter 5, is the ability to manage oneself and one's relationships in mature and constructive ways. Given that leadership is an influence process, it should come as no surprise that emotional intelligence is predicted to be associated with leadership effectiveness. While many consultants contend that they have evidence to support this conclusion,[11] it has not been published in scientific journals. We agree with others who contend that there presently is not enough research published in organizational behavior (OB) journals to substantiate the conclusion that emotional intelligence is significantly associated with leadership effectiveness.[12]

> **BACK TO THE CHAPTER-OPENING CASE** To what extent does Lynn Tilton fit your prototype of an effective leader?

What Traits Are Possessed by Bad Leaders?   Barbara Kellerman set out to study hundreds of contemporary cases involving bad leadership and bad followers in search of the traits possessed by bad leaders. Her qualitative analysis uncovered seven key traits:[13]

1. *Incompetent.* The leader and at least some followers lack the will or skill (or both) to sustain effective action. With regard to at least one important leadership challenge, they do not create positive change. For example, James Cayne, former CEO of Bear Stearns, was reportedly off playing golf and bridge as the company collapsed.

2. *Rigid.* The leader and at least some followers are stiff and unyielding. Although they may be competent, they are unable or unwilling to adapt to new ideas, new information, or changing times. Nokia's CEO, Stephen Elop, acknowledged that the company's significant drop in earnings in 2010 was partially due to this trait. He sent a letter to employees stating, "While competitors poured flames on our market share, what happened at Nokia? We fell behind, we missed big trends, and we lost time. At that time, we thought we were making the right decisions; but, with the benefit of hindsight, we now find ourselves years behind." For example, a lack of action on the company's part has allowed Apple's market share of $300 and up phones to go from 25 percent in 2008 to 61 percent in 2010.[14]

Tiger Woods has won more times (71) on the PGA tour than any other active player. Sadly, his image was tarnished when he had multiple affairs while being married. His former wife also felt betrayed by his handlers who failed to influence Tiger's intemperate behavior.

3. *Intemperate.* The leader lacks self-control and is aided and abetted by followers who are unwilling or unable to effectively intervene. Tiger Woods represents a widely known example of someone who displayed this trait by not controlling his sexual urges.

4. *Callous.* The leader and at least some followers are uncaring and unkind. Ignored or discounted

are the needs, wants, and desires of most members of the group or organization, especially subordinates. Steve Jobs is known for parking his car in handicapped spaces and for being so callous that he brings employees to tears.

5. *Corrupt.* The leader and at least some followers lie, cheat, or steal to a degree that exceeds the norm. They put self-interest ahead of the public interest.

6. *Insular.* The leader and at least some followers minimize or disregard the health and welfare of "the other," that is, those outside the group or organization for which they are directly responsible. Philip Schoonover, former CEO of Circuit City, fired 3,400 of the most experienced employees because he thought they made too much money.

7. *Evil.* Evil leaders such as Adolf Hitler and Saddam Hussein encourage their followers to commit atrocities. They tend to use pain as an instrument of power. The harm done to men, women, and children is severe rather than slight. The harm can be physical, psychological, or both.[15]

The above traits are not the only ones associated with ineffective leadership. Additional negative traits include insensitivity to others, inability to get along with others, overemphasizing personal goals at the expense of others' success, arrogance, or hubris, focusing on self-promotion rather than on promotion of others, high need for control, building an empire by hoarding resources, making abrupt decisions without asking for input, and micromanaging others.[16]

Do Women and Men Display the Same Leadership Traits?   The increase of women in the workforce has generated much interest in understanding the similarities and differences in female and male leaders. Three separate meta-analyses and a series of studies conducted by consultants across the United States uncovered the following differences: (1) Men and women were seen as displaying more task and social leadership, respectively;[17] (2) women used a more democratic or participative style than men, and men used a more autocratic and directive style than women;[18] (3) men and women were equally assertive;[19] and (4) women executives, when rated by their peers, managers, and direct reports, scored higher than their male counterparts on a variety of effectiveness criteria.[20]

What Are the Takeaways from Trait Theory?   We can no longer afford to ignore the implications of leadership traits. Traits play a central role in how we perceive leaders, and they ultimately impact leadership effectiveness. This list of positive traits shown in Table 14–1, along with the negative traits identified by Kellerman, provides guidance regarding the leadership traits you should attempt to cultivate if you want to assume a leadership role in the future. Personality tests, which were discussed in Chapter 5, and other trait assessments can be used to evaluate your strengths and weaknesses vis-à-vis these traits: The website for this book contains a host of such tests that you can take for this purpose.

There are two organizational applications of trait theory. First, organizations may want to include personality and trait assessments into their selection and promotion processes. For example, Nina Brody, head of talent for Take Care Health Systems in Conshohocken, Pennsylvania, used an assessment tool to assist in hiring nurses, doctors, medical assistants, and others. She wanted to hire people with traits that fit or matched the organization's culture.[21] It is important to remember that this should only be done with valid measures of leadership traits. Second, management development programs can be used to build a pipeline of leadership talent. This is a particularly important recommendation in light of results from corporate surveys showing that the majority of companies do not possess adequate leadership talent to fill future needs.[22]

TABLE 14–1   Key Positive Leadership Traits

> **Task competence** (intelligence, knowledge, problem-solving skills)
>
> **Interpersonal competence** (ability to communicate, demonstrate caring and empathy)
>
> **Intuition**
>
> **Traits of character** (conscientiousness, discipline, moral reasoning, integrity, and honesty)
>
> **Biophysical traits** (physical fitness, hardiness, and energy level)
>
> **Personal traits** (self-confidence, sociability, self-monitoring, extraversion, self-regulating, and self-efficacy)

SOURCE: These traits were identified in B M Bass and R Bass, *The Bass Handbook of Leadership* (New York: Free Press, 2008), p 135.

For example, both small and large companies such as EMC, McDonald's, and KPMG send targeted groups of managers to developmental programs that include management classes, coaching sessions, trait assessments, and stretch assignments.[23]

> **BACK TO THE CHAPTER-OPENING CASE**   Which of the positive and negative leadership traits were displayed by Lynn Tilton?

Behavioral Styles Theory

This phase of leadership research began during World War II as part of an effort to develop better military leaders. It was an outgrowth of two events: the seeming inability of trait theory to explain leadership effectiveness and the human relations movement, an outgrowth of the Hawthorne studies. The thrust of early behavioral leadership theory was to focus on leader behavior, instead of on personality traits. It was believed that leader behavior directly affected work-group effectiveness. This led researchers to identify patterns of behavior (called leadership styles) that enabled leaders to effectively influence others.

The Ohio State Studies   Researchers at Ohio State University began by generating a list of behaviors exhibited by leaders. Ultimately, the Ohio State researchers concluded there were only two independent dimensions of leader behavior: consideration and initiating structure. *Consideration* **involves leader behavior associated with creating mutual respect or trust and focuses on a concern for group members' needs and desires.** *Initiating structure* **is leader behavior that organizes and defines what group members should be doing to maximize output.** These two dimensions of leader behavior were oriented at right angles to yield four behavioral styles of leadership: low structure–high consideration, high structure–high consideration, low structure–low consideration, and high structure–low consideration.

It initially was hypothesized that a high-structure–high-consideration style would be the one best style of leadership. Through the years, the effectiveness of the high–high

Peter Drucker's Tips for Improving Leadership Effectiveness

1. Determine what needs to be done.
2. Determine the right thing to do for the welfare of the entire enterprise or organization.
3. Develop action plans that specify desired results, probable restraints, future revisions, check-in points, and implications for how one should spend his or her time.
4. Take responsibility for decisions.
5. Take responsibility for communicating action plans and give people the information they need to get the job done.
6. Focus on opportunities rather than problems. Do not sweep problems under the rug, and treat change as an opportunity rather than a threat.
7. Run productive meetings. Different types of meetings require different forms of preparation and different results. Prepare accordingly.
8. Think and say "we" rather than "I." Consider the needs and opportunities of the organization before thinking of your own opportunities and needs.
9. Listen first, speak last.

style has been tested many times. Overall, results have been mixed and there has been very little research about these leader behaviors until just recently. Findings from a meta-analysis of 20,000 individuals demonstrated that consideration and initiating structure had a moderately strong, significant relationship with leadership outcomes. Results revealed that followers performed more effectively for structuring leaders even though they preferred considerate leaders.[24] All told, results do not support the idea that there is one best style of leadership, but they do confirm the importance of considerate and structuring leader behaviors. Follower satisfaction, motivation, and performance are significantly associated with these two leader behaviors. Future research is needed to incorporate them into more contemporary leadership theories.

University of Michigan Studies   As in the Ohio State studies, this research sought to identify behavioral differences between effective and ineffective leaders. Researchers identified two different styles of leadership: one was employee centered, the other was job centered. These behavioral styles parallel the consideration and initiating structure styles identified by the Ohio State group.

What Are the Takeaways from Behavioral Styles Theory?   By emphasizing leader *behavior*, something that is learned, the behavioral style approach makes it clear that leaders are made, not born. Given what we know about behavior shaping and model-based training, leader *behaviors* can be systematically improved and developed.[25]

Behavioral styles research also revealed that there is no one best style of leadership. The effectiveness of a particular leadership style depends on the situation at hand. For instance, employees prefer structure over consideration when faced with role ambiguity. Finally, Peter Drucker, an internationally renowned management expert and consultant, recommended a set of nine behaviors (see Skills & Best Practices above) managers can focus on to improve their leadership effectiveness. The first two practices provide the knowledge leaders need. The next four help leaders convert knowledge into effective action, and the following two ensure that the whole organization feels responsible and accountable. Drucker refers to the last recommendation as a managerial rule.

Situational Theories

Situational leadership theories grew out of an attempt to explain the inconsistent findings about traits and styles. ***Situational theories* propose that the effectiveness of a particular style of leader behavior depends on the situation.** As situations change, different styles become appropriate. This directly challenges the idea of one best style of leadership. Let us closely examine two alternative situational theories of leadership that reject the notion of one best leadership style.

Fiedler's Contingency Model

LO14.2

Fred Fiedler, an OB scholar, developed a situational model of leadership. It is the oldest and one of the most widely known models of leadership. Fiedler's model is based on the following assumption:

> The performance of a leader depends on two interrelated factors: (1) the degree to which the situation gives the leader control and influence—that is, the likelihood that the leader can successfully accomplish the job; and (2) the leader's basic motivation—that is, whether [the leader's] self-esteem depends primarily on accomplishing the task or on having close supportive relations with others.[26]

With respect to a leader's basic motivation, Fiedler believes that leaders are either task motivated or relationship motivated. These basic motivations are similar to initiating structure/concern for production and consideration/concern for people.

Fiedler's theory also is based on the premise that leaders have one dominant leadership style that is resistant to change. He suggests that leaders must learn to manipulate or influence the leadership situation in order to create a "match" between their leadership style and the amount of control within the situation at hand. After discussing the components of situational control and the leadership matching process, we review relevant research and managerial implications.[27]

Situational Control   Situational control refers to the amount of control and influence the leader has in her or his immediate work environment. Situational control ranges from high to low. High control implies that the leader's decisions will produce predictable results because the leader has the ability to influence work outcomes. Low control implies that the leader's decisions may not influence work outcomes because the leader has very little influence. There are three dimensions of situational control: leader–member relations, task structure, and position power. These dimensions vary independently, forming eight combinations of situational control (see Figure 14–1).

The three dimensions of situational control are defined as follows:

- *Leader–member relations* reflect the extent to which the leader has the support, loyalty, and trust of the work group.

- *Task structure* is concerned with the amount of structure contained within tasks performed by the work group.

- *Position power* refers to the degree to which the leader has formal power to reward, punish, or otherwise obtain compliance from employees.

Representation of Fiedler's Contingency Model   FIGURE 14–1

Situational control	High control situations			Moderate control situations				Low control situations
Leader–member relations	Good	Good	Good	Good	Poor	Poor	Poor	Poor
Task structure	High	High	Low	Low	High	High	Low	Low
Position power	Strong	Weak	Strong	Weak	Strong	Weak	Strong	Weak
Situation	I	II	III	IV	V	VI	VII	VIII
Optimal leadership style	**Task-motivated leadership**			**Relationship-motivated leadership**				**Task-motivated leadership**

SOURCE: Adapted from F E Fiedler, "Situational Control and a Dynamic Theory of Leadership," in *Managerial Control and Organizational Democracy,* eds B King, S Streufert, and F E Fiedler (New York: John Wiley & Sons, 1978), p 114.

Linking Leadership Motivation and Situational Control   Fiedler's complete contingency model is presented in Figure 14–1. The last row under the Situational Control column shows that there are eight different leadership situations. Each situation represents a unique combination of leader–member relations, task structure, and position power. Situations I, II, and III represent high control situations. Figure 14–1 shows that task-motivated leaders are hypothesized to be most effective in situations of high control. Under conditions of moderate control (situations IV, V, VI, and VII), relationship-motivated leaders are expected to be more effective. Finally, the results orientation of task-motivated leaders is predicted to be more effective under the condition of very low control (situation VIII).

Takeaways from Fiedler's Model   Although research only provides partial support for this model,[28] there are three key takeaways from Fiedler's model. First, this model emphasizes the point that leadership effectiveness goes beyond traits and behaviors. It is a function of the fit between a leader's style and the situational demands at hand. As a case in point, a team of researchers examined the effectiveness of 20 senior-level managers from GE who left the company for other positions. The researchers concluded that

> not all managers are equally suited to all business situations. The strategic skills required to control costs in the face of fierce competition are not the same as those required to improve the top line in a rapidly growing business or balance investment against cash flow to survive in a highly cyclical business. . . . We weren't surprised to find that relevant industry experience had a positive impact on performance in a new job, but that these skills didn't transfer to a new industry.[29]

This study leads to the conclusion that organizations should attempt to hire or promote people whose leadership styles *fit* or *match* situational demands.

Second, this model explains why some people are successful in some situations and not in others. For example, the same hard-driving leadership style that led to Jack Griffin's success at Meredith Corporation resulted in his departure at Time Warner. His style and personality clashed with the culture and norms at Time Warner.[30] If a manager is failing in a certain context, management should consider moving the individual to another situation. Don't give up on a high-potential person simply because he or she was a poor leader in one context. Finally, leaders need to modify their style to fit a situation. Leadership styles are not universally effective.

Path–Goal Theory

LO14.3

Path–goal theory was originally proposed by Robert House in the 1970s.[31] He developed a model that describes how leadership effectiveness is influenced by the interaction between four leadership styles (directive, supportive, participative, and achievement oriented) and a variety of contingency factors. **Contingency factors are situational variables that cause one style of leadership to be more effective than another.** Path–goal theory has two groups of contingency variables. They are employee characteristics and environmental factors. Five important employee characteristics are locus of control, task ability, need for achievement, experience, and need for clarity. Two relevant environmental factors are task structure (independent versus interdependent tasks) and work-group dynamics. In order to gain a better understanding of how these contingency factors influence leadership effectiveness, we illustratively consider locus of control (see Chapter 5), task ability and experience, and task structure.

Employees with an internal locus of control are more likely to prefer participative or achievement-oriented leadership because they believe they have control over the work environment. Such individuals are unlikely to be satisfied with directive leader behaviors that exert additional control over their activities. In contrast, employees with an external locus tend to view the environment as uncontrollable, thereby preferring the structure provided by supportive or directive leadership. An employee with high task ability and experience is less apt to need additional direction and thus would respond negatively to directive leadership. This person is more likely to be motivated and satisfied by participative and achievement-oriented leadership. Oppositely, an inexperienced employee would find achievement-oriented leadership overwhelming as he or she confronts challenges associated with learning a new job. Supportive and directive leadership would be helpful in this situation. Finally, directive and supportive leadership should help employees experiencing role ambiguity. However, directive leadership is likely to frustrate employees working on routine and simple tasks. Supportive leadership is most useful in this context.

There have been about 50 studies testing various predictions derived from House's original model. Results have been mixed, with some studies supporting the theory and others not.[32] House thus proposed a new version of path–goal theory in 1996 based on these results and the accumulation of new knowledge about OB.

A Reformulated Theory   The revised theory is presented in Figure 14–2.[33] There are three key changes in the new theory. First, House now believes that leadership is more complex and involves a greater variety of leader behavior. He thus identifies eight categories of leadership styles or behavior (see Table 14–2). The need for an expanded list of leader behaviors is supported by current research and descriptions of business leaders.

A General Representation of House's Revised Path–Goal Theory   FIGURE 14–2

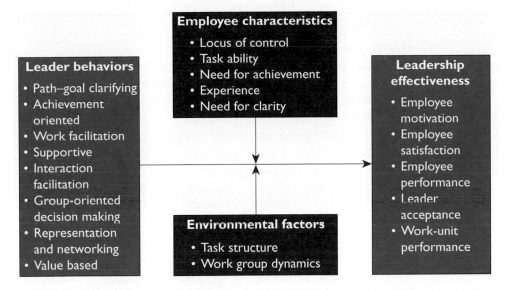

The second key change involves the role of intrinsic motivation (discussed in Chapter 6) and empowerment (discussed in Chapter 13) in influencing leadership effectiveness. House places much more emphasis on the need for leaders to foster intrinsic motivation through empowerment. Shared leadership represents the final change in the revised theory. That is, path–goal theory is based on the premise that an employee does not have to be a supervisor or manager to engage in leader behavior. Rather, House believes that leadership is shared among all employees within an organization. More is said about shared leadership in the final section of this chapter.

Takeaways from House's Theory   There are not enough direct tests of House's revised path–goal theory using appropriate research methods and statistical procedures to draw overall conclusions. Nonetheless, there are three important takeaways from this theory. First, effective leaders possess and use more than one style of leadership. Managers are encouraged to familiarize themselves with the different categories of leader behavior outlined in path–goal theory and to try new behaviors when the situation calls for them. Consider the leader behaviors exhibited by Bob Iger, CEO of Walt Disney Company. He prefers to work behind the scenes and does not host any Disney TV productions. He is known to say hello to everyone he encounters on the Disney campus and participates in a Disney team that competes in the Malibu, California, triathlon to raise money for charity. He loves to study operational statistics and is very interested in studying and using consumers' attitudes to make decisions. Since taking over the helm at Disney, Iger patched up the rocky relationship between Pixar and Disney and ultimately purchased Pixar for $7 billion. He also resolved several contentious issues with former director Roy Disney and Comcast. Iger empowers his employees and allows them plenty of freedom to make decisions. At that same time, he holds people accountable for their work.[34] This example illustrates that Iger uses path–goal clarifying behaviors, achievement-oriented behaviors, work-facilitation behaviors, supportive behaviors, interaction-facilitation behaviors, and representation and networking behaviors.

www.mcgrawhillconnect.com

Go to Connect for an interactive exercise to test your knowledge of House's Revised Path-Goal Theory.

TABLE 14–2   Categories of Leader Behavior within the Revised Path-Goal Theory

Category of Leader Behavior	Description of Leader Behaviors
Path–goal clarifying behaviors	Clarifying employees' performance goals; providing guidance on how employees can complete tasks; clarifying performance standards and expectations; use of positive and negative rewards contingent on performance
Achievement-oriented behaviors	Setting challenging goals; emphasizing excellence; demonstrating confidence in employees' abilities
Work-facilitation behaviors	Planning, scheduling, organizing, and coordinating work; providing mentoring, coaching, counseling, and feedback to assist employees in developing their skills; eliminating roadblocks; providing resources; empowering employees to take actions and make decisions
Supportive behaviors	Showing concern for the well-being and needs of employees; being friendly and approachable; treating employees as equals
Interaction facilitation behaviors	Resolving disputes; facilitating communication; encouraging the sharing of minority opinions; emphasizing collaboration and teamwork; encouraging close relationships among employees
Group-oriented decision-making behaviors	Posing problems rather than solutions to the work group; encouraging group members to participate in decision making; providing necessary information to the group for analysis; involving knowledgeable employees in decision making
Representation and networking behaviors	Presenting the work group in a positive light to others; maintaining positive relationships with influential others; participating in organizationwide social functions and ceremonies; doing unconditional favors for others
Value-based behaviors	Establishing a vision, displaying passion for it, and supporting its accomplishment; demonstrating self-confidence; communicating high-performance expectations and confidence in others' abilities to meet their goals; giving frequent positive feedback

SOURCE: Descriptions were adapted from R J House, "Path–Goal Theory of Leadership: Lessons, Legacy, and a Reformulated Theory," *Leadership Quarterly*, 1996, pp 323–52.

Second, the theory offers specific suggestions for how leaders can help employees. Leaders are encouraged to clarify the paths to goal accomplishment and to remove any obstacles that may impair an employee's ability to achieve his or her goals. The Skills & Best Practices feature on page 375 illustrates how the basic principles of this theory are used by Cascade Engineering in Grand Rapids, Michigan, to help transition welfare recipients to gainful employment. Cascade employs 900 people, and 40 are Welfare-to-Career participants. Cascade is implementing its third welfare to work program. The first two failed, and the current one has significantly reduced the turnover of participants. Finally, a small set of employee characteristics (i.e., ability, experience, and need for independence) and environmental factors (task characteristics of autonomy, variety, and significance) are relevant contingency factors.[35] Managers are advised to modify their leadership style to fit these various employee and task characteristics.

Cascade Engineering Uses the Principles of Path-Goal Theory to Help People Transition from Welfare to a Career

The Welfare-to-Career program has five key components.

1. A government case worker is on-site to assist and support participants.
2. An assessment tool is used to identify and remove barriers to employment.
3. Training and onboarding are used to help participants understand work-related norms and the "hidden rules" of different working classes (e.g., poverty vs. middle class).
4. A specific career track is used to motivate workers to develop their skills.
5. A culture grounded in the values of respect and dignity is reinforced.

"Michigan Department of Human Services caseworker Joyce Gutierrez-Marsh has an office on site. She explains that while many employees lose cash assistance as their incomes rise, they receive food stamps, child care assistance and Medicaid for children and continue to be her clients. She identifies barriers to work attendance and channels clients into assistance programs to overcome those barriers."

The most common barriers are lack of child care and transportation. To accommodate these barriers, Cascade changed its attendance policy to include sick children as a legitimate reason to miss work. For transportation, the company first appealed to local government officials to extend the bus route because it stopped a quarter-mile away. The route was extended and Welfare-to-Career participants are eligible for 90 days of free bus travel. The company also created a partnership with a taxi company to help employees get home when they were asked to go home at odd times. Supervisors call the cab company and the company pays the bill. Welfare-to-Career employees can also "take advantage of other programs, such as a $900 annual car repair benefit or a one-time $2,000 car purchase benefit."

SOURCE: Excerpted and derived from K Tyler, "From Dependence to Self-Sufficiency," *HR Magazine*, September 2010, pp 35–39.

Applying Situational Theories

Although researchers and practitioners support the logic of situational leadership, the practical application of such theories has not been clearly developed. A team of researchers thus attempted to resolve this problem by proposing a general strategy that managers can use across a variety of situations. The general strategy contains five steps.[36] We explain how to implement the steps by using the examples of a head coach of a sports team and a sales manager.

1. *Identify important outcomes.* This step entails a determination of the goals the leader is trying to achieve. For example, the head coach may have goals "to win" or "avoid injury to key players" whereas a sales manager's goals might be to "increase sales by 10%" or "decrease customers' complaints." It is important to identify the key goals that exist at a specific point in time.

2. *Identify relevant leadership types/behaviors.* This step requires the manager to identify the specific types of behaviors that may be appropriate for the situation at hand. The list of behaviors shown in Table 14–2 is a good starting point. A head coach in a championship game, for instance, might focus on achievement-oriented and work-facilitation behaviors. In contrast, a sales manager might find path–goal clarifying, work-facilitation, and supportive behaviors more

Eric Schmidt, former CEO of Google, uses situational leadership in these two photos. On the left, he uses his presentation skills and networking behaviors to communicate to global media executives in Abu Dhabi. On the right, he relies more on consideration and supportive behaviors while talking with an individual. Effective leaders change their behavior depending on the situation at hand.

relevant for the sales team. Don't try to use all available leadership behaviors. Rather, select the one or two that appear most helpful.

3. *Identify situational conditions.* Fiedler's contingency theory and House's path–goal theory both identify a set of potential contingency factors to consider. That said, there may be other practical considerations. For example, a star quarterback on a football team may be injured, which might require the team to adopt a different strategy toward winning the game. Similarly, managing a virtual sales team from around the world will affect the types of leadership that are most effective in this context.

4. *Match leadership to the conditions at hand.* This is the step in which research cannot provide conclusive recommendations because there simply are too many possible situational conditions. This means that you should use your knowledge about organizational behavior to determine the best match between leadership styles/behaviors and the situation at hand. The coach whose star quarterback is injured might use supportive and values-based behaviors to instill confidence that the team can win with a different quarterback. Our virtual sales manager also might find it useful to use the empowering leadership associated with work-facilitation behaviors (see Table 14–2) and to avoid directive leadership.

5. *Determine how to make the match.* It's now time to implement the leadership style or behaviors you determined were most appropriate in step 4. There are two basic approaches you can use according to contingency theory and House's path–goal theory. You can either change the person in the leadership role or the leader can change his or her style/behavior. Returning to our examples, it is not possible to change the head coach in a championship game. This means that the head coach needs to change his or her style/behavior. In contrast, the organization employing the sales manager might move him or her to another position because the individual is too directive and does not like to empower others. Alternatively, the sales manager could change his/her behavior.

> **BACK TO THE CHAPTER-OPENING CASE**   To what extent does Lynn Tilton display situational approaches toward leadership? Explain.

Caveat When Applying Situational Theories

Can you think of any downside to applying situational theories? Interestingly, they exist. A team of OB researchers recently tested the possibility that there are unintended negative consequences when managers use a situational approach with members from a team. Study findings revealed that treating group members differently resulted in some employees feeling that they were not among the leader's "in-group" (i.e., a partnership characterized by mutual trust, respect, and liking): The concept of in-groups and out-groups is discussed later in the chapter. These negative feelings in turn had a counterproductive effect on employees' self-efficacy and subsequent group performance. The point to remember is that leaders of teams need to be careful when treating individual team members differently. There are potential pros and cons to the application of situational theories in a team context.[37]

The Full-range Model of Leadership: From Laissez-faire to Transformational Leadership

One of the most recent approaches to leadership is referred to as a full-range model of leadership. The authors of this theory, Bernard Bass and Bruce Avolio, proposed that leadership behavior varied along a continuum from laissez-faire leadership (i.e., a general failure to take responsibility for leading) to transactional leadership to transformational leadership.[38] Examples of laissez-faire leadership include avoiding conflict, surfing the Internet during work, failing to assist employees in setting performance goals, failing to give performance feedback, or being so hands-off that employees have little idea about what they should be doing. Of course, laissez-faire leadership is a terrible way for any manager to behave and should be avoided. In contrast, transactional and transformational leadership are both positively related to a variety of employee attitudes and behaviors and represent different aspects of being a good leader. Let us consider these two important dimensions of leadership.

LO14.4

Transactional leadership **focuses on clarifying employees' role and task requirements and providing followers with positive and negative rewards contingent on performance.** Further, transactional leadership encompasses the fundamental managerial activities of setting goals, monitoring progress toward goal achievement, and rewarding and punishing people for their level of goal accomplishment.[39] You can see from this description that transactional leadership is based on using rewards and punishment to drive motivation and performance. Consider how Stephen Greer, founder of Hartwell Pacific, a scrap metal recycling business in Asia, used transactional leadership to combat several million dollars in fraud and theft from his employees in Mexico and his operations in Asia.

For Hartwell Pacific, the biggest strain was a lack of control systems. Greer was so focused on new markets that he glossed over niceties like accounting procedures, inventory audits, and reference checks for new hires. . . .

When he finally realized the extent of the fraud in his nascent empire, Greer pulled back, eventually liquidating the operation in Mexico. He also instituted a system of close oversight. He appointed local finance managers who reported directly to headquarters, creating checks and balances on local general managers. He started requiring three signatories for all company checks. He installed metal detectors to prevent theft. Once a month, the local managers flew to headquarters, where they compared revenues, costs, and overall performance. If one plant seemed to be overpaying for supplies, or if revenues seemed out of line with inventory, Greer began asking hard questions—ones he should have been asking all along.[40]

Jamie Dimon, CEO of J P Morgan Chase, is known to use both transactional and transformational leadership. He was instrumental in working with government officials during the 2009–10 economic crisis.

In contrast, ***transformational leaders*** **"engender trust, seek to develop leadership in others, exhibit self-sacrifice and serve as moral agents, focusing themselves and followers on objectives that transcend the more immediate needs of the work group."**[41] Transformational leaders can produce significant organizational change and results because this form of leadership fosters higher levels of employee engagement, trust, and loyalty from followers than does transactional leadership. That said, however, it is important to note that transactional leadership is an essential prerequisite to effective leadership, and that the best leaders learn to display both transactional and transformational leadership to various degrees. In support of this proposition, research reveals that transformational leadership leads to superior performance when it "augments" or adds to transactional leadership.[42] General Electric's CEO Jeff Immelt represents a good example of transformational leadership. The example below illustrates how Immelt is using it as a vehicle to improve the leadership talent within the company.

Immelt intends to spend this year exploring new ideas, which he describes as "wallowing in it," to decide how GE should shape and measure its leaders. He has solicited management suggestions from a broad range of organizations—from Google to China's Communist Party—and sent 30 of his top people to more than 100 companies worldwide. He's holding monthly dinners with 10 executives and an external "thought leader" to debate leadership. He launched a pilot program to bring in personal coaches for high-potential talent, a practice that GE once reserved mainly for those in need of remedial work. To increase exposure to the world beyond GE, Immelt is even reconsidering the age-old rule that employees can't sit on corporate boards. "I think about it all the time," he says. "You have to be willing to change when it makes sense."[43]

We now turn our attention to examining the process by which transformational leadership influences followers.

How Does Transformational Leadership Transform Followers?

Transformational leaders transform followers by creating changes in their goals, values, needs, beliefs, and aspirations. They accomplish this transformation by appealing to followers' self-concepts—namely their values and personal identity. Figure 14–3 presents a model of how leaders accomplish this transformation process.

Figure 14–3 shows that transformational leader behavior is first influenced by various individual and organizational characteristics. For example, research reveals that transformational leaders tend to have personalities that are more extraverted, agreeable, and proactive and less neurotic than nontransformational leaders. They also have higher emotional intelligence.[44] Female leaders also use transformational leadership more than male leaders.[45] It is important to note, however, that the relationship between personality traits and transformational leadership is relatively weak. This suggests that transformational leadership is less traitlike and more susceptible to managerial influence. Finally, Figure 14–3 shows that organizational culture influences the extent to which leaders are transformational. Cultures that are adaptive and flexible rather than rigid and bureaucratic are more likely to create environments that foster the opportunity for transformational leadership to be exhibited.

Transformational leaders engage in four key sets of leader behavior (see Figure 14–3).[46] The first set, referred to as *inspirational motivation,* involves establishing an attractive vision of the future, the use of emotional arguments, and exhibition of optimism and

FIGURE 14–3   A Transformational Model of Leadership

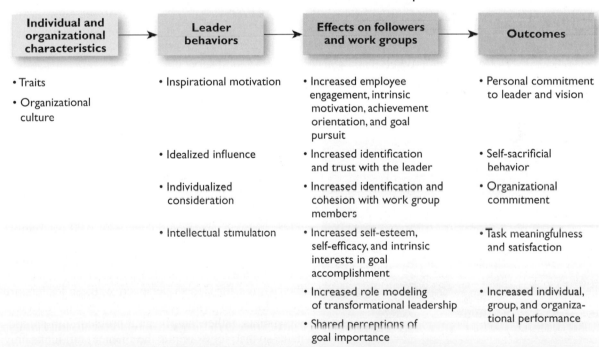

SOURCE: Based in part on D A Waldman and F J Yammarino, "CEO Charismatic Leadership: Levels of Management and Levels of Analysis Effects," *Academy of Management Review,* April 1999, pp 266–85; B Shamir, R J House, and M B Arthur, "The Motivational Effects of Charismatic Leadership: A Self-Concept Based Theory," *Organization Science,* November 1993, pp 577–94; and A E Colbert, A L Kristof-Brown, B H Bradley, and M R Barrick, "CEO Transformational Leadership: The Role of Goal Importance Congruence in Top Management Teams," *Academy of Management Journal,* February 2008, pp 81–96.

enthusiasm. A vision is "a realistic, credible, attractive future for your organization."[47] According to Burt Nanus, a leadership expert, the "right" vision unleashes human potential because it serves as a beacon of hope and common purpose. It does this by attracting commitment, energizing workers, creating meaning in employees' lives, establishing a standard of excellence, promoting high ideals, and bridging the gap between an organization's present problems and its future goals and aspirations. Carl-Henric Svanberg, current chairman of British Petroleum and former CEO of Ericsson, understands the importance of establishing an organization's vision. He concluded that in large organizations "you can't just tell everyone, 'Turn left and work fast,' You have to share with them the vision you want to accomplish and get everybody on board and enthusiastic about it. When you get them to march in the same direction, you can really move mountains together."[48]

Idealized influence, the second set of leader behaviors, includes behaviors such as sacrificing for the good of the group, being a role model, and displaying high ethical standards. Displaying ethical standards is very important because employees are more likely to report the questionable behavior of others when they believe that their boss sends positive messages about ethics.[49] Managers can send these positive messages by avoiding the barriers to an ethical work environment discussed in the Skills & Best Practices feature shown on page 381.

The third set, *individualized consideration,* entails behaviors associated with providing support, encouragement, empowerment, and coaching to employees. These behaviors necessitate that leaders pay special attention to the needs of their followers and search for ways to help people develop and grow. You can do this by spending time talking with people about their interests and by identifying new learning opportunities for them. For example, Jeff Immelt, CEO of General Electric, invites one of the company's officers to his home every other Friday for a casual evening of drinks, some laughs, dinner, and conversation about world events. On Saturday, they get back together to talk about the individual's career. This "high touch" approach is a great way for Immelt to get to know his employees and to serve as a mentor.[50] You can also protect people from time-wasting meetings and interruptions while fostering a culture that allows people to feel safe in speaking up and disagreeing with each other and the boss. Showing interest in people by remembering their names and previous conversations are other simple ways in which you can demonstrate individualized consideration.[51]

President Obama selected Jeff Immelt, General Electric's Chairman and CEO, to serve as an economic advisor regarding job creation. Time will tell whether Immelt's use of transformational leadership can help the country.

Intellectual stimulation, the fourth set of leadership behaviors, involves behaviors that encourage employees to question the status quo and to seek innovative and creative solutions to organizational problems. These behaviors are consistent with the finding by management expert Roger Martin that successful leaders tend to see problems and opportunities in all their complexity, rather than as either-or choices. In their search for a fresh perspective, these leaders are more likely to bring together people with different viewpoints, rather than break a problem into components so that, for example, the finance staff looks only at the financial implications while the sales managers look only for ways to push their product to new customers.[52]

Barriers to an Ethical Work Environment

	Ill-Conceived Goals	Motivated Blindness	Indirect Blindness	The Slippery Slope	Overvaluing Outcomes
Description	We set goals and incentives to promote a desired behavior, but they encourage a negative one.	We overlook the unethical behavior of others when it's in our interest to remain ignorant.	We hold others less accountable for unethical behavior when it's carried out through third parties.	We are less able to see others' unethical behavior when it develops gradually.	We give a pass to unethical behavior if the outcome is good.
Example	The pressure to maximize billable hours in accounting, consulting, and law firms leads to unconscious padding.	Baseball officials failed to notice they'd created conditions that encouraged steroid use.	A drug company deflects attention from a price increase by selling rights to another company, which imposes the increase.	Auditors may be more likely to accept a client firm's questionable financial statements if infractions have accrued over time.	A researcher whose fraudulent clinical trial saves lives is considered more ethical than the one whose fraudulent trial leads to deaths.
Remedies	Brainstorm unintended consequences when devising goals and incentives. Consider alternative goals that may be more important to reward.	Root out conflicts of interest. Simply being aware of them doesn't necessarily reduce their negative effect on decision making.	When handing off or outsourcing work, ask whether the assignment might invite unethical behavior and take ownership of the implications.	Be alert for even trivial ethical infractions and address them immediately. Investigate whether a change in behavior has occurred.	Examine both "good" and "bad" decisions for their ethical implications. Reward solid decision processes, not just good outcomes.

SOURCE. M H Bazerman and A E Tenbrunsel, "Ethical Breakdowns," *Harvard Business Review*, April 2011, p 63.

Research and Managerial Implications

Components of the transformational model of leadership have been the most widely researched leadership topic over the last decade. Overall, relationships outlined in Figure 14–3 generally were supported by previous research. For example, a meta-analysis of 49 studies indicated that transformational leadership was positively associated with measures of leadership effectiveness and employees' job satisfaction.[53] At the

> **BACK TO THE CHAPTER-OPENING CASE** Is Lynn Tilton more of a transactional or transformational leader?
> Which of the four types of transformational leadership behavior are displayed by Tilton? Provide examples.

organizational level, a second meta-analysis demonstrated that transformational leadership was positively correlated with organizational measures of effectiveness.[54]

Support for transformational leadership underscores six important managerial implications. First, the establishment of a positive vision of the future—inspirational motivation—should be considered a first step at applying transformational leadership. Why? Because the vision represents a long-term goal, and it is important for leaders to begin their influence attempts by gaining agreement and consensus about where the team or organization is headed. It also is critical to widely communicate the vision among the team or entire organization.[55] People can't get excited about something they don't know about or don't understand. Second, the best leaders are not just transformational; they are both transactional and transformational, and they avoid a laissez-faire or "wait-and-see" style.[56] We encourage you to use both transactional and transformational leadership.

Third, transformational leadership not only affects individual-level outcomes like job satisfaction, organizational commitment, and performance, but it also influences group dynamics and group-level outcomes.[57] Managers can thus use the four types of transformational leadership shown in Figure 14–3 as a vehicle to improve group dynamics and work-unit outcomes. This is important in today's organizations because most employees do not work in isolation. Rather, people tend to rely on the input and collaboration of others, and many organizations are structured around teams. The key point to remember is that transformational leadership transforms individuals as well as teams and work groups. We encourage you to use this to your advantage.

Fourth, transformational leadership works virtually. If you lead geographically dispersed people, then it is important to focus on how you can display the four transformational leader behaviors in your emails, tweets, webinars, and conference calls.[58] Fifth, employees at any level in an organization can be trained to be more transactional and transformational.[59] This reinforces the organizational value of developing and rolling out a combination of transactional and transformational leadership training for all employees. These programs, however, should be based on an overall corporate philosophy that constitutes the foundation of leadership development.

Finally, transformational leaders can be ethical or unethical. Whereas ethical transformational leaders enable employees to enhance their self-concepts, unethical ones select or produce obedient, dependent, and compliant followers. Top management can create and maintain ethical transformational leadership by

1. Creating and enforcing a clearly stated code of ethics.
2. Recruiting, selecting, and promoting people who display ethical behavior.
3. Developing performance expectations around the treatment of employees—these expectations can then be assessed in the performance appraisal process.
4. Training employees to value diversity.
5. Identifying, rewarding, and publicly praising employees who exemplify high moral conduct.[60]

Additional Perspectives on Leadership

This section examines four additional perspectives to leadership: leader–member exchange theory, shared leadership, servant-leadership, and a follower perspective. We spend more time discussing leader–member exchange theory because it has been more thoroughly investigated.

The Leader–Member Exchange Model of Leadership

The leader–member exchange (LMX) model of leadership revolves around the development of dyadic relationships between managers and their direct reports. This model is quite different from those previously discussed in that it focuses on the quality of relationships between managers and subordinates as opposed to the behaviors or traits of either leaders or followers. It also is different in that it does not assume that leader behavior is characterized by a stable or average leadership style as does behavioral styles theory and Fiedler's contingency theory. In other words, these models assume a leader treats all employees in about the same way. In contrast, the LMX model is based on the assumption that leaders develop unique one-to-one relationships with each of the people reporting to them. Behavioral scientists call this sort of relationship a *vertical dyad*. The forming of vertical dyads is said to be a naturally occurring process, resulting from the leader's attempt to delegate and assign work roles. As a result of this process, two distinct types of leader–member exchange relationships are expected to evolve.[61]

 LO14.5

One type of leader–member exchange is called the *in-group exchange*. **In this relationship, leaders and followers develop a partnership characterized by reciprocal influence, mutual trust, respect and liking, and a sense of common fates.** In the second type of exchange, referred to as an *out-group exchange,* **leaders are characterized as overseers who fail to create a sense of mutual trust, respect, or common fate.**[62]

Research Findings   If the leader–member exchange model is correct, there should be a significant relationship between the type of leader–member exchange and job-related outcomes. Research supports this prediction. For example, a positive leader–member exchange was positively associated with job satisfaction, intentions to stay employed at the company, job performance, commitment to organizational change, trust between managers and employees, procedural and distributive justice (recall our discussion in Chapter 7), willingness to help coworkers, and satisfaction with leadership.[63] Results from a recent meta-analysis of 50 studies also revealed a moderately strong, positive relationship between LMX and organizational citizenship behaviors—recall our discussion in Chapter 6.[64] You can see that a positive LMX is associated with a host of positive outcomes. Finally, studies also have identified a variety of variables that influence the quality of an LMX. For example, LMX was positively related to the extent to which employees identified with their managers and the breadth of a leader's social networks within the organization.[65]

Managerial Implications   There are three important implications associated with the LMX model of leadership. First, leaders are encouraged to establish high-performance expectations for all of their direct reports because setting high-performance standards fosters high-quality LMXs. Second, because personality and demographic similarity between leaders and followers is associated with higher LMXs, managers need to be careful that they don't create a homogeneous work environment in the spirit of having positive relationships with their direct reports. Our discussion of diversity in Chapter 4 clearly documented that there are many positive benefits of having a diverse workforce. The third implication pertains to those of us who find ourselves in a poor LMX. Before providing advice about what to do in this situation, we would like you to assess the quality of your current leader–member exchange. The Hands-On Exercise on page 385 contains a measure of leader–member exchange that segments an LMX into four subdimensions: mutual affection, loyalty, contribution to work activities, and professional respect.

What is the overall quality of your LMX? Do you agree with this assessment? Which subdimensions are high and low? If your overall LMX and associated subdimensions are all high, you should be in a very good situation with respect to the relationship between you and your manager. Having a low LMX overall score or a low dimensional score, however, reveals that part of the relationship with your manager may need improvement. A management consultant offers the following tips for improving the quality of leader–member exchanges.[66]

1. Stay focused on your department's goals and remain positive about your ability to accomplish your goals. An unsupportive boss is just another obstacle to be overcome.

2. Do not fall prey to feeling powerless, and empower yourself to get things done.

3. Exercise the power you have by focusing on circumstances you can control and avoid dwelling on circumstances you cannot control.

4. Work on improving your relationship with your manager. Begin by examining the level of trust between the two of you and then try to improve it by frequently and effectively communicating. You can also increase trust by following through on your commitments and achieving your goals.

5. Use an authentic, respectful, and assertive approach to resolve differences with your manager. It also is useful to use a problem-solving approach when disagreements arise.

Shared Leadership

A pair of OB scholars noted that "there is some speculation, and some preliminary evidence, to suggest that concentration of leadership in a single chain of command may be less optimal than shared leadership responsibility among two or more individuals in certain task environments."[67] This perspective is quite different from the previous theories and models discussed in this chapter, which assume that leadership is a vertical, downward-flowing process. In contrast, the notion of shared leadership is based on the idea that people need to share information and collaborate to get things done at work. This, in turn, underscores the need for employees to adopt a horizontal process of influence or leadership. ***Shared leadership* entails a simultaneous, ongoing, mutual influence process in which individuals share responsibility for leading regardless of formal roles and titles.**

HANDS-ON EXERCISE

Assessing Your Leader–Member Exchange

INSTRUCTIONS: For each of the items shown below, use the following scale to circle the answer that best represents how you feel about the relationship between you and your current manager or supervisor. If you are not currently working, complete the survey by thinking about a previous manager. Remember, there are no right or wrong answers. After circling a response for each of the 12 items, use the scoring key to compute scores for the subdimensions within your leader–member exchange.

1 = Strongly disagree
2 = Disagree
3 = Neither agree nor disagree
4 = Agree
5 = Strongly agree

1. I like my supervisor very much as a person.   1 2 3 4 5

2. My supervisor is the kind of person one would like to have as a friend.   1 2 3 4 5

3. My supervisor is a lot of fun to work with.   1 2 3 4 5

4. My supervisor defends my work actions to a superior, even without complete knowledge of the issue in question.   1 2 3 4 5

5. My supervisor would come to my defense if I were "attacked" by others.   1 2 3 4 5

6. My supervisor would defend me to others in the organization if I made an honest mistake.   1 2 3 4 5

7. I do work for my supervisor that goes beyond what is specified in my job description.   1 2 3 4 5

8. I am willing to apply extra efforts, beyond those normally required, to meet my supervisor's work goals.   1 2 3 4 5

9. I do not mind working my hardest for my supervisor.   1 2 3 4 5

10. I am impressed with my supervisor's knowledge of his or her job.   1 2 3 4 5

11. I respect my supervisor's knowledge of and competence on the job.   1 2 3 4 5

12. I admire my supervisor's professional skills.   1 2 3 4 5

SCORING KEY

Mutual affection (add items 1–3)
Loyalty (add items 4–6)
Contribution to work activities (add items 7–9)
Professional respect (add items 10–12)
Overall score (add all 12 items)

ARBITRARY NORMS

Low mutual affection = 3–9
High mutual affection = 10–15
Low loyalty = 3–9
High loyalty = 10–15
Low contribution to work activities = 3–9
High contribution to work activities = 10–15
Low professional respect = 3–9
High professional respect = 10–15
Low overall leader–member exchange = 12–38
High overall leader–member exchange = 39–60

SOURCES: From R C Liden and J M Maslyn, "Multidimensionality of Leader-Member Exchange: An Empirical Assessment Through Scale Development," *Journal of Management*, Vol. 24, No. 1, p. 56. Copyright © 1998. Reproduced with permission of Sage Publications, Inc. via Copyright Clearance Center.

Shared leadership is most likely to be needed when people work in teams, when people are involved in complex projects, and when people are doing knowledge work—work that requires voluntary contributions of intellectual capital by skilled professionals.[68] Interestingly, a group of management professors points out that these are the conditions in which leaders direct teams (often called guilds) in online role-playing games.[69] Interviews with and observations of people who excel as leaders in these games showed that they build expertise at assessing complex situations, making speedy decisions, taking risks, and moving in and out of leadership roles as the situation's needs match their capabilities and willingness to step forward or accept the group's nomination. The researchers found that this type of shared leadership was especially effective when leaders could offer nonmonetary incentives and information was available to the entire team—conditions that could readily exist in the modern workplace.

Researchers are just now beginning to explore the process of shared leadership, and results are promising. For example, shared leadership in teams was positively associated with group cohesion, group citizenship, and group effectiveness.[70] Table 14–3 contains a list of key questions and answers that managers should consider when determining how they can develop shared leadership.

Servant-Leadership

LO14.6

Servant-leadership is more a philosophy of managing than a testable theory. The term *servant-leadership* was coined by Robert Greenleaf in 1970. Greenleaf believes that great leaders act as servants, putting the needs of others, including employees, customers, and community, as their first priority. **Servant-leadership focuses on increased service to others rather than to oneself.**[71] Because the focus of servant-leadership is serving others over self-interest, servant-leaders are less likely to engage in self-serving behaviors that hurt others. Embedding servant-leadership into an organization's culture requires actions as well as words. For example, John Donahoe, CEO of eBay, is committed to serving customers, "specifically the companies and entrepreneurs who sell goods on the site. Then he visualizes a chain of command through which the CEO can deliver what customers need. On trips around the world he takes along a Flip Video camera and films interviews with eBay sellers to share their opinions with his staff. He has even tied managers' compensation to customer loyalty, measured through regular surveys."[72]

www.mcgrawhillconnect.com

Go to Connect for an interactive exercise to test your knowledge of the premises of servant-leadership.

According to Jim Stuart, cofounder of the leadership circle in Tampa, Florida, "Leadership derives naturally from a commitment to service. You know that you're practicing servant-leadership if your followers become wiser, healthier, more autonomous—and more likely to become servant-leaders themselves."[73] Servant-leadership is not a quick-fix approach to leadership. Rather, it is a long-term, transformational approach to life and work.

Servant-leaders have the characteristics listed in Table 14–4. An example of someone with these characteristics is Sam Palmisano, chairman and CEO of IBM. Here is what he had to say about his approach to leadership:

> Over the course of my IBM career I've observed many CEOs, heads of state, and others in positions of great authority. I've noticed that some of the most effective leaders don't make themselves the center of attention. They are respectful. They listen. This is an appealing personal quality, but it's also an effective leadership attribute. Their selflessness makes the people around them comfortable. People open up, speak up, contribute. They give those leaders their very best.[74]

Key Questions and Answers to Consider When Developing   **TABLE 14–3**
Shared Leadership

Key Questions	Answers
What task characteristics call for shared leadership?	Tasks that are highly interdependent.
	Tasks that require a great deal of creativity.
	Tasks that are highly complex.
What is the role of the leader in developing shared leadership?	Designing the team, including clarifying purpose, securing resources, articulating vision, selecting members, and defining team processes.
	Managing the boundaries of the team.
How can organizational systems facilitate the development of shared leadership?	Training and development systems can be used to prepare both designated leaders and team members to engage in shared leadership.
	Reward systems can be used to promote and reward shared leadership.
	Cultural systems can be used to articulate and to demonstrate the value of shared leadership.
What vertical and shared leadership behaviors are important to team outcomes?	Directive leadership can provide task-focused directions.
	Transactional leadership can provide both personal and material rewards based on key performance metrics.
	Transformational leadership can stimulate commitment to a team vision, emotional engagement, and fulfillment of higher-order needs.
	Empowering leadership can reinforce the importance of self-motivation.
What are the ongoing responsibilities of the vertical leader?	The vertical leader needs to be able to step in and fill voids in the team.
	The vertical leader needs to continue to emphasize the importance of the shared leadership approach, given the task characteristics facing the team.

SOURCE: From C L Pearce, "The Future of Leadership: Combining Vertical and Shared Leadership to Transform Knowledge Work," *Academy of Management Executive,* February 2004, p. 48. Copyright © 2004 with permission of Academy of management via Copyright Clearance Center.

Researchers have just begun to develop measures of servant-leadership and to examine relationships between this type of leadership and various outcomes. In support of Greenleaf's ideas, servant-leadership was found to be positively associated with employees' performance, organizational commitment, job satisfaction, creativity, organizational citizenship behaviors, and perceptions of justice. Servant-leadership also was negatively related to counterproductive work behavior.[75] These results suggest that managers would be well served by using the servant-leadership characteristics shown in Table 14–4.

TABLE 14–4   Characteristics of the Servant-Leader

Servant–Leadership Characteristics	Description
1. Listening	Servant-leaders focus on listening to identify and clarify the needs and desires of a group.
2. Empathy	Servant-leaders try to empathize with others' feelings and emotions. An individual's good intentions are assumed even when he or she performs poorly.
3. Healing	Servant-leaders strive to make themselves and others whole in the face of failure or suffering.
4. Awareness	Servant-leaders are very self-aware of their strengths and limitations.
5. Persuasion	Servant-leaders rely more on persuasion than positional authority when making decisions and trying to influence others.
6. Conceptualization	Servant-leaders take the time and effort to develop broader based conceptual thinking. Servant-leaders seek an appropriate balance between a short-term, day-to-day focus and a long-term, conceptual orientation.
7. Foresight	Servant-leaders have the ability to foresee future outcomes associated with a current course of action or situation.
8. Stewardship	Servant-leaders assume that they are stewards of the people and resources they manage.
9. Commitment to the growth of people	Servant-leaders are committed to people beyond their immediate work role. They commit to fostering an environment that encourages personal, professional, and spiritual growth.
10. Building community	Servant-leaders strive to create a sense of community both within and outside the work organization.

SOURCE: These characteristics and descriptions were derived from L C Spears, "Introduction: Servant-Leadership and the Greenleaf Legacy," in *Reflections on Leadership: How Robert K Greenleaf 's Theory of Servant-Leadership Influenced Today's Top Management Thinkers,* L C Spears, ed (New York: John Wiley & Sons, 1995), pp 1–14.

The Role of Followers in the Leadership Process

 LO14.7

All of the previous theories discussed in this chapter have been leader-centric. That is, they focused on understanding leadership effectiveness from the leader's point of view. We conclude this chapter by discussing the role of followers in the leadership process. Although very little research has been devoted to this topic, it is an important issue to consider because the success of both leaders and followers is contingent on the dynamic relationship among the people involved.[76]

We begin our discussion by noting that both leaders and followers are closely linked. You cannot lead without having followers, and you cannot follow without having leaders. The point is that each needs the other, and the quality of the relationship determines how we behave as followers. This is why it is important for both leaders

Nancy Lublin Believes That Her Followers Make Her Successful

We've overdone this whole leadership/founder/ entrepreneur thing. And we're not spending nearly enough time crediting the folks who turn all that visionary stuff into tangible reality. . . .

We degrade the very idea of followers— lemmings!—yet the world needs people who can follow intelligently. I am not talking about mindless armies that march in formation and shoot if their leader points down a dark hallway. The key word is "intelligently." Good followers ask good questions. They probe their leaders. They crunch the numbers to ensure that their visionary boss's gorgeous plan actually works. . . .

Honoring good followers isn't just a nice thing—it's necessary. It's the sanest, smartest way to run your company, for-profit or not. We have to recognize that your bright ideas—and mine— would go nowhere without the doers. Failing to do so will make us collectively poorer, not just in spirit but in money.

SOURCE: Excerpted from N Lublin, "Let's Hear It for the Little Guys," *Fastcompany*, April 2010, p 33.

and followers to focus on developing a mutually rewarding and beneficial relationship. The Skills & Best Practices feature above summarizes Nancy Lublin's view on this mutually reinforcing relationship. Lublin was founder of Dress for Success and CEO of DoSomething.

Followers vary in terms of the extent to which they commit, comply, and resist a leader's influence attempts. For example, one researcher identified three types of followers: helpers, independents, and rebels. *"Helpers* show deference and comply with the leadership; *independents* distance themselves from the leadership and show less compliance; and *rebels* show divergence from the leader and are at least compliant. Among other types of followers, moderate in compliance, are *diplomats, partisans,* and *counselors.*"[77] Leaders obviously want followers who are productive, reliable, honest, cooperative, proactive, and flexible. Leaders do not benefit from followers who hide the truth, withhold information, fail to generate ideas, are unwilling to collaborate, provide inaccurate feedback, or are unwilling to take the lead on projects and initiatives.[78]

In contrast, research shows that followers seek, admire, and respect leaders who foster three emotional responses in others: Followers want organizational leaders to create feelings of *significance* (what one does at work is important and meaningful), *community* (a sense of unity encourages people to treat others with respect and dignity and to work together in pursuit of organizational goals), and *excitement* (people are engaged and feel energy at work).[79]

A pair of OB experts developed a four-step process for followers to use in managing the leader–follower relationship.[80] First, it is critical for followers to understand their boss. Followers should attempt to gain an appreciation for their manager's leadership style, interpersonal style, goals, expectations, pressures, and strengths and weaknesses. One way of doing this is to ask your manager to answer the following seven questions:[81]

1. How would you describe your leadership style? Does your style change when you are under pressure?
2. When would you like me to approach you with questions or information? Are there any situations that are off limits (e.g., a social event)?
3. How do you want me to communicate with you?
4. How do you like to work?
5. Are there behaviors or attitudes that you will not tolerate? What are they?
6. What is your approach toward giving feedback?
7. How can I help you?

Second, followers need to understand their own style, needs, goals, expectations, and strengths and weaknesses. The next step entails conducting a gap analysis between the understanding a follower has about his or her boss and the understanding the follower has about him- or herself. With this information in mind, followers are ready to proceed to the final step of developing and maintaining a relationship that fits both parties' needs and styles.

This final step requires followers to build on mutual strengths and to adjust or accommodate the leader's divergent style, goals, expectations, and weaknesses.[82] For example, a follower might adjust his or her style of communication in response to the boss's preferred method for receiving information. Other adjustments might be made in terms of decision making. If the boss prefers a participative approach, then followers should attempt to involve their manager in all decisions regardless of the follower's decision-making style—recall our discussion of decision-making styles in Chapter 10. Good use of time and resources is another issue for followers to consider. Most managers are pushed for time, energy, and resources and are more likely to appreciate followers who save rather than cost them time and energy. Followers should not waste their manager's time discussing trivial matters.

There are two final issues to consider. First, a follower may not be able to accommodate a leader's style, expectations, or weaknesses and may have to seek a transfer or quit his or her job to reconcile the discrepancy. We recognize that there are personal and ethical trade-offs that one may not be willing to make when managing the leader–follower relationship. Second, we can all enhance our boss's leadership effectiveness and our employer's success by becoming better followers. Remember, it is in an individual's best interest to be a good follower because leaders need and want competent employees.

key terms

chapter summary

- *Review trait theory, and discuss the takeaways from both the trait and behavioral styles theories of leadership.* Historical leadership research does not support the notion that effective leaders possess traits unique from followers. More recent research shows that effective leaders possess the following traits: task competence, interpersonal competence, intuition, traits of character, biophysical traits, and personal traits. In contrast, bad leaders displayed the following characteristics: incompetent, rigid, intemperate, callous, corrupt, insular, and evil. Research also demonstrated that men and women exhibited different styles of leadership. The takeaways from trait theory are that (a) we can no longer ignore the implications of leadership traits; traits influence leadership effectiveness; (b) organizations may want to include personality and trait assessments into their selection and promotion processes; and (c) management development programs can be used to enhance employees' leadership traits.

  The takeaways from behavioral styles theory are as follows: (a) leaders are made, not born; (b) there is no one best style of leadership; (c) the effectiveness of a particular style depends on the situation at hand; and (d) managers are encouraged to apply Drucker's tips for effective leadership.

- *Explain, according to Fiedler's contingency model, how leadership style interacts with situational control, and discuss the takeaways from this model.* Fiedler believes leader effectiveness depends on an appropriate match between leadership style and situational control. Leaders are either task motivated or relationship motivated. Situation control is composed of leader–member relations, task structure, and position power. Task-motivated leaders are effective under situations of both high and low control. Relationship-motivated leaders are more effective when they have moderate situational control. The three takeaways are (a) leadership effectiveness goes beyond traits and behaviors,

(b) leaders are unlikely to be successful in all situations, and (c) leaders need to modify their style to fit a situation.

- *Discuss House's revised path–goal theory and its practical takeaways.* There are three key changes in the revised path–goal theory. Leaders now are viewed as exhibiting eight categories of leader behavior (see Table 14–2) instead of four. In turn, the effectiveness of these styles depends on various employee characteristics and environmental factors. Second, leaders are expected to spend more effort fostering intrinsic motivation through empowerment. Third, leadership is not limited to people in managerial roles. Rather, leadership is shared among all employees within an organization. There are three takeaways: (a) effective leaders possess and use more than one style of leadership, (b) the theory offers specific suggestions for how leaders can help employees, and (c) managers are advised to modify their leadership style to fit relevant contingency factors.

- *Describe the difference between transactional and transformational leadership and discuss how transformational leadership transforms followers and work groups.* There is an important difference between transactional and transformational leadership. Transactional leaders focus on clarifying employees' role and task requirements and provide followers with positive and negative rewards contingent on performance. Transformational leaders motivate employees to pursue organizational goals over their own self-interests. Both forms of leadership are important for organizational success. Individual characteristics and organizational culture are key precursors of transformational leadership, which comprises four sets of leader behavior. These leader behaviors, in turn, positively affect followers' and work-groups' goals, values, beliefs, aspirations, and motivation. These positive effects are then associated with a host of preferred outcomes.

- *Explain the leader–member exchange (LMX) model of leadership and the concept of shared leadership.* The LMX model revolves around the development of dyadic relationships between managers and their direct reports. These leader–member exchanges qualify as either in-group or out-group relationships. Research supports this model of leadership. Shared leadership involves a simultaneous, ongoing, mutual influence process in which individuals share responsibility for leading regardless of formal roles and titles. This type of leadership is most likely to be needed when people work in teams, when people are involved in complex projects, and when people are doing knowledge work.

- *Review the principles of servant-leadership.* Servant-leadership is more a philosophy than a testable theory. It is based on the premise that great leaders act as servants, putting the needs of others, including employees, customers, and community, as their first priority.

- *Describe the follower's role in the leadership process.* Followers can use a four-step process for managing the leader–follower relationship. Followers need to understand their boss and themselves. They then conduct a gap analysis between the understanding they have about their boss and themselves. The final step requires followers to build on mutual strengths and to adjust or accommodate the leader's divergent style, goals, expectations, and weaknesses.

discussion questions

1. Do you agree with Barbara Kellerman's conclusion that leadership is not a moral concept? Explain.
2. Is everyone cut out to be a leader? Discuss.
3. Does it make more sense to change a person's leadership style or the situation? How would Fred Fiedler and Robert House answer this question?
4. Have you ever worked for a transformational leader? Describe how she or he transformed followers.
5. In your view, which leadership theory has the greatest practical application? Why?

legal/ethical challenge

Is It Ethical to Use Subversive Approaches To Influence Others?

"Last week, National Public Radio's chief executive [Vivian Schiller] and senior fundraiser Ron Schiller resigned after off-the-cuff remarks were made to conservative activists posing as potential donors."[83] The Schillers are unrelated. The potential donors, headed by James O'Keefe, met with Ron Schiller at a posh restaurant for lunch under the guise that they wanted to donate $5 million as representatives from a Muslim organization. O'Keefe secretly recorded the interview and later released a doctored video clip that portrayed NPR in a very bad light. Schiller made negative and damaging comments about the Republican Party in general and the Tea Party in particular. You can imagine how this video was received by politicians, particularly those who vote on funding for National Public Radio (NPR).

A reporter from the *Washington Post* described the video as "selective and deceptive." He stated that "O'Keefe's final product excludes explanatory context, exaggerates [Ron] Schiller's tolerance for Islamist radicalism and attributes sentiments to Schiller that are actually quotes by others—all the hallmarks of a hit piece." The reporter concluded that "O'Keefe did not merely leave a false impression; he manufactured an elaborate lie. . . . The stingers bought access with fake money. There is no ethical canon or tradition that would excuse such deception on the part of a professional journalist."[84]

The video led some government officials to call for major, if not total funding cuts to NPR, which would threaten the organization's very existence. The end result is that the U.S. Senate voted in March 2011 to block public radio stations from spending federal money on programming. It appears that O'Keefe's attempts at influence had some success.[85]

Not everyone agrees that O'Keefe did anything wrong. Some think that subversive techniques are a good way to keep people accountable. After all, TV programs such as *20/20* have used hidden cameras for years to catch people doing bad things. The subversive trend is growing. For example, "[T]he subversive approach has become so popular that the Yes Men, anti-corporate jokers who have made two critically acclaimed movies, recently opened the Yes Lab, which trains others in the art of dirty work." Mike Bonanno, who cofounded Yes Men, concluded that "with mainstream media being defunded, there is less real reporting out there and more people are resorting to these kind of tactics to get the work out on stuff that should be obvious."[86] Further, "O'Keefe defenders contend he is not really a journalist but a new breed of 'citizen journalist.' This can be defined as the simultaneous demands for journalistic respect and for release from journalistic standards, including a commitment to honesty."[87]

What Do You Think Should Be Done about James O'Keefe?

1. Although O'Keefe did not violate any laws, he should be punished. His behavior was unethical. He lied about his identity to Ron Schiller and edited the video to present false impressions about NPR. His subversive actions also led to a negative vote about funding for public radio.

2. O'Keefe didn't break any laws, so he should be left alone. He actually is providing service to the public.

What Should Be Done about Citizen Journalism?

1. Given today's technology, we need regulations to govern this aspect of modern life. If people like James O'Keefe want to do journalistic work on their own, then they should be held to the same standards as professionals.

2. Wake up and smell the coffee. The only way to expose people like Ron Schiller is to use subversive techniques. I have no problem with what O'Keefe did. Besides, others are doing the same thing.

If you're looking for additional study materials, be sure to check out the Online Learning Center at

www.mhhe.com/kinickiob5e

for more information and interactivities that correspond to this chapter.

Designing Effective Organizations

Is Organizational Structure Related to How Organizations Make and Execute Decisions?

Organizational structure is not the only determinant of performance. In some cases, it is not even particularly important. That's why changing a company's structure to meet a particular strategic goal can actually exacerbate problems rather than help solve them. For example, an organization struggling to innovate may try to gather more and more creative input—and end up getting too many people involved, thereby slowing the pace of decision making and stifling innovation.

Take the case of Yahoo. In December 2006, then-CEO Terry Semel announced a sweeping reorganization of the company, replacing Yahoo's product-aligned structure with one focused on users and advertiser customers. Seven product units were merged into a group called Advertisers and Publishers. A unit dubbed Technology would provide infrastructure for the two new operating groups. The idea was to accelerate growth by exploiting economies of scope across Yahoo's rich collection of audience and advertiser products. Semel's team had thought they'd carefully defined roles and responsibilities under the new structure, but decision making and execution quickly became bogged down. Audience demanded tailored solutions that Technology could not provide at a reasonable cost. Advertisers and Publishers needed its own set of unique products and so was constantly competing with Audience for scarce developer time. In response, Yahoo executives created new roles and management levels to coordinate the units. The organization ballooned to 12 layers, product development slowed as decisions stalled, and overhead costs increased.

Yahoo's experience shows how a lack of attention to the decision-making process can thwart the best-intentioned reorganization and undermine performance....

The ongoing turnaround at Ford illustrates the power of explicitly delineating a company's critical decisions. When Alan Mulally became CEO at the automaker in 2006, the company was in dire need of change. Ford had been losing a point or more of market share every year since 2000 and was on the verge of collapse. But

Alan Mulally, CEO of Ford Motor Company

rather than change the company's structure first and then worry about decisions, Mulally took the opposite approach. He and his team outlined the decisions that were critical to a turnaround. Only then did they begin to build the new organization around those decisions.

Fixing the company's operations and restoring profitability centered on a schematic depicting Ford's critical decisions. It spelled out the key decisions that needed to be made at each stage in Ford's value chain, along with the infrastructure required to execute them effectively. Every week, Mulally and his team tracked their progress in making and executing these decisions.

They divested noncore brands such as Aston Martin, Jaguar, Land Rover, and Volvo; reduced the number of production platforms; began consolidating both suppliers and dealers; and so on. They also reorganized the company, moving from a structure based on regional business units to a global matrix of functions and geographies. This new structure enabled Mulally's team to make its most important decisions better and faster—creating global car platforms, for instance, which had been painfully difficult under the old structure. Set in this context, the reorg made perfect sense and helped restore the company to profitability in early 2010.[1]

VIRTUALLY EVERY ASPECT OF LIFE is affected at least indirectly by some type of organization. We look to organizations to feed, clothe, house, educate, and employ us. Organizations attend to our needs for entertainment, police and fire protection, insurance, recreation, national security, transportation, news and information, legal assistance, and health care. Modern organizations have one thing in common: They are the primary context for *organizational behavior.* In a manner of speaking, organizations are the chessboard upon which the game of organizational behavior is played. Therefore, present and future managers need a working knowledge of modern organizations to improve their chances of making the right moves when managing people at work.

The chapter-opening case illustrates that there is not one type of organizational design that works best in all situations. The best design depends on the extent to which it matches the demands of the situation at hand, including the key strategic decisions that must be made. This type of contingency design is discussed later in this chapter. The example of Ford in the chapter-opening case also reinforces a conclusion we made in Chapter 2. That is, organizational structure is related to an organization's culture. This underscores how important it is for managers to consider the interplay between organizational culture and organizational design. This chapter will help you to manage this dynamic and important relationship.

We begin by defining the term *organization,* discussing important dimensions of organization charts, and contrasting views of organizations as closed or open systems. Our attention then turns to the various ways organizations are designed, from traditional divisions of work to more recent, popular ideas about lowering barriers between departments and companies. Next, we discuss the contingency approach to designing organizations. We conclude by describing criteria for assessing an organization's effectiveness.

Organizations: Definition and Dimensions

As a necessary springboard for this chapter, we need to formally define the term *organization* and clarify the meaning of organization charts.

What Is an Organization?

LO15.1

According to Chester I Barnard's classic definition, an ***organization* is "a system of consciously coordinated activities or forces of two or more persons."**[2] Embodied in the conscious coordination aspect of this definition are four common denominators of all organizations: coordination of effort, a common goal, division of labor, and a hierarchy of authority.[3] Organization theorists refer to these factors as the organization's structure.

Coordination of effort is achieved through formulation and enforcement of policies, rules, and regulations. Division of labor occurs when the common goal is pursued by individuals performing different but related tasks. The hierarchy of authority, also called the chain of command, is a control mechanism dedicated to making sure the right people do the right things at the right time. Historically, managers have maintained the integrity of the hierarchy of authority by adhering to the unity of command principle. The ***unity of command principle* specifies that each employee should report to only one manager.** Otherwise, the argument goes, inefficiency would prevail because of conflicting orders and lack of personal accountability. (Indeed, these are problems in today's more fluid and flexible organizations based on innovations such as cross-functional and self-managed teams.) Managers in the hierarchy of authority also administer rewards and punishments. When operating in concert, the four definitional factors—coordination of effort, a common goal, division of labor, and a hierarchy of authority—enable an organization to come to life and function.

Organization Charts

An *organization chart* **is a graphic representation of formal authority and division of labor relationships.** To the casual observer, the term *organization chart* means the family tree-like pattern of boxes and lines posted on workplace walls. Within each box one usually finds the names and titles of current position holders. To organization theorists, however, organization charts reveal much more. The partial organization chart in Figure 15–1 reveals four basic dimensions of organizational structure: (1) hierarchy of authority (who reports to whom), (2) division of labor, (3) spans of control, and (4) line and staff positions.

Hierarchy of Authority   As Figure 15–1 illustrates, there is an unmistakable hierarchy of authority. Working from bottom to top, the 10 directors report to the two executive directors who report to the president who reports to the chief executive officer. Ultimately, the chief executive officer answers to the hospital's board of directors. The chart in Figure 15–1 shows strict unity of command up and down the line. A formal hierarchy of authority also delineates the official communication network.

Division of Labor   In addition to showing the chain of command, the sample organization chart indicates extensive division of labor. Immediately below the hospital's president, one executive director is responsible for general administration while another is responsible for medical affairs. Each of these two specialties is further subdivided as indicated by the next layer of positions. At each successively lower level in the organization, jobs become more specialized.

Spans of Control   The *span of control* **refers to the number of people reporting directly to a given manager.** Spans of control can range from narrow to wide. For example, the president in Figure 15–1 has a narrow span of control of two. (Staff assistants usually are not included in a manager's span of control.) The executive administrative director in Figure 15–1 has a wider span of control of five. Spans of control exceeding 30 can be found in assembly-line operations where machine-paced and repetitive work substitutes for close supervision. Historically, spans of five to six were considered best. Despite years of debate, organization theorists have not arrived at a consensus regarding the ideal span of control.

Generally, the narrower the span of control, the closer the supervision and the higher the administrative costs as a result of a higher manager-to-worker ratio. Recent emphasis on leanness and administrative efficiency dictates spans of control as wide as possible but guarding against inadequate supervision and lack of coordination. Wider spans also complement the trend toward greater worker autonomy and empowerment (see the Skills & Best Practices feature on page 399).

Line and Staff Positions   The organization chart in Figure 15–1 also distinguishes between line and staff positions. Line managers such as the president, the two executive directors, and the various directors occupy formal decision-making positions within the chain of command. Line positions generally are connected by solid lines on organization charts. Dotted lines indicate staff relationships. *Staff personnel* **do background research and provide technical advice and recommendations to their *line managers*, who have**

www.mcgrawhillconnect.com

Go to Connect for an interactive exercise to test your knowledge of organization charts.

FIGURE 15–1   Sample Organization Chart for a Hospital (executive and director levels only)

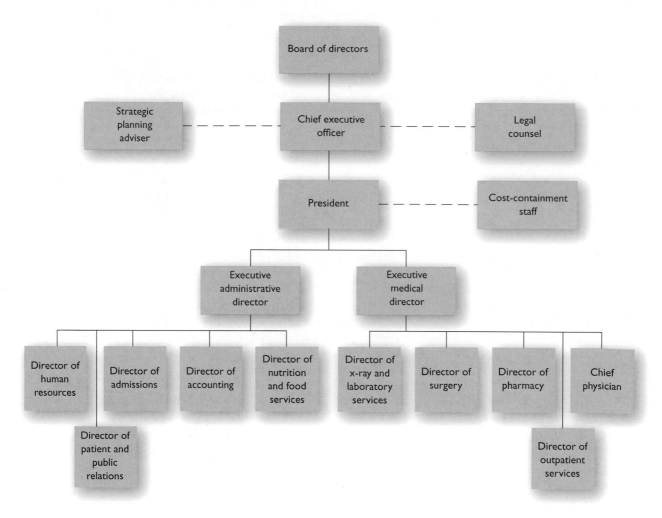

the authority to make decisions. For example, the cost-containment specialists in the sample organization chart merely advise the president on relevant matters. Apart from supervising the work of their own staff assistants, they have no line authority over other organizational members. Modern trends such as cross-functional teams and matrix structures are blurring the distinction between line and staff.

An Open-System Perspective of Organizations

LO15.2

To understand how organizations have evolved, we need to know the difference between closed and open systems. A *closed system* **is said to be a self-sufficient entity. It is "closed" to the surrounding environment.** In contrast, an *open system* **depends on constant interaction with the environment for survival.** The distinction

Managing a Wide Span

In some situations, a manager can successfully lead a group of 30 or even more employees. The following conditions and practices help.

- Jobs are similar to one another, so training and goal setting are simpler.
- Employees have the knowledge, talent, and motivation to work independently.
- Employees are empowered to make decisions.
- Pay is linked to results, so employees have an incentive to excel.
- Communication technology keeps managers in touch with their employees and helps everyone share knowledge.

At Gemesa, PepsiCo's cookie business in Mexico, supervisors are responsible for the work of 56 employees each. That span of control succeeds because employees are so familiar with company goals and processes that they can handle greater responsibility. Also, incentive pay is linked to productivity, quality, service, and teamwork. The efficiency of this organizational structure has enhanced Gemesa's business results.

SOURCE: Based on G Anders, "Overseeing More Employees—with Fewer Managers," *The Wall Street Journal,* March 24, 2008, p B6.

---

between closed and open systems is a matter of degree. Because every worldly system is partly closed and partly open, the key question is: How great a role does the environment play in the functioning of the system? For instance, a battery-powered clock is a relatively closed system. Once the battery is inserted, the clock performs its time-keeping function hour after hour until the battery goes dead. The human body, on the other hand, is a highly open system because it requires a constant supply of life-sustaining oxygen from the environment. Nutrients also are imported from the environment. Open systems are capable of self-correction, adaptation, and growth, thanks to characteristics such as homeostasis and feedback control.

Historically, management theorists downplayed the environment as they used closed-system thinking to characterize organizations as either well-oiled machines or highly disciplined military units. They believed rigorous planning and control would eliminate environmental uncertainty. But that proved unrealistic. Drawing on the field of general systems theory that emerged during the 1950s, organization theorists suggested a more dynamic model for organizations.[4] The resulting open-system model likened organizations to the human body.[5] Accordingly, the model in Figure 15–2 reveals the organization to be a living organism that transforms inputs into various outputs. The outer boundary of the organization is permeable. People, information, capital, and goods and services move back and forth across this boundary. Moreover, each of the five organizational subsystems—goals and values, technical, psychosocial, structural, and managerial—is dependent on the others. Feedback about such things as sales and customer satisfaction or dissatisfaction enables the organization to self-adjust and survive despite uncertainty and change. In effect, the organization is alive.

The 2011 tragedy in Japan is a good example of an open system. The crisis started with an earthquake, which led to a tsunami, and then to a nuclear accident. The effects of open systems then caused many different problems for the Japanese people (e.g., nuclear exposure, food shortages, contaminated water, death, and destruction) and for organizations located in Japan, such as Walmart.[6] "Of its 414 Seiyu stores—as Walmart's Japanese chain is called—24 were in the Sendai and Fukushima areas in northern Japan,

This is what an open system can do. The Japan tsunami sent cars and boats floating away to unforeseen locations, like a boat on top of a house. Experts estimate that the Japan tsunami caused about $60 billion in property damage and that it ultimately may lead to 10,000 deaths.

close to the epicenter. Stores were trashed as goods fell off shelves during the temblor. A massive power outage ensued. Two stores suffered extensive damage. Close to 2,000 employees worked in the stricken region and were unaccounted for."[7] The effects of open systems also go beyond physical and geographical boundaries. For example, Ford Motor Company "halted all new orders for trucks, SUVs and cars in 'tuxedo black' and a handful of other hues due to shortages of some pigments made in Japan."[8]

Organization Design in a Changing World

Organizational design is defined as "**the structures of accountability and responsibility used to develop and implement strategies, and the human resource practices and information and business processes that activate those structures.**"[9] The general idea behind the study of organizational design is that organizations are more effective or successful when their structure supports the execution of corporate strategies. This in turn has led researchers, consultants, and managers to consider how organizations might best structure themselves.[10] Many managers underestimate the complexity of this task. This was illustrated in the chapter-opening case example of Yahoo.

Unfortunately, changes in organizational design, such as the one at Yahoo, frequently produce bad results. For example, a McKinsey & Company survey of 1,890 executives

The Organization as an Open System   FIGURE 15–2

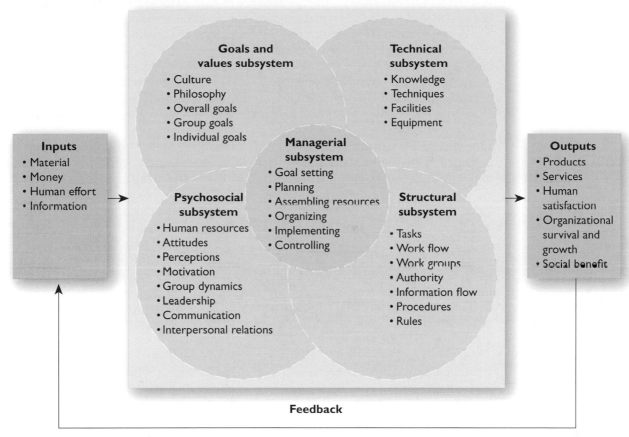

SOURCE: This model is a combination of Figures 5–2 and 5–3 in F E Kast and J E Rosenzweig, *Organization and Management: A Systems and Contingency Approach* 4th ed, McGraw-Hill, 1986, pp. 112, 114. Reprinted with permission of The McGraw-Hill Companies, Inc.

revealed that only 8% experienced positive results after making structural changes. This finding is consistent with a study of 57 reorganizations by consulting firm Bain & Company. Results revealed that most reorganizations had no effect, and some led to lower organizational performance.[11] What then is a manager supposed to do about determining the best organizational design?

Although there is no simple answer to this question, you will never be able to address this issue without understanding the different types of structures that exist. This section thus provides an overview of seven fundamental types of organizational structures. The following section then attempts to help you determine when these structures may be most effective.[12]

Traditional Designs

Organizations defined by a traditional approach tend to have functional, divisional, and/ or matrix structures. Each of these structures relies on a vertical hierarchy and attempts to define clear departmental boundaries and reporting relationships. Let us consider each type of structure.

Functional Structure   A functional structure groups people according to the business functions they perform, for example, manufacturing, marketing, and finance. A manager is responsible for the performance of each of these functions, and employees tend to identify strongly with their particular function, such as sales or engineering. The organization chart in Figure 15–1 illustrates a functional structure. Responsibility at this hospital is first divided into administrative and medical functions, and within each category, directors are responsible for each of the functions. This arrangement puts together people who are experts in the same or similar activities. Thus, as a small company grows and hires more production workers, salespeople, and accounting staff, it typically groups them together with a supervisor who understands their function.

Divisional Structure   In a divisional structure, the organization groups together activities related to outputs, such as type of product or type (or location) of customer. For example, General Electric has four businesses (major product divisions): GE Technology Infrastructure, GE Finance, GE Energy Infrastructure, and GE Consumer and Industrial. These major business areas are subdivided into either product or geographic divisions.[13] The people in a division can become experts at making a particular type of product or serving the particular needs of their customer group or geographic area. Typically, each division has a functional structure. Some organizations have concluded that using a functional or divisional structure divides people too much. Either employees don't collaborate across functions well enough to meet customer needs or they don't share expertise across divisions well enough to operate efficiently. One way to address this problem while still focusing on hierarchy is to create a matrix structure.

Matrix Structure   Organizations use matrix structures when they need stronger horizontal alignment or cooperation in order to meet their goals. A matrix structure combines functional and divisional chains of command to form a grid with two command structures, one shown vertically according to function, and the other shown horizontally, by product line, brand, customer group, or geographic region. In the example shown in Figure 15–3, Ford might set up vice presidents for each functional group and project managers for each make of car. Employees would report to two managers: one in charge of the function they perform and the other in charge of the project they are working on.

Focus on Collaboration: Horizontal Design

The traditional approach of dividing up work according to functions, products, and customers is dissatisfying to managers who want to focus on bringing people together without internal boundaries to keep them apart. If you want people to share knowledge and continually improve the way things are done, you need to create an environment in which collaboration feels easy and natural. Many organizations with this viewpoint have emphasized horizontal relationships among people who are working on shared tasks more than vertical relationships in a traditional organizational design.

This horizontal approach to organizational design tends to focus on work processes. A process consists of every task and responsibility needed to meet a customer need, such as developing a new product or filling a customer order. Completing a process requires input from people in different functions, typically organized into a cross-functional team (described in Chapter 9). Thus, teamwork is a feature of organizations designed horizontally. Two experts in organization design have identified five principles for designing a horizontal organization:

Sample Matrix Structure That Ford Might Use   FIGURE 15–3

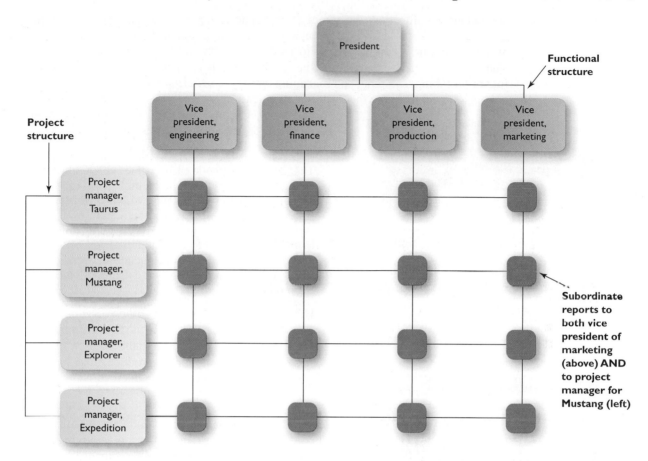

1. Organize around complete workflow processes rather than tasks.
2. Flatten hierarchy and use teams to manage everything.
3. Appoint process team leaders to manage internal team processes.
4. Let supplier and customer contact drive performance.
5. Provide required expertise from outside the team as required.[14]

Designs That Open Boundaries between Organizations

While the horizontal organization aims to break down barriers within organizations, some structures are based on the idea that not even barriers *between* organizations are always ideal. Sometimes organizations can perform better by creating structures in which they can pool their resources to work toward a shared goal. This strategic approach results in structures that are called hollow, modular, or virtual.

Hollow Structure   A hollow organization results from strategic application of the trend toward outsourcing. The organization's managers identify core competencies—functions the organization can do better and more profitably than other organizations. An athletic shoe company, for example, might decide that it can excel at developing new designs, owing to its design talent and knowledge of the market. Then it might find outsourcing partners to handle other activities such as manufacturing, order taking, shipping, and managing employee benefits. The more processes that are outsourced, the more the resulting organization is "hollow"—and focused on what

it does best. Furniture company Herman Miller goes outside the organization for design expertise. CEO Brian Walker explains the advantages:

> This external network ensures that we are always taking a fresh look at problems faced by our customers without subjecting it to our own filters. If you have only an internal design staff, even an enormously talented one, you are inherently limited by their existing world view and experiences. Our ability to tap into a broader outside network lets us. . . get a fresh perspective on existing or emerging problems.[15]

Herman Miller also uses other organizations for manufacturing; Walker says the company is "more. . . an integrator than a manufacturer," which makes it less resistant to new product ideas because it doesn't have to change manufacturing processes itself.

Nokia is the leading supplier of mobile phones around the world. Part of the company's success is related to its approach to product development. Nokia develops phones in partnership with AT&T and other phone carriers. What characteristics must this and other virtual organizations have in order to survive?

Modular Structure   A modular organization, like a hollow organization, uses outsourcing. But instead of outsourcing processes, it outsources parts of a product, such as components of a jet or subroutines of a software program. The modular organization is responsible for ensuring that the parts meet quality requirements, that the parts arrive in a timely fashion, and that the organization is capable of efficiently combining the parts into the final whole. A well-known example is Boeing, in its production of the 787 Dreamliner.

Virtual Structure   Finally, an organization may identify partners to create a virtual organization, "a company outside a company created specifically to respond to an exceptional market opportunity that is often temporary."[16] Just as "virtual memory" in a computer causes it to seem as if it has more memory, so a virtual organization does more than what its founding organization could do with the resources within the organization's boundaries. The organization identifies partners with the needed talents and negotiates an agreement in which the participants typically work in separate facilities. Instead of relying heavily on face-to-face meetings, however, members of virtual organizations send e-mail and voice-mail messages, exchange project information over the Internet, and convene videoconferences

Virtual Structures Are Being Used by Entrepreneurs

Growing numbers of Americans are striking out on their own as solo entrepreneurs. And a whole industrial complex has sprung up to support them.

Need a cubicle to put together a presentation or a conference room for a meeting? There are companies in most big cities that will rent you as much work space as you need. If you need someone to take your calls and arrange your appointments, a host of services will connect you with receptionists who work off-site. There's also help available online. Digital marketplaces make it easier to land clients and projects, while new software lets you access files on the road and track your finances. . . .

Online services can also help entrepreneurs track down work. There are numerous online platforms that connect consultants to clients, such as oDesk Corp. and Elance Inc.

SOURCE: Excerpted from R A Greenwald, "Solo Support," *The Wall Street Journal,* **February 14, 2011, p R8.**

among dispersed participants (recall our discussion of virtual teams in Chapter 9). Information technology clearly enables virtual organizations to work toward common goals, such as developing a new products or entering a new market. For instance, virtual organizations can help in developing cell phones for the U.S. market.

AT&T and Verizon dominate the market for wireless service to such a degree that phone producers must work with them to create compatible products and to develop a pipeline for selling them. Nokia, which had trouble gaining market share in the United States, shifted its strategy "to develop phones in partnership with U.S. carriers, in part by assigning 300 product developers each to AT&T and Verizon."[17] Salespeople and R&D personnel also are assigned to work with particular wireless carriers. In general, a virtual organization demands flexibility, and managers must be able to lead and motivate people in separate locations. This structure is valuable for organizations that want to grow through partnerships with other companies.[18] It also increasingly is being used by people starting their own companies (see Skills & Best Practices above).

> **BACK TO THE CHAPTER-OPENING CASE** What types of structures were used by Yahoo and Ford? Why did these companies adopt new designs?

The Contingency Approach to Designing Organizations

According to the *contingency approach to organization design*, **organizations tend to be more effective when they are structured to fit the demands of the situation.** The purpose of this section is to extend the previous one by introducing you to the contingency approach to organization design. We review a landmark study, drawing a distinction between centralized and decentralized decision making, and then discuss when each of the seven organization designs previously discussed is most likely to be effective.

Mechanistic versus Organic Organizations

A landmark contingency design study was reported by a pair of British behavioral scientists, Tom Burns and G M Stalker. In the course of their research, they drew a very instructive distinction between what they called mechanistic and organic organizations. *Mechanistic organizations* **are rigid bureaucracies with strict rules, narrowly defined tasks, and top-down communication.** A mechanistic organization generally would have one of the traditional organization designs described earlier in this chapter and a hierarchical culture—see the discussion of culture types in Chapter 2. The "orderliness" of this structure is expected to produce reliability and consistency in internal processes, thereby resulting in higher efficiency, quality, and timeliness. You can imagine how valuable this type of structure might be for a company in the nuclear power industry where mistakes and errors can be catastrophic. It is important to note that being mechanistic does not mean that an organization should not be responsive to employee and customer feedback. Toyota, a company noted for being more mechanistic, fell into this trap and ended up with recalls involving faulty accelerator pedals and rusted spare-tire carriers (see the Skills & Best Practices feature on page 407).

LO15.4   Oppositely, *organic organizations* **are flexible networks of multitalented individuals who perform a variety of tasks.** An example is Eileen Fisher, a company that designs and manufactures women's clothing. The firm's leadership includes Susan Schor, who—in the words of founder Eileen Fisher—"came in and created her own place": heading all aspects of "people and culture," including employee development, social consciousness, human resources, and internal communications. Schor's accomplishments include crafting an organizational structure in which all employees work in teams run by facilitators and "no one reports to anyone. Instead, we 'connect into' someone else."[19] These qualities of an organic organization are easiest to maintain with the lowered boundaries of horizontal and virtual organizations. Internet technology and social media has made such arrangements more practical by enabling individuals to develop networks of people with whom they can readily share information as needed.[20]

Toyota's Prius, a full hybrid which gets an estimated 50 miles per gallon, represents a good example of using customer feedback to design a vehicle. Contrary to stereotypes, mechanistic companies like Toyota will seek customer and employee feedback to improve their products or services.

A Matter of Degree   Importantly, as illustrated in the Hands-On Exercise, each of the mechanistic-organic characteristics is a matter of degree. Organizations tend to be *relatively* mechanistic or *relatively* organic. Pure types are rare because divisions, departments, or units in the same organization may be more or less mechanistic or organic. From an employee's standpoint, which organization structure would you prefer?

Different Approaches to Decision Making   Decision making tends to be centralized in mechanistic organizations and decentralized in organic organizations.

Has Toyota Become Too Mechanistic?

The *shusa* or chief engineer at Toyota wields much power and authority. This individual has "complete responsibility for a vehicle, beginning with its conception and sometimes lasting through its entire sales life." The *shusa* is accountable for the success of a vehicle and defines its intended market. He is also responsible for meeting goals related to cost, weight, performance, and quality. There are 38 *shusas* at Toyota and they are "highly respected and are granted near-absolute authority." You can see the mechanistic nature of Toyota's structure.

The role of *shusas* within Toyota's structure came under scrutiny when Katusake Watanabe was president from 2005 to 2009. Watanabe told the *shusas* to increase profitability by aggressively cutting costs. They pursued this goal with vigor around the world. "When they cut too deeply, feedback was not quick to reach them." . . .

"When Toyota customers began to raise questions about the quality of their vehicles, either because they performed unsafely or just looked cheap, Toyota brushed off the complaints and delayed finding solutions. Some current and former Toyota executives in the U.S. came to believe that the *shusas* were responsible for the company's defensiveness. They thought the *shusas* deflected questions about quality and were reluctant to take the problems to top management because they feared losing face." . . .

"As the company grew, its Japanese leaders never relinquished the iron grip they exercised over the company's operations . . . and continued to make all important decisions in Japan. Instead of globalizing, Toyota colonized."

SOURCE: Excerpted from A Taylor III, "How Toyota Lost Its Way," *Fortune*, July 26, 2010, p 110.

Centralized decision making **occurs when key decisions are made by top management.** *Decentralized decision making* **occurs when important decisions are made by middle- and lower-level managers.** Generally, centralized organizations are more tightly controlled while decentralized organizations are more adaptive to changing situations. Semco, a Brazilian manufacturer, turned to a more decentralized structure when it needed to spark dramatic change. Ricardo Semler became CEO when Semco was headed for bankruptcy; he eliminated most senior-management jobs and pushed decision making down to lower levels of self-managed teams. The outcomes have been promising.

> The move initially caused inefficiencies and higher costs but eventually allowed low-level innovation to flourish. . . . Inventory backlogs have eased, product lines have expanded, and sales have jumped. . . . After the company's reorganization, revenues climbed from $4 million to $212 million.[21]

Experts on the subject warn against extremes of centralization or decentralization. The challenge is to achieve a workable balance between the two extremes. A management consultant put it this way:

> The modern organization in transition will recognize the pull of two polarities: a need for greater centralization to create low-cost shared resources; and, a need to improve market responsiveness with greater decentralization. Today's winning organizations are the ones that can handle the paradox and tensions of both pulls. These are the firms that analyze the optimum organizational solution in each particular circumstance, without prejudice for one type of organization over another. The result is, almost invariably, a messy mixture of decentralized units sharing cost-effective centralized resources.[22]

connect™
www.mcgrawhillconnect.com

Go to Connect to take a self-assessment to determine your preferred organizational structure.

HANDS-ON EXERCISE

Mechanistic or Organic?

INSTRUCTIONS: Think of your current (or a past) place of employment and rate it on the following eight factors. Calculate a total score and compare it to the scale.

Characteristics

1. Task definition and knowledge required	Narrow, technical	1 2 3 4 5 6 7	Broad; general
2. Linkage between individual's contribution and organization's purpose	Vague or indirect	1 2 3 4 5 6 7	Clear or direct
3. Task flexibility	Rigid; routine	1 2 3 4 5 6 7	Flexible; varied
4. Specification of techniques, obligations, and rights	Specific	1 2 3 4 5 6 7	General
5. Degree of hierarchical control	High	1 2 3 4 5 6 7	Low (self-control emphasized)
6. Primary communication pattern	Top-down	1 2 3 4 5 6 7	Lateral (between peers)
7. Primary decision-making style	Authoritarian	1 2 3 4 5 6 7	Democratic; participative
8. Emphasis on obedience and loyalty	High	1 2 3 4 5 6 7	Low

Total score = _____

Scale

  8–24 = Relatively mechanistic
25–39 = Mixed
40–56 = Relatively organic

SOURCE: Adapted from discussion in T Burns and G M Stalker, *The Management of Innovation* (London: Tavistock, 1961), pp 119–25.

Centralization and decentralization are not an either-or proposition; they are an *and-also* balancing act.

> **BACK TO THE CHAPTER-OPENING CASE** Was Ford more mechanistic or organic in the approach it used to restructure? Explain.

Practical Research Insights When they classified a sample of actual companies as either mechanistic or organic, Burns and Stalker discovered one type was not superior to the other. Each type had its appropriate place, depending on the environment. When the environment was relatively stable and certain, the successful organizations tended to be *mechanistic. Organic* organizations tended to be the successful ones when the environment was unstable and uncertain.[23]

Another interesting finding comes from a study of 42 voluntary church organizations. As the organizations became more mechanistic (more bureaucratic) the intrinsic motivation of their members decreased. Mechanistic organizations apparently undermined the volunteers' sense of freedom and self-determination. Additionally, the researchers believe their findings help explain why bureaucracy tends to feed on itself: "A mechanistic organizational structure may breed the need for a more extremely mechanistic system because of the reduction in intrinsically motivated behavior."[24] Thus, bureaucracy begets greater bureaucracy.

Most recently, field research in two factories, one mechanistic and the other organic, found expected communication patterns. Command-and-control (downward) communication characterized the mechanistic factory. Consultative or participative (two-way) communication prevailed in the organic factory.[25]

www.mcgrawhillconnect.com

Go to Connect for a video case to view the One Smooth Stone company and how organizational design relates to their success.

Both Mechanistic and Organic Structures Have Their Places

Although achievement-oriented students of OB typically express a distaste for mechanistic organizations, not all organizations or subunits can or should be organic. For example, McDonald's could not achieve its admired quality and service standards without extremely mechanistic restaurant operations. Imagine the food and service you would get if McDonald's employees used their own favorite ways of doing things and worked at their own pace! On the other hand, mechanistic structure alienates some employees because it erodes their sense of self-control.

Getting the Right Fit

All of the organization structures described in this chapter are used today because each structure has advantages and disadvantages that make it appropriate in some cases. For example, the clear roles and strict hierarchy of an extremely mechanistic organization are beneficial when careful routines and a set of checks and balances are important, as at a nuclear power facility. In a fast-changing environment with a great deal of uncertainty, an organization would benefit from a more organic structure that lowers boundaries between functions and organizations. Let us consider each of the seven basic organization designs.

LO15.5

A functional structure can save money by grouping together people who need similar materials and equipment. Quality standards can be maintained because supervisors understand what department members do and because people in the same function develop pride in their specialty. Workers can devote more of their time to what they do best. These benefits are easiest to realize in a stable environment, where the organization doesn't depend on employees to coordinate their efforts to solve varied problems. Today fewer organizations see their environment as stable, so more are moving away from strictly functional structures.

Divisional structures increase employees' focus on customers and products. Managers have the flexibility to make decisions that affect several functions in order to serve customer needs. This enables the organization to move faster if a new customer need arises or if a competitor introduces an important product. However, duplicating functions in each division can add to costs, so this structure may be too expensive for some organizations. Also, divisions sometimes focus on their own customer groups or products to the exclusion of the company's overall mission. Ford Motor Company has struggled to unify its geographic and brand divisions to save money by sharing design, engineering, and manufacturing. Managers of geographic divisions have introduced new car models on different time lines and insisted that their customers want different features.[26]

In contrast, geographic divisions have helped McDonald's grow by freeing managers to introduce menu items and décor that locals appreciate.[27]

A matrix structure tries to combine the advantages of functional and divisional structures. This advantage is also the structure's main drawback: it violates the unity of command principle, described previously in the chapter. Employees have to balance the demands of a functional manager and a product or project manager. When they struggle with this balance, decision making can slow to a crawl, and political behavior can overpower progress. The success of a matrix organization therefore requires superior managers who communicate extensively, foster commitment and collaboration, manage conflict, and negotiate effectively to establish goals and priorities consistent with the organization's strategy. One organization that has made matrix structures work for decades is Procter & Gamble. To manage 138,000 employees in more than 80 countries, the company has a matrix structure in which global business units are responsible for a brand's development and production, while market development organizations focus on the customer needs for particular regions and the way the brands can meet those needs. Employees have to meet objectives both for the brand and for the market, with different managers responsible for each.[28]

Horizontal designs generally improve coordination and communication in organizations.[29] Cross-functional teams can arrive at creative solutions to problems that arise in a fast-changing environment. Teams can develop new products faster and more efficiently than can functions working independently in a traditional structure. Horizontal designs also encourage knowledge sharing. However, because lines of authority are less clear, managers must be able to share responsibility for the organization's overall performance, build commitment to a shared vision, and influence others even when they lack direct authority. This type of structure is a good fit when specialization is less important than the ability to respond to varied or changing customer needs. It requires employees who can rise to the challenges of empowerment. A horizontal design is a good fit for Research in Motion (RIM) because it builds on employees' deep product and customer knowledge. All employees use the company's BlackBerry pocket computers, so they know what works and what doesn't. RIM's chief executive maintains that because employees know the details of what makes the BlackBerry work, they are well positioned to continue improving it: "We didn't just buy an operating system from one company and a radio technology from another, and then have them assembled somewhere in Asia. We actually built the whole thing. . . . I don't mind investing in it because I know there's a return."[30] RIM applies that knowledge by creating teams to brainstorm new ideas in every aspect of the company's operations.

This $2,500 Tata Motors compact car is the result of an organization that adopted a modular structure. How did this structure enable the company to cut costs and inefficiencies?

Finally, organizations that open their boundaries to become hollow, modular, or virtual can generate superior returns by focusing on what they do best.[31] Like functional organizations, they tap people in particular specialties, who may be more expert than the generalists of a divisional or horizontal organization. The downside of these structures is that organizations give up expertise and control in the functions or operations that are outsourced. Still, like divisional and horizontal organizations, they can focus on customers or products, leaving their partners to focus on their own specialty area. In India, when Tata Motors wanted to develop a $2,500 compact car, it decided its own engineers needed assistance, so Tata adopted a modular structure. Each of its suppliers tackled designing particular components to be as inexpensive as possible while still meeting quality standards, and Tata focused on coordinating their work.[32] An example of a successful hollow organization is one global manufacturer that shifted its focus to developing products and contracted with outsourcing firms to make the products in the manufacturer's own facilities, handling the process from ordering materials to shipping the finished product. The arrangement maintained quality while cutting labor costs by 40% by avoiding inefficiency and duplication of work.[33]

The success of organizations that work across boundaries depends on managers' ability to get results from people over whom they do not have direct formal authority by virtue of their position in the organization. Boeing, for example, has been embarrassed by its setbacks in manufacturing the Dreamliner from components provided by a network of suppliers, which did not always meet their commitments to Boeing. Also, individuals in these organizations may not have the same degree of commitment as employees of a traditional organization, so motivation and leadership may be more difficult. Therefore, these designs are the best fit when organizations have suitable partners they trust; efficiency is very important; the organization can identify functions, processes, or product components to outsource profitably; and in the case of a virtual organization, when the need to be met is temporary. In a study of managers in 20 organizations that extensively collaborate with other companies, these efforts most often succeeded in companies that select and train for teamwork skills, invest in processes that promote collaboration, set up tools and systems for sharing information, and treat collaboration as one of the company's ongoing programs requiring leadership.[34]

> **BACK TO THE CHAPTER-OPENING CASE** Based on the contingency approach toward organizational design, where did Yahoo go wrong with its new structure?

Striving for Organizational Effectiveness

Assessing organizational effectiveness is an important topic for an array of people, including managers, stockholders, government agencies, and OB specialists. The purpose of this section is to introduce a widely applicable and useful model of organizational effectiveness.

Generic Effectiveness Criteria

A good way to better understand this complex subject is to consider four generic approaches to assessing an organization's effectiveness (see Figure 15–4). These effectiveness criteria apply equally well to large or small and profit or not-for-profit organizations. Moreover, as denoted by the overlapping circles in Figure 15–4, the four effectiveness criteria can be used in various combinations. The key thing to remember is "no single approach to the evaluation of effectiveness is appropriate in all circumstances or for all organization types."[35] What do Coca-Cola and France Télécom, for example, have in common, other than being large profit-seeking corporations? Because a multidimensional approach is required, we need to look more closely at each of the four generic effectiveness criteria before we can answer this question.

LO15.6

FIGURE 15–4   Four Dimensions of Organizational Effectiveness

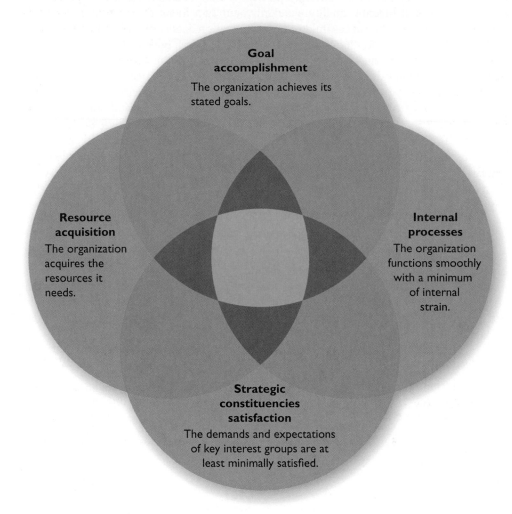

SOURCE: Adapted from discussion in K Cameron, "Critical Questions in Assessing Organizational Effectiveness," *Organizational Dynamics*, Autumn 1980, pp 66–80; and K S Cameron, "Effectiveness as Paradox: Consensus and Conflict in Conceptions of Organizational Effectiveness," *Management Science*, May 1986, pp 539–53.

Goal Accomplishment   Goal accomplishment is the most widely used effectiveness criterion for organizations. Key organizational results or outputs are compared with previously stated goals or objectives. Deviations, either plus or minus, require corrective action. This is simply an organizational variation of the personal goal-setting process discussed in Chapter 7. Effectiveness, relative to the criterion of goal accomplishment, is gauged by how well the organization meets or exceeds its goals.

Productivity improvement, involving the relationship between inputs and outputs, is a common organization-level goal. Goals also may be set for organizational efforts such as minority recruiting, sustainability, customer satisfaction, employee satisfaction, quality improvement, and output.[36] For example, Hyundai currently has capacity to produce 5.8 million cars and trucks and has established the goal of growing capacity to 6.5 million units by 2012. The company also is putting the goal of vehicle quality at the top of its list of strategic goals. Hyundai "developed a two-part quality target it calls GQ 3-3-5-5, as Joon-Sang Kim, executive vice president of Hyundai-Kia's Quality Division, explained in an interview. Hyundai aims to finish in the top three in actual quality within three years as measured by J D Power's dependability survey—and to finish in the top five in perceived quality in five years."[37] Given today's competitive pressures and e-commerce revolution, innovation and speed are very important organizational goals for many organizations.

Resource Acquisition   The second criterion, resource acquisition, relates to inputs rather than outputs. An organization is deemed effective in this regard if it acquires necessary factors of production such as raw materials, labor, capital, and managerial and technical expertise. Charitable organizations such as the Salvation Army and United Way judge their effectiveness in terms of how much money they raise from private and corporate donations.

Internal Processes   This dimension of effectiveness focuses on "what the organization must excel at" to effectively meet its financial objectives and customers' expectations. A team of researchers have identified four critical high-level internal processes that managers are encouraged to measure and manage. These processes influence productivity, efficiency, quality, safety, and a host of other internal metrics. The processes include organizational activities associated with (1) innovation, (2) customer service and satisfaction, (3) operational excellence, and (4) being a good corporate citizen.[38] Companies tend to adopt continuous improvement programs in pursuit of improving their internal processes. Consider what Hyundai has done to improve the quality of its internal processes.

> It installed Six Sigma at its engineering center to measure its improvement. It made quality a cross-functional responsibility, with involvement from procurement, finance, and sales and marketing. It enlisted outside suppliers and put them together with designers and engineers to work out problems before they occurred. Quality oversight meetings, which had been poorly attended, became must-go events after Chairman Chung began to show up for twice-monthly gatherings.[39]

Strategic Constituencies Satisfaction   Organizations both depend on people and affect the lives of people. Consequently, many consider the satisfaction of key interested parties to be an important criterion of organizational effectiveness.

A *strategic constituency* **is any group of individuals who have some stake in the organization—for example, resource providers, users of the organization's products or services, producers of the organization's output, groups whose cooperation is essential for the organization's survival, or those whose lives are significantly affected by the organization.**[40]

Strategic constituencies (or *stakeholders*) generally have competing or conflicting interests.[41] This forces executives to do some strategic juggling to achieve workable balances. For example, in recent years, it has been difficult for many organizations to satisfy the needs and preferences of employees, in part because of investors' pressure to operate more efficiently to withstand global competition at the same time many employees are demanding more flexibility so that they can fulfill competing roles. Sharon Allen, chairman of the board of Deloitte, believes that the company has balanced these competing interests by allowing employees more flexibility. Deloitte estimates that its flexibility programs saved the company about $45 million a year.[42] Besides employees and investors, another key constituency is, of course, customers.

www.mcgrawhillconnect.com

Go to Connect for an interactive exercise to test your knowledge of the generic organizational effectiveness criteria.

Mixing Effectiveness Criteria: Practical Guidelines

Experts on the subject recommend a multidimensional approach to assessing the effectiveness of modern organizations. This means no single criterion is appropriate for all stages of the organization's life cycle. Nor will a single criterion satisfy competing stakeholders. Well-managed organizations mix and match effectiveness criteria to fit the unique requirements of the situation. For example, Irdeto Holdings, which provides content protection for pay TV and video recordings, decided on a structural change after determining that sales were growing fastest in Asia, which already accounted for almost 40% of the company's revenues. To meet business goals for serving this important geographic market, Irdeto's executives decided to convert the company's Beijing office into a second headquarters (the first headquarters is located near Amsterdam). This change serves an important constituency—Asian customers—but raised concerns with Amsterdam employees. Responding to that second constituency, Irdeto's CEO, Graham Kill, announced plans to build a new Amsterdam office building and explained that employees can enjoy an exciting career path if they are willing to rotate between the two headquarters' cities. Management also has had to address internal processes, especially in developing Chinese managers to take initiative in decision making and to think about issues affecting the entire corporation, not just its Asian markets.[43]

Managers need to identify and seek input from strategic constituencies. This information, when merged with the organization's stated mission and philosophy, enables management to derive an appropriate *combination* of effectiveness criteria. The following guidelines are helpful in this regard:

- *The goal accomplishment approach* is appropriate when "goals are clear, consensual, time-bounded, measurable."[44]

- *The resource acquisition approach* is appropriate when inputs have a traceable effect on results or output. For example, the amount of money the American Red Cross receives through donations dictates the level of services provided.

Southwest Airlines is the envy of the beleaguered commercial airline industry because it is consistently effective at turning a profit by satisfying its customers and employees with a low-cost, on-time strategy and a no-layoff policy. Southwest's response to the accident with this plane is an example of its responsiveness to customer and safety issues. Southwest uses many of the theories and recommendations discussed in this book to pave the way toward its success.

- *The internal processes approach* is appropriate when organizational performance is strongly influenced by specific processes (e.g., cross-functional teamwork).

- *The strategic constituencies approach* is appropriate when powerful stakeholders can significantly benefit or harm the organization.

Unforeseen events or accidents represent another set of factors that should be considered when evaluating organizational effectiveness. For example, Southwest Airlines focused its attention on airplane safety after the fuselage ruptured on one of its Boeing 737 models causing a 5-foot-long tear in the plane's ceiling. Southwest canceled 300 flights as it voluntarily conducted inspections on 79 of its older planes.[45] This example illustrates how a company can quickly change its focus on specific goals in response to an accident.

key terms

chapter summary

- *Describe the four characteristics common to all organizations.* They are coordination of effort (achieved through policies and rules), a common goal (a collective purpose), division of labor (people performing different but related tasks), and a hierarchy of authority (the chain of command).

- *Explain the difference between closed and open systems.* Closed systems, such as a battery-powered clock, are relatively self-sufficient. Open systems, such as the human body, are highly dependent on the environment for survival.

- *Define seven basic ways organizations are structured.* Traditional designs include (1) functional structures, in which work is divided according to function; (2) divisional structures, in which work is divided according to product or customer type or location; and (3) matrix structures, with dual reporting structures based on product and function. Organizations also may be designed (4) horizontally, with cross-functional teams responsible for entire processes. Organization design also may reduce barriers between organizations, becoming (5) hollow organizations, which outsource functions; (6) modular organizations, which outsource the production of a product's components; or (7) virtual organizations, which temporarily combine the efforts of members of different companies in order to complete a project.

- *Discuss Burns and Stalker's findings regarding mechanistic and organic organizations.* British researchers Burns and Stalker found that mechanistic (bureaucratic, centralized) organizations tended to be effective in stable situations. In unstable situations, organic (flexible, decentralized) organizations were more effective. These findings underscored the need for a contingency approach to organization design.

- *Identify when each of the seven organization structures is the right fit.* Mechanistic organizations and functional structures may be necessary when tight control is important and the environment is stable. Organic organizations allow for innovation in a rapidly changing environment. Divisional structures are a good fit when the organization needs deep knowledge of varied customer groups and the ability to respond to customer demands quickly. A matrix organization can deliver the advantages of functional and divisional structures if the company has superior managers who communicate extensively, foster commitment and collaboration, and negotiate effectively to establish goals and priorities consistent with the organization's strategy. A horizontal design is a good fit when specialization is less important than the ability to respond to varied or changing customer needs. Hollow, modular, and virtual designs are best when organizations have suitable partners they trust; efficiency is very important; the organization can identify functions, processes, or product components to outsource; and in the case of a virtual organization, when the need to be met is temporary.

- *Describe the four generic organizational effectiveness criteria.* They are goal accomplishment (satisfying stated objectives), resource acquisition (gathering the necessary productive inputs), internal processes (building and maintaining healthy organizational systems), and strategic constituencies satisfaction (achieving at least minimal satisfaction for all key stakeholders).

discussion questions

1. What would an organization chart of your current (or last) place of employment look like? Does the chart you have drawn reveal the hierarchy (chain of command), division of labor, span of control, and line–staff distinctions? Does it reveal anything else? Explain.
2. Why is it appropriate to view modern organizations as open systems?
3. In a nutshell, what does contingency organization design entail?
4. If organic organizations are popular with most employees, why can't all organizations be structured in an organic fashion?
5. If you were president of your university, what criteria would you use to evaluate the university's effectiveness? Provide specific examples.

legal/ethical challenge

One of the Fastest Growing Businesses Involves Spying on Consumers: Is This Ethical?[46]

Many companies believe that the use of sophisticated software that tracks our internet behavior is an innovative way to get information that can be used to increase their revenue.

"Hidden inside Ashley Hayes-Beaty's computer, a tiny file helps gather personal details about her, all to be put up for sale for a tenth of a penny. The file consists of a single code . . . that secretly identifies her as a 26-year-old female in Nashville, Tennessee."

The code knows that her favorite movies include *The Princess Bride, 50 First Dates,* and *10 Things I Hate About You.* It knows she enjoys the *Sex and the City* series. "It knows she browses entertainment news and likes to take quizzes."

Upon learning about the file, Ashley concluded it was "eerily correct." Ms. Hayes's behavior is being monitored without her knowledge or permission by Lotame Solutions. The company uses special software called a "beacon" to track what people type on websites. "Lotame packages that data into profiles about individuals, without determining a person's name, and sells the profiles to companies seeking customers." That said, Eric Porres, Lotame's chief marketing officer, indicated that the profile can be segmented "all the way down to one person." Lotame also claimed that you can remove yourself from their system, assuming you even know that you are being tracked by the system.

"The information that companies gather is anonymous, in the sense that Internet users are identified by a number assigned to their computer, not by a specific person's name."

Many companies are unaware that their websites were tagged with beacons and that intrusive files were being attached to anyone who visited their website. The courts have not ruled on the legality of these complex tracking procedures.

How Do You Feel about the Practice of Someone Tracking Your Internet Behavior without Your Approval or Awareness?

1. Give me a break, this is the Internet age. Tracking is fair game and it provides useful information to companies so they can target products that meet our needs. Besides, you can get off Latame's system if you don't want to be tracked. Further, tracking can be used to catch pedophiles and other types of criminal behavior.

2. I can accept the idea of tracking, but companies like Latame should get our approval before they start collecting data.

3. This is an invasion of my privacy and it should be disallowed by the courts.

4. I am against any attempts to police what goes on when we use the Internet.

If you're looking for additional study materials, be sure to check out the Online Learning Center at

www.mhhe.com/kininckiob5e

for more information and interactivities that correspond to this chapter.

chapter 16

Managing Change and Organizational Learning

LEARNING OBJECTIVES

After reading the material in this chapter, you should be able to:

LO16.1 Discuss the external and internal forces that create the need for organizational change.

LO16.2 Describe Lewin's change model and the systems model of change.

LO16.3 Explain Kotter's eight steps for leading organizational change.

LO16.4 Review the 11 reasons employees resist change.

LO16.5 Identify alternative strategies for overcoming resistance to change.

LO16.6 Define the term *learning organization*.

LO16.7 Review the factors that hinder an organization's ability to learn from success and failure.

Why Was HCL Technologies' Transformation So Successful?

Vineet Nayar, CEO of HCL Technologies, a Delhi-based IT services provider, was interviewed by the *Harvard Business Review* regarding the company's transformation. His interview is summarized in this case.

Although the company's revenues were growing by about 30% a year, it was losing market share and mindshare. Our competitors were growing at the rate of 40% or 50% a year, and the IT services industry was changing rapidly. Customers didn't want to work with an undifferentiated services provider that offered discrete services; they wanted long-term partners that would provide end-to-end services. Could HCL become such a company?

History will tell you it did. By 2009, HCL had changed its business model, nearly tripled its annual revenues, doubled its market capitalization, been ranked India's best employer by Hewitt—and pioneered a unique management culture that I call Employees First, Customers Second (EFCS).

How did I do this? I didn't. One hundred senior managers and 55,000 employees, the people of our company, accomplished the transformation....

I realized that no one would jump into the future until the organization acknowledged that we needed to do so. So I spent the first few weeks of my tenure visiting HCL's offices around the world, meeting senior managers in small groups and at larger gatherings. I discussed the company's current situation—Point A, I call it....

I also met with customers during my travels, and it was from them that a potential Point B—where we should land—began to take shape. What struck me was that customers didn't talk much about our products, services, or technologies; they spoke mostly about HCL's employees. The value the company offered lay in the interface between customers and frontline employees—that was our value zone.

However, we weren't organized as if that was the case. HCL was a traditional pyramid, in which frontline people were accountable to a hierarchy of managers. The hierarchy usually made it more difficult for employees to add value....

I had told everyone that we would set a strategy collaboratively—and I meant it. In July 2005, I convened a meeting of our top 100 managers and proposed that HCL transform itself from an IT services vendor into an end-to-end global IT services partner that could compete against the likes of IBM, Accenture, and EDS....

The "Yes, buts ..." took three forms. Some managers feared that by taking on the major global players, we would forsake the position we had built over the past decade and would lose everything. Others raised issues I hadn't thought of, asking, for example, "The IT analysts favor the established players—how can we get them to recommend HCL?" A third group supported the proposed strategy and was exasperated with the status quo. These managers wanted us to act boldly, and often to ignore others' objections.

I said very little during these discussions.... Three days of debate later, we agreed to adopt the strategy I had proposed. Everyone was on board—at least in theory.

During this period I also held informal meetings with frontline employees, engaging them in discussions about the kind of company they wanted to work for and how they saw their jobs. These meetings became more formal in 2006, with a series of companywide meetings we called Directions. (We still hold them.) They involve thousands of employees and take place in large venues around the world.... Transformation requires action, not just words, but I don't believe in large-scale technology initiatives or massive reorganizations. We triggered change at HCL through small-scale catalysts....

Sharing financial data. At the time, employees had access to the financial information that pertained to their projects but didn't know how either their business unit or the organization was doing. Nor could they compare the performance of their team to that of others. We decided to share financial data extensively, within and across groups....

The smart service desk. I set up an online system that allows anyone in the organization to lodge a complaint or make a suggestion by opening a ticket. We have a defined process for handling tickets ... and the employee who opened the ticket determines whether its resolution is satisfactory. Not only does the system help resolve issues, but it effectively puts managers in the service of frontline employees.

The comprehensive 360-degree. Although HCL had a 360-degree performance review system in place, employees rarely reviewed managers because they didn't know what they stood to gain by doing so. I decided to allow anyone who had provided feedback to a manager to see the results.... I knew I couldn't force managers to make their reviews public; I could only encourage them to do so. The best way to do that was to lead by example. In 2006 I posted the results of my 360-degree appraisal on the intranet for all the company to see. Most managers followed suit....

The online planning process. Rather than reviewing the business plans of my 100 managers, as has been the case earlier, I asked managers to make video recordings summarizing their plans and post them on an online portal, where other managers could review them, share feedback, and discuss changes. This made a difference in how managers formulated and communicated ideas. Consequently, plans became more specific and executable....

I wanted passion. We developed a new survey, the Employee Passion Indicative Count, to identify the drivers of passion in the workplace. This led to the creation of Employees First Councils, groups that focus on specific passions, from art and music to philanthropy and social responsibility. The councils help employees break down the barriers between their personal and professional lives and bring more meaning to their work. These groups had one unexpected benefit: Some sprang up around business issues, such as cloud computing, which channelled personal passion into company innovation....

The most difficult decision to make about transformation is when to start. We began when HCL was still growing at a healthy clip. We may appear to have been early, but I'm convinced that if we hadn't made our move then, HCL, wouldn't be so successful today.[1]

WORLDWIDE COMPETITION AND rapid changes in technology are creating tremendous pressure on organizations to change. The chapter-opening case, for example, illustrated how HCL Technologies' CEO Vineet Nayar took a proactive approach toward leading change in the company. Other well-known companies such as GE, Intel, Toyota, and Pepsi have similarly implemented corporate-wide change initiatives to help compete in the marketplace.[2] We don't expect the need to change to go away any time soon. For example, IBM's annual survey of 1,541 CEOs, general managers, and senior public-sector leaders from 60 countries and 33 industries led to the conclusion "that incremental changes are no longer sufficient in a world that is operating in fundamentally different ways." These executives believe that life in general is becoming more complex and that managing complexity will differentiate those firms that survive in the long term.[3]

Moreover, any type of change, whether it be product driven, personal, or organizational, is likely to encounter resistance even when it represents an appropriate course of action. Even when employees don't actively resist a change, the goal of the change might not be realized if employees feel so negative about it that absenteeism and turnover rise. Peter Senge, a well-known expert on the topic of organizational change, made the following comment during an interview with *Fast Company* magazine:

> When I look at efforts to create change in big companies over the past 10 years, I have to say that there's enough evidence of success to say that change is possible—and enough evidence of failure to say that it isn't likely.[4]

If Senge is correct, then it is all the more important for current and future managers to learn how they can successfully implement organizational change.

This final chapter was written to help managers navigate the journey of change. Specifically, we discuss the forces that create the need for organization change, models of planned change, resistance to change, and creating a learning organization.

Forces of Change

 LO16.1

How do organizations know when they should change? What cues should an organization look for? Although there are no clear-cut answers to these questions, the "cues" that signal the need for change are found by monitoring the forces for change.

Organizations encounter many different forces for change. These forces come from external sources outside the organization and from internal sources. This section examines the forces that create the need for change. Awareness of the forces of change can help managers determine when they should consider implementing an organizational change.

External Forces

***External forces for change* originate outside the organization.** Because these forces have global effects, they may cause an organization to question the essence of what business it is in and the process by which products and services are produced. There are four key external forces for change: demographic characteristics, technological advancements, market changes, and social and political pressures. Each is now discussed.

Demographic Characteristics   Chapter 4 provided a detailed discussion of the demographic changes occurring in the U.S. workforce. You learned that organizations are changing employment benefits and aspects of the work environment in order to attract, motivate, and retain diverse employees.[5] Organizations also are changing the way in which they design and market their products and services and design their store layouts based on generational differences. For example, Ken Romanzi, North American chief operating officer for Ocean Spray Cranberries, told a *Wall Street Journal* reporter that "we don't do anything to remind boomers that they are getting older."[6] Further, persistently higher unemployment levels among young people around the world is creating a strong force for change by governments and organizations alike. For example, experts believe that much of the current unrest in the Middle East is being fueled by a younger population that cannot find meaningful employment opportunities.[7]

Technological Advancements   Both manufacturing and service organizations are increasingly using technology as a means to improve productivity, competitiveness, and customer service while also cutting costs. For example, more and more companies are using social networking as standard recruiting tools, and HR professionals indicate that they expect to use them more frequently in the future.[8] Information technology also is enabling more and more forms of self-service, from Internet stores and banks for customers to online help for employees who want to learn about their benefits packages. *Telepresence* **is a good example of a technology that enables organizations to change the way they deliver products, coordinate virtual workers, encourage employee collaboration, improve communication, and increase productivity.** It represents an advanced form of videoconferencing and robotics that in combination makes virtual conversations seem like they are taking place in one location. These systems, which can cost upward of $300,000, are used by companies such as Bank of America, PepsiCo, Procter & Gamble, and Royal Dutch Shell. They have been found to help companies significantly cut their travel expenses (see the Skills & Best Practices feature on page 422) and to improve communications among employees and customers.[9]

Under former CEO Robert Siegel, the venerable clothier Lacoste is responding to market forces. Shifting tastes among U.S. shoppers inspired the company to restore its brand's luxury image with better fabrics, higher prices, more exclusive distribution, and newly designed multiseason fashions like stylish boots and shearling jackets that appeal to a new generation of shoppers. "When you think back to Lacoste 10 years ago," says Siegel, "we never had the young customer that we have now."

Customer and Market Changes   Increasing customer sophistication is requiring organizations to deliver higher value in their products and services. Customers are simply demanding more now than they did in the past. Moreover, customers are more likely to shop elsewhere if they do not get what they want because of lower customer switching costs. This has led more and more companies to seek customer feedback about a wide range of issues in order to retain and attract

Telepresence Enhances Collaboration and Reduces Travel by Linking People around the Globe

Telepresence has even come to the coffee break: Four of Cisco's European offices have wall-size telepresence screens constantly on in the office canteen, so that co-workers hundreds of miles apart can "meet" there for a drink.

"You're able to virtualize people and resources," says Marthin De Beer, the Cisco executive who led the development of the company's telepresence offerings, in an interview conducted between two telepresence suites. De Beer now spends much of his time in a suite at Cisco's San Jose headquarters, clicking from one distant locale to another as if flipping through TV channels. "I'm frequently in five or six cities a day, and it would be impossible to get on that many planes," he says. "Rarely a day goes by when I'm not in at least three or four telepresence meetings."

While these systems are growing in popularity, the cost is prohibiting wide-scale application. That said, Autodesk has 20 telepresence rooms and social network game developer Zynga uses them to coordinate interactions between designers and programmers around the world. The CBS show *The Good Wife* also uses telepresence suites to conduct bicoastal writers' meetings. Hospitals also use this technology to link remote doctors with patients.

SOURCE: Excerpted from D Bennett, "I'll Have My Robots Talk to Your Robots," *Bloomberg Businessweek,* **February 21–27, 2011, p 54.**

customers. For example, General Motors has made it a point to seek customer feedback in the design and marketing of its vehicles and McDonald's actively collects information about consumer preferences and tastes and uses it to revise the menu. This led McDonald's to create more chicken offerings. The company now sells almost as much chicken as beef and its chicken sales are twice those of its leading competitors combined.[10]

With respect to market changes, companies are experiencing increased pressure to obtain more productivity because global competition is fierce. Swings in the economic cycle also spur a need to change in response to surging or falling demand for products, requiring companies to produce more or survive on less.

Social and Political Pressures   These forces are created by social and political events. For example, widespread concern about the impact of climate change and rising energy costs have been important forces for change in almost every industry around the world. Companies have gone "green," looking for ways to use less energy themselves and to sell products that consume less energy and are safer to use. For example, Esquel, one of the world's largest producers of premium cotton shirts, received pressure from retail customers such as Nike and Marks & Spencer to improve its environmental and social performance. These retail stores want Esquel to produce more cotton organically. This is very difficult to do because most of Esquel's cotton comes from "Xinjiang, an arid province in northwestern China that depends mainly on underground sources of water. The traditional method of irrigation there was to periodically flood the fields—an inefficient approach that created a perfect breeding ground for insects and diseases. Heavy pesticide use was a necessity." This pressure ultimately caused Esquel to closely work with farms to implement sustainable farming techniques. "For example, it assisted them in adopting drip irrigation to decrease their water use and in establishing natural pest and disease control programs such as breeding disease-resistant strains of cotton, to reduce reliance on pesticides. (The new variety of cotton plants also produced stronger fiber, resulting in less scrap during fabric manufacturing then conventional cotton did.)[11]

Internal Forces

***Internal forces for change* come from inside the organization.** These forces can be subtle, such as low job satisfaction, or can manifest in outward signs, such as low productivity, conflict, or strikes. In general, internal forces for change come from both human resource problems and managerial behavior/decisions. For example, Chinese employees from Honda Motor and Toyota Motor companies shocked management by striking in response to labor issues. Honda ultimately decided to increase salaries to a level that "would be roughly double the average amount paid to a factory worker in India or 33% higher than that in Thailand. Such higher labor costs would make it difficult for Honda to compete with vehicles exported from these countries by rivals including Toyota, which has a plant

Johnson & Johnson's product recalls are creating a strong force for change. Is your decision to purchase their products influenced by these recalls?

in Thailand, and Nissan Motor Co. and Suzuki Motor Co., which have plants in India."[12]

Managerial decisions also are a powerful force for change. Consider the case of Johnson & Johnson (J&J). The company has voluntarily recalled more than 50 products since 2010 and the 2010 annual report contained "eight pages detailing government criminal and civil investigations and thousands of private lawsuits covering a wide range of drugs, device, and business practices." A recent article in *Bloomberg Businessweek* suggested that cost-cutting decisions made by management along with a decentralized structure may be the root causes of these problems. J&J's CEO William Weldon believes that these issues are being blown out of proportion because most product-related problems originated at only 3 of 120 manufacturing facilities. Weldon believes that the company still puts patients ahead of profits and shareholders and he has no intention of stepping down because of the product recalls. The company is currently focused on fixing its manufacturing problems.[13]

> **BACK TO THE CHAPTER-OPENING CASE**   What were the external and internal forces for change at HCL?

Models of Planned Change

American managers are criticized for emphasizing short-term, quick-fix solutions to organizational problems. When applied to organizational change, this approach is doomed from the start. Quick-fix solutions do not really solve underlying causes of problems and they have little staying power. Researchers and managers alike thus have tried to identify effective ways to manage the change process. This section reviews three models of planned change—Lewin's change model, a systems model of change, and Kotter's eight steps for leading organizational change—and organizational development.

Lewin's Change Model

 LO16.2

Most theories of organizational change originated from the landmark work of social psychologist Kurt Lewin. Lewin developed a three-stage model of planned change which explained how to initiate, manage, and stabilize the change process.[14] The three stages are unfreezing, changing, and refreezing.

Unfreezing   The focus of this stage is to create the motivation to change. In so doing, individuals are encouraged to replace old behaviors and attitudes with those desired by management. Managers can begin the unfreezing process by disconfirming the usefulness or appropriateness of employees' present behaviors or attitudes. In other words, employees need to become dissatisfied with the old way of doing things. Managers frequently create the motivation for change by presenting data regarding levels of effectiveness, efficiency, or customer satisfaction. Declines in the stock price and same-store sales of Starbucks, along with the reappointment of Howard Schultz as CEO of the company he once built into an internationally known brand, signaled a need for change in how Starbucks operated. Schultz concluded that "the company had been hitting a home run in terms of growth every single year, but I could smell that things were wrong. We weren't creating a soulful, romantic experience anymore: We'd lost sight of the experience around the coffee, and we were too focused on ringing the register."[15]

To unfreeze the organization, Schultz began by apologizing to Starbucks employees about managerial decisions that led to the company's predicament. He then closed every store for retraining at a cost of $6 million. He then sent every store manager to New Orleans, which cost $30 million, for meetings and social bonding by having them volunteer in the Ninth Ward.[16]

Benchmarking is another technique that can be used to unfreeze an organization. *Benchmarking* **"describes the overall process by which a company compares its performance with that of other companies, then learns how the strongest-performing companies achieve their results."**[17] For example, one company for which we consulted discovered through benchmarking that its costs to develop software were twice as high as the best companies in the industry, and the time it took to get a new product to market was four times longer than the benchmarked organizations. These data were ultimately used to unfreeze employees' attitudes and motivate people to change the organization's internal processes in order to remain competitive. Managers also need to devise ways to reduce the barriers to change during this stage.

Changing   Organizational change, whether large or small, is undertaken to improve some process, procedure, product, service, or outcome of interest to management. Because change involves learning and doing things differently, this stage entails

Application of Lewin's Model: Creating Customer Focus within a Call Center

1. *Unfreezing:* Managers hold a meeting with all telephone representatives. During the meeting, customer survey results are discussed. Additionally, lost customer estimates are translated into dollars and cents so that telephone representatives can see how poor customer service results in overall company performance and lost jobs.

2. *Change:* After the meeting, telephone representatives are provided with customer service training that involves role-playing and group discussions. This allows the representatives to experience "poor" service and "good" service. Representatives are instructed to take their time with calls and to make sure they address all customer needs. A new peer support system is created whereby representatives spend 15 minutes every shift listening to other calls and providing feedback and support. Mirrors are placed on every call station so that representatives can make sure they "end the call with a smile." This becomes an unofficial slogan for the center.

3. *Refreezing:* The old compensation system rewarded representatives based on the number of calls made per hour. Clearly, this old system would not support the desired changes so the compensation system is changed. Representatives are now paid on an hourly rate and bonuses are based on customer satisfaction surveys. Additionally, the employees have the opportunity to nominate each other for "customer service guru of the week." The honor comes with a silly hat and certificate.

SOURCE: Excerpted from J H Mills, K Dye, and A J Mills, *Understanding Organizational Change* (New York: Routledge, 2009).

providing employees with new information, new behavioral models, new processes or procedures, new equipment, new technology, or new ways of getting the job done. How does management know what to change?

There is no simple answer to this question. Organizational change can be aimed at improvement or growth, or it can focus on solving a problem such as poor customer service or low productivity. Change also can be targeted at different levels in an organization. For example, sending managers to leadership training programs can be a solution to improving individuals' job satisfaction and productivity. In contrast, installing new information technology may be the change required to increase work-group productivity and overall corporate profits. The point to keep in mind is that change should be targeted at some type of desired end result. The systems model of change, which is the next model to be discussed, provides managers with a framework to diagnose the target of change.

Refreezing   Change is stabilized during refreezing by helping employees integrate the changed behavior or attitude into their normal way of doing things. This is accomplished by first giving employees the chance to exhibit the new behaviors or attitudes. Once these have been exhibited, positive reinforcement is used to reinforce the desired change. Additional coaching and modeling also are used at this point to reinforce the stability of the change. Extrinsic rewards, particularly monetary incentives (recall our discussion in Chapter 8), are frequently used to reinforce behavioral change. The Skills & Best Practices feature above illustrates the application of Lewin's theory to a call center that received negative evaluations from customers. Managers examined customer feedback and concluded that customers were unhappy about being rushed off the phone without having their concerns resolved. The focus of the change effort was to encourage employees to become more customer focused.

A Systems Model of Change

A systems approach takes a "big picture" perspective of organizational change. It is based on the notion that any change, no matter how large or small, has a cascading effect throughout an organization.[18] For example, promoting an individual to a new work group affects the group dynamics in both the old and new groups. Similarly, creating project or work teams may necessitate the need to revamp compensation practices. These examples illustrate that change creates additional change. Today's solutions are tomorrow's problems.

A systems model of change offers managers a framework or model to use for diagnosing *what* to change and for determining *how* to evaluate the success of a change effort. To further your understanding about this model, we first describe its components and then discuss a brief application. The four main components of a systems model of change are inputs, strategic plans, target elements of change, and outputs (see Figure 16–1).

Inputs   All organizational changes should be consistent with an organization's mission, vision, and resulting strategic plan. A **mission statement represents the "reason" an organization exists, and an organization's *vision* is a long-term goal that describes "what" an organization wants to become.** Consider how the difference between mission and vision affects organizational change. Your university probably has a mission to educate people. This mission does not necessarily imply anything about change. It simply defines the university's overall purpose. In contrast, the university may have a vision to be recognized as the "best" university in the country. This vision requires the organization to benchmark itself against other world-class universities and to create plans for achieving the vision. For example, the vision of the W. P. Carey School of Business at Arizona State University is to be among the top 25 business schools in the world. An assessment of an organization's internal strengths and weaknesses against its environmental opportunities and threats (SWOT) is another key input within the systems model. This SWOT analysis is a key component of the strategic planning process.

Strategic Plans   A *strategic plan* **outlines an organization's long-term direction and the actions necessary to achieve planned results.** Among other things, strategic plans are based on results from a SWOT analysis. This analysis aids in developing an organizational strategy to attain desired goals such as profits, customer satisfaction, quality, adequate return on investment, and acceptable levels of turnover and employee satisfaction and commitment.

Target Elements of Change   *Target elements of change* **are the components of an organization that may be changed.** They essentially represent change levers that managers can push and pull to influence various aspects of an organization. The choice of which lever to pull, however, is based on a diagnosis of a problem, or problems, or the actions needed to accomplish a vision or goal: A problem exists when managers are not obtaining the results they desire. The target elements of change are used to diagnose problems and to identify change-related solutions.

A Systems Model of Change   FIGURE 16–1

Target elements of change

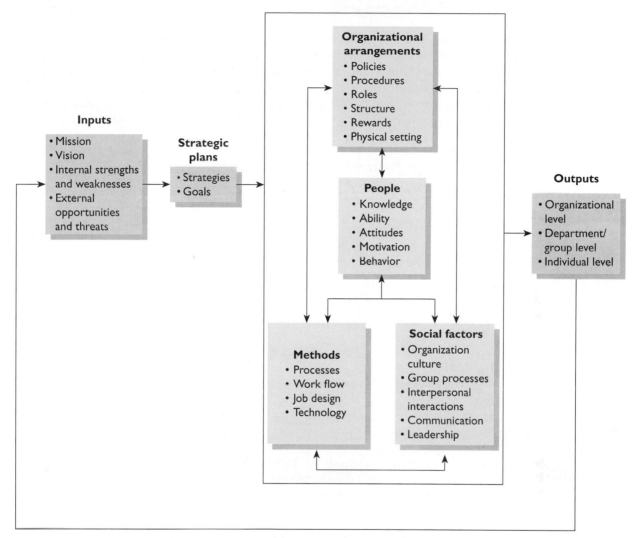

SOURCE: Adapted from D R Fuqua and D J Kurpius, "Conceptual Models in Organizational Consultation," *Journal of Counseling & Development*, July–August 1993, pp 602–18; and D A Nadler and M L Tushman, "Organizational Frame Bending: Principles for Managing Reorientation," *Academy of Management Executive*, August 1989, pp 194–203.

As shown in Figure 16–1, there are four targeted elements of change: organizational arrangements, social factors, methods, and people.[19] Each target element of change contains a subset of more detailed organizational features. For instance, the "social factors" component includes consideration of an organization's culture, group processes, interpersonal interactions, communication, and leadership. There are two final issues to keep in mind about the target elements of change shown in Figure 16–1. First, the double-headed arrows connecting each target element of change convey the message that change ripples across an organization. For example, changing a reward system to reinforce team rather than individual performance (an organizational arrangement) is likely to impact organizational culture (a social factor). Second, the "people" component is placed in the center of the target elements of change box because all organizational change ultimately impacts employees. Organizational change is more likely to succeed when managers proactively consider the impact of change on its employees.

Outputs   Outputs represent the desired end results of a change. Once again, these end results should be consistent with an organization's strategic plan. Figure 16–1 indicates that change may be directed at the organizational level, department/group level, or individual level. Change efforts are more complicated and difficult to manage when they are targeted at the organizational level. This occurs because organizational-level changes are more likely to affect multiple target elements of change shown in the model.

Applying the Systems Model of Change   There are two different ways to apply the systems model of change. The first is as an aid during the strategic planning process. Once a group of managers has determined its vision and strategic goals, the target elements of change can be considered when developing action plans to support the accomplishment of goals. For example, following the merger of Adolph Coors Company and Molson, the management team of Molson Coors Brewing established goals of cutting costs by $180 million, making Coors Light a global brand, and developing new high-end brands of beer. Target elements of change have included strengthening shared values of the predecessor companies (social factors), keeping production and distribution employees focused on their existing functions (motivation, a people factor), creating a general-management development program (another people factor), and establishing a subsidiary to specialize in new products (organizational arrangements).[20]

The merger between Coors and Molson involved several of the target elements of change. Based on the systems model of change, why do mergers frequently fail to meet management's expectations?

The second application involves using the model as a diagnostic framework to determine the causes of an organizational problem and to propose solutions. We highlight this application by considering a consulting project in which we used the model. We were contacted by the CEO of a software company and asked to figure out why the presidents of three divisions were not collaborating with each other—the problem. It turned out that two of the presidents submitted a proposal for the same $4 million project from a potential customer. Our client did not get the work because the customer was appalled at having received two proposals from the same company; hence the CEO's call to us. We decided to interview employees by using a structured set of questions that pertained to each of the target elements of change. For instance, we asked employees to comment on the extent to which the reward system, organizational culture, work flow, and physical setting contributed to collaboration across divisions. The interviews taught us that the lack of collaboration among the division presidents was due to the reward system (an organizational arrangement), a competitive culture and poor communications (social factors), and poor work flow (a methods factor). Our recommendation was to change the reward systems, restructure the organization, and redesign the work flow.

> **BACK TO THE CHAPTER-OPENING CASE**   Which of the target elements of change were affected by the changes at HCL Technologies?

Kotter's Eight Steps for Leading Organizational Change

John Kotter, an expert in leadership and change management, believes that organizational change typically fails because senior management makes a host of implementation errors. Kotter proposed an eight-step process for leading change (see Table 16–1) based on these errors.[21] Unlike the systems model of change, this model is not diagnostic in orientation. Its application will not help managers to diagnose *what* needs to be changed. Rather, this model is more like Lewin's model of change in that it prescribes *how* managers should sequence or lead the change process.

Kotter's eight steps shown in Table 16–1 subsume Lewin's model of change. The first four steps represent Lewin's "unfreezing" stage. Steps 5, 6, and 7 represent "changing," and step 8 corresponds to "refreezing." The value of Kotter's steps is that they provide specific recommendations about behaviors that managers need to exhibit to successfully lead organizational change. It is important to remember that Kotter's research reveals that it is ineffective to skip steps and that managers most often make mistakes at the beginning.[22] For instance, Yahoo cofounder and former CEO Jerry Yang was partially unsuccessful in creating change at Yahoo because "he was slow to consolidate redundant businesses (two photo-sharing properties, multiple social-media sites) and failed to explain the strategy behind his Get Google objective."[23] These errors pertain to steps one and three.

> **BACK TO THE CHAPTER-OPENING CASE**   To what extent did Vineet Nayar follow the change models proposed by Lewin and Kotter?

Creating Change through Organization Development

Organization development (OD) is different from the previously discussed models of change. OD does not entail a structured sequence as proposed by Lewin and Kotter, but it does possess the same diagnostic focus associated with the systems model of change. That said, OD is much broader in orientation than any of the previously

LO16.3

www.mcgrawhillconnect.com

Go to Connect for an interactive exercise to test your knowledge of Kotter's 8 Steps for Leading Organizational Change.

connect
www.mcgrawhillconnect.com

Go to Connect for a self-assessment to determine how ready an organization is ready for change.

TABLE 16–1   Steps to Leading Organizational Change

Step	Description
1. Establish a sense of urgency	Unfreeze the organization by creating a compelling reason for why change is needed.
2. Create the guiding coalition	Create a cross-functional, cross-level group of people with enough power to lead the change.
3. Develop a vision and strategy	Create a vision and strategic plan to guide the change process.
4. Communicate the change vision	Create and implement a communication strategy that consistently communicates the new vision and strategic plan.
5. Empower broad-based action	Eliminate barriers to change, and use target elements of change to transform the organization. Encourage risk taking and creative problem solving.
6. Generate short-term wins	Plan for and create short-term "wins" or improvements. Recognize and reward people who contribute to the wins.
7. Consolidate gains and produce more change	The guiding coalition uses credibility from short-term wins to create more change. Additional people are brought into the change process as change cascades throughout the organization. Attempts are made to reinvigorate the change process.
8. Anchor new approaches in the culture	Reinforce the changes by highlighting connections between new behaviors and processes and organizational success. Develop methods to ensure leadership development and succession.

SOURCE: The steps were developed by J P Kotter, *Leading Change* (Boston: Harvard Business School Press, 1996).

discussed models. Specifically, a pair of experts in this field of study and practice defined *organization development* as follows:

> **OD consists of planned efforts to help persons work and live together more effectively, over time, in their organizations.** These goals are achieved by applying behavioral science principles, methods, and theories adapted from the fields of psychology, sociology, education, and management.[24]

As you can see from this definition, OD constitutes a set of techniques or interventions that are used to implement "planned" organizational change aimed at increasing "an organization's ability to improve itself as a humane and effective system."[25] OD techniques or interventions apply to each of the change models discussed in this section. For example, OD is used during Lewin's "changing" stage. It also is used to identify and implement targeted elements of change within the systems model of change. OD also might be used during Kotter's steps 1, 3, 5, 6, and 7. Finally, OD is put into

practice by change agents. A ***change agent*** **is some-**
one who is a catalyst in helping organizations to
deal with old problems in new ways. Change agents
can be external consultants or internal employees. In
this section, we briefly review how OD works and its
research and practical implications.[26]

How OD Works   OD change agents follow a
medical-like model. They approach the organization
as if it were a "sick" patient, "diagnose" its ills, pre-
scribe and implement an "intervention," and "evaluate" progress. Let us consider the components of the
OD process shown in Figure 16–2.

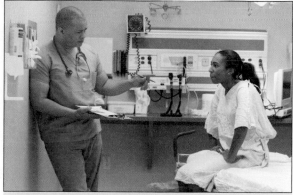

OD specialists use a medical-like model to diagnose and fix organizational problems. How would you like to be an organizational doctor?

1. *Diagnosis: What is the problem and its causes?*
   Change agents use a combination of interviews,
   surveys, meetings, written materials, and direct
   observation to determine the problem and its associated causes. We recommend
   using the target elements of change in the systems model of change as a vehicle
   to develop diagnostic questions aimed at identifying causes. For example, you
   might ask, "To what extent does the structure or reward system contribute to
   the problem?"

2. *Intervention: What can be done to solve the problem?* The treatment or intervention represents the changes being made to solve the problem. Treatments are
   selected based on the causes of the problem. For example, if the cause of low
   quality is poor teamwork, then team building (see Chapter 9) might be used as the
   intervention. In contrast, managers might be sent to some type of leadership training if bad leadership is the cause of low quality (see Chapter 14). The key thing
   to remember is there is not one "set" of intervention techniques that apply to all

The OD Process   **FIGURE 16–2**

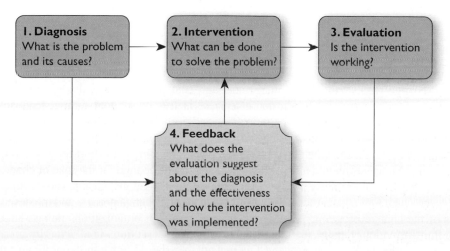

SOURCE: Adapted from W L French and C H Bell Jr. *Organization Development: Behavioral Interventions for Organizational Improvement* (Englewood Cliffs, NJ: Prentice Hall, 1978).

situations. Rather, you can use any number of interventions based on theories and models you studied in this book. A contingency approach allows you to select the intervention that seems best suited for the problem and causes at hand.

3. *Evaluation: Is the intervention working?* Evaluation requires the organization to develop measures of effectiveness—recall our discussion of organizational effectiveness in Chapter 15. The proper measure depends on the problem. For example, measures of voluntary turnover and productivity would be appropriate if the problem involved employee turnover and productivity, respectively. If possible, the final evaluation should be based on comparing measures of effectiveness obtained before and after the intervention.

4. *Feedback: What does the evaluation suggest about the diagnosis and the effectiveness of how the intervention was implemented?* If the evaluation reveals that the intervention worked, then the OD process is complete and the change agent can consider how best to "refreeze" the changes. Oppositely, a negative evaluation means one of two things: (1) either the initial diagnosis was wrong or (2) the intervention was not effectively implemented. Negative evaluations generally require the change agent to collect more information about steps 1 and 2 in the OD process shown in Figure 16–2.

OD Research and Practical Implications   Before discussing the application of OD research, it is important to note that OD-related interventions produced the following insights:

- A meta-analysis of 18 studies indicates that employee satisfaction with change is higher when top management is highly committed to the change effort.[27]

- A meta-analysis of 52 studies provides support for the systems model of organizational change. Specifically, varying one target element of change creates changes in other target elements. Also, there is a positive relationship between individual behavior change and organizational-level change.[28]

- A meta-analysis of 126 studies demonstrates that multifaceted interventions using more than one OD technique are more effective in changing job attitudes and work attitudes than interventions that rely on only one human-process or technostructural approach.[29]

- A survey of 1,700 firms from China, Japan, the United States, and Europe reveals that (1) U.S. and European firms use OD interventions more frequently than firms from China and Japan and (2) some OD interventions are culture free and some are not.[30]

Four practical implications can be derived from this research. First, planned organizational change works. However, management and change agents are advised to rely on multifaceted interventions. As indicated elsewhere in this book, goal setting, feedback, recognition and rewards, training, participation, and a challenging job design have good track records relative to improving performance and satisfaction. Second, change programs are more successful when they are geared toward meeting both short-term and long-term results. Managers should not engage in organizational change for the sake of change. Change efforts should produce positive results. Third, organizational change is more likely to succeed when top management is truly committed to the change process and the desired goals of the change program. This is particularly true when organizations pursue large-scale transformation. Finally, the effectiveness of OD interventions is affected by cross-cultural considerations. Managers and OD consultants should not blindly apply an OD intervention that worked in one country to a similar situation in another country.

Understanding and Managing Resistance to Change

No matter how technically or administratively perfect a proposed change may be, people make or break it because organizational change represents a form of influence. That is, organizational change is management's attempt to have employees behave, think, or perform differently. Viewing change from this perspective underscores what we discussed about influence techniques and outcomes in Chapter 13. You may recall that resistance is one of the three possible influence outcomes; the other two are commitment and compliance. This perspective has led many people to conclude that resistance to change represents a failed influence attempt by a change agent. Interestingly, recent research indicates a need to rethink this interpretation.

Resistance to change is not as obvious as it appears in this photo. Why do you think people resist change at work and at home?

Past research on resistance has been based on the assumption that "change agents are doing the right and proper things while change recipients throw up unreasonable obstacles or barriers intent on 'doing in' or 'screwing up' the change. . . . Accordingly, change agents are portrayed as undeserving victims of the irrational and dysfunctional response of change recipients."[31] This is why resistance is viewed as a negative outcome that is caused by irrational and self-serving recipients. While this can be true, it is equally likely that resistance is caused by two other key factors: the change agent's characteristics, actions, inactions, and perceptions and the quality of the relationship between change agents and change recipients. This section is based on the premise that resistance is a natural form of employee feedback and that it can serve a useful purpose. Managers are encouraged to understand the causes of resistance if they are to effectively manage change.[32] Accordingly, this section reviews the causes of resistance and practical ways of overcoming it.

Why People Resist Change in the Workplace

Resistance to change is an emotional/behavioral response to real or imagined threats to an established work routine. Resistance can be as subtle as passive resignation and as overt as deliberate sabotage. The causes of resistance to change tend to originate in either recipient characteristics or change agent characteristics. Let us now consider the reasons employees resist change in the first place: The first six primarily pertain to recipient characteristics and the last five to issues associated with change agent characteristics.[33]

LO16.4

1. *An individual's predisposition toward change.* Your predisposition toward change in a particular situation is a function of both personal traits and change agent behaviors. On the trait side, it is an outgrowth of how one learns to handle change and ambiguity as a child. While some people are distrustful and suspicious of change, others see change as a situation requiring flexibility, patience, and understanding.[34] Resilience to change is an important trait that affects how we respond to change. *Resilience to change,* which represents

a composite characteristic reflecting high self-esteem, optimism, and an internal locus of control, was positively associated with recipients' willingness to accommodate or accept a specific organizational change.[35] The U.S. Army is taking this research one step further. The Army designed a series of courses to help military personnel become more resilient to the demands of modern warfare, which is characterized by "demanding missions, extreme climates, sleep deprivation, cultural dissonance, physical fatigue, prolonged separation from family, and the ever-present threat of serious bodily injury or death."[36] The ultimate goal of this training is to make sure that military personnel are psychologically fit for the challenges of war.

The second personal characteristic, *commitment to change*, **is defined as a mind-set "that binds an individual to a course of action deemed necessary for the successful implementation of a change initiative."**[37] This characteristic is more subject to change than resilience because it is partly a function of both traits and change agent characteristics. To further illustrate the idea of commitment to change, complete the Hands-On Exercise on page 436, a shortened version of an instrument measuring this commitment. Were you committed to the change? Did this level of commitment affect your behavioral support for what management was trying to accomplish?

2. *Surprise and fear of the unknown.* When innovative or radically different changes are introduced without warning, affected employees become fearful of the implications. The same is true when managers announce new goals without spelling out specific plans for how the goals will be achieved. Imagine how you would feel if your boss stated that your department was going to increase sales by 25% without hiring any new employees. Failing to set expectations around a change effort or the setting of new goals is a key contributor to resistance.[38]

3. *Fear of failure.* Intimidating changes on the job can cause employees to doubt their capabilities. Self-doubt erodes self-confidence and cripples personal growth and development. Recall our discussion about self-efficacy in Chapter 5.

4. *Loss of status and/or job security.* Administrative and technological changes that threaten to alter power bases or eliminate jobs generally trigger strong resistance. For example, most corporate restructuring involves the elimination of managerial jobs. One should not be surprised when middle managers resist restructuring and participative management programs that reduce their authority and status.

5. *Peer pressure.* Someone who is not directly affected by a change may actively resist it to protect the interest of his or her friends and coworkers.

6. *Past success.* Success can breed complacency. It also can foster a stubbornness to change because people come to believe that what worked in the past will work in the future. Decades ago the Green Revolution alleviated hunger in Asia and Latin America by equipping farmers with more productive strains of wheat and rice. But in the words of Usha Tuteja, who heads the Agricultural Economics Research Center at Delhi University, "People got complacent." Governments, believing that the problem of feeding a growing population had been solved, stopped funding agricultural research. Unfortunately, today new

challenges have again made food supply a major problem, and the solutions will require years of investment in further research.[39]

7. *Decisions that disrupt cultural traditions or group relationships.* Whenever individuals are transferred, promoted, or reassigned, cultural and group dynamics are thrown into disequilibrium. It would be similar to your being moved from one team to another during the middle of a semester. Resistance would increase because of the uncertainty associated with dealing with new team members and their expectations.

8. *Personality conflicts.* Just as a friend can get away with telling us something we would resent hearing from an adversary, the personalities of change agents can breed resistance. Change agents that display any of the traits of bad leadership discussed in Chapter 14 are likely to engender resistance from recipients.

9. *Lack of tact and/or poor timing.* Undue resistance can occur because changes are introduced in an insensitive manner or at an awkward time. Proposed organizational changes are more likely to be accepted by others when change agents effectively explain or "sell" the value of their proposed changes. This can be done by explaining how a proposed change is strategically important to an organization's success.

10. *Leadership style.* Research shows that people are less likely to resist change when the change agent uses transformational leadership (see Chapter 14).[40]

11. *Failing to legitimize change.* Change must be internalized by recipients before it will be truly accepted. Active, honest communication and reinforcing reward systems are needed to make this happen. This recommendation underscores the need for change agents to communicate with recipients in a way that considers employees' point of view and perspective. It also is important for change agents to explain how change will lead to positive personal and organizational benefits. This requires that change agents have a clear understanding about how recipients' jobs will change and how they will be rewarded.[41] For example, an employee is unlikely to support a change effort that is perceived as requiring him or her to work longer with more pressure without a commensurate increase in pay.

Alternative Strategies for Overcoming Resistance to Change

We previously noted that resistance is a form of feedback and managers need to understand why it is occurring before trying to overcome it. This can be done by considering the extent to which each of the sources of resistance just discussed are contributing to the problem. Consider employee characteristics as an example. Employees are more likely to resist when they perceive that the personal costs of change overshadow the benefits. If this is the case, then managers are advised to (1) provide as much information as possible to employees about the change, (2) inform employees about the reasons/rationale for the change, (3) conduct meetings to address employees' questions regarding the change, and (4) provide employees the opportunity to discuss how the proposed change might affect them. Using these recommendations also will improve the change agent–recipient relationship because they enhance the level of

LO16.5

HANDS-ON EXERCISE

Does Your Commitment to a Change Initiative Predict Your Behavioral Support for the Change?

INSTRUCTIONS: First, think of a time in which a previous or current employer was undergoing a change initiative that required you to learn something new or to discontinue an attitude, behavior, or organizational practice. Next, evaluate your commitment to this change effort by indicating the extent to which you agree with the following survey items. Use the rating scale shown below. Finally, assess your behavioral support for the change.

	Strongly Disagree	Disagree	Neutral	Agree	Strongly Agree
1. I believe in the value of this change.	1	2	3	4	5
2. This change serves an important purpose.	1	2	3	4	5
3. This change is a good strategy for the organization.	1	2	3	4	5
4. I have no choice but to go along with this change.	1	2	3	4	5
5. It would be risky to speak out against this change.	1	2	3	4	5
6. It would be too costly for me to resist this change.	1	2	3	4	5
7. I feel a sense of duty to work toward this change.	1	2	3	4	5
8. It would be irresponsible of me to resist this change.	1	2	3	4	5
9. I feel obligated to support this change.	1	2	3	4	5
Total score	_____	_____	_____	_____	_____

SCORING NORMS

8–18 = Low socialization   19–29 = Moderate socialization   30–40 = High socialization

BEHAVIORAL SUPPORT FOR THE CHANGE

Overall, I modified my attitudes and behavior in line with what management was trying to accomplish.	1	2	3	4	5

SOURCES: Survey items were obtained from L Herscovitch and J P Meyer, "Commitment to Organizational Change: Extension of a Three-Component Model," *Journal of Applied Psychology*, June 2002, p 477.

trust between the parties. The Skills & Best Practices feature on page 437 illustrates how hospital administrators are using these recommendations to encourage medical doctors to incorporate PCs into their medical practice.

Hospitals Work to Overcome Docs 'Resistance to Using PCs

The U.S. government has offered $27 billion in incentives for hospitals to convert to electronic medical records. "But performing such tasks as entering orders for medication and taking patients' medical histories by computer requires significant changes in work habits." For example, a survey of 150 hospital executives revealed that 79% were concerned about how to best train doctors and staff to properly use the records.

"To get doctors and care givers—some of whom are skeptical about the ability of electronic records to improve productivity or patient care—on board, hospitals are taking a range of approaches, including offering training any hour of the day or night, converting vacant buildings into training facilities and using computer programs to get physicians up to speed quickly."

One resister to this approach is the fact that "many physicians aren't fans of large classroom settings. 'No one likes to feel that they're not masters of the material, and they're frankly uncomfortable about being perceived as less than masterful,' says George Reynolds, chief information officer at Children's Hospital & Medical Center."

Doctors also don't like to be trained by non-physicians, and they like trainers to come to them rather than vice versa. This can get quite expensive and inconvenient for those delivering the training. The training also can require a lot of time away from the job, which increases employee resistance. For example, labor and delivery nurses at Anne Arundel Health System required about 24 hours of training.

In the end, hospital administrators agree that it is "crucial to get key physicians behind the effort early." These physicians can play an important role in informally convincing their colleagues to "step up" and commit to taking the training.

SOURCE: Excerpted from K Hobson, "Getting Docs to Use PCs," *The Wall Street Journal*, March 15, 2011, p B5.

Moreover, managers should not to assume that people are consciously resisting change. Resistance has a cause and, according to John Kotter's research of more than 100 companies, the cause generally involves some obstacle in the work environment. He noted that obstacles in the organization's structure or in a "performance appraisal system [that] makes people choose between the new vision and their own self-interests" impeded change more than an individual's direct resistance.[42] This perspective implies that it is important for management to obtain employee feedback about any obstacles that may be affecting their ability or willingness to accept change. In the end, change agents should not be afraid to modify the targeted elements of change or their approach toward change based on employee resistance. If people are resisting for valid reasons, then a new change initiative is needed.

In addition to these suggestions, employee participation in the change process is another generic approach for reducing resistance. That said, however, organizational change experts have criticized the tendency to treat participation as a cure-all for resistance to change. They prefer a contingency approach because resistance can take many forms and, furthermore, because situational factors vary (see Table 16–2). As shown in Table 16–2, Participation + Involvement does have its place, but it takes time that is not always available. Also as indicated in Table 16–2, each of the other five methods has its situational niche, advantages, and

TABLE 16–2   Six Strategies for Overcoming Resistance to Change

Approach	Commonly Used in Situations	Advantages	Drawbacks
Education + Communication	Where there is a lack of information or inaccurate information and analysis.	Once persuaded, people will often help with the implementation of the change.	Can be very time-consuming if lots of people are involved.
Participation + Involvement	Where the initiators do not have all the information they need to design the change and where others have considerable power to resist.	People who participate will be committed to implementing change, and any relevant information they have will be integrated into the change plan.	Can be very time-consuming if participators design an inappropriate change.
Facilitation + Support	Where people are resisting because of adjustment problems.	No other approach works as well with adjustment problems.	Can be time-consuming, expensive, and still fail.
Negotiation + Agreement	Where someone or some group will clearly lose out in a change and where that group has considerable power to resist.	Sometimes it is a relatively easy way to avoid major resistance.	Can be too expensive in many cases if it alerts others to negotiate for compliance.
Manipulation + Co-optation	Where other tactics will not work or are too expensive.	It can be a relatively quick and inexpensive solution to resistance problems.	Can lead to future problems if people feel manipulated.
Explicit + Implicit coercion	Where speed is essential and where the change initiators possess considerable power.	It is speedy and can overcome any kind of resistance.	Can be risky if it leaves people angry at the initiators.

SOURCE: Reprinted by permission of *Harvard Business Review*. Exhibit from "Choosing Strategies for Change," by J P Kotter and L A Schlesinger, March/April 1979. Copyright 1979 by the Harvard Business School Publishing Corporation; all rights reserved.

www.mcgrawhillconnect.com

Go to Connect for a video case to view Hillerich and Bradsby, the manufacturers of the famous Louisville Slugger, and how they manage change.

drawbacks. For example, Manipulation + Co-optation may appear to be a negative approach, but it works in the right context. We once used co-optation, which involves giving a resistor a desirable role in the change process, in order to motivate the individual to endorse the change process. This approach ultimately led to a modification in the change process and the resistor's final endorsement. In short, there is no universal strategy for overcoming resistance to change. Managers need a complete repertoire of change strategies.[43]

BACK TO THE CHAPTER-OPENING CASE   What did Vineet Nayar do to overcome resistance to change? Could he have done anything differently? Explain.

Creating a Learning Organization

Organizations are finding that yesterday's competitive advantage is becoming the minimum entrance requirement for staying in business. This puts tremendous pressure on organizations to learn how best to improve and stay ahead of competitors. In fact, both researchers and practicing managers agree that an organization's capability to learn is a key strategic weapon because it helps it to innovate. It thus is important for organizations to enhance and nurture their capability to learn.

LO16.6

The notion that organizations learn is an outgrowth of the open-system model discussed in Chapter 15. Organizations are said to have human-like cognitive functions, such as the abilities to perceive and interpret, solve problems, store information, and learn from experience. Today, managers read and hear a good deal about learning organizations and team mental models. Peter Senge, a professor at the Massachusetts Institute of Technology, popularized the term *learning organization* in his best-selling book entitled *The Fifth Discipline.* He described a learning organization as "a group of people working together to collectively enhance their capacities to create results that they truly care about."[44] A practical interpretation of these ideas results in the following definition. A **learning organization is one that proactively creates, acquires, and transfers knowledge and that changes its behavior on the basis of new knowledge and insights.**[45] The creation of a learning organization requires that organizational members use team mental models. A **team mental model represents team members' "shared, organized understanding and mental representation of knowledge about key elements of the team's relevant environment."**[46] Retired Coast Guard Admiral Thad Allen is a good example of someone who used team mental models to create a learning organization when he was directing the federal response to Hurricanes Katrina and Rita (see the Skills & Best Practices feature on page 440).

Learning organizations actively try to infuse their organizations, and associated team mental models, with new ideas and information. They do this by constantly scanning their external environments, hiring new talent and expertise when needed, and devoting significant resources to train and develop their employees. Next, new knowledge must be transferred throughout the organization. Learning organizations strive to reduce structural, process, and interpersonal barriers to the sharing of information, ideas, and knowledge among organizational members. They also focus on learning from both success and failure. We now consider how organizations learn from success and failure and conclude by discussing the role of leadership in creating a learning organization.

Learning from Success

Success provides the *opportunity* to learn what an organization did right in terms of accomplishing a goal or implementing a project. We italicized the word *opportunity* because there are three key factors that distract or impede learning from success.[47] The first is the self-serving bias discussed in Chapter 4. This bias reflects the tendency to take more personal responsibility for success than failure and can lead managers to assume that success was due to their insights and talents and not random events or external factors outside of management's control. The second pertains to the decision-making bias of overconfidence, which was reviewed in Chapter 10. This bias leads to the inflated perception that management is better than it actually is, which in turn can cause managers to "dismiss new innovations, dips in customer satisfaction, and increases in quality problems, and to make overly risky moves." The final distracter

LO16.7

Admiral Thad Allen Changed Mental Models When Dealing with the Aftermath of Hurricane Katrina

Here is what Admiral Allen said to an interviewer from the *Harvard Business Review* in response to a question about how leaders create unity of effort when responding to a crisis with multiple constituents.

"I'm a big fan of Peter Senge ... who talks about learning organizations and the use of mental models. You have to understand at a very large, macro level what the problem is that you're dealing with and what needs to be done to achieve the effects you want—and you have to be able to communicate that.

With Katrina, it was clear to me after about 24 hours in New Orleans that we weren't dealing only with a natural disaster. Had the levees not collapsed, ground zero for Hurricane Katrina would have been Bay St. Louis and Waverland, Mississippi, which basically got wiped off the map. But when the levees were breached and New Orleans flooded, it became a different event, and I'm not sure we recognized that as a nation. We were still treating the entire issue as if it were just a hurricane."

Admiral Allen went on to explain how the initial mental model of "hurricane" needed to be changed because it was impeding progress in dealing with the crisis. For example, under the hurricane response the federal government released resources to the local government, which was problematic because there was no functional local government during this period. Allen thus reframed the mission or mental model to one of "mass effect." This led to a new response in which the federal government and U.S. military started to combine efforts to provide security, remove water from the city, conduct house-to-house searches, and so on.

SOURCE: Excerpted from "You Have to Lead From Everywhere," *Harvard Business Review,* **November 2010, p 77.**

pertains to the natural tendency of "not asking why" we succeeded at something. "Success is commonly interpreted as evidence not only that your existing strategy and practices work but also that you have all the knowledge and information you need," along with the necessary skills. The takeaway from this discussion is that managers can learn from success by avoiding these learning traps. It also is important to remember that short-term success will not guarantee long-term success. This means that it is important to be vigilant about studying the causes of success over time.[48]

Learning from Failure

A G Lafley, CEO of Procter & Gamble from 2000 to 2009, believes that managers can learn from their mistakes and failures. He told a reporter from *Harvard Business Review* that he made plenty of mistakes and that he had "my fair share of failure. But you have to get past the disappointment and the blame and really understand what happened and why it happened. And then, more important, decide what you have learned and what you are going to do differently next time."[49] Lafley's views on learning certainly contributed to P&G's success under his leadership: "Sales doubled, profits quadrupled, and P&G's market value increased by more than $100 billion."[50]

Lafley's success begs the question of why more organizations and managers don't make it a point to learn from failure. Why do you think this happens? Some experts suggest that the reason stems from our being programmed during childhood to believe that failure is bad and should be avoided. After all, who wants to talk about their weaknesses and failures? Although people may not like to talk about their failures, many managers believe that learning from failure is pretty easy. You simply need to ask people involved to meet and reflect on what went wrong and then encourage them to avoid these trappings on future projects. Unfortunately, this simplistic approach is unlikely to produce significant learning according to Amy Edmondson, professor at Harvard Business School.

Professor Edmonson studied organizational failures for 20 years and concluded that there are a host of factors that determine the extent to which organizations learn from failure (see Table 16–3).[51] She recommends that organizations need to focus on overcoming the barriers shown in Table 16–3 in order to maximize learning from failure. A review of these barriers reveals that managers need to use evidence-based decision making, which was discussed in Chapter 10, if they want to learn from failure. We conclude by noting results from a recent study on organizational learning. The researchers wanted to know if organizations learn more from success or failure. What do you think? Results indicated that organizations learned from both success and failure, but learning was stronger and longer lasting when it was based on failure.[52]

Leadership Is the Foundation of a Learning Organization

Leadership is the key to fostering an environment that creates a learning organization. The most effective leaders are those who use both transactional and transformational leadership (recall our discussion in Chapter 14) to facilitate organizational learning. To make this happen, however, leaders must adopt new roles and associated activities. Specifically, leaders perform four key functions in building a learning organization: (1) building a commitment to learning, (2) working to generate ideas with impact, (3) working to generalize ideas with impact, and (4) helping the organization to "unlearn" old mental models.[53]

Building a Commitment to Learning   Leaders need to instill an intellectual and emotional commitment to learning. Thomas Tierney, former CEO of Bain & Company, proposes that leaders foster this commitment by building a culture that promotes the concept of "teacher-learners." His concept is based on the idea that organizational learning and innovation are enhanced when employees behave like both teachers and learners.[54] Of course, leaders also need to invest the financial resources needed to create a learning infrastructure.

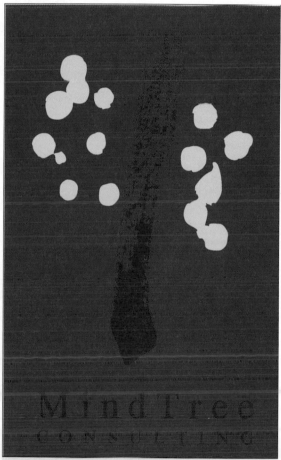

At MindTree Ltd., global IT services and product engineering company, learning was built in from the company's founding. Its corporate logo was designed by a child with Cerebral Palsy, which signifies, according to Executive Chairman and Gardener Subroto Bagchi, that "We believe there is much we can learn from everyone." To "break the engineering mind-set," the company invites people from widely diverse backgrounds such as dance, space exploration, and writing to present lectures for its 10,000 employees.

TABLE 16–3 Factors That Detract from an Organization's Ability to Learn from Failure

Factor	Description and Recommendation
1. The blame game	The tendency to blame failure on a person rather than internal processes, systems, or external events.
2. The inability to recognize that failures are not created equal	Failures range from preventable (e.g., a person did not follow an accepted procedure or process) to noncontrollable (e.g., Ford's inability to produce black-painted cars because it could not get materials from Japan during the 2011 crisis). It takes more time and effort to learn from failures caused by complex systems.
3. Not having a learning culture	People are afraid to point out or discuss failures. Managers are encouraged to create a psychologically safe culture that encourages employees to spot and discuss potential failures. It is critical to focus on processes and systems rather than on people.
4. Not detecting the lead indicators of failure	Analysis of failures focuses on people rather than on processes. Organizations are encouraged to identify and measure the status of short-term factors that lead to long-term success.
5. The self-serving bias	The tendency to blame failure on others or external events. It is important to consider the extent to which the causes of failure are controllable. It also is more beneficial to focus on controllable causes.
6. The reluctance to experiment.	When people are uncertain about the causes of failure they are reluctant to experiment with different solutions. Conduct experiments and accept the idea that failure is part of the improvement process.

SOURCE: Based on A C Edmonson, "Strategies for Learning from Failure," *Harvard Business Review*, April 2011, pp 48–55.

Working to Generate Ideas with Impact Ideas with impact are those that add value to one or more of an organization's three key stakeholders: employees, customers, and shareholders. Experts suggest the following ways to generate ideas with impact:

- Implement continuous improvement programs.
- Increase employee competence through training, or buy talent from outside the organization.
- Experiment with new ideas, processes, and structural arrangements.
- Go outside the organization to identify world-class ideas and processes.
- Instill systems thinking throughout the organization.

Working to Generalize Ideas with Impact Leaders must make a concerted effort to reduce interpersonal, group, and organizational barriers to learning. This can be done by creating a learning infrastructure.[55] This is a large-scale effort that includes the following activities:

- Measuring and rewarding learning.
- Increasing open and honest dialogue among organizational members.

- Reducing conflict.
- Increasing horizontal and vertical communication.
- Promoting teamwork.
- Rewarding risk taking and innovation.
- Reducing the fear of failure.
- Increasing the sharing of successes, failures, and best practices across organizational members.
- Reducing stressors and frustration.
- Reducing internal competition.
- Increasing cooperation and collaboration.
- Creating a psychologically safe and comforting environment.[56]

Helping the Organization to Unlearn Old Mental Models   In addition to implementing the ideas just discussed, organizations must concurrently unlearn organizational practices, paradigms, and team mental models that made them successful. Quite simply, traditional organizations and the associated organizational behaviors they created have outlived their usefulness. Management must seriously question and challenge the ways of thinking that worked in the past if they want to create a learning organization.[57] For example, the old management paradigm of planning, organizing, and control might be replaced with one of vision, values, and empowerment. The time has come for management and employees to think as owners, not as "us" and "them" adversaries.

key terms

chapter summary

- *Discuss the external and internal forces that create the need for organizational change.* Organizations encounter both external and internal forces for change. There are four key external forces for change: demographic characteristics, technological advancements, customer and market changes, and social and political pressures. Internal forces for change come from both human resource problems and managerial behavior/decisions.

- *Describe Lewin's change model and the systems model of change.* Lewin developed a three-stage model of planned change that explained how to initiate, manage, and stabilize the change process. The three stages were *unfreezing*, which entails creating the motivation to change, *changing*, and stabilizing change through *refreezing.* A systems model of change takes a big picture perspective of change. It focuses on the interaction among the key components of change. The three main components of change are inputs, target elements of change, and outputs. The target elements of change represent the components of an organization that may be changed. They include organizing arrangements, social factors, methods, goals, and people.

- *Discuss Kotter's eight steps for leading organizational change.* John Kotter believes that organizational change fails for one or more of eight common errors. He proposed eight steps that organizations should follow to overcome these errors. The eight steps are as follows: (a) establish a sense of urgency, (b) create the guiding coalition, (c) develop a vision and strategy, (d) communicate the change vision, (e) empower broad-based action, (f) generate short-term wins, (g) consolidate gains and produce more change, and (h) anchor new approaches in the culture.

- *Discuss the 11 reasons employees resist change.* Resistance to change is an emotional/behavioral response to real or imagined threats to an established work routine. Eleven reasons employees resist change are (a) an individual's predisposition toward change, (b) surprise and fear of the unknown, (c) fear of failure, (d) loss of status and/or job security, (e) peer pressure, (f) past success, (g) decisions that disrupt cultural traditions or group relationships, (h) personality conflicts, (i) lack of tact and/or poor timing, (j) leadership style, and (k) failure to legitimize change.

- *Identify alternative strategies for overcoming resistance to change.* Organizations must be ready for change. Assuming an organization is ready for change, the alternative strategies for overcoming resistance to change are education + communication, participation + involvement, facilitation + support, negotiation + agreement, manipulation + cooperation, and explicit + implicit coercion. Each has its situational appropriateness and advantages and drawbacks.

- *Define the term* learning organization. A learning organization is one that proactively creates, acquires, and transfers knowledge and that changes its behavior on the basis of new knowledge and insights.

- *Review the factors that hinder an organization's ability to learn from success and failure.* There are three factors that distract learning from success: the self-serving bias, overconfidence, and the natural tendency of "not asking why." Table 16–3 identifies six factors that inhibit learning from failure.

discussion questions

1. Do you think future organizational change will (a) stay about the same as it is now, (b) decrease, or (c) increase? Explain your rationale.
2. How would you respond to a manager who made the following statement? "Unfreezing is not important; employees will follow my directives."
3. Have you ever gone through a major organizational change at work? If yes, what type of organizational development intervention was used? Was it effective? Explain.
4. Which source of resistance to change do you think is the most common? Which is the most difficult for management to deal with?
5. How would you assess the extent to which an organization is truly a learning organization? Discuss different alternative methods.

legal/ethical challenge

Is There an Ethical Way to Implement Downsizing without Hurting Your Best Employees?[58]

Intel has restructured and eliminated about 10,500 jobs during the past 20 months. The company decided to make these cuts owing to declining revenue and market share. Intel used a quantitative approach in making the cuts. That is, the company studied workforce demographics and determined what areas were most in need of cuts and then reassigned people based on where they might best contribute to the company's future plans. The managerial ranks were reduced the most. Corporate executives are pleased with the process because the company is now more profitable and competitive.

In contrast, some employees believe that the company "botched the restructuring in ways that have harmed morale, employee development, and long-term leadership quality." Interviews with employees uncovered complaints that "Intel disregarded employees' passions in reorganizing, squandered the talents of HR specialists and unwisely shifted leadership training efforts from lower-level managers to upper-level executives." Disgruntled employees believe that Intel did not consider employees' interests during the restructuring. An internal memo obtained by *Workforce Management* indicated that senior management knew they would be losing quality employees. The memo states: "We know we are losing good people in this move. But we have too many managers, and this manager reduction is necessary to improve our decision making and communication and to resize the company. In addition, since we need to become a leaner company and are limiting job openings, redeploying their skills, as individual contributors or as managers, is not a reasonable option."

Solving the Dilemma: How Would You Have Handled the Layoffs at Intel?

1. Intel's approach sounds logical to me. Revenues are up, and the company just unveiled a new processing chip that *Time* called the best invention of the year. You can't make everyone happy when you let go more than 10,000 people.

2. Downsizing solely by the numbers is bad. Management should have accommodated employees' passions and interests when restructuring even if it resulted in fewer cuts than desired. In the long run, this will lead to higher employee satisfaction and performance.

3. It sounds like the criticisms are being leveled by people who don't like their new assignments. They should quit complaining and be happy they are still employed.

4. I am not sure that there is an optimum approach. It is impossible to balance the short-term goal of reducing costs while maintaining a positive work environment in which people are doing the type of work they are passionate about.

5. Invent other interpretations or options. Discuss.

If you're looking for additional study materials, be sure to check out the Online Learning Center at

www.mhhe.com/kinickiob5e

for more information and interactivities that correspond to this chapter.

Chapter 1

1 Excerpted from A Efrati and P W Tam, "Google Battles to Keep Talent," *The Wall Street Journal,* November 11, 2010.

2 As quoted in D Reed, "Kelly Must Build on Success," *USA Today,* August 16, 2004, p 4B. Also see "The Best Advice I Ever Got: Herb Kelleher, Founder and Chairman of Southwest Airlines," *Fortune,* March 21, 2005, pp 116, 118; and D Kirkpatrick, "Star Power: Kevin Johnson, Microsoft," *Fortune,* February 6, 2006, p 58.

3 Data from Southwest Airlines Co. Fact Sheet, http://www.swanfgpremium.com/html/about-southwest/history/fact-sheet.htm, accessed January 4, 2011.

4 J Pfeffer and J F Veiga, "Putting People First for Organizational Success," *Academy of Management Executive,* May 1999, p 37.

5 Adapted from ibid. Also see J K Harter, F L Schmidt, and T L Hayes, "Business-Unit-Level Relationship Between Employee Satisfaction, Employee Engagement, and Business Outcomes: A Meta-Analysis," *Journal of Applied Psychology,* April 2002, pp 268–79; J Pfeffer, "Producing Sustainable Competitive Advantage Through the Effective Management of People," *Academy of Management Executive,* November 2005, pp 95–106; J Pfeffer and R I Sutton, "Evidence-Based Management," *Harvard Business Review,* January 2006, pp 62–74.

6 C B Gibson, C L Porath, G S Benson, and E E Lawler III, "What Results When Firms Implement Practices: The Differential Relationship between Specific Practices, Firm Financial Performance, Customer Service, and Quality," *Journal of Applied Psychology* 92, pp 1467–80.

7 See J Pfeffer, "The Myth of the Disposable Worker," *Business 2.0,* October 2005, p 78; W F Cascio, "Strategies for Responsible Restructuring," *Academy of Management Executive,* November 2005, pp 39–50; and M Conlin, "The Shortsighted Solution," *BusinessWeek,* April 10, 2006, p 110.

8 See A Fox, "Raising Engagement," *HR Magazine,* May 2010, pp 35–40; and C D'Angela, "In Post-Recession World, Recognition Boosts Recovery," *The Power of Incentives: HR Magazine,* September 2010, pp 93–97.

9 See M Moskowitz, R Levering, and C Tkaczyk, "100 Best Companies to Work For," *Fortune,* February 7, 2011, p 91; and M Moskowitz, R Levering, and C Tkaczyk, "100 Best Companies to Work For," *Fortune,* February 8, 2010, p 75.

10 G Colvin, "How Are Most Admired Companies Different? They Invest in People and Keep Them Employed—Even in a Downturn," *Fortune,* March 22, 2010, p 82. See also I S Fulmer, B Gerhart, and K S Scott, "Are the 100 Best Better? An Empirical Investigation of the Relationship Between Being a 'Great Place to Work' and Firm Performance," *Personnel Psychology,* Winter 2003, pp 965–93.

11 For examples of predictors of a host of career success outcomes see S Y Todd, K J Harris, R B Harris, and A R Wheeler, "Career Success Implications of Political Skill," *Journal of Social Psychology* 2009 pp 179–204.

12 R Olson, J Verley, L Santos, and C Salas, "What We Teach Students about the Hawthorne Studies: A Review of Content within a Sample of Introductory I-O and OB Textbooks," *The Industrial-Organizational Psychologist* 41, 2004, 24–39.

13 Evidence indicating that the original conclusions of the famous Hawthorne studies were unjustified may be found in R G Greenwood, A A Bolton, and R A Greenwood, "Hawthorne a Half Century Later: Relay Assembly Participants Remember," *Journal of Management,* Fall–Winter 1983, pp 217–31. For a positive interpretation of the Hawthorne studies, see J A Sonnenfeld, "Shedding Light on the Hawthorne Studies," *Journal of Occupational Behavior,* April 1985, pp 111–30.

14 F Merrett, "Reflections on the Hawthorne Effect," *Educational Psychology* 26, 2006, pp 143–46.

15 See M Parker Follett, *Freedom and Coordination* (London: Management Publications Trust, 1949).

16 See D McGregor, *The Human Side of Enterprise* (New York: McGraw-Hill, 1960). Also see D Jacobs, "Book Review Essay: Douglas McGregor—The Human Side of Enterprise in Peril," *Academy of Management Review,* April 2004, pp 293–96.

17 See D Thomas and R Bostrom, "Building Trust and Cooperation through Technology Adaptation in Virtual Teams: Empirical Field Evidence," *Information Systems Management,* 2010, pp 45–56. For evidence related to measuring and using Theory X and Y, see R Kopelman, D Prottas, and A L Davis, "Douglas McGregor's Theory X and Y: Toward a Construct-valid Measure," *Journal of Managerial Issues,* Summer 2008, pp. 255–71.

18 J Hall, "Americans Know How to Be Productive If Managers Will Let Them," *Organizational Dynamics,* Winter 1994, p 38.

19 As quoted in P LaBarre, "The Industrialized Revolution," *Fast Company,* November 2003, pp 116, 118.

20 See J M Ivancevich, T N Duening, and W Lidwell, "Bridging the Manager-Organizational Scientist Collaboration Gap," *Organizational Dynamics,* 2005, pp 103–17; E W Ford, W J Duncan, A G Bedeian, P M Ginter, M D Rousculp, and A M Adams, "Mitigating Risks, Visible Hands, Inevitable Disasters, and Soft Variables: Management Research That Matters to Managers," *Academy of Management Executive,* November 2005, pp 24–38; and J M Bartunek, S L Rynes, and R D Ireland, "What Makes Management Research Interesting, and Why Does It Matter?" *Academy of Management Journal,* February 2006, pp 9–15.

21 For an interesting historical perspective on the behavioral sciences, see J Adler, "Freud in Our Midst," *Newsweek,* March 27, 2006, pp 42–49.

22 R E Ployhart, J A Weekley, and J Ramsey, "The Consequences of Human Resource Stocks and Flows: A Longitudinal Examination of Unit Service Orientation and Unit Effectiveness," *Academy of Management Journal,* 2009, pp 996–1015.

23 Ibid.

24 See B Groyseberg, L Eling Lee, and R Abrahams, "What It Takes to Make Star Hires Pay Off," *Sloan Management Review,* January 1, 2010; A Pomeroy, "C-Suite Worries Over Succession Planning," *HR Magazine,* December 2007, p 22.

25 S Pulliam and S Ng, "Buffett Flags Successor," *The Wall Street Journal,* October 26, 2010.

26 R E Ployhart and T P Moliterno, "Emergence of the Human Capital Resource: A Multilevel Model," *Academy of Management Review,* 2011, pp 127–50.

27 Inspired by P S Adler and S Kwon, "Social Capital: Prospects for a New Concept," *Academy of Management Review,* January 2002, pp 17–40.

28 P W Tam, "A Onetime 'Queen of the Net' Heads to Silicon Valley," *The Wall Street Journal,* November 30, 2010.

29 M Moskowitz, R Levering, and C Tkaczyk, "100 Best Companies to Work For," *Fortune,* February 8, 2010, p 82.

30 Derived from T W H Ng and D C Feldman, "The Effects of Organizational Embeddedness on Development of Social and Human Capital," *Journal of Applied Psychology,* 2010, pp 696–712.

31 M E P Seligman and M Csikszentmihalyi, "Positive Psychology: An Introduction," *American Psychologist,* January 2000, p 5. Also see the other 15 articles in the January 2000 issue of *American Psychologist.*

32 F Luthans and B J Avolio, "The 'point' of positive organizational behavior," *Journal of Organizational Behavior,* 2009, pp 291–307; also see F Luthans, "The Need for and Meaning of Positive Organizational Behavior," *Journal of Organizational Behavior,* September 2002, p 698. Ibid, F Luthans, 2002.

33 Ibid.

34 M Pearson and M Sharma, "Where Are India's Skilled Laborers?" *Bloomberg Businessweek,* January 16, 2011.

35 J E Michel and A Neuman, "Positive Psychology as a Catalyst for Change," *Harvard Business Review,* November 2010, pp 62–74.

36 See S Baker, "Wiser About the Web," *BusinessWeek,* March 27, 2006, pp 54–58.

37 M J De La Merced and E M Rusli, "LinkedIn Plans a Stock Offering this Year," *The New York Times,* January 6, 2011.

38 A Efrati and P W Tam, "Google Battles to Keep Talent" November 11, 2010; and Microsoft Fast Facts, www.microsoft.com/presspass/inside_ms.mspx, retrieved January 10, 2011.

39 De La Merced and E M Rusli. "LinkedIn Plans a Stock Offering this Year," January 6, 2011.

40 De La Merced and E M Rusli. "LinkedIn Plans a Stock Offering this Year," January 6, 2011. See also E Kelleher, "Work Is Changing as U.S. Companies Go Global," September 17, 2007, http://www.america.gov/st/peopleplace-english/2007/September/20070917165019berehellek1.978701e-02.html.

41 L C Latimer, "How Flexible Workspaces Can Transform Your Company's Culture," November 24, 2010, http://www.triplepundit.com/2010/11/how-flexible-workspaces-can-transform-your-company-culture/.

42 From "Office Workers, How Long Before you Hit the Breaking Point?" *The Wall Street Journal Online,* June 3, 2010.

43 T J Mullaney and A Weintraub, "The Digital Hospital," *BusinessWeek,* March 28, 2005, p 77.

44 See M A Tucker, "E-Learning Evolves," *HR Magazine,* October 2005, pp 74–78.

45 Quote found in "P&G Sets Two New Goals for Open Innovation Partnerships: Company Seeks to Triple the Impact of Connect + Develop," *PR Newswire,* October 28, 2010. Additional information can be found at the P&G website www.pgconnectdevelop.com.

46 S Oster, N Shirouzu, and P Glader, "China Squeezes Foreigners for Share of Global Riches," *The Wall Street Journal,* December 29, 2010.

47 J C Meister and K Willyerd, *The 2020 Workplace* (New York: HarperCollins Publishers, 2010).

48 G Bowley, "The New Speed of Money, Reshaping Markets," *The New York Times,* January 1, 2011.

49 See J Weber, "'Mosh Pits' of Creativity," *BusinessWeek,* November 7, 2005, pp 98–100.

50 J Bughin, M Chui, and J Manyika, "Clouds, Big Data, and Smart Assets: Ten Tech-Enabled Business Trends to Watch," *McKinsey Quarterly,* August 2010.

51 C Hall, "Don't Have Social Media Guidelines? Get Some," *The Dallas Morning News,* November 21, 2010, p D1.

52 Meister and Willyerd. *The 2020 Workplace.*

53 See T Demos, "Will Madoff's Enablers Get Hard Time?" *Fortune,* January 19, 2009, p 24; D Kansas, "Madoff Does Minneapolis," *Fortune,* February 2, 2009, pp 80–86; K McCoy, "Trading His Penthouse for Prison: Madoff Leaves Court Cuffed," *USA Today,* March 13, 2009, pp 1B–2B, R Parloff, "The Impostor," *Fortune,* April 13, 2009, pp 58–66; and J Bandler, N Varchaver, and D Burke, "How Bernie Did It," *Fortune,* May 11, 2009, pp 51–71.

54 See "50 People and Things that Took a Spill in 2010," *Bloomberg BusinessWeek,* January 2, 2011.

55 S Harrington, "Successful Companies Are Led by CEOs Who Take a People-Centered Approach," *Human Resources,* July–August 2010, p 4.

56 For an excellent description of the history of CSR and its application to the recent financial crisis, see A Kemper and R L Martin, "After the Fall: The Global Financial Crisis as a Test of Corporate Social Responsibility," *European Management Review,* 2010, pp 229–39.

57 A B Carroll, "Managing Ethically with Global Stakeholders: A Present and Future Challenge," *Academy of Management Executive,* May 2004, p 118.

58 Ibid.

59 E Levenson, "Citizen Nike," *Fortune,* November 24, 2008, p 166.

60 Based on M J Epstein, A R Buhovac, and K Yuthas, "Why Nike Kicks Butt in Sustainability," *Organizational Dynamics,* 2010, pp 353–56.

61 D Callahan, *The Cheating Culture: Why More Americans Are Doing Wrong to Get Ahead* (Orlando: Harcourt, 2004), pp 19–20. Also see S Block, "Americans May Be More Inclined to Cheat on Their Taxes," *USA Today,* February 5, 2009, p 3B.

62 Based on T Jackson, "Cultural Values and Management Ethics: A 10-Nation Study," *Human Relations,* October 2001, pp 1267–302.

63 Based on L K Trevino, G R Weaver, and M E Brown, "It's Lovely at the Top: Hierarchical Levels, Identities, and Perceptions of Organizational Ethics," *Business Ethics Quarterly,* April 2008, pp 233–52.

64 Results can be found in Matthew Boyle, "By the Numbers: Liar Liar!" *Fortune,* May 26, 2003, p 44.

65 P Babcock, "Spotting Lies," *HR Magazine,* October 2003, p 47. Also see D Macsai, ". . . And I Invented Velcro," *BusinessWeek,* August 4, 2008, p 15.

66 Also see the debate in L D Ordonez, M E Schweitzer, A D Galinsky, and M H Bazerman, "Goals Gone Wild: The Systematic Side Effects of Overprescribing Goal Setting," *Academy of Management Perspectives,* February 2009, pp 6–16.

67 B Tepper, "When Managers Pressure Employees to Behave Badly: Toward a Comprehensive Response," *Business Horizons* 53, 2010, pp 591–98.

68 S Jayson, "Teens Face Up to Ethics Choices—If You Can Believe Them," *USA Today,* December 6, 2006, p 6D.

69 Data and quotation from http://charactercounts.org/programs/reportcard/index.html, accessed March 14, 2009. Also see C L Grossman, "Almost All Denominations Losing Ground, Survey Finds," *USA Today,* March 9, 2009, pp 1A–2A.

70 See Chapter 6 in K Hodgson, *A Rock and a Hard Place: How to Make Ethical Business Decisions When the Choices Are Tough* (New York: AMACOM, 1992), pp 66–77.

71 P Brotherton, "Corporate Integrity Pays Off in Better Performance," *T&D,* January 2011, p 24.

72 L W Fry and J W Slocum Jr, "Maximizing the Triple Bottom Line through Spiritual Leadership," *Organizational Dynamics,* January–March 2008, pp 86–96.

73 For an excellent review of integrity testing, see D S Ones and C Viswesvaran, "Integrity Testing in Organizations," in *Dysfunctional Behavior in Organizations: Violent and Deviant Behavior,* ed R W Griffin et al. (Stamford, CT: JAI Press, 1998), pp 243–76. Also see J McGregor, "Background Checks That Never End," *BusinessWeek,* March 20, 2006, p 40.

74 P Loftus, "Whistleblower's Long Journey," *The Wall Street Journal,* October 28, 2010.

75 N Confessore, "Cuomo Plans One Year Freeze on State Worker's Pay," *The New York Times,* January 2, 2011.

76 Based on S J Reynolds, "Moral Attentiveness: Who Pays Attention to Moral Aspects of Life?" *Journal of Applied Psychology,* September 2008, pp 1027–41.

77 As quoted in D Jones, "Military a Model for Execs," *USA Today,* June 9, 2004, p 4B.

78 D Kirkpatrick, *The Facebook Effect: The Inside Story of the Company That Is Connecting the World* (New York: Simon & Schuster, 2010).

Chapter 2

1 Excerpted from K Linebaugh and J Bennett, "Marchionne Upends Chrysler's Ways," *The Wall Street Journal,* January 12, 2010, pp B1–B2.

2 E H Schein, "Culture: The Missing Concept in Organization Studies," *Administrative Science Quarterly,* June 1996, p 236.

3 This figure and related discussion are based on C Ostroff, A Kinicki, and M Tamkins, "Organizational Culture and Climate," in *Handbook of Psychology,* vol. 12, eds W C Borman, D R Ilgen, and R J Klimoski (New York: Wiley & Sons, 2003), pp 565–93.

4 This discussion is based on E H Schein, *Organizational Culture and Leadership,* 2nd ed (San Francisco: Jossey-Bass, 1992), pp 16–48.

5 H Walters, "Google Did," *Bloomberg BusinessWeek,* May 16, 2010, p 60.

6 S H Schwartz, "Universals in the Content and Structure of Values: Theoretical Advances and Empirical Tests in 20 Countries," in *Advances in Experimental Social Psychology,* ed M P Zanna (New York: Academic Press, 1992), p 4.

7 D Seidman, "Outgreening Delivers Sustainable Competitive Advantage," http://www.businessweek.com/managing/content/dec2008/ca2008125_029230-page-2.htm, accessed February 19, 2009.

8 A Ignatius, "We Had to Own the Mistakes," *Harvard Business Review,* July-August 2010, p 111.

9 Results are discussed in "Executing Ethics," *Training,* March 2007, p 8. Also see D Meinert, "Strong Ethical Culture Helps Bottom Line," *HR Magazine,* December 2010, p 21.

10 Statistics and data contained in the Southwest Airlines example can be found in the "Southwest Airlines Fact Sheet," updated November 7, 2010, http://www.southwest.com/html/about-southwest/history/fact-sheet.html.

11 K D Godsey, "Slow Climb to New Heights," *Success,* October 1996, p 21.

12 Southwest's mission statement can be found in "Customer Service Commitment," www.southwest.com.

13 See the related discussion in S Ten Have, W Ten Have, A F Stevens, M Vander Elst, and F Pol-Coyne, *Key Management Models: The Management Tools and Practices That Will Improve Your Business* (San Francisco: Jossey-Bass, 2003).

14 A thorough description of the CVF is provided in K S Cameron, R E Quinn, J Degraff, and A V Thakor, *Creating Values Leadership* (Northampton, MA: Edward Elgar, 2006).

15 Excerpted from K R Spors, "Top Small Workplaces 2008," *The Wall Street Journal,* October 13, 2008, p R4.

16 T Kelley and M F Cortez, "AstraZeneca's Risky Bet on Drug Discovery," *Bloomberg BusinessWeek,* January 3–9, 2011, p 21.

17 See M Arndt and B Einhorn, "The 50 Most Innovative Companies," *Bloomberg BusinessWeek,* April 25, 2010, p 39; and "Leadership With Trust," http://www.tata.com/aboutus/sub_index.aspx?sectid=8hOk5Qq3EfQ=.

18 B Stone, "Will Richard Branson's Virgin America Fly?" *Bloomberg BusinessWeek,* January 3–9, 2011, pp 64–68.

19 See D Welch, D Kiley, and M Ihlwan, "My Way or the Highway at Hyundai," *BusinessWeek,* March 17, 2008, pp 48–51.

20 J D Rockoff, "J&J Lapses Are Cited in Drugs for Kids," *The Wall Street Journal,* May 27, 2010, p B1; and J S Lublin, "Some CEOs Face Big Repair Jobs in 2011," *The Wall Street Journal,* January 4, 2011, p B6.

21 Results can be found in C Hartnell, Y Ou, and A Kinicki, "Organizational Culture and Organizational Effectiveness: A Meta-Analytic Investigation of the Competing Values Framework's Theoretical Suppositions," *Journal of Applied Psychology,* in press. Also see S A Sackman, "Culture and Performance," in *The Handbook of Organizational Culture and Climate* 2nd ed, ed N M Ashkanasy, C P M Wilderom, and M F Peterson (Los Angeles: Sage, 2011), pp 188–224.

22 Mergers are discussed by L Tepedino and M Watkins, "Be a Master of Mergers and Acquisitions," *HR Magazine,* June 2010, pp 53–56.

23 See C A Hartnell and F O Walumbwa, "Transformational Leadership and Organizational Culture," in *The Handbook of Organizational Culture and Climate,* 2nd ed, ed N M Ashkanasy, C P M Wilderom, and M F Peterson (Los Angeles: Sage, 2011), pp 225–48; and E F Goldman and A Casey, "Building a Culture that Encourages Strategic Thinking," *Journal of Leadership and Organizational Studies,"* May 2010, pp 119–28.

24 D W Young, "The Six Levers for Managing Organizational Culture," in *Readings in Organizational Behavior,* ed J A Wagner III and J R Hollenbeck (New York: Routledge, 2010), pp 533–46.

25 The mechanisms were based on material contained in E H Schein, "The Role of the Founder in Creating Organizational Culture," *Organizational Dynamics,* Summer 1983, pp 13–28.

26 See N Byrnes, "The Art of Motivation," *BusinessWeek,* May 1, 2006, pp 57–62.

27 A Fox, "Don't Let Silos Stand in the Way," *HR Magazine,* May 2010, p 51.

28 See M Kimes, "Fluor's Corporate Crime Fighter," *Fortune,* February 16, 2009, p 26.

29 D Moss, "Triage: Methodically Developing Its Employees," *HR Magazine,* July 2007, p 45.

30 L Freifeld, "Highway to Health," *Training,* May 2009, pp 52–53.

31 C Hymowitz, "New CEOs May Spur Resistance if They Try to Alter Firm's Culture," *The Wall Street Journal,* August 13, 2007, p B1.

32 G Chazan and D Mattioli, "BP Links Pay to Safety in 4th Quarter," *The Wall Street Journal,* October 19, 2010, p B5.

33 Hymowitz, "New CEOs May Spur Resistance if They Try to Alter Firm's Culture," p B1.

34 These examples are explored in B Roberts, "Social Networking at the Office," *HR Magazine,* March 2008, pp 81–83.

35 J Van Maanen, "Breaking In: Socialization to Work," in *Handbook of Work, Organization, and Society,* ed R Dubin (Chicago: Rand-McNally, 1976), p 67.

36 "Best Practices & Outstanding Initiatives: PricewaterhouseCoopers: 101: PwC Internship Experience," *Training,* February 2010, p 104.

37 Onboarding programs are discussed by D Moscato, "Using Technology to Get Employees on Board," *HR Magazine,* March 2005, pp 107–09.

38 M Weinstein, "ADP's ABCS of Training," *Training,* February 2010, pp 34–38.

39 H R Rafferty, "Social Media Etiquette: Communicate Behavioral Expectations," March 24, 2010. Retrieved January 5, 2011, from http://www.shrm.org.hrdisciplines/technology/Articles/Pages/SocialMedia Etiquette.aspx.

40 See D Cable and C Parsons, "Socialization Tactics and Person-Organization Fit," *Personnel Psychology,* Spring 2001, pp 1–23.

41 R Levering and M Moskowitz, "The 100 Best Companies to Work For: And the Winners Are . . ." *Fortune,* January 23, 2006, p 94.

42 See M M Smith, "Recognition ROI . . . Now More Than Ever," *HR Magazine: Special Advertisement Supplement—The Power of Incentives,* 2008, pp 87–94.

43 See J P Slattery, T T Selvarajan, and J E Anderson, "Influences of New Employee Development Practices on Temporary Employee Work-Related Attitudes," *Human Resource Development Quarterly,* 2006, pp 279–303.

44 See E H Offstein and R L Dufresne, "Building Strong Ethics and Promoting Positive Character Development: The Influence of HRM at the United States Military Academy at West Point," *Human Resource Management,* Spring 2007, pp 95–114.

45 For a thorough review of research on the socialization of diverse employees with disabilities see A Colella, "Organizational Socialization of Newcomers with Disabilities: A Framework for Future Research," in *Research in Personnel and Human Resources Management,* ed G R Ferris (Greenwich, CT: JAI Press, 1996), pp 351–417.

46 This definition is based on the network perspective of mentoring proposed by M Higgins and K Kram, "Reconceptualizing Mentoring at Work: A Development Network Perspective," *Academy of Management Review,* April 2001, pp 264–88.

47 Supportive results can be found in Monica L Forret and Thomas W Dougherty, "Networking Behaviors and Career Outcomes: Differences for Men and Women?" *Journal of Organizational Behavior,* May 2004, pp 419–37.

48 Career functions are discussed in detail in K Kram, *Mentoring at Work: Developmental Relationships in Organizational Life* (Glenview, IL: Scott Foresman, 1985).

49 T J DeLong, J J Gabarro, and R J Lees, "Why Mentoring Matters in a Hypercompetitive World," *Harvard Business Review,* January 2008, pp 115–21.

50 This discussion is based on Higgins and Kram, "Reconceptualizing Mentoring at Work."

51 See T D Allen, L T Eby, and E Lentz, "The Relationship between Formal Mentoring Program Characteristics and Perceived Program Effectiveness," *Personnel Psychology,* Spring 2006, pp 125–53.

52 See Chandler and Eby, "When Mentoring Goes Bad;" and S Wang, E D Tomlinson, and R A Noe, "The Role of Mentor Trust and Protégé Internal Locus of Control in Formal Mentoring Relationships," *Journal of Applied Psychology,* March 2010, pp 358–67.

53 J C Meister and K Willyerd, "Mentoring Millenials," *Harvard Business Review,* May 2010, pp 68–72.

54 DeLong et al., "Why Mentoring Matters," pp. 115–21.

55 Excerpted from J Silver-Greenberg, "The Credit-Card Blowup Ahead," *BusinessWeek,* October 20, 2008, pp 24–25.

Chapter 3

1 Excerpted and adapted from J. Wiscombe, "Tata Consultancy Services," *Workforce Management,* December 2010, p. 18. Reprinted with permission of Crain Communications, Inc.

2 Adapted from M Gunther, "The World's New Economic Landscape," *Fortune,* July 26, 2010, pp 104–6.

3 Adapted from D Court and L Narashimhan, "Capturing the World's Emerging Middle Class," *McKinsey Quarterly,* July 2010.

4 R Dye and E Stephenson, "McKinsey Global Survey Results: Five Forces Reshaping the Global Economy," *McKinsey Quarterly,* May 10, 2010.

5 Court and Narashimhan, "Capturing the World's Emerging Middle Class."

6 Gunther, "The World's New Economic Landscape," pp 104–6.

7 Excerpted and adapted from M Javidan, M Teagarden, and D Bowen, "Making It Overseas," *Harvard Business Review,* April 2010.

8 F Trompenaars and C Hampden-Turner, *Riding the Waves of Culture: Understanding Cultural Diversity in Global Business,* 2nd ed (New York: McGraw-Hill, 1998), pp 6–7.

9 See M Mendenhall, "A Painless Approach to Integrating 'International' into OB, HRM, and Management Courses," *Organizational Behavior Teaching Review,* no. 3 (1988–89), pp 23–27. For an example, see P Dvorak and L Abboud, "SAP's Plan to Globalize Hits Cultural Barriers," *The Wall Street Journal,* May 11, 2007, http://online.wsj.com.

10 See C L Sharma, "Ethnicity, National Integration, and Education in the Union of Soviet Socialist Republics," *The Journal of East and West Studies,* October 1989, pp 75–93.

11 H Tabuchi, "Facebook Wins Relatively Few Friends in Japan," *The New York Times,* January 9, 2011.

12 See G A Sumner, *Folkways* (New York: Ginn, 1906).

13 D A Heenan and H V Perlmutter, *Multinational Organization Development* (Reading, MA: Addison-Wesley, 1979), p 17.

14 Data from R Kopp, "International Human Resource Policies and Practices in Japanese, European, and United States Multinationals," *Human Resource Management,* Winter 1994, pp 581–99.

15 K J Templer, "Personal Attributes of Expatriate Managers, Subordinate Ethnocentrism, and Expatriate Success: A Host-Country Perspective," *The International Journal of Human Resources,* August 2010, p 1754.

16 H Nadiri and M Tumer, "Influence of Ethnocentrism on Consumers' Intentions to Buy Domestically Produced Goods: An Empirical Study in North Cyprus," *Journal of Business Economics and Management,* 2010, pp 444–61.

17 M Farkas and P De Backer, "There Are Only Five Ways to Lead," *Fortune,* January 15, 1996, p 111.

18 J S Osland and A Bird, "Beyond Sophisticated Stereotyping: Cultural Sensemaking in Context," *Academy of Management Executive,* February 2000, p 67.

19 H C Lin and S T Hou, "Managerial Lessons from the East: An Interview with Acer's Stan Shih," *Academy of Management Perspectives,* November 2010, pp 6–16.

20 P C Earley and E Mosakowski, "Cultural Intelligence," *Harvard Business Review,* October 2004, p 140; and I Alon and J M Higgins, "Global Leadership Success Through Emotional and Cultural Intelligences," *Business Horizons,* November–December 2005, pp 501–12.

21 R J House, N R Quigley, and M S de Luque, "Insights from Project GLOBE: Extending Global Advertising Research through a Contemporary Framework," *International Journal of Advertising,* 2010, pp 111–39. See also M Javidan and R J House, "Cultural Acumen for the Global Manager: Lessons from Project GLOBE," *Organizational Dynamics,* Spring 2001, p 292.

22 Ibid.

23 For related research, see G S Van Der Vegt, E Van De Vliert, and X Huang, "Location-Level Links Between Diversity and Innovative Climate Depend on National Power Distance," *Academy of Management Journal,* December 2005, pp 1171–182. See also V Taras, B L Kirkman, and P Steele, "Examining the Impact of Culture's Consequences: A Three Decade, Multilevel, Meta-Analytic Review of Hofstede's Cultural Value Dimensions," *Journal of Applied Psychology,* 2010, pp 405–39.

24 V Taras, P Steel, and B L Kirkman, "Negative Practice-Value Correlations in the GLOBE Data: Unexpected Findings, Questionnaire Limitations and Research Directions," *Journal of International Business Studies,* 2010, pp 1330–338.

25 M Irvine, "Young Workers Saving to Retire," *The Arizona Republic,* December 28, 2003, p D5.

26 L E Atwater, J F Brett, and A C Charles, "The Delivery of Workplace Discipline: Lessons Learned," *Organizational Dynamics,* 2007, pp 392–403.

27 M Edwards, "As Good as It Gets," *AARP: The Magazine,* November–December 2004, p 48.

28 Data from Trompenaars and Hampden-Turner, *Riding the Waves of Culture: Understanding Cultural Diversity in Global Business,* Ch 5. For relevant research evidence, see E G T Green and J Deschamps, "Variation of Individualism and Collectivism within and between 20 Countries," *Journal of Cross-Cultural Psychology,* May 2005, pp 321–39.

29 As quoted in E E Schultz, "Scudder Brings Lessons to Navajo, Gets Some of Its Own," *The Wall Street Journal,* April 29, 1999, p C12.

30 Data from Trompenaars and Hampden-Turner, *Riding the Waves of Culture: Understanding Cultural Diversity in Global Business,* Ch 5. For relevant research evidence, see E G T Green and J Deschamps, "Variation of Individualism and Collectivism within and between 20 Countries," *Journal of Cross-Cultural Psychology,* May 2005, pp 321–39.

31 See W L Adair, L Weingart, and J Brett, "The Timing and Function of Offers in U.S. and Japanese Negotiations," *Journal of Applied Psychology,* July 2007, pp 1056–68.

32 I Adler, "Between the Lines," *Business Mexico,* October 2000, p 24.

33 See C Saunders, C Van Slyke, and D R Vogel, "My Time or Yours? Managing Time Visions in Global Virtual Teams," *Academy of Management Executive,* February 2004, pp 19–31.

34 D J Lynch, "Building Explosion in China Pumps Up Exports from USA," *USA Today,* April 20, 2006, p 2B.

35 R W Moore, "Time, Culture, and Comparative Management: A Review and Future Direction," in *Advances in International Comparative Management,* vol. 5, ed S B Prasad (Greenwich, CT: JAI Press, 1990), pp 7–8.

36 See A C Bluedorn, C F Kaufman, and P M Lane, "How Many Things Do You Like to Do at Once? An Introduction to Monochronic and Polychronic Time," *Academy of Management Executive,* November 1992, pp 17–26.

37 O Port, "You May Have To Reset This Watch—In a Million Years," *BusinessWeek,* August 30, 1993, p 65.

38 See M Javidan, P W Dorfman, M S de Luque, and R J House, "In the Eye of the Beholder: Cross Cultural Lessons in Leadership from Project GLOBE," *Academy of Management Perspectives,* February 2006, pp 67–90.

39 B Becht, "Building a Company Without Borders," *Harvard Business Review,* April 2010.

40 A Fisher, "Five Ways to Ignite Your Career," *Fortune,* February 6, 2006, p 50.

41 C Geissler and L Kuhn, "Developing Your Global Know-How," *Harvard Business Review,* March 2011, pp 71–75.

42 L N Littrell, E Salas, K P Hess, M Paley, and S Riedel, "Expatriate Preparation: A Critical Analysis of 25 Years of Cross-Cultural Training Research," *Human Resource Development Review,* September 2006, pp 355–88.

43 Results are presented in A Maingault, L Albright, and V Neal, "Policy Tips, Repatriation, Safe Harbor Rules," *HR Magazine,* March 2008, pp 34–35.

44 Littrell, Salas, Hess, Paley, and Riedel, "Expatriate Preparation," pp 355–88.

45 An excellent reference book on this topic is J S Black, H B Gregersen, and M E Mendenhall, *Global Assignments: Successfully Expatriating and Repatriating International Managers* (San Francisco: Jossey-Bass, 1992).

46 For a review of cross-cultural training program content, structure and outcomes see J Selmer, "Expatriate Cross-cultural Training for China: Views and Experience of 'China Hands,'" *Management and Research Review,* 2010, pp 41–53.

47 Littrell, Salas, Hess, Paley, and Riedel, "Expatriate Preparation," pp 355–88.

48 See P C Earley, "Intercultural Training for Managers: A Comparison of Documentary and Interpersonal Methods," *Academy of Management Journal,* December 1987, pp 685–98; and J S Black and M Mendenhall, "Cross-Cultural Training Effectiveness: A Review and a Theoretical Framework for Future Research," *Academy of Management Review,* January 1990, pp 113–36.

49 M Harvey, H Mayerhofer, L Hartman, and M Moeller, "Corralling the 'Horses' to Staff the Global Organization of the 21st Century," *Organizational Dynamics,* 2010, pp 258–68.

50 Littrell, Salas, Hess, Paley, and Riedel, "Expatriate Preparation," pp 355–88.

51 T Lowry and F Balfour, "It's All About the Face-to-Face," *BusinessWeek,* January 28, 2008, pp 50–51.

52 Hay Group 2010 Best Companies for Leadership, http://www.haygroup
[unreadable]
medium=email&utm_campaign=BCL2010.

53 L Yuan, "Personal Lives, Office Lives," *The Wall Street Journal,* February 19, 2008, http://online.wsj.com.

[54] P Dvorak, "Plain English Gets Harder in Global Era," *The Wall Street Journal,* November 5, 2007, pp B1, B3.

[55] K L Miller, "How a Team of Buckeyes Helped Honda Save a Bundle," *BusinessWeek,* September 13, 1993, p 68.

[56] C I C Farh, K Bartol, D L Shapiro, and J Shin, "Networking Abroad: A Process Model of How Expatriates Form Support Ties to Facilitate Adjustment," *Academy of Management Review,* 2010, pp 434–54.

[57] B Newman, "For Ira Caplan, Re-Entry Has Been Strange," *The Wall Street Journal,* December 12, 1995, p A12.

[58] G K Stahl, C H Chua, P Caligiuri, J L Cerdin, and M Taniguchi, "Predictors of Turnover Intentions in Learning-Driven and Demand-Driven International Assignments: The Role of Repatriation Concerns, Satisfaction with Company Support, and Perceived Career Advancement Opportunities," *Human Resource Management,* January–February 2009, pp 89–109.

[59] D Barboza, "Rio Tinto Workers Admit Taking Bribes in China," *The New York Times,* March 22, 2010.

[60] Ibid.

Chapter 4

[1] Excerpted from G Jaffe, "Navy Condemns Raunchy Videos," *The Arizona Republic,* January 4, 2011, p A3.

[2] A Flaherty and P Jelinek, "Navy Fires Officer Years After Lewd Videos Made," *The Arizona Republic,* January 5, 2011, p A5.

[3] See "Bernard Madoff," January 5, 2011, http://en.wikipedia.org/wiki/Bernard_Madoff.

[4] The negative bias was examined by A Weinberg and G Hajcak, "Beyond Good and Evil: The Time-Course of Neural Activity Elicited by Specific Picture Content," *Emotion,* December 2010, pp 767–82.

[5] V Harnish, "Stop Doing These Five Business Killers Now: Here's How to Get Your Life in Order," *Fortune,* December 6, 2010, p 71.

[6] E Rosch, C B Mervis, W D Gray, D M Johnson, and P Boyes-Braem, "Basic Objects in Natural Categories," *Cognitive Psychology,* July 1976, p 383.

[7] C M Judd and B Park, "Definition and Assessment of Accuracy in Social Stereotypes," *Psychological Review,* January 1993, p 110.

[8] See J V Sanchez-Hucles and D D Davis, "Women and Women of Color in Leadership," *American Psychologist,* April 2010, pp 171–81; and S Bruckmüller and N R Branscombe, "How Women End Up On the 'Glass Cliff,'" *Harvard Business Review,* January–February 2011, p 26.

[9] See T DeAngelis, "Unmasking 'Racial Micro Aggressions,'" *Harvard Business Review,* February 2009, pp 42–46.

[10] See T W H Ng and D C Feldman, "The Relationship of Age to Ten Dimensions of Job Performance," *Journal of Applied Psychology,* March 2008, pp 392–423; and R W Griffeth, P W Hom, and S Gaertner, "A Meta-Analysis of Antecedents and Correlates of Employee Turnover: Update, Moderator Tests, and Research Implications for the Next Millennium," *Journal of Management,* 2000, pp 463–88.

[11] See E L Paluck and D P Green, "Prejudice Reduction: What Works? A Review and Assessment of Research and Practice," *Annual Review of Psychology,* 2009, pp 339–67.

[12] Implicit cognition is discussed by C E Drake, K K Kellum, K G Wilson, J B Luoma, J H Weinstein, and C H Adams, "Examining the Implicit Relational Assessment Procedure: Four Preliminary Studies," *The Psychological Record,* Winter 2010, pp 81–100.

[13] See M Orey, "White Men Can't Help It," *BusinessWeek,* May 15, 2006, pp 54, 57.

[14] See R C Mayer and J H Davis, "The Effect of the Performance Appraisal System on Trust for Management: A Field Quasi-Experiment," *Journal of Applied Psychology,* February 1999, pp 123–36.

[15] W H Bommer, J L Johnson, G A Rich, P M Podsakoff, and S B Mackenzie, "On the Interchangeability of Objective and Subjective Measures of Employee Performance: A Meta-Analysis," *Personnel Psychology,* Autumn 1995, pp 587–605.

[16] The effectiveness of rater training was supported by D V Day and L M Sulsky, "Effects of Frame-of-Reference Training and Information Configuration on Memory Organization and Rating Accuracy," *Journal of Applied Psychology,* February 1995, pp 158–67.

[17] Results can be found in J S Phillips and R G Lord, "Schematic Information Processing and Perceptions of Leadership in Problem-Solving Groups," *Journal of Applied Psychology,* August 1982, pp 486–92; and D D Cremer, M V Dijke, and D M Mayer, "Cooperating When 'You' and 'I' are Treated Fairly: The Moderating Role of Leader Prototypicality," *Journal of Applied Psychology,* November 2010, pp 1121–33.

[18] See P E Spector, J A Bauer, and S Fox, "Measurement Artifacts in the Assessment of Counterproductive Work Behavior and Organizational Citizenship Behavior: Do We Know What We Think We Know?" *Journal of Applied Psychology,* July 2010, pp 781–90; and B Schneider and K B Paul, "In the Company We Trust," *HR Magazine,* January 2011, pp 40–44.

[19] See M Beck, "Conquering Fear," *The Wall Street Journal,* January 4, 2011, pp D1, D2; and W Darr and G Johns, "Work Strain, Health, and Absenteeism: A Meta-Analysis," *Journal of Occupational Health Psychology,* October 2008, pp 293–318.

[20] See E C Baig, "Survey Offers a 'Sneak Peek' into Net Surfers' Brains," *USA Today,* March 27, 2006, p 4B.

[21] Kelley's model is discussed in detail in H H Kelley, "The Processes of Causal Attribution," *American Psychologist,* February 1973, pp 107–28.

[22] See J Reb and G J Greguras, "Understanding Performance Ratings: Dynamic Performance, Attributions, and Rating Purpose," *Journal of Applied Psychology,* January 2010, pp 213–20.

[23] Examples can be found in C Meyer and A Schwager, "Understanding Customer Experience," *Harvard Business Review,* February 2007, pp 117–26; and M S Hershcovis and J Barling, "Comparing Victim Attributions and Outcomes for Workplace Aggression and Sexual Harassment," *Journal of Applied Psychology,* September 2010, pp 874–88.

[24] B Leonard, "A Seldom-Seen World of Work," *HR Magazine,* June 2010, p 82.

[25] G Kolev, "The Stock Market Bubble, Shareholders' Attribution Bias and Excessive Top CEO Pay," *The Journal of Behavioral Finance,* April 2008, pp 62–71.

[26] R J Grossman, "What to Do about Substance Abuse," *HR Magazine,* November 2010, pp 33–38.

[27] J Metcalfe, "Recruiting Phone Calls at Center of NCAA Hearing," *The Arizona Republic,* August 13, 2010, p C7.

[28] See J Metcalfe, "NCAA Bans Arizona State University from 2011 Postseason," December 15, 2010, http://www.azcentral.com/sports/articles/2010/12/12/20101215ncaa-bans-arizona-state-asu.

[29] See S E Moss and M J Martinko, "The Effects of Performance Attributions and Outcome Dependence on Leader Feedback Behavior Following Poor Subordinate Performance," *Journal of Organizational Behavior,* May 1998, pp 259–74.

[30] See J Silvester, F Patterson, E Ferguson, "Comparing Two Attributional Models of Job Performance in Retail Sales: A Field Study," *Journal of Occupational and Organizational Psychology,* March 2003, pp 115–32.

[31] H Collingwood, "Who Handles a Diverse Work Force Best?" *Working Women,* February 1996, p 25.

[32] See M Moskowitz, R Levering, and C Tkaczyk, "100 Best Companies to Work For," *Fortune,* February 8, 2010, pp 75–88.

[33] Results can be found in D A Harrison, D A Kravitz, D M Mayer, L M Leslie, and D Lev-Arey, "Understanding Attitudes Toward Affirmative Action Programs in Employment: Summary and Meta-Analysis of 35 Years of Research," *Journal of Applied Psychology,* September 2006, pp 1013–36.

[34] For a thorough review of relevant research, see M E Heilman, "Affirmative Action: Some Unintended Consequences for Working Women," in *Research in Organizational Behavior,* vol 16, ed B M Staw and L L Cummings (Greenwich, CT: JAI Press, 1994), pp 125–69.

[35] M E Heilman, W S Battle, C E Keller, and R A Lee, "Type of Affirmative Action Policy: A Determinant of Reactions to Sex-Based Preferential Selection?" *Journal of Applied Psychology,* April 1998, pp 190–205.

[36] The survey process is described in "About the Diversity Inc Top 50 Companies for Diversity," May 6, 2010, http://www.diversityinc.com/article/7570/.

[37] A M Morrison, *The New Leaders: Guidelines on Leadership Diversity in America* (San Francisco: Jossey-Bass, 1992), p 78.

38 See J E O'Neill, "Washington's Equal Pay Obsession," *The Wall Street Journal,* November 16, 2010, p A19; and N M Carter and C Silva, "Women in Management: Delusions of Progress," *Harvard Business Review,* March 2010, pp 19–21.

39 See A H Eagly and L L Carli, *Through the Labyrinth* (Boston: Harvard Business School Press, 2007).

40 These statistics were obtained from "Women CEOs of the Fortune 1000," November 2010, http://www.catalyst.org/publication/322/women-ceos-of-the-fortune-1000.

41 See M J Perry, "Carpe Diem," February 2009, http://mjperry.blogspot.com/2009/02/degree-gap-will-continue-to-widen.html; "Women in Management in the United States, 1950–Present," April 2010, http://www.catalyst.org/publication/207/women-in-management-1950-present; "Women in the Board Room and in the President's Office: What Differences Does it Make?" Retrieved December 29, 2010, from http://www.agb.org/events/annual-meeting/2011/2011-agb-national-conference-trusteeship/sessions/women-board-room-and-pr; and L Jones, "8th Circuit Lags in Female Appointees," May 31, 2010, http://www.law.com/jsp/nlj/PubArticleNLJ.jsp?id=1202458929880&slreturn=1&hbxlogin=1.

42 Eagly and Carli, *Through the Labyrinth,* pp 26–27.

43 See G C Armas, "Almost Half of US Likely to Be Minorities by 2050," *The Arizona Republic,* March 18, 2004, p A5; US Census Bureau, Tbl. 1a., "Projected Population of the US by Race and Hispanic Origin: 2000–2050, March 2004, www.census.gov/ipc/www/usinterimproj/.

44 See Bureau of Labor Statistics, "Employed Persons by Occupation, Race, Hispanic or Latino Ethnicity, and Sex," retrieved February 5, 2009, www.bls.gov.

45 See U.S. Equal Employment Opportunity Commission, "Race-Based Charges FY 1997–FY 2009," retrieved December 29, 2010, from http://www.eeoc.gov/eeoc/statistics/enforcement/race.cfm.

46 See D-W Carmen, B D Proctor, and J C Smith, U.S. Census Bureau, Current Population Reports, P60-238, *Income, Poverty, and Health Insurance Coverage in the United States: 2009, Table 1-Income and Earnings Summary Measures by Selected Characteristics: 2008 and 2009,* retrieved December 29, 2010, from http://www.census.gov/prod/2010pubs/p60-238.pdf.

47 See "U.S. Census Bureau, Current Population Survey, 2009 Annual Social and Economic Supplement," April 2010, http://www.census.gov/hhes/socdemo/education/data/cps/2009/tables.html; and Bureau of Labor Statistics, "Education Projections," May 27, 2010, http://www.bls.gov.emp/ep_chart-001.htm.

48 See S Miller, "Skills Critical for a Changing Workforce," *HR Magazine,* August 2008, p 24; N Anderson, "High-School Graduation Rates Up in U.S.," *The Arizona Republic,* December 15, 2010, p A21; and "Illiteracy—Major U.S. Problem," January 20, 2009, http://www.enotalone.com/article/19273.html.

49 "Facts on Literacy," *National Literacy Facts,* August 27, 1998, www.svs.net/wpci/Litfacts.htm.

50 See R Strack, J Baier, and A Fahlander, "Managing Demographic Risk," *Harvard Business Review,* February 2008, pp 119–28.

51 H Jones, "CEOs Now Find That Principles and Profits Can Mix Well," *The Wall Street Journal,* November 22, 2010, p R5.

52 See A Joshi, J C Dencker, G Franz, and J J Martocchio, "Unpacking Generational Identities in Organizations," *Academy of Management Review,* July 2010, pp 392–414.

53 See "Demographics of Sexual Orientation," retrieved December 30, 2010, from http://en.wikipedia.org/wiki/Demographics_of_sexual_orientation; and L Visconti, "You're Gay? You're Fired!" retrieved December 28, 2010, from http://www.diversityinc.com/article/8206/Youre-Gay-Youre-Fired/.

54 R E Fassinger, S L Shullman, and M R Stevenson, "Toward an Affirmative Lesbian, Gay, Bisexual, and Transgender Leadership Program," *American Psychologist,* April 2010, pp 201–15.

55 These examples can be found in Moskowitz, R Levering, and C Tkaczyk, "100 Best Companies to Work For," pp 75–88.

56 S J Wells, "Say Hola! to the Majority Minority," *HR Magazine,* September 2008, p 38.

57 See S A Hewlett and R Rashid, "The Battle for Female Talent in Emerging Markets," *Harvard Business Review,* May 2010, pp 101–6.

58 C Hymowitz, "Women Tell Women: Life in the Top Jobs Is Worth the Effort," *The Wall Street Journal,* November 20, 2006, p B1.

59 S Boehle, "Voices of Opportunity," *Training,* January 2009, p 39.

60 See B Mirza, "Build Employee Skills, Help Nonprofits," *HR Magazine,* October 2008, p 30.

61 These recommendations were taken from G M McEvoy and M J Blahana, "Engagement or Disengagement? Older Workers and the Looming Labor Shortage," *Business Horizons,* September–October 2001, p 50.

62 See the related discussion in L Gratton, "The End of the Middle Manager," *Harvard Business Review,* January–February 2011, p 36; and A D Wright, "Millennials 'Bathed in Bits,'" *HR Magazine,* July 2010, pp 40–41.

63 These barriers were taken from discussions in Loden, *Implementing Diversity;* E E Spragins, "Benchmark: The Diverse Work Force," *Inc.,* January 1993, p 33; and Morrison, *The New Leaders: Guidelines on Leadership Diversity in America.*

64 C Chase, "ESPN Fires Announcer for Calling Female Colleague 'Sweet Baby,'" *Y! Sports Blog,* January 4, 2011, http://sports.yahoo.com/blogs/post/ESPN-fires-announcer-for-calling-female-colleague?urn=top-303299.

65 See the related discussion in A Fisher, "The Sky's the Limit," *Fortune,* May 1, 2006, pp 124B–H.

66 A C Homan, "Bridging Faultlines by Valuing Diversity: Diversity Beliefs, Information Elaboration, and Performance in Diverse Work Groups," *Journal of Applied Psychology,* September 2007, pp 1189–99.

67 See R J Crisp and R N Turner, "Cognitive Adaptation to the Experience of Social and Cultural Diversity," *Psychological Bulletin,* December 2010, pp 1–26.

68 This discussion is based on R R Thomas Jr, *Redefining Diversity* (New York: AMACOM, 1996).

69 D J Gaiter, "Eating Crow: How Shoney's, Belted by a Lawsuit, Found the Path to Diversity," *The Wall Street Journal,* April 16, 1996, pp A1, A11.

70 P Dass and B Parker, "Strategies for Managing Human Resource Diversity: From Resistance to Learning," *Academy of Management Executive,* May 1999, p 69.

71 Gaiter, "Eating Crow," pp A1, A11

72 E White, "Fostering Diversity to Aid Business," *The Wall Street Journal,* May 20, 2006, p B3.

73 See A Beard, "Surviving Twin Challenges—At Home and Work," *Harvard Business Review,* January–February 2011, p 164.

74 D Cadrain, "The Marijuana Exception," *HR Magazine,* November 2010, pp 40–41.

Chapter 5

1 Excerpted and adapted from L Grossman, "2010 Person of the Year," *Time,* December 27, 2010, pp 44–73; and D Kirkpatrick, *The Facebook Effect,* New York, NY: Simon & Schuster, 2010.

2 See E Krell, "Personality Assessments Are Being Used In New Ways Throughout the Employee Life Cycle," *HR Magazine,* November 1, 2005.

3 For interesting reading on intelligence, see J R Flynn, "Searching for Justice: The Discovery of IQ Gains over Time," *American Psychologist,* January 1999, pp 5–20; and E Benson, "Intelligent Intelligence Testing," *Monitor on Psychology,* February 2003, pp 48–54.

4 S Kanazawa, "Evolutionary Psychology and Intelligence Research," *American Psychologist,* May-June 2010, pp 279–289.

5 J W B Lang, M Kersting, U R Hulsheger, and J Lang, "General Mental Ability, Narrower Cognitive Abilities, and Job Performance: The Perspective of the Nested-Factor Model of Cognitive Abilities," *Personnel Psychology,* 63, 2010, pp 595–640.

6 S L Wilk, L Burris Desmarais, and P R Sackett, "Gravitation to Jobs Commensurate with Ability: Longitudinal and Cross-Sectional Tests," *Journal of Applied Psychology,* February 1995, p 79

7 B Azar, "People Are Becoming Smarter—Why?" *APA Monitor,* June 1996, p 20.

8 H Gardner, *Frames of Mind: The Theory of Multiple Intelligences,* 10th ed (New York: Basic Books, 1993). Also see H Gardner, *Intelligence Reframed: Multiple Intelligences for the 21st Century* (New York: Basic Books, 2000).

9 For a good overview of Gardner's life and work, see M K Smith, "Howard Gardner and Multiple Intelligences," *Encyclopedia of Informal Education,* 2002, www.infed.org/thinkers/gardner.htm. Also see B Fryer, "The Ethical Mind: A Conversation with Psychologist Howard Gardner," *Harvard Business Review,* March 2007, pp 51–56.

10 R J Sternberg, "WICS: A Model of Leadership in Organizations," *Academy of Management Learning and Education,* December 2003, p 388.

11 B Kidwell, D M Hardesty, B R Murtha, and S Sheng, "Emotional Intelligence in Marketing Exchanges," *Journal of Marketing,* January 2011, pp 78–95.

12 C J Ferguson, "A Meta-Analysis of Normal and Disordered Personality Across the Life Span," *Journal of Personality and Social Psychology,* 2010, pp 659–667. See also C J Hopwood, M B Donnellan, D M Blonigen, R F Krueger, M McGue, W G Iacono, and S A Burt, "Genetic and Environmental Influences on Personality Trait Stability and Growth During the Transition to Adulthood: A Three-Wave Longitudinal Study," *Journal of Personality and Social Psychology,* January 17, 2011, pp 1–12.

13 The landmark report is J M Digman, "Personality Structure: Emergence of the Five-Factor Model," *Annual Review of Psychology,* vol. 41, 1990, pp 417–40. Also see P Warr, D Bartram, and A Brown, "Big Five Validity: Aggregation Method Matters," *Journal of Occupational and Organizational Psychology,* September 2005, pp 377–86.

14 For more on personality measurement and assessment, see P Sackett and F Lievens, "Personnel Selection," *Annual Review of Psychology,* 2008, pp 419–50.

15 Data from S V Paunonen et al., "The Structure of Personality in Six Cultures," *Journal of Cross-Cultural Psychology,* May 1996, pp 339–53.

16 For supporting evidence see D P Schmitt, J Allik, R R McCrae, and V Benet-Martinez, "The Geographic Distribution of Big Five Personality Traits," *Journal of Cross-Cultural Psychology,* March 2007, pp 173–212.

17 J P Thomas, D S Whitman, and V Chockalingam, "Employee Proactivity in Organizations: A Comparative Meta-Analysis of Emergent Proactive Constructs," *Journal of Occupational & Organizational Psychology,* June 2010, pp 275–300.

18 Ibid.

19 D Hannah, "How I Did It: Joaquin Galan, CEO, Galypso International," *Inc.,* The 2007 Inc. 5000, www.inc.com/inc5000/, accessed March 26, 2008; and T Snyder, "How I Did It: Rachel Coleman, CEO, Two Little Hands Productions," *Inc.,* The 2007 Inc. 5000, www.inc.com/inc5000/, accessed March 26, 2008.

20 M R Barrick and M K Mount, "The Big Five Personality Dimensions and Job Performance: A Meta-Analysis," *Personnel Psychology,* Spring 1991, pp 1–26. See also I S Oh, G Wang, and M K Mount, "Validity of Observer Ratings of the Five-Factor Model of Personality Traits: A Meta-Analysis," *Journal of Applied Psychology,* December 13, 2010, pp. 1–12.

21 Ibid., Barrick and Mount. Also see D Kamdar and L Van Dyne, "The Joint Effects of Personality and Workplace Social Exchange Relationships in Predicting Task Performance and Citizenship Performance," *Journal of Applied Psychology,* September 2007, pp 1286–98.

22 B Marcus, K Lee, and M C Ashton, "Personality Dimensions Explaining Relationships between Integrity Tests and Counterproductive Behavior: Big Five, or One in Addition?" *Personnel Psychology,* Spring 2007, pp 1–34.

23 For details, see S Clarke and I T Robertson, "A Meta-Analytic Review of the Big Five Personality Factors and Accident Involvement in Occupational and Non-Occupational Settings," *Journal of Occupational and Organizational Psychology,* September 2005, pp 355–76.

24 Barrick and Mount, "The Big Five Personality Dimensions and Job Performance: A Meta-Analysis," p 21.

25 For details, see L A Witt and G R Ferris, "Social Skill as Moderator of the Conscientiousness-Performance Relationship: Convergent Results across Four Studies," *Journal of Applied Psychology,* October 2003, pp 809–20.

26 Lead researcher William Fleeson, as quoted in M Dittmann, "Acting Extraverted Spurs Positive Feelings, Study Finds," *Monitor on Psychology,* April 2003, p 17.

27 D Zielinski, "Effective Assessments," *HR Magazine,* January 2011, pp 61–64.

28 Oh, Wang, and Mount, "Validity of Observer Ratings of the Five-Factor Model of Personality Traits," pp. 1–12. For details on test bias see H Aguinis, S A Carpenter, and C A Pierce, "Revival of Test Bias Research in Pre-Employment Testing," *Journal of Applied Psychology,* 2010, pp 648–680. For a discussion and advice on using pre-employment tests see T Minton-Eversole, "Avoiding Bias in Pre-Employment Testing," *HR Magazine,* December 2010, pp 77–80.

29 Ibid., T Minton-Eversole. See also H Dolezalek, "Tests on Trial," *Training,* April 2005, p 34. Also see M Bolch, "Nice Work," *HR Magazine,* February 2008, pp 78–81; and M Weinstein, "Personalities & Performance," *Training,* July–August 2008, pp 36–40.

30 Based in part on T A Judge, "Core Self-Evaluations and Work Success," *Current Directions in Psychological Science,* 2009, pp 58–62.

31 Ibid.

32 Taken from D L Ferris, H Lian, D J Brown, F X J Pang, and L M Keeping, "Self-Esteem and Job Performance: The Moderating Role of Self-Esteem Contingencies," *Personnel Psychology,* 2010, pp 561–593.

33 E Diener and M Diener, "Cross-Cultural Correlates of Life Satisfaction and Self-Esteem," *Journal of Personality and Social Psychology,* April 1995, p 662.

34 See C Kobayashi and J D Brown, "Self-Esteem and Self-Enhancement in Japan and America," *Journal of Cross-Cultural Psychology,* September 2003, pp 567–80.

35 C Huang, "Mean-Level Change in Self-Esteem from Childhood through Adulthood: Meta-Analysis of Longitudinal Studies," *Review of General Psychology,* 2010, pp 251–260.

36 Based on data in F L Smoll, R E Smith, N P Barnett, and J J Everett, "Enhancement of Children's Self-Esteem through Social Support Training for Youth Sports Coaches," *Journal of Applied Psychology,* August 1993, pp 602–10.

37 W J McGuire and C V McGuire, "Enhancing Self-Esteem by Directed-Thinking Tasks: Cognitive and Affective Positivity Asymmetries," *Journal of Personality and Social Psychology,* June 1996, p 1124.

38 F Giblin and B Lakey, "Integrating Mentoring and Social Support Research within the Context of Stressful Medical Training," *Journal of Social and Clinical Psychology,* 2010, pp 771–796.

39 W B Swann Jr., C Chang-Schneider, and K L McClarty, "Do People's Self-Views Matter? Self-Concept and Self-Esteem in Everyday Life," *American Psychologist,* February–March 2007, pp 84–94.

40 Ferris, Lian, Brown, and Pang, and Keeping, "Self-Esteem and Job Performance," pp 561–593.

41 M E Gist, "Self-Efficacy: Implications for Organizational Behavior and Human Resource Management," *Academy of Management Review,* July 1987, p 472. Also see A Bandura, "Self-Efficacy: Toward a Unifying Theory of Behavioral Change," *Psychological Review,* March 1977, pp 191–215.

42 Giblin and Lakey, "Integrating Mentoring and Social Support Research within the Context of Stressful Medical Training," pp 771–796.

43 Based on D H Lindsley, D A Brass, and J B Thomas, "Efficacy-Performance Spirals: A Multilevel Perspective," *Academy of Management Review,* July 1995, pp 645–78.

44 See, for example, V Gecas, "The Social Psychology of Self-Efficacy," in *Annual Review of Sociology,* eds W R Scott and J Blake (Palo Alto, CA: Annual Reviews, Inc., 1989), vol. 15, pp 291–316.

45 For more on learned helplessness, see C R Campbell and M J Martinko, "An Integrative Attributional Perspective of Empowerment and Learned Helplessness: A Multimethod Field Study," *Journal of Management,* 2, 1998, pp 173–200.

46 For an update on Bandura, see D Smith, "The Theory Heard 'Round the World," *Monitor on Psychology,* October 2002, pp 30–32.

47 Research on this connection is reported in R B Rubin, M M Martin, S S Bruning, and D E Powers, "Test of a Self-Efficacy Model of Interpersonal Communication Competence," *Communication Quarterly,* Spring 1993, pp 210–20.

48 Excerpted from T Petzinger Jr, "Bob Schmonsees Has a Tool for Better Sales, and It Ignores Excuses," *The Wall Street Journal,* March 26, 1999, p B1.

49 T A Judge and J E Bono, "Relationship of Core Self-Evaluations Traits—Self-Esteem, Generalized Self-Efficacy, Locus of Control, and Emotional Stability—With Job Satisfaction and Job Performance: A Meta-Analysis," *Journal of Applied Psychology,* 2001, pp 80–92.

[50] Based in part on discussion in Gecas, "The Social Psychology of Self-Efficacy."

[51] See S K Parker, "Enhancing Role Breadth Self-Efficacy: The Roles of Job Enrichment and Other Organizational Interventions," *Journal of Applied Psychology,* December 1998, pp 835–52.

[52] The positive relationship between self-efficacy and readiness for retraining is documented in L A Hill and J Elias, "Retraining Midcareer Managers: Career History and Self-Efficacy Beliefs," *Human Resource Management,* Summer 1990, pp 197–217.

[53] See A D Stajkovic and Fred Luthans, "Social Cognitive Theory and Self-Efficacy: Going beyond Traditional Motivational and Behavioral Approaches," *Organizational Dynamics,* Spring 1998, pp 62–74.

[54] See P C Earley and T R Lituchy, "Delineating Goal and Efficacy Effects: A Test of Three Models," *Journal of Applied Psychology,* February 1991, pp 81–98.

[55] See P Tierney and S M Farmer, "Creative Self-Efficacy: Its Potential Antecedents and Relationship to Creative Performance," *Academy of Management Journal,* December 2002, pp 1137–48.

[56] See W S Silver, T R Mitchell, and M E Gist, "Response to Successful and Unsuccessful Performance: The Moderating Effect of Self-Efficacy on the Relationship between Performance and Attributions," *Organizational Behavior and Human Decision Processes,* June 1995, pp 286–99.

[57] For an instructive update, see J B Rotter, "Internal versus External Control of Reinforcement: A Case History of a Variable," *American Psychologist,* April 1990, pp 489–493.

[58] B K Fuller, M C Spears, and D F Parker, "Entrepreneurial Tendencies: Evidence from China and India," *International Journal of Management and Marketing Research,* 2010, pp 39–52.

[59] For an overall review of research on locus of control, see P E Spector, "Behavior in Organizations as a Function of Employee's Locus of Control," *Psychological Bulletin,* May 1982, pp 482–497.

[60] H Le, I S Oh, S B Robbins, R Illies, E Holland, and P Wstrick, "Too Much of a Good Thing: Curvilinear Relationships Between Personality Traits and Job Performance," *Journal of Applied Psychology,* 2011, pp 113–133.

[61] Ibid.

[62] K H Foulkrod, C Field, and C V R Brown, "Trauma Surgeon Personality and Job Satisfaction: Results from a National Survey," *The American Surgeon,* April 2010, pp 422–427.

[63] Judge, "Core Self-Evaluations and Work Success," pp 58–62. See also T A Judge, J E Bono, and C J Thoresen, "The Core Self-Evaluations Scale: Development of a Measure," *Personnel Psychology,* 2003, pp 303–331.

[64] Z Simsek, C Heavey, and J F Veiga, "The Impact of CEO Core Self-Evaluation on the Firm's Entrepreneurial Orientation," *Strategic Management Journal,* 2010, pp 110–119.

[65] These results are discussed in L Winerman, "A Healthy Mind, a Longer Life," *Monitor on Psychology,* November 2006, pp 42–44.

[66] See D A Harrison, D A Newman, and P L Roth, "How Important Are Job Attitudes? Meta-Analytic Comparisons of Integrative Behavioral Outcomes and Time Sequences," *Academy of Management Journal,* April 2006, pp 305–25.

[67] M Fishbein and I Ajzen, *Belief, Attitude, Intention and Behavior: An Introduction to Theory and Research* (Reading, MA: Addison-Wesley Publishing, 1975), p 6.

[68] Research on attitudes is thoroughly discussed by A P Brief, *Attitudes in and around Organizations* (Thousand Oaks, CA: Sage, 1998), pp 49–84.

[69] For details about this theory, see L Festinger, *A Theory of Cognitive Dissonance* (Stanford, CA: Stanford University Press, 1957).

[70] See B M Staw and J Ross, "Stability in the Midst of Change: A Dispositional Approach to Job Attitudes," *Journal of Applied Psychology,* August 1985, pp 469–80.

[71] Data from P S Visser and J A Krosnick, "Development of Attitude Strength over the Life Cycle: Surge and Decline," *Journal of Personality and Social Psychology,* December 1998, pp 389–410.

[72] This example is discussed in C Levinson and M Bradley, "Mubarak Digs In as Mobs Battle Police," *The Wall Street Journal,* January 29–30, 2011, pp A1, A12.

[73] I Ajzen, "The Theory of Planned Behavior," *Organizational Behavior and Human Decision Processes,* vol. 50 (1991), p 188.

[74] See R P Steel and N K Ovalle II, "A Review and Meta-Analysis of Research on the Relationship between Behavioral Intentions and Employee Turnover," *Journal of Applied Psychology,* November 1984, pp 673–86.

[75] Results can be found in M R Barrick and R D Zimmerman, "Reducing Voluntary Turnover through Selection," *Journal of Applied Psychology,* January 2005, pp 159–66.

[76] Drawn from I Ajzen and M Fishbein, *Understanding Attitudes and Predicting Social Behavior* (Englewood Cliffs, NJ: Prentice Hall, 1980); J Zikic, "Job Search and Social Cognitive Theory: The Role of Career-Related Activities," *Journal of Vocational Behavior,* February 2009, pp 117–27; F A White, M A Charles, and J K Nelson, "The Role of Persuasive Arguments in Changing Affirmative Action Attitudes and Expressed Behavior in Higher Education," *Journal of Applied Psychology,* November 2008, pp 1271–86; M-F Chen and P-J Tung, "The Moderating Effect of Perceived Lack of Facilities on Consumers," *Environment and Behavior,* November 2010, pp 824–844; L Luo, "Attitudes Toward Older People and Coworkers' Intention to Work with Older Employees: A Taiwanese Study," *The International Journal of Aging & Human Development,* 2010, pp 305–322; and P W Hom and C L Hulin, "A Competitive Test of the Prediction of Reenlistment by Several Models," *Journal of Applied Psychology,* February 1981, pp 23–39.

[77] Supportive research is presented in T L Webb and P Sheeran, "Does Changing Behavioral Intentions Engender Behavior Change: A Meta-Analysis of the Experimental Evidence," *Psychological Bulletin,* March 2006, pp 249–68.

[78] "Top Small Workplaces 2008," *The Wall Street Journal,* October 13, 2008, p 5.

[79] Colvin, "Spitzer's Bully Pulpit," *Fortune,* March 31, 2008, p 18.

[80] D Lieberman, "Fear of Failing Drives Diller," *USA Today,* February 10, 1999, p 3B.

[81] M Fugate, A J Kinicki, and G E Prussia, "Employee Coping with Organizational Change: An Examination of Alternative Theoretical Perspectives and Models," *Personnel Psychology,* 2008, pp 1–36.

[82] S D Pugh, M Groth, and T Hennig-Thurau, "Willing and Able to Fake Emotions: A Closer Examination of the Link Between Emotional Dissonance and Employee Well-Being," *Journal of Applied Psychology,* November 8, 2010.

[83] For more on crying at work, see M Diamond, S Shellenbarger, "Read This and Weep: Crying at Work Gains Acceptance," *The Wall Street Journal,* April 26, 2007, p D1.

[84] Fugate, Kinicki, and Prussia, "Employee Coping with Organizational Change," pp 1–36.

[85] R S Lazarus, *Emotion and Adaptation* (New York: Oxford University Press, 1991), Chs 6, 7.

[86] M Kornacki, "A Fine Balancing Act," *Training Journal,* June 2010, pp 21–23.

[87] D Goleman, *Emotional Intelligence* (New York: Bantam Books, 1995), p 34. For more, see B Wall, "Being Smart Only Takes You So Far," *Training and Development,* January 2007, pp 64–68.

[88] See the box titled "Get Happy Carefully" on p 49 of D Goleman, R Boyatzis, and A McKee, "Primal Leadership: The Hidden Driver of Great Performance," *Harvard Business Review,* Special Issue: Breakthrough Leadership, December 2001, pp 43–51.

[89] See J Mayer, R Roberts, and S Barsade, "Human Abilities: Emotional Intelligence," *Annual Review of Psychology,* 2008, pp 507–536.

[90] B Kidwell, D M Hardesty, B R Murtha, and S Sheng, "Emotional Intelligence in Marketing Exchanges," *Journal of Marketing,* January 2011, pp 78–95.

[91] J M Dienfendorff, R J Erickson, A A Grandey, and J J Dahling, "Emotional Display Rules as Work Unit Norms: A Multilevel Analysis of Emotional Labor Among Nurses," *Journal of Occupational Health Psychology,* January 2011, pp 1–17

[92] Mayer, Roberts, and Barsade, "Human Abilities," pp 507–536.

[93] F Walter, M S Cole, and R H Humphrey, "Emotional Intelligence: Sine Qua Non of Leadership or Folderol?" *Academy of Management Perspectives,* February 2011, pp 45–59.

[94] Data from S D Pugh, "Service with a Smile: Emotional Contagion in the Service Encounter," *Academy of Management Journal,* October 2001, pp 1018–27.

95 R Illies, D T Wagner, and F P Morgeson, "Explaining Affective Linkages in Teams: Individual Differences in Susceptibility to Contagion and Individualism–Collectivism," *Journal of Applied Psychology,* July 2007, pp 1140–48.

96 "Impact of Emotions in the Work Environment," Knowledge@ Wharton, April 23, 2007, reprinted in *News Journal,* Wilmington, DE, www.delawareonline.com.

97 N M Ashkanasy and C S Daus, "Emotion in the Workplace: The New Challenge for Managers," *Academy of Management Executive,* February 2002, p 79.

98 S G Barsade and D E Gibson, "Why Does Affect Matter in Organizations?" *Academy of Management Perspectives,* February 2007, pp 36–59; and "Impact of Emotions in the Work Environment."

99 U R Hulsheger, J W B Lang, and G W Maier, "Emotional Labor, Strain, and Performance: Testing Reciprocal Relationships in a Longitudinal Panel Study," *Journal of Occupational and Health Psychology,* 2010, pp 505–521.

100 M Sliter, S Jex, K Wolford, and J McInnerney, "How Rude! Emotional Labor as a Mediator Between Customer Incivility and Employee Outcomes," *Journal of Occupational and Health Psychology,* 2010, pp 468–481.

101 A G Sulzberger, "Hospitals Shift Smoking Bans to Smoker Ban," *The New York Times,* February 10, 2011.

Chapter 6

1 Excerpted from J Sandberg, "Cubicle Culture: For Many Employees, a Dream Job Is One That Isn't a Nightmare," *The Wall Street Journal,* April 15, 2008, p B1.

2 T R Mitchell, "Motivation: New Direction for Theory, Research, and Practice," *Academy of Management Review,* January 1982, p 81.

3 A review of motivation theories is provided by "Motivation in Today's Workplace: The Link to Performance," *Research Quarterly,* Second Quarter 2010, pp 1–9. Published by the Society for Human Resource Management.

4 Excerpted from C Tkaczyk, "100 Best Companies to Work For, No. 73 American Express," *Fortune,* August 16, 2010, p 14.

5 For a complete description of Maslow's theory, see A H Maslow, "A Theory of Human Motivation," *Psychological Review,* July 1943, pp 370–96.

6 M Hofman, "The Idea That Saved My Company," *Inc.,* October 2007, www.inc.com. Another application of Maslow's theory is provided by C Conley, *How Great Companies Get Their Mojo from Maslow* (San Francisco, CA: Jossey-Bass, 2007).

7 H A Murray, *Explorations in Personality* (New York: John Wiley & Sons, 1938), p 164.

8 See K G Shaver, "The Entrepreneurial Personality Myth," *Business and Economic Review,* April–June 1995, pp 20–23.

9 A Beard, "Life's Work," *Harvard Business Review,* July–August 2010, p 172.

10 Evidence for the validity of motivation training can be found in H Heckhausen and S Krug, "Motive Modification," in *Motivation and Society,* ed A J Stewart (San Francisco: Jossey-Bass, 1982).

11 Results can be found in D B Turban and T L Keon, "Organizational Attractiveness: An Interactionist Perspective," *Journal of Applied Psychology,* April 1993, pp 184–93.

12 For details see "Byrraju Ramalinga Raju," Wikipedia, last updated January 27, 2011, http://en.wikipedia.org.

13 J L Bowditch and A F Buono, *A Primer on Organizational Behavior* (New York: John Wiley & Sons, 1985), p 210.

14 A review of these approaches is provided by S Hornung, D M Rousseau, J Glaser, P Angerer, and M Weigl, "Beyond Top-Down and Bottom-Up Work Redesign: Customizing Job Content Through Idiosyncratic Deals," *Journal of Organizational Behavior,* February 2010, pp 187–215; and G R Oldham and J R Hackman, "Not What It Was and Not What It Will Be: The Future of Job Design," *Journal of Organizational Behavior,* February 2010, pp 463–79.

15 G D Babcock, *The Taylor System in Franklin Management,* 2nd ed (New York: Engineering Magazine Company, 1917), p 31.

16 See the related discussion in S Wagner-Tsukamoto, "An Institutional Economic Reconstruction of Scientific Management: On the Lost Theoretical Logic of Taylorism," *Academy of Management Review,* January 2007, pp 105–17.

17 This type of program was developed and tested by M A Campion and C L McClelland, "Follow-Up and Extension of the Interdisciplinary Costs and Benefits of Enlarged Jobs," *Journal of Applied Psychology,* June 1993, pp 339–51.

18 M Weinstein, "Foreign but Familiar," *Training,* January 2009, p 22.

19 See F Herzberg, B Mausner, and B B Snyderman, *The Motivation to Work* (New York: John Wiley & Sons, 1959).

20 See J Flint, "How to Be A Player," *Bloomberg Businessweek,* January 24–January 30, 2011, pp 108–9.

21 F Herzberg, "One More Time: How Do You Motivate Employees?" *Harvard Business Review,* January–February 1968, p 56.

22 For a thorough review of research on Herzberg's theory, see C C Pinder, *Work Motivation: Theory, Issues, and Applications* (Glenview, IL: Scott, Foresman, 1984).

23 M Moskowitz, R Levering, and C Tkaczyk, "100 Best Companies to Work For," *Fortune,* February 7, 2011, p 96.

24 J R Hackman, G R Oldham, R Janson, and K Purdy, "A New Strategy for Job Enrichment," *California Management Review,* Summer 1975, p 58.

25 Definitions of the job characteristics were adapted from J R Hackman and G R Oldham, "Motivation through the Design of Work: Test of a Theory," *Organizational Behavior and Human Performance,* August 1976, pp 250–79.

26 S E Humphrey, J D Nahrgang, and F P Morgeson, "Integrating Motivational, Social, and Contextual Work Design Features: A Meta-Analytic Summary and Theoretical Extension of the Work Design Literature," *Journal of Applied Psychology,* September 2007, pp 1332–56.

27 Moskowitz, Levering, and Tkaczyk, "100 Best Companies to Work For," p 93.

28 Productivity studies are reviewed in R E Kopelman, *Managing Productivity in Organizations* (New York: McGraw-Hill, 1986).

29 A Wrzesniewski and J E Dutton, "Crafting a Job: Revisioning Employees As Active Crafters of Their Work," *Academy of Management Review,* April 2001, p 179.

30 See J M Berg, A Wrzesniewski, and J E Dutton, "Perceiving and Responding to Challenges in Job Crafting at Different Ranks: When Proactivity Requires Adaptivity," *Journal of Organizational Behavior,* February 2010, pp 158–86.

31 Hornung, Rousseau, Glaser, Angerer, and Weigl, "Beyond Top-Down and Bottom-Up Work Redesign," p 188.

32 See T Hopke, "Go Ahead, Take a Few Months Off," *HR Magazine,* September 2010, pp 71–74; and "RSM McGladrey," Wikipedia, last updated December 6, 2010, http://en.wikipedia.org/wiki/RSM_McGladrey.

33 Hornung, Rousseau, Glaser, Angerer, and Weigl, "Beyond Top-Down and Bottom-Up Work Redesign," pp 187–215.

34 See A Fox, "Raising Engagement," *HR Magazine,* May 2010, pp 35–40; and C D'Angela, "In Post-Recession World, Recognition Boosts Recovery," *The Power of Incentives, HR Magazine,* September 2010, pp 93–97.

35 W A Kahn, "Psychological Conditions of Personal Engagement and Disengagement at Work," *Academy of Management Journal,* December 1990, p 695.

36 W A Macy, B Schneider, K M Barbera, and S A Young, *Employee Engagement: Tools for Analysis, Practice, and Competitive Advantage* (West Sussex, United Kingdom: Wiley-Blackwell, 2009), p 20.

37 See W H Macey and B Schneider, "The Meaning of Employee Engagement," *Industrial and Organizational Psychology,* March 2008, pp 3–30.

38 A L Kristof-Brown, R D Zimmerman, and E C Johnson, "Consequences of Individuals' Fit at Work: A Meta-Analysis of Person-Job, Person-Organization, Person-Group, and Person-Supervisor Fit," *Personnel Psychology,* Summer 2005, p 281.

39 Ibid, pp 281–342; and J P Meyer, T D Hecht, H Gill, and L Toplonytsky, "Person-Organization (Culture) Fit and Employee Commitment Under Conditions of Organization Change: A Longitudinal Study," *Journal of Vocational Behavior,* June 2010, pp 458–73.

40 C A Hartnell, A Y Ou, and A Kinicki, "Organizational Culture and Organizational Effectiveness: A Meta-Analytic Investigation of the Competing Values Framework's Theoretical Suppositions," *Journal of Applied Psychology,* in press.

41 See M Moskowitz, R Levering, and C Tkaczyk, "100 Best Companies to Work For," *Fortune,* February 7, 2011, p 95.

42 See K Thomas, *Intrinsic Motivation at Work: Building Energy and Commitment* (San Francisco: Berrett-Koehler Publishers, 2000).

43 See E L Deci and R M Ryan, "The 'What' and 'Why' of Goal Pursuits: Human Needs and Self-Determination of Behavior," *Psychological Inquiry,* December 2000, pp 227–68.

44 See Kahn, "Psychological Conditions of Personal Engagement and Disengagement at Work," p 695.

45 See B Schneider and K B Paul, "In the Company We Trust," *HR Magazine,* January 2011, pp 40–43; and P Yeramyan, "Building the (Workplace) Ties that Bind," *Fortune,* December 6, 2010, p 78.

46 See B L Rich, J A Lepine, and E R Crawford, "Job Engagement: Antecedents and Effects on Job Performance," *Academy of Management Journal,* June 2010, pp 617–35; J S Stoner and V C Gallagher, "Who Cares? The Role of Job Involvement in Psychological Contract Violation," *Journal of Applied Social Psychology,* June 2010, pp 1490–514.

47 R Zeidner, "Questing for Quality," *HR Magazine,* July 2010, p 27.

48 See J K Harter, F L Schmidt, and T L Hayes, "Business-Unit-Level Relationship between Employee Satisfaction, Employee Engagement, and Business Outcomes: A Meta-Analysis," *Journal of Applied Psychology,* April 2002, pp 268–79.

49 See J Robison, "Building Engagement in This Economic Crisis," *Gallup Management Journal,* February 19, 2009, http://gmj.gallup.com/content/115213/Building-Engagement-Economic-Crisis.aspx.

50 See Rich, Lepine, and Crawford, pp 617–35; D Fairhurst and J O'Connor, "Employee Well-Being: Taking Engagement and Performance to the Next Level," retrieved from towerswatson.com, April 13, 2010; and B Schneider, W H Macey, and K M Barbera, "Driving Customer Satisfaction and Financial Success Through Employee Engagement," *People & Strategy,* 2009, pp 22–27.

51 See J Robison, "How the Ritz-Carlton Manages the Mystique," *Gallup Management Journal,* December 11, 2008, http://gmj.gallup.com/content/112906.

52 M M Grynbaum, "Starbucks Takes a Three-Hour Coffee Break," *New York Times,* February 27, 2008, www.nytimes.com.

53 These examples were taken from Moskowitz, Levering, and Tkaczyk, "100 Best Companies to Work For," pp 93, 95.

54 Results can be found in "Generation Gap: On Their Bosses, Millennials Happier than Boomers," *The Wall Street Journal,* November 15, 2010, p B6; and J Schramm, "Post-Recession Job Dissatisfaction," *HR Magazine,* July 2010, p 88.

55 S P Smith, L M Kendall, and C L Hulin, *The Measurement of Satisfaction in Work and Retirement* (Skokie, IL: Rand-McNally, 1969); and D J Weiss, R V Dawis, G W England, and L H Lofquist, *Manual for the Minnesota Satisfaction Questionnaire* (Minneapolis: Industrial Relations Center, University of Minnesota, 1967).

56 S Miller, "HR, Employees Vary on Job Satisfaction," *HR Magazine,* August 2007, p 32.

57 See J P Wanous, T D Poland, S L Premack, and K S Davis, "The Effects of Met Expectations on Newcomer Attitudes and Behaviors: A Review and Meta-Analysis," *Journal of Applied Psychology,* June 1992, pp 288–97.

58 See "Most Employees Don't Speak Up," *HR Magazine,* September 2010, p 22.

59 M Weinstein, "Retention Redux," *Training,* October 2007, p 8.

60 Results can be found in J Cohen-Charash and P E Spector, "The Role of Justice in Organizations: A Meta-Analysis," *Organizational Behavior and Human Decision Processes,* November 2001, pp 278–321.

61 N A Bowling, E A Hendricks, and S H Wagner, "Positive and Negative Affectivity and Facet Satisfaction: A Meta Analysis," *Journal of Business Strategy,* December 2008, pp 115–25.

62 See R D Arvey, T J Bouchard, Jr, N L Segal, and L M Abraham, "Job Satisfaction: Environmental and Genetic Components," *Journal of Applied Psychology,* April 1989, pp 187–92.

63 See C Dormann and D Zapf, "Job Satisfaction: A Meta-Analysis of Stabilities," *Journal of Organizational Behavior,* August 2001, pp 483–504.

64 Results can be found in A J Kinicki, F M McKee-Ryan, C A Schriesheim, and K P Carson, "Assessing the Construct Validity of the Job Descriptive Index (JDI): A Review and Analysis," *Journal of Applied Psychology,* February 2002, pp 14–32.

65 See S P Brown, "A Meta-Analysis and Review of Organizational Research on Job Involvement," *Psychological Bulletin,* September 1996, pp 235–55.

66 Results can be found in A Cooper-Hakim and C Viswesvaran, "The Construct of Work Commitment: Testing an Integrative Framework," *Psychological Bulletin,* March 2005, pp 241–59.

67 D W Organ, "The Motivational Basis of Organizational Citizenship Behavior," in *Research in Organizational Behavior,* eds B M Staw and L L Cummings (Greenwich, CT: JAI Press, 1990), p 46.

68 B J Hoffman, C A Blair, J P Meriac, and D J Woehr, "Expanding the Criterion Domain? A Quantitative Review of the OCB Literature," *Journal of Applied Psychology,* March 2007, pp 555–66.

69 See N P Podsakoff, S W Whiting, P M Podsakoff, and B D Blume, "Individual- and Organizational-Level Consequences of Organizational Citizenship Behaviors: A Meta-Analysis," *Journal of Applied Psychology,* January 2009, pp 122–41; and D S Whitman, D L Van Rooy, and C Viswesvaran, "Satisfaction, Citizenship Behaviors, and Performance in Work Units: A Meta-Analysis of Collective Relations," *Personnel Psychology,* Spring 2010, pp 41–81.

70 Results can be found in P W Hom and A J Kinicki, "Toward a Greater Understanding of How Dissatisfaction Drives Employee Turnover," *Academy of Management Journal,* October 2001, pp 975–87.

71 See the related discussion in S Lau, "Positive Turnover, Disability Awareness, Employee Selection Guidelines," *HR Magazine,* January 2011, p 20.

72 Y Lermusiaux, "Calculating the High Cost of Employee Turnover," www.ilogos.com/en/expertviews/articles/strategic/200331007_YL.html, accessed April 15, 2005, p 1.

73 Ibid. An automated program for calculating the cost of turnover can be found at "Turnover Impacts Your Bottom Line," http://www.drakeintl.com/us/engage.turnovercost.aspx, accessed February 21, 2011.

74 Results can be found in R W Griffeth, P W Hom, and S Gaertner, "A Meta-Analysis of Antecedents and Correlates of Employee Turnover: Update, Moderator Tests, and Research Implications for the Next Millennium," *Journal of Management,* 2000, pp 463–88.

75 See A Nyberg, "Retaining Your High Performers: Moderators of the Performance-Job Satisfaction-Voluntary Turnover Relationship," *Journal of Applied Psychology,* May 2010, pp 440–53; and M A Maltarich, A J. Nyberg, and G Reilly, "A Conceptual and Empirical Analysis of the Cognitive Ability-Voluntary Turnover Relationship," *Journal of Applied Psychology,* November 2010, pp 1058–70.

76 See J McGregor, "Giving Back to Your Stars," *Fortune,* November 1, 2010, pp 53–54; and J Martin and C Schmidt, "How to Keep Your Top Talent," *Harvard Business Review,* May 2010, pp 54–61.

77 J Light, "Keeping 'Overqualifieds' on Board," *The Wall Street Journal,* November 15, 2010, p B6.

78 M Fiester, "What Is Meant by the Term 'Dual Career Ladder'?" *HR Magazine,* November 2010, p 21.

79 Meta-analytic results can be found in N P Podsakoff, J A LePine, and M A LePine, "Differential Challenge Stressor–Hindrance Stressor Relationships with Job Attitudes, Turnover Intentions, Turnover, and Withdrawal Behavior: A Meta-Analysis," *Journal of Applied Psychology,* March 2007, pp 438–54; also see A Novotney, "Boosting Morale," *Monitor on Psychology,* December 2010, pp 32–34; C Fritz, M Yankelevich, A Zarubin, and P Barger, "Happy, Healthy, and Productive: The Role of Detachment From Work During Nonwork Time," *Journal of Applied Psychology,* September 2010, pp 977–83; and S Sonnentag, C Binnewies, and E J Mojza, "Staying Well and Engaged When Demands Are High: The Role of Psychological Detachment," *Journal of Applied Psychology,* September 2010, pp 965–76.

80 See T A Judge, C J Thoresen, J E Bono, and G K Patton, "The Job Satisfaction–Job Performance Relationship: A Qualitative and Quantitative Review," *Psychological Bulletin,* May 2001, pp 376–407.

81 Results can be found in Whitman, Van Rooy, and C Viswesvaran, "Satisfaction, Citizenship Behaviors, and Performance in Work Units: A Meta-Analysis of Collective Relations." Also see R G Netemeyer,

J G Maxham III, and D R Lichtenstein, "Store Manager Performance and Satisfaction: Effects on Store Employee Performance and Satisfaction, Store Customer Satisfaction, and Store Customer Spending Growth," *Journal of Applied Psychology,* May 2010, pp 530–45.

[82] See P E Spector and S Fox, "Theorizing About the Deviant Citizen: An Attributional Explanation of the Interplay of Organizational Citizenship and Counterproductive Work Behavior," *Human Resource Management Review,* June 2010, pp 132–43; and K Tyler, "Helping Employees Cool It," *HR Magazine,* April 2010, pp 53–55.

[83] M Conlin, "To Catch a Corporate Thief," *BusinessWeek,* February 16, 2009, p 52.

[84] See B Leonard, "Survey: 10% of Employees Report Harassment at Work," *HR Magazine,* October 2010, p 18; and B Mirza, "Attorneys Advise Action to Prevent Bullying at Work," *HR Magazine,* 2010, p 16.

[85] See B J Tepper, C A Henle, L S Lambert, R A Giacalone, and M K Duffy, "Abusive Supervision and Subordinates' Organization Deviance," *Journal of Applied Psychology,* July 2008, pp 721–32.

[86] C Hymowitz, "Bosses Have to Learn How to Confront Troubled Employees," *The Wall Street Journal,* April 23, 2007, p B1.

[87] Ibid.

[88] B W Roberts, P D Harms, A Caspi, and T E Moffitt, "Predicting the Counterproductive Employee in a Child-to-Adult Prospective Study," *Journal of Applied Psychology,* September 2007, pp 1427–36.

[89] See P E Spector and J A Bauer, and S Fox, "Measurement Artifacts in the Assessment of Counterproductive Work Behavior and Organizational Citizenship Behavior: Do We Know What We Think We Know?" *Journal of Applied Psychology,* July 2010, pp 781–90; and L R Bolton, L K Becker, and L K Barber, "Big Five Trait Predictions of Differential Counterproductive Work Behavior Dimensions," *Personality and Individual Differences,* October 2010, pp 537–41.

[90] S Dilchert, D S Ones, R D Davis, and C D Rostow, "Cognitive Ability Predicts Objectively Measured Counterproductive Work Behaviors," *Journal of Applied Psychology,* May 2007, pp 616–27.

[91] J R Detert, L K Treviño, E R Burris, and M Andiappan, "Managerial Modes of Influence and Counterproductivity in Organizations: A Longitudinal Business-Unit-Level Investigation," *Journal of Applied Psychology,* July 2007, pp 993–1005.

[92] Excerpted from S Carey, "Cranky Skies: Fliers Behave Badly Again as 9/11 Era Fades," *The Wall Street Journal,* September 12, 2007, p A16.

Chapter 7

[1] Excerpted from S Banchero, "Teachers Lose Jobs Over Test Scores," *The Wall Street Journal,* July 24, 2010, p A3; W McGuran, "Giving Lousy Teachers the Boot," *The Wall Street Journal,* July 27, 2010, p A17; and R Whitmire, "Can Rhee's Reforms Work Without Rhee's Toughness?" *The Washington Post,* January 21, 2011, http://www.washingtonpost.com/opinions/can-rhees-reforms-work-without-rhees-toughness/2011/01/21/ABSQcKR_story.html

[2] See L Festinger, *A Theory of Cognitive Dissonance* (Stanford, CA: Stanford University Press, 1957).

[3] See R G Satter and J Lawless, "WikiLeaks Supporters Protest Via Cyberattacks," *The Arizona Republic,* December 10, 2010, p A15.

[4] See P Bamberger and E Belogolovsky, "The Impact of Pay Secrecy on Individual Task Performance," *Personnel Psychology,* Winter 2010, pp 965–96; and M C Bolino and W H Turnley, "Old Faces, New Places: Equity Theory in Cross-Cultural Contexts," *Journal of Organizational Behavior,* January 2008, pp 29–50.

[5] N Koppel and V O'Connell, "Pay Gap Widens at Big Law Firms as Partners Chase Star Attorneys," *The Wall Street Journal,* February 8, 2011, p A1.

[6] M N Bing and S M Burroughs, "The Predictive and Interactive Effects of Equity Sensitivity in Teamwork-Oriented Organizations," *Journal of Organizational Behavior,* May 2001, p 271.

[7] Types of equity sensitivity are discussed by ibid., pp 271–90; and K S Sauley and A G Bedeian, "Equity Sensitivity: Construction of a Measure and Examination of Its Psychometric Properties," *Journal of Management,* 2000, pp 885–910.

[8] J Bernoff and T Schadler, "Empowered," *Harvard Business Review,* July–August 2010, pp 95–101.

[9] For a thorough review of organizational justice theory and research, see R Cropanzano, D E Rupp, C J Mohler, and M Schminke, "Three Roads to Organizational Justice," in *Research in Personnel and Human Resources Management,* vol. 20, ed G R Ferris (New York: JAI Press, 2001), pp 269–329.

[10] J A Colquitt, D E Conlon, M J Wesson, C O L H Porter, and K Y Ng, "Justice at the Millennium: A Meta-Analytic Review of 25 Years of Organizational Justice Research," *Journal of Applied Psychology,* June 2001, p 426.

[11] E Tahmincioglu, "Electronic Workplace Vulnerable to Revenge," *Arizona Republic,* August 6, 2001, p D1.

[12] For recent studies of justice, see D De Cremer, J Brockner, A Fishman, M van Dijke, W van Olffen, and D M Mayer, "When Do Procedural Fairness and Outcome Fairness Interact to Influence Employees' Work Attitudes and Behaviors? The Moderating Effect of Uncertainty," *Journal of Applied Psychology,* March 2010, pp 291–304; and O Janssen, C K Lam, and X Huang, "Emotional Exhaustion and Job Performance: The Moderating Roles of Distributive Justice and Positive Affect," *Journal of Organizational Behavior,* August 2010, pp 787–809.

[13] Results from this study were reported in K Gurchiek, "Show Workers Their Value, Study Says," *HR Magazine,* October 2006, p 40.

[14] E Thornton, "Managing through a Crisis: The New Rules," *BusinessWeek,* January 19, 2009, pp 30–34.

[15] See T Menon and L Thompson, "Envy at Work," *Harvard Business Review,* April 2010, pp 74–79.

[16] The impact of groups on justice perceptions was investigated by D A Jones and D P Skarlicki, "The Effects of Overhearing Peers Discuss an Authority's Fairness Reputation on Reactions to Subsequent Treatment," *Journal of Applied Psychology,* March 2005, pp 363–72.

[17] J Berry, "EEOC Files Discrimination Lawsuit Against FedEx Freight," AZCentral.com, http://www.azcentral.com/business/articles/2010/09/14/20100914eeoc-files-discrimination-lawsuit-against-fedex-freight.html (February 16, 2011).

[18] Climate for justice was studied by S Tangirala and R Ramanujam, "Employee Silence on Critical Work Issues: The Cross Level Effects of Procedural Justice Climate," *Personnel Psychology,* Spring 2008, pp 37–68.

[19] For a complete discussion of Vroom's theory, see V H Vroom, *Work and Motivation* (New York: John Wiley & Sons, 1964).

[20] See J Chowdhury, "The Motivational Impact of Sales Quotas on Effort," *Journal of Marketing Research,* February 1993, pp 28–41; and C C Pinder, *Work Motivation* (Glenview, IL: Scott, Foresman, 1984), ch 7.

[21] B Becht, "Building a Company Without Borders," *Harvard Business Review,* April 2010, p 106.

[22] Excerpted from "Federal Express's Fred Smith," *Inc.,* October 1986, p 38.

[23] Results can be found in W van Eerde and H Thierry, "Vroom's Expectancy Models and Work-Related Criteria: A Meta-Analysis," *Journal of Applied Psychology,* October 1996, pp 575–86.

[24] See J Cameron and W D Pierce, *Rewards and Intrinsic Motivation: Resolving the Controversy* (Alberta, Canada: Cameron and Pierce, 2002); K L Scott, J D Shaw, and M K Duffy, "Merit Pay Raises and Organization-Based Self-Esteem," *Journal of Organizational Behavior,* October 2008, pp 967–80.

[25] See A Kinicki, K Jacobson, S Peterson, and G Prussia, "The Development and Validation of the Performance Management Competency Scale," manuscript under review.

[26] See "Bonuses Are Back, with Emphasis on Results," *HR Magazine,* September 2010, p 14.

[27] This issue is discussed by S J Dubner, "The Freaky Side of Business," *Training,* February 2006, pp 8–9.

[28] See D R Spitzer, "Power Rewards: Rewards That Really Motivate," *Management Review,* May 1996, pp 45–50; and A Kohn, *Punished by Rewards: The Trouble with Gold Stars, Incentive Plans, A's, Praise, and Other Bribes* (Boston: Houghton Mifflin, 1993).

[29] Result can be found in G D Jenkins, Jr, A Mitra, N Gupta, and J D Shaw, "Are Financial Incentives Related to Performance? A Meta-Analytic Review of Empirical Research," *Journal of Applied Psychology,* October 1998, pp 777–87.

[30] See S Bates, "Top Pay for Best Performance," *HR Magazine,* January 2003, pp 31–38.

[31] See S Miller, "Salary Increases, Variable Pay Lower than Expected for 2010," *HR Magazine,* October 2010, p 16.

[32] M Moskowitz, R Levering, and C Tkaczyk, "100 Best Companies to Work For," *Fortune,* February 7, 2011, p 94.

[33] M Dewhurst, M Gulhridge, and W Mohr, "Motivating People: Getting Beyond Money," *McKinsey & Company,* November 2009, http://www.mckinseyquarterly.com/Motivating_people_Getting_beyond_money_2460. Also see E Krell, "All For Incentives, Incentives for All," *HR Magazine,* January 2011, pp 35–38.

[34] See S Terlep, "GM Rethinks Pay for Unionized Workers," *The Wall Street Journal,* January 12, 2011, p B6; S Terlep, "GM's Profit Sharing Largest Amount Ever," *The Wall Street Journal,* February 9, 2011, p B2; and S Terlep, "GM Rebounds with Best Year Since 1999," *The Wall Street Journal,* February 25, 2011, pp B1, B2.

[35] E A Locke, K N Shaw, L M Saari, and G P Latham, "Goal Setting and Task Performance: 1969–1980," *Psychological Bulletin,* July 1981, p 126.

[36] Results from both studies can be found in R Rodgers and J E Hunter, "Impact of Management by Objectives on Organizational Productivity," *Journal of Applied Psychology,* April 1991, pp 322–36; and R Rodgers, J E Hunter, and D L Rogers, "Influence of Top Management Commitment on Management Program Success," *Journal of Applied Psychology,* February 1993, pp 151–55.

[37] The following discussion is based on E A Locke and G P Latham, "Building a Practically Useful Theory of Goal Setting and Task Motivation," *American Psychologist,* September 2002, pp 705–17.

[38] M Moskowitz, R Levering, and C Tkaczyk, "100 Best Companies to Work For," *Fortune,* February 7, 2011, p 95.

[39] The case of multiple goals is discussed by J B Vancouver, J M Weinhardt, and A M Schmidt, "A Formal, Computational Theory of Multiple-Goal Pursuit: Integrating Goal-Choice and Goal-Striving Processes," *Journal of Applied Psychology,* November 2010, pp 985–1008.

[40] R Weiss and B Kammel, "How Siemens Got Its Geist Back," *Bloomberg Businessweek,* January 31–February 6, 2011, pp 18–20.

[41] M Frese, S I Krauss, N Keith, S Escher, R Grabarkiewicz, S T Luneng, C Heers, J Unger, and C Friedrich, "Business Owners' Action Planning and Its Relationship to Business Success in Three African Countries," *Journal of Applied Psychology,* November 2007, pp 1481–98.

[42] Results can be found in P M Wright, "Operationalization of Goal Difficulty as a Moderator of the Goal Difficulty–Performance Relationship," *Journal of Applied Psychology,* June 1990, pp 227–34.

[43] See E A Locke and G P Latham, *A Theory of Goal Setting and Task Performance* (Englewood Cliffs, NJ: Prentice Hall, 1990).

[44] Ibid.

[45] D Morisano, J B Hirsh, J B Peterson, R O Pihl, and B M Shore, "Setting, Elaborating, and Reflecting on Personal Goals Improves Academic Performance," *Journal of Applied Psychology,* March 2010, pp 255–64.

[46] Supportive results can be found in S E Humphrey, J D Nahrgang, and F P Morgeson, "Integrating Motivational, Social, and Contextual Work Design Features: A Meta-Analytic Summary and Theoretical Extension of the Work Design Literature," *Journal of Applied Psychology,* September 2007, pp 1332–56.

[47] See J J Donovan and D J Radosevich, "The Moderating Role of Goal Commitment on the Goal Difficulty-Performance Relationship: A Meta-Analytic Review and Critical Reanalysis," *Journal of Applied Psychology,* April 1998, pp 308–15.

[48] See T Demos, "Motivate Without Spending Millions," *Fortune,* April 12, 2010, pp 37–38.

[49] See F M Moussa, "Determinants, Process, and Consequences of Personal Goals and Performance," *Journal of Management,* 2000, pp 1259–85.

[50] See "It's a Balancing Act," *Training,* May 2009, p 10.

[51] Results are presented in "Coming Up Short? Join the Club," *Training,* April 2006, p 14; and "Race Review," *Training,* September-October 2010, p 7.

[52] See J A Colquitt and M J Simmering, "Conscientiousness, Goal Orientation, and Motivation to Learn during the Learning Process: A Longitudinal Study," *Journal of Applied Psychology,* August 1998, pp 654–65.

[53] C L Porath and T S Bateman, "Self-Regulation: From Goal Orientation to Job Performance," *Journal of Applied Psychology,* January 2006, pp 185–86.

[54] Ibid., pp 185–92; and C O L H Porter, J W Webb, and C I Gogus, "When Goal Orientations Collide: Effects of Learning and Performance Orientation on Team Adaptability in Response to Workload Imbalance," *Journal of Applied Psychology,* September 2010, pp 935–43.

[55] L B Cattaneo and A R Chapman, "The Process of Empowerment," *American Psychologist,* October 2010, pp 646–59.

[56] Towers Watson, "Engaging and Retaining Top Performers," December 2009, towerswatson.com.

[57] M Weinstein, "Business Driven," *Training,* March 2007, pp 40, 42.

[58] T R Mitchell, "Motivation: New Directions for Theory, Research, and Practice," *Academy of Management Review,* January 1982, p 81.

[59] Details can be found in S Ng and J S Lublin, "AIG Pay Plan: Rank and Rile," *The Wall Street Journal,* February 11, 2010, pp C1, C4.

[60] J Welch and S Welch, "An Employee Bill of Rights," *BusinessWeek,* March 16, 2009, p 72.

[61] Excerpted from C Bellamy, "Teacher Resigns as School Backs Plagiarizing Kids," *Arizona Republic,* February 10, 2002, p A21.

Chapter 8

[1] Excerpted and adapted from E. Krell, "All for Incentives, Incentives for All," *HR Magazine,* January 2011, pp. 35–38. Reprinted with permission of the Society for Human Resource Management (www.shrm.org), Alexandria, VA, publisher of *HR Magazine.* © SHRM.

[2] B Tulgan, "The Under-Management Epidemic," *HR Magazine,* October 2004, p 119.

[3] See H Aguinis and C Pierce, "Enhancing the Relevance of Organizational Behavior by Embracing Performance Management Research," *Journal of Organizational Behavior,* January 2008, pp 139–45.

[4] See W F Cascio, "Global Performance Management Systems," in *Handbook of Research in International Human Resources Management,* eds I Bjorkman and G Stahl, (London, UK: Edward Elgar Ltd, 2006), pp 176–96; See also E D Pulakos, *Performance Management: A New Approach for Driving Business Results* (West Sussex, UK: Wiley-Blackwell, 2009).

[5] J Light, "Human Resource Executives Say Reviews Are Off Mark," *The Wall Street Journal,* November 7, 2010.

[6] Based on R Illies, T A Judge, and D T Wagner, "The Influence of Cognitive and Affective Reactions to Feedback on Subsequent Goals," *European Psychologist,* 2010, pp 121–31.

[7] As quoted in A D'Innocenzio and R Beck, "AP Interview: Wal-Mart CEO Talks Leadership, Life," The Associated Press, February 6, 2011.

[8] K Tyler, "One Bad Apple," *HR Magazine,* December 2004, p 85. Data taken from "Managers Are Ignoring Their Employees," *LeadershipIQ,* December 2, 2009.

[9] C D Lee, "Feedback, Not Appraisal," *HR Magazine,* November 2006, p 111.

[10] Both the definition of feedback and the functions of feedback are based on discussion in D R Ilgen, C D Fisher, and M S Taylor, "Consequences of Individual Feedback on Behavior in Organizations," *Journal of Applied Psychology,* August 1979, pp 349–71.

[11] See P C Earley, G B Northcraft, C Lee, and T R Lituchy, "Impact of Process and Outcome Feedback on the Relation of Goal Setting to Task Performance," *Academy of Management Journal,* March 1990, pp 87–105.

[12] Based on C C Rosen, P E Levy, and R J Hall, "Placing Perceptions of Politics in the Context of the Feedback Environment, Employee Attitudes, and Job Performance," *Journal of Applied Psychology,* January 2006, pp 211–20.

[13] For relevant research, see J S Goodman, "The Interactive Effects of Task and External Feedback on Practice Performance and Learning," *Organizational Behavior and Human Decision Processes,* December 1998, pp 223–52.

[14] D Debow, "When You're the Boss, Who Gives You Reviews?," *Fortune,* December 22, 2010.

[15] See B D Bannister, "Performance Outcome Feedback and Attributional Feedback: Interactive Effects on Recipient Responses," *Journal of Applied Psychology,* May 1986, pp 203–10.

[16] For complete details, see P M Podsakoff and J-L Farh, "Effects of Feedback Sign and Credibility on Goal Setting and Task Performance," *Organizational Behavior and Human Decision Processes,* August 1989, pp 45–67.

[17] W S Silver, T R Mitchell, and M E Gist, "Responses to Successful and Unsuccessful Performance: The Moderating Effect of Self-Efficacy on the Relationship between Performance and Attributions," *Organizational Behavior and Human Decision Processes,* June 1995, p 297; Ibid., Illies, Judge, and Wagner.

[18] L E Atwater, J F Brett, and A C Charles, "The Delivery of Workplace Discipline: Lessons Learned," *Organizational Dynamics,* 2007, pp 392–403.

[19] See T J DeLong and V Vijayaraghavan, "Let's Hear It for B Players," *Harvard Business Review,* June 2003, pp 96–102.

[20] A J Kinicki, G E Prussia, B Wu, and F M McKee-Ryan, "A Covariance Structure Analysis of Employees' Response to Performance Feedback," *Journal of Applied Psychology,* vol 89, no 6, December 2004, pp 1057–69.

[21] See J Smither, M London, and R Reilly, "Does Performance Improve Following Multisource Feedback? A Theoretical Model, Meta-analysis, and Review of Empirical Findings," *Personnel Psychology,* Spring 2005, pp 33–66.

[22] M Weinstein, "Study: HR Execs Don't Trust Employee Evaluations," *Training,* April 2006, p 11.

[23] See M R Edwards, A J Ewen, and W A Verdini, "Fair Performance Management and Pay Practices for Diverse Work Forces: The Promise of Multisource Assessment," *ACA Journal,* Spring 1995, pp 50–63.

[24] See G D Huet-Cox, T M Nielsen, and E Sundstrom, "Get the Most from 360-Degree Feedback: Put It on the Internet," *HR Magazine,* May 1999, pp 92–103.

[25] This list is based in part on discussion in H J Bernardin, "Subordinate Appraisal: A Valuable Source of Information about Managers," *Human Resource Management,* Fall 1986, pp 421–39.

[26] Data from D Antonioni, "The Effects of Feedback Accountability on Upward Appraisal Ratings," *Personnel Psychology,* Summer 1994, pp 349–56.

[27] See L Atwater, P Roush, and A Fischthal, "The Influence of Upward Feedback on Self- and Follower Ratings of Leadership," *Personnel Psychology,* Spring 1995, pp 35–59.

[28] Data from JW Smither, M London, NL Vasilopoulos, RR Reilly, RE Millsap, and N Salvemini, "An Examination of the Effects of an Upward Feedback Program over Time, *Personnel Psychology,* Spring 1995, pp 1–34.

[29] A Bryant, "He's Not Bill Gates, or Fred Astaire," *The New York Times,* February 14, 2010.

[30] A Bryant, "Defensive? It Leads to Destructive," *The New York Times,* November 27, 2010.

[31] See D E Coates, "Don't Tie 360-Feedback to Pay," *Training,* September 1998, pp 68–78.

[32] "Friendly Feedback," *Training,* May 2007, p 11.

[33] Adapted from C Bell and R Zemke, "On-Target Feedback," *Training,* June 1992, pp 36–44. A model feedback program is discussed by M Weinstein, "Leadership Leader," *Training,* February 2008, pp 41–46.

[34] For a comprehensive collection of articles and research related to feedback see, "Guide to Giving Effective Feedback," *Harvard Business Review,* February 9, 2011.

[35] For example, see B Nelson, *1001 Ways to Reward Employees,* 2nd ed (New York: Workman Publishing, 2005).

[36] Excerpted and adapted from R L Heneman and E E Coyne, "Implementing Total Rewards Strategies," *Society for Human Resource Management,* October 21, 2010, http://www.shrm.org/about/foundation/products/Pages/ImplementingTotalRewards.aspx.

[37] L Chenoweth, Y H Jeon, T Merlyn, and H Brodaty, "A Systematic Review of What Factors Attract and Retain Nurses in Aged and Dementia Care," *Journal of Clinical Nursing,* vol 19, no 1–2, January 2010, pp 156–67.

[38] A Zimmerman, "49: Carol Tomé," *The Wall Street Journal,* November 19, 2007, p R12.

[39] Adapted from S Miller, "Pay vs Intangibles: Which Rewards Best Motivate, Engage?," *Society for Human Resource Management,* July 20, 2010, http://www.shrm.org/hrdisciplines/compensation/Articles/Pages/IntangibleIncentives.aspx.

[40] Ibid.

[41] Ibid.

[42] M Von Glinow, "Reward Strategies for Attracting, Evaluating, and Retaining Professionals," *Human Resource Management,* Summer 1985, p 193.

[43] Six reward system objectives are discussed in E E Lawler III, "The New Pay: A Strategic Approach," *Compensation & Benefits Review,* July–August 1995, pp 14–22.

[44] For both sides of the "Does money motivate?" debate, see N Gupta and J D Shaw, "Let the Evidence Speak: Financial Incentives *Are* Effective!!" *Compensation & Benefits Review,* March–April 1998, pp 26, 28–32; A Kohn, "Challenging Behaviorist Dogma: Myths about Money and Motivation," *Compensation & Benefits Review;* March–April 1998, pp 27, 33–37; and B Ettorre, "Is Salary a Motivator?" *Management Review,* January 1999, p 8.

[45] J M Minami and M M May, "3rd Circuit: Employees Who Received Flat-Rate Payments Tied to Sales Are Exempt," *Society of Human Resource Management,* September 24, 2010, http://www.shrm.org/LegalIssues/FederalResources/Pages/3rdFlatRatePayments.aspx.

[46] Based on C S Moore, *The Confidence Game* (Hoboken NJ: John Wiley & Sons, 2010).

[47] C B Cadsby, F Song, and F Tapon, "Sorting and Incentive Effects of Pay for Performance: An Experimental Investigation," *Academy of Management Journal,* April 2007, pp 387–405.

[48] Data from M Bloom and G T Milkovich, "Relationships among Risk, Incentive Pay, and Organizational Performance," *Academy of Management Journal,* June 1998, pp 283–97.

[49] For details, see G D Jenkins, Jr, N Gupta, A Mitra, and J D Shaw, "Are Financial Incentives Related to Performance? A Meta-Analytic Review of Empirical Research," *Journal of Applied Psychology,* October 1998, pp 777–87.

[50] L A Bebchuk and J M Fried, "Pay without Performance: Overview of the Issues," *Academy of Management Perspectives,* February 2006, pp 5–24.

[51] Excerpted from "How Effective Is Incentive Pay?" *HR Magazine,* January 2008, p 12.

[52] S Miller, "Satisfaction with Pay, Benefits Falling," *HR Magazine,* January 2007, pp 38–39; and C Palmeri, "Workers Say: 'We Want an Upgrade," *BusinessWeek,* April 16, 2007, p 11.

[53] For a recent unconventional perspective, see R J DeGrandpre, "A Science of Meaning? Can Behaviorism Bring Meaning to Psychological Science?" *American Psychologist,* July 2000, pp 721–38.

[54] See E L Thorndike, *Educational Psychology: The Psychology of Learning,* vol. II (New York: Columbia University Teachers College, 1913).

[55] Discussion of an early behaviorist who influenced Skinner's work can be found in P J Kreshel, "John B Watson at J Walter Thompson: The Legitimation of 'Science' in Advertising," *Journal of Advertising,* no. 2, 1990, pp 49–59.

[56] For more recent discussion, see J W Donahoe, "The Unconventional Wisdom of B F Skinner: The Analysis-Interpretation Distinction," *Journal of the Experimental Analysis of Behavior,* September 1993, pp 453–56.

[57] See B F Skinner, *The Behavior of Organisms* (New York: Appleton-Century-Crofts, 1938).

[58] For modern approaches to respondent behavior, see B Azar, "Classical Conditioning Could Link Disorders and Brain Dysfunction, Researchers Suggest," *APA Monitor,* March 1999, p 17.

[59] For interesting discussions of Skinner and one of his students, see M B Gilbert and T F Gilbert, "What Skinner Gave Us," *Training,* September 1991, pp 42–48.

[60] See F Luthans and R Kreitner, *Organizational Behavior Modification and Beyond: An Operant and Social Learning Approach* (Glenview, IL: Scott, Foresman, 1985), pp 49–56.

[61] G C Hazan and D Mattioli, "BP Links Pay to Safety in Fourth Quarter," *The Wall Street Journal,* October 19, 2010.

[62] W Neuman, "Flights at JFK Sit on Tarmac for Hours," *The New York Times,* December 29, 2010.

63 See C B Ferster and B F Skinner, *Schedules of Reinforcement* (New York: Appleton-Century-Crofts, 1957).

64 See L M Saari and G P Latham, "Employee Reactions to Continuous and Variable Ratio Reinforcement Schedules Involving a Monetary Incentive," *Journal of Applied Psychology,* August 1982, pp 506–8.

65 M Moskowitz, R Levering, and C Tkaczyk, "Fortune 100 Best Companies to Work For: 2010," *Fortune,* February 7, 2011, p 93.

66 Data from M Rapoport, "Regulators to Target 'Window Dressing,'" *The Wall Street Journal,* September 16, 2010.

67 The topic of managerial credibility is covered in J M Kouzes and B Z Posner, *Credibility* (San Francisco: Jossey-Bass, 1993).

68 An on-the-job example of behavior shaping can be found in J Case, "Are Your Meetings Like This?" *Inc.,* March 2003, p 79.

69 S Gilbert, "Whole Foods CEO John Mackey to Staff: Get Slim, Save Money," DailyFinance.com, January 30, 2010.

70 Adapted from E Dash, "Stock-Hedging Lets Bankers Skirt Efforts to Overhaul Pay," *The New York Times,* February 5, 2011.

Chapter 9

1 Reprinted by permission of Harvard Business Review. Excerpt from "Turning Doctors into Leaders," by T.H. Lee, April 2010; and quote taken from A. Gawande, "Health Care Needs a New Kind of Hero," April 2010. Copyright 2010 by the Harvard Business School Publishing Corporation; all rights reserved.

2 E Van Velsor and J Brittain Leslie, "Why Executives Derail: Perspectives across Time and Cultures," *Academy of Management Executive,* November 1995, p 62.

3 J Zenger and J Folkman, "Ten Fatal Flaws that Derail Leaders," *Harvard Business Review,* June 2009, p 18.

4 This definition is based in part on one found in D Horton Smith, "A Parsimonious Definition of 'Group': Toward Conceptual Clarity and Scientific Utility," *Sociological Inquiry,* Spring 1967, pp 141–67.

5 E H Schein, *Organizational Psychology,* 3rd ed (Englewood Cliffs, NJ: Prentice Hall, 1980), p 145. For more, see L R Weingart, "How Did They Do That? The Ways and Means of Studying Group Process," in *Research in Organizational Behavior,* vol. 19, eds L L Cummings and B M Staw (Greenwich, CT: JAI Press, 1997), pp 189–239.

6 See R Cross, N Nohria, and A Parker, "Six Myths about Informal Networks—and How to Overcome Them," *MIT Sloan Management Review,* Spring 2002, pp 67–75; and C Shirky, "Watching the Patterns Emerge," *Harvard Business Review,* February 2004, pp 34–35.

7 Excerpted from S Armour, "Company 'Alumni' Groups Keep Word Out after Workers Go," *USA Today,* August 30, 2005, p 4B.

8 See J Janove, "FOB: Friend of Boss," *HR Magazine,* June 2005, pp 153–56.

9 Taken from K Gurchiek, "Gap Exists Between What Workers Need and Get from the Boss," *Society for Human Resource Management,* November 22, 2010, http://www.shrm.org/Publications/HRNews/Pages/NeedGetFromBoss.aspx.

10 See Schein, *Organizational Psychology,* pp 149–53.

11 M Moskowitz, R Levering, and C Tkaczyk, "Fortune's 100 Best Companies to Work For, 2010," *Fortune,* February 7, 2011, p 96.

12 For an instructive overview of five different theories of group development, see J P Wanous, A E Reichers, and S D Malik, "Organizational Socialization and Group Development: Toward an Integrative Perspective," *Academy of Management Review,* October 1984, pp 670–83.

13 See B W Tuckman, "Developmental Sequence in Small Groups," *Psychological Bulletin,* June 1965, pp 384–99; and B W Tuckman and M A C Jensen, "Stages of Small-Group Development Revisited," *Group & Organization Studies,* December 1977, pp 419–27.

14 See T Postmes, R Spears, A T Lee, and R J Novak, "Individuality and Social Influence in Groups: Inductive and Deductive Routes to Group Identity," *Journal of Personality and Social Psychology,* November 2005, pp 747–63.

15 Based in part on J L Bunn, J Lin, and J T Chou, "Task Conflict and Team Creativity: A Question of How Much and When," *Journal of Applied Psychology,* 2010, pp 1173–80.

16 J McGregor, "Forget Going with Your Gut," *BusinessWeek,* March 20, 2006, p 112.

17 For related research, see M Van Vugt and C M Hart, "Social Identity as Social Glue: The Origins of Group Loyalty," *Journal of Personality and Social Psychology,* April 2004, pp 585–98.

18 S E Humphrey, F P Morgeson, and M J Mannor, "Developing a Theory of the Strategic Core of Teams: A Role Composition Model of Team Performance," *Journal of Applied Psychology,* 2009, pp 48–61.

19 G Graen, "Role-Making Processes within Complex Organizations," in *Handbook of Industrial and Organizational Psychology,* ed M D Dunnette (Chicago: Rand McNally, 1976), p 1201.

20 See D J McAllister, D Kamdar, E W Morrison, and D B Turban, "Disentangling Role Perceptions: How Perceived Role Breadth, Discretion, Instrumentality, and Efficacy Relate to Helping and Taking Charge," *Journal of Applied Psychology,* September 2007, pp 1200–11.

21 See K D Benne and P Sheats, "Functional Roles of Group Members," *Journal of Social Issues,* Spring 1948, pp 41–49.

22 "B of A's Krawcheck Sets Her Team: The Memo," *The Wall Street Journal Online,* September 29, 2009, http://blogs.wsj.com/deals/2009/09/29/bofas-krawcheck-sets-her-team-the-memo/.

23 E C Dierdorff and F P Morgeson, "Consensus in Work Role Requirements: The Influence of Discrete Occupational Context on Role Expectations," *Journal of Applied Psychology,* September 2007, pp 1228–41.

24 See H J Klein and P W Mulvey, "Two Investigations of the Relationships among Group Goals, Goal Commitment, Cohesion, and Performance," *Organizational Behavior and Human Decision Processes,* January 1995, pp 44–53; and D Knight, C C Durham, and E A Locke, "The Relationship of Team Goals, Incentives, and Efficacy to Strategic Risk, Tactical Implementation, and Performance," *Academy of Management Journal,* April 2001, pp 326–38.

25 A Zander, "The Value of Belonging to a Group in Japan," *Small Group Behavior,* February 1983, pp 7–8.

26 Adapted from K Goetz, "How 3M Gave Everyone Days Off and Created an Innovation Dynamo," *Fast Company,* February 1, 2011.

27 See J Pfeffer, "Bring Back Shame," *Business 2.0,* September 2003, p 80.

28 D Michaels, "Airbus, Amid Turmoil, Revives Troubled Plane," *The Wall Street Journal,* October 15, 2007, pp A1, A19.

29 L Meckler, "How 10 People Reshaped Massachusetts Health Care," *The Wall Street Journal,* May 30, 2007, pp A1, A13.

30 D C Feldman, "The Development and Enforcement of Group Norms," *Academy of Management Review,* January 1984, pp 50–52.

31 Ibid.

32 "Top 10 Leadership Tips from Jeff Immelt," *Fast Company,* April 2004, p 96.

33 As quoted in A Sellers, "Jamie Dimon's Full Disclosure," *Fortune,* April 13, 2010.

34 J Dixon, C Belnap, C Albrecht, and K Lee, "The Importance of Soft Skills," *Corporate Finance Review,* May–June 2010, pp 35–38.

35 "How Three Bosses Got to the Top," *Arizona Republic,* August 5, 2007, p D5.

36 J R Katzenbach and D K Smith, *The Wisdom of Teams: Creating the High-Performance Organization* (New York: HarperBusiness, 1999), p 45.

37 Condensed and adapted from ibid., p 214. Also see R Rico, M Sánchez-Manzanares, F Gil, and C Gibson, "Team Implicit Coordination Processes: A Team Knowledge-Based Approach," *Academy of Management Review,* January 2008, pp 163–84.

38 "Company Is a Team, Not a Family," *HR Magazine,* April 2007, p 18.

39 J R Katzenbach and D K Smith, "The Discipline of Teams," *Harvard Business Review,* March–April 1993, p 112.

40 M Hoegl, "Smaller Teams—Better Teamwork: How to Keep Project Teams Small," *Business Horizons,* 2005, pp 209–14.

41 "A Team's-Eye View of Teams," *Training,* November 1995, p 16; and L Gratton and T J Erickson, "Eight Ways to Build Collaborative Teams," *Harvard Business Review,* November 2007, pp 101–9.

42 D Coutu, "Why Teams Don't Work," *Harvard Business Review,* May 2009.

43 M Hoegl, "Smaller Teams—Better Teamwork," pp 209–14.

44 Excerpted from *Harvard Business Essentials: Creating Teams with an Edge,* February 19, 2004.

45 M Ridley, "Are You Wasting Money on L&D?," *Training Journal,* February 2011, trainingjournal.com.

46 A Leigh, "Prove It! Making Sense of the ROI from Developing People," *Training & Management Development Methods,* 2009, pp 1–7.
47 Adapted from M Rosenberg, "Beyond the Basics of Experiential Learning," *Training and Development,* December 2007, pp 26–28.
48 J Garfield and K Stanton, "Building Effective Teams in Real Time," *Harvard Management Update,* November 2005; also see D Ancona and H Bresman, *X-Teams: How to Build Teams That Lead, Innovate, and Succeed* (Boston: Harvard Business School Press, 2007).
49 Found in B Kiviat, "Which Companies Do People Respect?," *Time,* April 5, 2010.
50 L Prusak and D Cohen, "How to Invest in Social Capital," *Harvard Business Review,* June 2001, p 90.
51 M van Dijke, D De Cremer, and D M Mayer, "The Role of Authority Power in Explaining Procedural Fairness Effects," *Journal of Applied Psychology,* 2010, pp 488–502.
52 J A Colquitt, B A Scott, and J A LePine, "Trust, Trustworthiness, and Trust Propensity: A Meta-Analytic Test of Their Unique Relationships with Risk Taking and Job Performance," *Journal of Applied Psychology,* July 2007, pp 909–27.
53 From R Hastings, "Broken Trust Is Bad for Business," *Society of Human Resource Management,* March 7, 2011.
54 See R Zemke, "Little Lies," *Training,* February 2004, p 8.
55 Adapted from F Bartolomé, "Nobody Trusts the Boss Completely—Now What?" *Harvard Business Review,* March–April 1989, pp 135–42.
56 Data from J P Millikin, P W Hom, and C C Manz, "Self-Management Competencies in Self-Managing Teams: Their Impact on Multi-Team System Productivity," *The Leadership Quarterly,* 2010, pp 687–702.
57 K McKeough, "1: The Best of the Best—Google," *Crain's Chicago Business,* March 3, 2008, downloaded from General Reference Center Gold, http://find.galegroup.com.
58 See A E Randal and K S Jaussi, "Functional Background Identity, Diversity, and Individual Performance in Cross-Functional Teams," *Academy of Management Journal,* December 2003, pp 763–74.
59 Quote from K Pattison, "How Herman Miller Has Designed Employee Loyalty," *Fast Company,* September 2010.
60 Millikin, Hom, and Manz, "Self-Management Competencies in Self-Managing Teams," pp 687–702.
61 See P S Goodman, R Devadas, and T L Griffith Hughson, "Groups and Productivity: Analyzing the Effectiveness of Self-Managing Teams," in *Productivity in Organizations,* eds J P Campbell, R J Campbell and Associates (San Francisco: Jossey-Bass, 1988), pp 295–327; see also S Kauffeld, "Self-Directed Work Groups and Team Competence," *Journal of Occupational and Organizational Psychology,* March 2006, pp 1–21.
62 See C Saunders, C Van Slyke, and D R Vogel, "My Time or Yours? Managing Time Visions in Global Virtual Teams," *Academy of Management Executive,* February 2004, pp 19–31.
63 D Clemons and M Kroth, *Managing the Mobile Workforce* (Burr Ridge, IL: McGraw-Hill, 2011).
64 P E Bierly, E M Stark, and E H Kessler, "The Moderating Effects of Virtuality on the Antecedents and Outcome of NPD Team Trust," *Journal of Product Innovation Management,* 2009, pp 551–65.
65 Adapted from F Siebdrat, M Hoegl, and J Ernst, "How to Manage Virtual Teams," *MIT Sloan Management Review,* Summer 2009, pp 63–68; see also B L Kirkman, B Rosen, C B Gibson, P E Tesluk, and S O McPherson, "Five Challenges to Virtual Team Success: Lessons from Sabre, Inc.," *Academy of Management Executive,* August 2002, pp 67–79.
66 "The Challenges of Working in Virtual Teams," RW3 Culture Wizard, http://rw-3.com/VTSReportv7.pdf.
67 Clemons and Kroth, *Managing the Mobile Workforce.*
68 Ibid.
69 N Lockwood, "Successfully Transitioning to a Virtual Organization: Challenges, Impact, and Technology," *Society of Human Resource Management—Research Quarterly,* First Quarter 2010.
70 E Meyer, "The Four Keys to Success with Virtual Teams," Forbes.com, August 19, 2010, http://www.forbes.com/2010/08/19/virtual-teams-meetings-leadership-managing-cooperation_print.html; see also R F Maruca, "How Do You Manage an Off-Site Team?" *BusinessWeek,* September 30, 2007, www.businessweek.com.
71 For a comprehensive update on groupthink, see the entire February–March 1998 issue of *Organizational Behavior and Human Decision Processes.*

72 I L Janis, *Groupthink,* 2nd ed (Boston: Houghton Mifflin, 1982), p 9. Alternative models are discussed in K Granstrom and D Stiwne, "A Bipolar Model of Groupthink: An Expansion of Janis's Concept," *Small Group Research,* February 1998, pp 32–56.
73 Ibid. For an alternative model, see R J Aldag and S Riggs Fuller, "Beyond Fiasco: A Reappraisal of the Groupthink Phenomenon and a New Model of Group Decision Processes," *Psychological Bulletin,* May 1993, pp 533–52.
74 Adapted from Janis, *Groupthink,* pp 174–75. Also see J M Wellen and M Neale, "Deviance, Self-Typicality, and Group Cohesion: The Corrosive Effects of the Bad Apples on the Barrel," *Small Group Research,* April 2006, pp 165–86.
75 A Stuart, "Group Therapy," *CFO,* November 2007, pp 31–33.
76 D D Henningsen, M L M Henningsen, J Eden, and M G Cruz, "Examining the Symptoms of Groupthink and Retrospective Sensemaking," *Small Group Research,* February 2006, pp 36–64.
77 "Group Think Takes a Back Seat," *Journal of Financial Planning,* July 2010; the article refers to the study by K Girota, C Terwiesch, and K T Ulrich, "Idea Generation and the Quality of the Best Idea," http://knowledge.wharton.upenn.edu/papers/download/051210_Terwiesch_Ulrich_Creativity.pdf
78 Stuart, "Group Therapy," pp 31–33.
79 Based on discussion in B Latane, K Williams, and S Harkins, "Many Hands Make Light the Work: The Causes and Consequences of Social Loafing," *Journal of Personality and Social Psychology,* June 1979, pp 822–32; and D A Kravitz and B Martin, "Ringelmann Rediscovered: The Original Article," *Journal of Personality and Social Psychology,* May 1986, pp 936–41.
80 O A Alnuaimi, L P Robert, and L M Maruping, "Team Size, Dispersion, and Social Loafing in Technology-Supported Teams: A Perspective on the Theory of Moral Disengagement," *Journal of Management Information Systems,* Summer 2010, pp 203–30.
81 M Pearsall, M S Christian, and A P J Ellis, "Motivating Interdependent Teams: Individual Rewards, Shared Rewards, or Something in Between?," *Journal of Applied Psychology,* 2010, pp 183–91; see also S J Karau and K D Williams, "Social Loafing: Meta-Analytic Review and Theoretical Integration," *Journal of Personality and Social Psychology,* October 1993, pp 681–706.
82 Pearsall, Christian, and Ellis, "Motivating Interdependent Teams," pp 183–91.
83 Data from J A Wagner III, "Studies of Individualism-Collectivism: Effects on Cooperation in Groups," *Academy of Management Journal,* February 1995, pp 152–72. Also see P W Mulvey, L Bowes-Sperry, and H J Klein, "The Effects of Perceived Loafing and Defensive Impression Management on Group Effectiveness," *Small Group Research,* June 1998, pp 394–415.
84 S Buchold and T Roth, *Creating the High-Performance Team* (New York: John Wiley & Sons, 1987).
85 Based on J E Mathieu and T L Rapp, "Laying the Foundation for Successful Team Performance Trajectories: The Roles of Team Charters and Performance Strategies," *Journal of Applied Psychology,* 2009, pp 90–103.
86 Derived from K R Randall, C J Resick, and L A DeChurch, "Building Team Adaptive Capacity: The Roles of Sensegiving and Team Composition," *Journal of Applied Psychology,* February 14, 2011.
87 The final paragraph is based loosely on J Eisinger, "Postcrisis, a Struggle Over Mortgage Bond Ratings," *The New York Times,* January 5, 2011.

Chapter 10

1 Excerpted from R Gold, "Rig's Final Hours Probed," *The Wall Street Journal,* July 19, 2010, pp A1, A4.
2 See S Goldenberg, "BP Cost-Cutting Blames for 'Avoidable' Deepwater Horizon Oil Spill," *The Guardian,* January 6, 2011, http://www.guardian.co.uk/environment/2011/jan/06/bp-oil-spill-deepwater-horizon?INTCMP=SRCH.
3 D Brady, "Etc. Hard Choices," *Bloomberg Businessweek,* February 7–13, 2011, p 92.

[4] A thorough discussion of the rational model can be found in M H Bazerman, *Judgment in Managerial Decision Making* (Hoboken, NJ: John Wiley & Sons, 2006).

[5] J L Yang, "Mattel's CEO Recalls a Rough Summer" (interview with Bob Eckert), *Fortune,* January 22, 2008, http://money.cnn.com/2008/01/21/news/companies/mattel.fortune/index.htm.

[6] M V Copeland, "Reed Hastings: Leader of the Pack," *Fortune,* December 6, 2010, pp 121–30.

[7] This study was conducted by P C Nutt, "Expanding the Search for Alternatives during Strategic Decision-Making," *Academy of Management Executive,* November 2004, pp 13–28.

[8] Yang, "Mattel's CEO Recalls a Rough Summer," http://money.cnn.com/2008/01/21/news/companies/mattel.fortune/index.htm

[9] H A Simon, "Rational Decision Making in Business Organizations," *American Economic Review,* September 1979, p 510.

[10] R Brown, *Rational Choice and Judgment* (Hoboken, NJ: John Wiley & Sons, 2005), p 9.

[11] Results can be found in J P Byrnes, D C Miller, and W D Schafer, "Gender Differences in Risk Taking: A Meta-Analysis," *Psychological Bulletin,* May 1999, pp 367–83.

[12] Bounded rationality is discussed by A R Memati, A M Bhatti, M Maqsal, I Mansoor, and F Naveed, "Impact of Resource Based View and Resource Dependence Theory on Strategic Decision Making," *International Journal of Business Management,* December 2010, pp 110–15; and H A Simon, *Administrative Behavior* 2nd ed (New York: Free Press, 1957).

[13] These conclusions were excerpted from "Poor Decisions Hurt Company Performance," *HR Magazine,* February 2007, p 16.

[14] See M D Cohen, J G March, and J P Olsen, "A Garbage Can Model of Organizational Choice," *Administrative Science Quarterly,* March 1981, pp 1–25.

[15] Ibid., p 2.

[16] See G Fioretti and A Lomi, "Passing the Buck in the Garbage Can Model of Organizational Choice," *Computational and Mathematical Organization Theory,* June 2010, pp 113–43; and A Styhre, L Wikmalm, S Olilla, and J Roth, "Garbage-Can Decision Making and the Accommodation of Uncertainty in New Drug Development Work," *Creativity and Innovation Management,* June 2010, pp 134–46.

[17] See A Carter, "Lighting a Fire under Campbell," *BusinessWeek,* December 4, 2006, pp 96, 99.

[18] Example of a garbage can process can be found in K A Strassel, "Mr. Fairness," *The Wall Street Journal,* August 7–8, 2010, p A11; and S Carey, "United Pulls Back on Growth Plans," *The Wall Street Journal,* March 8, 2011, p B4.

[19] D J Snowden and M E Boone, "A Leader's Framework for Decision Making," *Harvard Business Review,* November 2007, pp 69–76.

[20] See P M Tingling and M J Brydon, "Is Decision-Based Evidence Making Necessarily Bad? *MIT Sloan Management Review,* Summer 2010, pp 71–76.

[21] See A Tversky and D Kahneman, "Judgment under Uncertainty: Heuristics and Biases," *Science,* September 1974, pp 1124–31.

[22] See L Landro, "What the Doctor Missed," *The Wall Street Journal,* September 28, 2010, pp D1, D4.

[23] R A Lowe and A A Ziedonis, "Overoptimism and the Performance of Entrepreneurial Firms," *Management Science,* February 2006, pp 173–86.

[24] See B Borenstein, "Disasters Often Stem from Hubris," *The Arizona Republic,* July 12, 2010, p A4.

[25] This scenario was taken from Bazerman, *Judgment in Managerial Decision Making,* p 41.

[26] M Spector and J S Lublin, "Blockbuster Asks for More Cash," *The Wall Street Journal,* January 18, 2011, p B1.

[27] See J Ross and B M Staw, "Organizational Escalation and Exit: Lessons from the Shoreham Nuclear Power Plant," *Academy of Management Journal,* August 1993, pp 701–32; and G Pan, and L Shan, "Transition to IS Project De-Escalation: An Exploration Into Management Executives' Influence Behaviors," *IEEE Transactions on Engineering Management,* February 2011, pp 109–23.

[28] The definition comes from J Pfeffer and R I Sutton, "Evidence-Based Management," *Harvard Business Review,* January 2006, pp 112. Case applications can be found in S Birk, "The Evidence-Based Road," *Healthcare Executive,* July–August 2010, pp 28–36.

[29] The model was proposed by R B Briner, D Denyer, and D M Rousseau, "Evidence-Based Management: Concept Cleanup Time?" *Academy of Management Perspectives,* November 2009, pp 19–32.

[30] The following definitions and discussion were derived from Tingling and Brydon, "Is Evidence- Based Decision Making Necessarily Bad?" pp 71–76.

[31] The quotes and discussion were based on J Pfeffer and R I Sutton, "Profiting from Evidence-Based Management," *Strategy & Leadership,* 2006, vol 34, no 2, pp 35–42.

[32] For details, see E T Anderson and D Simester, "Every Company Can Profit from Testing Customers' Reactions to Changes. Here's How to Get Started," *Harvard Business Review,* March 2011, pp 99–105.

[33] See D Meinert, "Top Performers Boast Analytics Over Intuition," *HR Magazine,* February 2011, p 18; and D Rich, "Power of Predictive Analytics," *Malaysian Business,* December 1, 2010, p 66.

[34] K Naughton, "The Happiest Man in Detroit," *Bloomberg Businessweek,* February 7–13, 2011, p 68.

[35] From Pfeffer and Sutton, "Profiting from Evidence-Based Management," pp 35–42; also see J Griffin, "Who's Responsible for Analytics?" *Information Management,* January 1, 2011, p 29.

[36] This definition was derived from A J Rowe and R O Mason, *Managing with Style: A Guide to Understanding, Assessing and Improving Decision Making* (San Francisco: Jossey-Bass, 1987).

[37] The discussion of styles was based on material contained in Rowe and Mason, *Managing with Style.*

[38] Excerpted from B Gimbel, "Keeping Planes Apart," *Fortune,* June 27, 2005, p 112.

[39] B Bremner and D Roberts, "A Billion Tough Sells," *BusinessWeek,* March 20, 2006, p 44.

[40] Y I Kane and P Dvorak, "Howard Stringer, Japanese CEO," *The Wall Street Journal,* March 3–4, 2007, pp A1, A6.

[41] Norms were obtained from Rowe and Mason, *Managing with Style.*

[42] See M Gupta, A Brantley, and V P Jackson, "Product Involvement as a Predictor of Generation Y Consumer Decision Making Styles," *The Business Review,* Summer 2010, pp 28–33; and S S Wang, "Why So Many People Can't Make Decisions," *The Wall Street Journal,* September 28, 2010, pp D1, D2.

[43] D Kahneman and G Klein, "Conditions for Intuitive Expertise: A Failure to Disagree," *American Psychologist,* September 2009, p 519.

[44] See R Lange, and J Houran, "A Transliminal View of Intuitions in the Workplace," *North American Journal of Psychology,* December 2010, pp 501–16.

[45] C C Miller and R D Ireland, "Intuition in Strategic Decision Making: Friend or Foe in the Fast-Paced 21st Century," *Academy of Management Executive,* February 2005, p 20.

[46] See Kahneman and Klein, "Conditions for Intuitive Expertise," p 519.

[47] E Dane and M G Pratt, "Exploring Intuition and Its Role in Managerial Decision Making," *Academy of Management Review,* January 2007, pp 33–54.

[48] See Kahneman and Klein, "Conditions for Intuitive Expertise," p 519.

[49] This definition was based on R J Sternberg, "What Is the Common Thread of Creativity?" *American Psychologist,* April 2001, pp 360–62.

[50] F Werner, "Obama Urges Budget Deal," *The Arizona Republic,* March 6, 2011, p A10.

[51] J Y Kim, "A Lifelong Battle against Disease," *US News & World Report,* November 19, 2007, pp 62, 64.

[52] D Coutu, "Creativity Step by Step," *Harvard Business Review,* April 2008, pp 47–51 (interview with Twyla Tharp).

[53] See J Lehrer, "Bother Me, I'm Thinking," *The Wall Street Journal,* February 19–20, 2011, p C12.

[54] These recommendations were derived from E Catmull, "How Pixar Fosters Collective Creativity," *Harvard Business Review,* September 2008, pp 65–72; "Keeping Creatives Happy," *Fortune,* March 16, 2009, p 40 (interview with Jeffrey Katzenberg), and L Tischler, "A Designer Takes on His Biggest Challenge Ever," *Fast Company,* February 2009, pp 78–83.

[55] See A Oke, N Munshi, and F O Walumbwa, "The Influence of Leadership on Innovation Processes and Activities," *Organizational Dynamics,* January–March 2009, pp 64–72.

[56] D A Peluso, "Preserving Employee Know How," *HR Magazine,* May 2010, p 99.

57 See *Ethics Resource Center,* 2010, "Reporting: Who's Telling You What You Need to Know, Who Isn't, and What You Can Do About It." Retrieved March 5, 2011, from www.ethics.org/nbes; and *Ethics Resource Center,* 2010, "Ethics and Employee Engagement." Retrieved March 5, 2011, from www.ethics.org/nbes.

58 The decision tree and resulting discussion are based on C E Bagley, "The Ethical Leader's Decision Tree," *Harvard Business Review,* February 2003, pp 18–19.

59 Details of this example can be found in E E Schultz and T Francis, "Financial Surgery: How Cuts in Retiree Benefits Fatten Companies' Bottom Lines," *The Wall Street Journal,* March 1, 2004, p A1.

60 Results can be found in C K W De Dreu and M A West, "Minority Dissent and Team Innovation: The Importance of Participation in Decision Making," *Journal of Applied Psychology,* December 2001, pp 1191–201.

61 G Park and R P DeShon, "A Multilevel Model of Minority Opinion Expression and Team Decision-making Effectiveness," *Journal of Applied Psychology,* September 2010, pp 824–33.

62 These recommendations were derived from R Y Hirokawa, "Group Communication and Decision-making Performance: A Continued Test of the Functional Perspective," *Human Communication Research,* October 1988, pp 487–515.

63 These guidelines were derived from G P Huber, *Managerial Decision Making* (Glenview, IL: Scott, Foresman, 1980), p 149.

64 G W Hill, "Group versus Individual Performance: Are $N + 1$ Heads Better than One?" *Psychological Bulletin,* May 1982, p 535.

65 See T Connolly and L Ordóñez, "Judgment and Decision Making," in *Handbook of Psychology,* vol. 12, eds W C Borman, D R Ilgen, and R J Klimoski (Hoboken, NJ: John Wiley & Sons, 2003), pp 493–518. Also see R Adams and D Ferreira, "Moderation in Groups: Evidence from Betting on Ice Break-Ups in Alaska," *The Review of Economic Studies,* July 2010, pp 882–913.

66 G M Parker, *Team Players and Teamwork: The New Competitive Business Strategy* (San Francisco: Jossey-Bass, 1990).

67 These recommendations were obtained from ibid.

68 See A F Osborn, *Applied Imagination: Principles and Procedures of Creative Thinking,* 3rd ed (New York: Scribners, 1979).

69 P Sanders, "Boeing Brings in Old Hands, Gets an Earful," *The Wall Street Journal,* July 19, 2010, pp B1, B5. Also see K German, "Boeing Resumes Dreamliner Testing," December 23, 2010, http://news.cnet.com/8301-11386_3-20026583-76.html?tag=contentMain;contentBody;1n.

70 See J Castaldo, "Getting Drowned Out By the Brainstorm," *Canadian Business,* July 19, 2010, p 91; and K Girotra and C Terwiesch, "Idea Generation and the Quality of the Best Idea," *Management Science,* April 2010, pp 591–605.

71 See W H Cooper, R Brent Gallupe, S Pollard, and J Cadsby, "Some Liberating Effects of Anonymous Electronic Brainstorming," *Small Group Research,* April 1998, pp 147–78.

72 These recommendations and descriptions were derived from B Nussbaum, "The Power of Design," *BusinessWeek,* May 17, 2004, pp 88–94.

73 An application of the NGT can be found in S Lloyd, "Applying the Nominal Group Technique to Specify the Domain of a Construct," *Qualitative Market Research,* January 2011, pp 105–21.

74 See L Thompson, "Improving the Creativity of Organizational Work Groups," *Academy of Management Executive,* February 2003, pp 96–109.

75 See N C Dalkey, D L Rourke, R Lewis, and D Snyder, *Studies in the Quality of Life: Delphi and Decision Making* (Lexington, MA: Lexington Books: D C Heath and Co., 1972).

76 An application of the Delphi technique can be found in A Graefe and J S Armstrong, "Comparing Face-to-Face Meetings, Nominal Groups, Delphi and Prediction Markets on an Estimating Task," *International Journal of Forecasting,* January–March 2011, pp 183–95.

77 A thorough description of computer-aided decision-making systems is provided by M C Er and A C Ng, "The Anonymity and Proximity Factors in Group Decision Support Systems," *Decision Support Systems,* May 1995, pp 75–83.

78 M Weinstein, "So Happy Together," *Training,* May 2006, p 38.

79 Supportive results can be found in S S Lam and J Schaubroeck, "Improving Group Decisions by Better Polling Information: A Comparative Advantage of Group Decision Support Systems," *Journal of Applied Psychology,* August 2000, pp 565–73.

80 Excerpted from N Timiraos, "Seeing the Allure of 'Can Pay, Won't Pay,'" *The Wall Street Journal,* December 29, 2010, p A4.

Chapter 11

1 Excerpted and adapted from D Hechler, "The Insiders," *Legal Week,* March 3, 2011, pp 12–13.

2 P E Spector, "Introduction: Conflict in Organizations," *Journal of Organizational Behavior,* January 2008, p 3.

3 J A Wall, Jr, and R Robert Callister, "Conflict and Its Management," *Journal of Management,* no. 3, 1995, p 517.

4 Ibid., p 544.

5 See O Jones, "Scientific Management, Culture and Control: A First-Hand Account of Taylorism in Practice," *Human Relations,* May 2000, pp 631–53.

6 C G Donald, J D Ralston, and S F Webb, "Arbitral Views of Fighting: An Analysis of Arbitration Cases, 1989-2003," *Journal of Academic and Business Ethics,* July 2009, pp 1–19.

7 K Duncum, "Turning Conflict into Cooperation," *Bloomberg Businessweek,* October 15, 2010.

8 G R Massey and P L Dawes, "The Antecedents and Consequence of Functional and Dysfunctional Conflict between Marketing Managers and Sales Managers," *Industrial Marketing Management,* 2007, pp 1118–129. See also S Alper, D Tjosvold, and K S Law, "Interdependence and Controversy in Group Decision Making: Antecedents to Effective Self-Managing Teams," *Organizational Behavior and Human Decision Processes,* April 1998, pp 33–52.

9 Adapted in part from discussion in A C Filley, *Interpersonal Conflict Resolution* (Glenview, IL: Scott, Foresman, 1975), pp 9–12; and B Fortado, "The Accumulation of Grievance Conflict," *Journal of Management Inquiry,* December 1992, pp 288–303. Also see D Tjosvold and M Poon, "Dealing with Scarce Resources: Open-Minded Interaction for Resolving Budget Conflicts," *Group & Organization Management,* September 1998, pp 237–55.

10 Excerpted from T Ursiny, *The Coward's Guide to Conflict: Empowering Solutions for Those Who Would Rather Run than Fight* (Naperville, IL: Sourcebooks, 2003), p 27.

11 Adapted from discussion in Tjosvold, *Learning to Manage Conflict,* pp 12–13.

12 Data from "Do I Have It?" *BusinessWeek,* July 7, 2003, p 14.

13 Novations Group, "Sharp Rise Seen in Sexual Remarks in Workplace," news release, February 25, 2008, www.novations.com.

14 S Lim and A Lee, "Work and Nonwork Outcomes of Workplace Incivility: Does Family Support Help?" *Journal of Occupational and Health Psychology,*" 2011, pp 95–111.

15 Data found in C H Kraemer, "Like the Schoolyard, the Workplace Has Its Bully," *Employment Law Alliance,* August 30, 2010; see also Workplace Bullying Institute, *2010 U.S. Bullying Survey,* http://www.workplacebullying.org/research/WBI-NatlSurvey2010.html.

16 C Porath, D Macinnis, and V Folkes, "Witnessing Incivility among Employees: Effects on Consumer Anger and Negative Inferences about Companies," *Journal of Consumer Research,* August 2010, pp 292–304; see also C Pearson and C Porath, *The Cost of Bad Behavior: How Incivility Is Damaging Your Business and What to Do About It* (New York: Portfolio Hardcover, 2009).

17 W Liu, S C S Chi, R Friedman, and M H Tsai, "Explaining Incivility in the Workplace: The Effects of Personality and Culture," *Negotiation and Conflict Management Research,* May 2009, pp 164–84.

18 See J. B. Olson-Buchanan and W R Boswell, "An Integrative Model of Experiencing and Responding to Mistreatment at Work," *Academy of Management Review,* January 2008, pp 76–96; and C Hymowitz, "Bosses Have to Learn How to Confront Troubled Employees," *The Wall Street Journal,* April 23, 2007, p B1.

19 L M Cortina and V J Magley, "Patterns and Profiles of Responses to Incivility in the Workplace," *Journal of Occupational Health Psychology,* 2009, pp 272–288.

20 T Maxon, "American Airlines Pilot Union Chief. We Asked for Too Much, Put Too Many Items on the Table," *The Dallas Morning News,* February 8, 2011.

21 Based on discussion in G Labianca, D J Brass, and B Gray, "Social Networks and Perceptions of Intergroup Conflict: The Role of Negative Relationships and Third Parties," *Academy of Management Journal,* February 1998, pp 55–67.

22 J Binder, H Zagefka, R Brown, R Funke, T Kessler, A Mummendey, A Maquil, S Demoulin, and J P Leyens, "Does Contact Reduce Prejudice or Does Prejudice Reduce Contact? A Longitudinal Test of the Contact Hypothesis Among Majority and Minority Groups in Three European Countries," *Journal of Personality and Social Psychology,* 2009, pp 843–56.

23 For example, see S C Wright, A Aron, T McLaughlin-Volpe, and S A Ropp, "The Extended Contact Effect: Knowledge of Cross-Group Friendships and Prejudice," *Journal of Personality and Social Psychology,* July 1997, pp 73–90.

24 Based on and adapted from research evidence in G Labianca, D J Brass, and B Gray, "Social Networks and Perceptions of Intergroup Conflict: The Role of Negative Relationships and Third Parties," *Academy of Management Journal,* February 1998, pp 55–67; C D Batson et al., "Empathy and Attitudes: Can Feeling for a Member of a Stigmatized Group Improve Feelings toward the Group?" *Journal of Personality and Social Psychology,* January 1997, pp 105–18; and S C Wright et al., "The Extended Contact Effect: Knowledge of Cross-Group Friendships and Prejudice," *Journal of Personality and Social Psychology,* July 1997, pp 73–90.

25 See R L Tung, "American Expatriates Abroad: From Neophytes to Cosmopolitans," *Journal of World Business,* Summer 1998, pp 125–44.

26 P L Perrewé and W A Hochwarter, "Can We Really Have It All? The Attainment of Work and Family Values," *Current Directions in Psychological Science,* February 2001, p 31.

27 See M Wang, S Liu, Y Zhan, and J Shi, "Daily Work–Family Conflict and Alcohol Use: Testing the Cross-Level Moderation Effects of Peer Drinking Norms and Social Support," *Journal of Applied Psychology,* March 2010, pp 377–86; and P Wang, J J Lawler, and K Shi, "Work–Family Conflict, Self-Efficacy, Job Satisfaction, and Gender: Evidences from Asia," *Journal of Leadership & Organizational Studies,* May 2010, pp 298–308.

28 See S R Ezzedeen and K G Ritchey, "Career and Family Strategies of Executive Women: Revisiting the Quest to 'Have it All'," *Organizational Dynamics,* October–December 2009, pp 270–80; and F M Cheung and D F Halpern, "Women at the Top," *American Psychologist,* April 2010, pp 182–93.

29 "Flexible Work Plans Key to Retention," *HR Magazine,* December 2010, p 105.

30 See D A Major, T D Fletcher, D D Davis, and L M Germano, "The Influence of Work–Family Culture and Workplace Relationships on Work Interference with Family: A Multilevel Model," *Journal of Organizational Behavior,* October 2008, pp 881–97; and D P Bhave, A Kramer, and T M Glomb, "Work–Family Conflict in Work Groups: Social Information Processing, Support, and Demographic Dissimilarity," *Journal of Applied Psychology,* January 2010, pp 145–58.

31 See J M Twenge, S M Campbell, B J Hoffman, and C E Lance, "Generational Differences in Work Values: Leisure and Extrinsic Values Increasing, Social and Intrinsic Values Decreasing," *Journal of Management,* September 2010, pp 1117–42; and J M Twenge, "A Review of the Empirical Evidence on Generational Differences in Work Attitudes," *Journal of Business Strategy,* June 2010, pp 201–10.

32 See J M Hoobler, J Hu, and M Wilson, "Do Workers Who Experience Conflict between the Work and Family Domains Hit a 'Glass Ceiling'?: A Meta-Analytic Examination," *Journal of Vocational Behavior,* December 2010, pp 481–94; and G N Powell and J H Greenhaus, "Sex, Gender, and the Work-to-Family Interface: Exploring Negative and Positive Interdependencies," *Academy of Management Journal,* June 2010, pp 513–34.

33 See M Moskowitz, R Levering, and C Tkaczyk, "100 Best Companies to Work For," *Fortune,* February 8, 2010, p 88.

34 R A Cosier and C R Schwenk, "Agreement and Thinking Alike: Ingredients for Poor Decisions," *Academy of Management Executive,* February 1990, p 71.

35 R T Hartwig, "Facilitating Problem Solving: A Case Study Using the Devil's Advocacy Technique," *Group Facilitation: A Research and Applications Journal,* January 2010, pp 17–29.

36 T Greitemeyer, S Schulz-Hardt, and D Frey, "The Effects of Authentic and Contrived Dissent on Escalation of Commitment in Group Decision Making," *European Journal of Social Psychology,* 2009, vol 39, pp 639–47.

37 See G Katzenstein, "The Debate on Structured Debate: Toward a Unified Theory," *Organizational Behavior and Human Decision Processes,* June 1996, pp 316–32.

38 See J S Valacich and C Schwenk, "Devil's Advocacy and Dialectical Inquiry Effects on Face-to-Face and Computer-Mediated Group Decision Making," *Organizational Behavior and Human Decision Processes,* August 1995, pp 158–73.

39 See D M Schweiger, W R Sandberg, and P L Rechner, "Experiential Effects of Dialectical Inquiry, Devil's Advocacy, and Consensus Approaches to Strategic Decision Making," *Academy of Management Journal,* December 1989, pp 745–72.

40 A statistical validation for this model can be found in M A Rahim and N R Magner, "Confirmatory Factor Analysis of the Styles of Handling Interpersonal Conflict: First-Order Factor Model and Its Invariance across Groups," *Journal of Applied Psychology,* February 1995, pp 122–32.

41 M Dixit and D Mallik, "Assessing Suitability of Rahim Organizational Conflict Inventory-II in Indian Family Owned and Managed Businesses," *International Journal of Business Insights & Transformation,* October–March 2009, pp 28–38.

42 D Salin, "Ways of Explaining Workplace Bullying: A Review of Enabling, Motivating and Precipitating Structures and Processes in the Work Environment," *Human Relations,* October 2003, pp 1213–32.

43 P K Lam and K S Chin, "Managing Conflict in Collaborative New Product Development: A Supplier Perspective," *International Journal of Quality and Reliability Management,* 2007, vol 24, pp 891–907.

44 Dixit and Mallik, "Assessing Suitability of Rahim Organizational Conflict Inventory-II in Indian Family Owned and Managed Businesses," pp 28–38.

45 J Morrison, "The Relationship between Emotional Intelligence Competencies and Preferred Conflict Handling Styles," *Journal of Nursing Management,* August 2008, pp 974–83.

46 F Aquila, "Taming the Litigation Beast," *Bloomberg Businessweek,* April 6, 2010.

47 B Morrow and L M Bernardi, "Resolving Workplace Disputes," *Canadian Manager,* Spring 1999, p 17. For related research, see J M Brett, M Olekalns, R Friedman, N Goates, C Anderson, and C Cherry Lisco, "Sticks and Stones: Language, Face, and Online Dispute Resolution," *Academy of Management Journal,* February 2007, pp 85–99.

48 Aquila, "Taming the Litigation Beast,"

49 Adapted from the discussion in K O Wilburn, "Employment Disputes: Solving Them Out of Court," *Management Review,* March 1998, pp 17–21; and Morrow and Bernardi, "Resolving Workplace Disputes," pp 17–19, 27.

50 For more, see M M Clark, "A Jury of Their Peers," *HR Magazine,* January 2004, pp 54–59.

51 Wilburn, "Employment Disputes," p 19.

52 For an excellent description of the pros and cons from both employee and employer perspectives see C D Coleman, "Is Mandatory Employment Arbitration Living Up to Its Expectations? A View from the Employer's Perspective," *ABA Journal of Labor & Employment Law,* Winter 2010, pp 227–39.

53 Based on a definition in M A Neale and M H Bazerman, "Negotiating Rationally: The Power and Impact of the Negotiator's Frame," *Academy of Management Executive,* August 1992, pp 42–51.

54 R L Pinkley, "The Effect of Cognitive Biases on Judgments about Fair Pay: Implications for Negotiators as Price-Justifiers." In *The Psychology of Negotiations for the 21st Century,* ed B Goldman and D Shapiro (SIOP Frontiers Series, in press); for the quote and related information see P H Kim, R L Pinkley, and A R Fragale, "Power Dynamics in Negotiation," *Academy of Management Review,* October 2005, pp 799–822.

55 Pinkley, "The Effect of Cognitive Biases on Judgments about Fair Pay;" also good win–win negotiation strategies can be found in R R Reck and D G Long, *The Win–Win Negotiator: How to Negotiate Favorable Agreements That Last* (New York: Pocket Books, 1987); and N Brodsky, "The Paranoia Moment: Are They Stalling? Is This Deal about to Fall Apart?" *Inc,* April 2007, pp 67–68.

56 B Schulte, "Teaming Up with the Enemy," *U.S. News & World Report,* November 19, 2007, pp 54, 56.

57 Pinkley, "The Effect of Cognitive Biases on Judgments about Fair Pay,"

58 Adapted from K Albrecht and S Albrecht, "Added Value Negotiating," *Training,* April 1993, pp 26–29.

59 J R Curhan, H A Elfenbein, and G J Kilduff, "Getting Off on the Right Foot: Subjective Value versus Economic Value in Predicting Longitudinal Job Outcomes from Job Offer Negotiations*," Journal of Applied Psychology,* 2009, pp 524–34.

60 Excerpted and adapted from S Craig, "Financial Fraud Case Pits Arbitration vs. Class Action," *The New York Times,*" March 4, 2011.

Chapter 12

1 Reprinted by permission of *Harvard Business Review.* Excerpt from "Best Buy's CEO on Learning to Love Social Media," by BJ Dunn, December 2010. Copyright 2010 by the Harvard Business School Publishing Corporation; all rights reserved.

2 J L Bowditch and A F Buono, *A Primer on Organizational Behavior,* 4th ed (New York: John Wiley & Sons, 1997), p 120.

3 For a detailed discussion about selecting an appropriate medium, see B Barry and I Smithey-Fulmer, "The Medium and the Message: The Adaptive Use of Communication Media in Dyadic Influence," *Academy of Management Review,* April 2004, pp 272–92.

4 J Adamy, "38: Janice Fields, Executive Vice President and Chief Operating Officer, McDonald's USA," *The Wall Street Journal,* November 19, 2007, p R10.

5 How to lay-off employees is discussed in L Rubis, "Laying Off Employees Still Best Done Face-to-Face," *Society of Human Resource Management,* June 30, 2009.

6 "Radio Shack Email to Employees: Pink Slip Attached," *Associated Press,* August 30, 2006.

7 J Pollack and J Neff, "Notebook: Krugman a Downer, Few Practicing What They Tweet," *Advertising Age,* October 18, 2010, p 22.

8 "Managing Organizational Communication," *Society of Human Resource Management,* March 26, 2010.

9 G A Fowler, "In China's Offices, Foreign Colleagues Might Get an Earful," *The Wall Street Journal,* February 13, 2007, p B1.

10 "Leading Now, Leading the Future: What Senior HR Leaders Need to Know," *Society for Human Resource Management,* June 16, 2009.

11 For a thorough discussion of these barriers, see C R Rogers and F J Roethlisberger, "Barriers and Gateways to Communication," *Harvard Business Review,* July–August 1952, pp 46–52.

12 Ibid., p 47.

13 R Cross, P Gray, S Cunningham, M Showers, and R J Thomas, "The Collaborative Organization: How to Make Employee Networks Work," *MIT Sloan Management Review,* Fall 2010, pp 83–91.

14 L Buchanan, "Do Not Disturb," *Inc,* November 2007, p 144.

15 E Ekpenyong, "Translating and Interpreting," *Babel,* 2010, pp 328–40.

16 J Sandberg, "It Says Press Any Key; Where's the Any Key?" *The Wall Street Journal,* February 20, 2007, p B1.

17 Results can be found in J D Johnson, W A Donohue, C K Atkin, and S Johnson, "Communication, Involvement, and Perceived Innovativeness," *Group & Organization Management,* March 2001, pp 24–52.

18 A R Sanchez, A Pico, and L B Comer, "Salespeople's Communication Competence," *Journal of Business & Economic Studies,* Spring 2010.

19 1. *False.* Clients always take precedence, and people with the greatest authority or importance should be introduced first.

2. *False.* You should introduce yourself. Say something like "My name is. I don't believe we've met."

3. *False.* It's OK to admit you can't remember. Say something like "My mind just went blank, your name is?" Or offer your name and wait for the other person to respond with his or hers.

4. *False.* Business etiquette has become gender neutral.

5. *a. Host.* This enables him or her to lead their guest to the meeting place.

6. *False.* Not only is it rude to invade public areas with your conversation, but you never know who might hear details of your business transaction or personal life.

7. *b. 3 feet.* Closer than this is an invasion of personal space. Farther away forces people to raise their voices. Because communication varies from country to country, you should also inform yourself about cultural differences.

8. *True.* An exception to this would be if your company holds an event at the beach or the pool.

9. *False.* Just wave your hand over it when asked, or say "No thank you."

10. *True.* The person who initiated the call should redial if the connection is broken.

11. *True.* If you must use a speakerphone, you should inform all parties who's present.

12. *True.* You should record a greeting such as "I'm out of the office today, March 12. If you need help, please dial _____ at extension . . ."

20 B Kupperschmidt, E Kientz, J Ward, and B Reinholz, "A Healthy Work Environment Begins with You," *Online Journal of Nursing Issues,* 2010; see also F Timmins and C McCabe, "How Assertive Are Nurses in the Workplace? A Preliminary Pilot Study," *Journal of Nursing Management,* January 2005, pp 61–67; for application to financial planning see C Nelson, "Practice Trends: Communication Styles and Business Growth," *Journal of Financial Planning,* September 2010, pp 8–11.

21 J A Waters, "Managerial Assertiveness," *Business Horizons,* September–October 1982, p 25.

22 R E de Vries, A Bakker-Pieper, and W Oostenveld, "Leadership = Communication? The Relations of Leaders' Communication Styles with Leadership Styles, Knowledge Sharing and Leader Outcomes," *Journal of Business Psychology,* 2010, pp 367–80.

23 "Doctor Report Cards Not Last Word on Physician Performance," *U.S. News and World Report,* September 13, 2010.

24 J Edmondson, "Let's Be Clear: How to Manage Communication Styles," *Training and Development,* September 2009, pp 30–31.

25 Waters, "Managerial Assertiveness," p 27. Also see C Binkley, "Want to Be CEO? You Have to Dress the Part," *The Wall Street Journal,* January 10, 2008, pp D1, D12.

26 Sanchez, Pico, and Comer. Quote and statistics from L Talley, "Body Language: Read It or Weep," *HR Magazine,* July 1, 2010.

27 H Elfbenbein and N Eisenkraft, "The Relationship Between Displaying and Perceiving Nonverbal Cues of Affect: A Meta-Analysis to Solve an Old Mystery," *Journal of Personality and Social Psychology,* 2010, pp 301–18.

28 Quote taken from J Grumet, "Reading Between the Lines: Interpreting Body Language Can Improve Care," *Medical Economics,* February 25, 2011.

29 Talley. See also D B Rane, "Effective Body Language for Organizational Success," *Journal of Soft Skills,* 2010, pp.17–26.

30 Related research is summarized by J A Hall, "Male and Female Nonverbal Behavior," in *Multichannel Integrations of Nonverbal Behavior,* eds A W Siegman and S Feldstein (Hillsdale, NJ: Lawrence Erlbaum, 1985), pp 195–226.

31 Data found in L Fitzpatrick, "Are Hugs the New Handshakes?," *Time,* February 12, 2009.

32 See R E Axtell, *Gestures: The Do's and Taboos of Body Language around the World* (New York: John Wiley & Sons, 1991); and E Flitter, "Touchy Subject: Doing Business Where Hugs Replace Handshakes," *The Wall Street Journal,* December 19, 2007, http://online.wsj.com.

33 Rane, "Effective Body Language for Organizational Success," pp.17–26. See also B Azar, "A Case for Angry Men and Happy Women," *Monitor on Psychology,* April 2007, pp 18–19.

34 N O Rule, N Ambady, R B Adams, H Ozono, S Nakashima, S Yoshikawa, and M Watabe, "Polling the Face: Prediction and Consensus Across Cultures," *Journal of Personality and Social Psychology,* 2010, pp 1–15.

35 Norms for cross-cultural eye contact are discussed by C Engholm, *When Business East Meets Business West: The Guide to Practice and Protocol in the Pacific Rim* (New York: John Wiley & Sons, 1991).

36 See D Knight, "Perks Keeping Workers out of Revolving Door," *The Wall Street Journal,* April 30, 2005, p D3; and G Rooper, "Managing Employee Relations," *HR Magazine,* May 2005, pp 101–4.

37 J Beeson, "Why You Didn't Get that Promotion," *Harvard Business Review,* June 2009.

38 D Aarts, "The 5 Most Essential Sales Skills," *Profit,* November 2010, p 37.

39 The discussion of listening styles is based on "5 Listening Styles," June 19, 2004, http://www.crossroadsinstitute.org/listyle.html.
40 These recommendations were excerpted from J Jay, "On Communicating Well," *HR Magazine,* January 2005, pp 87–88.
41 D Tannen, "The Power of Talk: Who Gets Heard and Why," *Harvard Business Review,* September–October 1995, p 139.
42 A L Gonzales, J T Hancock, and J W Pennebaker, "Language Style Matching as a Predictor of Social Dynamics in Small Groups," *Communication Research,* 2010, pp 3–19.
43 K Coussement and D Van den Poel, "Improving Customer Complaint Management by Automatic Email Classification Using Linguistic Style," *Decision Support Systems,* March 2008.
44 For a thorough review of the evolutionary explanation of sex differences in communication, see A H Eagly and W Wood, "The Origins of Sex Differences in Human Behavior," *American Psychologist,* June 1999, pp 408–23.
45 See D Tannen, "The Power of Talk: Who Gets Heard and Why," in *Negotiation: Readings, Exercises, and Cases,* 3rd ed, eds R J Lewicki and D M Saunders (Boston, MA: Irwin/McGraw-Hill, 1999), pp 160–73; also see J Ewers, "Ladies, Cool It if You Want Cash," *U.S. News & World Report,* September 24, 2007, p 57.
46 See M Dainton and E D Zelley, *Applying Communication Theory for Professional Life: A Practical Introduction* (Thousand Oaks, CA: Sage, 2005).
47 E Melero, "Are Workplaces with Many Women in Management Run Differently?" *Journal of Business Research,* 2011, pp 385–93.
48 J R Fine, "Enhancing Gen Y Communication Skills," *Society for Human Resource Management,* March 13, 2009.
49 Ibid. For an excellent, detailed description of generational differences and implications at work see J C Meister and K Willyerd, *The 2020 Workplace* (New York: HarperCollins, 2010).
50 Based on C Houck, "Multigenerational and Virtual: How Do We Build a Mentoring Program for Today's Workforce?," *Performance Improvement,* February 2011, pp 25–30.
51 Fine, "Enhancing Gen Y Communication Skills."
52 Ibid.
53 Data from ComScore press release April 1, 2011, http://www.comscoredatamine.com/2011.
54 Ibid.
55 S E Jackson, "New Media: Debunking the Myths," *Journal of Business Strategy,* 2010, pp 56–58.
56 ComScore, April 1, 2011, http://www.comscoredatamine.com/2011.
57 Meister and Willyerd, *The 2020 Workplace,* pp 31–32.
58 B A Lautsch and E E Kossek, "Managing a Blended Workforce: Telecommuters and Non-Telecommuters," *Organizational Dynamics,* 2011, pp 10–17.
59 J Bughin and M Chui, "The Rise of the Networked Enterprise: Web 2.0 Finds its Payday," *McKinsey Quarterly,* December 2010.
60 L Grensing-Pophal, "Efficiency Boosters: Making the Most of Your Time Resources," *Society for Human Resource Management Consultants Forum,* 2011.
61 Ibid.
62 D Clemons and M Kroth, *Managing the Mobile Workforce* (Burr Ridge, IL: McGraw-Hill).
63 See R S Gajendran and D A Harrison, "The Good, the Bad, and the Unknown About Telecommuting: Meta-Analysis of Psychological Mediators and Individual Consequences," *Journal of Applied Psychology,* November 2007, pp 1524–41.
64 Lautsch and Kossek, "Managing a Blended Workforce."
65 Ibid.
66 Data from "Global Publics Embrace Social Networking," *Pew Research Center Publications,* December 15, 2010, http://pewglobal.org/files/2010/12/Pew-Global-Attitudes-Technology-Report FINAL December-15-2010.pdf
67 M K Foster, A Francescucci, and B C West, "Why Users Participate in Online Social Networks," *International Journal of e-Business Management,* 2010, pp 3–19.
68 J T Arnold, "Twittering and Facebooking While They Work," *HR Magazine,* December 1, 2009.

69 N Savage, "Twitter as Medium and Message," *Communications of the ACM,* March 2011, pp 18–20.
70 B A Hackworth and M B Kunz, "Health Care and Social Media: Building Relationships Via Social Networks," *Academy of Health Care Management Journal,* 2010, pp 55–68.
71 Quote from "The Revolution Will Be Shared: Social Media and Innovation," *Research and Technology Management,* February 2011, pp 64–66.
72 Ibid., and T Wasserman, "Pepsi Snafu Illustrates Dangers of Crowd Sourcing," Crowdsourcing.org, January 7, 2011, http://www.crowdsourcing.org/document/pepsico-snafu-illustrates-dangers-of-crowd-sourcing/2249.
73 Arnold, "Twittering and Facebooking While They Work."
74 Excerpted and adapted from M Ramsay, "Social Media Etiquette: A Guide and Checklist to the Benefits and Perils of Social Marketing," *Database Marketing & Customer Strategy Management,* 2010, pp 257–61.
75 "German Workplaces Ban Social Media," *Information Management,* January–February 2011.
76 Arnold, "Twittering and Facebooking While They Work."
77 J Deschenaux, "Employee Use of Social Media: Laws Fail to Keep Pace with Technology," *Society of Human Resource Management,* March 16, 2011.
78 Ibid., and "Online Reputation: Putting Your Firm's Reputation on the Line," *Recruiter,* February 3, 2010.
79 M Meece, "Who's the Boss, You or Your Gadget?" *The New York Times,* February 5, 2011.
80 "Online Reputation: Putting Your Firm's Reputation on the Line."
81 E Steel and G A Fowler, "Facebook in Privacy Breach," *The Wall Street Journal,* October 18, 2010.
82 Dunn, "How I Did It . . ." pp 43–48.
83 "Fired Over Facebook: Employer Regulation of Speech on Social Media Sites," *Media Law and Freedom of Expression Blog: Global Networking for Media Lawyers,* February 25, 2011, http://ibamedialaw.wordpress.com/2011/02/25/fired-over-facebook-employer-regulation-of-speech-on-social-media-sites/.
84 J Borzo, "Employers Tread a Minefield," *The Wall Street Journal,* January 21, 2011.

Chapter 13

1 Adapted from R Gupta, "How I Did It . . . Rohm and Haas's Former CEO on Pulling Off a Suite to deal in a Down Market," *Harvard Business Review,* November 2010, pp 49–54.
2 See D Kipnis, S M Schmidt, and J Wilkinson, "Intraorganizational Influence Tactics: Explorations in Getting One's Way," *Journal of Applied Psychology,* August 1980, pp 440–52.
3 For related reading, see K D Elsbach, "How to Pitch a Brilliant Idea," *Harvard Business Review,* September 2003, pp 117–23.
4 Based on discussion in G Yukl, H Kim, and C M Falbe, "Antecedents of Influence Outcomes," *Journal of Applied Psychology,* June 1996, pp 309–17.
5 See R E Boyatzis, M L Smith, and N Blaize, "Developing Sustainable Leaders through Coaching and Compassion," *Academy of Management Learning and Education,* March 2006, pp 8–24.
6 C Tkaczyk, "Follow These Leaders," *Fortune,* December 12, 2005, p 125.
7 C F Seifert and G Yukl, "Effects of Repeated Multi-Source Feedback on the Influence Behavior and Effectiveness of Managers: A Field Experiment," *The Leadership Quarterly,* 2010, pp 856–66.
8 Supportive results can be found in S Hysong, "The Role of Technical Skill in Perceptions of Managerial Performance," *The Journal of Management Development,* 2008, pp 275–90; and R W Kolodinsky, D C F Treadway, and G R Ferris, "Political Skill and Influence Effectiveness: Testing Portions of an Expanded Ferris and Judge (1991) Model," *Human Relations,* December 2007, pp 1747–78. Also see T R Clark, "Engaging the Disengaged," *HR Magazine,* April 2008, pp 109–12.
9 Data from G Yukl and J B Tracey, "Consequences of Influence Tactics Used with Subordinates, Peers, and the Boss," *Journal of Applied*

Psychology, August 1992, pp 525–35. Also see C M Falbe and G Yukl, "Consequences for Managers of Using Single Influence Tactics and Combinations of Tactics," *Academy of Management Journal,* August 1992, pp 638–52.

[10] Data from Yukl, Kim, and Falbe, "Antecedents of Influence Outcomes," pp 309–17.

[11] Based on C Pornpitakpan, "The Persuasiveness of Source Credibility: A Critical Review of Five Decades' Evidence," *Journal of Applied Social Psychology,* February 2004, pp 243–81.

[12] S A Furst and D M Cable, "Employee Resistance to Organizational Change: Managerial Influence Tactics and Leader–Member Exchange," *Journal of Applied Psychology,* March 2008, pp 453–62.

[13] S Chakrabarty, G Brown, and R E Widing, "Closed Influence Tactics: Do Smugglers Win in the Long Run?" *Journal of Personal Selling & Sales Management,* Winter 2010, pp 23–32.

[14] I Stern and J D Westphal, "Stealthy Footsteps to the Boardroom: Executive's Backgrounds, Sophisticated Interpersonal Influence Behavior, and Board Appointments," *Administrative Science Quarterly,* 2010, pp 278–319.

[15] Seifert and Yukl, "Effects of Repeated Multi-Source Feedback on the Influence Behavior and Effectiveness of Managers," pp 856–66.

[16] Adapted from R B Cialdini, "Harnessing the Science of Persuasion," *Harvard Business Review,* October 2001, pp 72–79.

[17] Ibid., p 77.

[18] See A D Wright, "Survey: Nonprofits Fall Short on Ethics," *HR Magazine,* May 2008, p 24; and R. Riney, "Heal Leadership Disorders," *HR Magazine,* May 2008, pp 62–66.

[19] M W McCall Jr, *Power, Influence, and Authority: The Hazards of Carrying a Sword,* Technical Report No. 10 (Greensboro, NC: Center for Creative Leadership, 1978), p 5. For an excellent overview of power, see E P Hollander and L R Offermann, "Power and Leadership in Organizations," *American Psychologist,* February 1990, pp 179–89.

[20] See J R P French and B Raven, "The Bases of Social Power," in *Studies in Social Power,* ed D Cartwright (Ann Arbor: University of Michigan Press, 1959), pp 150–67.

[21] S Berfield, "A Pistachio Farmer, Pom Wonderful, and the FTC," *Bloomberg Businessweek,* November 11, 2010.

[22] B Worthen and J S Lublin, "Hurd Deal Inflamed Directors," *The Wall Street Journal,* August 16, 2010.

[23] S Forbes, "Deficit Size Egos," *Forbes,* April 11, 2011.

[24] B Stone, "The New New Andreessen," *Bloomberg Businessweek,* November 3, 2010.

[25] P Kaipa and M Kriger, "Empowerment, Vision, and Positive Leadership: An Interview with Alan Mulally, Former CEO, Boeing Commercial— Current CEO, Ford Motor Company," *Journal of Management Inquiry,* June 2010, p 110.

[26] See B Gupta and N K Sharma, "Compliance with Bases of Power and Subordinates' Perception of Superiors: Moderating Effect of Quality of Interaction," *Singapore Management Review,* 2008, pp 1–24; P M Podsakoff and C A Schriesheim, "Field Studies of French and Raven's Bases of Power: Critique, Reanalysis, and Suggestions for Future Research," *Psychological Bulletin,* May 1985, p 388.

[27] See T R Hinkin and C A Schriesheim, "Relationships between Subordinate Perceptions and Supervisor Influence Tactics and Attributed Bases of Supervisory Power," *Human Relations,* March 1990, pp 221–37.

[28] J Zheng, "Cross-Cultural Study of French and Chinese Managers' Use of Power Sources," *International Journal of Business and Management,* May 2010, pp 219–25.

[29] S S Standifird, F Pons, and D Moshavi, "Influence Tactics in the Classroom and Relationship to Student Satisfaction," *Decision Sciences Journal of Innovative Education,* January 2008, pp 135–49.

[30] J Galante and D MacMillan, "Meg Whitman Joins Venture Firm Kleiner Perkins as Advisor," *Bloomberg Businessweek,* March 29, 2011.

[31] See C L Pearce and C C Manz, "The New Silver Bullets of Leadership: The Importance of Self- and Shared Leadership in Knowledge Work," *Organizational Dynamics,* no. 2, 2005, pp 130–40.

[32] W A Randolph and M Sashkin, "Can Organizational Empowerment Work in Multinational Settings?" *Academy of Management Executive,* February 2002, p 104. Also see N R Lockwood, "Leveraging Employee Engagement for Competitive Advantage: HR's Strategic

Role," *HR Magazine,* 2007 SHRM Research Quarterly, March 2007, pp 1–12. Also see R C Liden and S Arad, "A Power Perspective of Empowerment and Work Groups: Implications for Human Resources Management Research," in *Research in Personnel and Human Resources Management,* vol. 14, ed G R Ferris (Greenwich, CT: JAI Press, 1996), pp 205–51.

[33] K. Greasley, A Bryman, A Dainty, and A Price, et al., "Understanding Empowerment from an Employee Perspective; What Does It Mean and Do They Want It?" *Team Performance Management,* 2008, pp 39–55; see also G M Spreitzer, "Social Structural Characteristics of Psychological Empowerment," *Academy of Management Journal,* April 1996, pp 483–504.

[34] H Liao, K Toya, D P Lepak, and Y Hong, "Do They See Eye to Eye? Management and Employee Perspectives of High-Performance Work Systems and Influence Processes on Service Quality," *Journal of Applied Psychology,* 2009, pp 371–91.

[35] L Shaper Walters, "A Leader Redefines Management," *Christian Science Monitor,* September 22, 1992, p 14.

[36] Y Atanasova and C Senn, "Global Customer Team Design: Dimensions, Determinants, and Performance Outcomes," *Industrial Marketing Management,* 2011, pp 278–89.

[37] See S Zuboff, "Ranking Ourselves to Death," *Fast Company,* November 2004, p 125.

[38] L Lorber, "An Open Book: When Companies Share Their Financial Data with Employees the Results Can Be Dramatic," *The Wall Street Journal,* February 23, 2009.

[39] R Rayasam, "Equal Exchange Serves Up a Cup of Cooperation," *U.S. News & World Report,* April 24, 2008, http://find.galegroup.com.

[40] P Benoleil and A Somech, "Who Benefits from Participative Management?" *Journal of Educational Administration,* 2010, pp 285–308.

[41] For an extended discussion of this model, see M Sashkin, "Participative Management Is an Ethical Imperative," *Organizational Dynamics,* Spring 1984, pp 4–22; see also X Huang, J Iun, A Liu, and Y Gong, "Does Participative Leadership Enhance Work Performance by Inducing Empowerment or Trust? The Differential Effects on Managerial and Nonmanagerial Subordinates," *Journal of Organizational Behavior,* 2010, pp 122–43.

[42] C Edwards, "Bosch Maps Out Future in UK," *Engineering and Technology Magazine,* August 2, 2010.

[43] X Zhang and K M Bartol, "Linking Empowering Leadership and Employee Creativity: The Influence of Psychological Empowerment, Intrinsic Motivation, and Creative Process Engagement," *Academy of Management Journal,* 2010, pp 107–128.

[44] G Chen, P N Sharma, S K Edinger, D L Shapiro, and J L Farh, "Motivating and Demotivating Forces in Teams: Cross-Level Influences of Empowering Leadership and Relationship Conflict," *Journal of Applied Psychology,* December 2010, pp 1–17.

[45] S Seibert, G Wang, and S H Courtright, "Antecedents and Consequences of Psychological and Team Empowerment in Organizations: A Meta-Analytic Review," *Journal of Applied Psychology,* March 28, 2011, pp 1–23.

[46] Ibid.

[47] G N Gotsis and Z Kortezi, "Ethical Considerations in Organizational Politics: Expanding the Perspective," *Journal of Business Ethics,* 2010, pp 497–517.

[48] G Atinc, M Darrat, B Fuller, and B W Parker, "Perceptions of Organizational Politics: A Meta-Analysis of Theoretical Antecedents," *Journal of Managerial Issues,* Winter 2010, pp 494–513.

[49] Ibid.

[50] Ibid; see also discussion in D R Beeman and T W Sharkey, "The Use and Abuse of Corporate Politics," *Business Horizons,* March–April 1987, pp 26–30.

[51] Quote and data from "The Big Picture: Reasons for Raises," *BusinessWeek,* May 29, 2006, p 11.

[52] A Raia, "Power, Politics, and the Human Resource Professional," *Human Resource Planning,* no. 4, 1985, p 203.

[53] A J DuBrin, "Career Maturity, Organizational Rank, and Political Behavioral Tendencies: A Correlational Analysis of Organizational Politics and Career Experience," *Psychological Reports,* October 1988, p 535.

[54] This three-level distinction comes from A T Cobb, "Political Diagnosis: Applications in Organizational Development," *Academy of Management Review,* July 1986, pp 482–96.

[55] An excellent historical and theoretical perspective of coalitions can be found in W B Stevenson, J L Pearce, and L W Porter, "The Concept of 'Coalition' in Organization Theory and Research," *Academy of Management Review,* April 1985, pp 256–68.

[56] M Gordon, "Farmers, Airlines Exempt from Derivatives Rules," *Bloomberg Businessweek,* April 12, 2011.

[57] G Steinhauser and M Liedtke, "Microsoft Skewers Google in EU Antitrust Complaint," *Bloomberg Businessweek,* March 31, 2011.

[58] R Whelan, "St. Joe CEO, 3 Directors Resign," *The Wall Street Journal,* February 28, 2011.

[59] D Faber, "Goldman Sachs—Power and Peril," *CNBC,* October 6, 2010. For more on networks and influence see J Pfeffer, *Power—Why Some People Have It and Others Don't* (New York: HarperCollins, 2010).

[60] See D A Buchanan, "You Stab My Back, I'll Stab Yours: Management Experience and Perceptions of Organization Political Behavior," *British Journal of Management,* March 2008, pp 49–64; and Allen, Madison, Porter, Renwick, and Mayes, "Organizational Politics," p 77.

[61] N D Schwartz, "Facing Threat from WikiLeaks, Bank Plays Defense," *The New York Times,* January 2, 2011.

[62] Pfeffer. *Power—Why Some People Have It and Others Don't.*

[63] B Dattner and R Hogan, "Can You Handle Failure?" *Harvard Business Review,* April 2011.

[64] H Zhao and R C Liden, "Internship: A Recruitment and Selection Perspective," *Journal of Applied Psychology,* 2011, pp 221–29.

[65] M R Barrick, B W Swider, and G L Stewart, "Initial Evaluations in the Interview: Relationships with Subsequent Interviewer Evaluations and Employment Offers," *Journal of Applied Psychology,* 2010, pp 1163–72.

[66] S Friedman, "What Do You Really Care About? What Are You Most Interested In?" *Fast Company,* March 1999, p 90.

[67] J D Westphal and M E Graebner, "A Matter of Appearances: How Corporate Leaders Manage the Impressions of Financial Analysts About the Conduct of Their Boards," *Academy of Management Journal,* 2010, pp 15–43.

[68] See S J Wayne and G R Ferris, "Influence Tactics, Affect, and Exchange Quality in Supervisor-Subordinate Interactions: A Laboratory Experiment and Field Study," *Journal of Applied Psychology,* October 1990, pp 487–99. For another version, see Table 1 (p 246) in S J Wayne and R C Liden, "Effects of Impression Management on Performance Ratings: A Longitudinal Study," *Academy of Management Journal,* February 1995, pp 232–60.

[69] See R A Gordon, "Impact of Ingratiation on Judgments and Evaluations: A Meta-Analytic Investigation," *Journal of Personality and Social Psychology,* July 1996, pp 54–70.

[70] See Y-Y Chen and W Fang, "The Moderating Effect of Impression Management on the Organizational Politics-Performance Relationship," *Journal of Business Ethics,* May 2008, pp 263–77.

[71] See, for example, D C Treadway, G R Ferris, A B Duke, G L Adams, and J B Thatcher, "The Moderating Role of Subordinate Political Skill on Supervisors' Impressions of Subordinate Ingratiation and Ratings of Subordinate Interpersonal Facilitation," *Journal of Applied Psychology,* May 2007, pp 848–55.

[72] R A Giacalone and J W Beard, "Impression Management, Diversity, and International Management," *American Behavioral Scientist,* March 1994, pp 621–36.

[73] For a humorous discussion of making a bad impression, see P Hellman, "Looking BAD," *Management Review,* January 2000, p 64; see also T E Becker and S L Martin, "Trying to Look Bad at Work: Methods and Motives for Managing Poor Impressions in Organizations," *Academy of Management Journal,* February 1995, p 191.

[74] Excerpted and adapted from R Hosking, "Poor Behaviors: Could You Be Making a Bad Impression With Your Boss?" *OfficePro,* August–September 2010, p 5.

[75] P S Goodman, "In Case of Emergency: What Not to Do," *The New York Times,* August 21, 2010.

[76] Ibid.

[77] Ibid.

[78] Adapted from Ibid.

[79] K T Dirks, P H Kim, D L Ferrin, and C D Cooper, "Understanding the Effects of Substantive Responses on Trust Following Transgression," *Organizational Behavior and Decision Processes,* 2011, pp 87–103.

[80] B Kellerman, "When Should a Leader Apologize—And When Not?" *Harvard Business Review,* April 1, 2006.

[81] Ibid.

[82] L A Helmchen, M R Richards, and T B McDonald, "Successful Remediation of Patient Safety Incidents: A Tale of Two Medication Errors," *Health Care Management Review,* 2011, pp 114–23.

[83] B K Miller, M A Rutherford, and R W Kolodinsky, "Perceptions of Organizational Politics: A Meta-Analysis of Outcomes," *Journal of Business and Psychology,* March 2008, pp 209–23.

[84] A Zaleznik, "Real Work," *Harvard Business Review* January–February 1989, p 60.

[85] C M Koen Jr, and S M Crow, "Human Relations and Political Skills," *HR Focus,* December 1995, p 11.

[86] L Story, "A Secretive Banking Elite Rules Trading in Derivatives," *The New York Times,* December 11, 2010.

Chapter 14

[1] Excerpted and adapted from R Frank, "Tilton Flaunts Her Style at Patriarch," *The Wall Street Journal,* January 8–9, 2011, pp B1, B17.

[2] C A Schriesheim, J M Tolliver, and O C Behling, "Leadership Theory: Some Implications for Managers," *MSU Business Topics,* Summer 1978, p 35.

[3] The different levels of leadership are thoroughly discussed by A J Kinicki, K J L Jacobson, B M Galvin, and G E Prussia, "A Multilevel Systems Model of Leadership," *Journal of Leadership & Organizational Studies,* in press.

[4] B Kellerman, "Leadership: Warts and All," *Harvard Business Review,* January 2004, p 45.

[5] For a review see B M Bass and R Bass, *The Bass Handbook of Leadership: Theory, Research, and Managerial Applications,* 4th ed (New York: Free Press, 2008), pp 103–35.

[6] Implicit leadership theory is discussed by Bass and Bass, *The Bass Handbook of Leadership,* pp 46–78; and J S Mueller, J A Goncalo, and D Kamdar, "Recognizing Creative Leadership: Can Creative Idea Expression Negatively Relate to Perceptions of Leadership Potential?" *Journal of Experimental Social Psychology,* in press.

[7] Results can be found in R G Lord, C L De Vader, and G M Alliger, "A Meta-Analysis of the Relation between Personality Traits and Leadership Perceptions: An Application of Validity Generalization Procedures," *Journal of Applied Psychology,* August 1986, pp 402–10.

[8] See A H Eagly and J L Chin, "Diversity and Leadership in a Changing World," *American Psychologist,* April 2010, pp 216–24; and D D Cremer, M van Dijke, and D M Mayer, "Cooperating When 'You' and 'I' Are Treated Fairly: The Moderating Role of Leader Prototypicality," *Journal of Applied Psychology,* November 2010, pp 1121–33.

[9] Results can be found in T A Judge, J E Bono, R Ilies, and M W Gerhardt, "Personality and Leadership: A Qualitative and Quantitative Review," *Journal of Applied Psychology,* August 2002, pp 765–80.

[10] See T A Judge, A E Colbert, and R Ilies, "Intelligence and Leadership: A Quantitative Review and Test of Theoretical Propositions," *Journal of Applied Psychology,* June 2004, pp 542–52.

[11] R S Nadler, *Leading with Emotional Intelligence* (New York: McGraw-Hill, 2011).

[12] See D L Joseph and D A Newman, "Emotional Intelligence: An Integrative Meta-Analysis and Cascading Model, "*Journal of Applied Psychology,* January 2010, pp 54–78; and J Antonakis, N M Ashkanasy, and M T Dasborough, "Does Leadership Need Emotional Intelligence?" *The Leadership Quarterly,* April 2009, pp 247–61.

[13] Kellerman's research can be found in B Kellerman, *Bad Leadership* (Boston: Harvard Business School Press, 2004).

[14] "Nokia CEO's Letter to Employees," February 9, 2011, http://articles.timesofindia.indiatimes.com/2011-02-09/telecom/28546254_1_oil-platform-strategy-and-financial-briefing-nokia-ceo.

[15] The trait definitions were quoted from ibid., pp 40–46. Some of the personal examples were taken from "The Worst Managers," *BusinessWeek,* January 19, 2009, p 42.

[16] See A Morriss, R J Ely, and F X Frei, "Stop Holding Yourself Back," *Harvard Business Review,* January–February 2011, pp 160–64; and L Wiseman and G McKeown, "Bringing Out the Best In Your People," *Harvard Business Review,* May 2010, pp 117–21.

[17] Gender and the emergence of leaders was examined by A H Eagly and S J Karau, "Gender and the Emergence of Leaders: A Meta-Analysis," *Journal of Personality and Social Psychology,* May 1991, pp 685–710; and R Ayman and K Korabik, "Leadership: Why Gender and Culture Matter," *American Psychologist,* April 2010, pp 157–70.

[18] See A H Eagly, S J Karau, and B T Johnson, "Gender and Leadership Style among School Principals: A Meta-Analysis," *Educational Administration Quarterly,* February 1992, pp 76–102.

[19] Supportive findings are contained in J M Twenge, "Changes in Women's Assertiveness in Response to Status and Roles: A Cross-Temporal Meta-Analysis, 1931–1993," *Journal of Personality and Social Psychology,* July 2001, pp 133–45.

[20] For a summary of this research, see H Ibarra and O Obodaru, "Women and Vision Thing," *Harvard Business Review,* January 2009, pp 62–70.

[21] D Zielinski, "Effective Assessments," *HR Magazine,* January 2011, pp 61–64.

[22] See J Helyar and C Hymowitz, "Companies & Industries: The Recession Is Gone, and The CEO Could Be Next," *Bloomberg Businessweek,* February 7–13, 2011, pp 24–26; and "What Happened to Your Future Leaders?" *Training,* February 2010, p 11.

[23] See N Doss, "Fast Food: East Meets West at Hamburger University," *Bloomberg Businessweek,* January 31–February 6, 2011, pp 22–23; and H Dolezalek, "Talent Scout," *Training,* February 2010, pp 52–56.

[24] Results can be found in T A Judge, R F Piccolo, and R Ilies, "The Forgotten Ones? The Validity of Consideration and Initiating Structure in Leadership Research," *Journal of Applied Psychology,* February 2004, pp 36–51.

[25] See S T Hannah and B J Avolio, "Ready or Not: How Do We Accelerate the Developmental Readiness of Leaders?" *Journal of Organizational Behavior,* November 2010, pp 1181–87; and J M Leigh, E R Shapiro, and S H Penney, "Developing Diverse, Collaborative Leaders: An Empirical Program Evaluation," *Journal of Leadership & Organizational Studies,* November 2010, pp 370–79.

[26] F E Fiedler, "Job Engineering for Effective Leadership: A New Approach," *Management Review,* September 1977, p 29.

[27] For more on this theory, see F E Fiedler, "A Contingency Model of Leadership Effectiveness," in *Advances in Experimental Social Psychology,* vol 1, ed L Berkowitz (New York: Academic Press, 1964); and F E Fiedler, *A Theory of Leadership Effectiveness* (New York: McGraw-Hill, 1967).

[28] See L H Peters, D D Hartke, and J T Pohlmann, "Fiedler's Contingency Theory of Leadership: An Application of the Meta-Analyses Procedures of Schmidt and Hunter," *Psychological Bulletin,* March 1985, pp 274–85; and C A Schriesheim, B J Tepper, and L A Tetrault, "Least Preferred Co-Worker Score, Situational Control, and Leadership Effectiveness: A Meta-Analysis of Contingency Model Performance Predictions," *Journal of Applied Psychology,* August 1994, pp 561–73.

[29] B Groysberg, A N McLean, and N Nohria, "Are Leaders Portable?" *Harvard Business Review,* May 2006, pp 95, 97.

[30] See R Adams and L Schuker, "Time Inc.'s CEO Shown the Door," *The Wall Street Journal,* February 18, 2011, p B1.

[31] For more detail on this theory, see R J House, "A Path–Goal Theory of Leader Effectiveness," *Administrative Science Quarterly,* September 1971, pp 321–38.

[32] This research is summarized by R J House, "Path–Goal Theory of Leadership: Lessons, Legacy, and a Reformulated Theory," *Leadership Quarterly,* Autumn 1996, pp 323–52.

[33] See ibid.

[34] See R Siklos, "Bob Iger Rocks Disney," *Fortune,* January 19, 2009, pp 80–86.

[35] Results can be found in P M Podsakoff, S B MacKenzie, M Ahearne, and W H Bommer, "Searching for a Needle in a Haystack: Trying to Identify the Illusive Moderators of Leadership Behaviors," *Journal of Management,* 1995, pp 422–70.

[36] The steps were developed by H P Sims Jr, S Faraj, and S Yun, "When Should a Leader Be Directive or Empowering? How to Develop Your Own Situational Theory of Leadership," *Business Horizons,* March–April 2009, pp 149–58.

[37] See J B Wu, A S Tsui, and A J Kinicki, "Consequences of Differentiated Leadership in Groups," *Academy of Management Journal,* February 2010, pp 90–106.

[38] For a complete description of this theory, see B J Bass and B J Avolio, *Revised Manual for the Multi-Factor Leadership Questionnaire* (Palo Alto, CA: Mindgarden, 1997).

[39] A definition and description of transactional leadership is provided by J Antonakis and R J House, "The Full-Range Leadership Theory: The Way Forward," in *Transformational and Charismatic Leadership: The Road Ahead,* ed B J Avolio and F J Yammarino (New York: JAI Press, 2002), pp 3–34.

[40] Excerpted from D McGinn, "Battling Back from Betrayal," *Harvard Business Review,* December 2010, p 131.

[41] U R Dumdum, K B Lowe, and B J Avolio, "A Meta-Analysis of Transformational and Transactional Leadership Correlates of Effectiveness and Satisfaction: An Update and Extension," in *Transformational and Charismatic Leadership: The Road Ahead,* ed B J Avolio and F J Yammarino (New York: JAI Press, 2002), p 38.

[42] Supportive research is summarized by Bass and Bass, *The Bass Handbook of Leadership,* pp 618–48.

[43] Excerpted from D Brady, "Can GE Still Manage?" *Bloomberg Businessweek,* April 25, 2010, p 28.

[44] Supportive results can be found in P D Harms and M Credé, "Emotional Intelligence and Transformational and Transactional Leadership: A Meta-Analysis," *Journal of Leadership & Organizational Studies,* February 2010, pp 5–17; and J E Bono and T A Judge, "Personality and Transformational and Transactional Leadership: A Meta-Analysis," *Journal of Applied Psychology,* October 2004, pp 901–10.

[45] See Eagly, Johannesen-Schmidt, and van Engen, "Transformational, Transactional, and Laissez-Faire Leadership Styles."

[46] These actions are derived from R Kark, B Shamir, and C Chen, "The Two Faces of Transformational Leadership: Empowerment and Dependency," *Journal of Applied Psychology,* April 2003, pp 246–55.

[47] B Nanus, *Visionary Leadership* (San Francisco: Jossey-Bass, 1992), p 8.

[48] T Bisoux, "Making Connections," *BizEd,* January–February 2009, p 22. Also see "Carl-Henric Svanberg," *The New York Times,* March 16, 2011, http://topics.nytimes.com/top/reference/timestopics/people/s/carlhenric_svanberg/index.html?8qa&scp=1-spot&sq=carl+henric+svanberg&st=nyt.

[49] See S Bates, "View of Senior Managers Critical to Whistle-Blowers," *HR Magazine,* March 2011, p 11.

[50] See Brady, "Can GE Still Manage?" p 28.

[51] Supportive examples are discussed in R I Sutton, "The Boss as Human Shield," *Harvard Business Review,* September 2010, pp 106–9.

[52] R Martin, "How Successful Leaders Think," *Harvard Business Review,* June 2007, pp 60–67.

[53] Results can be found in U R Dumdum, K B Lowe, and B J Avolio, "A Meta-Analysis of Transformational and Transactional Leadership Correlates of Effectiveness and Satisfaction: An Update and Extension," in *Transactional and Charismatic Leadership: The Road Ahead,* ed B J Avolio and F J Yammarino (New York: JAI, 2002), pp 35–66.

[54] See K B Lowe, K G Kroeck, and N Sivasubramaniam, "Effectiveness Correlates of Transformational and Transactional Leadership: A Meta-Analytic Review of the MLQ Literature," *The Leadership Quarterly,* 1996, pp 385–425.

[55] Visionary leadership is studied by C A Hartnell and F O Walumbwa, "Transformational Leadership and Organizational Culture," in *The Handbook of Organizational Culture and Climate,* 2nd ed, ed N M Ashkanasy, C P M Wilderom, and M F Peterson (Thousand Oaks, CA: Sage, 2011), pp 225–48; and M A Griffin, S K Parker, and C M Mason, "Leader Vision and the Development of Adaptive and Proactive Performance: A Longitudinal Study," *Journal of Applied Psychology,* January 2010, pp 174–82.

[56] Supportive results can be found in T A Judge and R F Piccolo, "Transformational and Transactional Leadership: A Meta-Analytic Test of Their Relative Validity," *Journal of Applied Psychology,* October 2004, pp 755–68.

57 X-H Wang and J M Howell, "Exploring the Dual-Level Effects of Transformational Leadership on Followers," *Journal of Applied Psychology,* November 2010, pp 1134–44.

58 T Whitford and S A Moss, "Transformational Leadership in Distributed Work Groups: The Moderating Role of Follower Regulatory Focus and Goal Orientation," *Communication Research,* December 2009, pp 810–37.

59 See A J Towler, "Effects of Charismatic Influence Training on Attitudes, Behavior, and Performance," *Personnel Psychology,* Summer 2003, pp 363–81.

60 These recommendations were derived from J M Howell and B J Avolio, "The Ethics of Charismatic Leadership: Submission or Liberation?" *Academy of Management Executive,* May 1992, pp 43–54.

61 See F Dansereau, Jr, G Graen, and W Haga, "A Vertical Dyad Linkage Approach to Leadership within Formal Organizations," *Organizational Behavior and Human Performance,* February 1975, pp 46–78.

62 These descriptions were taken from D Duchon, S G Green, and T D Taber, "Vertical Dyad Linkage: A Longitudinal Assessment of Antecedents, Measures, and Consequences," *Journal of Applied Psychology,* February 1986, pp 56–60.

63 Supportive results can be found in B Erodogan and T N Bauer, "Differentiated Leader–Member Exchanges: The Buffering Role of Justice Climate," *Journal of Applied Psychology,* November 2010, pp 1104–20; and L W Hughes, J B Avey, and D R Nixon, "Relationships Between Leadership and Followers' Quitting Intentions and Job Search Behaviors," *Journal of Leadership & Organizational Studies,* November 2010, pp 351–62.

64 Results can be found in R Ilies, J D Nahrgang, and F P Morgeson, "Leader–Member Exchange and Citizenship Behaviors: A Meta-Analysis," *Journal of Applied Psychology,* January 2007, pp 269–77.

65 See V Venkataramani, S G Green, and D J Schleicher, "Well-Connected Leaders: The Impact of Leaders' Social Network Ties on LMX and Members' Work Attitudes," *Journal of Applied Psychology,* November 2010, pp 1071–84; R Eisenberger, G Karagonlar, F Stinglhamber, P Neves, T E Becker, M G Gonzalez-Morales, and M Steiger-Mueller, "Leader-Member Exchange and Affective Organizational Commitment: The Contribution of Supervisor's Organizational Embodiment," *Journal of Applied Psychology,* November 2010, pp 1085–103.

66 These recommendations were derived from G C Mage, "Leading Despite Your Boss," *HR Magazine,* September 2003, pp 139–44.

67 R J House and R N Aditya, "The Social Scientific Study of Leadership: Quo Vadis?" *Journal of Management,* 1997, p 457.

68 Thorough discussion of shared leadership is provided by C L Pearce, "The Future of Leadership: Combining Vertical and Shared Leadership to Transform Knowledge Work," *Academy of Management Executive,* February 2004, pp 47–57.

69 B Reeves, T W Malone, and T O'Driscoll, "Leadership's Online Labs," *Harvard Business Review,* May 2008, pp 59–66.

70 This research is summarized in B J Avolio, J J Soskik, D I Jung, and Y Berson, "Leadership Models, Methods, and Applications," in *Handbook of Psychology,* ed W C Borman, D R Ilgen, R J Klimoski (Hoboken, NJ: John Wiley & Sons, 2003), vol 12, pp 277–307.

71 An overall summary of servant-leadership is provided by L C Spears, *Reflections on Leadership: How Robert K Greenleaf's Theory of Servant-Leadership Influenced Today's Top Management Thinkers* (New York: John Wiley & Sons, 1995).

72 D MacMillan, "Survivor. CEO Edition," *Bloomberg Businessweek,* March 1, 2010, p 35.

73 J Stuart, *Fast Company,* September 1999, p 114.

74 "The Best Advice I Ever Got," *Fortune,* May 12, 2008, p 74.

75 Supportive results can be found in F O Walumbwa, C A Hartnell, and A Oke, "Servant Leadership, Procedural Justice Climate, Service Climate, Employee Attitudes, and Organizational Citizenship Behavior: A Cross-Level Investigation," *Journal of Applied Psychology,* May 2010, pp 517–29, and R C Liden, S J Wayne, H Zhao, and D Henderson, "Servant Leadership: Development of a Multidimensional Measure and Multi-Level Assessment," *The Leadership Quarterly,* April 2008, pp 161–77.

76 The role of followers is discussed by D S DeRue and S J Ashford, "Who Will Lead and Who Will Follow? A Social Process of Leadership Identity Construction in Organizations," *Academy of Management Review,* October 2010.

77 Bass and Bass, *The Bass Handbook of Leadership,* p 408.

78 See L Bossidy, "What Your Leader Expects of You and What You Should Expect in Return," *Harvard Business Review,* April 2007, pp 58–65.

79 See R Goffee and G Jones, "Followership: It's Personal, Too," *Harvard Business Review,* December 2001, p 148.

80 This checklist was proposed by J J Gabarro and J P Kotter, "Managing Your Boss," *Harvard Business Review,* January 2005, pp 92–99.

81 These ideas were partially based on B Dattner, "Forewarned Is Forearmed," *BusinessWeek,* September 1, 2008, p 50; and P Drucker, "Managing Oneself," *Harvard Business Review,* January 2005, pp 2–11.

82 The following suggestions were discussed by Gabarro and Kotter, "Managing Your Boss." Also see J Banks and D Coutu, "How to Protect Your Job in a Recession," *Harvard Business Review,* September 2008, pp 113–16.

83 N Justin, "Political Pranksters Keep Getting Savvier," *The Arizona Republic,* March 17, 2011, p A10.

84 M Gerson, "No Journalism Ethic Justifies NPR Video Attack," *The Arizona Republic,* March 17, 2011, p B5.

85 J Hook and D Yadron, "Spending Bill Passes, NPR Targeted," *The Wall Street Journal,* March 18, 2011, p A4.

86 Justin, "Political Pranksters Keep Getting Savvier," p A10.

87 Gerson, "No Journalism Ethic Justifies NPR Video Attack," p B5.

Chapter 15

1 Reprinted by permission of *Harvard Business Review*. Excerpt from "The Decision-Driven Organization" by M C Mankins and P Rogers, June 2010. Copyright 2010 by the Harvard Business School Publishing Corporation; all rights reserved.

2 C I Barnard, *The Functions of the Executive* (Cambridge, MA: Harvard University Press, 1938), p 73.

3 Drawn from E H Schein, *Organizational Psychology,* 3rd ed (Englewood Cliffs, NJ: Prentice Hall, 1980), pp 12–15.

4 For a management-oriented discussion of general systems theory, see K E Boulding, "General Systems Theory: The Skeleton of Science," *Management Science,* April 1956, pp 197–208. For a more recent discussion see A J Kinicki, K J L Jacobson, B M Galvin, and G E Prussia, "A Multi-Systems Model of Leadership," *Journal of Leadership & Organizational* Studies, in press.

5 See L Buchanan, "No More Metaphors," *Harvard Business Review,* March 2005, p 19; and L Prusak, "The Madness of Individuals," *Harvard Business Review,* June 2005, p 22.

6 See J Bussey, "Nation Will Rebuild From Quake But Faces Other Daunting Tests," *The Wall Street Journal,* March 25, 2011, pp B1, B5; and A Dowell, "Japan: The Business Aftershocks," *The Wall Street Journal,* March 25, 2011, pp B1, B4.

7 M Sanchanta, "Wal-Mart's Local Team Shifts Into Crisis Mode," *The Wall Street Journal,* March 25, 2011, p B1.

8 N E Boudette and J Bennett, "Henry Ford Maxim Is Reversed," *The Wall Street Journal,* March 25, 2011, p B5.

9 R Greenwood and D Miller, "Tackling Design Anew: Getting Back to the Heart of Organizational Theory," *Academy of Management Perspectives,* November 2010, p 78.

10 Reviews of organizational design are provided by R E Miles, C C Snow, Ø D Fjeldstad, G Miles, and C Lettl, "Designing Organizations to Meet 21st-Century Opportunities and Challenges," *Organizational Dynamics,* April–June 2010, pp 93–103; and J R Galbraith, "The Multi-Dimensional and Reconfigurable Organization," *Organizational Dynamics,* April–June 2010, pp 115–125.

11 See M C Mankins and P Rogers, "The Decision-Driven Organization," *Harvard Business Review,* June 2010, pp 56–57; and "Full Speed Ahead," *HR Magazine,* March 2011, p 18.

12 The following discussion is based on N Anand and R L Daft, "What Is the Right Organization Design?" *Organizational Dynamics,* 2007, pp 329–44.

13 "GE Businesses," Retrieved March 26, 2011, from http://www.ge.com/ citizenship/about-citizenship/ge-citizenship-facts/ge-businesses.html.

14 Anand and Daft, "What Is the Right Organization Design?" p 332.

[15] P Lawrence, "Herman Miller's Creative Network," *BusinessWeek*, February 15, 2008, www.businessweek.com (interview with Brian Walker).

[16] Anand and Daft, "What Is the Right Organization Design?" p 338.

[17] D Kiley, "Nokia Starts Listening," *BusinessWeek*, May 5, 2008, p 30.

[18] See "Successfully Transitioning to a Virtual Organization: Challenges, Impact and Technology," *SHRM Research Quarterly*, First Quarter 2010, pp 1–9.

[19] A Pomeroy, "Passion, Obsession Drive the 'Eileen Fisher Way,'" *HR Magazine*, July 2007, p 55.

[20] A Bruzzese, "Employers Can Harness Social Media," *The Arizona Republic*, July 21, 2010, p CL1.

[21] J Ewers, "No Ideas? You're Not Alone," *U.S. News & World Report*, June 18, 2007, pp 50–52, quoting from p 51.

[22] P Kaestle, "A New Rationale for Organizational Structure," *Planning Review*, July–August 1990, p 22.

[23] Details of this study can be found in T Burns and G M Stalker, *The Management of Innovation* (London: Tavistock, 1961).

[24] J D Sherman and H L Smith, "The Influence of Organizational Structure on Intrinsic versus Extrinsic Motivation," *Academy of Management Journal*, December 1984, p 883.

[25] See J A Courtright, G T Fairhurst, and L E Rogers, "Interaction Patterns in Organic and Mechanistic Systems," *Academy of Management Journal*, December 1989, pp 773–802.

[26] A Taylor III, "Can This Car Save Ford?" *Fortune*, April 22, 2008, http://money.cnn.com/2008/04/21/news/companies/saving_ford.fortune/index.htm.

[27] P Gumbel, "Big Mac's Local Flavor," *Fortune*, May 2, 2008, http://money.cnn.com/2008/04/29/news/companies/big_macs_local.fortune/index.htm.

[28] See Galbraith, "The Multi-Dimensional and Reconfigurable Organization," pp 115–125.

[29] Anand and Daft, "What Is the Right Organization Design?" pp 331–33.

[30] A Hesseldahl, "BlackBerry: Innovation behind the Icon," *BusinessWeek*, April 4, 2008, http://www.businessweek.com/innovate/content/apr2008/id2008044_416784.htm.

[31] Anand and Daft, "What Is the Right Organization Design?" pp 333–40.

[32] M Kripalani, "Inside the Tata Nano Factory," *BusinessWeek*, May 9, 2008, http://www.businessweek.com/innovate/content/may2008/id2008059_312111.htm.

[33] J Holland, "Innovative Outsourcing Model Saves Company Millions," *Industry Week*, April 25, 2007, http://www.industryweek.com/articles/innovative_outsourcing_model_saves_company_millions_14018.aspx?Page=1?ShowAll=1.

[34] MacCormack and T Forbath, "Learning the Fine Art of Global Collaboration," *Harvard Business Review*, January 2008, pp 24, 26.

[35] K Cameron, "Critical Questions in Assessing Organizational Effectiveness," *Organizational Dynamics*, Autumn 1980, p 70.

[36] See S C Voelpel and C K Streb, "A Balanced Scorecard for Managing the Aging Workforce," *Organizational Dynamics*, January–March 2010, pp 84–90.

[37] A Taylor III, "Hyundai Smokes the Competition," *Fortune*, January 18, 2010, p 69.

[38] See R S Kaplan and D P Norton, "Having Trouble with Your Strategy? Then Map It," *Harvard Business Review*, September– October 2000, pp 167–76.

[39] Taylor III, "Hyundai Smokes the Competition," pp 66, 68.

[40] Cameron, "Critical Questions in Assessing Organizational Effectiveness," p 67.

[41] See R K Mitchell, B R Agle, and D J Wood, "Toward a Theory of Stakeholder Identification and Salience: Defining the Principle of Who and What Really Counts," *Academy of Management Review*, October 1997, pp 853–96.

[42] See H G Jackson, "Flexibility Workplaces: The Next Imperative," *HR Magazine*, March 2011, p 8.

[43] P Dvorak, "How Irdeto Split Headquarters," *The Wall Street Journal*, January 7, 2008, p B3.

[44] K S Cameron, "Effectiveness as Paradox: Consensus and Conflict in Conceptions of Organizational Effectiveness," *Management Science*, May 1986, p 542.

[45] See B Christie, "Southwest Finds Jet Cracks," *The Arizona Republic*, April 4, 2011, pp B4, B5; and A Pasztor and T W Martin, "Mystery Still Surrounds Cause of Rupture Aboard Southwest Jet," *The Wall Street Journal*, April 4, 2011, pp B1, B4.

[46] Excerpted from J Angwin, "The Web's New Gold Mine: Your Secrets," *The Wall Street Journal*, July 31–August 1, 2010, p W1.

Chapter 16

[1] Reprinted by permission of *Harvard Business Review*. Excerpt from "A Maverick CEO Explains How He Persuaded His Team to Leap Into the Future," by V Nayar, June 2010. Copyright 2010 by the Harvard Business School Publishing Corporation; all rights reserved.

[2] See J McGregor, "From Great to Good," *BusinessWeek*, April 13, 2009, pp 32–35; I Rowley and H Tashiro, "There's Even Trouble in Toyota City," *BusinessWeek*, April 27, 2009, pp 50–51; and B Helm, "Blowing Up Pepsi," *BusinessWeek*, April 27, 2009, pp 32–36.

[3] "Capitalizing on Complexity," IBM corporation, May 2010.

[4] A M Webber, "Learning for a Change," *Fast Company*, May 1999, p 180.

[5] See "Training Top 125," *Training*, January–February 2011, pp 54–93.

[6] E Byron, "How to Market to an Aging Boomer: Flattery, Subterfuge and Euphemism," *The Wall Street Journal*, February 2, 2011, pp A1, A12.

[7] P Coy, "A Message from the Street," *Bloomberg Businessweek*, February 7–13, 2011, pp 58–65.

[8] See "Social Networking Comes to Fore As Regular Recruiting Tool," *HR Trendbook HR Magazine*, 2011, p 63.

[9] See D Bennett, "I'll Have My Robots Talk to Your Robots," *Bloomberg Businessweek*, February 21–27, 2011, pp 52–61.

[10] See D Welch, "For Dan Akerson, A Magic Moment to Remake GM," *Bloomberg Businessweek*, January 24–30, 2011, pp 21–22; and J Shambora, A Lashinsky, B Gimbel, and J Schlosser, "A View from the Top," *Fortune*, March 16, 2009, p 110.

[11] H L Lee, "Don't Tweak Your Supply Chain—Rethink It End to End," *Harvard Business Review*, October 2010, pp 64–65.

[12] Y Takahashi, "Strikes in China Roil Honda's Strategy," *The Wall Street Journal*, June 24, 2010, p B3.

[13] See D Voreacos, A Nussbaum, and G Farrell, "Johnson & Johnson Fights to Clear Its Once-Trusted Name," *Bloomberg Businessweek*, April 4–10, 2011, pp 64–71; and A Nussbaum and D Voreacos, "J&J CEO Weldon Has 'No Plans' to Retire, Focuses on Recalls," *Bloomberg Businessweek*, April 9, 2011. Retrieved from http://www.bloomberg.com/news/2011-03-18/j-j-ceo-weldon-has-no-plans-to-retire-focuses-on-fixing-manufacturing.html.

[14] For a thorough discussion of the model, see K Lewin, *Field Theory in Social Science* (New York: Harper & Row, 1951).

[15] D Brady, "Etc. Hard Choices: Howard Schultz," *Bloomberg Businessweek*, April 4 – April 10, 2011, p 102.

[16] See ibid.

[17] C Goldwasser, "Benchmarking: People Make the Process," *Management Review*, June 1995, p 40.

[18] See T A Stewart, "Architects of Change," *Harvard Business Review*, April 2006, p 10; also see D Shaner, *The Seven Arts of Change* (New York: Union Square Press, 2010).

[19] A thorough discussion of the target elements of change can be found in M Beer and B Spector, "Organizational Diagnosis: Its Role in Organizational Learning," *Journal of Counseling & Development*, July–August 1993, pp 642–50.

[20] D Kesmodel, "How 'Chief Beer Taster' Blended Molson, Coors," *The Wall Street Journal*, October 1, 2007, pp B1, B5.

[21] These errors are discussed in J P Kotter, "Leading Change: The Eight Steps to Transformation," in *The Leader's Change Handbook*, ed J A Conger, G M Spreitzer, and E E Lawler III (San Francisco: Jossey-Bass, 1999), pp 87–99.

[22] See L Freifeld, "Changes with Penguins," *Training*, June 2008, pp 24–28.

[23] J Fortt, "Yahoo's Taskmaster," *Fortune*, April 27, 2009, p 83.

[24] P G Hanson and B Lubin, "Answers to Questions Frequently Asked about Organization Development," in *The Emerging Practice of Organization Development*, ed W Sikes, A Drexter, and J Grant (Alexandria, VA: NTL Institute, 1989), p 16; and Society for Human

Resource Management, "Organization Development: A Strategic HR Tool," *Research Quarterly,* Third Quarter 2007, pp 1–9.

[25] Different stage-based models of OD are discussed by R A Gallagher, "What Is OD?" www.orgdct.com/what_is_od.htm, accessed May 12, 2005.

[26] Reviews of organizational development are provided by L Martins, "Organizational Change and Development," *Handbook of Industrial and Organizational Psychology,* 2011, pp 691–728.

[27] See R Rodgers, J E Hunter, and D L Rogers, "Influence of Top Management Commitment on Management Program Success," *Journal of Applied Psychology,* February 1993, pp 151–55.

[28] Results can be found in P J Robertson, D R Roberts, and J I Porras, "Dynamics of Planned Organizational Change: Assessing Empirical Support for a Theoretical Model," *Academy of Management Journal,* June 1993, pp 619–34.

[29] Results from the meta-analysis can be found in G A Neuman, J E Edwards, and N S Raju, "Organizational Development Interventions: A Meta-Analysis of Their Effects on Satisfaction and Other Attitudes," *Personnel Psychology,* Autumn 1989, pp 461–90.

[30] Results can be found in C-M Lau and H-Y Ngo, "Organization Development and Firm Performance: A Comparison of Multinational and Local Firms," *Journal of International Business Studies,* First Quarter 2001, pp 95–114.

[31] J D Ford, L W Ford, and A D'Amelio, "Resistance to Change: The Rest of the Story," *Academy of Management Review,* April 2008, p 362.

[32] See J D Ford and L W Ford, "Stop Blaming Resistance to Change and Start Using It," *Organizational Dynamics,* January–March 2010, pp 24–36.

[33] Adapted in part from J D Ford, L W Ford, and A D'Amelio, "Resistance to Change: The Rest of the Story," *Academy of Management Review,* April 2008, pp 362–77; and A S Judson, *Changing Behavior in Organizations: Minimizing Resistance to Change* (Cambridge, MA: Blackwell, 1991).

[34] An individual's predisposition to change was investigated by E Lamm and J R Gordon, "Empowerment, Predisposition to Resist Change, and Support for Organizational Change," *Journal of Leadership & Organizational Studies,* November 2010, pp 426–37.

[35] Research regarding resilience is discussed by K Kersting, "Resilience: The Mental Muscle Everyone Has," *Monitor on Psychology,* April 2005, pp 32–33.

[36] R Cornum, M D Matthews, and M E P Seligman, "Comprehensive Soldier Fitness," *American Psychologist,* January 2011, p 4; also see K J Reivich, M E P Seligman, and S McBride, "Master Resilience Training in the U.S. Army," *American Psychologist,* January 2011, pp 25–34.

[37] L Herscovitch and J P Meyer, "Commitment to Organizational Change: Extension of a Three-Component Model," *Journal of Applied Psychology,* June 2003, p 475.

[38] See R H Schaffer, "Mistakes Leaders Keep Making," *Harvard Business Review,* September 2010, pp 86–91.

[39] L Goering, "Land of Plenty No Longer," *Chicago Tribune,* May 20, 2008, sec 1, p 8.

[40] See D M Harold, D B Fedor, S Caldwell, and Y Liu, "The Effects of Transformational and Change Leadership on Employees' Commitment to Change: A Multilevel Study," *Journal of Applied Psychology,* March 2008, pp 346–57.

[41] See R H Miles, "Accelerating Corporate Transformations (Don't Lose Your Nerve!)," *Harvard Business Review,* January–February 2010, pp 69–75.

[42] J P Kotter, "Leading Change: Why Transformation Efforts Fail," *Harvard Business Review,* 1995, p 64.

[43] J P Kotter and L A Schlesinger, "Choosing Strategies for Change," *Harvard Business Review,* July–August 2008, pp 130–39.

[44] R M Fulmer and J B Keys, "A Conversation with Peter Senge: New Development in Organizational Learning," *Organizational Dynamics,* Autumn 1998, p 35.

[45] This definition was based on D A Garvin, "Building a Learning Organization," *Harvard Business Review,* July–August 1993, pp 78–91.

[46] S Mohammed, L Ferzandi, and K Hamilton, "Metaphor No More: A 15-Year Review of the Team Mental Model Construct," *Journal of Management,* July 2010, p 879.

[47] This discussion and quotes come from F Gino and G P Pisano, "Why Leaders Don't Learn from Success," *Harvard Business Review,* April 2011, pp 68–74.

[48] A Zolli and A M Healy, "Vision Statement: When Failure Looks Like Success," *Harvard Business Review,* April 2011, pp 30–31.

[49] K Dillon, "I Think of My Failures as a Gift," *Harvard Business Review,* April 2011, p 86.

[50] A G Lafley, Wikipedia. Last updated January 13, 2011, http://en.wikipedia.org/wiki/A._G._Lafley.

[51] See A C Edmondson, "Strategies For Learning From Failure," *Harvard Business Review,* April 2011, pp 48–55.

[52] See P M Madsen and V Desai, "Failing to Learn? The Effects of Failure and Success on Organizational Learning in the Global Orbital Launch Vehicle Industry," *Academy of Management Journal,* June 2010, pp 451–76.

[53] This discussion is based in part on D Ulrich, T Jick, and M Von Glinow, "High-Impact Learning: Building and Diffusing Learning Capability," *Organizational Dynamics,* Autumn 1993, pp 52–66.

[54] See J W Lorsch and T J Tierney, *Aligning the Stars: Organizing Professionals to Win* (Boston: Harvard Business School Press, 2002).

[55] The creation of learning infrastructure is discussed by C R James, "Designing Learning Organizations," *Organizational Dynamics,* 2003, pp 46–61.

[56] See J B Quinn, "Leveraging Intellect," *Academy of Management Executive,* November 2005, pp 78–94; and M T Hansen, M L Mors, and B Lovås, "Knowledge Sharing in Organizations: Multiple Networks, Multiple Phases," *Academy of Management Journal,* October 2005, pp 776–93.

[57] See the related discussion in D Lei, J W Slocum, and R A Pitts, "Designing Organizations for Competitive Advantage: The Power of Unlearning and Learning," *Organizational Dynamics,* Winter 1999, pp 24–38.

[58] This case was based on material contained in E Frauenheim, "Culture Crash: Lost in the Shuffle," *Workforce Management,* January 14, 2008, pp 1, 12–17.